# West Bengal TET

## Paper 1

Latest Edition
Practice Kit

**10 Tests**

10 Practice Test

Based On Real Exam Pattern

✓ Thoroughly Revised and Updated

✓ Detailed Analysis of all MCQs

<table>
<tr><td>Title</td><td>: West Bengal TET Paper 1</td></tr>
<tr><td>Author Name</td><td>: Mr. Rohit Manglik</td></tr>
<tr><td>Published By</td><td>: EduGorilla Community Pvt. Ltd.</td></tr>
<tr><td>Publishers Address</td><td>: 12/651, First Floor Opp. Arvindo Park, Near Jama Masjid,<br>Indira Nagar, Lucknow, Uttar Pradesh-226016, India</td></tr>
</table>

## Copyright EduGorilla

**ISBN : 978-93-55569-97-4**

**First Edition**

No part of this book may be reproduced, distributed, or transmitted in any form by any means, without the prior written permission of the publisher.

**All Right Reserved**

© **by EduGorilla Community Pvt. Ltd**

## Disclaimer EduGorilla

Although the author and publisher have made every effort to ensure the accuracy of information in this book, we do not assume any responsibility to errors and hereby disclaim any liability to any party for any loss, damage, or disruption caused by errors or omissions, whether such errors or omissions result from negligence, accident, or any other cause.

**Compiled and created by EduGorilla Community Pvt. Ltd**

**Printed By EduGorilla Community Pvt. Ltd.**

# TABLE OF CONTENTS


| Practice Test | 1-194 |
|---|---|
| **1.** Practice Test - 1 | 1-21 |
| **2.** Practice Test - 2 | 22-43 |
| **3.** Practice Test - 3 | 44-63 |
| **4.** Practice Test - 4 | 64-84 |
| **5.** Practice Test - 5 | 85-103 |
| **6.** Practice Test - 6 | 104-122 |
| **7.** Practice Test - 7 | 123-142 |
| **8.** Practice Test - 8 | 143-157 |
| **9.** Practice Test - 9 | 158-179 |
| **10.** Practice Test - 10 | 180-194 |

## Child Development and Pedagogy

1. Which of the following is the characteristic of the stage of later childhood?
   (a) Self-assertion
   (b) Time concept
   (c) Social tendency
   (d) Hero worship

2. Understanding the principles of development of a child helps a teacher in:
   (a) Rationalizing why the learner ought to be taught.
   (b) Effectively catering to the different learning styles of learners
   (c) Identifying the social status of the learner
   (d) Identifying the economic background of the learner

3. The other name of heredity is:
   (a) Genes      (b) Nature
   (c) Zygote     (d) Nurture

4. Which of the following is a passive agency of socialization?
   (a) Health club
   (b) Family
   (c) Eco club
   (d) Public library

5. "Reasoning of child is not logical and is based on intuition rather than on systematic logic." According to Piaget this stage of cognitive development is called:
   (a) Sensory motor period
   (b) Preoperations period
   (c) Concrete operations period
   (d) Formal operations period

6. As a teacher you firmly believe in saying no to ragging and bullying' and put up posters and form committees in schools. The young adolescents who join you with strong beliefs, are at which of the following stages?
   (a) The conventional level
   (b) The pre-conventional level
   (c) The post-conventional level
   (d) Social order maintaining level

7. Which of the following strategy is problem centered?
   (a) Project
   (b) Heuristic
   (c) Discovery
   (d) All of the above

8. Ability to understand oneself, appreciate one's feelings, fears and motivations. There are the characteristics of ______ intelligence.
   (a) Linguistic
   (b) Interpersonal
   (c) Intrapersonal
   (d) Spatial

9. Who said that children have an innate ability to acquire language?
   (a) B.F. Skinner
   (b) McWhinney
   (c) Noam Chomsky
   (d) J. B. Watson

10. Which of the following do not help in understanding the ethnic individual differences?
    (a) Value system
    (b) Verbal and non-verbal communication
    (c) Difference learning arrangements & processes
    (d) Intelligence

11. As a teacher, you have collected information about intelligence, personality and classroom behaviour of a student by using appropriate test and check-list. This process is called as:
    (a) Assessment
    (b) Measurement
    (c) Evaluation
    (d) All the above

12. The elements of the teaching model are:
    (a) Goals and Objectives
    (b) Objective and Structure
    (c) Social System and Evaluation
    (d) All of the above

13. All of the following are characteristics of morons except:
    (a) They are restricted to unskilled or semi skilled occupations
    (b) They are likely to be delinquent more easily
    (c) They have stronger sex drives than the normals
    (d) They are educable upto normal level but at a slower rate

14. Educationally, learning disabled look similar to:
    (a) Dullers

    (b) Backward children
    (c) Both (A) and (B)
    (d) None of these

15. The type of education where teaching learning programme is imparted to children with special needs along with normal children in the same school is:
    (a) Special Education
    (b) Integrated Education
    (c) Inclusive Education
    (d) Non-formal Education

16. Who introduces 'Learning Disable' word very first for the children suffered from various learning problems ?
    (a) Heward      (b) Samuel Kirk
    (c) Van Riper   (d) Birch

17. Divergence in 'learning styles' among learners may be attributed to:
    (a) Social environment of the child
    (b) Economic conditions of the child
    (c) Parenting of the child
    (d) Thinking strategies adopted by the learner.

18. Students are engaged in the classroom through different learning tasks. This phase is known as:
    (a) Engagement phase
    (b) Exploration phase
    (c) Explanation phase
    (d) Evaluation phase

19. Major drawback of multigrade teaching is:
    (a) It puts more responsibility on learners
    (b) It may create indiscipline
    (c) It allows less individual attention
    (d) It makes teachers inactive

20. Which of the following is not the characteristics of the emotions?
    (a) Emotions have wide range of degree
    (b) Affection play a key role in emotions
    (c) Emotions accompany instincts
    (d) Emotions and reasoning go together

21. Which one of the following teaching practices is consistent with cognitive perspective of motivation?

   (a) Providing Mid-Day Meal at school for all students.

   (b) Making sure students don't bring weapons to school.

   (c) Encouraging students to "try, try again" when they run into difficulty on challenging tasks.

   (d) Giving students special incentives whenever they do something well.

**22. Physical and emotional health of children _____ their learning.**

   (a) is not related to

   (b) has an insignificant role in

   (c) does not have any influence on

   (d) plays an important role in

**23. When students are given an opportunity to discuss a problem in groups, their learning curve:**

   (a) Remains stable

   (b) Declines

   (c) Remains the same

   (d) Become better

**24. Ashok, is very fond of playing cricket and he is very good at it too. He is the captain of his college team. He spends long hours playing or watching cricket and never gets tired or bored. Which personal factor is affecting the learning in this example?**

   (a) Maturation

   (b) Motivation

   (c) Self-concept

   (d) Levels of Aspiration

**25. Which factors affect learning?**

   (a) Personal factor

   (b) Environmental factor

   (c) Social factor

   (d) All of the above

**26. Which is not an example of scaffolding?**

   (a) Giving assignments which students cannot do on their own but can do with some help

   (b) Administering standardized IQ tests

   (c) Otherwise gifted students being taught about the correct way of taking notes

   (d) All of the above

**27. According to Vygotsky, child's language and thought develop _______.**

   (a) Independently of each other, then merge

   (b) Independently of each other

   (c) Universally across the culture

   (d) Together as child grows

**28. Christina took her class for a field trip before starting a new chapter in the class and after coming back, she discussed the trip with her students. It may be connoted as:**

   (a) Learning for Assessment

   (b) Learning of Assessment

   (c) Assessment of Learning

   (d) Assessment for Learning

**29. A science teacher has joined a rural school at the beginning of the academic session. Which of the following tests he should use?**

   (a) Situational

   (b) Diagnostic test

   (c) Achievement test

   (d) In basket test

**30. Stereotyped behaviour can usually be observed in children who are?**

   (a) Restless

   (b) Autistic

   (c) Hearing-impaired

   (d) None of these

## Language - I: English

**Ques (31-39): Direction** : Read the following passage carefully and answer the questions given below it in the context of the passage.

The world is fast becoming a global village due to the increasing daily requirement of energy by all population across the world but, the earth in its form cannot change. The need for energy and its related services to satisfy human social and economic development, welfare, and health is increasing. Returning to renewables to help mitigate climate change is an excellent approach that needs to be sustainable in order to meet the energy demand of future generations. The study reviewed the opportunities associated with renewable energy sources which include: Energy Security, Energy Access, Social and Economic Development, Climate Change Mitigation, and reduction of environmental and health impacts. Despite these opportunities, there are challenges that hinder the sustainability of renewable energy sources towards climate change mitigation. These challenges include Market failures, lack of information, access to raw materials for future renewable resource deployment, and our daily carbon footprint. The study suggested some measures and policy recommendations which when considered would help achieve the goal of renewable energy thus reducing emissions, mitigate climate change and provide a clean environment as well as clean energy for all and future generations.

Energy is a requirement in our everyday life as a way of improving human development leading to economic growth and productivity. The return-to-renewables will help mitigate climate change is an excellent way but needs to be sustainable in order to ensure a sustainable future and bequeath future generations to meet their energy needs. Knowledge regarding the interrelations between sustainable development and renewable energy, in particular, is still limited. The world is fast becoming a global village due to the increasing daily requirement of energy by all population across the world while the earth in its form cannot change. The need for energy and its related services to satisfy human social and economic development, welfare and health is increasing.

**31. What is the magnificent perspective that needs to be maintained?**

   (a) Challenging the requirements of energy

   (b) Looking back to renewable sources to reduce the changes in climate

   (c) Looking back to non- renewable sources to reduce the changes in climate

   (d) Looking back to renewable sources to increase the changes in climate

**32. The word 'hinder' means:**

   (a) Persuade    (b) Hamper

   (c) Instruct    (d) Help

**33. What are Market failures, lack of information, access to raw materials for future renewable resource deployment, and our daily carbon footprint as used in the passage?**

   (a) These are the challenges that create obstructions to reduce climatic changes

   (b) These are the factors that are necessary for uplifting energy consumption

   (c) These are the names of various studies

   (d) These are the challenges that helps to reduce climatic changes

**34. What are the opportunities which are connected to renewable sources of energy?**

   (a) Fuel Security, Fuel Access, Political Development and an increase in environmental impacts

   (b) Market profits, abundance of knowledge and daily carbon

traces

(c) Market failures, lack of information, access to raw materials for future renewable resource deployment, and our daily carbon footprint

(d) Energy Security, Energy Access, Social and Economic Development, Climate Change Mitigation, and reduction of environmental and health impacts

**35.** 'Improving' in the sentence, "Energy is a requirement in our everyday life as a way of improving human development leading to economic growth and productivity." is:

(a) Adverb    (b) Adjective

(c) Preposition    (d) Conjunction

**36.** Why is energy required in our day to day life?

(a) Because it is helpful for controlling population

(b) Because it is helpful for the development of human beings that further leads to productivity

(c) Because it is helpful for digesting foods

(d) Because it is helpful for digesting foods

**37.** Energy is a requirement in our everyday life as a way of improving human development leading to:

(a) Reduction of environmental and health impacts

(b) Meet the energy demand of future generations

(c) Economic growth and productivity

(d) None of these

**38.** The main purpose of the passage is to:

(a) Inform    (b) Apologize

(c) Claim    (d) Praise

**39.** The word 'mitigate' means:

(a) Harm    (b) Alleviate

(c) Hurt    (d) Injure

**Ques (40-45): Direction** : Read the poem carefully and answer the questions.
Tyger Tyger, burning bright,
In the forests of the night;
What immortal hand or eye,
Could frame thy fearful symmetry?
In what distant deeps or skies.
Burnt the fire of thine eyes?
On what wings dare he aspire?
What the hand, dare seize the fire?
And what shoulder, & what art,
Could twist the sinews of thy heart?

And when thy heart began to beat,
What dread hand? & what dread feet?

**40.** Whom does the "he" used in the following lines refer to?
On what wings dare he aspire?
What the hand, dare seize the fire?

(a) Immortals    (b) Ironsmith

(c) God    (d) Tiger

**41.** Which of the following statements are false?

(a) Which immortal being could have created the Tiger

(b) Tiger's eyes are fiery

(c) Did the Tiger's creator have wings?

(d) No one was strong enough to create the Tiger

**42.** What the expression 'Could frame thy fearful symmetry' means?

(a) Could create the fearsome figure of a tiger

(b) Could have given symmetry to Tiger

(c) Could have made him so fearless

(d) Why he was made fearless

**43.** Name the figure of speech in the following line.
"Tyger Tyger, burning bright, "

(a) Oxymoron    (b) Alliteration

(c) Consonance    (d) Simile

**44.** Who has the poet addressed in the poem?

(a) Deep skies

(b) Fearful symmetry

(c) Immortal being

(d) Tiger

**45.** The literary device used in the following line is:
Burnt the fire of thine eyes

(a) Oxymoron    (b) Simile

(c) Metaphor    (d) Assonance

**46.** The conduction of debate in a language classroom is useful for:
(i) Acquisition of new words
(ii) Fluency practice
(iii) Acquisition of grammatical rules
(iv) Developing the ability to express one's ideas

(a) (i) and (ii)    (b) (ii) and (iii)

(c) (ii) and (iv)    (d) (i) and (iii)

**47.** Collection and organisation of ideas, sequencing, cohesion and use of vocabulary are subskills of ———-.

(a) listening    (b) speaking

(c) reading    (d) writing

**48.** A child is not able to pay attention in a language classroom and shows irrelevant and inappropriate behavior. Which of the following can be considered as the possible reason for this type of behavior of child?

(a) Dyspraxia    (b) Autism

(c) Aphasia    (d) ADHD

**49.** Authentic material can be used in the classroom:

(a) To expose students to real language

(b) To make the language learning experience more meaningful

(c) To make language learning enjoyable

(d) All of the above

**50.** Teachers can remediate for the student with language learning difficulty by:

(a) Focusing on individual progress with individualized instruction

(b) Providing notes that are summarized and simplified

(c) Initially, giving information as reading only, no writing

(d) Conduct extra classes for the student to 'catch up' with others

**51.** Which of the following is not the advantage of teaching by story telling students?

(a) Enhances a child's vocabulary

(b) Enhances speaking skills of children

(c) Encourage development of emotions and feeling in a child

(d) Makes learning easier

**52.** In language teaching, creative expressions develop the ability to assimilate the concept efficiently by building creative thinking skills. Which is the best method to develop creative expression among students?

(a) Write summary of the story that has read

(b) Write your experiences about the earthquake

(c) Write a letter for leave for two days

(d) Write an essay on - My Ideal School (in 100 words)

**53.** Which of the following statement does not follow the principle of language teaching?

(a) Enhance motivation to learn

(b) Create an active learning environment

(c) Maintain high expectations with

student

(d) Help students organize their knowledge

**54. Which of the following would be considered as the primary difference between language acquisition and language learning?**

(a) Fluency and accuracy

(b) The level of spoken expressions

(c) Accuracy and fluidity

(d) Fluidity and pronunciation

**55. Which of the following should be the main focus when evaluating student writing?**

(a) Accurate spelling and grammar

(b) Presentation of ideas

(c) Limited word count

(d) Use of proverbs and phrases

**56. A child has the symptom of repetitive behaviors like hand-flapping, rocking, jumping, or twirling. This shows the child is suffering from:**

(a) Dyslexia    (b) Dysgraphia

(c) Autism    (d) Apraxia

**57. Which statement is not correct?**

(a) The teacher who is providing remedial teaching must understand the learner's strength and weaknesses.

(b) The pupil needing remedial teaching are generally talented learners.

(c) Pupils needing remedial teaching are temporarily low academic achievers.

(d) Remedial teaching helps learner to develop positive attitude.

**58. The teacher can have a number of language activities connected with the topic such as oral drill, reading, sentence writing, composition, grammar, translation, language exercises etc. This example deal with principle of:**

(a) Oral approach

(b) Graded patterns

(c) Multiple approach

(d) Spiral approach

**59. Which of the following is considered for developing skills in language studies?**

(a) To explain the statement

(b) To read various literature forms

(c) To use language effectively in various forms in day-to-day life

(d) To write an article on language studies

**60. 'Pedagogical Grammar' means that:**

(a) Begin from form and move on to use

(b) Teaching through immersion

(c) All grammar teaching should be rule focussed

(d) Teaching grammar in context

## Mathematics

**61. The sum of twice a number and thrice its reciprocal is $\frac{25}{2}$. What is the number?**

(a) 7    (b) 6

(c) 5    (d) 4

**62. Find the wrong number in the sequence $5, 10, 17, 26, 38, 50, 65$.**

(a) 10    (b) 26

(c) 38    (d) 65

**63. The ratio of age of two boys is $5 : 6$, after two years the ratio will be $7 : 8$. The ratio of their age after 12 years will be:**

(a) $\frac{21}{22}$    (b) $\frac{15}{16}$

(c) $\frac{17}{18}$    (d) $\frac{11}{12}$

**64. If the diameter of a wire is decreased by $10\%$, by how much percent (approx) will the length be increased to keep the vol. constant?**

(a) $5\%$    (b) $17\%$

(c) $20\%$    (d) $23\%$

**65. The ratio of the outer and inner perimeters of a circular path is $23 : 22$. If the path is $5$ wide, the diameter of the inner circle is:**

(a) 55 m    (b) 110 m

(c) 220 m    (d) 230 m

**66. Find the value of $2.8 + (5.2 \div 1.3 \times 2) - 6 \times 3 \div 8 + 2$.**

(a) 6.45    (b) 4.55

(c) 8.45    (d) 10.55

**67. If the opposite sides of a quadrilateral and also its diagonal are equal, then each of the angles of quadrilateral is:**

(a) $90°$    (b) $105°$

(c) $120°$    (d) $60°$

**68. Find length of the arc whose central angle is $45°$ and radius of the circle is $28$ cm.**

(a) 11    (b) 22

(c) 33    (d) 44

**69. A man covered a certain distance by a train running at the speed of $50$ km/h and covers the same distance by walking back at the speed of $5$ km/h. If the whole journey took $5$ hr and $30$ min, then what was the distance (in km) of one side?**

(a) 18    (b) 20

(c) 25    (d) 30

**70. The curved surface area of a cylinder is $594cm^2$ and its vol is $1336.5cm^3$. What is the height (in cm) of the cylinder?**

(a) 114    (b) 21

(c) 24.5    (d) 10.5

**71. Which of the following is not a characteristic of effective mathematics pedagogy?**

(a) Following strict time rules when introducing a new concept.

(b) Focusing patterns of students errors.

(c) Making connections with everyday experiences.

(d) Using various teaching-learning strategies for a single concept.

**72. Out of the following which is not the characteristic of reasoning in Mathematics?**

(a) Accuracy

(b) Certainty of result

(c) Originality

(d) Originality

**73. In the textbook of mathematics the content should be developed:**

(a) In the order of exercise

(b) In logical order

(c) In problematic order

(d) All of the above

**74. Which of the following aligns with the overall objective of achieving 'Mathematics for All' as per NCF-2005?**

(a) It should be acknowledged that mathematics is meant for selected few students

(b) Textbooks should only include problems of average difficulty

(c) Contributions of mathematicians from different region and different social groups should be highlighted

(d) Mathematically talented students should be groomed in isolation

**75. According to NCF 2005, school Mathematics takes place in a situation where:**

(a) Mathematics is a part of children's life experience.

(b) Children are forced to learn all concepts by daily practice.

(c) Children are listeners and the teacher is an active narrator.

(d) Children are involved in the chorus drill of formulae and pressure of performance in the examination.

**76. The step(s) describe the error analysis process is/are:**
(a) Collect a sample
(b) Record all responses
(c) Interview the student
(d) All of the above

**77. Gautam wakes in the morning at 06 : 20 am. After completing his breakfast, he starts to go to the market at 06 : 45 am. He arrives at the market 35 minutes before his friend Ananya who came to the market at 08 : 30 am. How long did it take him to go to the market after waking up in the morning (in minutes)?**
(a) 90 minutes   (b) 95 minutes
(c) 100 minutes   (d) 105 minutes

**78. The weight of one liter of pure ghee is 960 grams. The weight of 800 milliliters of ghee will be:**
(a) 798 grams   (b) 878 grams
(c) 868 grams   (d) 768 grams

**79. Tanuja drinks $250ml$ of water at a time. She drinks water seven times a day. How much water (in litre) will she drink in the month of April in 2022 ?**
(a) 52 litre   (b) 52.5 litre
(c) 53 litre   (d) 53.5 litre

**80. Two-third part of a number is 42 more than one-fifth of a number. What is the number?**
(a) 60   (b) 90
(c) 40   (d) 100

**81. Arun and Meena recently celebrated their golden anniversary and their daughter Seema's birthday. If the age of Seema is 18 years after her parent's marriage and her age at their golden anniversary is in the ratio 5 : 21, how many years after the marriage was Seema born?**
(a) 8 years   (b) 15 years
(c) 12 years   (d) 10 years

**82. Which type of test is usually used to check the ability of critical evaluation?**
(a) Essay type test
(b) Prognostic test
(c) Standardised test
(d) Diagnostic test

**83. Which of the following is true in context of evaluation in mathematics?**
(a) It is merely for giving scores
(b) It involves decisions regarding the effectiveness of the total instructional programme
(c) It does not supports improvement of instruction
(d) It means giving test

**84. The main purpose of the remedial teaching of mathematics is:**
(a) To develop the talents of the students.
(b) To change the behavior of students.
(c) Teaching outside the curriculum.
(d) Helping backward students individually.

**85. One of the objectives of teaching mathematics is that the student will able to:**
(a) Substitute appropriate values in the formula
(b) Get a higher position
(c) Develop the skill to use algorithms in problems solving
(d) Follow the correct procedure

**86. What is the mean of the range and median of the given data?**
$11, 16, 14, 7, 11, 23, 10, 30, 20, 33, 19, 12, 17, 14$
(a) 25.5   (b) 20.5
(c) 24   (d) 19

**87. How many lines of symmetry does a Rhombus have?**
(a) 1   (b) 2
(c) 3   (d) 4

**88. Study the following pattern**
$9 \times 9 + 7 = 88$
$98 \times 9 + 6 = 888$
$987 \times 9 + 5 = 8888 \dots \dots$ What is
$987654 \times 9 + 2?$
(a) 88888   (b) 888888 A
(c) 8888888   (d) 8898988

**89. Let $x$ be the least number which when divided by $8, 12, 20, 28, 35$ leaves a remainder 5 in each case. What is the sum of digits of $x$ ?**
(a) 11   (b) 14
(c) 15   (d) 17

**90. The twice of a number when added to 15 gives 121.When the digits of this number is reversed, then the twice of new number formed is greater than the original number by a. Then the square of a is:**

(a) 256   (b) 289
(c) 324   (d) 361



**91. Bipinnaria is the larval stage of:**
(a) Coelenterata
(b) Mollusca
(c) Echinodermata
(d) Hemichordata

**92. The application of water-soluble fertilizers through irrigation water is known as?**
(a) Fertigation
(b) Foliar application
(c) Injection into soil
(d) Aerial application

**93. _____ was discovered by the Scottish physician Daniel Rutherford in 1772.**
(a) Helium   (b) Hydrogen
(c) Chlorine   (d) Nitrogen

**94. Which of the following hormones is associated with the Stomatal movement?**
(a) Auxin   (b) Gibberellins
(c) Cytokinin   (d) Abscisic acid

**95. Name the excretory products in plants?**
(a) Carbon dioxide
(b) Water vapour
(c) Oxygen
(d) All of the above

**96. Which of the following foods can be eaten both raw and cooked?**
(a) Cabbage and Carrot
(b) Broccoli and Rajma
(c) Spinach and Potato
(d) Chilly and Brinjal

**97. For vermicomposting, this species of earthworm is not apt:**
(a) Perionyx excavatus
(b) Pheretima posthuma
(c) Eudrilus eugeniae
(d) Eisenia fetidae

**98. Which of the following limits the number of trophic levels in a food chain?**
(a) Deficient food supply
(b) Polluted air
(c) Decrease in the available energy at higher trophic levels
(d) Parasitic organisms

**99. Which of the following is not an insectivorous plant?**

(a) Drosera

(b) Venus Flytrap

(c) Nepenthes

(d) Dischidia

**100.** The Haryana canal and Drainage Act, was passed in which year for providing all the water irrigation services?

(a) 1970      (b) 1971

(c) 1972      (d) 1974

**101.** What is called for the method of removing dust and other particles from water using filters?

(a) Filtration

(b) Sublimation

(c) Rainwater harvesting

(d) Evaporation

**102.** The group of diseases carried by insects is:

(a) typhoid, jaundice, dysentery

(b) mumps, measles, smallpox

(c) rabies, ringworm, scarlet fever

(d) malaria, filaria, yellow fever

**103.** The child looks at his/her environment and learns in a holistic or integrated manner. This statement justifies the _____ nature of EVS at primary level.

(a) Sensitive

(b) Interdisciplinary

(c) Primary

(d) Thematic

**104.** The teaching of important issues of water like its importance and usage comes under which of the following aspects of environmental education as suggested in the EVS syllabus?

(a) Food and nutrition

(b) Conservation of resources

(c) Problems of population

(d) Health and hygiene

**105.** Environmental education help us to realize:

(a) Environment conservation is Government responsibility

(b) Environment conservation is nature's resposibility

(c) Along with Government, environmental conservation is our responsibility as well

(d) All of the above

**106.** Which of the following is not a disadvantage of using project method in the teaching of EVS?

(a) Difficult to implement

(b) Requires skillful teacher

(c) Self-directed learning

(d) Tough to understand

**107.** Why is Environmental Education is more relevant to the primary classes?

(a) To make the children aware of their environment.

(b) Enable the children to understand their environment.

(c) To make them behave responsibly to protect their environment from degradation.

(d) All of the above

**108.** The following are the methods to teach EVS except

(a) Explaining through lectures

(b) Problem-solving

(c) Cooperative learning

(d) Guided enquiry

**109.** Which of the following is not a form of discussion?

(a) Debate

(b) Symposium

(c) Brain storming

(d) Interview

**110.** To introduce the concept of water scarcity nowadays, the EVS teacher usually asks "what if there will be no water on earth?". Which of the following can be the alternate way to present the concept of "water scarcity"?

(a) To ask them about different resources of water

(b) To ask them to observe and discuss the availability of water

(c) To ask them about the natural disasters due to water

(d) To ask them about the different usage of water

**111.** In an EVS class, the steps of the problem-solving method include:

(a) Analyse the problem

(b) Define the problem

(c) Evaluate the result

(d) All of the above

**112.** **Direction:** Radha uses travel tickets of different types. Which of the following concepts could be effectively discussed by using such tickets?

**A. The cost of travel by different means is different.**

**B. The cost of travel depends upon the fuel used by the vehicle.**

**C. We need tickets to travel by public transport from one place to another.**

**D. Understanding the reservation**

process.

**Choose the most appropriate option:**

(a) A and D      (b) A and C

(c) B and C      (d) C and D

**113.** Penalty for conservation of the provisions of the Forest Act is under:

(a) Section 3A    (b) Section 4A

(c) Section 12A   (d) Section 8A

**114.** One of the important pedagogical principle of environmental studies is:

(a) Maximum use of environment related books

(b) use of environment as learning resource

(c) Maximum homework to students

(d) All the above

**115.** The branch of science that deals with the institutions and activities of human society and studies the interactions of individuals as members of society is known as:

(a) Social science

(b) Educational Sociology

(c) Social studies

(d) Civics

**116.** Which of the following is the MOST appropriate critical question a teacher can ask while teaching the topic of 'People and Environment'?

(a) Define environment?

(b) Are people affected by their environment?

(c) What are the features of environment?

(d) How will the earth be if there are no forests at all?

**117.** While teaching the topic on 'Water' in her EVS classroom, Anjali organizes role-play on different sources of water and individual actions to conserve water. The activity is primarily aimed at:

(a) improving social skills of students

(b) breaking monotony in the process of learning

(c) ensuring active participation of students in the process of learning

(d) enhancing students' knowledge on sources of water

**118.** A teacher of Class IV told her students – "Ask some old people if there were plants they had seen

**when they were young but are not seen these days."**
**Which of the following skills is not likely to be assessed by asking this question?**
(a) Questioning
(b) Expression
(c) Experimentation
(d) Discussion

119. **Which of the following can/are tools of the trade?**
I. Paper doll
II. Puppets
III. Picture card
(a) Only II    (b) II and III
(c) Only I    (d) I, II, III

120. **Features of school-based assessment include _________.**
(a) term end assessment
(b) continuous assessment
(c) assisting special children
(d) educational aspects of development

## // Hints and Solutions //

**1(C).** The development process passes through different stages. Each stage of development has certain distinct and specific characteristics.
Later childhood is the time period from the age of 'seven to twelve years'. The signs of puberty usually begin to appear in this stage. It is also known as troublesome age, gang age, play age, etc.
Social tendency is the characteristics of later childhood as in this stage there is an increased capacity to appreciate the need for rules in life and in relationships.
Other Characteristics of late childhood:
• Increased logical reasoning.
• High Interest in science fiction.
• Use of analogies in explanation.
• Development of problem-solving skills.
• Powers of perception and observation become keen.
• Ability to exercise their own power of memory and imagination.
So, we can conclude that Social tendency is the characteristic of the stage of later childhood.

**2(B).** Importance of Understanding Principle of Development: It necessary for the teachers to understand the need and importance to study them.
• Knowledge of the development patterns for different age groups helps us to know what to expect of a child and when to expect it. We may often expect too much from a child too early. Your own experience in teaching will help you to understand this fact. For example. you know that trying to teach algebra to a III standard child will be a hostile exercise

The concepts are too complicated for the child to comprehend.
• It helps parents and teachers to give timely guidance to children as they grow from one stage to the other. whcn a child is showing an increased curiosity in things around, parents/teachers can facilitate this development by providing more opportunities. For example, answering the child's questions, giving suitable books to browse through, Iielping to observe letters, etc.
• It helps the teachers in effectively catering to the different learning styles and diverse needs of learners.
• Normal development pattern makes it possible for parents and teachers to prepare children ahead of time for changes that will take place in their bodies, their interests or their behaviour. For example, cliildren can be prepared for what will be expected from them when they enter school. Similarly, older children call be explained the reasons for physiological changes during puberty.
So, we can conclude that Understanding the principles of development of a child helps a teacher in effectively catering to the different learning styles of learners.

**3(B).** The very old debate in psychology is nature versus nurture. The debate centres around the question of whether human behaviour is the result of nature (heredity) or nurture (environment). There is a relationship between heredity and environment factors in determining development.
• The word nature is used synonymously with heredity . Nature refers to the biological predispositions which mark our inborn traits and abilities.
• The term 'nature' stands for what comes to children through genetic influences and heredity, i.e. it denotes the influence of factors inherent in the child himself from the time he is conceived.
• On the other hand, the term 'nurture' stands for the influence of the environment on child development, i.e. all the contextual factors that influence who we are, including our perceptions of early childhood, our social relationships, and the society around us.
• Nature refers to heredity , influenced by inherited characteristics of personality, physical growth, intellectual growth and social interaction.
• Nurture refers to the influence of the environment of all of those same things and includes parenting style, physical surroundings, economic factor and anything that can have an influence and development that does not come from within the person.
So, it could be concluded that the other name of heredity is Nature .

**4(D).** Socialization is the process through which communities transact or educate their members about the norms and values of society to be socially acceptable.
• Socialization is a process by which an individual becomes a member of society through a mechanism of interaction . Its purpose is to prepare individuals for future roles.
• Public library is a passive agency of socialization because here we are not interacting directly with someone but we follow the norms and learn how to behave in public .
So, it could be concluded that Public library is passive agency of socialization.

**5(B).** 'Jean Piaget ' , a swiss psychologist, is famous for his work on child development. He made a systematic study of cognitive development in his theory that is categorized in four stages.
The above-mentioned characteristics belong to the ' preoperational period ' which lasts around 2 to 6 years of age. In this stage, the child doesn't reason logically but begins to think symbolically.
Characteristics of the preoperational period:
• Egocentrism takes place.
• Develops the skills of language acquisition.
• Faces problem with the concept of conservation.
• Struggles with the idea of centration and reversibility.
• Learns to compare objects through external characteristics.
So, it could be concluded the above-mentioned stage of cognitive development is called the Preoperations period .

**6(C).** Lawrence Kohlberg , an American psychologist, has propounded the 'Theory of Moral Development' .
He has made a systematic study of moral development in his theory that is categorized into 3 levels and 6 stages .
He has studied moral development by posing moral dilemmas to groups of children as well as adolescents and adults.
The three-level of Moral Development is:
Pre-conventional Level:
• At this level, the child is not responsive to cultural rules and labels of good and bad, right or wrong but interprets these labels in terms of physical or hedonistic consequences of actions or in terms of physical powers of those who communicate the rules and labels.
Conventional level:
• At this level maintaining the expectations of the individual, family, group, or nation is perceived of value in its own right regardless of the immediate and obvious consequences.
Post-conventional Level:
• At this level, there is a clear effort to define moral values and principles that

have validity and application apart from the authority of the groups or persons.

- If young adolescents who join their teacher with strong beliefs in saying no to ragging and bullying are at the post-conventional level. As he believes in morals and values.
- In this stage, the social rules and laws get in conflict with moral principles.
- They agree to obey laws and social rules of conduct that promote respect and acknowledges their moral value.
- They obey laws and social rules that fall in line with these universal principles.

Thus from the above-mentioned points, it is clear that the young adolescent is at a post-conventional level.

**7(D).** The teaching method i s a way to put theory in practice with the help of principles, pedagogy, and management strategies. It helps the teachers to plan and present the lesson coherently. There are a variety of teaching methods that can be used by the teacher for teaching theory and skills in the classroom setting.

Project method:
- The project method of teaching is one of the problem-centered methods of teaching in which the curriculum content is considered from the child's point of view and is related to his needs and interest in the context of real-life situations.
- The Project method emphasizes active learning by association and mutual co-operation of a group of peers to complete a specific project effectively. It relates learning with real-life and promotes learners' active participation.

Heuristic method:-
- The term 'Heuristic' has its origin in the Greek word 'Heurisco' means "I find out'. In this method, learners are independent investigators. It is a problem-centered strategy that is good for developing scientific skills and scientific temper among learners.
- It has a distinguished difference from the project method where learners do their work in continuous observation and guidance of the teacher but in the heuristic me thod, no help or guidance is provided by teachers once the problem is identified.

Discovery method:
- The expression 'discovery learning' refers to those situations in which the learner achieves the instructional objectives by testing hypotheses and developing generalizations and with little or no guidance from the teacher.
- The effectiveness of discovery learning as a problem-centered method lies in the fact that it requires the individual learner to find out the solution to a problem.

Thus, it is concluded that Project, Heuristic, and Discovery all are problem-centered

strategies .

**8(C).** Intelligence refers to a set of different cognitive abilities to think rationally, act purposefully, resolve problems and deal with the demands of the environment.

To define intelligence more broadly, Gardner established several criteria for defining intelligence:
- the potential for brain isolation by brain damage
- its place in evolutionary history
- the presence of core operations
- susceptibility to encoding
- a distinct developmental progression
- the existence of idiot-savants, prodigies and other exceptional people
- support from experimental psychology
- support from psychometric findings

So, we can conclude that the above characteristics are the characteristics of Intrapersonal intelligence.

**9(C).** Noam Chomsky , the linguist who gave an explanation that children have an innate ability to acquire language . He put forth the innate proposition of the development of language. This knowledge is given to them by nature – the rules that govern language are part of a biologically based human language faculty. This is called the Language Acquisition Device (LAD) .

Some major points of his theory are:
- The rate at which children acquire words and grammar without being taught can not be explained by learning principles.
- Children also create all sorts of sentences they have never heard and, therefore, could not be imitating.
- Chomsky believes language development is just like physical maturation - given adequate care, it "just happens to the child".
- Children are born with "universal grammar". They readily learn the grammar of any language they hear.
- Children throughout the world seem to have a critical period , a period when learning must occur if it is to occur successfully, for learning the language.
- Children across the world also go through the same stages of language development.
- Chomsky's emphasis on our innate readiness to learn grammar helps explain why children acquire language so readily without direct teaching.

So, we can conclude that Noam Chomsky said that children have an innate ability to acquire language.

**10(D).** The term individual differences refer to the fact that people vary in many ways. People differ from one another in their physiological and bodily conditions, in their past experiences and background, in

their abilities, personality pattern as well as in psychological variables.

We Can Understand The Ethnic Individual Differences By The Following Technique/Methods:
- Value System: Each ethnic group has its value system, which they follow, such as truthfulness, transparency, honesty, compassion, and charity, etc. also there value system different among different ethnic groups.
- It is important to understand the difference in ethnic groups to know about their value system.
- Verbal and Non-Verbal Communication: Verbal and non-verbal communication is a direct method to understand the ethnicity of a particular group.
- Difference Learning Arrangements & Processes: It also helps to understand an ethnic group, and by that, we can compare them with others.

So, from the above points, it can be concluded that intelligence does not help in understanding the ethnic individual differences

**11(A).** Assessment is a process of collecting relevant information on student learning. It is an integral part of the teaching-learning process. Assessment is conducted in different phases of the teaching-learning process.
- Assessment process measures personality, attitude, cognitive, social functioning, and intelligence .
- Psychological assessment is the process of testing that uses a combination of tests or techniques to get an idea of persons and their behaviors, personalities, capabilities.
- Some assessments are conducted before the beginning of the teaching-learning process, some are carried out during the process, and others are conducted at the end of the instructional process.
- In the above-mentioned phenomenon, the teacher is collecting information about the intelligence, personality, and classroom behaviour of a student by using appropriate test and check-list, hence it is the process of assessment.

Therefore, it can be concluded that the above-mentioned process is called assessment.

**12(D).** Model of teaching enables students to engage in robust cognitive and social tasks and teach students how to use them productively. It provides comprehensive blueprints for the curriculum to design instructional materials, planning lessons, teacher-pupils roles, supporting aids and so forth. These are designed to meet specific objectives or goals . Helps in creating a proper teaching-learning environment, it ensures maximum achievement of instructional objectives .

There are five components of teaching

models:
1. Focus: Focus is the main point in a teaching model. It is an objective and specifies the reason for teaching a particular topic. The focus of the teaching model is related to instructional objectives which are achieved through the teaching-learning process.
2. Syntax : Syntax refers to the phase of stages or the sequence of activities. It explains the structure of activities involved in the teaching-learning process which are to be followed strictly.
3. Social System: It describes the role of students and teachers and the relationship between them.
4. Support System : It helps in making teaching-learning effective and refers to material such as audio-visual aids, articles, books, journals, etc. It also helps in evaluating teaching on basis of acquired knowledge.
5. Application: It refers to the use and application of models for specific objectives.

So, it can be concluded that all the given points are the elements of the teaching models.

**13(C).** Mental retardation refers to an intellectual disability characterized by low Intelligence Quotient (IQ) and impairments in adaptive daily life skills. It is one of the most well-known social problems.
- The mentally retarded are those whose normal intellectual growth is arrested before birth , during the birth process, or in the early years of development. The impact of this disorder may vary in different individuals, ranging from mild to profound.
- Morons are children with mild intellectual disability. They are educable mentally retarded individuals as they are capable to learn with appropriate help and guidance.

Characteristics of Moron Learners:
- IQ score of 50-69.
- Need limited support.
- Can't be diagnosed easily.
- Able to learn but learn slowly.
- Likely to be delinquent more easily.
- Educable upto normal level but at a slower rate.
- Restricted to unskilled or semi-skilled occupations.

So, it could be concluded that all of the following are characteristics of morons except they have stronger sex drives than the normals.

**14(C).** Learning Disability is an umbrella term that encompasses a variety of specific kinds of learning problems. Children with learning disabilities experience difficulty in learning and using certain skills namely reading, writing, listening, etc.
- Usually learning disability is not identified until they enter schools. A child with a learning disability has difficulty mastering one or more academic subjects, has normal intelligence, and is not suffering from any sensory impairment or inadequate instructions.
- Learning disability is an invisible disability. The child usually appears normal in every aspect except that his learning difficulties limit his progress in school .
- Learning disability is believed to be present if there is a 'substantial' difference between expected and actual performance based on intelligence, ruling out other contributing factors such as poor learning-teaching environment, second language, etc.

Educationally, learning disabled look similar to both dullers and backward children as:
- The backward child is also called a slow learner. The child is unable to cope with routine work normally expected of his/her age group . He finds it difficult to keep pace with the normal child in his school work.
- Dullers are slow in thinking and understanding. These are the learners with below-average ability. They have cognitive problems, language-related problems , auditory perceptual problems, visual-motor problems, and social-emotional problems.

So, it could be concluded that educationally, the learning disabled look similar to both dullers and backward children .

**15(C).** Inclusive Education means education for all children in school as It refers to the inclusion of all children in the education system, regardless of their differences and disabilities.
- It values the diversity, each child brings to the classroom and facilitates all with equal opportunities to learn and grow.
- Inclusive education improves the quality and making provisions of education for all.
- Inclusive education welcomes and celebrates diversity.
- It provides a provision to include disabled children along with normal children in a regular classroom environment.
- It refers to an education system that accommodates all children regardless of their physical, intellectual, social, emotional, linguistic, or other conditions.

So, it could be concluded that the type of education where teaching learning programme is imparted to children with special needs along with normal children in the same school is Inclusive Education.

**16(B).** Learning Disable is any of various conditions (such as dyslexia or dysgraphia) that interfere with an individual's ability to learn and so result in impaired functioning in language, reasoning, or academic skills (such as reading, writing, and mathematics) and that are thought to be caused by difficulties in processing and integrating information.
- 1963 In Chicago, psychologist Samuel A. Kirk becomes the first to use the term "learning disability" at an education conference.
- The term "learning disability" was at first used by Samuel Kirk in 1963 to refer to children with normal intellectual ability, but afflicted by a covert, brain-based disability that affected their learning.
- The term disability was a brilliant stroke for advocacy, as it put these children on par with others with overt disabilities, and allowed for legislation, policies, and funding to be established to help them.

So, Samuel kirk introduced the 'Learning Disable' word very first for the children suffering from various learning problems.

**17(D).** Learning styles represent those characteristics that determine and characterize a person's preferred approach to learning and its use in problem-solving. Different learners display different preferences in terms of their learning styles.

Divergence in 'learning styles' among learners may be attributed to thinking strategies adopted by the learner as:
- Thinking is the mental process of manipulating information to draw a conclusion or to generate ideas. It is a higher cognitive function that allows beings to produce thought.
- Thinking is a mental activity in the cognitive aspect which refers to the process by which one acquires knowledge through experience, thought, and sensory input.
- It involves seeing and observing things in an open-minded way and examining an idea or concept in a way to forms as many angles as possible. It helps in making logical connections between ideas by thinking rationally.

Thus, it is concluded that divergence in 'learning styles' among learners may be attributed to thinking strategies adopted by the learner.

**18(A).** 5E's Learning Model: In this model of learning, students learn in five sequential phases in order to have learning viable. The phases are Engagement, Exploration, Explanation, Elaboration, Evaluation.
- Engagement phase: In this, students are engaged in the classroom through different learning tasks . This learning task may be an activity, showing any surprising event, peculiar examples etc, where students will get an opportunity to relate their previous knowledge with

the existing ideas.

- Exploration Phase: In this phase, the students have an opportunity to get directly involved with the phenomena and materials . Involving themselves in these activities they develop a grounding of experiences with the phenomenon .
- Explanation Phase: The third stage is the point at which the learner begins to put the abstract experience and clarify their misconception through discussion in the classroom. You will explain the concept only after students have got the common experiences through collaboration.
- Elaboration Phase: This phase of this learning cycle provides an opportunity for students to apply their knowledge to new situations , which may include raising new questions and hypotheses to explore.
- Evaluation Phase: The fifth 'E', is an on-going diagnostic process that allows you to determine, whether the learner has attained understanding of concepts and knowledge .

So, we conclude that the above statement relates to the Engagement Phase.

**19(C).** Multigrade teaching refers to a teaching situation in which a teacher has to teach the students of two or more grade levels in the same classroom .

The major drawback of multigrade teaching is that it allows less individual attention as in multigrade classroom:

- every child has their own individual learning needs and styles.
- every child is unique that's why no teaching method will be applicable to all.
- every child brings a wide range of aptitudes, developmental stages, experiences, etc.
- every child differs from the others on psychological aspects such as intelligence, personality, etc.

So, addressing those needs of different level students of different grades simultaneously , is the most important issue of multigrade teaching.

So, it could be concluded that the major drawback of multigrade teaching is that it allows less individual attention.

**20(D).** Emotions are a complex pattern of arousal, subjective feeling, and cognitive interpretation. Emotions, as we experience them, move us internally, and this process involves physiological as well as psychological reactions. Emotion is a subjective feeling and the experience of emotions varies from person to person.

Characteristics of emotions

- Affection plays a key role in emotions. Every experience has three modes – cognition, affection, and conation. It is the affection mode of mind that dominates the emotion.
- Emotions accompany instincts.

Emotions occur when associated with some instinct or biological drive.

- Emotions have a hedonic tone. Emotions are accompanied by pleasure or pleasantness. But they give us pain also.
- Universal acceptance. Emotions are found in everybody. There are no exceptions. They are found in young and old.
- Varying intensity. The expression of emotion and its intensity may vary from person to person based on levels of education, training, and intelligence.
- Emotions have a wide range of degrees. Emotions are aroused at all stages of mental development. An emotion can last for a very short moment but it can persist for a long time also.
- Emotions and reasoning do not go together. During emotional outbursts, thinking and reasoning power is decreased.

So, we can conclude that emotions and reasoning go together statement is not the characteristics of emotions.

**21(C).** Motivation has been mainly termed as a factor that drives or pushes one in a certain direction or to behave in a certain way. Motivation can be termed as a driving force or it can also be stated as a process that starts and drives various activities, whether physical or psychological.

The cognitive perspective of motivation:- This perspective states that "motivation is a result of people's thoughts, beliefs, expectations, and goals". Thus, a student will be motivated to study for examination based on his/ her expectation whether studying will lead to obtaining good marks in the examination.

- Cognitive behaviour represents another approach to understanding the effects of learning on the instigation of behaviour. In the process of learning that particular behaviours can lead to particular goals, expectations about the goals are established and the goals acquire values.
- Individuals are more likely to work on a certain task or towards achieving a certain goal when they are intrinsically motivated as opposed to extrinsically motivated. And it may so happen that attempts to increase extrinsic motivation may lead to a decrease in intrinsic motivation.
- Encouraging students to "try, try again" when they run into difficulty on challenging tasks is a consistent teaching practice.
- In this practice, the teacher is motivating or encouraging students to try again and again when they encounter challenging tasks.

Thus, it is concluded that encouraging students to "try, try again" when they run into difficulty on challenging tasks teaching practices is consistent with the cognitive

perspective of motivation.

**22(D).** Learning may be defined as " any relatively permanent change in behaviour or behavioural potential produced by experience ". Learning is not a mere addition to the knowledge or acquisition of facts and skills through drill and repetition. It involves reorganization of experience.

Factors affecting learning:

Physiological Factors:

- Among the organic factors considered to cause learning problems are genetics, brain injury. biochemical imbalances, intake of toxic substances like lead, oxygen deprivation, infectious diseases, drug intoxication, malnutrition and congenital defects. While considering these as factors influencing learning, it may be mentioned that attempts to correlate specific physiological factors with learning problems are not successful.
- Unless the body is physiologically mature and ready, academic learning cannot take place.

Psychological Factors:

- Several psychological factors such as intelligence, personality, attitude, interest, and aptitude have considerable influence on the learning of a child.

Socio-emotional Factors:

- The family the child belongs to has a considerable influence on the learning. Family factors such as child-rearing practices, reward and punishment, the scope for freedom and independence in activities, play and study facilities, the ambitiousness of the parents, disorganization and discord among members, degree of maturity expected of the boy or the girl child, birth position such as eldest, youngest or single child have their definite influence on learning.
- Working mothers who also experience marital discord are not only physically absent from their children, they are also emotionally absent. Learner from such a home is usually found self-absorbed and inattentive.

Thus from above-mentioned points, it is clear that the physical and emotional health of children plays an important role in their learning.

**23(D).** Learning curve is a graphic representation of how learning takes place in a particular situation. In all types of learning situations, the course of learning can be depicted and described graphically by drawing learning curves against the x and y-axis.

When students are given an opportunity to discuss a problem in groups, their learning curve becomes better as discussion is a teaching methodology which facilitates meaningful learning by emphasizing upon:

- Sharing ideas and experiences with peers and teachers.

- Learning through meaningful interaction in group settings.
- Looking at any issues from different angles and points of view.
- Developing a democratic way of thinking and the spirit of tolerance.
- Increasing the maximum participation of students in the learning process.

So, it could be concluded that when students are given an opportunity to discuss a problem in groups, their learning curve becomes better.

**24(B).** Ashok is very fond of playing cricket and he is very good at it too. He is the captain of his college team. He spends long hours playing or watching cricket and never gets tired or bored. Motivation personal factor is affecting the learning in this example.

Ashok is intrinsically motivated i.e. he derives internal satisfaction from the game. Intrinsic motivation is closely related to one's need for self-fulfillment, and achievement.

These needs impel us to become better by learning more, interacting with our environment, and developing ourselves.

Learning is most effective when there is intrinsic motivation - a desire to learn from within, which finds satisfaction in the achievement itself and does not bother about other factors.

Thus, it is concluded motivation is the personal factor that affects learning in the given example.

**25(D).** Learning is a comprehensive process that refers to a change in behavior, knowledge and skills as a result of practice and experience. There are many factors that affect learning.

**Factors Affecting Learning:**

**Environmental factors affecting learning:**

The phrase "social environment" describes how a classroom environment affects or encourages interactions between young children, instructors, and family members.

A well-designed social environment fosters positive peer relationships, promotes pleasant interactions between adults and children, and allows adults to assist children in achieving their social objectives.

**Personal factors affecting learning:**

Personal factors are the elements of one's personality that limit or enhance the ways that one learns and thinks.

Personal factors that affect learning include Physical health, Age and maturation, Emotional conditions, Interest and motivation, Readiness and willingness, etc.

**Social factors affecting learning:**

Regardless of the differences, most students learn best when they live in a culture that values not just education but understanding the material well.

So students should be encouraged to question and test concepts when they are learning and not on cultural backgrounds.

**26(B).** Administering standardized IQ tests is not an example of scaffolding.

**Scaffolding:** It is the help or motivation that is provided by MKO to that child. For example, help when they make the assignment, teaching them (helping them with) the correct way of taking notes.

**27(A).** According to Vygotsky, child's language and thought develop independently of each other, then merge.

Lev Vygotsky was a Russian psychologist and a social constructivist. He has propounded 'Socio-cultural Theory' which emphasizes the role of social interaction in cognitive development.

Lev Vygotsky emphasized that the acquisition of speech is the major activity in cognitive development.

He believed that cognitive skills and patterns of thinking are the product of the interaction between the individual and the socio-cultural institution where the individual grows up.

**28(D).** Christina took her class for a field trip before starting a new chapter in the class and after coming back, she discussed the trip with her students. It may be connotated as assessment for Learning.

**Assessment for Learning:**

- It occurs during, rather than after, the teaching-learning process as it has its primary focus on the ongoing improvement of learning for all students.
- This assessment is school-based and integral to teaching-learning. As a school-based activity integrated with the teaching-learning, CCE helps in doing away with examination-related fear, anxiety, or trauma.
- It is multiple evidence-based as no single strategy of assessment is capable of providing complete information about a child's progress and learning.
- It includes assessment of all aspects of students' personality, i.e., knowledge, performance, skills, interests, dispositions, and motivation.
- It is sensitive to individual learning needs as this requires identifying individual and specific needs of all children.
- It helps the teacher to probe what a child can or cannot do and explore the reasons behind the learning gaps.
- After observing the gaps and determining the possible causes, the teacher builds logical connections between the existing and the new knowledge to address learning gaps.

**29(A).** A science teacher has joined a rural school at the beginning of the academic session. He should use situational test.

**Situational Tests:** One gets a sample of how people respond to their day-to-day situations amid friends and families without the contrived atmosphere of a laboratory or interview. A situational test is a kind of compromise between a standardized test and observational methods of assessing personality.

**30(B).** Ritualistic and compulsive phenomena are common in early and middle childhood, especially in children who are autistic since they are resistant to transition and change. These children are ritually compulsive about certain routines and activities.

**Stereotyped Behaviour:**

- It is also known as stimming or self-stimulatory behaviours.
- It refers to repetitive, stereotyped, functionally autonomous behaviours seen in normal and special children.
- These behaviours include body-rocking, head-nodding, flapping hands, feet tapping, eye movements and fixations, jaw-clicking, spinning objects, self-talk, etc.
- Psychologists also uses various terms to describe such behaviours, viz. 'abnormal stereotyped acts', 'mannerisms', 'motility disturbances', 'rhythmic habit patterns', 'ritualistic acts', etc.
- Identifying and addressing the underlying cause of such behaviours is necessary for the proper management of such individuals.
- This can be done through positive behavioural approach or an approach that rewards appropriate behaviour. This appropriate behaviour will be repeated and help in replacing the undesirable behaviour.
- So, considering the above-mentioned points, it is clear that stereotyped behaviours are usually observed in autistic children.

**31(B).** According to the passage, "Returning to renewables to help mitigate climate change is an excellent approach that needs to be sustainable in order to meet the energy demand of future generations."

It can be concluded from the above line that the magnificent perspective that needs to be maintained is looking back to renewable sources to reduce the changes in climate.

**32(B).** The meaning of the given words:

- Hinder: to make it difficult for (someone) to do something or for (something) to happen.
- Hamper: to prevent someone doing something easily.
- Persuade: to make someone do or believe something by advising or urging him.
- Instruct: to teach somebody something
- Help: to do something for somebody in order to be useful or to make something easier for him/her

Thus, it is concluded that hinder means to hamper.

**33(A).** According to the passage, "Despite these opportunities, there are challenges that hinder the sustainability of renewable energy sources towards climate change mitigation. These challenges include Market failures, lack of information, access to raw materials for future renewable resource deployment, and our daily carbon footprint."

It can be concluded from the above lines that Market failures, lack of information, access to raw materials for future renewable resource deployment, and our daily carbon footprint as used in the passage are the challenges that create obstructions to reduce climatic changes.

**34(D).** According to the passage, "The study reviewed the opportunities associated with renewable energy sources which include: Energy Security, Energy Access, Social and Economic Development, Climate Change Mitigation, and reduction of environmental and health impacts."

It can be concluded from the above lines that the opportunities which are connected to renewable sources of energy are Energy Security, Energy Access, Social and Economic Development, Climate Change Mitigation, and reduction of environmental and health impacts.

**35(B).** Improving is a adjective which means to raise to a more desirable or more excellent quality or condition; make better.

Here, improving is modifying our noun 'human development'.

Adjectives are words that are used to describe or modify nouns or pronouns.

**36(B).** According to the passage, "Energy is a requirement in our everyday life as a way of improving human development leading to economic growth and productivity."

It can be concluded from the above lines that energy is required in our day-to-day life because it is helpful for the development of human beings that further leads to productivity.

**37(C).** According to the passage, "Energy is a requirement in our everyday life as a way of improving human development leading to economic growth and productivity."

**38(A).** The passage provides us information regarding how world is becoming a global village due to the increasing daily requirement of energy, studies that have been done, suggestions, need of the hour and much more.

Thus, we can infer that the main purpose of the passage is to 'inform'.

**39(B).** The meaning of the given words:
- Mitigate: to make something less

harmful, unpleasant, or bad.
- Alleviate: to make something less severe.
- Harm: damage or injury
- Hurt: to feel painful
- Injure: to harm or hurt yourself or somebody else physically, especially in an accident

Thus, mitigate means to alleviate.

**40(C).** According to the given lines,
"On what wings dare he aspire?
What the hand, dare seize the fire?"
The poet is questioning that whether the creator of the Tiger had wings or whose hands were so daring to create the Tiger?
In the previous stanza poet stated "What immortal hand or eye"
The immortal being referred to God.
Thus, from all the points given above, we can infer that the "he" used by the poet refers to "God".

**41(D).** The statement 'No one was strong enough to create the Tiger' is incorrect.
The whole poem talks about the Tiger and Its creator.

**42(A).** The poet addresses the Tiger and asks him various rhetorical questions to express his marvel.
Here the poet is questioning the Tiger about his fearsome figure that poet elaborates in later lines.
Thus, the expression 'Could frame thy fearful symmetry' means 'Could create the fearsome figure of a tiger'.

**43(B).** As we can see that the letters t and b are repeated multiple times in the line.
- When words begin with the same sound and are placed next to one another are called alliteration.
- It's a literary device commonly used to make the poem sounds better and also to make provide a natural rhythm to poetry.
- Examples of alliteration: And the s ilken, s ad, uncertain ru s tling of each purple curtain

Therefore, the device used in the given lines is 'Alliteration.'

**44(D).** Throughout the poet he asks different rhetorical questions to the Tiger about his figure and his creator:
- Could frame thy fearful symmetry?
- Burnt the fire of thine eyes?
- And when thy heart began to beat
- Here thy and thine refers to the Tiger.
Therefore, the poet addresses the Tiger in the poem.

**45(C).** A metaphor is a figure of speech where two dissimilar things or entities are compared.
- The poet has compared the bright eyes of the Tiger to fire.
- Fire and eyes have nothing common but to emphasize the brightness of the tiger's eyes, the poet has compared it to

fire.
Therefore, The line; Burnt the fire of thine eyes? contains a metaphor.

**46(C).** When a teacher uses the debate as a framework for language learning, s/he hopes to get students to look at any issues from different angles, gather supporting evidence, engage in collaborative learning, delegate tasks, improve communication skills, and develop leadership and team skills - all at one go.

Co-curricular activities in language learning are those activities that are usually organized in the classroom to provide opportunities for students to develop their special talents and to creatively express themselves through various forms. These activities are like debates, discussions, etc.
- Debates are a great way to express and exchange ideas. They can help in improving language fluency and reasoning skills.
- Debates always help to develop essential critical thinking skills which help the learner to look at any issues from different angles.
- It is a learner-centered activity that refers to make learning enliven by engaging them in real activities. However, sometimes debates and discussions can end up being closed-minded long talks.

So, from the above points, we can infer that the conduction of debate in a language classroom is useful for fluency practice and for developing the ability to express one's ideas.

**47(D).** Sub-skill: A skill that makes up a part of a larger skill. The language skills of speaking, listening, writing, and reading is often divided into sub-skills, which are specific behaviors that language users do to be effective in each of the skills.

Sub-skills of writing:
- Writing accurately.
- Use of vocabulary.
- Use appropriate word order.
- Use good grammar.
- Know how to express a particular meaning using different grammatical forms.
- Benefit from the use of synonyms, antonyms, and other literary devices.
- Use cohesive devices.
- Be able to organize ideas.
- Use writing strategies such as writing drafts or asking for peer correction.
- Be able to structure a text into paragraphs and use devices such as thesis statements.
- Be able to write purposefully and meaningfully.

Thus, it is concluded that collection and organization of ideas, sequencing, cohesion, and use of vocabulary are subskills of writing.

**48(D).** Attention Deficit Hyperactivity Disorder (ADHD): It is a complex neurodevelopmental disorder that leads to hyperactivity in a child's behavior.
- The child who is suffering from ADHD will show irrelevant and inappropriate behavior i.e., he will be constantly in motion, tapping fingers, poking others for no apparent reason, talking out of turn, and fidgeting is often called hyperactive.
- These children also have difficulty in concentrating i.e., they would not be able to pay attention in class for long. So, they may not be able to complete the task on time and shy away from taking independent charge of doing tasks.
- ADHD leaves a negative impact on language learning as children can be easily distracted. Due to this, they are unable to learn and comprehend the language.
- They will continuously face problems like restlessness and impulsiveness. Their activities and movements seem haphazard which can be observable through their behavior in the classroom.

Therefore, it is concluded that ADHD is the main reason behind the irrelevant and inappropriate behavior of child.

**49(D).** TLM generally includes all the collections of things and objects which help the teacher and student in the learning process.
- Such material can be used to make the language learning experience more meaningful and to make it more enjoyable.
- It is an important component of the teaching-learning process which helps the teacher to make the teaching of a specific lesson/unit interesting.
- It is most important that while using TLM, a teacher should have to make sure that the material should be contextualized and fit to be used in an integrated manner.
- For example, to teach language to the students of class III, the teacher uses cartoons to teach language in class III, that will be more contextualized and relevant.
- It will also expose the students to real language which we used normally while communicating with others.
- The use of TLM in the teaching process makes the teaching-learning process more stimulating, more reinforcing, and more effective. TLM used to provide direct and hands-on learning experiences to the students.

Therefore, it is concluded that all of the above are correct.

**50(A).** Objectives of Remedial Teaching in the English language:
- To provide individualized teaching with intensive remedial support.
- To eliminate ineffective habits.
- To make learners learn better by giving additional help.
- To provide learning activities and practical experiences to pupils according to their abilities and requirements.
- To teach again the language items not properly learned.
- To arise learners' interest in learning with stimulating approaches.
- Help the pupils to get rid of their common or specific weaknesses.
- To transmit practical experiences to learners according to their diverse needs.

So, teachers can remediate for the student with language learning difficulty by focusing on individual progress with individualized instruction.

**51(B).** Storytelling is the best teaching method to develop morals, values, and cultural norms among children at the primary level.

To develop morals, values, and cultural norms among children at the primary level Storytelling is the best teaching method, Because:
- Stories are universal in that they can bridge cultural, linguistic, and age-related divides.
- Storytelling can be used as a method to teach ethics, values and cultural norms, and differences.
- Stories function as a tool to pass on knowledge in a social context.
- Stories are effective educational tools because listeners become engaged and therefore remember which also makes learning easier.
- Storytelling is used as a tool to teach children the importance of respect through the practice of listening.
- As well as connecting children with their environment, through the theme of the stories, and giving them more autonomy by using repetitive statements, which improve their learning to learn competence.
- It is also used to teach children to have respect for all life, value interconnectedness, and always work to overcome adversity which also encourages the development of emotions and feelings in a child.
- Children in indigenous communities can also learn from the underlying message of a story.
- It increases the child's vocabulary as they learn so many new words from the stories in different contexts.

So, we can conclude that story-telling does not enhance the speaking skills of students.

**52(A).** Creative expression helps children articulate their feelings and thoughts. They think critically about their world and practice visual communication.
- Stories are magic, they can create other worlds, emotions, ideas and make every day seem incredible. Students will express their ideas in writing the summary.
- While writing summary children have opportunities to write in their own language so their creative expressions will be increased. It will enhance the ability to use the language appropriately.

Thus, it is concluded that writing the summary of the story that has been read is the best method to develop creative expression among students.

**53(C).** Language teaching is the process whereby a child gains communicative comprehension or fluency over a language. It involves practice by learners where facilitation is provided by a teacher.

Principles of effective teaching-learning language:
- focus attention
- provide timely feedback
- enhance motivation to learn
- connect knowledge to the outer world
- help students organize their knowledge
- create an active learning environment
- balance high expectations with student support
- communicate your message in a variety of ways

So, we can conclude that maintaining high expectations with students does not follow the principle of language teaching.

**54(B).** The level of spoken expressions can be considered as the primary difference between language acquisition and language learning.
- As the learner will not be speak acquired and learned the language with the same expressions with precise intonations.
- A learner can speak the learned language easily with fluency and accuracy whereas it will be difficult for him to speak the acquired language with fluency and accuracy.

Thus, it is concluded that the level of spoken expressions would be considered as the primary difference between language acquisition and language learning.

**55(B).** Writing should be self-expressive and original. It should create unique ideas that are imaginative and innovative.

Presentation of ideas should be the main focus when evaluating student writing as:
- it will encourage children to exercise their creative minds by using their imaginations.
- it will help children to express their experiences and thoughts beautifully and to convey the information in the best way.
- it will develop creative writing skills which go beyond the simple academic or technical form of literature that attracts people.

Thus, it is concluded that the presentation of ideas should be the main focus when evaluating student writing.

**56(C).** Autism spectrum disorder (ASD) can look different in different people. It's a developmental disability that affects the way people communicate, behave, or interact with others. There's no single cause for it, and symptoms can be very mild or very severe.

Patterns of Behavior: Children with ASD also act in ways that seem unusual or have interests that aren't typical. Examples of this can include:

- Repetitive behaviors like hand-flapping, rocking, jumping, or twirling
- Constant moving (pacing) and "hyper" behavior
- Fixations on certain activities or objects
- Specific routines or rituals (and getting upset when a routine is changed, even slightly)
- Extreme sensitivity to touch, light, and sound
- Not taking part in "make-believe" play or imitating others' behaviors
- Fussy eating habits
- Lack of coordination, clumsiness

So, we can conclude that A child has the symptom of repetitive behaviors like hand-flapping, rocking, jumping, or twirling. This shows the child is suffering from autism.

**57(B).** Remedial language teaching is meant for the:

- discovery of causal factors of slow learning.
- development of areas left by regular teaching.
- development of positive attitude in learners.
- reteaching of incorrectly learnt skills by the students.
- development of particular skills left by regular teaching.
- identification of low academic achievers or slow learners.
- identification of the students who are facing trouble or need help.
- transmission of practical experiences to learners as per their diverse needs.

So, it becomes clear that the statement 'pupil needing remedial teaching are generally talented learners' is not correct.

**58(C).** Multiple Approach: The term "multiple" implies that one is to proceed simultaneously from many different points towards the same end.

- We should reject nothing except the useless material and should select judiciously and without prejudice all that is likely to help in our work".
- Teaching a language implies attacking the problem from all fronts.
- Say, for example, there is a lesson on 'Holidays' in the textbook. The teacher can have several language activities connected with the topic such as oral drill, reading, sentence writing, composition, grammar, translation, language exercises, etc.

So, we can conclude that the teacher can have a number of language activities connected with the topic such as oral drill, reading, sentence writing, composition, grammar, translation, language exercises, etc. This example deals with the principle of multiple approach.

**59(C).** In order to communicate effectively, it is important that one should be able to listen and read with understanding, speak with a degree of fluency and accuracy, and write effectively.

- These can be referred to as language abilities or language skills. Developing a skill can be done in the only way, that is by practicing and using language effectively in various forms.
- Practicing a skill regularly and rigorously with patience and perseverance makes an individual proficient in that particular skill. Language is a very important part of everyday life.

Using language effectively in various forms in day-to-day life is considered for developing skills in language studies as it:

- facilitates the learning process in a meaningful and productive way.
- making learning more interesting by bringing the class to the real world.
- encourages classroom interaction and helps in meeting individual differences.

Thus, it is concluded that using language effectively in various forms in day-to-day life is considered for developing skills in language studies.

**60(D).** Pedagogical Grammar: It is a grammatical analysis and instruction designed for language students.

- It is a description of how to use the grammar of a language to communicate, for people wanting to learn the target language.
- Pedagogical grammar is grammar in context to connect grammar points with real-life context.
- It focuses on how grammatical items may be made more learnable and teachable for meaningful learning.
- It is the study of the grammatical problems of learners or on a combination of approaches.
- Pedagogical grammar is the learning of grammar in context through use.
- Pedagogic grammars contain assumptions about how learners learn, follow certain linguistic theories in their descriptions, and are written for a specific target audience.

So, from the above-mentioned points, it becomes clear that Pedagogical grammar means that teaching grammar in context.

**61(B).** Let number be $x$ then its reciprocal be $\frac{1}{x}$.

According to the question,

$$2x + \frac{3}{x} = \frac{25}{2}$$
$$\Rightarrow 2x^2 + 3 = \frac{25x}{2}$$
$$\Rightarrow 4x^2 + 6 = 25x$$
$$\Rightarrow 4x^2 - 25x + 6 = 0$$
$$\Rightarrow (4x - 1)(x - 6) = 0$$
$$\Rightarrow x = 6, \frac{1}{4}$$

Value of number cannot be a fraction. So, the number is 6.

**62(C).** The series follows the following pattern:

$5 + 5 = 10$
$10 + 7 = 17$
$17 + 9 = 26$
$26 + 11 = 37 \neq 38$
$37 + 13 = 50$
$50 + 15 = 65$

So, 38 is the wrong number in the sequence.

**63(B).** Let the ages of the two boys be $5x$ and $6x$.

According to the question,

$$\frac{5x+2}{6x+2} = \frac{7}{8}$$
$$\Rightarrow 40x + 16 = 42x + 14$$
$$\Rightarrow 2x = 2$$
$$\Rightarrow x = 1$$

$\therefore$ Required ratio $= (5x + 10) : (6x + 10)$
$= (5 \times 1 + 10) : (6 \times 1 + 10)$
$= 15 : 16$
$= \frac{15}{16}$

**64(D).** Since the wire is cylindrical in shape, its volume $= \frac{1}{4}\pi d^2 l$

Where, $d$ is the diameter, $l$ is the length.

Also, $r^2 = \left(\frac{d}{2}\right)^2$
$= \frac{d^2}{4}$

Decreased diameter $= d - 10\%$ of $d$
$= d\left(1 - \frac{10}{100}\right)$
$= \frac{9d}{10}$

New length $= l_n$

New volume = original volume (given)

$$\Rightarrow \frac{1}{4}\pi\left(\frac{9d}{10}\right)^2 l_n = \frac{1}{4}\pi d^2 l$$
$$\Rightarrow \frac{l_n}{l} = \frac{10^2}{9^2}$$
$$\Rightarrow \frac{l_n}{l} = \frac{100}{81}$$
$$\Rightarrow l_n = \frac{100}{81}l$$

$\therefore$ % increase in length $= \left(\frac{\frac{100}{81}l - l}{l} \times 100\right)$
$= \frac{19}{81} \times 100$
$= 23\%$ (approx)

**65(C).** Let the radius of inner perimeter be $r_1$ and the outer perimeter be $r_2$.

So, $\frac{2r_2\pi}{2r_1\pi} = \frac{23}{22}$

$\Rightarrow r_2 = \frac{23}{22}r_1$

Now from the question, we have
$r_2 - r_1 = 5$

$\frac{23}{22}r_1 - r_1 = 5$

$\Rightarrow r_1 = 110$

So, the diameter of the inner circle
$= r \times 2 = 110 \times 2 = 220$ m

**66(D).** Given,
$2.8 + (5.2 \div 1.3 \times 2) - 6 \times 3 \div 8 + 2$
$= 2.8 + (4 \times 2) - \frac{18}{8} + 2$
$= 2.8 + 8 - 2.25 + 2$
$= 10.8 - 0.25$
$= 10.55$

**67(A).** According to question, we draw a figure of rectangle ABCD,

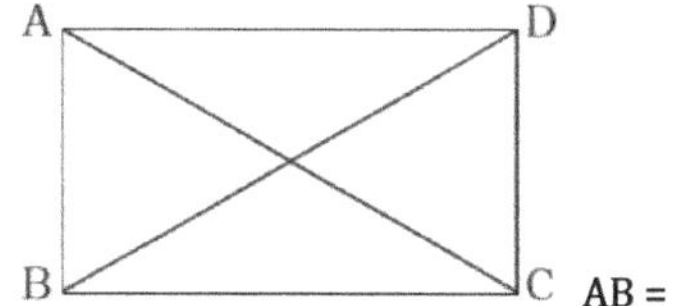

$AB = CD$
$BC = AD$
$AC = BD$
It will be a rectangle and each angle will be a (right angle) $90°$.

**68(B).** Given,
$r = 28$ cm
As we know,
Circumference $= 2\pi r$ for a central angle of $360°$
For a central angle of $45°$, length of arc
$= 2\pi r \times \frac{45}{360} = \frac{\pi r}{4}$
$= \frac{22}{7} \times \frac{28}{4}$
$= 22$ cm

**69(C).** Given,
Distance cover by the man with 50 km/hr by train.
Same distance return back with 5 km/hr by walking.
Whole journey time = 5 hours 30 minutes
As we know,
Time $= \frac{\text{Distance}}{\text{Speed}}$
Let the distance be $D$.
Total time = 5 hours 30 minutes $= \frac{11}{2}$ hours
Time taken by train + time taken by walking $= \frac{11}{2}$
According to the question,
$\Rightarrow \frac{D}{50} + \frac{D}{5} = \frac{11}{2}$
$\Rightarrow \frac{(D+10D)}{50} = \frac{11}{2}$
$\Rightarrow \frac{11D}{50} = \frac{11}{2}$
$\Rightarrow D = 25$ km
$\therefore$ The distance of one side is 25 km.

**70(B).** Curved surface area of cylinder
$= 2\pi rh = 594$
$\Rightarrow rh = 594 \times \frac{7}{44}$
$\Rightarrow rh = 94.5$
Volume of cylinder $= \pi r^2 h$
$= 1336.5$
$\Rightarrow r^2 h = 425.25$
$\Rightarrow \frac{r^2 h}{rh} = \frac{425.25}{94.5}$

$\Rightarrow r = 4.5$
$\Rightarrow h = \frac{94.5}{4.5}$
$\Rightarrow h = 21cm$
$\therefore$ Height of cylinder $= 21cm$

**71(A).** Mathematical concepts are abstract in nature and helping learners construct these meaningfully has always been a challenge for teachers. Teaching mathematics requires thinking about concepts, learner-centred pedagogy and diversified creative assessment.
It should be remembered that:
- Focusing patterns of students errors helps to understand the level of thinking and thought pattern of students and it is considered as an effective mathematics pedagogy.
- Making connections with everyday experiences helps students to understand basic concepts easily and is durable. It also helps students to visualize the topics. Hence, it is also a characteristic of effective mathematics pedagogy.
- One of the basic characteristics of effective mathematics pedagogy is using various teaching-learning strategies for a single concept according to needs and individual differences of students.
- There are no such strict time rules when introducing new concepts since qualitative learning is important and not quantitative.
So, f ollowing strict time rules when introducing a new concep t is not an characteristic of effective math pedagogy.

**72(D).** Mathematics is a branch of science which deals with counting, calculating, and studying numbers, shapes, and structures. The following are the characteristics of reasoning in mathematics:
- Simplicity: It is simple in the way that it involves problem-solving by following specific steps and nothing is rocket science.
- Accuracy: This property can be understood by the example that two and two are four in every part of the world, hence it does not change merely owing to perception.
- Certainty of Results: The beauty of maths is that every result is certain and can be derived using some logic and concept.
- Originality: It makes one to think independently and have novel ideas.
- Verification: Each statement in maths can be verified and if not, they are self-evident (axioms).
So, we conclude that subjectivity is not the characteristic of reasoning in mathematics.

**73(B).** Textbooks are predominantly textual with some images. Normally, content in a textbook is organized under chapters, units, and lessons. Most textbooks are written in factual or information giving style with little or no interactivity inbuilt in the text. Thus, most of them do not serve the purpose of self-learning materials for learners.
Organization of content in Mathematics Textbook:
- The textbook should provide authentic content knowledge;
- Contents in the textbook should be logical, coherent, and sequential;
- The language used in the textbook needs to be simple, and comprehensible by elementary students;
- Presentation of contents needs to be conversational and based on sound pedagogic principles;
- Concepts and propositions need to be explained with examples and illustration;
- There need to be a lot of activities, cases built into the textbook;
- Presentation of contents needs to motivate the learners throughout the process of learning.
So, we can conclude that in the textbook of mathematics the content should be developed in a logical order.

**74(C).** As Per NCF - 2005 , the teaching of mathematics should enhance the child's resources to think and reason, to visualize and handle abstractions, to formulate and solve problems. This broad spectrum of aims can be covered by teaching relevant and important mathematics embedded in the child's experience. Succeeding in mathematics should be seen as the 'Right of every child'.
Vision For School Mathematics:
- Children learn to enjoy mathematics rather than fear it.
- Teachers engage every child in the class with the conviction that everyone can learn mathematics and enrich them with examples of achievements and contributions of mathematicians from different regions and different social groups who created history.
- Children learn mathematics is more than formulas and mechanical procedures.
- Children see mathematics as something to talk about, to communicate through, to discuss among themselves, to work together on. and relating it to other subjects is essential.
- The infrastructural challenge involved in making available computer hardware, and software and connectivity to every school should be pursued.
- Children pose and solve meaningful problems.
- Children use abstractions to perceive relationships, to see structures, to reason out things, to argue the truth or falsity of statements.
- Children understand the basic structure of Mathematics: Arithmetic, algebra, geometry, and trigonometry, the basic

content areas of school mathematics, all offer a methodology for abstraction, structuration, and generalization.

So, contributions of mathematicians from different region and different social groups should be highlighted aligns with the overall objective of achieving 'Mathematics for All' as per NCF-2005.

**75(A).** The National Council for Educational Research and Training (NCERT) published a document called the National Curriculum Framework (NCF). NCF 2005 has been translated into 22 languages and influenced the syllabi in 17 states.

According to National Curriculum Framework-2005:

- The main goal of Mathematics education in school is the mathematization of the child's thought process.
- Children should learn to think about any situation using the language of Mathematics.
- The aim of teaching mathematics is to develop the child to think and reason mathematically, to pursue assumptions to their logical conclusions, and to handle abstractions.
- The school Mathematics curriculum should help the children learn to enjoy Mathematics.
- Mathematics takes place in a situation where mathematics is a part of children's life experience.
- Mathematics subject to be learned in order to perform daily life activities in a better way.
- Constructing the Mathematics curriculum we need to consider those topics Mathematics or themes, which would help children to succeed in their everyday life.
- The curriculum of mathematics should be introduced by connecting it to real-life situations and through its use in solving various life problems.

So, it becomes clear that according to NCF 2005, mathematics takes place in a situation where mathematics is a part of children's life experience.

**76(D).** Error analysis is a method commonly used to identify the cause of student errors when they make consistent mistakes. It is a process of reviewing a student's work and then looking for patterns of misunderstanding. Errors in mathematics can be factual, procedural, or conceptual, and may occur for a number of reasons.

The following steps describe the error analysis process, applied to mathematics:

- Collect a sample of student work for each type of problem.
- Have the student verbalize or think aloud as he solves the problems without providing any type of cues or prompting.
- Record all student responses in written and verbal format.
- Analyze the responses and look for patterns among common problem types.
- Look for examples of "exceptions" to an apparent pattern.
- Describe the patterns observed in simple language and the possible reasons for the student's problems.
- Interview the student by asking him/her to explain how s/he solved the problem to confirm suspected error patterns.

Thus from the above-mentioned points, it is clear that all of these are true.

**77(B).** Given,

Gautam wakes in the morning at $06:20$ am. Ananya came to the market at $08:30$ am.

As we know,

1 hour = 60 minutes

Gautam arrives at the market 35 minutes before his friend Ananya.

Ananya came to the market at $08:30$ am.

Gautam came to the market = $08:30$ am $-35$ minutes

= $07:55$ am

Time is taken by Gautam to arrives market = $07:55$ am $-06:20$ am

= 1 hour 35 minutes

1 hour 35 minutes = $(1 \times 60 + 35)$ minutes

= 95 minutes

∴ Gautam takes 95 minutes to go to the market after waking up in the morning.

**78(D).** Given,

1 liter of pure ghee = 960 grams

As we know,

1 litre = 1000 millilitres

1 litre of pure ghee = 960 grams

1000 millilitre of pure ghee = 960 grams

1 millilitre of pure ghee = $\frac{960}{1000}$ grams

800 millilitres of pure ghee = $\left(\frac{960}{1000}\right) \times 800$

= 768 grams

∴ The weight of 800 milliliters of ghee will be 768 grams.

**79(B).** Given,

Tanuja drinks water at a time = $250ml$

Total number of times she drinks water in a day = 7

Total number of days in April, 2022 = 30

Tanuja drinks water at a time = $250ml$

The total amount of water drinks in a day

= $(7 \times 250)ml$

= $1750ml$

$1750ml = \left(\frac{1750}{1000}\right)$ litre = 1.75 litre

She will drink a total amount of water in April, 2022 = $30 \times 1.75$

= 52.5 litre

∴ She will drink 52.5 litre of water in the month of April in 2022.

**80(B).** Given,

Two-third part of a number = 42 more than one-fifth of a number

Let, the number = $x$

According to the question,

$\Rightarrow \left(\frac{2}{3}\right)x = \left(\frac{1}{5}\right)x + 42$

$\Rightarrow \left(\frac{2}{3}\right)x - \left(\frac{1}{5}\right)x = 42$

$\Rightarrow \frac{7x}{15} = 42$

$\Rightarrow 7x = (42 \times 15)$

$\Rightarrow x = \frac{(42 \times 15)}{7}$

$\Rightarrow x = 90$

∴ required number = 90

**81(A).** Given,

The age of Seema 18 years after her parent's marriage be $5k$ years

Therefore,

Age of Seema at golden anniversary of her parents = $(5k + 32)$ years

According to question,

$\frac{5k}{(5k+32)} = \frac{5}{21}$

$\Rightarrow 21 \times 5k = 5(5k + 32)$

$\Rightarrow 105k = 25k + 160$

$\Rightarrow 105k - 25k = 160$

$\Rightarrow 80k = 160$

$\Rightarrow k = \frac{160}{80}$

$k = 2$

Now,

Age of seema = $5k$

= $5 \times 2$

= 10

So, Seema's age was 10, when her parents had completed 18 years of marriage.

So, Seema was born 8 years after her parent's marriage.

**82(A).** Essay type test is usually used to check the ability of critical evaluation.

Essay type Test: The essay type test is known as the long answer test. Long answer or essay type tests are used to measure such learning outcomes that are complex rather than simple and higher-order learning rather than lower-order learning demanding understanding and reflection. Therefore, these are another variety of response construction type tests. The teacher critically evaluates the answer to essay-type tests.

**83(B).** A teacher of mathematics aims at making sure that his pupils learn mathematics and learn it well. The final test of a curriculum is its effectiveness in fostering learning. Every teacher has to find out the progress pupils have made towards accepted objectives. Note that evaluation:

- is concerned with the improvement of instruction.
- involves decisions regarding the effectiveness of the total instructional programme.

So, we conclude that the evaluation involves decisions regarding the effectiveness of the total instructional programme.

**84(D).** The main purpose of the remedial teaching of mathematics is helping backward students individually.

Remedial teaching: During learning, a child makes mistakes. It is the job of a teacher to help students to correct those mistakes after diagnosing them. The method is known as remedial teaching. It helps the teacher to provide learners with the necessary help and guidance to overcome the problems.

**85(C).** One of the objectives of teaching mathematics is that the student will able to develop the skill to use algorithms in problems solving.

**Following are the general objectives of teaching Mathematics:**

The students will be able to:

- Acquire knowledge of facts, concepts, theories, laws, principles, proofs of Mathematics
- Develop the ability to communicate mathematical ideas with precision and accuracy
- Develop a most inert and positive attitude towards Mathematics Aims and Objectives of
- Apply mathematical knowledge to solve real-life problems
- Develop the skill to use algorithms in problems solving
- Appreciate the contributions of mathematicians
- Develop mastery of algebraic skills, drawing skills, deducing interpretations, finding patterns, making connections, analyse, organise data, reasoning, critical thinking, etc.

**86(B).** Given
$11, 16, 14, 7, 11, 23, 10, 30, 20, 33, 19, 12, 17, 14$
Arrange the data in ascending order
$= 7, 10, 11, 11, 12, 14, 14, 16, 17, 19, 20, 23, 30, 33$
Range $= 33 - 7$
$= 26$
Median
$= \dfrac{\{(\frac{14}{2})\text{ th term} + [(\frac{14}{2})+1]\text{ th term}\}}{2}$
$= \dfrac{(7\text{ th term} + 8\text{ th term})}{2}$
$= \dfrac{(14+16)}{2}$
$= \dfrac{30}{2}$
$= 15$
Mean $= \dfrac{(26+15)}{2}$
$= \dfrac{41}{2}$
$= 20.5$
∴ The mean of the range and median of the given data is 20.5 .

**87(B).** Given:
A rhombus
A line of symmetry is a line that cuts a shape into half and both halves match exactly.
In the Rhombus ABCD

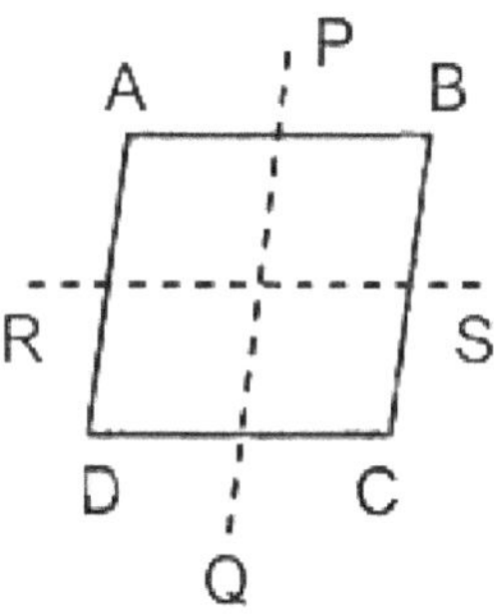


$PQ$ and RS are the lines of symmetry.
∴ The rhombus has 2 lines of symmetry.

**88(C).** Logic:
$9 \times 9 + 7 = 88$
$98 \times 9 + 6 = 888$
$987 \times 9 + 5 = 8888$
Similarly,
$9876 \times 9 + 4 = 88888$
$98765 \times 9 + 3 = 888888$
$987654 \times 9 + 2 = 8888888$

**89(D).** Given,
$x$ is the least number which when divided by $8, 12, 20, 28$ , and $35$ always leaves the remainder $5$ .
As we know,
Required number $=$ LCM of given number $+$ Equal remainder
LCM of $8, 12, 20, 28$ , and $35 = 840$
840 is the least factor which is divisible by $8, 12, 20, 28$ , and $35$ leaves remainder $0$ .
According to the question,
There is always remainder $= 5$
Required number $= 840 + 5 = 845$
Sum of the digits of the number
$= 8 + 4 + 5 = 17$

**90(B).** Let the number be x.
$\Rightarrow 2x + 15 = 121$
$\Rightarrow x = 53$
On reversing the digits, the number formed is $35$ .
According to question:
$\Rightarrow 2 \times 35 - x = a$
$\Rightarrow 2 \times 35 - 53 = a$
$\Rightarrow 70 - 53 = a$
$\Rightarrow a = 17$
∴ Square of a = 289

**91(C).** Bipinnaria is the larval stage of e chinodermata.
The larva is a stage in the development of many animals, occurring after birth or hatching and before the adult form is reached. These immature, active forms are structurally different from the adults and are adapted to a different environment.
There are different types of larvas like Tonaria larva , Muller's larva, Tadpole larva, etc.
The five classes of existing echinoderms are these:

1. Crinoidea - Body form is plant-like i.e. fixed. Larva: Dololaria
2. Asteroidea - Body form is flat & star-like. Larva: Bipinnaria, dipleura
3. Ophiuroidea - Body form is flat & star-like. Larva: Ophiopluteus
4. Echinoidea - Body form is globular & disc-like. Larva: Echinopleutus
5. Holothuroidea - Body form is long & cylindrical. Larva: Auricularia

**92(A).** The application of water-soluble fertilizers through irrigation water is known as Fertigation.
Fertigation is the injection of fertilizers, used for soil amendments, water amendments and other water-soluble products into an irrigation system.
Fertigation is related to chemigation, the injection of chemicals into an irrigation system. The two terms are sometimes used interchangeably however chemigation is generally a more controlled and regulated process due to the nature of the chemicals used. Chemigation often involves insecticides herbicides, and fungicides, some of which pose health threat to humans, animals, and the environment.

**93(D).** Nitrogen was discovered by the Scottish physician Daniel Rutherford in 1772.

- Nitrogen was discovered by the Scottish physician Daniel Rutherford .
- Rutherford discovered nitrogen by the isolation of the particle in 1772 .
- Nitrogen is the chemical element with the symbol N and atomic number 7 .
- The name nitrogen was suggested by French chemist Jean-Antoine-Claude Chaptal in 1790.
- Nitrogen is the fifth most abundant element in the Universe, it constitutes 78% of Earth's air.

**94(D).** Abscisic acid hormones is associated with the Stomatal movement.
Stomata are tiny pores present on the surface of the leaves.

- Massive amounts of gaseous exchange take place in the leaves through these pores for the purpose of photosynthesis.
- But it is important to note here that the exchange of gases occurs across the surface of stems, roots, and leaves as well.
- Since large amounts of water can also be lost through these stomata , the plant closes these pores when it does not need carbon dioxide for photosynthesis.
- The opening and closing of the pore is a function of the guard cells.
- The guard cells swell when water flows into them, causing the stomatal pore to open. Similarly, the pore closes if the guard cells shrink.

Abscisic acid (ABA) was discovered for its role in regulating abscission and dormancy.

- But like other PGRs , it also has other wide-ranging effects on plant growth and development.
- It acts as a general plant growth

inhibitor and an inhibitor of plant metabolism.

- ABA stimulates the closure of stomata in the epidermis and increases the tolerance of plants to various kinds of stresses.
- Therefore, it is also called the stress hormone .

**95(D).** The excretory products in plants is c arbon dioxide, water vapour and oxygen.
Plants use completely different strategies for excretion than those of animals.

- During the process of photosynthesis, plants utilize carbon dioxide and water for the formation of carbohydrates. Oxygen is formed as a bi-product. This oxygen is of no use to the plants and is an excretory product.
- Carbon dioxide is the waste product of aerobic respiration in plant cells.
- Plants get rid of excess water by transpiration .
- Thereby, the correct option is all of these.

**96(A).** Cabbage and Carrot can be eaten both raw and cooked.
People eat different types of fruits and vegetables.

- Different parts or all parts of various plants can be eaten as food.
- In different places, different parts of a plant are eaten.
- Some food items can be eaten raw whereas some need to be cooked before taking it.

Cabbage:

- Can be eaten raw in salads.
- Can be cooked as a vegetable.

Carrot:

- Can be eaten raw in salads.
- Can be cooked as a vegetable.

**97(B).** For vermicomposting, this species of earthworm is not apt Pheretima posthuma.
All earthworms are not used for vermicompost. Earthworms are classified as humus formers and humus feeders. Among which humus formers are good for vermicompost and they include Eudrilus eugenics, Eisenia fetidae, Perionyx excavators. Pheretima posthuma is not recommended for vermicomposting as it is a humus feeder.

**98(C).** Decrease in the available energy at higher trophic levels limits the number of trophic levels in a food chain.
According to the 10 percent law, the amount of energy decreases at each trophic level, and hence the number of trophic levels in a food chain is limited.

- The 10% Rule means that when energy is passed in an ecosystem from one trophic level to the next, only ten percent of the energy will be passed on.
- A trophic level is the position of an organism in a food chain or energy pyramid.

- Reymond Lindeman gave ten percent of the energy transfer law or Lindeman's trophic efficiency rule in food chains.
- The 10 percent energy is transferred from one trophic level to the next successive trophic level according to this rule.
- During energy transfer and respiration, the majority of the energy is lost.
- The maximum energy is in the first trophic stage.
- All ecosystems are characterized by two basic features- the unidirectional flow of energy and the cycling of materials.
- At each trophic level, most of the energy available is utilized for life processes and only ten percent of the available energy is passed on to the next level.
- Because only ten percent of the available energy can be passed on to the next trophic level, the higher trophic levels have substantially less energy content and the number of trophic levels in a food chain is limited.

**99(D).** Dischidia is a non-insectivorous plant from the family of Apocynaceae.

- They are epiphytes native to tropical areas of China and India.
- Insectivorous plants are those that derive most of their nutrition from the insects they trap and consume.
- They are mostly found in places where there is a lack of nitrogen.
- They are mostly found in wet, damp, humid, and acidic soil deficient in nutrients.
- Some of the examples of insectivorous plants are - Drosera, Venus Flytrap, Nepenthes, Pinguicula, and Genlisea.

**100(D).** The Haryana Canal and Drainage Act, was passed in 1974 for providing all the water irrigation services.

- Under this act, all canal, channels, and reservoirs constructed, maintained or controlled by the State Government for the supply of water.
- All drains, works, embankments, and structures, connected with drains, maintained or controlled by the State Government.
- All tube wells, field drains are maintained by the state government.

**101(A).** Filtration is called for the method of removing dust and other particles from water using filters.
Filtration is a process that removes particles from suspension in water. Removal of particles takes place by a number of mechanisms that include straining, flocculation, surface capture and more types.

**102(D).** The group of diseases carried by insects is: malaria, filaria, yellow fever
Mosquitoes (insects) are carriers of malaria, filaria and yellow fever.

- Malaria – Anopheles (female mosquito)
- Filariasis – Culex (female mosquito)
- Yellow fever – Aedes (female mosquito)

**103(B).** The child looks at his/her environment and learns in a holistic or integrated manner. This statement justifies the interdisciplinary nature of EVS at primary level.
Environmental studies or EVS is the study of the environment in the context of earth and living things. It is more concerned with the scientific attitude to explore, investigate, and develop an understanding of our natural, human, social and cultural dimensions of local and wider environments. At the primary level , children must be taught through an integrated approach so that they could explore the other aspects of a specific subject matter and could find the connection among them. At the primary level, we shouldn't teach students the concepts in isolation.

- The interdisciplinary nature of EVS means the teacher aims to develop the different dimensions of one's personality (social, emotional, mental, moral) by teaching one or two subjects together in a collective manner.
- It feels less burdened by the learners as they can learn more comprehensively and they will also able to connect two subjects or topics with each other in several domains.
- It helps to integrate knowledge from different disciplines by using a real process of synthesis.
- This approach tries to create holistic knowledge by integrating knowledge from different disciplines.
- For example, the child looks at his environment and learns in a holistic or integrated manner. It is justifying the interdisciplinary nature of EVS.
- This approach is learner-centred and in this approach, a learner gets ample opportunity to achieve unified knowledge, which is meaningfully drawn from different disciplines.
- Integrating the concepts or issues of social sciences with the concepts or issues of other disciplines like mathematics, general sciences, languages, etc. is an example of an interdisciplinary approach to the integration of concepts or issues of social sciences.

**104(B).** Environmental Studies are the study of the environment in the context of earth and living things. It includes the study of humans with other aspects affecting their life.
Conservation of resources: Resource is anything useful or can be made useful to humans to meet their needs. The resource that is directly available for use from nature is called natural resource, which includes

air, water from rainfall in lakes, rivers, and wells, soil, land, forest, biodiversity, minerals, fossil fuels, etc. Thus natural resources are supplied by our environment. These resources must be used carefully and judiciously so that they are conserved for the future.

In general, conservation means preserving and restore all kinds of objects getting to deteriorate. To conserve and protect the environment from harmful effects by natural and manual acts.

- Forest conservation: The conservation of forests as well as its resources is forest conservation which is one of the major content of EVS. Afforestation and reforestation are major steps taken for forest conservation.
- Water conservation: Conservation of water and water resources is water conservation. It is also one of the major content of EVS. Example, Rainwater harvesting.
- Soil conservation: Conservation of soil along with its resources is soil conservation. Different modern farming techniques like crop rotation, mixed cropping, terrace farming, etc are examples activity to conserve soil. hence it is also one of the major content of EVS.

So, we can conclude that the teacher is teaching the conservation of resources as suggested in the EVS syllabus.

**105(C).** Environmental education help us to realize a long with Government, environmental conservation is our responsibility as well.

Environmental education describes the interrelationships among organisms, the environment and all the factors, which influence life on earth, including atmospheric conditions, food chains, the water cycle, etc. It is a basic science about our earth and its daily activities, and therefore, this science is important for everyone.

Environmental responsibility is one of such aspects of our life that most people are aware of, but tend to ignore at some level of consciousness. Of course, there are activists who voice their concern and try to change this world for the better, making it more nature-friendly, but the number of such people is still too little to make a difference.

**106(C).** Self-directed learning is not a disadvantage of using project method in the teaching of EVS.

Project-based learning is a student-centered pedagogy that involves a dynamic classroom approach in which it is believed that students acquire a deeper knowledge through active exploration of real-world challenges and problems.

The disadvantages of project-based learning:

- Potentially Poorer Performance on Tests: Devoting too much time to problem-based learning can cause issues when students take standardized tests, as they may not have the breadth of knowledge needed to achieve high scores.
- Needs Trained Teachers: If supervising a problem-based learning activity is a new experience, you may have to prepare to adjust some and be prepared beforehand.
- Time-Consuming Assessment: Assessing a student's performance throughout a problem-based learning exercise demands constant monitoring and note-taking.
- Varying Degrees of Relevancy and Applicability: It can be difficult to implement and to identify a tangible problem that students can solve with the content they're studying and skills they're mastering. As some students might have difficulty understanding the method.

**107(D).** The NPE 1986 and the subsequent educational policies (NCFSE, 2000, NCF 2005) have given environmental education an explicit place in school education. As a consequence, today, the infusion of environmental awareness and understanding has become an integral part of the curriculum (formal or non-formal), with a view to enabling them to explore and understand their environment.

Aims of Environmental Education at primary level:

- It helps children connect with their natural and human-made environment and in understanding our dependence on the various components of the environment (biotic, abiotic, and human-made) which makes children aware of their environment.
- It helps children develop a holistic understanding of their environment including the socio-cultural environment, enables them to understand their environment.
- It helps children in maintaining a multidisciplinary perspective to understand our environmental issues or problems and appreciate the impact of our daily activities on its integrity, which later helps them protect their environment from degradation by encouraging them to take steps to conserve the environment.

To put the above in a nutshell, the teaching-learning of EVS aims to:

- Expose children to the real-life world (natural and socio-cultural).
- Enable them to analyze, evaluate and draw inferences about problems and concerns related to the environment.
- Help them understand environmental issues.
- Foster and nurture favorable attitudes and values towards the environment.

Thus, it is clear that all of the above are correct about environmental education in primary classes.

**108(A).** The teaching of environmental education involves both practical (hands-on) and theoretical (understanding) aspects. The major objectives of environmental education are creating awareness, changing attitudes, and bringing people into action towards environmental conservation and protection.

Lecture Method:

- Information tends to be forgotten quickly when students are passive.
- Lectures presume that all students learn at the same pace and are at the same level of understanding.
- Lectures are not suited for teaching higher orders of thinking such as application, analysis, synthesis, or evaluation; for teaching motor skills, or for influencing attitudes or values.
- Lectures are not well suited for teaching complex, abstract material.
- Lectures require effective speakers.
- Lectures emphasize learning by listening.

Holistic thinking or integrated perspective is the heart of EVS. Holistic education aims at helping children be the 'most that they can be', which amounts to the development of a child's intellectual, emotional, social, physical, artistic, creative, and spiritual potentials . That is why Lecture Method is not the correct method to teach EVS. Because EVS is a subject where we have to focus on children and focuses on "experiential learning" rather than "teaching".

So, Explaining through lecture is not the suitable method to teach EVS.

**109(D).** Interview is not a form of discussion.

The exchange of ideas between individuals is known as discussion. Discussion helps learners process the information rather than being only at the receiving end of the spectrum. It is an important aspect of the teaching and learning process. The discussion provides the opportunity to the students to help them express their opinions orally on a certain topic . The discussion doesn't need to always involve the presentation of new information but it can also involve sharing of experiences and ideas, solving problems, and promoting tolerance .

Interview- It is a structured/ unstructured or semi-structured form of conversation where one participant asks questions and other participants answer the questions. The questions are typically designed to obtain information from a person and hence negligible discussions are involved.

**110(B).** Here, the teacher is using the question what if there is no water on earth, this way children can imagine the importance of water in daily life.

- To present the concept of water scarcity in an alternate way, the teacher can ask the students to observe and discuss the availability of water.
- As the students will discuss the availability of water in their respective regional areas, they will become more aware of the water scarcity and how they should use it smartly.
- Discussion among peers about the availability of water will make the students responsible for its use.
- Also, the students will observe the water resources in their surroundings and how people are misusing or polluting them.

Thus, it is clear that to present the concept of water scarcity in an alternate way, the teacher can ask the students to observe and discuss the availability of water.

**111(D).** EVS class helps children to develop desirable attitudes, values, and behaviour pattern necessary for an environment-friendly lifestyle.

Problem-Solving Method:

- In this approach, teachers create a problematic situation for students and then assist them in perceiving, defining, and stating the problems in a fear-free classroom environment.
- It provides children with an opportunity to solve problems quite independently or through a guided approach by following systematic steps.
- It is a learner-centered approach that emphasizes the learner's active involvement in the learning process.
- Steps involved in the problem-solving method:
- Identify and define the problem
- Analyze and scrutinize the problem
- Anticipate outcomes and set subgoals
- Explore possible strategies/solution
- Select and implement the best solution
- Evaluate the result/outcome

So, we conclude that all the given steps are included in the problem-solving method.

**112(B).** Travelling tickets are used by people to go from one place to another. A travel ticket is obtained after booking a reservation.

It gives various information about our travel, i.e. date, seat number, time of arrival etc. The cost of different travelling tickets is different. The cost of travelling ticket depends on the type of transport used, i.e. busses, trains, planes etc. The cost of a travelling ticket also depends on the distance on travel, i.e., regional, national or international. When using public transport we always have to buy tickets.

Thus,

A. The cost of travel by different means is different: Correct

B. The cost of travel depends upon the fuel used by the vehicle: Incorrect

C. We need tickets to travel by public transport from one place to another: Correct

D. Understanding the reservation process: Incorrect

**113(A).** Penalty for conservation of the provisions of the Forest Act is under Section 3A.

Penalty for contravention of the provisions of the Act- Whoever contravenes or abets the contravention of any of the provisions of section 2, shall be punishable with simple imprisonment for a period which may extend to fifteen days.

**114(B).** One of the important pedagogical principle of environmental studies is use of environment as learning resource.

Environmental studies describe the interrelationships among organisms, the environment and all the factors, which influence life on earth, including atmospheric conditions, food chains, the water cycle, etc. It is a basic science about our earth and its daily activities, and therefore, this science is important for everyone.

Pedagogical principles in teaching-learning of EVS:

- Active participation of children is important in constructing knowledge. Opportunities should be given for observations using a variety of learning resources such as visits to parks, museums, water bodies and various places in the community. If learning occurs beyond the walls of classrooms, the quality of learning is better.
- Efforts should be made by teachers to relate the child's local knowledge to the school knowledge - this would discourage rote memorization and encourage developmentally age-appropriate learning in EVS.
- Children in early grades learn through a variety of ways, therefore opportunities should be given to explore, observe, draw, categorise, discuss/ speak, ask questions and enlist, etc. to develop various skills /processes.
- Pictures /illustrations play a very important role in EVS learning as these support the written material.

**115(A).** The branch of science that deals with the institutions and activities of human society and studies the interactions of individuals as members of society is known as Social Science.

Social Sciences constitute a broad field of knowledge and deal with human beings in relation to their social behavior.

- Social Sciences study the concepts or issues like culture, tradition, lifestyles, places and environment, power and authority, governance, economy, civic sense, etc. which have social implications.
- Social sciences are basically concerned with human relationships. The study of the nature of human society is the ultimate goal of all social sciences.
- Social sciences have their own/distinct content areas and methodologies for approaching and understanding knowledge. Some of the common methods used in social sciences for understanding knowledge are historical, thematic, participatory, non-coercive, quasi-experimental, etc.

Thus, it is concluded that The branch of science that deals with the institutions and activities of human society and studies the interactions of individuals as members of society is known as Social Science.

**116(D).** Critical pedagogy is a teaching approach which attempts to help students question and challenge domination, beliefs and practices that dominate. It helps students to achieve critical consciousness. As reflected in NCF (2005), critical pedagogy provides an opportunity to reflect critically on issues in terms of their political, social, economic and moral aspects. It entails the acceptance of multiple views on social issues and a commitment to democratic forms of interaction.

So, we conclude that the most appropriate critical question a teacher can ask while teaching the topic of 'People and Environment' is "How will the earth be if there are no forests at all?"

**117(C).** While teaching the topic on 'Water' in her EVS classroom, Anjali organizes role-play on different sources of water and individual actions to conserve water. The activity is primarily aimed at ensuring active participation of students in the process of learning.

Role Play Method: In a role-play, the student has to act out a person or character. It is an activity which is often taken up in classrooms to promote learning of different kinds. The following are its characteristics:

- Develops skill in leadership, interviewing and social interaction, group discussions
- Provides an opportunity for the student to put herself in another's place and to become more sensitive to another's feelings. For example, 'Sources of Water' can be taught by using this method to enable student's active participation.
- Develops skills in group problem-solving. It helps the student in identifying critical issues and to come to a neutral agreement.
- Develops the ability to observe and analyse situations
- Gives an opportunity to the student to practice selected behaviour in a real-life situation without the stress of making a mistake.

- Whatever they have learnt previously can be used in a different context by means of a role play.
- While learning a language, it gives a safe environment for students to rehearse what they have learnt .

**118(C).** Questioning Skills refer to one's ability to formulate and respond to questions about situations, objects, concepts, and ideas. Questions may derive from oneself or from other people. It arousing curiosity in the classroom. Note that:

Here, questioning, discussion and expression skills could be assessed, because by asking questions students will get involved in the discussion and will express their view regarding the answers of the old people.

Experimentation skill is not likely to be assessed here, because experimentation skills refer to be carried out experiments appropriately, using a range of apparatus and methods.

So, we conclude that experimentation is not likely to be assessed in the above situation.

**119(D).** The concept of the word "TRADE" , simply and effectively means a voluntary act done by and between two or more persons for the exchange of two or more items in between them, wherein all the parties to the transaction "believe" that the said transaction is for their benefit.

On the other hand, trade is a vast world in itself and it includes innumerable types of relations between 'persons' in the eyes of law. Trade can be executed in-kind versus kind (barter system) or in-kind versus currency (modem day trade).

Handicraft Trade: Handicraft items are made by hand, like Paper doll, Puppets, Picture card, pottery items, etc. , and the use of these simple tools generally artistic and traditional in nature. They include objects of utility and objects of decoration. Also Note:

An invaluable, and integral part of the Nation's heritage, handicrafts command importance, both cultural and economic. The handicrafts sector yields a number of economic, social and cultural benefits such as:

- Highly dispersed and centralized, spread all over the country in rural and urban areas,
- Highly labour-intensive, especially helping weaker sections of the society.
- High employment potential in relation to capital employed.
- High output to investment ratio
- Generation of subsidiary off-season employment
- Generation of foreign Exchange from exports
- High ratio of value addition
- Large scale involvement of women, weaker sections and minorities

So, we conclude that all the three are tools of the trade.

**120(B).** Features of school-based assessment include continuous assessment.

School-based assessment refers to the process of regularly assessing students by teachers in a school.

Therefore, we can say that the characteristics of school-based assessment include continuous assessment.

## Child Development and Pedagogy

1. Combination of Physical, Social, Emotional, Moral and Mental aspects refers to the principle of development:
   (a) Principle of Differentiation of rate.
   (b) Principle of integration.
   (c) Principle of Interrelation.
   (d) Principle of continuity.

2. After seeing a cat a child says it is a dog, because the child learn that dog has 4 legs. This view is a representation of:
   (a) Schema formation
   (b) Assimilation
   (c) Adaptation
   (d) Accommodation

3. Which one of the following is correct about the principle of developmental sequences of a child-
   (i) The development of a child spreads over the body from head to foot is called the Proximodistal sequence.
   (ii) The development of a child spreads over the body from the central part to the whole peripheral is called the Cephalo-caudal sequence.
   (a) Only (i)
   (b) Only (ii)
   (c) Both (i) and (ii) are correct.
   (d) Both (i) and (ii) are incorrect.

4. Which of the following teaching methods are adopted under progressive education?
   (a) Project-Method and Problem-Method
   (b) Project-Method and Interpretation-Method
   (c) Problem-Method and Q & A-Method
   (d) All of the above

5. Which of the following principle is not given by Lev Vygotsky?
   (a) Children construct their own knowledge.
   (b) Acquisition of knowledge can take place without social context.
   (c) Learning is mediated.
   (d) Language plays a central role in cognitive development.

6. Poorvi analyzes that the eyes and nose of her child are the same as her husband, according to your view how can it be possible?
   (a) This happened due to nutrition given to the child.
   (b) There is no reason, this is only a coincident.
   (c) This is due to a transfer of genes from the parents to the child.
   (d) Child live with their parents so that's why he is looking as same as his parents.

7. Direction: Consider the correct statement.
   (I) Gender discrimination is prohibited by the constitution of India under Article 15 (1).
   (II) Biological differences among men and women are termed as "gender discrimination".
   (a) Both I & II
   (b) Only I
   (c) Only II
   (d) None of these

8. According to Piaget, language development occurs rapidly during which stage?
   (a) Concrete operational
   (b) Formal operational
   (c) Sensorimotor
   (d) Preoperational

9. In assessment, self-assessment is _______.
   (a) assessment for learning
   (b) assessment of learning
   (c) assessment as learning
   (d) evaluation through learning

10. Direction: The following question consist of two statements, one labelled as Assertion and the other Reason. Examine both the statements carefully and mark the correct choice according to the instructions given below.
    Assertion (A): Mohan believes that learning with the help of someone is much more effective, so he helps their students in their learning by using various methods.
    Reason (R): Scaffolding is the term with defined the difference between learning by self and with the help of others.
    (a) Both (A) and (R) are true and (R) is the correct explanation of (A).
    (b) Both (A) and (R) are true but (R) is not the correct explanation of (A).
    (c) (A) is true but (R) is false.
    (d) Both (A) and (R) are false.

11. Anu is reluctant to do homework. Which of the following strategies can be used to overcome the problem?
    (a) Provide special coaching
    (b) Analyse the reason and take remedial measures
    (c) Neglect the problem
    (d) Inform parents

12. Direction: The following question consist of two statements, one labelled as Assertion and the other Reason. Examine both the statements carefully and mark the correct choice according to the instructions given below.
    Assertion (A): The class teacher engaged his students in various activities where students can get creative and use their intellectual abilities.
    Reason (R): Creativity and intellectual abilities do not depend on the heredity and environmental factor during the development of the child.
    (a) Both (A) and (R) are true and (R) is the correct explanation of (A).
    (b) Both (A) and (R) are true but (R) is not the correct explanation of (A).
    (c) (A) is true but (R) is false.
    (d) Both (A) and (R) are false.

13. Which of the following is not the characteristics of learning?
    (a) Learning is the change in behaviour.
    (b) Learning helps in proper adjustment.
    (c) Learning is the product of activity and environment.
    (d) Learning is a product, not a process.

14. In which context Piaget and Vygotsky's views are different from each other?
    (a) Piaget believed that the language development is done by social interaction and Vygotsky believed the language developed by own cognition.
    (b) Piaget believed that language is developed in the child by their own cognition and Vygotsky's believed that language is developed by social interaction.
    (c) Both (A) and (B)

(d)  None of these

**15.  A teacher can catch the thoughts of children towards morality by __________.**
(a)  telling the same story of H einz dilemma and ask their opinion.
(b)  By engaging them into different curriculum activities.
(c)  making them emotional to get their moral views.
(d)  punishing the students.

**16.  Which of the following are not the characteristics of the development of a child?**
(a)  Child develops many abilities through the interaction with the people.
(b)  Environmental factor doesn't have any role in the development of the child.
(c)  Both (A) and (B)
(d)  None of these

**17.  A teacher always helps his students to link the knowledge acquired from one subject area with the knowledge of other subject areas. What does it promote?**
(a)  To reinforce
(b)  Correlation and transfer of knowledge
(c)  Individual differences
(d)  Students' autonomy

**18.  "Development is a life long process", this statement refers to which principle of development?**
(a)  Principle of interaction.
(b)  Principle of predictability.
(c)  Principle of individual differences.
(d)  Principle of continuity.

**19.  A child is a social animal, he becomes a member of society after he is born. According to you, where does the child first get his social education?**
(a)  From school
(b)  From friends
(c)  From relatives
(d)  From family

**20.  A student makes errors. As a teacher you should not:**
**A. provide the student the correct answer.**
**B. allow the student to copy answer from other students.**
**C. ask the student to use an alternative method or redo it to find out errors on his/her own.**
**D. show the student where the errors were made and ask the student to redo it.**
(a)  B and C　　(b)  C and D
(c)  D and A　　(d)  A and B

**21.  Pupils can be taught to ask themselves questions about their learning in order to reflect on the content and process is called __________.**
(a)  Self assessment
(b)  Comparing
(c)  Hypothesising
(d)  Self-questioning

**22.  As per NPE 2020, age of 5 year child will move to __________**
(a)  Agandwadis
(b)  Constructive class
(c)  Preparatory class
(d)  Vocational class

**23.  "Right behavior consists of doing one's duty, showing respect for established or lawful authority, and maintaining given social order for its own sake" is explained in which stage of Kohlberg's moral development theory?**
(a)  Good boy - Nice Girl Orientation
(b)  The Universal Ethical Principle Orientation
(c)  The Social Contract, Legalistic Orientation
(d)  Law and order orientation

**24.  Motivation to learn can be sustained by __________.**
(a)  Focusing on mastery-oriented goals
(b)  Giving very easy tasks to children
(c)  Focusing on rote-memorisation
(d)  Punishing the child

**25.  Once a teacher learned that his South Indian English-language learners students consider it rude to ask the teacher questions because questioning implies that the teacher has done a poor job of teaching, he could generalize to which one of the following assumptions?**
(a)  If his English language learners are not asking questions, he needs to ask them why.
(b)  He should always quiz his South Indian students because they may not be able to understand.
(c)  South Indian students are always very polite, but their silence can mean they do not respect him as a teacher.
(d)  Teacher cannot make any generalizations about culture

and learning.

**26.  Pratiksha, who has just moved house; her household goods including her furniture, etc. are lying outside, all in a pile; she enters the living room, then the bedrooms, kitchen, toilet, etc. She examines the spaces available in different rooms and figures out where she would keep his beds, washing machine, dryer, sofas, etc. She suddenly notices the comer where she can keep the TV and the big table lamp. This phenomenon emphasizes that:**
(a)  Thought is independent of language.
(b)  Language is independent of thought.
(c)  Language and thought are interrelated.
(d)  Language is only one tool for communicating thoughts.

**27.  Assertion (A): Parents of Radha observe that the development of a child depends on many factors, such as physical environment, social environment, biological abilities, etc.**
**Reason (R): Jean Piaget's theory of the development of a child is based on physical environment and biological abilities, he ignores social aspects.**
(a)  Both (A) and (R) are true and (R) is the correct explanation of (A).
(b)  Both (A) and (R) are true but (R) is not the correct explanation of (A).
(c)  (A) is true but (R) is false.
(d)  Both (A) and (R) are false.

**28.  A child with visual impairment maximizes learning with the help of:**
(a)  Tactile inputs
(b)  Kinaesthetic system
(c)  Auditory system
(d)  Learning aids

**29.  What kind of pedagogy would enable a teacher to cater to individual differences among learners in her class?**
(a)  Standard and uniform
(b)  Totally centered around exams
(c)  Totally centered around textbooks
(d)  Engaging and contextual

**30.  Which of the following advertisements is not an example of gender stereotype?**

(a) A girl playing football in an advertisement for a sports shoe.

(b) A boy playing tennis in an advertisement for tennis racquets.

(c) A girl doing makeup in an advertisement for lipsticks.

(d) A woman being dropped by her husband to the office in an advertisement for a car.

## Language - I: English

**Ques (31-39): Direction** : Read the passage given below and answer the questions by choosing the correct/most appropriate options.

By all considerations, Ashoka is one of the greatest kings not only in the history of India but that of the whole world. In the beginning, like all other Kings, Ashoka was also given to kingly pleasures and military conquests but after the battle of Kalinga, a powerful Kingdom on the Bay of Bengal, Ashoka was completely transformed. In this battle, lakhs of people were slain, wounded, which produced a profound reaction on the mind of Ashoka. The era of military conquests was now over and an era of spiritual conquests as Dharma Vijay began. Ashoka was converted to Buddhism and devoted the rest of his life to spread and put into practice the teachings of Buddhism. For the welfare of his subjects, Ashoka planted trees along the roads for providing shade, built rest houses for travellers and established hospitals for human beings and animals. He had also opened a separate department for distributing charity to the poor.

Ashoka also followed the Law of Piety or Dharma in his personal life; he gave up hunting and curbed slaughter of animals for the royal kitchen. A new class of officials called the 'Dharma-Mahamatras' was created for enforcing Law of Piety among people. For spreading Buddhism, Ashoka also despatched missions to foreign countries like Egypt, Syria, Macedonia etc. Ashoka's son Mahendra and daughter Sanghmitra went to Ceylon where they became successful in converting the Ceylonese king to Buddhism. Ashoka also got the teachings of Buddhism engraved on many rocks and pillars in different parts of his empire.

Ashoka was the son of the Mauryan emperor Bindusara. He ascended the Magadha throne in 273 B.C., Buddhist records tell that he captured the throne after killing his 99 brothers, but this is hot supported by any other evidence. It seems certain that he had to contend with his elder brother Susima.

For his qualities and character, Ashoka as a king is still unparalleled in the history of the world.

31. Who is considered to be one of the greatest kings not only in the history of India but also for the whole world?

(a) Ashoka     (b) Bindusara

(c) Susima     (d) Mahendra

32. Which of the following things had been done by Ashoka for the welfare of his subjects?
A. Planted trees along the roads for providing shade.
B. Built rest houses for travellers.
C. Established hospitals for human beings and animals.
D. Opened a separate department for distributing charity to the poor.

(a) A, B and C

(b) A, B and D

(c) A, C and D

(d) All of the above

33. Select the most appropriate antonym of the the word, ' unparalleled ' as used in the passage(para 3)?

(a) Rare     (b) Unique

(c) Exceptional    (d) Ordinary

34. Read the following statements:
A. Ashoka got the teachings of Buddhism engraved on many rocks and pillars in different parts of his empire.
B. Ashoka was the son of the Mauryan emperor Bindusara.
Which of the following statement/ statements is/are true?

(a) A is true and B is false

(b) B is true and A is false

(c) Both A and B are true

(d) Both A and B are false

35. Identify the parts of speech of the underlined segment in the given sentence.
Ashoka as a king, is still <u>unparalleled</u> in the history of the world.

(a) Noun     (b) Pronoun

(c) Adjective    (d) Adjective

36. Which battle had transformed Ashoka and converted him to Buddhism?

(a) Battle of Plassey

(b) Battle of Panipat

(c) Battle of Kalinga

(d) Battle of Khanwa

37. Select the most appropriate synonym of the the word, 'contend' as used in the passage(para 3)?

(a) Engrave     (b) Compete

(c) Capture     (d) Ascend

38. What Ashoka had done for following the Law of Piety or Dharma?

(a) Planted trees along the roads for providing shade.

(b) Built rest houses for travellers.

(c) Gave up hunting and curbed slaughter of animals.

(d) Established hospitals for human beings and animals.

39. When was Ashoka ascended the Magadha throne?

(a) 373 B.C.     (b) 253 B.C.

(c) 273 B.C.     (d) 270 B.C.

**Ques (40-45): Direction:** Read the following poem and answer the questions by choosing the correct/most appropriate options:

Now we will count to twelve
and we will all keep still
for once on the face of the earth,
let's not speak in any language;
let's stop for a second,
and not move our arms so much.
It would be an exotic moment
without rush, without engines;
we would all be together
in a sudden strangeness.
Fishermen in the cold sea
would not harm whales
and the man gathering salt
would not look at his hurt hands.
Those who prepare green wars,
wars with gas, wars with fire,
victories with no survivors,
would put on clean clothes
and walk about with their brothers
in the shade, doing nothing.
What I want should not be confused
with total inactivity.
Life is what it is about;
I want no truck with death.

40. What does 'green wars' signify in the poem?

(a) Wars against the humen

(b) Wars against the environment

(c) Wars against the animals

(d) None of these

41. The overall tone of the poem is:

(a) Optimistic    (b) Bitter

(c) Challenging    (d) Gloomy

42. Which figure of speech has been used in the line?
in the shade, doing nothing.

(a) Alliteration

(b) Metaphor

(c) Personification

(d) Simile

43. Which figure of speech has been used in the line?
would not look at his hurt hands.

(a) Metaphor
(b) Personification
(c) Simile
(d) Alliteration

**44. What are the people urged to maintain?**
(a) Universal brotherhood and peace
(b) Universal brotherhood and war
(c) Universal war
(d) Universal death and war

**45. The poem tells us about:**
(a) Suffering and distress
(b) Arms and war
(c) Peace and silence
(d) Life and death

**46. Nitesh, a 4 years old child, understands grammatical rules without being told about the rules or without giving attention to them. This happens in a natural manner, thus it is an example of:**
(a) Language acquisition
(b) Language learning
(c) Language development
(d) Language competence

**47. Consider the statements (A) and (B) regarding grammar translation method.**
**(A) It focus on translating the sentence correctly.**
**(B) The role of teacher is to follow the lesson and role of students is to memorize the words.**
(a) (A) is true, (B) is false.
(b) (A) is false, (B) is true.
(c) Both (A) and (B) are true.
(d) Both (A) and (B) are false.

**48. Using gestures, expressions and actions is one of the techniques used to teach ____.**
(a) grammar
(b) spelling
(c) vocabulary
(d) pronunciation

**49. One of the following helps us to get 'a bird's eye view' of the book. Identify it.**
(a) Jacket
(b) Front page
(c) Blurb
(d) The preface

**50. Learning disabled children are:**
(a) Deficient in using potentials
(b) Low in intelligence
(c) Slow in activity
(d) None of these

**51. Remedial teaching is ___________**

(a) nothing but re-teaching.
(b) something where achievement is expected to be very low.
(c) need not be highly specific and need based.
(d) more like a crash course.

**52. Questions such as, 'What is the main theme of the passage?' is an example of:**
(a) Factual question
(b) Inferential question
(c) Comprehension question
(d) Hypothetical question

**53. In a language classroom, which skill, among the ones listed below, cannot be tested in a formal written examination?**
(a) Reading for information
(b) Meaning of words and phrases
(c) Reading for pleasure
(d) Inferential comprehension

**54. A $2\frac{1}{2}$ years old child picks up his sibling's book and looking at the pictures tells a story. The child is ________.**
(a) emergent student
(b) emergent reader
(c) emergent story writer
(d) emergent writer

**55. Which one of the following statements is true?**
(a) All formative tasks are meant for assessment.
(b) Assignments need to be given as classwork followed by homework every day to provide variety and practice.
(c) Formative assessment, to be effective, must be conducted only after teaching a lesson.
(d) While all formative tasks are meant for improving teaching-learning, some are used for assessment too.

**56. Dyslexia is associated mainly with difficulties in ________.**
(a) reading
(b) speaking
(c) listening
(d) writing

**57. From the following which one is the most important pre-requisite for language learning, whether first or second?**
(a) A structural-situational approach
(b) Skills-based instruction
(c) A multi-lingual approach
(d) Language rich environment

**58. Which among the following says that English should be continued to be used in official works of the Union?**
(a) Article 343 (1)
(b) Article 343 (2)
(c) The Official Language Act
(d) Three language formula

**59. What is the role of grammar in language teaching?**
(a) To acquire the ability to speak and write the language correctly.
(b) To acquire the ability to read 'poetry'
(c) To get higher position in the society
(d) All of the above

**60. English textbook at primary level should most importantly focus on ___________**
(a) age and interest of the learners and objective of the language.
(b) proper binding of book.
(c) attractive cover page and illustrations.
(d) grammatical forms.



**61. The cost of 40 coins of Rs 5 and 22 coins of Rs 2 will be equal to?**
(a) 2 notes of Rs 100 + 4 notes of Rs 10 + 4 coins of Rs 1
(b) 4 notes of Rs 50 + 4 notes of Rs 20 + 2 notes of Rs 1
(c) 2 notes of Rs 100 + 2 notes of Rs 10 + 2 coins of Rs 1
(d) 4 notes of Rs 50 + 4 notes of Rs 10 + 4 notes of Rs 2

**62. The perimeter of a square is double the perimeter of a rectangle. The area of the rectangle is 480 sq cm. Find the area of the square.**
(a) 162 sq m
(b) 72 sq m
(c) 12 sq cm
(d) Cannot be determined

**63. Tom's weight is 45000 g. What is his weight in kg?**
(a) 450 kg
(b) 45 kg
(c) 4.5 kg
(d) None of these

**64. Number 36005023 will be read as:**
(a) Three crore sixty lakh five hundred twenty three
(b) Thirty six crore five thousand twenty three

(c) Three crores sixty lakh five thousand twenty three

(d) Three crore sixty thousand five hundred twenty three

**65.** If 6 years is subtracted from the present age of Randheer and the remainder is divided by 18 , then the present age of his grandson Anup is obtained, If Anup is 2 year younger than Mahesh whose age is 5 Years, then what is the age of Randheer?

(a) 70 years     (b) 45 years

(c) 60 years     (d) 55 years

**66.** What is the difference between the face value of the number 7 in the numbers 4782 and 32170 .

(a) 630         (b) 712

(c) 0           (d) 770

**67.** Which of the following is the smallest fraction number?
$$\frac{6}{11}, \frac{13}{18}, \frac{15}{22}, \frac{19}{36}, \frac{5}{6}$$

(a) $\frac{19}{36}$       (b) $\frac{13}{18}$

(c) $\frac{6}{11}$        (d) $\frac{5}{6}$

**68.** **Direction:** Study the following data and answer the following question.
The following table shows the population information of three villages $A, B$ and $C$ .

| Populat ion% | Village | | |
|---|---|---|---|
| | $A$ | $B$ | $C$ |
| Men | 55% | 45% | 30% |
| Women | 30% | 35% | 45% |
| Childre n | 15% | 20% | 25% |
| Total Po pulation | 5000 | 6500 | 4500 |

**Find the ratio between the number of children in village $A$ and $B$ .**

(a) 27 : 16     (b) 26 : 18

(c) 15 : 26     (d) 5 : 9

**69.** If angles of a triangle are in the ration of 2 : 3 : 4 , then the measure of the smallest angle is:

(a) 30°        (b) 50°

(c) 40°        (d) 20°

**70.** A person crosses a $900\,m$ long street in 5 minutes. What is his speed in $km/hr$ ?

(a) 10.8      (b) 3.6

(c) 7.82      (d) 24

**71.** Sides of a triangle are $15m, 16m$ and $11m$ , then area of the triangle is:

(a) $31\sqrt{2}m^2$     (b) $41\sqrt{3}m^2$

(c) $40\sqrt{5}m^2$     (d) $30\sqrt{7}m^2$

**72.** If an 8– digit number $1862383A$ is divisible by 22 , find the value of $A$ .

(a) 6         (b) 4

(c) 2         (d) 8

**73.** If the time at present is $7 : 42\,am$ , what will be the time after 72332 minutes?

(a) $1 : 16pm$     (b) $2 : 24pm$

(c) $9 : 42pm$     (d) $1 : 14pm$

**74.** Which of the following statements is NOT correct with regards to the nature of mathematics?

(a) It is a subject in which previous knowledge has a greater influence.

(b) In mathematics there is no place for logical sequence.

(c) Mathematics is abstract in nature.

(d) Mathematics have its own language and symbolism.

**75.** Learning objective for fourth-grade students is given as:
"Students are able to order and compare two decimal numbers up to two decimal places".
This learning objectives refers to:

(a) Content goal

(b) Process goal

(c) Disposition goal

(d) Social goal

**76.** While teaching comparison subtraction, a teacher says, "Whenever you read keywords like 'more/less' 'increasing/ decreasing', 'exceeds', there is always subtraction." The teacher is trying to:

(a) Make mathematical language tough

(b) Make mathematical language easy

(c) Confusing students

(d) Teaching experimentation

**77.** A child having problems in addition is likely to develop problems in:

(a) Factorisation

(b) Multiplication

(c) Division

(d) Generalisation

**78.** For teaching the concept of volume of a cone, which mathematical manipulative should be used by the teacher?

(a) Geo board     (b) 3D models

(c) Dienes block   (d) Tessellation

**79.** Which of the following activities is most likely to build the concept of 'Area' among students?

(a) Geo board     (b) Graph paper

(c) Scale         (d) Thread

**80.** In which phase of 5E's learning model, students get chance to reflect on their knowledge?

(a) Exploration Phase

(b) Evaluation Phase

(c) Explanation Phase

(d) Elaboration Phase

**81.** The process of assessment in Mathematics includes the following except _____.

(a) concepts and procedures

(b) mathematical reasoning

(c) communication

(d) verbal skills

**82.** Which of the following is correct with regards to the purpose of the question bank?
I. They are used to evaluating learning process
II. Can be used for self-evaluation

(a) Only I

(b) Only II

(c) Neither I nor II

(d) Both I and II

**83.** Most effective teaching aids in mathematics is:

(a) Activity aids

(b) Projected aids

(c) Non-projected aids

(d) None of these

**84.** Which of the following issue(s) is/ are particularly relevant for planning of the mathematics curriculum?

(a) Use of new topics for enrichment of traditional ones.

(b) New knowledge of mathematics for adaptation at the primary stage.

(c) The developmental needs of the pupil, his/her intellectual development and capability of learning at different stages.

(d) All of the above

**85.** What is the biggest problem in learning mathematics for students?

(a) Lack of practice in solving mathematics problems

(b) Lack of interest in mathematics subject

(c) Fear about mathematics subject

(d) Teachers' attitude about teaching mathematics

86. **Direction: Consider the following statements:**
**(i) Accuracy and speed cannot go together**
**(ii) Accuracy and speed can go together**
**(iii) Accuracy and speed must be developed separately**
**Which of the statements given above is/are true?**
(a) Only (i)
(b) Only (ii)
(c) Only (iii)
(d) (i), (ii) and (iii)

87. **Out of following which statement does not show nature of mathematics?**
(a) Mathematics is the queen of all science.
(b) Its presence is there in all the subjects.
(c) Mathematics is more than computation.
(d) Its knowledge is only conceptual.

88. **A mathematical learning disability may occur due to all of the following except:**
(a) Cerebral dysfunction
(b) Emotional disturbance
(c) Behavioural disturbance
(d) Cultural factors

89. **If $15 - 15 \div 15 \times 6 = x$, then $x$ is:**
(a) 6
(b) 0
(c) 9
(d) 84

90. **What should come in place of the question mark '?' in the following number series?**
$32, 8, 64, 16, 128, ?$
(a) 32
(b) 36
(c) 34
(d) 30

## Environmental Studies

91. **Ragdoll and Somali are the breeds of:**
(a) Dogs
(b) Cats
(c) Elephants
(d) None of these

92. **Which of the following is a carnivorous plant?**
(a) Pitcher plant
(b) Venus fly-trap
(c) Sundew

(d) All of the above

93. **Which country is the second-largest producer of sugarcane in the world?**
(a) China
(b) India
(c) Pakistan
(d) Brazil

94. **The most effective farming method for returning minerals to the soil is:**
(a) Contour ploughing
(b) Terracing
(c) Crop rotation
(d) Furrowing

95. **Which substance gives heat and light after combustion?**
(a) Flame
(b) Fuel
(c) Combustion
(d) None of these

96. **The mountaineers carry oxygen with them because:**
(a) At an altitude of more than 5 km there is no air.
(b) The amount of air available to a person is less than that available on the ground.
(c) The temperature of air is higher than that on the ground.
(d) The pressure of air is higher than that on the ground.

97. **Pulses are a good source of:**
(a) Carbohydrates
(b) Proteins
(c) Fats
(d) Vitamins

98. **What is the collection of rainwater for use called?**
(a) Rain collection
(b) Rain water harvesting
(c) Rain digging
(d) Rain water pumping

99. **Which of the following insects is the carrier of grassy stunt pathogenic virus?**
(a) Red ants
(b) Pink ants
(c) Leafhoppers
(d) All of the above

100. **Who among the following did many experiments and found out many secrets about digestion?**
(a) Dr. Beaumont
(b) Robert Hooke
(c) Gregor Mendel
(d) Dr. Jonas Salk

101. **Match List-I with List-II and select the correct answer using the codes given below:**

| List-I (Plant) | List-II (Uses) |
| --- | --- |
| (a) Jamun | (i) Cough and cold |
| (b) Clove | (ii) Cure eyesore |
| (c) Babool | (iii) Controlling diabetes |
| (d) Tulsi | (iv) Toothache |

(a) (a) - (i), (b) - (iv), (c) -(iii), (d) - (ii)
(b) (a) - (ii), (b) - (iv), (c) -(iii), (d) - (i)
(c) (a) - (iii), (b) - (iv), (c) -(ii), (d) - (i)
(d) (a) - (ii), (b) - (iv), (c) -(i), (d) - (iii)

102. **The art of growing short plants is called as:**
(a) Bonsai
(b) Horticulture
(c) Topiary
(d) None of these

103. **What is the major advantage of three-tire vermiculture technology?**
(a) It can be applied to both solid and liquid wastes
(b) It cannot be applied to both solid and liquid wastes
(c) It involves chemical treatment
(d) It can degrade organic wastes

104. **Which of the following disease is spread by flies?**
(a) Cholera
(b) Typhoid
(c) Anthrax
(d) All of the above

105. **Carbon monoxide poisoning can be cured by:**
(a) Drinking lemon-water
(b) Eating butter
(c) Exposing the affected person to fresh oxygen
(d) Consuming multi-vitamin tablet

106. **Hamida is a teacher in primary school. She wants to develop the concept of water conversation among Class V students. Which activity is most suitable for this?**
(a) Creating a group of some students for group discussion
(b) To organize a debate

competition for this

(c) Encouraging students to participate in a painting competition related to this

(d) Getting students to travel to different sources of water and giving examples of how life is not possible without water.

**107. If you want children in your school to encourage them to take interest in a class in environmental studies, which of the following methods would be appropriate for you?**

(a) You should explain to the children about maximum environmental studies.

(b) The child should be instructed for different tasks in the classroom.

(c) Environmental studies should be linked to real life through different types of stories.

(d) According to the syllabus, the child should be read and asked to memorize it.

**108. The biggest goal and objective of teaching environmental studies is:**

(a) Human welfare and development of all organisms

(b) Understanding and preserving nature's work style

(c) To adjust to the environment and live a systematic life

(d) All of the above

**109. Teachers use teaching aids, because:**

(a) Some teachers are incapable of teaching on their own

(b) Students require some change while learning

(c) It is necessary to reach the students' level of understanding

(d) To use the updated technology of teaching

**110. Which of the following statements regarding teaching of environmental studies to the child is not correct?**

(a) This topic gives the child a chance to discover the events happening around him

(b) This topic helps children to memorize concepts and definitions of different facts

(c) It is a matter of a unified nature

(d) Child centric education can enhance environmental studies better

**111. If you are appointed as a teacher** of environmental studies in a primary school and you want that environmental education is necessary for everyone, what would be the most important reason for this?

(a) To give a green environment to the students

(b) Students need environmental education to make sports a place

(c) To develop knowledge and consciousness about the environment in students

(d) None of these

**112. There are different types of special needs and backward children in your school, which of the following types of education will you pay attention to while using environmental education?**

(a) Inclusive education

(b) Subject based education

(c) Disabled education

(d) None of these

**113. If you are a teacher of environmental studies in a school. So what would you not do with the following ideas while creating a group activity in your classroom?**

(a) Give everyone in the class a chance to work together equally.

(b) Make small groups to work.

(c) Boys and girls will not work equally.

(d) Will tell the children about group education how the work is done easily by staying in the group.

**114. If you are the headmaster of a school, then what should be required for conducting a class of environmental studies in the school?**

(a) Class based on the activities given in the textbook.

(b) Class based on rigid rules for children.

(c) Classroom based on overall activity.

(d) None of these

**115. Which of the following text book of environmental studies will be useful for the students?**

(a) Activities given at the end of unit

(b) Activities given at the end of chapter

(c) Activities given along with the topic

(d) Activities given at different places in book

**116. There is an effective teaching-learning process in the classroom when the teacher helps to connect the knowledge of the children with the new concept being taught, its objectives whom to promote?**

(a) Reinforcement

(b) Individual variation

(c) Learner-autonomy

(d) Correlation and transfer of knowledge

**117. TLM should be chosen based on:**
**I. Contextualisation**
**II. Exemplars**
**III. Related to real-life experience**
**IV. Relevancy**

(a) I, III and IV

(b) I, II, III and IV

(c) I, II and III

(d) I, II and IV

**118. Which of these provide learning opportunities to students in developing analytical and communication skills?**

(a) Group discussion

(b) Infrequent assessment

(c) Writing from rote memory

(d) Didactic lecture

**119. The main reason behind grouping the EVS content into different themes is:**

(a) To bring a change in curriculum

(b) To make content more lively for students

(c) To make it different from other subjects

(d) None of these

**120. In EVS concepts and issues have not been compartmentalized into science and social science. Why?**

(a) The child looks at his/her environment in a holistic manner.

(b) It is a good teaching-learning strategy.

(c) It is for decreasing the syllabus load.

(d) Syllabus of EVS has been prescribed as such by CBSE.

**// Hints and Solutions //**

**1(B).** Combination of physical, social, emotional, moral and mental aspects refers to the principle of integration.
**Development leads to integration -** All

types of developments, i.e. physical, mental, social and emotional, are related to each other e.g. a child, who is physically healthy is likely to have superior sociability and emotional stability. The child develops as a unified whole. Each area of development is dependent on the other and thus influences the other developments.

- Sufi has appropriate weight and height for her age. She also has well developed language ability that enables her to communicate with everyone. She is loved by all and has positive self esteem.
- Once the child learns specific or differentiated responses, then, as development continues, she can synthesise or integrate these specific responses to form a whole. For example, the young child learns to speak single, discrete words in the beginning. Later, he can join together these sentences in the form of language.

**2(B).** After seeing a cat a child says it is a dog, because the child learn that dog has 4 legs. This view is a representation of a ssimilation.

**Assimilation:** The process of taking in new information into our previously existing schemas is known as assimilation.

The child who now 'knows' the animal-type called dog, sees a cat for the first time. He sees that the animal has a tail, is furry, and has four legs – just like his scheme to understand a dog. He now calls the cat a dog. He has used an existing scheme/ knowledge of dogs to make sense of a new animal he sees. Despite the fact that the cat does not look exactly the same like the dog he understands the cat as a dog. This fitting of new experience into an already existing scheme is called assimilation.

**3(D).** **Development follows a fixed pattern/sequence:** Each child may have a different rate of development. However, the development of all human beings follows a similar pattern, similar sequence or direction.

**Sequential pattern of development can be seen in two directions:**

**Cephalo-caudal sequence :** Means that development spreads over the body from head to foot i.e. individual begins to grow from head region down wards. Sufi first gained control on her head, then she could catch hold of objects, sit, crawl and later she could stand and walk.

**Proximodistal sequence :** Means that the development proceeds from central part of the body towards peripheries. In this sequence, the spinal cord of the individual develops first and then outward development takes place. For example, babies cut their front teeth before they cut their side ones. Functionally, Sufi could use her arms before her hands and use her hands before she could control the movement of her fingers.

**4(D).** All the above methods are adopted under progressive education.

**Progressive education:** Emphasizes enhancing skills and understanding of the learners by engaging with the contents and experiences. Promotes 'learning by doing to make children self-reliant and productive to use their knowledge and talents effectively. Ensures the active participation of students by working in a group and applying practical knowledge to complete an activity.

**Following teaching methods are adopted under Progressive Education:**

- **Project method:** Children learn by doing.
- **Problem-solving method:** Children learn by working on different problems.
- **Interpretation method:** Children by interpreting their thoughts or learnings.
- **Q & A method:** Children learn by putting questions and finding answers on their own or by asking the teacher.

**5(B).** Acquisition of knowledge can take place without social context, is not given by Lev Vygotsky.

**Lev Vygotsky gives these principles in his theory:**

- Society and Culture help a child in their development.
- Children/ Learner construct their knowledge through social interaction (with help of society, peers, etc).
- Language plays an important role in the cognitive development of a learner/ child.
- Learning is mediated or Learning is done by the learner and with the interaction between him and his mediator or facilitator who facilitates the environment or learning for him.
- Learning is done with help of social interaction or in the social context.

**6(C).** Poorvi analyzes that the eyes and nose of her child are the same as her husband's due to a transfer of genes from the parents to the child.

Human growth and development are influenced by both ' Heredity and Environment' as they are the elements that play a vital role in determining the growth and development of an individual. Genetics is a broad field of study that is concerned with heredity and how particular qualities or traits are passed on from parents to offspring.

- Genetics is the study of heredity.
- Heredity is what a person is born with. It is a specific combination of genes we inherit and is shown in characteristics like height and certain habits.
- Heredity is a biological process where a parent passes certain genes onto their children or offspring.
- Every child inherits genes from both of their biological parents and these genes, in turn, express specific traits.
- Some of these traits may be physical for

example hair and eye color and skin color etc.

**7(B).** Gender is a social construct . It refers to the socially and culturally constructed system that attributes meaning to what it means to be a male or a female in a particular society. A society comprises males and females.

- Gender discrimination is not about the biological differences among men and women but it's about how we treat them i.e., the way they are given respect, work opportunities, and opportunities to express themselves, and so on.
- It is prohibited by the constitution of India under Article 15 (1) which says that the State shall not discriminate against any citizen on grounds only of religion, race, caste, sex, place of birth, or any of them.
- Every individual will be provided with equal opportunities in terms of education, employment, freedom, labor, socialization, etc.
- Unequal gender relations not only perpetuate domination but also create anxieties and stunt the freedom of both boys and girls to develop their human capacities to their fullest.
- Gender discrimination will have an adverse effect on the performance and achievement of students. So, the teacher should encourage gender equality in the teaching-learning activities.

**8(D).** According to Piaget, language development occurs rapidly during the preoperational stage.

**The development and properties of Piaget's Preoperational Stage( 2-7 years) of Cognitive Development are given below:**

- Lake of understanding the Logic behind the things.
- Lack of reversibility of thoughts.
- Showing animistic behavior with things.
- The child supposes himself the center of the universe.
- Language Development occurs rapidly during this stage.
- In this stage, the child can see only one side of things.

**9(A).** In assessment, self-assessment is assessment for learning.

**Self-assessment is an assessment for learning as:**

- It helps learners to look into their own mistakes and correct them.
- Makes the learner his ability and the level of learning and understanding he has.
- Doesn't provide any final marks or grades so there will be no opportunity for the learner to improve.
- Makes learners realize their strengths and weaknesses and work on the weaknesses for better results.

- Provides learner maximum time to evaluate his work and act accordingly.

**10(C).** Socio-cultural Development theory concludes that learning is based on interacting with other people, society, etc.

**Some important terms and points of socio-cultural theory.**

- This theory states that learning with the help of someone is much more effective and learners can easily learn.
- Scaffolding - It is a process in which More Knowledgeable Others model or demonstrate how to solve a problem, and then step back, offering support as needed.
- Zone of Proximal Development (Z.P.D.) - It is the difference between learning by self and with the help of others.

**11(B).** Anu is reluctant to do home work. Analyse the reason and take remedial measures strategies can be used to overcome the problem.

**Remedial teaching:** The type of teaching where instructional corrective measures are used to understand the needs of the learners is known as remedial teaching. It is a common phenomenon that in a class different kinds of learners exists. Some may be very sharp and can learn very fast, however there are many learners who are not very sharp to get the work done. In such cases, where the learners are not very sharp the teachers need to analyze the reasons for the lag. Many a times the learners faces problems due to family issues at home, or parents quarrelling and hence that impacts the learning levels. The duty of a teacher in such a case becomes that the reasons for the slow learners needs to be understood and then accordingly remedial measures need to be taken.

**The objectives of remedial classes are discussed below:**

- The objective of the Remedial Teaching Program is to offer learning support to students who are not doing well compared to their peers.
- Using the school curriculum and teaching methods, a teacher delivers learning exercises and practical experiences to students based on their skills and needs.
- A teacher also creates individualized instructional programs with intense remedial assistance to assist students in consolidating their fundamental knowledge in various subjects, mastering learning processes, and their trust, and improving their learning effectiveness.
- Teachers should have formal instruction to help students improve generic skills such as interpersonal relationships, communication, problem-solving, self-management, self-learning, critical thought, imagination, and information technology use.

- Remedial education lays the groundwork for students' life-long learning, assisting them in the development of healthy attitudes and values, and preparing them for future studies and careers.

**12(C).** Creativity is defined as something different from intelligence and as a parallel construct to intelligence, but it differs from intelligence in that it is not restricted to cognitive or intellectual functioning or behavior. Instead, it is concerned with a complex mix of motivational conditions, personality factors, environmental conditions, chance factors, and even products.

- To keep the students engaged class teachers can use various activities where the students can become creative and apply their abilities to solve the task.
- For example:- Riddles, fun games, mystery stories, etc.
- Students use their intellectual abilities for working on the activities.

Thus, assertion (A) statement is correct.

- The two factors that could be responsible for affecting intelligence and creativity are- heredity and environment.
- Heredity consists of genetic materials and codes that we inherit from our parents. The environment consists of the socio-cultural conditions and experiences of people in the course of their lives.
- So, creativity and intellectual abilities depend on heredity and environment.

Thus, reason (R) statement is incorrect.

**13(D).** Learning is a product, not a process, is not the characteristic of learning. Learning represents progressive changes in behaviour. It also involves the acquisition of knowledge, habits, and attitude.

Characteristics of learning:

- Learning is the change in behaviour or the strengthening or weakening of old behaviour as a result of experience.
- Learning helps in proper adjustment as it makes an individual mature enough to tackle real-life problems in a more effective and sensitive way.
- Learning is the product of activity and environment as students learn through various activities and by interacting with their physical environment.
- Learning is an active process. Learning is an active process as it takes place in a better way when learners are actively involved in it.
- Learning is individualistic. You might have observed that in a class there are some students who learn more quickly while others learn slowly.

**14(B).**

Piaget believed that language is developed in the child by their own cognition and

Vygotsky believed that language is developed by social interation.

Jean Piaget and Lev Vygotsky both are constructivists. Jean Piaget gave the theory of "Cognitive Development" and Lev Vygotsky gave the theory of "Social and cultural development".

| Jean Piaget | Lev Vygotsky |
| --- | --- |
| He believed that the child is the active constructor of knowledge. | He believed that learning support is necessary for every child. |
| He considered that after maturity, the child can learn anything easily. | He considered that Group or Peer is important for learning anything. |
| This theory is based on Cognitive Development. | Vygotsky emphasized the role of culture in cognitive development. |
| The first thought came then Language comes. | First Language came then Thoughts come. |

**15(A).** A teacher can catch the thoughts of children towards morality by telling the same story of H einz dilemma and ask their opinion.

Moral dilemmas occur only when there is a conflict between two moral reasons. A moral reason is a moral requirement just in case it would be morally wrong not to act on it without an adequate justification or excuse. Lawrence Kohlberg studied moral development by posing moral dilemmas to groups of children as well as adolescents and adults.

- These dilemmas take the form of stories, one of Kohlberg's best-known dilemmas involves a man named Heinz , who must choose between stealing medicine and letting his wife die.
- Instead of the answer, Kohlberg analyzed the reasons children gave for their answers. He identified three general levels of moral reasoning: pre-conventional, conventional, and post-conventional, and described two stages at each level.
- The moral reasoning of preschool children was influenced by a concern for obedience and punishment and for satisfying personal needs. When children enter the stage of concrete operations, they are able to turn away from their egocentric thinking, growing more concerned about appearing 'good'.

**16(B).** Environmental factor doesn't have any role in the development of the child, not the characteristics of the development of a child.

Development is a wide and continuous process that refers to an increase in structure for better and enhanced functioning of organs. It is a process of interaction between a person and his environment.

**Following are the characteristics of development:-**

- **The child develops many abilities through interaction with people:-** A child's learning occurs when he interacts with the people and the environment. Following abilities the child can develop through interaction:-
  1. Ability to learn and problem-solving skills.
  2. Ability to understand and communicate.
  3. Physical skills
  4. Social, emotional, and development skills, etc.
- Children can learn much from their environment as such, from school culture, their society, their peer groups, etc.
- Development depends on many factors such as environment, nutrition, physical abilities, disabilities, biological factors, etc.

**17(B).** A teacher always helps his students to link the knowledge acquired from one subject area with the knowledge of other subject areas. C orrelation and transfer of knowledge promote it.

**Transfer of Knowledge:**

- Knowledge transfer is the process of exchanging or disseminating information and providing input into problem-solving. Knowledge transfer is the challenge of moving information from one section of an organization to another, according to organizational theory.
- It refers to learning in one circumstance and applying the acquired learning in a real-life or practical condition.
- There are three kinds of transfer of learning or transfer of knowledge namely, from prior knowledge to learning, from learning to new learning, and from learning to application. Thus, application to learning is the odd one out.
- A teacher will constantly assist his students in making connections between the knowledge they have gained in one topic area and the knowledge they have gained in other subject areas.

**18(D).** "Development is a life long process", this statement refers to p rinciple of continuity.

Although all individuals grow and develop in their own unique way and in their own contexts, there are some basic principles which underlie the process of development and can be observed in all human beings. These are called the principles of development.

**Principle of continuity -** Principle of Continuity states that the 'Development is never-ending process'.

- The development follows the principle of continuity which starts with conception and ends with death. It is a never-ending process in life.
- The child, through the developmental process, passes continuously with changes although the pace and quantity of change vary from stage to stage.For example, a child at the age of four has learned some words but later on, s/he will learn to prepare sentences out of it. So, development never ends but it continues till death.
- Development is continuous No development whether physical, mental or speech, occurs suddenly. It takes place at a slow, regular pace. Growth starts from the time of conception of the baby and continues till maturity. Physical and mental traits continue to develop until they reach their maximum level of growth. Growth occurs at a continuous rate and does not take place in "jerks and stops". It is the continuous nature of development which accounts for one stage of growth and development influencing the next.

**19(D).** A child is a social animal, he becomes a member of society after he is born, the child first get his social education from family.

Social development is essentially a matter of integration of one's purposes with those of the social order as it refers to:

- The development of social skills and values in an individual across the lifespan.
- The individuals' ability to act and respond according to the circumstances and culture of the society.
- The way an individual adapts social norms, values, culture, etc and internalizes the attitudes and customs of society.

**Family:**

- A family is a unit of the system, which is Universal.
- The family have a hierarchical structure based on the age and sex of the members
- The family has a set of rules, follow certain values and belief systems.
- Family perpetuates values and culture that supports authorities.
- The family helps in learning of roles in the family.

**20(D).** According to NCF 2005, errors are important because they provide an insight into the child's thinking and help to identify solutions.

Errors are the window of a child's thinking, the error they make represent the way they are thinking. Errors are not just careless answers but sometimes they are intelligent generalizations making by students with their previous experience.

**As a teacher, you should adopt the following strategies-**

**View mistakes as a source of understanding:** When students remember the concepts of wrong solutions while working on a problem, they are able to deal with the problem at a much deeper level than someone who has already been given the right solution and has to memorize it. Also, we must not only correct the error but also make sure that the students see and understand the reason for the error.

**Develop motivation and confidence by responding and overcoming mistakes:** A student who successfully corrects something wrong is experiencing personal success. They see firsthand how valuable their efforts are and how well their skills are being developed. Such a successful experience leads to greater motivation and motivation in the future as they work towards achieving the learning goal because they know they can achieve it.

**Provide timely feedback to correct mistakes:** If a cognitive problem is identified too late in the learning process and too long before the student is found to have to re-read the topic, negative thinking processes can become firmly entrenched in the student's mind. The learning process usually follows these steps this way: do the tasks, make mistakes, get the answer, think about the answer, and then try again.

**Analyze causes and sources:** There are different types of errors. Ignorant errors, systematic errors, misconceptions - the cause of errors can have many sources.

**21(D).** Pupils can be taught to ask themselves questions about their learning in order to reflect on the content and process is called self-questioning.

Learning strategies refer to the various approaches, processes, and actions that the learner applies to learn a concept. These are the learner's own way of organizing and using specific sets of skills to achieve expected learning outcomes.

- Pupils can be taught to ask themselves questions about their learning in order to reflect on the content and process is called self-questioning.
- In self-questioning, pupils ask questions to themselves about their learning in order to reflect on the content and process.
- It helps children in learning by allowing them to introspect themselves and identify their weaknesses and strengths.

So, we conclude that the above statement is about self-questioning.

**22(C).** As per NPE 2020, age of 5 year child will move to p reparatory class.

**National Education Policy 2020:**

As per NPE 2020, learning should be holistic, integrated, enjoyable, and engaging. Therefore, the current 10+2 system is to be replaced by a four-stage 5+3+3+4 structure.

- The curricular and pedagogical structure of school education will be reconfigured to make it responsive and relevant to the developmental needs and interests of learners at different stages of their development, corresponding to the age ranges of 3-8, 8-11, 11-14, and 14-18 years, respectively.

- It is envisaged that prior to the age of 5 every child will move to a " Preparatory Class" or "Balavatika" (that is, before Class 1), which has an ECCE-qualified teacher.
- The learning in the preparatory class shall be based primarily on play-based learning with a focus on developing cognitive, affective, and psychomotor abilities and early literacy and numeracy.
- The mid-day meal program shall also be extended to the preparatory classes in primary schools.
- Health check-ups and growth monitoring that are available in the Anganwadi system shall also be made available to preparatory class students of Anganwadi as well as of primary schools.

**23(D).** "Right behavior consists of doing one's duty, showing respect for established or lawful authority, and maintaining given social order for its own sake" is explained in the Conventional Level - Law and Order Orientation stage of Kohlberg's moral development theory.

Kohlberg proposed the Theory of Moral Development that had three levels and each level is split into two stages. According to Kohlberg, each individual passes through each stage in a fixed order, and how moral development is linked with intellectual and cognitive development.

By considering a child's responses to moral dilemmas, Kohlberg tried to establish the reasoning behind the decision as a major indicator of moral development.

**24(A).** Motivation to learn can be sustained by focusing on mastery-oriented goals.

As teachers, we are deeply concerned about classroom learning. Your understanding of classroom motivation would enhance the probability of students' learning better.

- Affiliation motivation had hit rock bottom. As children grow, the need for peer affiliation becomes stronger.
- Creating a lot of opportunities for exploration for learners, so they can motivate each other and learn effectively.
- The healthy competition between students, motivated them to excel in their work. When they were separated and put into two different sections, the competition motivation became very low and their performance suffered.
- Project work on various topics can also motivate learners. The 'knowledge of results is a stronger motivator for

learning than an offhand word of praise. Thus from the above-mentioned points, it is clear that motivation to learn can be sustained by focusing on mastery-oriented goals.

**25(A).** Once a teacher learned that his South Indian English-language learners students consider it rude to ask the teacher questions because questioning implies that the teacher has done a poor job of teaching, he could generalize this assumption: If his English language learners are not asking questions, he needs to ask them why.

As the question states that the teacher has "learned" about few students have an ideology where it is considered rude to ask teacher questions. It means that he has gained this information which is truth or the ground reality through some source, it is not an assumption or an implication of actions, but information that holds true. On the basis of this information, he has to generalize one of the assumptions stated in the question.

- If his English language learners are not asking questions, he needs to ask them why. This is the correct option as it is a general methodology to find the root cause of a problem.
- In some industries, such type of analysis is also known as Why-Why Analysis which aims to not only find the root cause of the problem but also to prevent such problem from occurring in the future.

**26(A).** Pratiksha, who has just moved house; her household goods including her furniture, etc. are lying outside, all in a pile; she enters the living room, then the bedrooms, kitchen, toilet, etc. She examines the spaces available in different rooms and figures out where she would keep his beds, washing machine, dryer, sofas, etc. She suddenly notices the comer where she can keep the TV and the big table lamp. This phenomenon emphasizes that t hought is independent of language.

There are diametrically opposed views about the relationship between language and thought. At the one extreme end, we have the view that thought is language; at the other extreme, we have the view that thought is independent of language.

- There is no doubt that language conditions our thinking in a very substantial way. We internalize a considerable part of our conceptual world and knowledge through language.
- We should also note that for most people language is the only frequently used medium of articulating thoughts and ideas.
- On the other hand, we also need to recognize that a lot o f language-independent thought is possible and that language-independent thought is at the source of a considerable part of

normal human activity and of poetry, mathematics, and science.

**27(B).** Heredity and environment are the elements that play a pivotal role in determining the personality development of an individual. The individual's personality is a product of both heredity and the environment. Heredity determines the potential of a child while the environment influences the extent to which the potential is achieved.

**Let us first understand about assertion statement:**

- The term ' development ' refers to qualitative changes in an individual such as changes in personality or other mental and emotional aspects.
- Developmen t depends on many factors such as environment, nutrition, physical abilities, disabilities, biological factors, etc.
- Stimulation to the development of innate abilities comes from the environment. Environment influences this potential only to a limited extent favorably or unfavorably.

Thus, the assertion statement is correct.

**Now, let us understand about reason statement:**

- Piaget did not just describe but rather explained the cognitive development of children. He gave accounts of various biological, environmental, and psychological factors responsible for it.
- Careful observation adopted by Piaget became an important tool to study children and their behavior. His emphasis on studying shifts from one stage to another (for example, from preoperational to concrete operations) and the process involved in that also paved way for many new concepts and theories. Another important aspect that can be learned is that the concepts do not emerge suddenly, there is a gradual mastery involved, thus recognizing the steps in it.
- It seems Piaget overlooked the effect of cultural and social groups while studying cognitive development in children. For instance, in many cultures such as Wolof in West Africa, central Australia, and New Guinea, many 10–13-year-old are not able to attain conservation successfully.

Thus, the reason statement is also correct but it is not the explanation of assertion statement.

**28(C).** A child with visual impairment maximizes learning with the help of a uditory system.

Visual impairment is a term used to describe any kind of vision loss, whether it's someone who cannot see or someone who has partial vision loss.

- It can range from no vision, blindness, or very low vision to not being able to see particular colours.

- A child with visual impairment maximizes learning with the help of the auditory system .
- So, the audio CD of the textbook should be provided to the child with low vision to enrich their knowledge by providing information about different subjects and boost their self-confidence and independence.

**29(D).** Engaging and contextual would enable a teacher to cater to individual differences among learners in her class.
Individual difference refers to the differen ce which distinguishes an individual from another on the basis of psychological characteristics. Individual differences could be seen in all domains of development such as physical, emotional, mental, etc.

- Engaging and contextual pedagogy would enable a teacher to cater to individual differences among learners in her class.
- Pedagogy refers to the techniques used in the teaching process and is influenced by the development of learners.
- It helps a teacher to conduct the teaching-learning activities more efficiently and appropriately to the level and needs of the students.
- Engaging and contextual pedagogy makes education more experiential, holistic, integrated, inquiry-driven, discovery-oriented , learner-centered, discussion-based, and, of course, enjoyable.
- Under engaging and contextual pedagogies, the teacher emphasizes the use of contextual materials so the students could relate words in the context. Using such materials develop contextual understanding in depth.

**30(A).** ' A girl playing football in an advertisement for a sports shoe ' is not an example of gender stereotype.
Gender stereotyping refers to the relatively fixed and overgeneralized attitudes and behaviors that are considered normal and appropriate for a person in a particular culture based on his or her biological sex.
**Example:**
- Presenting women doing make-up.
- Being dropped by her husband.
- Doing some household chores given that when a woman is capable of doing much more.

**31(A).** As we can see in the first paragraph of the passage, it is clearly mentioned that "By all considerations, Ashoka is one of the greatest kings not only in the history of India but that of the whole world".
Thus, it can be concluded that Ashoka is considered to be one of the greatest kings not only in the history of India but also for the whole world.

**32(D).** As we can see in the first paragraph of the passage, it is clearly mentioned that " For the welfare of his subjects, Ashoka planted trees along the roads for providing shade, built rest houses for travellers and established hospitals for human beings and animals. He had also opened a separate department for distributing charity to the poor ".
Thus, it can be concluded that Ashoka had done all the things mentioned above for the welfare of his subjects.

**33(D).** 'Ordinary' is the most appropriate antonym of the the word, ' unparalleled '.
**Unparalleled:** Unparalleled means having no parallel or equal; exceptional.
**Example:** War crimes of this type are unparalleled in history.
**Ordinary:** Ordinary means with no special or distinctive features; normal.
**Example:** Her paintings are of ordinary everyday objects.

**34(C).** As we can see in the first paragraph of the passage, it is clearly mentioned that " Ashoka also got the teachings of Buddhism engraved on many rocks and pillars in different parts of his empire ". Thus, it can be concluded that statement (A) is true.
As we can see in the second paragraph of the passage, it is clearly mentioned that " Ashoka was the son of the Mauryan emperor Bindusara ". Thus, it can be concluded that statement (B) is true.

**35(C).** Here the underlined word ' unparalleled ' is an adjective i.e., a word naming an attribute of a noun, such as sweet, red, or technical.
- Unparalleled means having no parallel or equal; exceptional.
- **For example:** War crimes of this type are unparalleled in history.

**36(C).** As we can see in the first paragraph of the passage, it is clearly mentioned that " In the beginning, like all other Kings, Ashoka was also given to kingly pleasures and military conquests but after the battle of Kalinga, a powerful Kingdom on the Bay of Bengal, Ashoka was completely transformed. In this battle, lakhs of people were slain, wounded, which produced a profound reaction on the mind of Ashoka. The era of military conquests was now over and an era of spiritual conquests as Dharma Vijay began. Ashoka was converted to Buddhism and devoted the rest of his life to spread and put into practice the teachings of Buddhism ".
Thus, it can be concluded that battle of Kalinga had transformed Ashoka and converted him to Buddhism.

**37(B).** 'Compete' is the most appropriate synonym of the the word, ' contend '.
**Contend:** Contend means struggle to surmount (a difficulty); compete with

others in a struggle to achieve (something).
**Example:** To obtain custody of her children in the divorce, Bridgett will contend her husband is an abusive man.
**Compete:** Compete means strive to gain or win something by defeating or establishing superiority over others.
**Example:** The boys would compete with each other to impress her.

**38(C).** As we can see in the second paragraph of the passage, it is clearly mentioned that " Ashoka also followed the Law of Piety or Dharma in his personal life; he gave up hunting and curbed slaughter of animals for the royal kitchen ".
Thus, it can be concluded that Ashoka had gave up hunting and curbed slaughter of animals for following the Law of Piety or Dharma.

**39(C).** Ashoka was ascended the Magadha throne in 273 B.C.
Buddhist records tell that he captured the throne after killing his 99 brothers, but this is hot supported by any other evidence. It seems certain that he had to contend with his elder brother Susima.

**40(B).** The meaning of this word 'green wars' is wars against the environment.
- It acts of violence that are masked behind seemingly earth-friendly actions.
- It refers the nuclear wars and armed activities which harms the nature to a great extent.
- The environment is polluted excessively and increasingly and the resources get wasted.
- **Example :** Those who prepare green wars,
wars with gas, wars with fire,
victories with no survivors.

**41(A).** From reading the poem we can clearly see that the tone of this poem is full of hope and optimistic and calm throughout .
Since the poet is urging his readers to stay silent and still, he himself adopts a very tranquil serene tone, to set the poem's mood.
According to the poet, if a person introspects himself, then he will be able to understand himself, the world well and then there will be generosity among the people and they will stop looking at each other with the spirit of violence.
He calls on people around the world to unite in stability and The poet does not want there to be any kind of war. He is an optimist and promoting universal brotherhood and peace.

**42(B).** Metaphor figure of speech has been used in the line, "in the shade, doing nothing."
**Metaphor:** An expression, often found in literature, that describes a person or object by referring to something that is considered

to have similar characteristics to that person or object.
**Example:** Life is a highway.

**43(D).** Alliteration figure of speech has been used in the above line.
**Alliteration:** A literary device that reflects repetition in two or more nearby words of initial consonant sounds.
Alliteration does not refer to the repetition of consonant letters that begin words, but rather the repetition of the consonant sound at the beginning of words.
**Example :**
• W in 'we would'
• S in 'sudden strangeness

**44(A).** The poem is an optimistic one and is promoting universal brotherhood and peace.
The poem urges people to stop all sorts of aggression, including that towards the environment. If we think of ourselves as the hands of the clock on the face of this earth, moving in our routine ways and introspects himself, then he will be able to understand himself, the world well.
**Example :** We would all be together in a sudden strangeness.
In the third paragraph the poet is requesting the people not to join the war and is telling about the disadvantages of war.
• Rather, he wants people to take a new approach towards life and mankind.

**45(C).** The poem tells us about p eace and silence.
The poet stresses upon being quiet and harmless to the human beings, animals and environment.
According to the poet, if a person introspects himself, then he will be able to understand himself, the world well. It tells us how a moment of silent introspection will make us realize the utter of our aggressive endeavours.
He suggests that in order to maintain peace and harmony, it is required to stop and introspect ourselves.
• Fishermen in the cold sea
  would not harm whales.

**46(A).** Nitesh, a 4 years old child, understands grammatical rules without being told about the rules or without giving attention to them. This happens in a natural manner, thus it is an example of l anguage acquisition.
**Language acquisition :**
• It refers to the subconscious process of learning a native or second language because of the innate capacity of the human brain.
• It is a natural process whereby children acquire language by observing and repeating what they hear in their native environment.
• Language acquisition does not require any formal instruction, children acquire

the language without being taught.
• Language acquisition is a natural process so, one does not forget one's native language.

**47(C).** Grammar translation method is one of the methods of language teaching. It was a way of learning a language through a detailed study of its grammar.
**Features of grammar-translation method:**
• The learner applied the rules of grammar in translating sentences and parts of text from the mother tongue into the target language and vice versa.
• Its focus is on translating the sentence correctly.
• The learner's role was passive; she/he did not play an active role in the use of the language.
• Vocabulary was taught through bilingual word lists and there was a lot of stress on memorization of words.
• The teacher was totally dependent on the text as she had to rigidly follow the lesson.

**48(C).** Using gestures, expressions and actions is one of the techniques used to teach v ocabulary .
Vocabulary refers to the set of words an individual uses as a tool for communication. It is a collection of familiar words used or understood by an individual or group of people.
• The core vocabulary of the first language is learned quite naturally at home. Neither the child nor his/her family has much to say about the words that must be learned - those are given by the immediate environment and the culture.
• The vocabulary of a second language can thus be decided by the teacher, the textbook, or the school. The development of vocabulary is very important for the students.

**49(D).** The preface help s us to get a bird's eye view of the book.
The textbook is a tool to be used in the teaching-learning process to facilitate effective and meaningful learning. A good textbook should primarily provide comprehensible inputs to develop a good understanding of the concept for better academic outcomes.
• The textbook contains detailed data, information, facts, and knowledge about a certain topic with visuals, flowcharts, and practice questions in a systematic order.
• Also, new words should be introduced while keeping in mind the age, class, and previous knowledge of students . All the concepts and topics must be interrelated and should be based on psychological approaches.
• In the beginning of a textbook, there is a preface that helps us to get a bird's

eye view of the book. The author's own statement about the work is called a preface.
• The author's preface generally consists of reasons for undertaking the work , method of research, etc for compiling the work, acknowledgments, and sometimes, permissions granted for the use of previously published materials in the book.

**50(A).** Learning disabled children are d eficient in using potentials.
Learning disability is a syndrome found in children of normal or above intelligence characterized by specific difficulties in learning to read (dyslexia), to write (dysgraphia) and to do grade appropriate mathematics (dyscalculia).
**Learning Disabled children may show following characteristics-**
• It influences individual's self-concept.
• It primarily excludes other disability categories.
• An untreated or poorly treated LD can have adverse effects on educational, vocational, social and activities of daily living.
• Children feel deficient in using their potentials.
• LD can also be defined as one or more significant defects in essential learning processes.

**51(A).** Remedial teaching is nothing but re-teaching.
Remedial teaching is used for 'learning disabled children' as the objective of the remedial method is to give additional help to learners who have fallen behind the rest of the class in any topic or subject.
Remedial teaching is nothing but re-teaching the incorrectly learned skills to the students. It is the process of identifying slow learners and improving their ability to learn something. It is a teaching or instructional approach to provide the remedial measures to help students to get assistance on their weaknesses. In this view, the general or specific nature of weakness of the pupil is identified and appropriate steps are taken.

**52(B).** Questions such as, 'What is the main theme of the passage?' is an example of i nferential question.
To test the reading comprehension, a teacher provides a number of different questions. We can arrange these questions into two categories:
**Big picture questions (based on the complete passage):**
• Main Idea Question
• Primary Purpose Question
• Title Question
• Structure & Organization
**Specific purpose questions (based on some particular section of the passage):**
• Fact-based/Specific            Detail/Target

Question
- Inference Question
- 'Must be true' Question
- Paraphrase Question
- Vocabulary Question

**Inferential question :** The term 'inference' means something derived by reasoning-something, that is not directly stated but only suggested in the text. This may be a logical conclusion that is drawn from statements through deduction or induction.

**53(C).** In a language classroom, r eading for pleasure skill, among the ones listed below, cannot be tested in a formal written examination.

The formal written examination is a test that can be half-yearly, yearly. They are designed for some designated time. It is conducted under the supervision of the teacher.

Reading refers to the practice of comprehending and interpreting the written text to perceive the text meaningfully. In a language classroom, these skills can be tested in a formal written examination:
- Reading for information is a skill that can be tested. Reading for information can be from different sources such as tables, figures, magazines, calendars, diaries, and other texts. While reading for information we use different skills and sub-skills of reading depending on the nature of the information we need.
- Meaning of words and phrases can be tested in the written examination by involving learners in such questions.
- Inferential comprehension - The term 'inference' means something derived by reasoning-something, that is not directly stated but only suggested in the text. This may be a logical conclusion that is drawn from statements through deduction or induction. Inferential comprehension is demonstrated by the learner when he/she successfully synthesizes the content of the selected reading matter. This can be also be tested in the written examination.

**54(B).** A $2\frac{1}{2}$ years old child picks up his sibling's book and looking at the pictures tells a story. The child is emergent reader. The word 'emergent' means prominent or to have expertise in some specific field. Emergent readers are those who grasp the basic concept of books by images or picture or some brief ideas. Emergent literacy has the following skills:
- **Print motivation :** Being interested in and enjoying books.
- **Vocabulary:** Knowing the names of things.
- **Print awareness:** Noticing print, knowing how to handle a book, and knowing how to follow words on a page.
- **Narrative skills:** Being able to describe

things and events and to tell stories (Emergent reader)
- **Letter knowledge:** Understanding letters are different from each other, knowing their names and sounds, and recognizing letters everywhere (Emergent writer)
- **Phonological awareness:** Being able to hear and play with the smaller sounds in words.

**55(D).** Statement "While all formative tasks are meant for improving teaching-learning, some are used for assessment too", is true.

Assessment is a process of collecting relevant information on student learning. It is one of the crucial components of the teaching-learning process. Assessment does more than just measuring learning.

**Formative Assessment:**
- It is a type of assessment that refers to monitor the child's progress throughout the learning and teaching process.
- Oral testing, anecdotal records, portfolios, class test, etc are the tools of formative assessment.
- It provides feedback to the teachers regarding the effectiveness of their teaching.

**56(A).** Dyslexia is associated mainly with difficulties in reading.

Dyslexia is associated with the 'Reading disorder' as it refers to a difficulty in Reading, Writing, and Spelling.

**Dyslexia is the most common learning disability (Reading disorder) which makes learners:**
- Confuse with the same shapes and sounds of the alphabet.
- Unable to read, interpret, and understand letters and words.
- Bewilder in identifying and relating speech sounds with letters and words.

**57(D).** Language rich environment is the most important pre-requisite for language learning, whether first or second.

Language rich environment refers to the environment which ensures language development by containing features that involve all five senses and provokes open-ended outcomes. It provides learners an opportunity where the language is seen, noticed and used by children.

**A Language rich environment is the most important pre-requisite for language learning as it:**
- Lays the foundation for spontaneous language growth and development.
- Nurtures the expressiveness, creativity and imagination skill of the learners.
- Addresses learner's diverse need by a variety of learning models and techniques.
- Consists of visual and performance arts which engage students in creative activity.

**58(C).** T he Official Language Act says that english should be continued to be used in official works of the Union.

The Official Language Act allows for the continuation of English alongside Hindi in the Indian government indefinitely until legislation decides to change it.

**Continuation of English Language for official purposes of the Union and to use in Parliament:**
- Notwithstanding the expiration of the period of fifteen years from the commencement of the Constitution, the English language may, as from the appointed day, continue to be used in addition to Hindi,
- for all the official purposes of the Union for which it was being used immediately before that day; and for the transaction of business in Parliament.
- Provided that the English language shall be used for purposes of communication between the Union and a State which has not adopted Hindi as its Official Language.

**59(A).** To acquire the ability to speak and write the language correctly, is the role of grammar in language teaching.

**Grammar should always be taught by enabling practice in context:**
- Here, the teacher is not concerned with teaching grammar - either in the form of rules or drills.
- His/her major objective is to provide context for the learners to communicate in English.
- It is believed that by engaging in the process of communication, the students will implicitly master the rules of grammar .
- It will allow the learners to use these grammar patterns in a situation .
- So, the more opportunities learners get for communication, the better their proficiency.

**60(A).** English textbook at primary level should most importantly focus on age and interest of the learners and objective of the language.
- At the primary level, english textbooks must be primarily focused on the age, the interest of the learners, and objectives of the subject matter i.e., the content of the textbook should be within the cognitive reach of the students of that specific age group for which it is designed.
- And the textbook should also be according to the objectives to be achieved in the learning of a particular class.
- Also, if the textbook is not focused on the interests of learners then they will not take interest in reading it. So, f ocusing on the age and interest of the learners, and the objectives of the language should be the primary priority while

designing an english textbook.

**61(A).** Given,

40 coins of Rs 5 and 22 coins of Rs 2

Total cost of 40 coins of Rs 5 and 22 coins of Rs 2 $= (40 \times 5) + (22 \times 2)$

$= 200 + 44$

$= $ Rs 244 .

To solve this question we have check all the options:

Option (A) 2 notes of Rs 100 + 4 notes of Rs 10 + 4 coins of Rs 1 $= (200 + 40 + 4)$

$= $ Rs 244

Option (B) 4 notes of Rs 50 + 4 notes of Rs 20 + 2 notes of Rs 1 $= (200 + 80 + 2)$

$= $ Rs 282

Option (C) 2 notes of Rs 100 + 2 notes of Rs 10 + 2 coins of Rs 1 $= (200 + 20 + 2)$

$= $ Rs 222

Option (D) 4 notes of Rs 50 + 4 notes of Rs 10 + 4 notes of Rs 2 $= (200 + 40 + 8)$

$= $ Rs 248

**62(D).** Given,

The perimeter of a square is double the perimeter of a rectangle.

Let the side of the Square be $'a'\ cm$ and the length and breadth of the rectangle be $'L'\ cm$ and $'B'\ cm$

$\Rightarrow 4a = 2(L + B)$

$\Rightarrow 2a = (L + B)$

$\Rightarrow L \times B = 480$ sq m

We cannot find $L + B$ only with the help of $L \times B$

$\therefore a$ cannot be found

Therefore, the area of the square cannot be determined.

**63(B).** Given,

Tom's weight $= 45000$ g

As we know,

$1$ kg $= 1000$ g

Tom's weight $= 45000 \div 1000$

$= 45$ kg

**64(C).** $36005023$ can be written as $3,60,05,023$ .

As we know,

1 ones

10 Tens

100 Hundred

1000 Thousand

$10,000$ Ten thousand

$1,00,000$ Lacs

$10,00,000$ Ten lacs

$1,00,00,000$ Crore

$\therefore 3,60,05,023$ can be written as three crores sixty lakh five thousand twenty three.

**65(C).** Given,

Mahesh's present age $= 5$ years

Anup's present age $= 5 - 2$

$= 3$ years

Let the present age of Randheer be $x$ .

Then, Anup's present age $= \dfrac{x-6}{18}$

Now, according to the question.

$\dfrac{x-6}{18} = 3$

$\Rightarrow x - 6 = 54$

$\Rightarrow x = 54 + 6$

$= 60$ years

**66(C).** As we know,

- Place value is defined as the digit multiplied by wherever it is placed, either by hundreds or thousands.
- Face value is simply defined as the digit itself within a number.

The face value of 7 in 4782 is 7 .

The face value of 7 in 32170 is 7 .

Difference $= 7 - 7$

$= 0$

**67(A).** Given,

$\dfrac{6}{11}, \dfrac{13}{18}, \dfrac{15}{22}, \dfrac{19}{36}, \dfrac{5}{6}$

After converting the fractions into decimals,

$\Rightarrow \dfrac{6}{11} = 0.54$

$\Rightarrow \dfrac{13}{18} = 0.72$

$\Rightarrow \dfrac{15}{22} = 0.68$

$\Rightarrow \dfrac{19}{36} = 0.52$

$\Rightarrow \dfrac{5}{6} = 0.83$

$\therefore$ The smallest fraction number is $\dfrac{19}{36}$ .

**68(C).** Given,

Total number of children in village $A = 5000 \times \dfrac{15}{100}$

$= 750$

Total number of children in village $B = 6500 \times \dfrac{20}{100}$

$= 1300$

Required ratio $= 750 : 1300$

$= 15 : 26$

$\therefore$ The ratio between the number of children in village $A$ and $B$ is $15 : 26$ .

**69(C).** Given,

Angles of a triangle are in the ration of $2 : 3 : 4$ .

As we know,

Sum of all three angles of a triangle is 180 .

Ratio of three angles of a triangle $= 2 : 3 : 4$

$2 + 3 + 4 = 9$ unit

$\Rightarrow 9$ unit $= 180$

$\Rightarrow 1$ unit $= 20$

$\Rightarrow 2$ unit $= 20 \times 2$

$= 40$

**70(A).** Given,

Length of street $= 900\ m$

Taken time $= 5$ minutes

As we know,

Speed $= \dfrac{\text{Distance}}{\text{Time}}$

Speed $= \left(\dfrac{900}{5 \times 60}\right) m/sec.$

$= 3 m/sec$

Converting $m/sec$ to $km/hr$

$= \left(3 \times \dfrac{18}{5}\right) km/hr$

$= 10.8\ km/hr$

**71(D).** Given,

Sides of a triangle are $15m, 16m$ and $11m$ .

As we know,

When lengths of all three sides are given $a, b$

and $c$ , then

Area of the triangle $= \sqrt{[s(s - a)(s - b)(s - c)]}$

Here, $s = \dfrac{(a+b+c)}{2}$

Where , $s = $ Semi perimeter of the triangle,

$s = \dfrac{(15+16+11)}{2}$

$\Rightarrow s = \dfrac{42}{2}$

$\Rightarrow s = 21$

Area of the triangle $=$

$\sqrt{[21 \times (21 - 15) \times (21 - 16) \times (21 - 11)]}$

$= \sqrt{[21 \times 6 \times 5 \times 10]}$

$= \sqrt{(3 \times 7 \times 2 \times 3 \times 5 \times 2 \times 5)}$

$= 30\sqrt{7}m^2$

$\therefore$ Area of the triangle $= 30\sqrt{7}m^2$

**72(A).** Given,

An $8-$ digit number $1862383A$ is divisible by 22 .

As we know,

Divisibility rule for 2 : The last digit of any digit number is an even number.

Divisibility rule for 11 : The difference for the sum of the digits in the odd and even places of the given number is 0 or divisible by 11 .

Divisibility rule for 22 : The required number is divisible by 2 and 11 then the number is divisible by 22 .

Prime factorization of $22 = 2 \times 11$

As we know, If the required number $1862383A$ is divisible by 2 and 11 then the number is divisible by 22 .

As per the divisibility rule for 2 , the value of $A$ must be an even number.

The possible value of $A : 2, 4, 6, 8, 0$

As per the divisibility rule for 11 ,

$\Rightarrow (8 + 2 + 8 + A) - (1 + 6 + 3 + 3) = 0$ or multiple of 11

$\Rightarrow 18 + A - 13 = 0$ or multiple of 11

$\Rightarrow 5 + A = 0$ or multiple of 11

For $5 + A$ to be a multiple of 11 , the value of $A$ must be 6 .

$\therefore$ The required value of $A$ is 6 .

**73(D).** Given,

If the time at present is $7 : 42\ am$ .

As we know,

Minutes in 24 hours $= 1440$ minutes

Minutes in 50 days $= 1440 \times 50$

$= 72000$

$72332$ minutes $= 72000$ minutes $+ 300$ minutes $+ 32$ minutes (time will be same after 24 hours)

$\Rightarrow 72332$ minutes $= 7 : 42\ am + 1200$ hours $+5$ hours $+32$ minutes (5 hours $= 300$ minutes)

$= 7 : 42\ am + 24 \times 50 + 5$ hours $+32$ minutes

$= 12 : 42\ pm + 32$ minutes

$= 1 : 14\ pm$

**74(B).** The basic structure of mathematics includes arithmetic, algebra, geometry, and trigonometry that helps in learning the techniques to handle abstractions and structures.

- The teaching of mathematics must develop attitudes to think, reason, analyze, and articulate logically.
- The nature of mathematics highly influences the nature of the teaching-learning process in mathematics.

**Nature of mathematics:**

- Just like we use letters, alphabets, and words to write or speak a language, mathematical language uses symbols, numbers, diagrams, and graphics to express, define, or prove the mathematical statements and concepts.
- The symbols that are generally used in mathematics are $+, -, <, =, >, \%, \times$, etc. So, mathematics has its own language and symbolism.
- At the primary level, the teaching of concrete concepts helps in developing the basic mathematical skills that are required to handle abstractions in the later level of learning.
- And then in the upper primary and higher classes the abstract concepts of mathematics are taught like algebra, trigonometry, etc.
- So, mathematics basically prepares the children to handle its complex abstractions that will also help in solving real-life problems. Therefore, mathematics aims at abstraction.
- It is a subject in which previous knowledge has a greater influence i.e., if the learners are not aware of the geometrical shapes then they will not be able to understand the concept of "area" and "perimeter".

**75(A).** "Students are able to order and compare two decimal numbers up to two decimal places".

This learning objectives refers to c ontent goal.

**Learning Objectives:** In the process of education, the aims of education are clear from the 'why' aspect of education. These are broad and long-term objectives are the smaller steps, achievable through the teaching-learning process in the classroom and the achievement of objectives helps us in moving closer to the aim. Objectives are the well-defined purposes of education that are achieved through various subjects taught in the school.

The content goal includes an understanding of the content like words, geometrical shapes, ordering of numbers (in different series like ascending and descending), comparison of numbers (greater or larger), etc. For example, students can order and compare two decimal numbers up to two decimal places.

**76(B).** While teaching comparison subtraction, a teacher says, "Whenever you read keywords like 'more/less' 'increasing/decreasing', 'exceeds', there is always

subtraction." The teacher is trying to m ake mathematical language easy.

**Comparison subtraction:** In this, we subtract to find out how much bigger (or smaller) one set is compared to another . For example , Ashima, mother of a 7-year-old child, says to his husband, "Tomorrow we have to travel 96 km". After which her child replies, 4 km less than 100.

**The main characteristics of mathematical language are:**

- The simplicity of the concepts so that the learner can easily understand them.
- Accuracy is also needed in mathematics so that students can learn to commit fewer mistakes and be accurate in doing calculations.
- Through precision, students learn exactly how to use formulas and under what situations these formulas are correct.

**77(B).** A child having problems in addition is likely to develop problems in multiplication.

A child having problems, also, is likely to develop problems in multiplication as multiplication is considered as repeated addition.

- Multiplication is simply a form of repeated addition. Its purpose is to simplify equations and to help execute the problems more quickly.
- Repeated addition is the repetition of equal groups of a number, added together to get an answer.
- Repeated addition helps students build a foundational knowledge of multiplication.

**78(B).** For teaching the concept of volume of a cone, 3D models should be used by the teacher.

Teaching aid is an important component of the teaching-learning process which helps the teacher to make the teaching of a specific lesson/unit interesting. The use of teaching aids in the teaching process makes the teaching-learning process more stimulating, more reinforcing, and more effective.

- It is also known as the TLM ( Teaching-Learning Materials) which helps in enhancing the teaching and facilitates the learner as well.
- They are instructional materials which are helping in achieving desired learning objectives.

**3D models:**

- They are the representation of the 3D shapes of mathematics which may or may not be proportionately scaled down.
- These are the objects with suitable size, complexity, timing, safety, and cost factors for carrying out the desired instructional purpose.
- These are the substitute for real things and sometimes they are more effective

than in reality.

- Generally, they are used to explain abstract concepts in reality and to make teaching interesting .
- For example, It is more effective in teaching the 3d shapes, the similarities and dissimilarities among them, the concept of volume, and so on.
- The volume of the cone can be easily demonstrated and understandable by the use of 3D models.
- The 3D model of the cone will be used to make it easier for the teacher to explain the slant and straight height of the cone and also it will be easier to show how we calculate the radius of the cone.

**79(B).** Graph paper is most likely to build the concept of 'Area' among students.

**Graph paper:**

- It has a network of grids that form small squares that are used to represent mathematical data.
- Two straight lines, one horizontal and the other vertical (known as the X-axis and Y-axis, respectively), are drawn on the graph paper, which intersects at a point called the origin.
- The given data are represented as points on the graph paper which helps the children to understand the points in a plane surface.
- Let's take an example, the following image is showing a figure to find the area of this figure we have to count the number of squares it is fitting into.

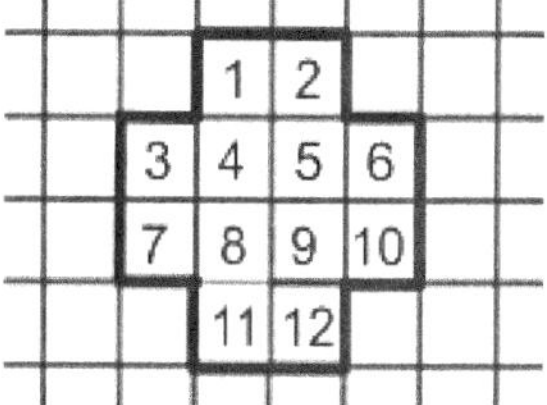


- So, a total of 12 squares of graph paper are occupied in the given figure which means that the area of the given figure is 12 squares.
- As the area of an object or shape is the space enclosed by it in a plane surface. Therefore, the graph paper can be used to teach the concept of area effectively.

**80(D).** In elaboration phase of 5E's learning model, students get chance to reflect on their knowledge.

The 5E's learning model, developed by 'Rodger Bybee' is an instructional model based on five stages which are engaging, exploration, explanation, elaboration, and evaluation. This constructivist model of learning ensures the active involvement of learners in the teaching-learning process.

Elaboration Phase:

- It provides an opportunity for students to apply their knowledge to new situations and reflect upon it , which may include raising new questions and hypotheses to explore.

- The teacher guides the students in applying the concepts they have learned from the earlier three phases.
- They make connections to other related concepts and apply their understanding to the real world around them.

**81(D).** The process of assessment in mathematics includes the following except verbal skills.

**Dimensions of assessment of mathematical learning:**

The process of assessment in mathematics includes the following dimensions of mathematical learning at the elementary school level (NCERT, 2009):

**Concepts and procedures:**

- It is expected that every teacher while teaching mathematics in the classroom, should explore the nature of their students development of the concepts and procedures.
- This is because every child has his/her own uniqueness in development of the concepts and procedures in his/her context which is different from those reading in other schools.
- In such exploration of children's nature of learning mathematical concepts procedures, assessment has crucial importance.
- For ensuring comprehensive assessment of mathematics learning, appropriate tools and methods should be properly planned for assessing the concepts, skills, procedural knowledge, thinking skills, etc.

**Mathematical reasoning:**

- Inductive and Deductive reasoning, is dominantly employed in the mathematics learning at the elementary stage.
- The emphasis on reasoning in mathematics learning influences the ways of solving and presenting the solutions of mathematical problems.
- It also impacts learners' language, ways of presenting communications logically, and even different activities conducted by the learners in their daily life.
- Therefore, assessment of mathematics learning cannot exclude this important aspect. Assessing mathematical reasoning shall include several methods including the tests, both oral, written, and performance, observation of learners' activities etc.

**Communication :**

- One of the important outcomes of mathematics learning is the development of the way of communication which is typically precise, logical, relevant and disciplined.
- Both in oral and written communications, these characteristics can be observed. In addition, use of symbols, figures, graphs and charts makes the written communications more precise, and orderly.
- These aspects of mathematical communication have to be included in both formal and informal modes of assessment.

**82(D).** **Purposes of question bank:** The question bank is useful for the teachers in bringing reform in the traditional evaluation system.

- The National Curriculum Framework (2005) rightly observed that the present evaluation system can be described as "one-exam fits-all," as one question paper is employed to all students during the examination.
- This is because the teacher has no other option but to use some questions which are available to him.
- But, if the teacher has a variety of questions in the question bank then he can prepare different question papers and use them for different learners as per their requirement.

**The other purposes of question bank are:**

- The question bank is useful to prepare a test for instant testing of the learners
- Though the test items in a question bank are objective-based, those are helpful for the teachers to evaluate the learning progress concerning learning objectives.
- The learners can prepare themselves for the questions available in the question bank.
- The learners can also self-evaluate themselves by using the question bank.
- Questions not only help in the assessment of learning but also aid in classroom transactions for helping the students to learn better. Therefore, a variety of items on different learning outcomes should be available to you and your students in the classroom. Question bank in the classroom serves this purpose effectively.

**83(A).** Most effective teaching aids in mathematics is a ctivity aids.

Teaching aids are the materials used for effective teaching and enhancing the learning of students. It can be anything readymade or made by the teacher or made by students. Different teaching aids are used by me in teaching mathematics like charts, manipulatives, Programmed Learning materials (PLM), computers, etc.

**Activity aids:**

- Learning by Activity is a very effective methodology in the teaching-learning mathematics as the experience gained meticulously, remains permanently affixed in the minds of the children.
- So innovative teaching aids & projects of math's laboratory play a vital role in the conceptualization process as recommended by NCF 2005 also.
- As the NCF 2005 emphasizes that children's experience of school education must be linked with life outside the school so that the learning experience is joyful.
- Having had this in mind, several opportunities are provided to students to construct their systematic knowledge by engaging them in activities, experiment, projects field visits, discussion with peers & teachers, group work, brainstorming sessions, collecting information from different sources, enquiring, listening, thinking, etc.
- The students are provoked & allowed to share & explain their ideas & to ask, raise, pose & frame questions. Appropriate innovative tools & techniques are applied depending upon the situation & requirement of the underlying concepts.

**84(D).** Mathematics is a subject that finds application in every walk of our life. Knowingly or unknowingly, people use concepts of mathematics in their daily life. Considering the relevance of mathematics, it is treated as one of the basic and compulsory subjects in the school curriculum. In the elementary school curriculum, learning basic concepts of mathematics is emphasised. As and when children reach higher classes, the complexity of mathematical concepts gets widened.

**Stages for the planning of the mathematics curriculum:**

**Aim of Education:** It would be difficult to imagine any curriculum in the absence of general educational aims. Therefore general educational aims have to be kept in mind while framing curriculum.

**Subject-wise Objectives or Specific objectives -** The Specific objectives should include knowledge, skills, attitude, application and interest so that expected changes in mathematics should be brought in student.

**Content Selection and Organization:** On the basis of principles of content selection and organization, a selection of well-connected concepts, information, knowledge, skills, value, attitude etc should be made and formed in an organized way. For example Statistic consist of mean, median, mode, the average should be introduced in consideration of growing usefulness in life. The teacher should use new topics for the enrichment of traditional ones also.

**Organization of Content:** The content selected for inclusion in the curriculum should have a proper order and arrangement to facilitate the teaching and learning of subject like mathematics.

**Teaching-learning Experiences:** The learning experiences selected in any curriculum should be judged on the following criterion:

- They should bring designed behavioural changes to the learner.

- The developmental needs of the pupil, his/her intellectual development and capability of learning at different stages.
- They should be suitable for the concerned area or topic.
- Teaching-learning Experiences should be effective.
- New knowledge of mathematics for adaptation at the primary stage.
- They should be practicable.

**I nstructional Aid and Material:** These materials should guide the teachers to select the appropriate teaching aids for specific content.

**Evaluation of Learning Outcome:** In the framing of the curriculum, the suitable evaluation system for students should be definitely mentioned in the curriculum.

Thus from the above-mentioned points, it is clear that all of the given options are particularly relevant for planning of the mathematics curriculum.

**85(C).** Fear about mathematics subject is the biggest problem in learning mathematics for students.

**Problems in teaching and learning of mathematics:**

**Fear and Failure:** Feat about mathematics subject about mathematics is the biggest problem in learning mathematics for students. Because of fear, they are unable to understand the concept and due to this they lack interest in the subject. Most of the students, peers, teachers, parents, etc. have given priority to teaching and learning mathematics at the elementary level although most of them thought that it is a difficult subject. Lack of awareness of objectives is also another cause of fear and failure.

**Disappointing Curriculum:** An unattractive and Loaded mathematics curriculum created disappointment among the students. Most of the mathematics curriculum emphasizes procedure, formulas, mathematical facts, and memorization of concepts. The textbook and syllabi on mathematics are rigidly prescribed. The mathematics curriculum is far away from real life.

**Inadequate Learning Materials:** For the majority of children in elementary schools textbook in mathematics is the only resource material available to them. Further, most of the textbooks, mathematics textbooks as well, are mostly content loaded and prescriptive. The student finds very little scope for pleasure and fun in learning mathematics from the textbooks.

**Crude Assessment:** Most of our mathematics curriculum emphasized on memorization of formulas. Our classroom teaching process is also examination-oriented. In our school, different tests are designed to assess student's knowledge of procedure and memory of formulas and facts. Questions are set not to expose student's experiences but to get a fixed answer. For example students free to answer — + — = 8 than 2 + 6 = —? Moreover, similar types of assessment procedures are applied in the formative assessment as well as a summative assessment.

**Inadequate teacher preparation:** Teaching and learning mathematics at the elementary level purely depends on the preparation of teachers, her own understanding, the preparation of teachers on pedagogic techniques, and the student's preparedness. As there is an acute dearth of mathematics teachers, it forced other teachers to teach mathematics in the classes in compulsion.

**The teaching-learning process:** The teaching-learning process in mathematics at the elementary level are not attractive because:

- Bookish knowledge in the class creates dissatisfaction,
- School mathematics learning becomes charmless, dull, uninteresting, and stereotype,
- Emphasis on rote learning,
- Emphasis on teaching, not on learning,
- Development of Understanding, Application, and skill are ignored.

**Lack of interest:** Most school children find learning mathematics difficult and lose their confidence in mathematics. The teaching-learning process in mathematics is not joyful and attractive. Even the students don't know what benefit they will get after learning mathematics. So students lack their interest and attitude towards mathematics.

**86(B).** Mathematics develops the ability to perform necessary computations with accuracy and reasonable speed . It also develops an understanding of the processes of measurement and the skill needed in the use of instruments of precision.

- One of the major objectives of teaching primary mathematics is to enable children to solve speedily and accurately the numerical and spatial problems which they encounter at home, in the school, and the community.
- It should help children develop an understanding of key mathematical concepts through appropriate experiences with the physical world and the immediate environment.
- These include subject matter which must be thoroughly mastered so that speed and accuracy are ensured on which future learning can be based.

Speed in mathematics can be defined as the time taken to solve the problem. Accuracy in mathematics can be defined as how close the obtained value (answer) to the acute (true) value.

Thus from the above-mentioned points, it is clear that Accuracy and speed can go together.

**87(D).** Mathematics is a science that involves dealing with numbers, different kinds of calculations, measurement of shapes and structures, organisation and interpretation of data and establishing relationship among variables, etc.

- Mathematics is the "queen of all sciences" and its presence is there in all the subjects.
- Mathematics acts as the basis and structure of other subjects.
- These views have brought in the relevance of Mathematics to be considered as one of the core subjects of the school curriculum. Second, Mathematics is more than computation.
- Mathematics gives us clear and correct answers through calculations.
- Mathematical ideas grow from concrete to abstract, particular to general and their knowledge is conceptual as well procedural.
- Mathematics is associated with our day-to-day activities. This helps us to understand its nature.

Thus from the above-mentioned points, it is clear that "its knowledge is only conceptual" this statement does not show the nature of mathematics.

**88(D).** A mathematical learning disability may occur due to all of the following except cultural factors.

Learning disability- A learning disability is a neurological disorder. In simple terms, a learning disability will give different results just the way a person's brain is wired. Children with learning disabilities are equally smart as their peer group, but they may have difficulty reading, writing, spelling, reasoning, recalling, and/or organizing information.

**89(C).** Given:
$$15 - 15 \div 15 \times 6 = x$$
$$x = 15 - 15 \times \frac{1}{15} \times 6$$
$$x = 15 - 15 \times \frac{1}{15} \times 6$$
$$x = 15 - 6$$
$$x = 9$$

**90(A).** Given,
$$32, 8, 64, 16, 128, ?$$
The series follows the following pattern:
$$32 \div 4 = 8$$
$$8 \times 8 = 64$$
$$64 \div 4 = 16$$
$$16 \times 8 = 128$$
$$128 \div 4 = 32$$
$\therefore$ 32 will come in place of the question mark '?'.

**91(B).** Ragdoll and Somali are the breeds of cats.

Ragdoll:

- Ragdolls are among the younger siblings in the family of cat breeds.
- This breed was first developed by breeder Ann Baker in Riverside, California, in the 1960s.

- They are characterised with large and muscular semi-longhairs and blue eyes.

Somali:

- The Somali cat is described as a long-haired African cat.
- It is medium-large in size and is recognized for their bushy tails, large almond eyes and large pointed ears. It is nicknamed as "Fox Cat."

**92(D).** Pitcher plant, s undew and v enus fly-trap are carnivorous plant.

Carnivorous plants obtain the essential nutrients from the heterotrophs . These plants trap insects and obtain the nutrients which they do not get from the soil. They are not called heterotrophs or consumers, because they only derive nutrients from insects. These plants get energy from the process of photosynthesis.

**Pitcher plant:** Leaves transformed into a slippery deep pool containing digestive juices. Insects fall into these pools and plant digests them.

**Venus Flytrap:** It has snap traps, which snap shut when touched by insects.

**Sundew:** It has a sticky substance on its surface which looks like dews. The insect gets stuck on it and digestive juices digest it by the time.

**93(B).** India is the second-largest producer of sugarcane in the world.

- The sugar industry is the second largest agro-based industry after the textile industry in India.
- India is known as the homeland of Sugar.
- Brazil is the largest sugarcane-producing country in the world followed by India, China and Thailand.
- Brazil produces around 768 million tonnes of sugarcane every year.

**94(C).** The most effective farming method for returning minerals to the soil is crop rotation.

- Each crop uses different types of minerals in the soil. If the same crop is planted each year, over time the soil is depleted of minerals essential for plant growth and health.
- Rotating different crops, helps return depleted minerals to the soil as the plant dies and decomposes.

**95(B).** Fuel gives heat and light after combustion.

Fuels release heat on burning: Heat of combustion is the total amount of heat released when a fuel is burnt when there is complete combustion with oxygen. It is a chemical reaction in which hydrocarbon is burnt and it produces carbon dioxide, heat and water.

**96(B).** The mountaineers carry oxygen with them because the amount of air available to a person is less than that available on the ground.

The climate at higher elevations is not the same as at sea level, and therefore the mountaineers face the following difficulty:

- Lack of oxygen.
- Low atmospheric pressure.
- Very low freezing/sub-freezing temperatures.
- Very high chilly winds.

Other than climatic factors, the topography adds another difficulty to the climbers as:

- At the high mountain, slopes are steep and walking becomes difficult.
- Snow on the mountain makes it slippery.
- Avalanches and landslides are common in the mountains.

**97(B).** Pulses are a great source of proteins. They can be particularly important for people who do not eat meat, fish, or dairy products. Pulses include beans, lentils, and peas.

Proteins are made up of hundreds or thousands of smaller units called amino acids, which are attached to one another in long chains. There are 20 different types of amino acids that can be combined to make a protein.

**98(B).** Rainwater harvesting is a technique of collecting and storing rainwater in natural reservoirs or tanks. Rainwater can be collected from rivers, terraces and many other places. The stored water can be used in any necessary condition.

**99(C).** Leafhoppers is the carrier of grassy stunt pathogenic virus.

Leafhoppers are a destructive pest as they suck the sap from plants and transmit plant diseases. Small numbers of leafhoppers are usually not a matter for concern, but they can grow into large infestation that cause significant damage

**100(A).** Dr. Beaumont did many experiments and found out many secrets about digestion.

**Willi am Beaumont :**

- William Beaumont (November 21, 1785 – April 25, 1853) was a surgeon in the U.S. Army.
- He became known as the "Father of Gastric Physiology" following his research on human digestion.
- Dr. Beaumont did many experiments and found out many secrets about digestion.
- He found that food digests faster in the stomach than outside.
- In 1822, an employee of the American Fur Company named Alexis St. Martin was accidentally shot.
- Dr. Beaumont treated his wound but expected St. Martin to die from his injuries.
- Despite this dire prediction, St. Martin survived but with a hole in his stomach that never fully healed.
- He was hired as a handyman by Dr. Beaumont to observe digestive processes.

**101(C).** Many plants have medicinal benefits that have long been exploited by humans. Medicinal plants usually have a characteristic fragrance and are hence known as aromatic plants. Example of aromatic plants is turmeric, cinnamon, fennel, clove and tulsi. These plants have been employed in Ayurveda, a form of traditional medicine system.

**Babool:** It is commonly known as Gum Arabic tree. It is a hardwood tree. It belongs to the Fabaceae family. Its wood has a density of about 1170 kg/meter cube. It is suitable for making charcoal. It is a medicinal plant also with amazing health benefits.

**Clove:** Clove buds have medicinal properties. The buds are used to heal a toothache.

**Tulsi:** Tulsi is another aromatic plant that is an immunity booster and cough, cold. Tulsi holds an important place in the Hindu religion.

**Jamun:** The powder of its seeds is used for controlling diabetes. The juice prepared from its ripe fruit is used to prepare vinegar.

| List-I (Plant) | List-II (Uses) |
|---|---|
| (a) Jamun | (iii) Controlling diabetes |
| (b) Clove | (iv) Toothache |
| (c) Babool | (ii) Cure eyesore |
| (d) Tulsi | (i) Cough and cold |

**102(A).** The art of growing short plants is called Bonsai.

A bonsai is a specific tree grown as a miniature tree in a pot cultivated by special methods. Growing Bonsai trees requires utmost care as there is minimum soil required and moisture also needs to be adequate. The tree foliage and shape of the tree are guided by the grower by the following methods:

- Pruning the roots
- Wiring the branches
- Leaf trimming

**103(A).** The three-tire vermi-culture technology developed by biotechnology resource center is so inexpensive with respect to the conventional method. Also, the operational costs are negligible. But the major advantage is it can be applied to both solid and liquid wastes. It doesn't involve chemical treatment and degradation of organic wastes is not a specialty of vermicomposting.

**104(D).** Flies spread dysentery, cholera, typhoid, anthrax etc. Flies are easily attracted by filth. They sit on dirty and filthy matters. Again when these sit upon the food, microbes are deposited on the food from there these can enter the human body.

**105(C).** Carbon monoxide poisoning can

be cured by exposing the affected person to fresh oxygen. It is because Carbon monoxide poisoning leads to oxygen starvation of body cells. This therapy involves breathing pure oxygen in a chamber in which the air pressure is about two to three times higher than normal. This speeds the replacement of carbon monoxide with oxygen in your blood. Hyperbaric oxygen therapy may be used in cases of severe carbon monoxide poisoning.

**106(D).** Hamida is a teacher in primary school. She wants to develop the concept of water conversation among class V students. Getting students to travel to different sources of water and giving examples of how life is not possible without water, is most suitable for this.

**Importance of using innovative methods in environmental science-**

- To establish environmental science as a discipline that lays emphasis on inductive learning, the method of teaching used by the students and teachers should be the experimental or the discovery approach.
- Child-centered teaching-learning.
- The role of a teacher should be as an organizer, facilitator, moderator, and guide. In these roles, the teacher has to use various teaching-learning strategies such as discussion, group activity, teacher-discussion, and group discussion.
- Different approaches to the teaching of environmental studies/science especially relating to the child's environment and use of community resources need to be properly emphasized.
- The development of scientific temper may have significance in the methods of teaching-learning environmental studies/science at the elementary level in die elementary teacher education curriculum.

**107(C).** Environmental Science (EVS) is not a new subject in our school curriculum. It is rather a new approach and perspective for handling a curricular area that earlier went under such varied names as general knowledge, social studies, general science, nature knowledge/study, citizenship education for the young, and others.

**Importance of Using Innovative Methods in Environmental Science -**

- To establish environmental science as a discipline which lays emphasis on inductive learning, the method of teaching used by the students and teachers should be the experimental or the discovery approach.
- The role of a teacher should be as an organizer, facilitator, moderator and guide. In these roles, the teacher has to use various teaching-learning strategies such as discussion, group activity,

teacher-discussion, and group discussion.

- Different approaches to the teaching of environmental studies/science especially relating to the child's environment and use of community resources need to be properly emphasized.
- The development of scientific temper may have significance in the methods of teaching-learning environmental studies/science at the elementary level in die elementary teacher education curriculum.

Therefore, we can conclude that to bring a realistic approach, Environmental Science should be linked to real life through different types of stories.

**108(D).** The biggest goal and objective of teaching environmental studies are h uman welfare and development of all organisms, Understanding and preserving nature's work style and t o adjust to the environment and live a systematic life.

**Objectives of Teaching Environmental Studies are-**

- Education about the environment has the purpose of developing knowledge and understanding of values and attitudes.
- It should enhance the natural curiosity of the child.
- It should help the child in developing attitudes and qualities such as self-confidence, the spirit of inquiry, initiative, and courage to ask questions.
- It should encourage the child to think of solutions to problems in his/her day-to-day life.
- It should develop the desired skills in children.
- It should help a child to develop logical thinking.
- It should help a child to take an active interest and participate in solving some simple problems in a limited way.
- Education in or through the environment involves the use of the environment as a resource for learning. This helps in the development of knowledge and understanding along with skills of investigation and communication.

**109(C).** Teaching aids are the additional teaching equipment that helps learners to improve comprehension skills, illustrate or reinforcement of concepts, and relieve boredom by the presentation of information in an interactive and exciting way.

The benefits of using teaching aids:

- It supplements lesson discussion by engaging the student with live demonstrations and engaging content.
- Teaching aids such as graphs, charts, flashcards, videos enable visual stimulation to the learners which allows

them to access the content as per their individual level of understanding.

- It generates constant excitement and curiosity in the students who have little patience for lecture-style teaching
- It improves the quality of education by providing students with the sense of excitement they desire.
- It is helpful in meeting the individual differences of the learners.
- It enables abstract ideas to be concrete thus helping the learning process more effectively and retention of knowledge for a longer time.

**110(B).** This topic helps children to memorize concepts and definitions of different facts regarding teaching of environmental studies to the child is not correct.

**Objectives of Teaching Environmental Studies are:**

- Education about the environment has the purpose of developing knowledge and understanding of values and attitudes.
- It should enhance the natural curiosity of the child.
- It should help the child in developing attitudes and qualities such as self-confidence, the spirit of inquiry, initiative, and courage to ask questions.
- It should encourage the child to think of solutions to problems in his/her day-to-day life.
- It should develop the desired skills in children.
- It should help a child to develop logical thinking.
- It should help a child to take an active interest and participate in solving some simple problems in a limited way.
- Education in or through the environment involves the use of the environment as a resource for learning. This helps in the development of knowledge and understanding along with skills of investigation and communication.
- Environmental studies have been regarded as a life-long process concerned with the total environment aimed at developing and sharpening awareness, knowledge, skills, attitudes, values, and concern for environmental improvement and protection. It will help to adjust to the environment and help in understanding nature's work styles along with human development.

**111(C).** If you are appointed as a teacher of environmental studies in a primary school and you want that environmental education is necessary for everyone, t o develop knowledge and consciousness about the environment in students will the most important reason for this.

Environmental studies mean education about the environment through the environment and for the environment. Environmental studies is a major area of curriculum at the primary stage. It aims at developing active well-informed citizens who are aware of their environment, its problems, and their responsibilities for protecting and conserving environmental resources. It should be regarded as an integral part of education at all levels. Education for the environment encourages children to explore their environment, so as to form an idea about their relationship with the environment and environmental issues.

**112(A).** Inclusion refers to a process by which efforts are made to ensure equal opportunities for all, regardless of their background, be it money, class, ethnicity, gender, race, or whatever the index of diversity is, to enable full and active participation in all aspects of life, including civic, social, economic, and political activities, as well as participation in decision-making processes. Social inclusion can be approached as a goal, an objective, and a process. Its process affects almost all societal activities, and should therefore be approached from various dimensions.

Inclusive Education Classrooms bring all students together in one classroom and school, regardless of their strengths or limitations in any area, and it seeks to maximize the potential of all students. Diversity in a group with respect to any aspect is appreciated and everyone is recognized and respected for what he/she is worth. Efforts are made to make sure that diverse learners are taught using teaching-learning strategies adapted to individual learning needs. Every individual is helped to feel accepted, valued, and safe, thus enhancing the well-being of every member of the community.

Social inclusion is the process to ensure equal opportunities for all, regardless of their background, be it money, class, ethnicity, gender, race or whatever the index of diversity is, to enable full and active participation in all aspects of life, including civic, social, economic, and political activities, as well as participation in decision-making processes.

**113(C).** As a teacher of environmental studies in a school, while creating a group activity in your classroom we would not discriminate between boys and girls.

**Group activity:** When the activity at some stage in a lesson calls for discussion or active collaboration among a group of students, a number of such groups are formed and each given a relevant task to work on. This is called group work or group activity.

**While designing a group activity in the EVS class, a teacher should:**
- Be conscious of the interests of all learners

- Choose topic equally appealing to children of all religious and cultural background
- Not discriminate between boys and girls
- Concerned about individual differences of learners
- Equal status Interactions among the team members is essential for smooth teamwork.

**114(C).** As a headmaster of the school classroom based on overall activity should be required for conducting a class of environmental studies in the school.

**Activity-based:** The activities included in the curriculum should meet the basic learning needs of children and should provide such essential tools of learning as knowledge, skills, value, and attitude which can make them self-reliant.

**While designing a activity in the EVS class, a headteacher should:**
- Play the role of philosopher, friend, and counselor.
- Teach concepts, procedures, and convictions to the students.
- Create a learning environment that promotes the development of a child's imagination power and encourages them to think of multiple ways of approaching a problem.
- Be conscious of the interests of all learners
- Choose topic equally appealing to children of all religious and cultural background
- Concerned about individual differences of learners
- Focus on all-round development.

**115(B).** Activities given along with the topic of text book of environmental studies will be useful for the students.

Features for environmental studies textbooks for it to be useful for students:
- Steers clear of rote learning
- Encourages child's thought and intuition
- Equal balance of group and individual activities
- Graded complexity of concepts
- The moral and emotional tone of concepts

Hence, the correct option is (C).

**116(D).** There is an effective teaching-learning process in the classroom when the teacher helps to connect the knowledge of the children with the new concept being taught, its objectives are c orrelation and transfer of knowledge to promote.
- Use the previous knowledge of whatever students know from their environment by connecting it with the topic of teaching.
- Make linkages between children's experiential informal knowledge
- Connect concepts with the objects around the students is considered a successful teacher..

- Every moment in their life children are experiencing many things, and as a result of that, they are learning.

**117(B).** Teaching-learning materials (TLMs) also known as instructional aids, facilitate a teacher in achieving the learning objectives formulated by her/him prior to teaching-learning activities start. The materials should be chosen on the following considerations besides ensuring their characteristics:
- Since, in the primary grades, the learning activities are totally related to the real-life experiences of the learners, the materials need to be chosen from their world of real-life activities.
- The materials need to be relevant to the learning of a particular concept dealt with in the learning activity.
- Direct experiences like participating in exhibitions, field trips, study tours, visiting important institutions/ organizations.
- Mere collection of a large number of materials is not enough for conducting an activity effectively. Their contextualization at the appropriate stage of activity is also important.
- In the learning activities where a new concept is being introduced, both the materials that are exemplars of the concept and non-exemplars of the same concept need to be used for clear discrimination of the characteristics of the concept.
- The adequate quantities of the chosen materials for the learning activity are to be ensured much before the commencement of the activity.

**118(D).** Group discussions provide learning opportunities to students in developing analytical and communication skills.

The discussion takes place whenever there is a difference of opinion concerning the situation. It involves an interchange of questions and ideas among the students.
- The purpose of the discussion is to encourage an exchange of ideas and viewpoints.
- Discussion methods may be superior to lectures or reading for the retention of information.
- This method is superior in building attitudes that are important in shaping behaviour patterns.

Hence, the correct option is (A).

**119(B).** The main reason behind grouping the EVS content into different themes is t o make content more lively for students.

The teaching of EVS also helps students to develop desirable attitudes, values, and behavior patterns necessary for an environment-friendly lifestyle.
- The EVS syllabus of class III to V is

connected and integrated within broad themes and sub-themes.

- The main reason behind grouping the EVS content into different themes is to make content more lively for students so that they can make the best of their educational experiences.

**120(A).** In EVS concepts and issues have not been compartmentalized into science and social science because t he child looks at his/her environment in a holistic manner.

The integrated nature of EVS means the teacher aims to develop the different dimensions of one's personality (social, emotional, mental, moral) by teaching one or two subjects together in a collaborative manner because of the following reasons:

- To create cognitive capacity and resourcefulness and to make the child curious.
- To nurture the creativity of the child particularly in relation to the natural and human environment (including artifacts and people).
- To develop an understanding based on observation and illustration, drawn from lived experiences and physical, biological, social, and cultural aspects of life.
- It feels less burdened by the learners as they can learn more comprehensively and they will also able to connect two subjects or topics.
- The child looks at his environment and learns in a holistic or integrated manner. because of the interdisciplinary nature of EVS.
- This approach is learner-centered and in this approach, a learner gets ample opportunity to achieve unified knowledge, which is meaningful.
- Integrating the concepts or issues of environmental studies with other disciplines like social sciences, mathematics, general sciences, languages, etc.

## Child Development and Pedagogy

1. Do children acquire language because they are genetically predisposed to do so or because parents intensively teach them from an early age? This question essentially highlights:
   (a) The nature-nurture debate
   (b) The discussion on development as a multi-factor ability.
   (c) Whether development is a continuous process or discontinuous one?
   (d) The influence of cognition on development of laguage.

2. A child coming to pre-school for the first time cries profusely. After two years when the same child goes to the primary school for the first time, he does not express his tension by crying rather his shoulder and neck muscles become tense. This change in his behaviour can be explained on the basis of which of the following principles?
   (a) Development proceeds in a sequential manner.
   (b) Development is gradual.
   (c) Development is different in different people.
   (d) Development is characterized by differentiation and integration.

3. Which one of the following statements is true about the role of heredity and the environment?
   (a) Certain aspects of development are influenced more by heredity and others more by the environment.
   (b) A child's ability to learn and perform is completely decided by the genes.
   (c) Good care and a nutritious diet can fight off any disorder a child is born with.
   (d) The environment plays a significant role only in the child's language development.

4. Social development of a child actually begins _____.
   (a) in early school stage
   (b) in infancy
   (c) in early childhood
   (d) in later childhood

5. According to Vygotsky, when adults adjust the support to extend the child's current level of performance, it is called:
   (a) discovery learning
   (b) zone of proximal development
   (c) scaffolding
   (d) inter-subjectivity

6. Which of the following is not true about the socio-cultural theory of Vygotsky?
   (a) Children learn very little from performing tasks they can already do independently
   (b) Concept of Zone of Proximal Development (ZPD) is a part of it
   (c) It ignores the importance of language in cognitive development
   (d) It emphasizes the role of the socio-cultural environment in cognitive development

7. Individualized Education Programme is planned from the perspective of _______.
   (a) child-centred education programme
   (b) open School educational programme
   (c) e-Learning education programme
   (d) special education programme

8. Students who can effectively express their thoughts show _____ intelligence.
   (a) Emotional
   (b) Linguistic
   (c) Inter-personal
   (d) Cognitive

9. Which of the characteristics in classroom teaching behaviour as given below will be classified as a part of formative assessment?
   (A) The teacher asks questions to elicit classification from students.
   (B) The teacher specifies the level of mastery attained by students.
   (C) The teacher prompts and probes the students while making a presentation.
   (D) The teacher pauses for a few seconds, looks at students, and asks questions.
   (E) The teacher indicates performance criteria and given judgemental values.
   Choose the correct answer from the options given below:
   (a) (A), (B) and (C) only
   (b) (A), (C) and (D) only
   (c) (B), (C) and (D) only
   (d) (C), (D) and (E) only

10. A teacher wants to diagnose the weaknesses of students to give them feedback so that their learning difficulties can be removed. Which of the following types of assessment should be adopted by him?
    (a) Assessment as learning
    (b) Assessment for learning
    (c) Assessment of learning
    (d) Assessment from learning

11. Which one of the following is a critique of theory of multiple intelligences ?
    (a) Multiple intelligence are only the 'talents' present in intelligence as a whole.
    (b) Multiple intelligence provides students to discover their propensities.
    (c) It over emphasises practical intelligence.
    (d) It cannot be supported by empirical evidence at all.

12. What kind of errors are common between a learner who is learning his mother tongue and the learner who learns the same language as a second language?
    (a) Overgeneralization
    (b) Simplification
    (c) Developmental
    (d) Hypercorrection

13. Which one of the following many be the criteria of gender parity in a society?
    (a) Comparison of number of male and female teachers in school
    (b) Equal number of distinctions achieved by boys and girls in Class 12
    (c) Comparison of number of boys and girls who survive up to Class 12
    (d) Whether the girl students are allowed to participate in competitions organized outside the school

14. Which of the following provision is not suitable to meet individual differences among learners?
    (a) Labelling them
    (b) Making Individualisation necessary
    (c) Adequate facilities and material should be provided
    (d) Their abilities should be

assessed

**15.** Which one of the following types of evaluation assesses the learning progress to provide continuous feedback to both teachers and students during instruction?
(a) Placement evaluation
(b) Formative evaluation
(c) Diagnostic evaluation
(d) Summative evaluation

**16.** A child 'who is in the middle of his school (that is about ten and half years) is unable to do the work of the class below that which is normal for his age" is known as which type of children?
(a) Mentally retarded
(b) Educationally retarded
(c) Moron
(d) Idiot

**17.** In order to address learners from diverse backgrounds, a teacher should:
(a) draw examples from diverse settings.
(b) use standardized assessment for all
(c) use statements that strengthen negative stereotypes
(d) avoid talking about aspects related to diversity.

**18.** Which one of the following behaviours is an identifier of a child with learning disability?
(a) Abusive behaviour
(b) Writing 'b' as 'd', 'was' as 'saw', '21' as '12'
(c) Low attention span and high physical activity
(d) Frequent mood swings

**19.** Ruby has hearing impairment and all the students in her school have many such difficulties and disabilities. What do you call such schools?
(a) Private schools
(b) Comprehensive school
(c) Government school
(d) Special school

**20.** "The needs of children with special needs will vary from child to child depending on the disability he/she has." With respect to this given statement, which of the following statement is correct?
I. A child with mental retardation will not need concrete material but will need repeated instruction to understand a concept.
II. A child with motor disabilities will need physician support depending on the need.
(a) Only I
(b) Neither I nor II
(c) Only II
(d) Both I and II

**21.** Misconceptions among students represent their _______.
(a) extremely flawed and irrational thinking process.
(b) higher-order emotional and intellectual abilities.
(c) native and intuitive understanding about concepts.
(d) severe cognitive deficiencies and neurological disorders.

**22.** Which step is prominent in the syntax of teaching model of memory level and understanding level?
(a) Planning
(b) Exploration
(c) Generalization
(d) Presentation

**23.** If a teacher finds a problematic child in the class, what should he does?
(a) Send the child back to home immediately
(b) Ignore the child
(c) Punish the child
(d) Provide counselling to the child

**24.** Which of the following type of discipline is developed as a revolt against the authoritarian discipline many adults had been subjected to during their childhood?
(a) Authoritarian discipline
(b) Democratic discipline
(c) Motivational discipline
(d) Permissive discipline

**25.** Which theory of educational psychology deals with prior knowledge of the child and takes into consideration the social and cultural determinants in the process of learning?
(a) Behaviorism
(b) Social cognitivism
(c) Cognitivism
(d) Constructivism

**26.** Children often form alternative conceptions and misconceptions about various concepts. Which of the following statement is NOT correct in this context?
(a) Alternative conceptions and misconceptions formed by students should be highly discouraged by the teacher.
(b) Formation of alternative conceptions and misconceptions is very natural among children as well as adults.
(c) A teacher should definitely attend to these alternative conceptions and misconceptions as they are significant in process of teaching - learning.
(d) Alternative conceptions about misconceptions are not always baseless rather these represent children's intuitive ideas about world around them.

**27.** Perception about your bodily changes, following an event, brings forth emotion is:
(a) Activation theory
(b) Hypothalamic theory
(c) Cannon Bard theory
(d) James Lange theory

**28.** What type of factor motivation is:
(a) Physical
(b) Social
(c) Psychological
(d) Cultural

**29.** The period of learning, where no improvement in performance is made, is called:
(a) learning curve
(b) plateau of learning
(c) memory
(d) attention

**30.** Which characteristics of community influence education?
I. Demographics
II. Occupational patterns
III. Customs and traditions
(a) I and III  (b) I and II
(c) II and III  (d) I, II and III

## Language - I: English

Ques (31-39): Direction : Read the passage given below and answer the questions by selecting the correct/most appropriate options:

The Indian Premier League's suspension effective from Tuesday was an inevitable full stop considering India's continuing trauma with COVID-19 and the breach of the tournament's much-vaunted bio-bubble. Until the emergence of the COVID-positive results of Kolkata Knight Riders' Sandeep Warrier and Varun Chakravarthy; Sunrisers Hyderabad's Wriddhiman Saha; Delhi Capitals' Amit Mishra, Chennai Super Kings' bowling coach L. Balaji and a member of the squad's logistics staff, the

Board of Control for Cricket in India (BCCI) was in denial-mode, firmly believing that its bio-bubble protocols cannot be breached. BCCI officials also insisted that the league is not a super-spreader like election rallies or other permitted activities where crowds were allowed to assemble. That both fans and the media were kept away from the venues was cited as an example of how strict the IPL management was with regard to social-distancing. Besides this, the constant testing of everyone in the bubble was seen as another fail-safe method to ensure that the league did not turn into a coronavirus hotspot. But before the final denouement, what jarred was the tone-deafness of having matches in Delhi while beyond the ground, the accompanying note was that of ambulances blaring their sirens while patients gasped for oxygen. Even if the league has its share of a massive television audience and offers a diversion to the viewers, having Delhi as a host was extremely insensitive.

The IPL's 14th edition is at the crossroads, a reality which it had avoided since its launch in 2008. The cash-rich league always found a way to sidestep obstacles. During three general elections, the championship either fully or partially leant on neutral venues. There was also the incident of low intensity blasts just outside Bengaluru's M. Chinnaswamy Stadium on April 17, 2010, ahead of a match featuring Royal Challengers Bangalore and Mumbai Indians. It is an event that has faded from public memory but on that ominous day, two bombs went off, injuring a few and a third was found, which was immediately defused. The contest started an hour late and the IPL continued unhindered. But the latest crisis due to a pandemic is something that humankind has never faced since the Spanish Flu in 1918. Meanwhile, the board officials are hinting about resuming the league later this year in the United Arab Emirates, which also hosted the 13th leg. But for that the virus should wane and most countries have suspended flights from India, with the Australian Prime Minister Scott Morrison not even permitting a chartered flight with the IPL's Aussie players. To find a window in a packed international cricket schedule will be arduous even if the last word on the IPL's tenuous resumption is yet to be spoken.

**31. Read the following statements:**
   **A. During an ongoing match between Royal Challengers Bangalore and Mumbai Indians, some bomb blasts were occurred outside the stadium on April 17, 2010.**
   **B. The IPL had started in 2008.**

(a) Both A and B are true.

(b) A is true but B is false

(c) B is true but A is false

(d) Both A and B are false

**32. How many people had been found COVID-19 positive according to the passage due to which the IPL was suspended?**

(a) 6; 4 cricketers, 1 coach, 1 member of logistic staff

(b) 6; 3 cricketers, 1 coach, 2 members of logistic staff

(c) 8; 4 cricketers, 2 coach, 2 members of logistic staff

(d) 4; 2 cricketers, 2 coaches

**33. What arguments were put forward By BCCI in support of organizing IPL despite adverse Covid-19 situation in the country?**
**A. Its bio-bubble protocols can't be breached.**
**B. Both fans and media were not allowed at he venues.**
**C. the constant testing of everyone in the bubble to prevent the league from being a coronavirus hotspot.**

(a) Only A

(b) Only B and C

(c) Only A and C

(d) All A, B and C

**34. What can be inferred from the following lines?**
**"in Delhi while beyond the ground, the accompanying note was that of ambulances blaring their sirens while patients gasped for oxygen".**

(a) Delhi's air is polluted and there is a scarcity of oxygen available in the air.

(b) Delhi's is facing a glooming situation because the surge in COVID positive cases.

(c) There is an earthquake in Delhi causing deaths.

(d) A bridge has been collapsed near the ground due to which some people has died.

**35. Choose the antonym of the word 'tenuous' as used in the passage.**

(a) substantial    (b) flimsy

(c) fragile    (d) delicate

**36. Which of the following statements is true?**

(a) The United Arab Emirates hosted the 13th season of the Indian Premier League.

(b) This season of IPL won't be resumed further.

(c) IPL has a limited television audience.

(d) It is being hinted that the league might resume this year in South Africa.

**37. What has been regarded as insensitive by the author?**

(a) resuming the match even after bomb blasts

(b) having Delhi as a venue of matches

(c) resuming the match even after COVID positive results of several players and staff

(d) not allowing the fans and media at the venues

**38. Choose the synonym of the word 'ominous' as used in the passage:**

(a) auspicious    (b) sinister

(c) benign    (d) unlucky

**39. Choose the correct synonym of the word 'resumption'.**

(a) resuscitation   (b) abeyance

(c) dormancy    (d) quiescence

**Ques (40-45): Direction** : Read the passage carefully and answer the questions that follow:
Beloved of the rivers, beset
By azure water and transparent drops,
Like a tree of veins your spectre
Of dark goddess biting apples:
And then awakening naked
To be tattooed by the rivers,
And in the wet heights your head
Filled the world with new dew.
Water rose to your waist,
You are made of wellsprings
And lakes shone on your forehead.
From your sources of density you drew
Water like vital tears
And hauled the riverbeds to the sand
Across the planetary night,
Crossing rough, dilated stone,
Breaking down on the way
All the salt of geology,
Cutting through forests of compact walls
Dislodging the muscles of quartz.

**40. Which of the following traits do not apply to the river?**

(a) Vital tears

(b) Dark goddess

(c) Naked

(d) Mortal

**41. Identify the figure of speech in, "Water like vital tears".**

(a) Metaphor

(b) Metonymy

(c) Simile

(d) Personification

**42. What does 'vital' mean?**

(a) Refuse    (b) Slow

(c) Important    (d) Obstruct

**43. In the first stanza, the poet says that:**
(a) River fills the world with new dew.
(b) River is the image of Mother Nature.
(c) River shows wrath.
(d) Both (A) and (B)

**44. Identify the figure of speech in, "You are made of wellsprings".**
(a) Oxymoron    (b) Assonance
(c) Imagery    (d) Simile

**45. Which of the following is TRUE?**
(a) River doesn't flow through forests
(b) River is the giver of new life
(c) River brings apples to the earth
(d) All of the above

**46. While studying class 6 Saurabh reads the sequence of letters in reverse order, which learning disorder is he suffering from?**
(a) dyslexia    (b) dysgraphia
(c) dysphagia    (d) dyscalculia

**47. This is assumed to be a major difference between language acquisition and learning.**
(a) Language acquisition happens at an early stage while language learning takes place later.
(b) Language acquisition always happens in mother tongue and language learning happens in the second language.
(c) Language acquisition is meaning formation and language learning is making meaning.
(d) Language acquisition is natural and language learning is deliberate/instructed.

**48. Which principle of teaching English creates a zeal to learn something new in language?**
(a) The principle of proper order
(b) The principle of habit formation
(c) The principle of motivation
(d) The principle of selection

**49. A child in Class II writes, "I laik tu red a buk" instead of writing "I like to read a book". What does the child's writing show?**
(a) He needs remedial classes to improve spelling
(b) He has used invented spellings
(c) He is not paying any attention in the class
(d) He needs to work on phonetics

**50. Students' hearing ability is assessed in the following manner.**
(a) Practice conversation with students.
(b) Telling the story to the students and asking comprehensible questions on it.
(c) Giving students extra reading opportunities.
(d) Taking students on a trip.

**51. Learning in the mother-tongue helps a student to _____ what is being taught.**
(a) reproduce
(b) create
(c) interpret
(d) easily comprehend

**52. A teacher collects the instances of learning and performances of learners and makes a note of them to report in the assessment record. What is this assessment process known as?**
(a) Portfolio assessment
(b) Summative assessment
(c) Comprehensive assessment
(d) Non formal assessment

**53. Which of the following is not necessary while assessing speaking task?**
(a) pronunciation of words
(b) using words contextually in correct structure
(c) using sources and dictionaries
(d) clarity of the speech

**54. A teacher divides her class students into pairs (As and Bs). The "A Partner" should dictate the words to "Partner B" and "Partner B" should fill the gaps without watching the "Partner A" worksheet to get the full content. What is this task known as?**
(a) Punctuation dictation
(b) Mutual dictation
(c) Composition dictation
(d) Real dictation

**55. One of the principles of materials preparation for language learning is that _____.**
(a) complex materials should be chosen for each age group
(b) materials need to be graded appropriately
(c) any kind of materials can be selected
(d) materials should be short and limited

**56. A reader uses her prior knowledge, makes semantic cues and syntactic cues then moves to other more specific information. What model of reading the reader here adopts?**
(a) Bottom up model
(b) Top down model
(c) Interactive model
(d) Whole language model

**57. Grammatical units should be presented in a clear and interesting way through activities, this helps to ___.**
(a) It helps the learners to do only then and understand the rules
(b) Helps learners to memorize rules
(c) Helps the learner feel free to do or not to do it
(d) Helps learners to 'monitor' their work

**58. A student is not able to solve those word problems which involve transposition in algebra. The best remedial strategy is to:**
(a) give lot of practice questions on transposition of numbers.
(b) give lot of practise questions of word problems in another language.
(c) explain him/her word problem in simple language.
(d) explain concept of equality using alternate method.

**59. A device for finding out what pupils understand and can do with the purpose of adapting future teaching to the needs of the individual or the class is known as:**
(a) Summative Assessment
(b) Information Assessment
(c) Diagnostic Assessment
(d) Testing

**60. A good paragraph writing in English involves:**
(a) Legible handwriting
(b) Correct punctuation marks
(c) Ideas, presentation and coherence
(d) Flowery language

## Mathematics

**61. The ultimate aim of remedial teaching is:**
(a) To help pupils who have fallen behind to learn
(b) To help pupils who have high IQ

(c) To help pupils who have health issues

(d) All of the above

**62. Which of the following could not be a contributing factor towards underachievement in mathematics?**

(a) Nature of mathematics and gender

(b) School climate and language differences

(c) Students' attitudes toward mathematics

(d) Educational background of the family

**63. Evaluation should be done in teaching of Mathematics _____.**

(a) at the time of providing experiences of learning

(b) at the time of clarification of objectives

(c) after the classification of objectives and providing the experiences of learning

(d) at all the above levels

**64. Mathematics is hierarchical in nature and the concepts are logically structured and connected. Which of the following statements most appropriately explains this?**
**(A) Multiplication follows and builds on the concept of addition.**
**(B) Addition and multiplication are distinct concepts independent of each other.**
**(C) Mathematical concepts should only be assessed through summative assessments.**
**(D) Number sense needs to be developed before the concept of addition and subtraction.**
**Choose the correct option.**

(a) (B) and (C)

(b) (A) and (D)

(c) (A), (B) and (D)

(d) (C) and (D)

**65. Who stated this definition: "Mathematics is the indispensable instrument of all physical researches"?**

(a) Gauss      (b) Kant

(c) Aristotle      (d) Bacon

**66. The main feature(s) of the language of mathematics is(are):**

(a) Accuracy

(b) Authenticity

(c) Both (A) and (B)

(d) None of these

**67. Identify the correct statement with respect to the mathematics curriculum.**

(a) The concept of symmetry should be introduced only at upper primary level.

(b) The concept of tessellation should be introduced at upper primary level for better understanding.

(c) The concept of ratio should be introduced only at upper primary level.

(d) The foundation of linear equation can be laid at primary level.

**68. Activity-Centred Curriculum is based on:**

(a) The premise that child loves to play and activity will help to create motivation

(b) Help the child to enjoy Mathematics, to make him realize its beauty, and to remove the fear of difficulty of the subject

(c) The premise that whenever a child encounters a new experience, he/she can either easily connect it

(d) The role of students in this approach is to repeat what teacher transacted in the classroom

**69. According to Van Hiele Theory, there are five levels of thinking in geometry. Rigour represent which level of Van Hiele Theory?**

(a) 1st level      (b) 2nd level

(c) 3rd level      (d) 4th level

**70. While introducing the concept of multiplication Ms Neetu, a class II teacher, started with word problems such as "There are 4 members in a family and if each member requires 3 rotis for lunch, how many rotis are required? What is the objective of using this type of word problems to introduce the concept?**

(a) To improve the communication skills of children

(b) To develop the ability to connect real life situation with mathematical problems.

(c) To integrate mathematics and language classes

(d) To focus only on developing mathematical language among children

**71. To asses the students competency on solving of word problems based on addition and subtraction, rubrics of assessment are:**

(a) understanding of problem and writing of correct solution

(b) identification of problem, performing correct operation

(c) incorrect, partially correct, completely correct

(d) comprehension of problem, identification of operation to be performed, representation of problem mathematically, solution of problem and presentation of problem

**72. Identify the correct statement about the ability to conserve different physical quantities in 'measurement' as proposed by Piaget.**

(a) Conservation of volume is grasped before conservation of mass.

(b) Conservation of weight is grasped before conservation of number.

(c) Conservation of length is grasped before conservation of number.

(d) Conservation of weight is grasped before conservation of volume.

**73. A mathematics teacher asks the students to identify all the rectangles in a tangram. The above activity is appropriate for assessing the learners at which level of geometric reasoning according to the Van-Hiele**

(a) Visualization

(b) Axiomatic

(c) Establishing relationships between different shapes

(d) Recognition of shapes

**74. Some students of your class are repeatedly not able to do well in mathematics examinations and tests. As a teacher you would:**

(a) make them sit with high achievers

(b) explain the consequences of not doing well

(c) give more tests for practice

(d) diagnose the causes and take steps for remediation

**75. Knowing the nature and characteristics of error by the students while solving mathematics problems is called _______.**

(a) Content analysis in Mathematics

(b) Error analysis in Mathematics

(c) Content synthesis in Mathematics

(d) Error synthesis in Mathematics

**76.** Find the value of $x$ :
$$2^3 \times 3^4 \times 1080 \div 15 = 6^x$$
(a) 4      (b) 6
(c) 8      (d) 2

**77.** A class II student reads 203 as twenty three. As a teacher, which one of the following activities would you do so that the student realises his error?
(a) Writing numbers in numeral form
(b) Drill and practise worksheets
(c) Using beads and strings
(d) Reading number chart

**78.** Direction: Following pie chart shows the percentage break up of students who participated in the CAT entrance test for MBA from different states.
Total Number of students is 8800 .

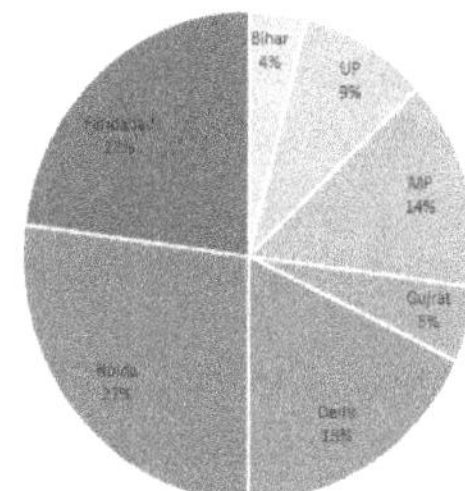

Find the ratio of students from UP to Students from MP.
(a) 1 : 8      (b) 9 : 14
(c) 10 : 14      (d) 2 : 5

**79.** What will come next $24, 20, 16, 12$
(a) 8      (b) 10
(c) 9      (d) 11

**80.** How many times is 400 g contained in 49.2 kg?
(a) 153      (b) 133
(c) 123      (d) 113

**81.** Ranjan can cycle from point A to point B in 40 minutes 20 seconds. She returns back from point B to A in 1 hour 20 minutes. She cycles for _______ seconds.
(a) 7,220 seconds
(b) 7,620 seconds
(c) 6,220 seconds
(d) 7,240 seconds

**82.** From each of the four corners of a rectangular sheet of dimensions 48 cm × 27 cm, a square of side 3.5 cm is cut off and a box is made. The volume of the box is:
(a) $2880 \text{ cm}^3$      (b) $2780 \text{ cm}^3$
(c) $2870 \text{ cm}^3$      (d) $2860 \text{ cm}^3$

**83.** The difference between the length and the breadth of a rectangle is 10 cm and the perimeter is 80 cm. Which of the following can be the length and breadth of this rectangle?
(a) L = 15 cm, B = 15 cm
(b) L = 15 cm, B = 25 cm
(c) L = 15 cm, B = 35 cm
(d) L = 25 cm, B = 15 cm

**84.** The radius of a metallic solid sphere is 21.6 cm. It is melted and drawn into a wire of uniform cross section. If the length of the wire is 259.2 m, then the radius of the wire is:
(a) 0.72 cm      (b) 0.9 cm
(c) 0.54 cm      (d) 0.8 cm

**85.** Ratio of Present age of A and B is 5 : 3 . If the difference between the age of A, 10 years hence and the age of B, 4 years ago is 20 years, then find Present age of A.
(a) 11 years      (b) 15 years
(c) 17 years      (d) 20 years

**86.** Which of the following is the largest fraction: $\frac{3}{4}, \frac{5}{8}, \frac{7}{9}, \frac{1}{2}$ ?
(a) $\frac{5}{8}$      (b) $\frac{3}{4}$
(c) $\frac{7}{9}$      (d) $\frac{1}{2}$

**87.** If the length and breadth of a rectangle are in the ratio 3 : 2 and its perimeter is 20 cm, then the area of the rectangle is:
(a) $24 \text{ cm}^2$      (b) $22 \text{ cm}^2$
(c) $20 \text{ cm}^2$      (d) $48 \text{ cm}^2$

**88.** Two persons are standing on opposite ends of a field of length 1500 meters. If they are running towards each other at 10 km/hr and 20 km/hr respectively, after how much time will they meet each other?
(a) 220 seconds    (b) 120 seconds
(c) 150 seconds    (d) 180 seconds

**89.** If the sum of two positive numbers is 65 and the square root of their product is 26 , then the sum of their reciprocals is:
(a) $\frac{5}{52}$      (b) $\frac{7}{52}$
(c) $\frac{1}{52}$      (d) $\frac{3}{52}$

**90.** The weights of 3 boxes are 4, 5 & 11 kilograms. Which of the following cannot be the total weight, in kilograms, of any combination of these boxes?
(a) 20      (b) 16
(c) 17      (d) 15



**91.** Which is NOT an example of one-sided symbiotic relationship?
(a) Cattle egrets and cattle
(b) A hermit crab and an empty seashells
(c) A spider on a tree
(d) Tapeworm in host's stomach

**92.** Which act seeks to consolidate the law relating to forests, the transit of forest produce and the duty that can be levied on timber and other forest produce?
(a) Indian Forest Act, 1927
(b) The Forest Conservation Act, 1980
(c) Indian Forest Act, 1865
(d) Wildlife Protection Act, 1972

**93.** Wheat requires _____ of annual rainfall evenly distributed over the growing season.
(a) 25 to 50 cm    (b) 75 to 100 cm
(c) 50 to 75 cm    (d) 85 to 130 cm

**94.** _______ is the famous scientist from Sweden, known as the inventor of dynamite.
(a) Thomas Alva Edison
(b) Neils Bohr
(c) Alfred Nobel
(d) Marie Curie

**95.** At school level, the important objective of environmental education is to build and develop skills of _____ that concern humans and the world around them.
a. adjustment
b. reasoning
c. evaluating
d. making decisions
(a) a, d and b      (b) a, c and d
(c) a, c and d      (d) b, c and d

**96.** Green algae are green because of:
(a) phycoerythrin
(b) chlorophyll
(c) xanthophylls
(d) phycobilin

**97.** Which of the following is a plant hormone that helps in cell division?
(a) Auxin      (b) Abscisic acid
(c) Cytokinin      (d) Gibberellin

**98.** Which of the following food components give energy to our body?
(a) Carbohydrates
(b) Cholesterol

(c) Fat

(d) All of the above

**99. What is the most abundant element found in human body?**

(a) Oxygen    (b) Carbon

(c) Iron    (d) Nitrogen

**100. Which vitamin is chemically called ascorbic acid?**

(a) Vitamin D    (b) Vitamin C

(c) Vitamin K    (d) Vitamin E

**101. Fossil fuels are used in:**

(a) Non-conventional energy production

(b) Conventional energy production

(c) Wind energy production

(d) Solar fuel cells

**102. Which of the following type of irrigation system is practiced on small scale in India?**

(a) Lift Irrigation

(b) Flood Irrigation

(c) Natural sub-irrigation

(d) Artificial sub-irrigation

**103. The bacterium which provides nitrogen to the leguminous plants is:**

(a) Rhizobium    (b) Yeast

(c) Fungi    (d) Lichens

**104. Water harvesting is a method which:**

(a) Increase ground water level

(b) Not practised in modern days

(c) Has no relation with ground water

(d) Decrease ground water level

**105. Ascaris infection is transmitted by:**

(a) mosquito bite

(b) Tse-tse fly

(c) consuming uncooked pork

(d) drinking contaminated water with eggs of Ascaris

**106. The integrated nature of EVS helps to:**

(a) reduce curriculum load and help children to learn meaningfully.

(b) follow child-centered approach and introduce larger number of concepts.

(c) learn from information and description provided.

(d) reduce the curriculum load and introduce specific topics.

**107. EVS for classes-III to V is a subject**

area which integrates __________.

(a) the concepts and issues of Science.

(b) the concepts and issues of Science, Social studies and Environmental education.

(c) the concepts and issues of Social science and Science.

(d) the concepts and issues of Science and Environmental education.

**108. Giving importance to individual experiences of child will help teacher in EVS classroom:**

(a) In knowing some special experience of child

(b) Help in improving language and communication skill of child

(c) Helps them in maintaining discipline in class

(d) Helps them in connecting with the children and enable them in teaching EVS by relating it with their experiences

**109. Which one of the following is not an objective of the study of EVS in relation to Social Sciences?**

(a) It should enable children to question existing ideas and practices.

(b) It should enable children to grow up as a responsible member of society.

(c) It should enable children to respect differences in cultural practices.

(d) It should enable children to learn the correct definition of key terms.

**110. Which one of the following will be a more effective learning experience to emphasize more on social inequalities in an EVS class?**

(a) Showing video films on related issue

(b) Organizing special lectures on related issue

(c) Conducting a quiz contest on the issue

(d) Asking the students to undertake group projects

**111. Learning of mathematical tables by children is an example of:**

(a) Paired-Associate Learning

(b) Concept Learning

(c) Classical Conditioning

(d) Serial Learning

**112. A science exhibition was organized in Rohan's school. It was organized with an objective.**

Which in your view is the most appropriate objective?

(a) establish a name for the school

(b) satisfy the parents

(c) trained students for various professions

(d) provide a creative channel for learners

**113. A teacher asks every child to use some waste material from their homes and make something useful out of it.**

The pedagogical intention of the teacher is not to:

(a) judge the best student in the class

(b) develop creativity among children

(c) make children understand the concept of recycling, reuse and reduce

(d) organize an exhibition of best articles made out of waste

**114. Which of the following is not included in Emotional skills under CCE?**

(a) Reduction in fear

(b) Increase in learning

(c) Increase in empathy

(d) Reduction in anger

**115. Which one of the following is not an objective of including poems and stories in EVS textbooks?**

(a) To develop an interest in the subject

(b) To have a change in routine and monotonous content

(c) To provide fun and enjoyment for learners

(d) To promote imaginative and creative ability in the learners

**116. Which of the following statements is true?**

(a) Audio-visual aids are useful for students

(b) Chart and graphs are audio-visual aids

(c) Charts are useful only in social studies

(d) Audio-visual aids are not important for efficiency in teaching

**117. Laboratory experiment in science will be classified as __________.**

(a) Audio aid

(b) Visual aid

(c) Activity aid

(d) Audio-visual aid

**118. The moisture level required for**

vermicomposting should be between _____.
(a) Below 30 per cent
(b) 40 and 50 per cent
(c) 70 and 80 per cent
(d) Above 90 per cent

119. **Which of these elements is present in the drinking water that can lead to numerous fatal diseases?**
(a) Phosphorus
(b) Calcium
(c) Arsenic
(d) None of the above

120. **In which of these years was the Forest Conservation Act amended?**
(a) 1978     (b) 1988
(c) 1963     (d) 1952

## // Hints and Solutions //

**1(A).** The growth and development of an individual is greatly affected by heredity and environment as well as the interaction between heredity and environment. However, there are certain issues and controversies related to this phenomena. The above-mentioned question essentially highlights the nature-nurture debate as:
- The nature versus nurture debate is one of the oldest issues in psychology. The debate centers on the relative contributions of genetic inheritance and environmental factors to human development.
- The term 'nature' stands for what comes to children through genetic influences and heredity, i.e. it denotes the influence of factors inherent in the child himself from the time he is conceived.
- On the other hand, the term 'nurture' stands for the influence of the environment on child development, i.e. all the contextual factors that influence who we are, including our perceptions of early childhood, our social relationships, and the society around us.
- In other words, the controversy on nature versus nurture concerns whether human behaviour is influenced by the environment or by genes of an individual.
- Heredity and environment both play a significant role in the development of children. Any individual trait is the 'result' of both genetics and the environment. Heredity determines the probable biological limits, whereas the environment determines the level up to which the development is possible.

So, it could be concluded that the above-mentioned question essentially highlights the nature-nurture debate.

**2(D).** Development is the pattern of progressive, orderly, and predictable changes that begin at conception and continue throughout life . Development mostly involves changes both growth and decline, as observed during old age.

A child coming to pre-school for the first time cries profusely. After two years when the same child goes to the primary school for the first time, he does not express his tension by crying rather his shoulder and neck muscles become tense. This change in his behaviour is due to the principle of diffrentiation and integration of development.

Development is characterized by differentiation and integration-
- Werner proposed that development consisted of two processes: integration and differentiation .
- Integration refers to the idea that development consists of the integration of more basic, previously acquired behaviours into new, higher level structures.
- Differentiation refers to the idea that development also involves the progressive ability to make more distinctions among things.
- So when a child starts from crying then changes his behaviour to does not express his tension by crying rather his shoulder and neck muscles become tense. This shows that he learns to successfully reach for objects has learned to coordinate a variety of skills.

Thus from above-mentioned points, it is clear that child's this behaviour shows the principle of integration and differentiation od development.

**3(A).** Certain aspects of development are influenced more by heredity and others more by the environment statements is true about the role of heredity and the environment.

Development describes the growth of humans throughout the lifespan, from conception to death. Development does not just involve the biological and physical aspects of growth, but also the cognitive and social aspects associated with development.

Role of Heredity and the Environment in Development:
- Each individual is a product of the interaction between heredity and environment.
- A child born with a rich intellectual background cannot become a full-fledged personality if he/she does not get suitable environmental conditions.
- Similarly, there is the least chance of development, if you provide better environmental conditions in the form of schooling to a child who does not inherit a good intellectual ability.
- There exists a controversy regarding whether the heredity (nature) or environment (nurture) as the determining factor in the growth and development of the child.

**4(C).** Social development of a child actually begins in early childhood.

Social development: It refers to the way a child learns to interact with others and develop social relationships with others. It is the trust the child develops through early experiences at home and the independence that developed in exploring things around that impacts the social development of a child.

Social development in infancy: As an infant, strong ties are established between the child and his/her caretaker, generally mother, father, or family members.

Social development in early childhood: At this stage, most children typically begin to:
- Develop friendships with other kids
- Compare themselves to other children and adults
- Understand other people's thoughts and feelings
- Initiate or join in play with other children and makeup games
- Show an understanding of right and wrong
- Listen while others are speaking

Social development during late childhood: At this stage, he learns to get along with his age-mates.

From the above, we can conclude that the social development of a child actually begins in early childhood.

**5(C).** Scaffolding is a teaching method that enables a student to solve a problem, carry out a task, or achieve a goal through a gradual shedding of outside assistance. Scaffolding literally means the structure which is made to support the work crew while a building is constructed or repaired.

Vygotsky's Sociocultural Theory of Learning:
- Vygotsky was a Russian psychologist who believed that social interactions play a key role in development. According to him, learning occurs when children interact with people and the environment.
- He asserted that the cognitive development of children is enhanced through social interaction with other people, particularly those who are more skilled.
- He explains this with the concept of the Zone of Proximal Development (ZPD), which refers to a range of tasks that a child can achieve only with assistance from a more skilled adult or peer called the More Knowledgeable Other (MKO). Adult assistance is provided wherever necessary which is called Scaffolding.

Discovery learning is a technique of inquiry-based learning and is considered a constructivist based approach to education. It can occur whenever the student is not provided with an exact answer but rather the materials in order to find the answer themselves.

Inter-subjectivity is the process where two participants begin a task with a different understanding and arrive at a shared understanding. It is essential that participants work towards the same goal.

So, according to Vygotsky, when adults adjust the support to extend the child's current level of performance, it is called Scaffolding.

**6(C).** 'Lev Vygotsky', a Soviet psychologist, has propounded the "Socio-cultural Theory". This theory implies the idea that social interaction plays a crucial role in the development of a learner's cognitive ability. His theory emphasizes that children learn through interaction and collaboration with skilled and knowledgeable people.

Z one of Proximal Development:
- It refers to the difference between what a learner can do on his/her own and what he/she can do with someone's help.
- It is a distance between the learner's actual development level and his/her level of development under someone's guidance.

Role of Socio-cultural environment in cognitive development:
- This theory implies the idea that social interaction is a primary cause and plays a crucial role in the learner's cognitive development.
- Children learn through interaction and collaboration with skilled and knowledgeable people.

Vygotsky's view on Language:
- Lev Vygotsky emphasized that the acquisition of speech is the major activity in cognitive development.
- He believed by acquiring language, the child modifies its higher mental functions.

So, it could be concluded that the statement 'It ignores the importance of language in cognitive development' is not true about the socio-cultural theory of Vygotsky.

**7(A).** Individualized Education Programme is planned from the perspective of child-centred education programme.

An Individualized Education Program is a legal document under United States law that is developed for each public school child in the U.S. who needs special education. It is created through a team of the child's parent and district personnel who are knowledgeable about the child's needs. IEPs must be reviewed every year to keep track of the child's educational progress.

**8(B).** Students who can effectively express their thoughts show Linguistic intelligence. Howard Gardner proposed the theory of multiple intelligences. According to him, intelligence is not a single entity; rather distinct types of intelligence exist. Each of this intelligence is independent of each other. Gardner also put forth that different types of intelligence interact and work together to find a solution to a problem. Gardner studied extremely talented persons, who had shown exceptional abilities in their respective areas.

Emotional intelligence (otherwise known as emotional quotient or EQ):
- It is the ability to understand, use, and manage your own emotions in positive ways to relieve stress, communicate effectively, empathize with others, overcome challenges, and defuse conflict.
- Emotional intelligence helps you build stronger relationships, succeed at school and work, and achieve your career and personal goals.
- It can also help you to connect with your feelings, turn intention into action, and make informed decisions about what matters most to you.

**9(B).** The correct answer is:
- The teacher asks questions to elicit classification from students.
- The teacher prompts and probes the students while making a presentation.
- The teacher indicates performance criteria and given judgemental values.

Formative evaluation is developmental, not judgemental in nature. Its purpose is to improve students learning and instruction. Therefore, its major function is feedback to the teacher and students to locate strengths and weaknesses in the teaching-learning process in order to improve it. It operates during instruction and ideally, should not be limited to the assessment of cognitive behaviours. All classroom assessments which are not used for grading purpose, whether these are unit tests, informal tests, questioning during teaching, home assignments, or teacher classroom observations of pupils' responses are examples of formative evaluation.

**10(B).** A teacher wants to diagnose the weaknesses of students to give them feedback so that their learning difficulties can be removed. Assessment for learning of assessment should be adopted by him.

Assessment is done to determine the outcomes (what students have learned), process (the way they learned), and their approach to the learning before, during, or after the program or course. During instruction, the assessment can be used to determine what students are learning so that if there is a need, the teacher can adjust their teaching method. It is a process-oriented approach that is used to identify the areas for improvement in the learning process.

**11(A).** The theory of multiple intelligences was first proposed by Howard Gardner in his 1983 book "Frames of Mind", where he broadens the definition of intelligence and outlines several distinct types of intellectual competencies.

Howard Gardner's theory of multiple intelligences proposes that people are not born with all of the intelligence they will ever have. This theory challenged the traditional notion that there is one single type of intelligence, sometimes known as "g" for general intelligence, that only focuses on cognitive abilities.
- The theory of multiple intelligences proposes the differentiation of human intelligence into specific "modalities of intelligence", rather than defining intelligence as a single, general ability.
- To broaden this notion of intelligence, Gardner introduced eight different types of intelligence consisting of: Linguistic, Logical/Mathematical, Spatial, Bodily-Kinesthetic, Musical, Interpersonal, Intrapersonal, and Naturalist.

We can conclude that "it can certainly be stated that the different types of intelligence included in Gardener's system of multiple intelligences is consistent with investigations of distinct talents and skills in individuals.

So, Multiple intelligence is only the 'talents' present in intelligence as a whole is a critique of the theory of multiple intelligences.

**12(C).** Developmental errors are common between a learner who is learning his mother tongue and the learner who learns the same language as a second language.

The developmental errors are of four types. They are as follows:
- Overgeneralization: It covers instances where the learner creates a deviant structure based on his experience of both structures in the target language.
- Ignorance of rule restriction: It is the failure to observe the restrictions of existing structures, that is, the application of rules to contexts where they do not apply.
- Incomplete application of rules: It is the failure to observe the application of complete rules in a particular context.
- False concepts hypothesized: In this, the errors derive from faulty comprehension of distinctions In the target language. These are sometimes due to poor gradation of teaching items.
- Simplification- In this students use simple rules instead of more complex ones.
- Hypercorrection- It shows the over-application of rules in language learning.

Thus from the above-mentioned points, it is clear that developmental errors are common between a learner who is learning his mother tongue and the learner who learns the same language as a second language.

**13(C).** Gender is a social construct that impacts attitudes, roles, responsibilities, and behaviour patterns of boys and girls, men, and women in all societies.

Gender Parity refers:
- To a statical representation of boy and girl data in a group.
- To assess the state of gender equality within a group or organization.
- When we divide the number of female students at a given level of education by the number of male students at the same level, the resulting value is called a gender parity score.

Thus from the above-mentioned points, it is clear that a comparison of the number of boys and girls who survive up to class 12 shows the criteria of gender parity in society.

**14(A).** Labelling them is not suitable to meet individual differences among learners.

Individual difference refers to the difference which distinguishes an individual from another on the basis of physical, emotional, or psychological characteristics.

A teacher should know the differences in each and every one of his students. He should know their value of perspectives and should satisfy his students' needs.

Steps to meet individual differences among learners:
- Ability grouping.
- Enrichment of curriculum.
- Individualization of instruction.
- Identification of special talents.
- Assessing learners' abilities.
- Making Individualisation necessary.
- Adoption of modern method of teaching.
- Providing adequate facilities and material.

**15(B).** Formative evaluation assesses the learning progress to provide continuous feedback to both teachers and students during instruction.

Formative assessment, formative evaluation, formative feedback, or assessment for learning, including diagnostic testing, is a range of formal and informal assessment procedures conducted by teachers during the learning process in order to modify teaching and learning activities to improve student attainment.
- Formative assessment is a bridge between learning and teaching. It allows instructors to gather real data about students as they work, then adjust their instruction to better serve students at their current learning level.
- Examples of formative assessments include asking students to: draw a concept map in class to represent their understanding of a topic, submit one or two sentences identifying the main

point of a lecture, turn in a research proposal for early feedback.

**16(B).** A child 'who is in the middle of his school (that is about ten and half years) is unable to do the work of the class below that which is normal for his age" is known as educationally retarded type of children.

Exceptional children are those who deviate from the normal population and need special education services to meet their needs. It includes children who are gifted, backward, creative, learning disabled, educationally retarded, etc.

The above-mentioned characteristic is related to 'Educationally retarded children' as a class consists of students with varying learning abilities as some learn fast and some learn slowly.
- An educationally retarded child is not mentally retarded or physically disabled.
- He may have a neurological handicap or emotional disorder which hinders their abilities.
- Appropriate training required to make educationally retarded children learn some self-care and communication skills.
- Educationally retarded children show the inability to do the work of the class below that which is normal for their age.

**17(A).** The term diversity used in discourse related to people or communities or in social contexts is more specific, indicates that a group of people is made up of individuals who are different from each other in some way or the other or it means collective differences among people. They can be diverse socially, educationally, economically, culturally, etc.

Effective strategies to address learners from disadvantaged and deprived backgrounds-
- Inclusive education is a movement to empower the vulnerable and marginalized groups to overcome the disadvantages of unequalized socialization and give them examples from diverse settings.
- The curriculum should to be specific and related to the needs and real-life experiences. Emphasis should be on learning manual skills, life skills and technical efficiency.
- Sometime the teacher should talk to the learners to understand their needs and challenges faced by them.
- Interest in learning has to be, created by the teache r, effort should be towards developing self-confidence, self-respect and a sense of cultural identity.
- Form collaborative groups to work on activities and encourage students to support each other.
- Motivate the students to set moderately challenging goals and provide appropriate instructional support.

Thus from above-mentioned points, it is clear that in order to address learners from diverse backgrounds, a teacher should draw examples from diverse settings.

**18(B).** Dyslexia has been used to refer to the specific learning problem of reading. Dyslexia is associated with the 'Reading disorder' as it refers to a difficulty in Reading, Writing, and Spelling.

Dyslexia is the most common learning disability(Reading disorder) which makes learners:
- confuse with the same shapes and sounds of the alphabet.
- unable to read, interpret, and understand letters and words.
- bewilder in identifying and relating speech sounds with letters and words.
- Dyslexia is a disorder in children who, despite conventional classroom experience, fail to attain the language skills of reading, writing, and spelling commensurate with their intellectual abilities.

Here it is clear that if a child writes 'b' as 'd', 'was' as 'saw', '21' as '12' then he/she has a language-based learning disability called Dyslexia.

**19(D).** Ruby has hearing impairment and all the students in her school have many such difficulties and disabilities. You call such schools special schools.

Special school: The meaning of special school is a school for children who have physical or mental problems. Special education or special needs education is the practice of educating students with special needs in a way that addresses their individual differences, disability, and special needs.

So, The nation is committed to provide equal opportunity to every child for optimal development. "Inclusive Education" has emerged as a guiding principle to envisage this vision. But, sometimes it is not possible to teach students with special needs in the general classroom. For such students, t he government has provided with special schools and special education, so that it could cater to their individual differences and disability.

**20(C).** I. A child with mental retardation will not need concrete material but will need repeated instruction to understand a concept.
- Children with learning disabilities show greater learning when techniques like task analysis, peer teaching, cooperative learning, learning corners, and multisensory approach are used. The following strategies would be helpful to both the parents and teachers when trying to teach such children
- Creating a social climate conducive to writing development. Teachers need to be encouraging in a non-threatening

environment and should try to develop a sense of community by promoting student sharing and collaboration.

- Integrate writing with subjects such as language and arts so as to stimulate writing skills.
- It is not only instruction that is required for children with special needs, in fact, but concrete materials also enhance the learning speed and efficiency.

II. A child with motor disabilities will need physician support depending on the need.

- Motor impairment is the partial or total loss of function of a body part, usually a limb or limb. This may result in muscle weakness, poor stamina, lack of muscle control, or total paralysis. Motor impairment is often evident in neurological conditions such as cerebral palsy, Parkinson's disease, stroke, and multiple sclerosis.
- A child with motor disabilities requires special attention and often needs a physician's support.

So, A child with motor disabilities will need physician support depending on the need is correct.

**21(C).** Misconceptions among students represent their native and intuitive understanding about concepts.

- A misconception is a thought process that goes in the wrong direction due to a lack of complete information or just ignorance.
- Misconceptions are not always baseless rather they represent children's native and intuitive understanding about concepts and the world around them as it shows their thinking and they can think and put forward their views.
- The formation of misconceptions is very natural among children as well as adults because it is a natural thought process and no two minds can think alike exactly.
- A teacher should definitely attend to misconceptions as they are significant in process of teaching-learning because they are very helpful; in developing critical thinking. Without this, a child would not be able to put forward one's own views and would end up mugging things.

Hence, the correct option is (B).

**22(D).** Presentation step is prominent in the syntax of teaching model of memory level and understanding level.

Presentation step is prominent in the syntax of the teaching model of memory level and understanding level. It is the most important step as it gives the major status to the subject matter.

In the Presentation Step:

- The teacher introduces new knowledge in an interactive manner before the learners.
- The teacher tries to connect the previous knowledge of the learners with

a new set of knowledge.

- The teacher believes that when any topic is presented properly to the students they learn them in a coherent way.

**23(D).** Problematic children are those children who are difficult to raise or educate. They have a tendency to disrupt class as they are not self-controlled. Also, they are infamous for their anti-social behaviour.

Teacher have to tackle many problems associated with students as children with numerous problems of behaviour are found in every educational programme.

In the above-mentioned situation, the teacher should p rovide counselling to the child as it will help the teacher to:

- become more vigilant towards the child.
- recognize the root of the child's problem.
- better relate to child's unacceptable behaviour.
- assist the child with proper guidance in the right way.

So, it could be concluded that if a teacher finds a problematic child in the class, he should p rovide counselling to the child.

**24(D).** Permissive discipline is developed as a revolt against the authoritarian discipline many adults had been subjected to during their childhood.

The role of discipline is to teach children to behave per the expectations of their age. Throughout babyhood, babies begin to make correct specific responses to specific situations at home as well as in the neighborhood.

- When strict discipline is followed, involving emphasis on punishment for wrongdoing even very young babies can be forced into a pattern of behavior.
- Punishment for wrong behavior and rewarding with approval and affection for appropriate behavior will begin the education of values and moral standards in babyhood.
- Disciplining is society's way of teaching children the moral behavior approved by the social group

**25(D).** Constructivism theory of educational psychology deals with prior knowledge of the child and takes into consideration the social and cultural determinants in the process of learning.

Constructivism is the theory that says learners construct knowledge rather than just passively take in information. As people experience the world and reflect upon those experiences, they build their own representations and incorporate new information into their pre-existing knowledge (schemas).

**26(A).** The correct answer is: Alternative conceptions and misconceptions formed by students should be highly discouraged by the teacher.

Alternative conceptions (misconceptions) can really impede learning for several reasons. First, students generally are unaware that the knowledge they have is wrong. Moreover, misconceptions can be very entrenched in student thinking. In addition, students interpret new experiences through these erroneous understandings, thereby interfering with being able to correctly grasp new information. Also, alternative conceptions (misconceptions) tend to be very resistant to instruction because learning entails replacing or radically reorganizing student knowledge. So, conceptual change has to occur for learning to happen. This puts teachers in the very challenging position of needing to bring about significant conceptual change in student knowledge. Generally, ordinary forms of instruction, such as lectures, labs, discovery learning, or simply reading texts, are not very successful at overcoming student misconceptions. For all these reasons, misconceptions can be hard nuts for teachers to crack. However, several instructional strategies have proven to be effective in achieving conceptual change and helping students leave their alternative conceptions behind and learn correct concepts or theories.

**27(D).** Perception about your bodily changes, following an event, brings forth emotion is James Lange theory.

The James Lange theory is a hypothesis on the origin and nature of emotions and is one of the earliest theories of emotion within modern psychology. It was developed by philosopher John Dewey and named for two 19th-century scholars, William James and Carl Lange. The basic premise of the theory is that physiological arousal instigates the experience of emotion. Instead of feeling an emotion and subsequent physiological response, the theory proposes that the physiological change is primary, and emotion is then experienced when the brain reacts to the information received via the body's nervous system. It proposes that each specific category of emotion is attached to a unique and different pattern of physiological arousal and emotional behaviour in the reaction due to an exciting stimulus.

**28(C).** Motivation is considered a psychological factor.

Learning is a process that refers to a change in behaviour, knowledge and skill as a result of practice and experience. There are many factors that affect learning and the 'psychological aspect' is one of them. Psychological Factors are the elements of one's personality that limit or enhance the ways that one learn and thinks. Some Psychological factors that affect learning are :

- Physical Health (Age)
- Readiness
- Maturation and Ability
- Motivation and Interest
- Learning Desire
- Positive Learning Environment

Motivation is the psychological factor that initiates, guides and maintains goal oriented behaviour. It is the process of stimulating people to action for accomplishing the goal. Motivation is an urge to behave or act in a way that will satisfy certain conditions, such as wishes, desires, or goals.

**29(B).** The period of learning, where no improvement in performance is made, is called plateau of learning.

Learning Curve: A learning curve visualizes changes in pupil overall performance over time. The line graph displays opportunities across the x-axis, and a measure of student performance along the y-axis.

Learning Plateau:

- If the learner arrives at a plateau in his learning process, imperfect linguistic items, rules, and subsystems will become relatively permanently incorporated into the learning system of a second language learner, in spite of further experience, explanation, or instruction.
- The period of learning, where no improvement in performance is made,
- A learning plateau occurs when you stop learning quickly . It's easy to make quick progress early on, when you learn more, you naturally slow down. Because of this, learning plateau frequently occurs when learners reach an intermediate level of learning.

**30(D).** The characteristics of community influence education:

- Demographics
- Occupational Patterns and Financial position
- Customs and Traditions

When individuals live together in a common territory, have the feeling of mutuality, develop organized interaction among them, it is called the community spirit. The community is a social group characterized by the community spirit. The examples are a village, a town, a city etc. The community, therefore, is an expression of the unity of the common life of a group of people. In other words, the life of members of a community is wholly lived in it and there is very little they need to share with outside.

**31(C).** According to the second paragraph of the passage, which states "There was also the incident of low intensity blasts just outside Bengaluru's M. Chinnaswamy Stadium on April 17, 2010, ahead of a match featuring Royal Challengers Bangalore and Mumbai Indians".

- The highlighted word 'ahead' means 'earlier than or before someone or something'. So we can conclude that the blasts were occurred before the match not during the ongoing match. Thus, statement A is false.

According to the first line of the second paragraph of the passage, which states "The IPL's 14th edition is at the crossroads, a reality which it had avoided since its launch in 2008".

- In the above line, it is clearly mentioned that IPL was launched in 2008. Thus, statement B is true.

**32(A).** According to the first paragraph of the passage, which states "Until the emergence of the COVID-positive results of Kolkata Knight Riders' Sandeep Warrier and Varun Chakravarthy; Sunrisers Hyderabad's Wriddhiman Saha; Delhi Capitals' Amit Mishra, Chennai Super Kings' bowling coach L. Balaji and a member of the squad's logistics staff, the Board of Control for Cricket in India (BCCI) was in denial-mode".

- It can be understood that 4 players (Wriddhiman Saha, Amit Mishra, Sandeep Warrier, Varun Chakravarthy), a coach (L. Balaji) and a member of logistics staff has been tested positive.

Therefore, there are total 6; 4 cricketers, 1 coach, 1 member of logistic staff people had been found COVID-19 positive according to the passage due to which the IPL was suspended.

**33(D).** According to the first paragraph of the passage, which states "the Board of Control for Cricket in India (BCCI) was in denial-mode, firmly believing that its bio-bubble protocols cannot be breached. BCCI officials also insisted that the league is not a super-spreader like election rallies or other permitted activities where crowds were allowed to assemble. That both fans and the media were kept away from the venues was cited as an example of how strict the IPL management was with regard to social-distancing. Besides this, the constant testing of everyone in the bubble was seen as another fail-safe method to ensure that the league did not turn into a coronavirus hotspot".

Upon perusal of the above lines it is clear that all three arguments given in the question were put forward by the BCCI in support of its decision.

**34(B).** The correct answer is 'Delhi's is facing a glooming situation because the surge in COVID positive cases'.

The passage talks about the suspension of IPL due to COVID positive results of several players and staff.

According to the last line of the first paragraph of the passage, which states "But before the final denouement, what jarred was the tone-deafness of having matches in

Delhi while beyond the ground, the accompanying note was that of ambulances blaring their sirens while patients gasped for oxygen".

In above mentioned lines, the author criticizes the decision of the board to organize IPL matches in Delhi where people are badly hit by the virus and there is a abject scarcity of oxygen supplies.

Thus, we can infer that the situation in Delhi is absolutely grim due to the surge in COVID cases.

**35(A).** The antonym of the word 'Tenuous' as used in the passage is 'substantial'.

'Tenuous' means 'weak, unimportant, or in doubt'

- Example: The aging dictator's hold on power is tenuous.

The marked option 'substantial' means 'large in size, value, or importance'

- Example: She inherited a substantial fortune from her grandmother.

From the above explanation it is clear that 'substantial' is opposite in meaning to 'tenuous'.

**36(A).** According to the second paragraph of the passage, which states "Meanwhile, the board officials are hinting about resuming the league later this year in the United Arab Emirates, which also hosted the 13th leg".

Two conclusions can be drawn from the above lines;

- (1) The 13th season was hosted by the United Arab Emirates.
- (2) The board officials are hinting that the league might resume in the United Arab Emirates.

Thus, the statement in option (A) is true while that in option (B) is false. Also, the statement in option (D) is false.

According to the last line of the first paragraph of the passage, which states "Even if the league has its share of a massive television audience and offers a diversion to the viewers, having Delhi as a host was extremely insensitive".

From the above line, it is clear that IPL has a massive television audience (not limited). Thus, the statement in option (C) is also false.

**37(B).** The correct answer is 'having Delhi as a venue of matches'.

According to the last line of the first paragraph, which states "Even if the league has its share of a massive television audience and offers a diversion to the viewers, having Delhi as a host was extremely insensitive".

Upon perusal of above line, it can be understood that the situation in Delhi is grim due to the COVID-19 spread and the infected people are suffering from the scarcity of oxygen supply. In such a disturbing atmosphere, according to the author, having Delhi as a venue of the matches was highly insensitive.

**38(B).** The synonym of the word 'Ominous' as used in the passage is 'Sinister'.
'Ominous' means 'suggesting that something unpleasant is likely to happen'
- Example: There were ominous dark clouds gathering overhead.

The marked option 'sinister' means 'making you feel that something bad or evil might happen'
- Example: The ruined house had a sinister appearance.

From the above explanation, it is clear that 'sinister' is similar in meaning to 'ominous'.

**39(A).** The correct synonym of the word 'resumption' is 'resuscitation'.
'Resumption' means 'the start of something again after it has stopped'
- Example: The president called for an immediate ceasefire and a resumption of negotiations between the two sides.

The marked option 'resuscitation' means 'the act of bringing someone or something back to life or waking them'
- Example: The prime minister said that small businesses would play a full part in the resuscitation of the economy.

From the above explanation, it is clear that 'resuscitation' is the most similar in meaning to 'resumption'.

**40(D).** According to the lines:
- Of dark goddess biting apples
- And then awakening naked
- Water like vital tears

Thus, we can conclude that Mortal doesn't apply to the river as it is not mentioned anywhere in the poem.

**41(C).** A simile is a device used to compare two different objects to understand meanings by comparing these object's qualities with the help of 'like' or 'as'.
In the lines, "Water like vital tears." The poet compares water with tears.
Thus, a simile has been used.

**42(C).** Vital: absolutely necessary; essential
- Example: Our skin is one of the most vital parts of the body.

Important: of great significance or value
- Example: Fish is an important food source for people.

Thus, the synonym of 'vital' is 'important'.

**43(D).** According to the lines:
Like a tree of veins your spectre
Of dark goddess biting apples:
And then awakening naked
To be tattoed by the rivers,
And in the wet heights your head
Filled the world with new dew.
Thus, upon the perusal of the above lines, it can be deduced that the poet says that the river is the image of Mother Nature(as implied by the words 'goddess' and fills the world with new dew).

**44(C).** Imagery: the formation of mental images, figures, or likenesses of things, or of such images collectively
It is language used by poets, novelists and other writers to create images in the mind of the reader. Imagery includes figurative and metaphorical language to improve the reader's experience through their senses.
Similarly, in the line, "You are made of wellsprings" , a mental image has been created to say that water rose up to your waist and you are made of wellsprings.
Thus, imagery has been used.

**45(B).** The poet describes the river as a giver of life, of a goddess; the river is the image of Mother Nature. The force of the river is mighty.
He says that river cuts through the forests and finds it's way to flow.
Thus, the true statement is that "River is the giver of new life".

**46(A).** While studying class 6 Saurabh reads the sequence of letters in reverse order, he is suffering from dyslexia.
Dyslexia: This reading disability arises when there is a disorder or problem in reading which is called dyslexia. Dyslexia is a combination of two Greek words dos and lexis which literally mean speech language, it is the most common type of learning disability. Affects written form, oral form and linguistic proficiency of co-language.
Symptoms of dyslexia-
- Difficulty learning alphabet.
- Difficulty learning the sounds of letters.
- Difficulty in concentration.
- He gets stuck again and again while reading.
- Reversing words or reversing the sequence of letters, e.g. recognizing a name, reading doubts to a cub.
- Suffering from spelling defects.
- Decreased memory power. Not being able to recognize sounds with similar pronunciation.
- Lack of dictionary.

**47(D).** The correct answer is: Language acquisition is natural and language learning is deliberate/instructed.
Language is the medium of communication. People share their inner feelings and opinions with the help of language. Language development is continuous and recursive. Thus, language is either acquired or learned.
Language acquisition is the process by which humans acquire the capacity to perceive and comprehend language as well as to produce and use words and sentences to communicate.
Language learning is a conscious process, is the product of either a formal learning situation or a self-study programme.

**48(C).** The principle of motivation principle of teaching English creates a zeal to learn something new in language.
Principle of Language Teaching: To achieve the desired goals in English language teaching, a teacher uses the various principles. Each of them is listed below along with their characteristics.
It includes motivating the learners intrinsically to learn the language, guiding them to achieve the specific goals of language learning, and emphasizing learner's satisfaction to learn and improve the language.

**49(A).** A remedial teaching class is one that is meant to improve a learning skill or rectify a particular problem area in a student.
- In the above situation, the child needs remedial classes to improve spellings.
- Students who have trouble spell may need remedial teaching in English.
- There are many reasons why children may have difficulty in spelling such as memory problems resulting in letter reversals, lack of understanding letter-sound relationships, not reading or writing enough or trouble remembering sight words.
- If proper guidance and help are given to such children, they can overcome their difficulty with time and practice.

So, we conclude that in the above situation, the child needs He needs remedial classes to improve spelling.

**50(B).** The correct answer is: Telling the story to the students and asking comprehensible questions on it.
Listening or hearing is the process of receiving messages from oral, verbal, and nonverbal communication and interpreting the same.
- Hearing is a part of listening. We listen through ears, eyes, mind, and heart (empathy).
- Listening task not only the current input but also the matter that is already existing in the memory.
- Hearing in a classroom is different from hearing to the same from the same teacher privately.
- Hearing ability can be assured by telling a story and then asking comprehensible questions based on it as it involves the students in listening or hearing the story carefully and will make students think, analyze, and criticize the story before answering the questions.

**51(D).** The new National Education Policy of India mentioned that the mode of instruction at the primary level of classes must be the mother-tongue of children as they are already familiar with their native language.
In terms of a child's personal growth, the shift to learning in the mother tongue at

the primary level of learning will do a lot of good. Here's why:

- A child's learning begins at home in the mother tongue and when a child comes to school to learn in a foreign language, it does slow down the learning process.
- Continuing the learning in the mother tongue will ensure faster learning and retention by comprehending easily.
- Exposure to more than one language leads to higher synaptic activity in the brain of a child and multi-language processing leads to higher mental agility. This mental flexibility transfers to all areas of brain functioning.
- The use of the mother tongue as a medium of instruction will also result in a higher rate of parental participation in a child's learning . In India due to a lack of knowledge of English, many parents are unable to participate in their child's schooling effectively.

So, Learning in the mother tongue helps a student to easily comprehend what is being taught.

**52(A).** A teacher collects the instances of learning and performances of learners and makes a note of them to report in the assessment record. What is this assessment process known as Portfolio assessment.

Assessment is a process of collecting, receiving, and using data for the purpose of improvement in the learning process. It is one of the crucial components of the teaching-learning process.

A portfolio is a tool for assessing a variety of skills not usually testable in a single setting of the traditional written paper and pencil tests. It keeps the students' work of language use and uses it for assessing the learners' achievement.

**53(C).** Speaking is the process of transmitting information from the source to the receiver. The form or method of transmission of information when occurs through verbal communication is known as speaking.

Following things are necessary for assessing speaking tasks:

- While speaking assessment the teachers will consider pronunciation as incorrect pronunciation leads to ambiguity in communication.
- Teachers would also consider the assessment of the usage of words in the correct structure in a context as correct structure is the essence of any language.
- Clarity of the speech is also assessed while evaluating speaking because, without the clarity of the speech, communication is not going to be effective.

Thus, from the above-mentioned points, it is clear that using sources and dictionaries is not necessary while assessing speaking tasks.

**54(B).** A teacher divides her class students into pairs (As and Bs). The "A Partner" should dictate the words to "Partner B" and "Partner B" should fill the gaps without watching the "Partner A" worksheet to get the full content. What is this task known as Mutual dictation.

Dictation refers to the practice of speaking or reading aloud words to be noted down by others. It is of various types as explained below:

Mutual dictation: The main aim of the activity is to target the reading and writing skills by dictating the information to each other in order to get the complete text. This is one of the great activities to develop listening, reading, and writing skills integratively. Mutual dictation will help the children to develop writing skills as well as reading very effectively.

**55(B).** Language teaching is less about the school and more about the process of learning English. The modern approach to all language learning and teaching is the scientific one and is based on sound linguistic principles.

- Principle of Graded Patterns is one of the principles of materials preparation for language learning that emphasizes that materials need to be graded appropriately .
- "To teach a language is to impart a new system of complex habits, and habits are acquired slowly." So, language patterns should be taught gradually , in cumulative graded steps.
- This means the teacher should go on adding each new element or pattern to previous ones . New patterns of language should be introduced and practiced with vocabulary that students already know.

So, we can conclude that one of the principles of materials preparation for language learning is that materials need to be graded appropriately.

**56(B).** There are different kinds of teaching models in fashion to facilitate language teaching which include Top-down model, Bottom-up model, etc.

**T op-down model:**

In this approach, the learner utilizes the background or previous knowledge to figure out the meaning of language. It is a reading approach that focuses on:

- looking at language as a whole rather than individual sounds, words and phrases.
- concentrating on the meaning rather than grammatical structures and individual words.
- understanding the subject matter without necessarily going into detail of the particular topic.

So, we conclude that the above statement refers to the top-down model.

**57(A).** Grammatical units should be presented in a clear and interesting way through activities, this helps to the learners to do only then and understand the rules.

The psychological methods of teaching grammar are the inductive method, the language-contagion method. In the inductive method, the teacher reaches the rules of grammar with the help of examples, whereas in the language conjugation method, the grammatical rules coming in the context of the sentence are clarified.

The following steps can be adopted to present grammatical units in a clear and interesting way:

- Determination of objectives according to the sub-topic.
- Mention suitable examples and questions based on them.
- Collection of examples required for the topic or sub-topic of the topic with the help of the students.
- Analysis of examples by Q&A.
- Synthesizing words to arrive at regularization,
- Generalization on the basis of equality.
- To draw conclusions from the students by suitable comparison and interpretation.
- To use the rule in new situations as a test of the knowledge acquired by the students.
- Finding new examples.
- Using an understanding of grammar rules and examples.

**58(D).** A student is not able to solve those word problems which involve transposition in algebra. The best remedial strategy is to explain concept of equality using alternate method.

During the teaching-learning process, a child makes mistakes willingly-unwillingly or due to some alternative conceptions. It is the job of the teacher to help students to correct those mistakes after diagnosing them.

- Remedial strategy refers to the method of teaching that helps the teacher to provide learners with the necessary help and guidance to overcome the problems which are determined through diagnosing them.

**59(C).** A device for finding out what pupils understand and can do with the purpose of adapting future teaching to the needs of the individual or the class is known as Diagnostic Assessment.

Techniques, strategies, or methods used as an assessment to know the problems faced by the students and their weak points are called diagnostic assessments. Diagnostic assessments find out the ability, skill, speed, and amount of learning of a student. It helps in future-learning and outcomes according to the objective.

**60(C).** A good paragraph writing in

English involves Ideas, presentation and coherence.

A Paragraph is a collection of sentences that helps you fulfill your thesis. A paragraph should be clearly written and specific: and it should not wander or make irrelevant remarks. A paragraph can introduce a thesis statement, explain specific details, persuade or argue present points for or against an issue.

Characteristics of a Good Paragraph:

- It is not the number of sentences that constitute a paragraph but the unity and coherence of ideas among these sentences.
- A good paragraph writing in English involves Ideas, Presentation, Unity, Completeness, and Coherence.

**61(A).** The word 'remedial' means 'to rectify, improve or remedy something.' Remedial teaching is teaching which is designed to bring students who are lagging behind up to the level of achievement realized by their peers. Remedial teaching means necessary learning support will be provided to pupils who need pedagogical or didactic assistance. There are often children who receive a lower grade because of certain learning or behavioral problems/disorder.

The ultimate aim of remediation or remedial teaching is to help pupils who have fallen behind to learn to the best of their ability and to bring them back into the mainstream of the teaching-learning process as far as possible.

- Remedial teaching in which a teacher is required to prepare instructional material for quality learning and adopting different methodologies as per the needs of the learner or a particular group.
- During the process of remediation, a teacher is expected to devise some strategy to remove problems in learning and the causes due to which the learner has faced the difficulties.
- Teachers provide pupils clear instructions to avoid confusion, summarize the main points and encourage pupils' active participation in class activities.
- Teachers should prepare a rich, pleasant and comfortable learning environment for pupils during remedial classes.

So, we can conclude that the ultimate aim of remedial teaching is to help pupils who have fallen behind to learn.

**62(A).** Nature of mathematics and gender could not be a contributing factor towards underachievement in mathematics.

Underachievement is defined as a large discrepancy between the child's performance (at school) and his innate ability.

- When a child with a high I.Q. level is performing poorly, he is said to be an underachiever.
- A child who has average intelligence, but whose performance is below average is also said to be a low achiever.
- Factors are those related to the underachievement in mathematics, which surrounds the individual as well as to his unique persona (e.g., socio-economic level and educational background of the family, the school climate, the language background, and students' attitudes toward mathematics).
- Among social variables, the factors which were considered very widely are socio-economic status, parental involvement, and parent's education.

**63(C).** Evaluation should be done in teaching of Mathematics after the classification of objectives and providing the experiences of learning.

Evaluation refers to a continuous process of making value judgments based on both qualitative and quantitative data collected over a while. It is closely related to learning objectives since it tells if the student is good or poor in performance. It is done to find out the achievement level of the learning objectives as it:

- makes reliable decisions about educational planning.
- determines the effectiveness of the learning process or program.
- helps the teachers in evaluating teaching methodology regarding the expected objectives.
- is done after the classification of objectives and providing the experiences of learning

**64(B).** Nature of mathematics- The mathematical concepts are hierarchical, which means that they are built on the practical and conceptual knowledge from one class to the next, i.e. they are taught in a predetermined order such as arithmetic first, then algebra, trigonometry, and calculus.

- Relationship between addition and multiplication- Addition is the process of combining different elements to generate a new total. Multiplication, on the other hand, is the process of using repeated addition. The addition is the precursor of multiplication and multiplication follows and builds on the concept of addition. They are interdependent.
- Number sense is a person's ability to understand, relate and connect numbers. Children having strong number sense can think flexibly and fluently about numbers. It helps children to understand what numbers mean, improves their mental mathematics and it should be developed the concept of addition and subtraction.

So, we conclude that the statement that most appropriately explained this is (A) and (D).

**65(B).** Kant stated this definition: "Mathematics is the indispensable instrument of all physical researches".

- Mathematics is accepted as a branch of logic. All concepts of mathematics i.e. arithmetic, algebra, and analysis can be defined in terms of concepts of logic.
- The use of symbols makes mathematical expressions brief and clear, provided you understand the notations.
- Precision is the nature of mathematics that deals with accuracy and exactness and leaves no scope for doubt and ambiguity.
- The precise quality of mathematics helps in doing correct calculations.
- It deals with the quantitative facts and data to develop critical thinking and to bring abstraction into the thoughts of the learner.
- Abstraction is essential in mathematics. It converts the abstract concepts into concrete forms to bring clarity and understanding.
- The results of mathematics theorems and theories are both significant and useful and mathematics has place for logic or creativity.
- It refers to the science of space, numbers, magnitude, and measurement because mathematical operations help to deal with these concepts and solving their problems.

Hence, the correct option is (A).

**66(A).** The main feature(s) of the language of mathematics is(are) a ccuracy.

- Mathematical language walks hand in hand with the growth of mathematical understanding, permeating the general linguistic development of children.
- In teaching mathematics, the teacher uses ordinary language to communicate mathematical concepts and to clarify thoughts. Language is a means of gradually internalizing experience to the point where actions can proceed in imagination without recourse to their physical repetition.
- The main feature of mathematical language is simplicity, accuracy, and precision so that students can understand the mathematical language well and use it correctly in learning it.
- Effective learning of mathematical concepts does not result from mastery over activities alone. It depends on how far teachers are successful in developing language or other symbolic representations, building links with past experiences to formulate. corresponding abstractions or laws.

**67(C).** The concept of ratio should be introduced only at upper primary level is the correct statement with respect to the mathematics curriculum.

The Mathematics curriculum at the upper primary level aims to develop a number of mathematical skills and processes in children such as handling abstraction, problem-solving, mathematical communication, conjecturing and searching for proofs. At the upper primary stage, children get the first taste of the power of Mathematics through the application of powerful abstract concepts that compress previous learning and experience. This enables them to revisit and consolidate basic concepts and skills learnt at the primary stage, which is essential from the point of view of achieving universal mathematical literacy. Children are introduced to algebraic notation and its use in solving problems and in generalisation, to the systematic study of space and shapes, and to consolidating their knowledge of measurement. Data handling, representation and interpretation form a significant part of the ability to deal with information in general, which is a fundamental 'life skill'. The learning at this stage also offers an opportunity to enrich children's spatial reasoning and visualisation skills.

**68(A).** Activity-Centred Curriculum is based on the premise that child loves to play and activity will help to create motivation.

Activity-Centred Curriculum:

- This is also very similar to a learner-centred curriculum.
- The role of the learner is very important and should be very active.
- This is based on the premise that a child loves to play and activity will help to create motivation.
- When curricular material is presented in terms of activity, it is known as activity centred curriculum.
- Learning of the prescribed material included in the curriculum takes place through appropriate activities.
- Another benefit of this approach is that throughout the teaching period, the students should be active participants in the process of learning.
- A goal-directed activity should end in a productive experience. In an activity-centred curriculum, the content is presented through activities and knowledge is the outcome of these activities in terms of experiences.

**69(D).** According to Van Hiele Theory, there are five levels of thinking in geometry. Rigour represent 4th level of Van Hiele Theory.

Five levels of thinking are as follow:

- Visualization Level 0: Describe and sort out shapes on the basis of appearance.
- Descriptive/Analytic/Analysis Level 1: Students start analyzing and naming the properties of geometrical figures.

- Abstract/Relational/Informal Deduction Level 2: Perceive the relationship between properties and figures and create meaningful definitions.
- Formal Deduction Level 3: At this level students can provide deductive geometrical proofs and are able to differentiate between necessary and sufficient conditions.
- Mathematical Rigor Level 4: This is the final step where geometry is understood as a mathematician.

**70(B).** To develop the ability to connect real life situation with mathematical problems is the objective of using this type of word problems to introduce the concept. Real-life connections: When we take information and relate it to something we have already seen or done we have made a real-life connection.

Connecting real-life situations with mathematic problems -

- Teachers should relate the concept with the everyday experiences of the children so that the children would be more attentive towards the topic and it will also generate interest in the concept.
- Each student brings their own set of experiences to the class. Connections between student lives and topics boost student engagement in the class.
- According to John Dewey school activities and the real-life experiences of the students should be connected or else real under learning would be impossible.

**71(D).** To asses the students competency on solving of word problems based on addition and subtraction, rubrics of assessment are comprehension of problem, identification of operation to be performed, representation of problem mathematically, solution of problem and presentation of problem.

**Steps involved in solving a word problems based on addition and subtraction:**

| Steps | Characteristics |
|---|---|
| Comprehension of problem | • Identify the problem<br>• State the problem specifically<br>• Categorise Problem: Addition or Subtraction<br>• Identify what standard or expectation is violated<br>• Determine in which process the problem lies<br>• Avoid trying to solve the problem without data |
| Identification of operation to be performed | • Select the method/technique to solve the problem<br>• Identify the mathematical Operation (Addition |

| | & Subtraction ) |
|---|---|
| | • Specify alternatives consistent with organizational goals<br>• Brainstorm on others' ideas<br>• Seek alternatives that may solve the problem |
| Representation of problem mathematically | • Evaluate alternatives relative to established problem<br>• Evaluate both proven and possible outcomes<br>• State the selected alternative explicitly<br>• Represent the problem mathematically |
| Solution of problem and presentation of problem | • Select a method to solve the problem<br>• Solve the problem with the appropriate method<br>• Arrange Solution in steps<br>• Representation solution according to problem |
| Evaluation/Verification | • Verify or Evaluate Solution |

**72(D).** According to the psychologist Jean Piaget , Conservation refers to a logical thinking ability that allows a person to determine that a certain quantity will remain the same despite adjustment of the container, shape, or apparent size. Note that:

- Conservation of mass/length : 7 years
- Conservation of weight : 9 years
- Conservation of volume : 11 years

So, Conservation of weight is grasped before conservation of volume but not before conservation of number.

**73(C).** The correct answer is: Establishing relationships between different shapes Mathematics is not just the study of numbers and statistical data but also studies the different types of shapes, figures, and patterns.

- Van Heile's theory provides an insight to the teacher about how the students learn geometry at different levels.
- It helps in describing how the students learn at each level and pass to another level and shapes their learning of geometry at each level of learning.

**74(D).** Some students of your class are repeatedly not able to do well in mathematics examinations and tests. As a teacher you would diagnose the causes and take steps for remediation.

Diagnosis and Remedial Steps for Those Who were not Consistently Doing well in the Mathematics Class:

- Understanding the problems of students
- Find out the causes of problems
- Adopting a collective remedial method

for weakness in mathematics
- Directing study methods and making changes according to situation
- To arrange learning by dividing students into small groups on the basis of weakness
- Repeat the specific text and identify and remove the weakness

**75(B).** Knowing the nature and characteristics of error by the students while solving mathematics problems is called error analysis in Mathematics.
Mathematics deals with data analysis, integration of various fields of knowledge, involves proofs, deductive and inductive reasoning, and generalizations.
Error analysis is a method commonly used to identify the cause of student errors when they make consistent mistakes. It is a process of reviewing a student's work and then looking for patterns of misunderstanding. Errors in mathematics can be factual, procedural, or conceptual, and may occur for several reasons.

**76(B).** Given,
$2^3 \times 3^4 \times 1080 \div 15 = 6^x$
$\Rightarrow 2^3 \times 3^4 \times 72 = 6^x$
$\Rightarrow 2^3 \times 3^4 \times (2 \times 6^2) = 6^x$
$\Rightarrow 2^4 \times 3^4 \times 6^2 = 6^x$
$\Rightarrow (2 \times 3)^4 \times 6^2 = 6^x$
$[\because x^m \times y^m = (xy)^m]$
$\Rightarrow 6^4 \times 6^2 = 6^x$
$\Rightarrow 6^{(4+2)} = 6^x$
$\Rightarrow x = 6$

**77(C).** The correct answer is: Using beads and strings
Bead strings are ideal for helping to maintain student interaction in the classroom.
If a student reads 203 as twenty-three then a teacher can use beads and strings activity. This activity is great for emergent learners during maths lessons. They are perfect for both group as well as individual led work, encouraging problem-solving, number exploration, and familiarity with multiples of ten.
Beads and Strings activity:
- Bead strings are used for visualizing numbers with a moveable object.
- A teacher can hide or cover certain parts of a bead string so the students find it easier to count each bead by counting it one by one.
- We can Use bag tags to label the beginning and end of the string as 0 and 100.
- A 10 bead string contains five white and five red beads.

**78(B).** Given:
Students from UP $= 9\%$
Students from MP $= 14\%$
Required Ratio = Students from UP : Students from MP
$= 9 : 14$

**79(A).** Given:
$24, 20, 16, 12$
This series pattern is:
$24 - 4 = 20$
$20 - 4 = 16$
$16 - 4 = 12$
$12 - 4 = 8$
So, next term is $8$.

**80(C).** $1 \text{ kg} = 1000$ gram
Therefore,
$49.2 \text{ kg} = 49.2 \times 1000$ g
$49.2$ g $= 49200$ g
Now find how many $400$ g is in $49200$ g
$\Rightarrow \dfrac{49200}{400} = 123$
So, $123$ times $400$ g is in $49.2$ kg.

**81(A).** Given:
Time taken by Ranjan from point A to point B = 40 minutes 20 seconds
Time taken by Ranjan from point B to point A = 1 hour 20 minutes
Calculation:
Time taken by Ranjan from point A to point B = 40 minutes 20 seconds
Time taken by Ranjan from point B to point A = 1 hour 20 minutes
$\Rightarrow$ Total time taken = 1 hour 20 minutes + 40 minutes 20 seconds
$\Rightarrow$ Total time taken = 1 hour 60 minutes 20 seconds
$\Rightarrow$ Total time taken = 2 hour 20 seconds
1 hour = 3600 Seconds
$\Rightarrow$ 2 hours = 2 × 3600 = 7200 Seconds
$\Rightarrow$ 2 Hours 20 Seconds = 7200 Seconds + 20 Seconds = 7,220 Seconds
$\therefore$ She cycles for 7,220 seconds.

**82(C).** Given:
Length = 48 cm
Breadth = 27 cm
Height = 3.5 cm
Formula:
Volume of the box = l × b × h

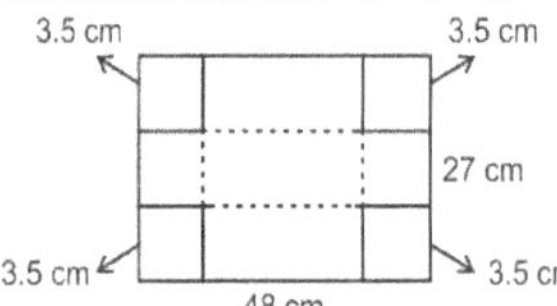


Length of the box = [48 – (2 × 3.5)] = (48 – 7)
= 41 cm
Breadth of the box = [27 – (2 × 3.5)] = (27 – 7)
= 20 cm
Height of the box = 3.5 cm
Now,
Volume of the box = (41 × 20 × 3.5) cm$^3$
= 2870 cm$^3$
$\therefore$ The volume of the box is 2870 cm$^3$.

**83(D).** Given:
The difference between the length and the breadth of the rectangle = 10 cm
The perimeter = 80 cm
Let the Length of rectangle $= x$ cm and Breadth of rectangle $= (x - 10)$ cm

$\Rightarrow$ Perimeter of rectangle
$= 2(x + x - 10) = 2(2x - 10)$
$\Rightarrow 2(2x - 10) = 80$
$\Rightarrow 2x = 50$ and $x = 25$
$\Rightarrow L = 25$ cm, B $= 25 - 10 = 15$ cm

**84(A).** Given:
Radius of a metallic solid sphere is 21.6 cm
Length of the wire is 259.2 m
Formula:
Volume of a sphere $= \dfrac{4}{3}\pi r^3$
Volume of a cylinder $= \pi r^2 h$
Calculation:
Here volume of solid sphere will be equal of the cross section
So,
$\dfrac{4}{3}\pi r^3 = \pi r^2 h$
$\Rightarrow \dfrac{4}{3} \times 21.6 \times 21.6 \times 21.6 = 25920 r^2$ [ 1 m = 100 cm]
$\Rightarrow 28.8 \times 21.6 \times 21.6 = 25920 r^2$
$\Rightarrow 0.5184 = r^2$
$\Rightarrow r = 0.72$ cm
$\therefore$ The radius of the wire is 0.72 cm.

**85(B).** Given:
Ratio of Present age of A and B $= 5 : 3$
The difference between the age of A, 10 years hence and eth age of B, 4 years ago $= 20$ years
Let the Present age of A and B be $5x$ and $3x$ respectively
$\Rightarrow$ The age of A, 10 years hence $= 5x + 10$
$\Rightarrow$ The age of B, 4 years ago $= 3x - 4$
Now, the difference:
$(5x + 10) - (3x - 4) = 20$
$\Rightarrow 2x + 14 = 20$
$\Rightarrow 2x = 6$
$\Rightarrow x = 3$
$\therefore$ The present age of A $= 5x = 5 \times 3 = 15$ years

**86(C).** Given fractions are $\dfrac{3}{4}, \dfrac{5}{8}, \dfrac{7}{9}, \dfrac{1}{2}$
L.C.M of denominator is 72
Now, we have to make the denominator the same, we get
$\dfrac{54}{72}, \dfrac{45}{72}, \dfrac{56}{72}, \dfrac{36}{72}$
Now, compare the numerator, we get
$\dfrac{36}{72} < \dfrac{45}{72} < \dfrac{54}{72} < \dfrac{56}{72}$
$\dfrac{1}{2} < \dfrac{5}{8} < \dfrac{3}{4} < \dfrac{7}{9}$
$\therefore$ The largest fraction is $\dfrac{7}{9}$.

**87(A).** Given:
If the length and breadth of a rectangle are in the ratio 3 : 2 and its perimeter is 20 cm.
Formula:
Area of rectangle = Length × Breadth
Perimeter of rectangle $= 2$ (Length + Breadth)
Calculation:
Let the length of the rectangle be $3x$.
Breadth of the rectangle be $2x$.
Area of the rectangle will be $6x^2$.
Perimeter of the rectangle is $2(L + B)$
Perimeter $= 2(3x + 2x)$
Perimeter $= 10x$

$\Rightarrow 10x = 20$
$\Rightarrow x = 2$
Length = 6 cm and Breadth = 4 cm
Area of rectangle $= 6x^2$
$\Rightarrow$ Area $= 6 \times 4$
$\therefore$ Area $= 24$ cm$^2$

**88(D).** Relative speed, if opposite directions $= (x + y)$km/hr
Relative speed of both men, if they running opposite direction.
$= 10 + 20 = 30$ km/hr
$= 30 \times \frac{5}{18}$ m/s
Time taken to meet each other
$= \frac{1500}{\left(30 \times \frac{5}{18}\right)} = 180$ seconds

**89(A).** Given:
The sum of two positive numbers = 65
The square root of their product = 26
Calculation:
Let the two numbers be a and b respectively
According to the question
$\Rightarrow$ a + b = 65
And, $\sqrt{ab} = 26$
$\Rightarrow$ ab $= (26 \times 26) = 676$
Now,
The sum of the reciprocals $= \frac{1}{a} + \frac{1}{b}$
$= \frac{a+b}{ab}$
$= \frac{65}{676}$
$= \frac{5}{52}$
$\therefore$ The sum of their reciprocals $\frac{5}{52}$ .

**90(C).** Given,
The weights of 3 boxes are 4, 5 & 11 kilograms.
Calculation:
Possible combinations of the weight
All 3 boxes $= 4 + 5 + 11 = 20$ kg
2 boxes ( 4 kg, 11 kg) $= 4 + 11 = 15$ kg
2 boxes ( 5 kg, 11 kg) $= 5 + 11 = 16$ kg
$\therefore$ Any combination of the boxes cannot make weight 17 kg.

**91(D).** Tapeworm in host's stomach is not an example of one-sided symbiotic relationship.
- Tapeworm in the host's stomach is NOT an example of a one-sided symbiotic relationship (Commensalism).
- Tapeworm in the host's stomach is an example of Parasitism.

**92(A).** Indian Forest Act, 1927 seeks to consolidate the law relating to forests, the transit of forest produce and the duty that can be levied on timber and other forest produce.
- The preamble to the Indian Forest Act, of 1927 states that the Act seeks to consolidate the law relating to forests, the transit of forest produce and the duty that can be levied on timber and other forest produce.
- It was largely based on previous Indian Forest Acts implemented under the British. Indian Forest Act of 1878 was the most famous one.
- The Indian Forest Act, 1927 was enacted after repealing the Indian Forest Act, 1878 for the purpose of consolidating the law relating to forests, the transit of forest produce and the duty leviable on timber and other forest produce.

**93(C).** Wheat requires 50 to 75 cm of annual rainfall evenly distributed over the growing season.
It requires a cool growing season and at the time of ripening needs bright sunshine. This rabi crop requires 50 to 75 cm of annual rainfall evenly distributed over the growing season. And annual rainfall of about 100 cm is the upper limit for its cultivation.

**94(C).** Alfred Nobel is the famous scientist from Sweden, known as the inventor of dynamite.
Alfred Nobel was born in Stockholm on 21 October 1833. His father, Immanuel Nobel, was an engineer and inventor who built bridges and buildings in Stockholm. In connection with his construction work Immanuel Nobel also experimented with different techniques for blasting rocks.

**95(D).** At school level, the important objective of environmental education is to build and develop skills of reasoning, evaluating and making decisions that concern humans and the world around them.
- The teaching of environmental education is inculcated in the school curriculum beginning from the primary classes because it is important to teach them the value of natural resources and sustainable development.
- It helps the students to develop skills of reasoning, evaluating, and decision-making because of human activities like overpopulation, industrialization, emission through vehicles. These actions are causing pollution and exploiting nature and its resources.
- They can save the mother earth from reaching the worst phase by changing their actions of using resources. For example, traveling from public transport instead of private transport, plantation.
- Major concerns cannot be avoided like the greenhouse effect, acid rain, global warming therefore students shall be made aware of them so that they can use their decision-making ability to tackle such environmental issues.
Hence, the correct option is (A).

**96(B).** Green algae are green because of chlorophyll.
- Chlorophyll is a green color pigment found in plants, algae
- Plants are perceived as green because chlorophyll absorbs mainly the blue and red wavelengths but the green light is reflected and not absorbed by plant structures like cell walls.
- The only metal present in chlorophyll is Magnesium.
- Photosynthesis is the process by which green plants produce carbohydrates by absorbing sunlight in the presence of chloroplast.
- Sunlight is the main source of energy for photosynthesis.

**97(C).** Cytokinin is a plant hormone that helps in cell division.
Cytokinins are a class of plant growth substances (phytohormones) that promote cell division or cytokinesis in plant roots and shoots.
There are two types of Cytokinins:
Adenine-type Cytokinins represented by Zeatin, Kinetin and 6-Benzylaminopurine and Phenylurea-type Cytokinins like Diphenylurea and Thidiazuron (TDZ).

**98(A).** Carbohydrates food components give energy to our body.
Carbohydrates are a source of energy. Carbohydrates are converted into energy by combining with oxygen obtained by respiration. The byproducts are water and carbon dioxide.
Carbohydrates are found in a wide array of both healthy and unhealthy foods-bread, beans, milk, popcorn, potatoes, cookies, spaghetti, soft drinks, corn, and cherry pie. They also come in a variety of forms. The most common and abundant forms are sugars, fibers, and starches.

**99(A).** The most abundant element found in human body is Oxygen.
Oxygen is the most abundant element found in the human body and it consists of 65% of the total weight.
96 percent of all atoms atom of the human body is made up of four important elements - hydrogen, oxygen, carbon, and nitrogen. Other elements found in the human body is – calcium (for bones), sulfur, phosphorus, sodium, etc. Carbon is the second most abundant element found in the human body and consists of 18.5% of the total weight. Hydrogen consists of 9.5% of the total weight of the human body.

**100(B).** Vitamin C is chemically called ascorbic acid.
Ascorbic acid is the chemical term for vitamin C. The name, ascorbic acid, is derived from the disease (meaning no) and scorbutus (scurvy), caused by a vitamin C deficiency.
Ascorbic Acid belongs to monosaccharide family and has a chemical formula $C_6H_8O_6$. Vitamin C (ascorbic acid) is a key vitamin to animals and plants. It is present in citrus fruits, strawberries, broccoli, raw bell pepper, kiwifruit, brussels sprouts, leafy vegetables, potatoes, and tomatoes etc. It is soluble in water.
It is widely used in treating and preventing

the common cold. It is applied to the skin to protect it from sun and pollution. People suffering from depression and Alzheimer's also take vitamin C. The body requires ascorbic acid to shape and hold the bones, blood vessels and skin.

**101(B).** Fossil fuels are used in conventional energy production.
The term conventional means not unusual or extreme or ordinary. For conventional energy production traditional sources of energy like coal and petroleum is used. Conventional energy sources are finite. They will not last forever. Conventional energy sources causes environmental pollution.

**102(D).** Artificial sub-irrigation system is practiced on small scale in India.
It is a system in which open joint drains is artificially laid below the soil, to supply water to the soil by capillarity. So, therefore it is very costly and can only be practiced in special cases, like favorable soil conditions and for cash crops of good return.

**103(A).** The bacterium which provides nitrogen to the leguminous plants is rhizobium
These bacteria, named Rhizobium, evidently attach themselves to the roots of leguminous plants, forming nodules. They are also able to absorb elemental nitrogen from the air and transform it into ammonia, which can then be made available to the host plants.

**104(A).** Water harvesting is a method which raises the ground water level.
Rainwater harvesting is basically the collection of rainwater on the roof of the building and then its underground storage and conservation for further use. Doing so not only prevents depletion of ground water, but it also increases the level of the depleting water table.

**105(D).** Ascaris infection is transmitted by drinking contaminated water with eggs of Ascaris.
Ascariasis is caused by ingesting infective eggs. This can happen when hands or fingers that have contaminated dirt on them are put in the mouth or by consuming vegetables or fruits that have not been carefully cooked, washed or peeled.

**106(A).** Environmental Studies is a multidimensional subject that covers important principles from various academic fields. It is a broad field that studies the basic principles of EVS as well as associated subjects such as social science , science , language , mathematics , etc. EVS emphasizes the following points:
- The contents of EVS are organized thematically. Topics of both social studies and science are integrated because at the primary level students are not matured enough to study 'heavy'

subjects like science and social science. Also, the reduced curriculum makes learning meaningful at primary stage.
- Provides scope for children's expressions–oral and written and other creative expressions, etc.
- Children learn about their environment through exploring and experiencing it, gathering and analysing information based on their observations and experiences, and constructing their own knowledge, enriching and enhancing it.
- Learning is planned to progress from what the child already knows, to what is to be learnt, from local to global, or from the immediate environment to community and society and beyond.
- Chapters begin with key questions initiating children into thinking and constructing their own knowledge .

So, we conclude that the integrated nature of EVS helps to reduce curriculum load and help children to learn meaningfully.

**107(B).** EVS for classes-III to V is a subject area which integrates the concepts and issues of Science, Social studies and Environmental education.
EVS is a multidimensional subject that covers important principles from various academic fields. EVS for class III to V is a subject area that integrates the concepts and issues of Science, Social studies and Environmental education because of early childhood.
- children look at their environment in a holistic manner.
- children couldn't compartmentalize any topic into 'science' and 'social science'.
- children are not mature enough to interpret the aspects of science and social science in a graded manner.

**108(D).** Giving importance to individual experiences of child will help teacher in EVS classroom to helps them in connecting with the children and enable them in teaching EVS by relating it with their experiences.
EVS class helps children to develop desirable attitudes, values, and behaviour pattern necessary for an environment-friendly lifestyle. The active participation and involvement of children play a very vital role in learning and shaping the personality of a child.
Individual Experiences of Children in an EVS Class will Benefit the Teacher:-
- To connect the subject to the learners' experiential world
- Promote reflection and learning
- To explore different ideas
- Help in the assessment of students
- Enhancing individual knowledge and skills
- Increase confidence and motivation in children

**109(A).** EVS class helps children to develop desirable attitudes, values, and

behaviour pattern necessary for an environment-friendly lifestyle.
EVS is a multidimensional subject that covers important principles from various academic fields. It is a broad field that studies the basic principles of environmental education as well as associated subjects such as social sciences, sciences, etc.
**Objectives of the Study of EVS Concerning Social Sciences:**
- Enabling children to respect differences in cultural practices.
- Enabling children to question existing ideas and practices.
- Enabling children to grow up as a responsible member of society.
- Enabling children to study human behaviour and diverse languages.
- Enabling children to address social issues and becoming socially acceptable.

So, from the above-mentioned points, it becomes clear that Enabling children to learn the correct definition of key terms is not an objective.

**110(D).** Asking the students to undertake group projects will be a more effective learning experience to emphasize more on social inequalities in an EVS class.
Project-based learning gives a thorough practical exposure to a problem upon which the project is based. Projects are developed generally in groups where students can learn various things such as working together, problem-solving, decision making, and investigating activities. So it can be known as group project-based learning. It can be used to emphasize social inequalities in an EVS class.
Main Principles of Project-based learning:
- The Principle of Purpose: Knowledge of purpose is a great stimulus that motivates the child to realize his/her goal. The student must have a purpose. 'Why is he doing certain things?' Purpose motivates learning. Interest cannot be aroused by aimless and meaningless activities. Due to motivation, the student develops an Individual sense of achievement.
- The Principle of Activity: Opportunities should be provided to students that make them active and learn things by doing. Physical, as well as mental activities, is to be provided to them. They are to be allowed to 'do' and to 'live through doing'.
- The Principle of Experience : Experience is the best teacher. What is learned must be experienced. The children learn new facts and information through experience.
- The Principle of Social Experience : The child is a social being and we have to prepare the student for social life. Training for a corporate life must be given to him. In the project method, the students work in groups to develop the

strong intra-group competition, collaboration and problem-solving skills.

- **The Principle of Reality:** Life is real and education to be meaningful must be real. The project method is a method of educating the child and therefore, it must also be real. Real-life situations should be presented in the life of the school.

**111(D).** Learning of mathematical tables by children is an example of Serial Learning. Children begin to learn mathematics much before they enter school. Starting from infancy children develop skills, concepts, and misconceptions about numbers and mathematics.

- Children learn mathematics as a series of disconnected and meaningless facts and rules to be blindly memorized and applied. (For example: Multiplication tables).
- Learning of tables is an example of serial learning. In serial learning, the learner is asked to recall the way the words were presented to him.
- It is a learning that occurs in a sequence manner. Free recall requires the learner to recall the words without regard to their order of presentation.

**112(D).** A science exhibition was organized in Rohan's school. It was organized with an objective. Provide a creative channel for learners in your view is the most appropriate objective.

Exhibition: It a large-scale showing in which objects and products are kept open. It can help learners to learn about objects, models and arts. Hence, a science exhibition is something that exhibits objects, models and artistic works related to science.

- Science exhibition plays an important role in the learning and teaching of science as it provides learners with a platform to show their talents and creativity.
- Science exhibition mainly deals with different scientific, innovative and creative ideas and helps students to apply their science knowledge in everyday life. In the exhibition, students are motivated to discover different scientific materials and objects using concepts of science.

**113(A).** **Activity-based learning:** As the name suggests, actively involves learners in the construction and re-construction of knowledge based on his or her individual experiences. Activity-based approach helps to achieve hands-on experience effectively.

- The activity of making something useful out of waste materials is intended to develop creativity among learners and to make them understand the concept of 3R which includes recycling, reuse and reduce in it .

- This activity will also help to organize an exhibition of best articles made out of waste.
- It provides opportunities to use multiple senses.
- Text-books themselves have a number of suggested activities, so that higher levels of retention can be achieved through active involvement in learning .
- There is an acknowledged need for students to be actively involved in the process of learning, and to develop practical skills which will be useful to them in their later lives.

So, we conclude that the pedagogical intention of the teacher is not to judge the best student in the class.

**114(B).** An increase in learning is not included in Emotional skills under CCE.

CCE refers to a school-based evaluation, which covers all aspects of school activities related to a child's development. It emphasizes two fold objectives such as continuity of evaluation and assessment of learning outcomes in a comprehensive manner.

It covers all the domains of learning i.e. cognitive, affective, and psychomotor domains. CCE introduces Life Skills in education for the development of co-scholastic areas in learning.

Life skill are abilities for adaptive and positive behavior that enable individuals to deal effectively with the demands and challenges of everyday life. These skills are:

- Thinking skills
- Emotional Skills
- Social skills

**115(B).** To have a change in routine and monotonous content is not an objective of including poems and stories in EVS textbooks.

EVS class helps children to develop desirable attitudes, values, and behaviour pattern necessary for an environment-friendly lifestyle.

An EVS textbook is a tool to be used in the teaching-learning of EVS to facilitate effective learning. It supports children to construct knowledge through active participation.

- Poems and stories are effective tools of the teaching-learning process.
- They are also used as a method of teaching to broaden learner's reading choices.

**116(A).** Audio-visual aids are useful for students statements is true.

Teaching Aids help in teaching-learning programme. It helps the teacher to present effectively and students to learn and retain the concepts better and for longer duration.

Audio-Visual Aids: These are sensory devices, they provide a sensory experience to the learner, i.e. the learners can see and hear simultaneously using their senses.

These are instructional devices which are used to communicate messages more effectively through sound and visuals. These may be used for literate as well as for illiterate people.

Benefits of Audio-Visual Aids:

- Audio-visual aids help to capture and sustain the attention of students.
- Audio-visual aids are useful for students and teachers as well, these are objects which initiate, stimulate and reinforce learning of students.
- Audio-visual aids help in saving energy and time of both the teachers and students.

**117(C).** Laboratory experiment in science will be classified as Activity aid.

Laboratory Method: In the laboratory method students perform laboratory experiments by their own hands individually or in small groups, under the supervision and guidance of their science teacher.

The role of the teacher when using this method in teaching science is that of a facilitator. The teacher goes to different individuals or small groups, observes them what they are doing, corrects them if they are doing something wrong, and he is always available to students when they really need him for any guidance.

**118(C).** The moisture level required for vermicomposting should be between 70 and 80 per cent.

Moisture must be maintained above 50%, as lower moisture content will not support worm respiration and can increase worm mortality. Operating moisture-content range should be between 70 and 90%, with a suggested content of 70-80% for vermicomposting operations.

Hence, the correct option is (D).

**119(C).** Arsenic elements is present in the drinking water that can lead to numerous fatal diseases.

Long-term exposure to arsenic from drinking-water and food can cause cancer and skin lesions. It has also been associated with cardiovascular disease and diabetes. In utero and early childhood exposure has been linked to negative impacts on cognitive development and increased deaths in young adults.

**120(B).** In 1988 was the Forest Conservation Act amended.

The Forest Conservation Act, 1980 an Act of the Parliament of India to provide for the conservation of forests and for matters connected therewith or ancillary or incidental thereto. It was further amended in 1988. This law extends to the whole of India. It was enacted by Parliament of India to control further deforestation of Forest Areas in India. The act came into force on 25 October 1980.

## Child Development and Pedagogy Environmental Studies

1. **By motor development we mean the development of in the use of arms and legs' by:**
   (a) Mind and Spirit
   (b) Learning and Education
   (c) Training and Learning
   (d) Strength and speed

2. **Which of the principles of development is defined by the below given example?**
   **Sufi has appropriate weight and height for her age. She also has a well-developed language ability that enables her to communicate with everyone. She is loved by all and has positive self-esteem.**
   (a) Development involves change.
   (b) Development follows a fixed pattern/sequence.
   (c) Development proceeds from general to specific.
   (d) Development is correlated.

3. **Which of the following is not true regarding heredity and environment?**
   (a) Influence personality
   (b) Influence physical and intellectual development
   (c) Influence health
   (d) Influence the economy

4. **Schools teach new behaviours and rules to children and expect them to act accordingly. The school is acting as an agency of _____ socialisation.**
   (a) primary     (b) constructive
   (c) secondary   (d) analytic

5. **"At a particular stage children begin to use primitive reasoning and want to know the answer to all sorts of questions." Piaget called this "intuitive". As per Piaget, which of the following stage, he means?**
   (a) Concrete operation
   (b) Pre-operation
   (c) Formal operation
   (d) None of these

6. **Lawrence Kohlberg's theory of moral reasoning has been criticized on several counts. Which of the following statements is correct in the context of this criticism?**
   (a) Kohlberg has based his study primarily on a male sample.
   (b) Kohlberg has not given typical responses to each stage of moral reasoning.
   (c) Kohlberg has duplicated Piaget's methods of arriving at his theoretical framework.
   (d) Kohlberg's theory does not focus on children's responses.

7. **Which one of the following statements is about progressive education?**
   (a) Given the freedom to learn according to students preferences and likes
   (b) Given the freedom to learn according to students behaviour
   (c) Given the freedom to learn according to students home environment
   (d) All of the above

8. **Howard Gardner's multiple intelligences theory impacts classroom today in the schools based upon its reflection of which current classroom strategy?**
   (a) Differentiated instruction
   (b) Inclusive Education
   (c) Socialization
   (d) Discovery Learning

9. **A child has ability to understand and effectively interact with others. He is showing which type of intelligence?**
   (a) Verbal
   (b) Mathematical
   (c) Interpersonal
   (d) Intrapersonal

10. **In _____ thinking, a child do simplification/ generalization on the one hand and truth and accuracy on the other.**
    (a) Reflective     (b) Critical
    (c) Aesthetic      (d) Creative

11. **'There is something wrong with a woman who doesn't want children' this statement is a prominent example of :**
    (a) Gender biasing
    (b) Gender stereotype
    (c) Gender socialization
    (d) All of the above

12. **A teacher should _________ if learners display individual differences.**
    (a) Enforce strict discipline in the class
    (b) Increase the number of tests / examinations
    (c) Provide a variety of learning experience
    (d) Provide a variety of learning materials

13. **Which one of the following would be the most effective way of conducting an assessment?**
    (a) Assessment is an inbuilt process in teaching-learning
    (b) Assessment should be done twice in an academic session at the beginning and at the end
    (c) Assessment should be done by an external agency and not by the teacher
    (d) Assessment should be at the end of the session

14. **A teacher asks his/her students to draw a concept map to reflect their comprehension of a topic. He/She is:**
    (a) Jogging the memory of the students
    (b) Conducting formative assessment
    (c) Testing the ability of the students to summarise the main points
    (d) Trying to develop rubrics to evaluate the achievement of the students

15. **Which of the following is a method to teach Autistic children?**
    (a) PECS
    (b) Braille
    (c) Taylor Frame
    (d) None of these

16. **What instructional adaptations should a teacher make while working with students who are 'Visually Challenged'?**
    (a) Use a variety of visual presentations.
    (b) Orient herself so that the students can watch her closely.
    (c) Focus on a variety of written tasks especially worksheets.
    (d) Speak clearly and use a lot of touches and feel materials

17. **Which of the following enrichment programmes is suitable for gifted children in the school?**
    (a) Mathematics or Science Olympiad
    (b) Challenging home assignments

(c) Map work during studies

(d) All of the above

**18. Which of the following is the best example of creativity?**

(a) Writing a script for role play in class

(b) Preparing an origami structure

(c) Making a Rangoli

(d) Making a painting

**19. Characteristics of thinking are:**

(a) It depends on both - perception and memory

(b) Thinking i s a mental process that starts with a problem and concludes with its solution

(c) It is a symbolic behavior

(d) All of the above

**20. Which of the following is not correct regarding teaching-learning process?**

(a) Processes of learning move from the simple to the complex

(b) Readiness and motivation to learn are the important to designing instructional activities

(c) Skills of problem solving are integral parts of the internal conditions of learning

(d) None of these

**21. As a teacher, what will you do if students do not attend your class?**

(a) Blame students for their absence from the class.

(b) Ponder over the present attitude of students in a calm manner.

(c) Think about using some interesting techniques for teaching.

(d) Try to understand the reasons and try to eliminate them.

**22. Alternate conceptions and misconceptions hold by children represent:**

(a) Inability to learn

(b) Intuitive ideas about particular concept

(c) Baseless assertions

(d) Permanent conceptional stagnation

**23. Which of the following statements about students' errors is correct?**

(a) Errors help the teachers in labelling students as 'weak' or 'bright'.

(b) On the basis of their errors, the teacher can fail students and save her time.

(c) Errors offer an opportunity for the teachers to understand students' thinking.

(d) Errors should be immediately rectified by asking the students to repeatedly rewrite the 'correct answers'.

**24. Which of the following is correct regarding emotion ?**

(a) Emotion is subjective in nature

(b) Emotion is both subjective and objective

(c) Physiological changes in emotions may not be noticed

(d) Emotions are basically an affective process that is simple in nature

**25. Which of the following example shows that intrinsic motivation is better than extrinsic motivation for learning?**

(a) A student want to participate in a sport because it's fun and she enjoys it.

(b) A student did homework because he did not want to get scolded by teacher

(c) A teacher in a private school is taking more responsibility at work in order to receive a raise or promotion.

(d) A child is speaking wrong English in the school to avoid fine.

**26. Which of the following factors influence learning?**
**(i) emotional**
**(ii) cultural content**
**(iii) maturation**
**(iv) interest**

(a) (iii), (iv)

(b) (ii), (iii), (iv)

(c) (i), (ii), (iii), (iv)

(d) (ii), (iv)

**27. Which one of these factors plays a very important role in learning?**

(a) Genetic make-up alone

(b) Physical infrastructure

(c) Social context and emotions

(d) Maturation and physical appearance

**28. Which of the following best describes the effect of heredity upon development?**

(a) Heredity determines how far we will go

(b) It determines how far we can go

(c) It is the prime determinant of how far we will go

(d) It is the prime determinant of how far we can go

**29. Which of the following is a property of "Deductive method"?**

(a) In this method, there is no opportunity to develop powers like logic, thinking and investigation.

(b) In this method, children work mechanically because they do not know why they are doing such a thing.

(c) By this method all the children of the class can be taught at the same time.

(d) All of the above

**30. In progressive-education children are seen as:**

(a) Passive imitators

(b) Active explorers

(c) Blank slates

(d) Miniature adults

## Language - I: English

**Ques (31-39): Direction** : Read the passage carefully and answer the questions that follow.

The Indus Waters Treaty is a water-distribution treaty between India and Pakistan, brokered by the World Bank, then the International Bank for Reconstruction and Development. The treaty was signed in Karachi on September 19, 1960, by Prime Minister of India Jawaharlal Nehru and President of Pakistan Ayub Khan.

According to this agreement, control over the three "eastern" rivers — the Beas, the Ravi, and the Sutlej — was given to India, while control over the three "western" rivers — the Indus, the Chenab, and the Jhelum — to Pakistan. In aftermath of the 2016 Uri attack, India reviewed the treaty and its provisions and proposed several changes. The treaty was reviewed by India to explore possible ways to use its share of water from rivers, including the Jhelum, flowing into Pakistan.

According to the IWT, India is permitted to construct water storage on western rivers -Indus, Jhelum, and Chenab -up to 3.6 million acre-feet for various purposes, including domestic use.

India is currently building 3 hydro projects on the rivers that flow to Pakistan in their course. One of this projects is the 1000 MW Pakul Dul dam on Chenab. Another one includes a 120 MW on Miyar, which would be located across Miyar Nalla, a right-bank tributary of the river Chenab and a 43 MW hydro project on the Lower Kalnai Nalla; another tributary of Chenab. Pakistan objected to these projects stating that these projects are in violation of the Indus Water Treaty of 1960.

India refused to countenance any change

of design of the Miyar dam in J&K, as asked by Pakistan and plans to continue utilization of its allocation under the Indus Waters Treaty.

**31. Which of the following river is not included according to IWT for the construction of water storage for India?**
- (a) Indus
- (b) Beas
- (c) Jhelum
- (d) Chenab

**32. Which of the following is not a correct pair of the eastern and western rivers according to the passage?**
**(a) Beas, Jhelum**
**(b) Ravi, Chenab**
**(c) Sutlej, Indus**
**(d) Chenab, Jhelum**
- (a) (b) is false
- (b) (a) is false
- (c) (d) is false
- (d) (c) is false

**33. Which of the following is refused by India as asked by Pakistan?**
- (a) 1000 MW Pakul Dul dam construction on Chenab.
- (b) Permit to construct the water storage in eastern rivers.
- (c) To allow the access to all the three eastern rivers.
- (d) To countenance any change of design of the Miyar dam in J&K.

**34. Choose the word which is most nearly the OPPOSITE in meaning to the word 'permit'.**
- (a) Allow
- (b) Back
- (c) Ban
- (d) Authorize

**35. Choose the word which is most nearly the SAME in meaning to the word 'explore'.**
- (a) Initiate
- (b) Investigate
- (c) Intimate
- (d) Neglect

**36. In aftermath of the 2016 Uri attack, India reviewed the treaty and its provisions and proposed several changes.**
**The part of speech ' aftermath ' is a/ an:**
- (a) Adverb
- (b) Adjective
- (c) Noun
- (d) Preposition

**37. What is the theme of the passage?**
- (a) Rivalry between India and Pakistan
- (b) River issues in both the countries
- (c) Indus Waters Treaty
- (d) Construction issues of Dam

**38. Find an error in a part of the sentence and mark the corresponding option.**
**One of this/ projects is /the 1000**

**MW/ Pakul Dul dam on Chenab.**
- (a) One of this
- (b) projects is
- (c) the 1000 MW
- (d) Pakul Dul dam on Chenab.

**39. Which of the following river is included which is reviewed by India to use its share of water from rivers?**
- (a) Beas
- (b) Sutlej
- (c) Ravi
- (d) Jhelum

**Ques (40-45): Direction** : Read the following poem and answer the question by choosing the correct/most appropriate option.
I love to rise in a summer morn,
When the birds sing on every tree;
The distant huntsman winds his horn,
And the skylark sings with me.
O! what sweet company.
But to go to school in a summer morn,
O! it drives all joy away;
Under a cruel eye outworn,
The little ones spend the day,
In sighing and dismay.
Ah! then at times I drooping sit,
And spend many an anxious hour.
Nor in my book can I take delight,
Nor sit in learning's bower,
Worn thro' with the dreary shower.
How can the bird that is born for joy,
Sit in a cage and sing.
How can a child when fears annoy,
But droop his tender wing,
And forget his youthful spring.

**40. How does the school boy feel when he goes to school?**
- (a) Very happy
- (b) Cheerful
- (c) Romantic
- (d) Unhappy

**41. Whom is the school boy compared to?**
- (a) A bird
- (b) Summer
- (c) Winds
- (d) Dreary shower

**42. Which figure of speech has been used in the line?**
**sky-lark sings**
- (a) Apostrophe
- (b) Alliteration
- (c) Assonance
- (d) Simile

**43. Which figure of speech has been used in the line?**
**Under a cruel eye outworn.**
- (a) Anaphora
- (b) Apostrophe
- (c) Alliteration
- (d) Metaphor

**44. What does the sweet company refer to in the first stanza?**
- (a) Skylark
- (b) Summer morning

- (c) Huntsman horn
- (d) Both (A) and (C)

**45. What takes away all the happiness of the child?**
- (a) Going to the school in the winter morning
- (b) Getup early in the morning
- (c) Going to the school in the summer morning
- (d) When skylark sings with him

**46. A child learns his/her first language in a:**
- (a) Friendly setting
- (b) Tutored setting
- (c) Formal setting
- (d) Natural setting

**47. Language learning is _____.**
- (a) Not a conscious attempt by the learner.
- (b) Conscious attempt by the learner.
- (c) An act which occurs naturally.
- (d) Conscious attempt by the teacher.

**48. Teaching a lesson, through a number of language activities connected with the topic, refers to which principle of second language teaching?**
- (a) Structural Approach
- (b) Multiple Line of Approach
- (c) Circular Approach
- (d) Bilingual approach

**49. "From small utterances, the students can easily pass on to longer sentences." Which principle of second language teaching could be associated with this statement?**
- (a) Give Priority to Sounds
- (b) Language Habit through Language Using
- (c) Present Language in Basic Sentence Patterns
- (d) Individual Differences

**50. 'Decorum' in spoken language pertains to:**
- (a) Correct grammatical usage
- (b) Voice quality or loudness
- (c) Clarity and purity of style
- (d) Appropriate gestures

**51. Teaching of grammar will help the learners to:**
- (a) Differentiate the phoneme
- (b) Have a basic knowledge of phonetics
- (c) Have a good conversational skill
- (d) Know the structure of the

language

**52. The principle of which of the following method is to memorize the rules of grammar?**
(a) Structural Approach
(b) Direct Method
(c) Grammar Translation Method
(d) Natural Approach

**53. What is the main challenge of teaching language in a diverse classroom?**
(a) Challenge of a mixed-ability group of learners.
(b) Challenge of teaching-learning materials.
(c) Challenges to curriculum design.
(d) All of the above

**54. Language skills can be learnt better:**
(a) If they are taught in an integrated manner
(b) With the help of challenging drills
(c) Through written tests and practices
(d) If taught in isolation

**55. Which of the following skills comes under the productive category of language skills?**
(a) Speaking and Listening
(b) Listening and Reading
(c) Reading and Writing
(d) Writing and Speaking

**56. Evaluation of speaking consists of:**
(a) Evaluation of pronunciation
(b) Evaluation of intonation
(c) Evaluation of stress
(d) All of the above

**57. Which of the following is not a useful activity of evaluating listening skills?**
(a) Dictations
(b) Oral presentations
(c) Vocabulary assessment task
(d) Listen and Draw

**58. Flannel board is useful for:**
(a) Teaching picture composition
(b) Developing reading skill
(c) Developing acting skill
(d) Improving thinking skill

**59. What can be used as props for dialogues to teach new lexical or structural items?**
(a) Textbook
(b) Reference book
(c) Realia
(d) Dictionary

**60. Remedial teaching is a:**
(a) Preparation of teaching
(b) Systematic process
(c) Pre-teaching program
(d) Random process

## Mathematics

**61. The length of a pendulum is $60cm$. The angle through which it swings when its tip describes an arc of length $16.5cm$ will be:**
(a) $15°30'$
(b) $15°45'$
(c) $16°15'$
(d) $16°45'$

**62. A wooden box measures $10$ cm by $6$ cm by $5$ cm. Thickness of wood is $2$ cm. Find the volume of wood required to make the box.**
(a) $206$ cm $^3$
(b) $207$ cm $^3$
(c) $204$ cm $^3$
(d) $288$ cm $^3$

**63. Circumference of the base of a $9m$ high conical tent is $44m$. Find the volume of air contained in it.**
(a) $430m^3$
(b) $462m^3$
(c) $472m^3$
(d) $492m^3$

**64. If sum of five consecutive integers is '$S$', then largest of these integers in terms of $S$ Will be :**
(a) $\dfrac{(S-10)}{5}$
(b) $\dfrac{(S+4)}{4}$
(c) $\dfrac{(S+5)}{4}$
(d) $\dfrac{(S+10)}{5}$

**65. What is the value of $13\frac{1}{5}+12\frac{2}{3}+13\frac{1}{3}+15\frac{4}{5}?$**
(a) $51$
(b) $53$
(c) $55$
(d) $49$

**66. If a man travels with a speed of $\frac{2}{5}$ times of his original speed and he reached his office 15 minutes late to the fixed time, then the time taken with his original speed will be:**
(a) $10$ min
(b) $15$ min
(c) $20$ min
(d) $25$ min

**67. One year ago ratio of age of Rohit and Sahil was $6:7$, their ratio four years from now will be $7:8$. How old is Sahil?**
(a) $40$
(b) $39$
(c) $37$
(d) $36$

**68. Direction :** In the following question a number of series is given with one term missing. Choose the correct alternative that will continue the same pattern.

$23, 48, 99, 203, 413$ ___

(a) $927$
(b) $837$
(c) $937$
(d) $437$

**69. Direction :** Study the given graph and answer the question that follows.

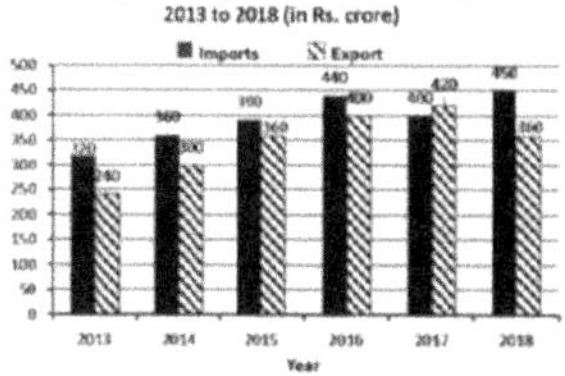


What is the ratio of the total exports in $2014$ and $2017$ to the total imports in $2015$ and $2018$?
(a) $6:7$
(b) $3:2$
(c) $5:6$
(d) $14:15$

**70. Jadu's flight is at $02:14$ pm. He wants to go to the airport $65$ minutes before the scheduled time of the flight to complete his lunch. He goes to the airport at the time and completes his lunch in $25$ minutes. How much time before Jadu completes his lunch before the scheduled time of his flight?**
(a) $40$ minutes
(b) $45$ minutes
(c) $50$ minutes
(d) $55$ minutes

**71. The weight of oranges is $4$ kg $455$ gm and that of some mangoes is $3$ kg and $100$ gm. The weight of orange is more than that of mangoes by:**
(a) $1$ kg $555$ gm
(b) $1$ kg $455$ gm
(c) $2$ kg $555$ gm
(d) $1$ kg $355$ gm

**72. Which of the following length is arranged in descending order?**
(a) $6km > 5.6km > 5455m > 4\frac{3}{4}km$
(b) $4\frac{3}{4}km > 6km > 5.6km > 5455m$
(c) $6km > 5.6km > 4\frac{3}{4}km > 5455m$
(d) $6km > 5455m > 4\frac{3}{4}km > 5.6km$

**73. The denominator of a fraction is $2$ more than the numerator. When the numerator is multiplied by $3$ and the denominator is multiplied by $2$ the fraction becomes $\frac{1}{2}$. The given fraction is:**
(a) $\frac{2}{5}$
(b) $\frac{1}{4}$
(c) $\frac{2}{3}$
(d) $\frac{1}{3}$

**74. Which of the following statements is incorrect about nature of mathematics?**

(a) Mathematics has its own language.

(b) Mathematics is an exact science.

(c) Mathematics is changeable in the universe.

(d) Mathematics is the science of logical reasoning.

75. **Which of the following options is/ are correct in the context of nature of Mathematics?**

(a) 'Mathematics' is a broad term that encompasses many branches and components.

(b) Mathematics is a way of thinking and it is related to our life on daily basis.

(c) Mathematics should be visualised as the vehicle to train a child to think, reason, analyse, and articulate logically.

(d) All of the above

76. **Which among the following statement is true regarding mathematics?**

(a) Boys easily learn mathematics in comparison to girls.

(b) Mathematics is very hard to understand at the primary stage.

(c) Everyone can learn and succeed in mathematics.

(d) Mathematics takes a lot of time to be understood in comparison to other subjects.

77. **The important role of Mathematics in the syllabus is:**

(a) Intellectual value

(b) Moral development

(c) Cultural development

(d) All of the above

78. **The subject Mathematics is important in curriculum since it:**

(a) Helps in the study of science subjects

(b) Improves logical thinking

(c) Is useful in daily life

(d) All of the above

79. **Which of the following is/are characteristics of language of mathematics?**

(a) Simplicity

(b) Accuracy

(c) Precision

(d) All of the above

80. **Which of the following is not one of the merits of mathematical language?**

(a) It is well defined

(b) It is clear

(c) It is highly compact and focussed

(d) It does not require other ordinary languages for its use

81. **Students often make a mistake in comparing the decimal numbers. For example, 0.50 is larger than 0.5. The most probable reason for this error is**

(a) Lack of practice of these types of questions in the class.

(b) Lack of concrete experience of representation of decimal number on the number line.

(c) Careless attempt by the students.

(d) Misconception regarding the significance of zero in ordering decimal.

82. **A learner has not understood certain concepts in a maths subject, to help him/her understand these concepts, the teacher will conduct:**

(a) Diagnostic Assessment

(b) Formative Assessment

(c) Placement Assessment

(d) Summative Assessment

83. **We may say that ________ implies a detailed study of learning difficulties to locate and identify the areas of learning difficulties.**

(a) Drill work

(b) Remedial testing

(c) Diagnostic testing

(d) Evaluation and assessment

84. **Direction** : What will come in the place of the question mark '?' in the following question?

$$\sqrt{324} + 9^2 - 7^2 = 2 \times (?)^2$$

(a) 25      (b) 10

(c) 20      (d) 5

85. **On dividing 13501 by a certain number, we get 78 as quotient and 7 as remainder. What is the divisor?**

(a) 163

(b) 173

(c) 153

(d) None of these

86. **A teacher asked the students to collect leaves and to identify symmetry patterns. This task reflects the teacher's efforts to:**

(a) Relate real life experience with mathematical concepts

(b) Introduce an intradisciplinary approach

(c) Enhance creativity amongst students

(d) Improve mathematical communication

87. **Evaluation in mathematics is necessary as it helps in:**

(a) Test mathematization abilities rather than procedural knowledge.

(b) Provides qualitative and quantitative information.

(c) Providing constructive feedback to both the students and the teachers.

(d) All of the above

88. **In which type of test, the teacher assess communication skills besides logical ability and precision in thinking in mathematics?**

(a) Essay type

(b) Objective type

(c) Diagnostic test

(d) Prognostic test

89. **A students is asked to draw a cube in the class or to show the example of it from among the classroom after the chapter on shapes has been completed. Which type of evaluation is represented by the above example?**

(a) Summative Assessment

(b) Formative Assessment

(c) Both (A) and (B)

(d) None of these

90. **Shreepriya is a mathematics teacher. Every Monday she takes a test. On upcoming Monday she has the plan to take a test on "Addition and Subtraction of fractions". This test can be categorized as:**

(a) Summative Assessment

(b) Formative Assessment

(c) Remedial Teaching

(d) Diagnostic Method of Teaching

## Environmental Studies

91. **Mammals have _____.**

(a) glandular skin with hairs

(b) dry and non-glandular skin with feathers

(c) dry and non-glandular skin with scales

(d) dry and glandular skin with feathers

92. **The crops depends on the onset of South-West monsoon are known as:**

(a) Kharif crop

(b) Rabi crop

(c) Zaid crop

(d) None of these

**93. Indian Satellite Series 'INSAT' is an example of:**
(a) Military Satellite
(b) Polar orbiting Satellite
(c) Meteorological Satellite
(d) Resource Satellite

**94. The tusks of male elephants are their:**
(a) Molars
(b) Lower incisors
(c) Upper incisors
(d) Incisors

**95. In a pitcher plant the pitcher is made by the modification of:**
(a) Leaf     (b) Branches
(c) Stem     (d) Flower

**96. Consider the following statements.**
**A. People of Maharashtra love to eat pakoras made of sahjan flowers.**
**B. In Jammu and Kashmir people like to eat vegetables made of banana flowers.**
**C. In Uttar Pradesh people enjoy eating a vegetable made of kachnar flowers.**
**The correct statement(s) is/are:**
(a) Only B     (b) A and C
(c) only C     (d) A and B

**97. Vermicompost is a/an:**
(a) Toxic material
(b) Organic biofertilizer
(c) Inorganic fertilizer
(d) Synthetic fertilizer

**98. A student was doing an experiment on increasing the elongation of the stem. He asked his supervisor to suggest the specific plant hormone for the same. Had you been his supervisor, which plant hormone would you suggest?**
(a) Auxins     (b) Gibberellins
(c) Abscisic acid     (d) cytokinins

**99. Which of the following is an effect of burning fossil fuels?**
(a) Air pollution
(b) Water pollution
(c) Climate change
(d) All of the above

**100. This system of irrigation supplies water to the plant equivalent to its consumptive use**
(a) Furrow irrigation system
(b) Flood irrigation system
(c) Drip irrigation system
(d) Check-basin irrigation system

**101. Which one of the following is an essential macro nutrient for plant growth?**
(a) Iron     (b) Copper
(c) Potassium     (d) Nickel

**102. Which one of the following is the benefit of rainwater harvesting?**
(a) Flood mitigation
(b) Provide a lot of water to play
(c) Create good aesthetic view
(d) Decrease the ground water level

**103. Kala-azar is transmitted by:**
(a) Dragon fly     (b) Housefly
(c) Tse-tse fly     (d) Sand fly

**104. The concept of environmental study should be integrated which includes:**
(a) Integration of teaching method
(b) Integration of Assessment Methods
(c) Integration of learning methods
(d) All of the above

**105. Which of the following activities should not be encouraged by EVS teacher while teaching at the primary level?**
(a) Acquisition of values for environmental protection
(b) Linkage with children's real life experiences
(c) To memorize maximum concepts in EVS
(d) To inculcate right attitude towards environment

**106. Why do we need gardening activities in school?**
(a) To improve environmental attitude
(b) To engage the students in their spare time period
(c) To make students aware about Horticulture
(d) To improve the school garden area

**107. Which of the following principle should be borne in mind while constructing curriculum for Environmental Studies?**
(a) Teacher centred curriculum
(b) Child centred curriculum
(c) Textbook centred curriculum
(d) Project based curriculum

**108. Rashmi is poking others for no apparent reason and has trouble paying attention in the EVS classroom. She is suffering from:**
(a) Dementia     (b) ADHD
(c) Otosclerosis     (d) Dysthymia

**109. Why, teaching of environmental studies is essential for children?**
(a) To develop understanding of morality.
(b) To develop deep understanding of concepts.
(c) To provide knowledge and importance of environment.
(d) All of the above

**110. Which of the following is NOT a scope of EVS?**
(a) Adoption of environment friendly practices and habits
(b) Promoting a conservation ethic
(c) Generating positive and proactive actions in improving the quality of the environment
(d) Developing positive values for non-living things

**111. If map is in front of you, the East direction is shown:**
(a) At the top of the map
(b) At the bottom of the map
(c) Towards your right hand
(d) Towards your left hand

**112. Why does the EVS teacher lay emphasis on using CCE to evaluate all the aspects of child development?**
(a) It reduces stress
(b) It prepares learners for future
(c) It reduces the drop out rate
(d) All of the above

**113. Children should be encouraged to tap sources other than textbooks and teachers in EVS. Why?**
**A. Textbook and teacher are not the only sources of EVS learning.**
**B. It will promote the involvement of parents and communities.**
**C. It will provide opportunities to teachers to know the child's background.**
**D. It will develop psychomotor skills and aesthetic sense of the children.**
(a) A, B and C     (b) B, C and D
(c) C and D only     (d) B and C only

**114. In many schools, EVS is still taught in the traditional method where either children are engaged in reading the textbooks in a louder voice in the chorus, underlining the important terms and definitions, or teacher lecturing about certain concepts. These kinds of learning processes create problems and challenges in EVS learning. **Which one of the following ways should be attempted by the teacher to address problems related to EVs learning?**

(a) Encourage children to discuss their concrete experience and ensure that children are involved in real-world situations.

(b) Encourage children for no or very less interaction with teacher in the classroom and to focus more on study

(c) Encourage children to be largely dependent on help books and guides to note down the answers which could be asked in the examination.

(d) Encourage children to don't take initiative and ownership for their own learning as any wrong step could be problematic.

115. **EVS is based on which of the following principle of learning?**

(a) Concrete to abstract

(b) Abstract to concrete

(c) Global to local

(d) Unknown to known

116. **It is often believed that girls do not play motor sports including bike and car racing. The EVS teacher conducts a discussion on discrimination in games on the basis of gender, caste and class. What is the main aim of this discussion?**

(a) To allow girls to play motor sports

(b) To remove gender stereotypes

(c) To allow girls play any sport

(d) To remove discrimination in sports

117. **Assertion (A): Environmental education includes the study of the relationship of humans with other aspects affecting their life for the development of human life. Reasoning (R): Through teaching about the environment, the teacher should sensitize the children about the protection and conservation of the enviro nment.**

(a) Both (A) and (R) are correct and (R) is the correct explanation of (A)

(b) Both (A) and (R) are correct, but (R) is not the correct explanation of (A)

(c) (A) is correct, but (R) is not the correct

(d) (A) is not correct, but (R) is correct

118. **Two of the statements given below are false. Identify these statements.**
**A. Natural and physical basis of scientific inquiry can be used in Social Science also.**
**B. The teaching of Social Science has responsibility for value education only.**
**C. The same methodology can be used to teach different disciplines of Social Science.**
**D. The teaching of Social Science concerns more with involvement with complexities rather than information.**

(a) B and C   (b) B and D

(c) C and D   (d) A and C

119. **Which of the following statement(s) is/are correct about the relationship between social studies and social sciences?**

(a) Social studies is integrated study of social sciences

(b) Social studies and social science are two sides of same coin

(c) Social studies and social science are two entirely different disciplines

(d) Social studies is a small part of social science

120. **______ of The Indian Forest Act 1927 deals with Power to stop ways and water-courses in reserved forests.**

(a) Section 24   (b) Section 25

(c) Section 23   (d) Section 22

---

**// Hints and Solutions //**

**1(D).** Motor development refers to the development of motor skills that makes children able to explore and manipulate their immediate environment.
Motor development is divided into two groups:
- Gross motor development: Development of gross motor skills is concerned with strength and speed as it refers to the development of larger muscles like arms and legs for bigger movements such as walking, jumping, etc.
- Fine motor development: Development of fine motor skills is concerned with flexibility and dexterity as it refers to the development of small muscles like wrists and fingers fir smaller movements such as writing, grasping small objects, etc.

So, it becomes clear that by motor development we mean the development of in the use of arms and legs strength and speed.

**2(D).** Principles of development define the basic process of human development. It will assess the role and importance of growth processes and levels and the principles of growth and behavior in the total life span.
Development is correlated: A ll types of developments, i.e. physical, mental, social, and emotional, are related to each other e.g. a physically healthy child is likely to have superior sociability and emotional stability. The child develops as a unified whole. Each area of development is dependent on the other and thus influences the other developments. Sufi has appropriate weight and height for her age. She also has a well-developed language ability that enables her to communicate with everyone. She is loved by all and has positive self-esteem.
So, we can conclude that Development is correlated is the correct answer.

**3(D).** The growth and development of the child influenced by heredity and environment. Heredity is discussed as an internal factor and environment as an external factor .
Heredity:
- Heredity is the sum total of the traits potentially present in the fertilized ovum. All the qualities that a child has inherited from the parents are called heredity.
- Heredity consists of all the structures, physical characteristics, functions or capacities derived from parents and other ancestors

Environment:
- Environment means the totality of the stimuli that impinge on the organism from without whatever found around the individual may be called by the term environment.
- The environment consists of various types of forces like physical, social, moral, economic, political cultural and emotional forces.

Thus from the above-mentioned points, it is clear that influence the economy is not true regarding heredity and environment .

**4(C).** Socialization is the process through wh ich communities transact or educate their members about the norms and values of society to be socially acceptable.
Secondary Socialization:
- It occurs once the infant passes into the childhood phase and continues into maturity. It refers to the process that begins in the later years through agencies such as schools and peer groups.
- During this phase more than the family, some other agents of socialization like the school and peers' group begin to play a role in socializing the child.
- For example, Schools help children in

learning the importance of social cohesion and unity and inculcating the informal cues about social roles through interaction. Schools teach new behaviors and rules to children and expect them to act accordingly.

So, it could be concluded that the school acts as an agency of secondary socialization.

**5(B).** Jean Piaget , a Swiss psychologist, has made a systematic study of cognitive development in his theory that is categorized in four stages. He observed his children and their process of making sense of the world around them and developed a model of how the mind processes new information encountered.

Piaget's Pre-operational stage is from 2 - 7 years. In this stage, the child faces problems with the concept of conservation and struggles with the idea of centration and irreversibility.

Preoperational stage (2-7 yrs): It is categorized into two parts:

- Pre-conceptual stage (2-4 yrs): In this, they began to pretend play; egocentrism and animism are controlled.
- Intuitive (4-7 yrs): In this, the child begins to be curious, wants to use primitive reasoning to know the things work.

So, we conclude that by the intuitive stage, Piaget refers to the pre-operational stage.

**6(A).** Criticisms of Kohlberg's Theory of Moral Development:

- Carol Gilligan has suggested that Kohlberg's theory was gender-biased since all of the subjects in his sample were male.
- Kohlberg has based his study primarily on a male sample.
- Critics have pointed out that Kohlberg's theory of moral development overemphasizes the concept of justice when making moral choices.

So, the statement 'Kohlberg has based his study primarily on a male sample', is correct in the context of this criticism.

**7(A).** The progressive education promotes 'learning by doing to make children self-reliant and productive to use their knowledge, talents, and skills to sustain themselves and to promote economic growth.

Qualities of a Teacher in Progressive Classroom:

- Focuses attention on student-centered learning where the teacher encourages them to indulge in self-learning techniques.
- Employs minimum effort and resources on teaching and motivates the learner to actively construct knowledge.
- The teacher should promote discovery in the classroom.
- Prepare students for active participation

in a democratic society.

- Progressively refining the learning experiences based on reflection and feedback.

So, we can conclude that given the freedom to learn according to student's preferences and likes is right regarding progressive education.

**8(A).** Howard Gardner's multiple intelligences theory:

- He was a psychologist who did not believe there was "one form of cognition" which cuts across all human thinking.
- There are multiple intelligences with autonomous "intelligence capacities" and he divided the intelligence into different types which are known as Gardner's theory of multiple intelligence.
- He believed that different individuals have different levels of abilities to work with these different types of intelligence in different circumstances as per their life.
- The theory of multiple intelligences offers support for instructional approaches that incorporate a variety of connections for teaching and learning that validate the unique experiences, interests, and cultures of all students.
- Given that individuals gravitate to the areas in which they have strengths and can incorporate these areas into their learning, the concept of multiple intelligences is uniquely suited to support and enhance a differentiated classroom.
- This theory of multiple intelligence given by Gardner is useful in giving differentiated instruction to the students as they all are different in their capabilities so they are required to be instructed differently.
- Gardner initially formulated a list of seven types of intelligence and visual-Spatial Intelligence is one of them. Later, two more types of intelligence are added by Gardner.

So, it is concluded that Howard Gardner's multiple intelligences theory impacts classrooms today in schools in terms of differentiated instruction.

**9(C).** Interpersonal skills: The ability to understand and effectively interact with others . It is an ability to notice and make distinctions among the moods, temperaments, motivations, and intentions of other people and potential to act on this knowledge (teachers, mental health professionals, parents, religious and political leaders)

So, we can conclude that a child has the ability to understand and effectively interact with others. The child is showing interpersonal intelligence.

**10(B).** Critical thinking aims at simplification/ generalization on the one hand and truth and accuracy on the other. It adheres to establish canons of logic. Logic is the science of thinking. It offers general rules for thinking.

- Knowledge of these rules for thinking helps us to verify whether our thinking in a particular instance is right. Mastery of these rules, assimilating them into the bloodstreams of our brain will ensure that our thinking does not go astray.
- The process of critical thinking should be strictly according to the established canons of logic if it is to be valid. In critical thinking, the road leading to truth is already well laid out.
- Further, there is only one royal road - the road of logic - to truth in critical thinking. And, truth is already waiting to be discovered.
- Critical thinking is described in psychology as convergent thinking because anyone and everyone who wants to arrive at truth must conform to the canons of logic.

So, we can conclude that In critical thinking, a child does simplification/ generalization on the one hand and truth and accuracy on the other.

**11(B).** Gender is a social construct.

- A gender stereotype is a generalized view or preconception about attributes or characteristics, or the roles that are or ought to be possessed by, or performed by, women and men .
- A gender stereotype is harmful when it limits women's and men's capacity to develop their personal abilities, pursue their professional careers, and/or make choices about their lives.
- Wrongful gender stereotyping is a frequent cause of discrimination against women .
- It is a contributing factor in violations of a vast array of rights such as the right to health, adequate standard of living , education, marriage and family relations, work, freedom of expression, freedom of movement, political participation and representation, effective remedy, and freedom from gender-based violence.

These are all examples of gender stereotypes.

- Not criminalizing marital rape, perceiving that women are the sexual property of men
- Failing to investigate, prosecute and sentence sexual violence against women, believing that victims of sexual violence agreed to sexual acts, as they were not dressing and behaving "modestly"
- There is something wrong with a woman who doesn't want children etc.
- In religious texts even in grammar, the existence of women was either denied

or they were told to fight.
- Even today the heir of the family is considered to be the child, while the child is being a victim of infanticide.
- Boys don't cry, when they cry, say don't behave like girls.

So, we can conclude that the right answer is a gender stereotype.

**12(C).** Individual difference refers to the difference which distinguishes an individual from another on the basis of psychological characteristics. Individual differences could be seen in all domains of development such as physical, emotional, mental, etc .

A teacher should provide a variety of learning experience if learners display individual differences as it will help in:
- selecting relevant prompts to be suitable for their ability level.
- combining different types of prompts to make them inculcate skills.
- catering to the range of learning needs and requirements of diverse learners.
- making learning effective for students who learn differently either visually, auditory, etc.

So, it could be concluded that a teacher should provide a variety of learning experience if learners display individual differences.

**13(A).** In order to know what children understand and are able to know, assessment is done. It is a systematic process of using data to measure skills and knowledge. By assessment, a teacher documents the improvements by a student and his endeavors towards learning.

With assessments as an inbuilt process in teaching-learning , teachers can understand the needs of the learners better and accordingly change or adjust the quality of their instruction during the process of teaching the unit itself.
- It is better when the assessments are conducted by the teacher himself, as the external agency might not be able to understand the needs of the individual learners or proper feedback might not be conveyed to the teacher.
- With assessments conducted at the end or twice in an academic session , teachers don't get immediate feedback about the progress of the learners and their quality of instruction.

So, we can conclude that assessment is an inbuilt process in teaching-learning.

**14(B).** From the above-mentioned situation, it could be interpreted that the teacher is assessing the students by conducting the formative assessment as it refers to monitor the child's progress throughout the teaching-learning process. In this case, it will help the teacher to know the children's learning needs regarding that topic and then meet the needs by remedial

teaching.

Assessment for Learning (Formative Assessment):
- It is also referred to as internal evaluation.
- In this form of assessment, a teacher embeds various forms of assessment all through the teaching and learning process. Therefore, it is an ongoing assessment that allows teachers to monitor students on a day-to-day basis and modify their teaching based on what the students need to be successful.
- Formative assessment refers to a wide variety of methods that teachers use to conduct in-process evaluations of student comprehension, learning needs, and academic progress during a lesson, unit, or course.
- Effective formative assessment strategies involve asking students to answer well-thought-out, higher-order questions such as "why" and "how."
- This assessment provides students with timely and specific feedback that they need to make adjustments to their learning.
- For students, it identifies learning errors that need to be corrected and for teachers, it provides information for modifying instructions.
- It helps the student to actively and continuously engage in learning in a non-threatening and supportive environment.
- Questionnaires, quizzes, oral discussions, unit tests are some tools used for formative evaluation.

So, we can conclude that a teacher asks his/her students to draw a concept map to reflect their comprehension of a topic. He/She is conducting the formative assessment.

**15(A).** PECS is a method to teach Autistic children.
- It is a type of augmentative and alternative communication technique where individuals with little or no verbal ability learn to communicate using picture cards.
- Children use the pictures to "vocalize" a desire, observation, or feeling.
- Many children with autism learn visually, and therefore, this type of communication technique has been shown to be effective in improving independent communication skills.

Thus from above-mentioned points, it is clear that PECS is a method to teach Autistic children.

**16(D).** A visually challenged child is the one who has a problem seeing with the naked eyes or is not able to see completely. Instruction adaptations that a teacher can follow while working with students who are 'visually challenged' are:
- Should speak clearly and audibly to help

them learn through listening or auditory learning
- Use a lot of touches and feel materials.
- Make use of material adaptations according to the individual needs, the actual degree of functional vision, presence of any other disabilities
- Using a variety of tactile materials like rough or smooth, cold or hot, wet or dry, vibrate or stationary helps the students to touch, feel, and understand the differences between the materials
- Break the entire learning process into smaller units
- Provide ample time for the challenged learner to learn in his/her own way
- Provide support and independence wherever necessary
- Braille, tactile symbols, large prints, recorded materials, etc. can be used as teaching aids for visually challenged learners
- A touch and feel tool for the visually challenged person

So, we can conclude that a teacher should speak clearly and use a lot of touches and feel materials while working with students who are 'Visually Challenged'.

**17(D).** A gifted child is the one who displays consistently remarkable performance in various physical or cognitive aspects and exhibits superiority in general intelligence levels.

Map work during studies, Challenging home assignments, and Mathematics or Science Olympiad are the enrichment programs that are suitable for gifted children in the school as these programs:
- can satisfy and utilize their intelligence.
- can give enriched learning experiences to them.
- Can develop the ability to visualize the spatial relationship.
- Can allow students to express their interests in the subject.
- Can give students the opportunity to try new things and explore.

So, it could be concluded that all of these are true in the context of the question.

**18(A).** Creativity is a mental and social process involving the generation of new ideas or concepts , or new associations of the creative mind between existing ideas or concepts. An alternative conception of creativeness is that it is simply the act of making something new.
- From a scientific point of view, the products of creative thought (sometimes referred to as divergent thought ) are usually considered to have both originality and appropriateness.
- Creativity is defined as the tendency to generate or recognize ideas, alternatives, or possibilities that may be useful in solving problems, communicating with others, and entertaining ourselves and others.

Ability to generate, create, or discover new ideas, solutions, and possibilities. divergent thinking: the opposite of convergent thinking, the capacity for exploring multiple potential answers or solutions to a given question or problem (e.g., coming up with many different uses for a common object)

So, it is concluded that writing a script for role play in class is the best example of creativity.

**19(D).** Thinking is a pattern of behaviour in which we make use of internal representations (symbols, signs, etc.) of things and events for the solution of some specific, purposeful problem.

Characteristics of thinking are:

- It is one of the most important aspects of one's cognitive behaviour.
- It depends on both – perception and memory.
- It involves trial and error; analysis and synthesis; foresight and hindsight.
- It is a symbolic behaviour.
- It is always directed to achieve some purpose.
- Thinking is a symbolic activity. (e.g.: engineers use mental symbols to design the plan for buildings).
- Thinking is a mental process that starts with a problem and concludes with its solution.
- There is mental exploration instead of motor exploration.

So, we can conclude that all of the above is true.

**20(D).** The teaching-learning process is the heart of extension education, and the fulfillment of the aims and objectives of development depends on it.

- Prerequisite behavior: Gagne advocated that processes of learning move from the simple to the complex . The learner has to develop, prerequisite capabilities before s/he acquires new terminal behavior. Thus the use of a hierarchy of learning and task analysis are integral parts of instructional transactions.
- Learners' characteristics : Learners' individual differences, readiness, and motivation to learn are the important issues to be considered before designing instructional activities.
- Cognitive process and instruction: The transfer of learning, the self-management skills of the learner, and teaching learners the skills of problem-solving are integral parts of the internal conditions of learning, applicable to instruction. The skill of learning 'how to learn' should be developed in the learner and the emphasis should be on the learner's individuality.

So, we can conclude that none of the above is incorrect regarding teaching-learning process.

**21(C).** Effective teaching occurs when a teacher is successful in keeping the students actively involved in learning. A few of the effective teaching practices include:

- Delivering lessons in an interesting manner by connecting the content being taught with real-life situations
- Using appropriate teaching techniques such as brainstorming, group learning, activity method, role plays, etc. that allows students to actively participate in the learning process
- Making use of audio/visual aids to cater to all the different senses
- Motivating students to learn more effectively through inquiry, experimentation, questioning, application, and reflection, leading to the creation of ideas.
- Providing opportunities to question, enquire, debate, reflect, and arrive at concepts or create new ideas.
- Employing flexibility and creativity while imparting knowledge rather than being rigid.

So, students can be encouraged to attend regular classes if teachers ensure to make use of interesting techniques.

**22(B).** Alternative conceptions are generated as a concept is understood from different aspects, while the misconception is a thought process that goes in the wrong direction due to a lack of complete information or just ignorance.

- Alternative conceptions and misconceptions are not always baseless rather they represent children's intuitive ideas about particular concepts and the world around them as it shows their thinking and they can think and put forward their views.
- The formation of alternative conceptions and misconceptions is very natural among children as well as adults because it is a natural thought process and no two minds can think alike exactly.
- A teacher should definitely attend to these alternative conceptions and misconceptions as they are significant in process of teaching-learning because they are very helpful; in developing critical thinking. Without this, a child would not be able to put forward one's own views and would end up mugging things.

Thus, it is concluded that alternate conceptions and misconceptions hold by children represent intuitive ideas about particular concepts.

**23(C).** All learners make mistakes. As someone has said: "You can't learn without goofing". Whether you are learning how to ride a bicycle, how to fly a kite or learn a language, everyone does make mistakes.

- An error is an incorrect form and a sure indication that the learner has not mastered the core of the selective topic in a learning process.
- Errors offer an opportunity for the teachers to understand students' thinking or thought processes since they are a window to children's thinking.
- Errors are necessary for the learning process to give insight into children's thinking. It helps the teacher to be aware of learners' learning styles and to cater to them according to their needs.
- Making an error cannot be just due to negligence and carelessness. It may be so that students are thinking about it in a different manner other than what is the right process.
- To understand this, a teacher should analyze what mistake the students are doing, how the mistake is generated, and where exactly they tend to make mistakes.

So, it is clear that errors offer an opportunity for the teachers to understand students' thinking.

**24(B).** Emotions have a great role to play in our lives. It involves feelings of pleasantness and unpleasantness. It can be expressed in various ways, like facial expressions on the face, like gestures, like volume and tone of speech, by the behavioral display or motives of a person. There is no moment in our life when we do not experience emotions. They can result from a variety of external or internal stimulations.

Characteristics of emotions

- Emotions are comparatively more complex in nature.
- Any emotional experience is preceded and accompanied by feelings. For example, the feeling of pleasure will lead or will be accompanied by the emotion of happiness/ joy.
- Emotion is an effective process that is much more active.
- Emotion is both subjective and objective.
- Emotions are of different types, for example, anger, joy, jealousy, and so forth.
- Physiological changes are experienced.

So, we can conclude that emotion is both subjective and objective statement is correct regarding emotion.

**25(A).** Learning is most effective when there is intrinsic motivation - a desire to learn from within, which finds satisfaction in the achievement itself and does not bother about other factors.

- Intrinsic Motivation refers to motivation that is driven by an interest or enjoyment in the task itself, and exists within the individual rather than relying on any external pressure. Intrinsic Motivation is based on taking pleasure in an activity rather working towards an external reward. Intrinsic motivation results in high-quality learning and creativity For example; preparing any project in science/ mathematics, participating in a sport may give pleasure to the pupil as a result of which he/she is motivated to undertake similar activities on his/her own.

Thus, it is concluded that student wants to participate in a sport because it's fun and she enjoys it is an example that shows Intrinsic motivation is better than extrinsic motivation for learning.

**26(C).** Factors influencing learning includes:

- Cultural content: Cultural content and its value are significant influencers in the process of learning. A child who is aware of his culture and is motivated to preserve the cultural integrity of the society develops an interest in learning more about the society and thinks about the ways towards the betterment of the society.
- Maturation: Maturation is the process by which we change, grow, and develop throughout life. The maturation of the learner affects learning because maturation is related to the structure and potential capacity.
- Interest: Interest refers to a feeling that keeps learners involved and attentive while learning or doing a specific task. Subjects in which a learner is interested reflect his motivation, attraction, and attentiveness in favor of that subject. If a learner is disinterested in learning a particular subject it shows that he/she has a feeling of demotivation against that subject.
- Emotional factor/Emotions: Emotion impacts our levels of motivation. Positive emotions can help a student engage with learning longer because they stay motivated. Emotions during learning also impact our feelings toward education. If we have positive experiences, we are more likely to enjoy our schooling and develop a love for learning.

So, it is clear that all (i), (ii), (iii) and (iv) factors influence learning.

**27(C).** Characteristics of Social-emotional Development

- The social context involves the interpersonal relationships of an individual, her acquired social skills, values, and how an individual adjusts to society. learning such qualities as sharing, cooperation, waiting for one's turn, respecting other people and things, and so on, forms a part of learning through social context.
- Emotions are the feelings or affect of an individual towards a person, object, or situation, which may generate physiological arousal, conscious experience, and/or behavioral expressions.

- Learning involves the acquisition of new knowledge, skills, values, and dispositions and as it takes shape in the young child's life it is more than intellectual in nature. It is a process located in and influenced by the social and emotional experiences and characteristics of the environment.
- The nature and quality of emotional experiences and the sense of security and belongingness at home and in the immediate surroundings at the early stages in life and attachments developed are crucial for the learning to take place.

Thus from the above-mentioned points, it is clear that social context and emotions play a very important role in learning.

**28(B).** Heredity refers to the traits that pass down from the parents to their offspring . It is the most important personality determinant that determines how far we can go.

- For example: If both the parents of a child are of short height, then the chance for being the short height of the child naturally is nearly 100% sure.
- How a person will develop depends on the environment but how far a person can develop depends on heredity.
- In the above question, option 3rd is neglected because it contains a word for the surety in the future, i.e 'will' and we cannot be 100% sure of some indefinite event in the future.

So, from the above points, we can clearly infer that the effect of heredity upon development is best defined by how far we can go.

**29(D).** Deductive learning is a more teacher-centered approach to education. Introduction of Generalizations and concepts is firstly given to learners, and to support the learning examples and activities are suggested. Minimum interaction is there between teacher and student, and the teaching method which is generally used is the lecture method.

Features of the Deductive method are:

- General to particular or abstract to concrete.
- Facts are given to the child and the principle of growth is not considered.
- The formula is decided and children are made to memorize it without applying logic to it.
- Children are made to learn and a lot of emphasis is given to the rote learning process.
- It starts with a rule and the application part is more in it, does not appreciate or follow the principle of learning by doing.
- It requires individual learning and in this process, the child is inactive and is a one-way process.
- Less interaction between teacher and student, the student only listens but does not know why we are doing this or

following this.

From the above points, we can conclude that all the above-mentioned properties are of the deductive method.

**30(B).** In progressive-education children are seen as active explorers as progressive education:

- emphasizes to enhance skills and understanding of the learners by engaging with the contents and experiences.
- promotes 'learning by doing' to make children self-reliant and productive to use their knowledge and talents effectively.
- ensures the active participation of students by working in a group and applying practical knowledge to complete an activity.

So, it could be concluded that in progressive-education children are seen as active explorers.

**31(B).** According to the passage, " According to the IWT, India is permitted to construct water storage on western rivers -Indus, Jhelum, and Chenab -up to 3.6 million acre-feet for various purposes, including domestic use."

So, it is concluded that Beas is not included according to the Indus Water Treaty for the construction of water storage for India.

**32(C).** According to the passage, "According to this agreement, control over the three "eastern" rivers — the Beas, the Ravi, and the Sutlej — was given to India, while control over the three "western" rivers — the Indus, the Chenab, and the Jhelum — to Pakistan. In aftermath of the 2016 Uri attack, India reviewed the treaty and its provisions and proposed several changes. The treaty was reviewed by India to explore possible ways to use its share of water from rivers, including the Jhelum, flowing into Pakistan."

So, it can be concluded that Chenab, Jhelum is not the correct pair of the eastern and western rivers.

**33(D).** According to passage,

Refer to the lines from the passage:

- 'India refused to countenance any change of design of the Miyar dam in J&K, as asked by Pakistan, and plans to continue utilization of its allocation under the Indus Waters Treaty.'
- Upon the perusal of the above lines, it can be concluded that 1000 MW Pakul Dul dam construction on Chenab, permits to construct the water storage in the eastern rivers is correct as mentioned in the passage so both are not the one which is refused by India as asked by Pakistan.
- To allow access to all the three eastern rivers is wrong because why did India refuse it as according to the Indus Water Treaty agreement, control over the three

"eastern" rivers — the Beas, the Ravi, and the Sutlej was given to India.
- So, we can't consider it as our answer.

The only option (D) is correct which is refused by India is to countenance any change of design of the Miyar dam in J&K as asked by Pakistan.

**34(C).** The meaning of the given words:
- Permit: to allow somebody to do something or something to happen, authorize, sanction, grant, license, and power.
- Ban: to officially say that something is not allowed, often by law, prohibition, forbid, veto, proscribe, outlaw, and embargo.

From the above meaning, it is evident that Ban is the opposite meaning of the word Permit.

**35(B).** The meaning of the given words:
- Explore: to travel around a place, etc, in order to learn about it, traverse, survey, inspect, scout, reconnoiter, prospect and recce.
- Investigate: trying to find out all facts about something, probe, scrutinize, look into, and explore.

From the above meaning, it is evident that Investigate is the same meaning as the word Explore.

**36(C).** 'Aftermath' is a noun.
- A noun is a part of speech that is a name of a thing, a place, or a person. Example: Slovakia.
- Here, "in" is the preposition that is used before the noun "aftermath" to show the time of happening of the Uri attack.
- Aftermath means the consequences or after-effects of a significant unpleasant event.

**37(C).** According to the passage, "The Indus Waters Treaty is a water-distribution treaty between India and Pakistan, brokered by the World Bank, then the International Bank for Reconstruction and Development. The treaty was signed in Karachi on September 19, 1960, by Prime Minister of India Jawaharlal Nehru and President of Pakistan Ayub Khan."

So, it can be concluded that the only option Indus Waters Treaty is the correct theme of the passage as it is mentioned in the passage and is also signed between the two countries in order to solve the issues related to water distribution and also the construction of the Dam and also the complete story of the passage revolves around the treaty between these two countries.

**38(A).** "One of" refers to a single entity of a group or subject.

A noun or pronoun or subject of such phrase will be in the plural form and the verb in such cases will always be singular as it refers to only a single subject.

The rule for such sentences:
- One/Every/Each/Neither/Either + of + Noun (Plural) + Verb (Singular).
- Example: One of the best students in the class is Manish.

Here, the error lies in "One of this" as the noun "projects" is in the plural form we need demonstrative adjectives "these" instead of "this" to define the plural noun "projects".

**39(D).** According to the passage, "The treaty was reviewed by India to explore possible ways to use its share of water from rivers, including the Jhelum, flowing into Pakistan."

So, it is concluded that Jhelum is included which is reviewed by India to use its share of water from rivers.

**40(D).** According to the given lines,
"O! what sweet company.
But to go to school in a summer morn,
O! it drives all joy away;
Under a cruel eye outworn,"
So, it is concluded that the school boy feels unhappy when he goes to school.

**41(A).** According to the given lines,
"How can the bird that is born for joy,
Sit in a cage and sing.
How can a child when fears annoy,
But droop his tender wing,"
So, it is concluded that the school boy is compared to a bird.

**42(B).** Alliteration: T he repetition of an initial consonant sound in words that are in close proximity to each other.

Alliteration does not refer to the repetition of consonant letters that begin words, but rather the repetition of the consonant sound at the beginning of words. Ex: Piper picked a peck

Here, sky-lark sings. The sound of s represents Alliteration figure of speech in the above line.

**43(D).** Metaphor: An expression, often found in literature, that describes a person or object by referring to something that is considered to have similar characteristics to that person or object. Ex: I'm feeling red.

Here, 'Under a cruel eye outworn' represents the teacher who keeps a close eye on students. The child hates to be under scrutiny. He dislikes the fact that he had to spend his day in the supervision of an inconsiderate person.

**44(D).** According to the given lines,
"I love to rise in a summer morn,
When the birds sing on every tree;
The distant huntsman winds his horn,
And the skylark sings with me.
O! what sweet company."
So, it is concluded that sweet company refer skylark and huntsman horn.

**45(C).** According to the given lines,
"But to go to school in a summer morn,

O! it drives all joy away;"
So, it is concluded that going to school in the summer morning takes away all the happiness of the child.

**46(D).** Language acquisition: It refers to the subconscious process of learning a native or second language because of the innate capacity of the human brain.
- It is a natural process whereby children acquire language by observing and repeating what they hear in the natural setting of their native environment.
- Language acquisition does not require any formal instruction, children acquire the language without being taught. It is a natural process so, one does not forget one's native language.

So, it could be concluded that a child learns his/her first language in a natural setting.

**47(B).** Language learning: When a child learns a language as a second or third language , it is assumed as language learning.
- It refers to having a basic knowledge of grammatical rules and their use in communication.
- It is effectively done by providing comprehensible inputs to make the learners actively involved in real communication.
- It refers to the result of deliberate and conscious effort in a formal environment, for a better understanding of foundational skills of language learning.

So, it could be concluded that language learning is a conscious attempt by the learner.

**48(B).** Multiple Line of Approach:
- The term "multiple line" implies that one is to proceed simultaneously from many different points towards the one and the same end. In teaching a language, it implies attacking the problem from all fronts.
- It means a lesson that is to be taught by the teacher should be tackled from many side s. So, it reflects that the Multi-line approach consists of reaching the same target from different directions and means.
- For example, there is a lesson on 'Holidays' in the textbook. The teacher can have a number of language activities connected with the topic such as oral drill, reading, sentence writing, composition, grammar, translation, language exercises, etc.

So, we can conclude that Teaching a lesson, through a number of language activities connected with the topic, refers to Multiple Line of Approach .

**49(C).** Present Language in Basic Sentence Patterns:
- Present, and have the students' memories, basic sentence patterns used

in day-to-day conversation. From small utterances, the students can easily pass on to longer sentences .

• In the case of learning mother-tongue, the student's memory span can retain much longer sentences than those of a foreign language.

• The facility thus gained in a foreign language enables the learners to expand the grasp of the language material in respect of sounds and vocabulary items.

So, we can conclude that the 'Present Language in Basic Sentence Patterns' principle of second language could be associated with the above-mentioned statement.

**50(D).** 'Decorum' in spoken language pertains to appropriate gestures.

Decorum was a principle of classical rhetoric, poetry and theatrical theory that was about fitness or otherwise of a style to a theatrical subject. The concept of decorum is also applied to prescribed limits of appropriate social behavior within set situations.

**51(C).** The teaching of grammar will help the learners to have good conversational skills as the ultimate aim of every language learner is to acquire the ability to speak and write the language correctly.

• In order to do this, he/she requires knowledge of grammar in some form or the other.

• So, any course in language teaching assigns an important role to grammar.

• The more we are aware of how it works, the more we can monitor the meaning and effectiveness of the way we and others use language.

From the above, we can conclude that Teaching of grammar will help the learners to have good conversational skills.

**52(C).** Grammar-translation method:

• The Grammar-Translation method of learning a language is through the detailed study of its grammar.

• In this method, the learner first learns grammatical rules and then applies those rules in translating sentences from the target language into the mother tongue.

• Primarily, the mother tongue or native language is used to teach the rule of grammar to the learners so that translations become easier.

• Vocabulary is built using bilingual word lists i.e., to teach the meaning of words in the mother tongue and in the target language.

• Rote learning or memorization plays a vital role when it comes to learning the rules of grammar.

So, the principle of the grammar-translation method is to memorize the rules of grammar.

**53(D).** The Main Challenges of Teaching

Language in a Diverse Classroom are:

• Issues and challenges to curriculum design.

• Challenge and issues of the teaching-learning process.

• Challenge of teaching-learning materials.

• Challenge of a mixed-ability group of learners.

• Challenge maintaining justice and democracy in the classroom.

So, we can conclude that all of the above are the main challenges of teaching language in a diverse classroom.

**54(A).** Language skills can be learned better in an integrated manner since it exploits all the skills. For example, when we speak, we also listen simultaneously, when we write we are also reading.

This engagement with language enables us to internalize the underlying grammaticality of the language. This leads to language learning.

So, from the above-mentioned points, it becomes clear that language skills can be learned better if they are taught in an integrated manner.

**55(D).** Listening and Reading comes under the receptive category while speaking and writing comes under the productive category of language skills.

• Speaking and writing come under the productive category of language skills because these generate output in form of oral and written. This why these are known as productive skills.

• Listening and Reading comes under the receptive category because the learner receives the inputs given by the teacher. That is why these are known as receptive skills.

So, we can conclude that speaking and writing comes under the productive category of language skills.

**56(D).** Components in the evaluation of speaking:

• Articulation: While evaluating the speaking of students, the teacher must pay attention to their articulation of words i.e., how they join words including their way of speaking.

• Intonation, stress, and voice quality: The power of persuasion often depends on convincing voice quality. Intonations (Ups and downs in the voice), stressing on important words, and voice quality (change in sound as per the mood and requirement) are an important part of speaking. So, it is important for a teacher to assess the intonations and voice quality of students while they are speaking during their evaluation of speaking skills.

• Vocabulary and Pronunciation: While evaluating the speaking skills, it is important to note down the kind of

vocabulary used by the speaker and how he is pronouncing the words. It reflects the proficiency of the speaker in the target language.

• Body language: Using hand and body movements while speaking helps the speaker to connect with the audience and to gain attention. Thus, the body language of students should also be evaluated along with the evaluation of speaking skills.

• Concentration: Children need to know that clear thought in an organized manner keeps the attention of the listener. So, they should speak by organizing their thoughts by concentrating on the main idea of the topic.

Thus, it is clear that evaluation of speaking consists of the evaluation of pronunciation, intonation, and stress.

**57(C).** Followings are some great activities in which teachers can evaluate students listening skills:

• Listen and Draw: this particular activity can be used with students who struggle to express themselves in English, Listen and Draw isolates listening from speaking. Simply have your students take out a blank piece of paper and give them instructions on what to draw.

• Dictations: with this activity, the teacher can easily evaluate students listening skills. The teacher just needs to select a couple of words and then call the words one by one and repeat at least once after calling the words. After calling all the words which the students have to write on a separate piece of paper. The teacher collects the papers and from there he can start evaluating each student based on their listening comprehension.

• Oral Presentations: It is more viewed in academic courses where the test takers have to talk about a given or selected topic, nevertheless, that doesn't mean that it cannot be used to assess other learners. Scoring is also easy because the test-taker speaks about a specific topic.

So, we can conclude that the vocabulary assessment task is not the activity of evaluating listening skills.

Hence, the correct option is (D).

**58(A).** Flannel boards can be used in classrooms in a variety of situations.

• The advantage of using a flannel board is that it provides the flexibility of using a material to teach students.

• Flannel boards are used to display pictures, messages .

• In the English Language classroom, it can be used to teach picture composition .

• It allows children to explore stories, apply their imagination, boost fine motor skills, and enhance their

creativity .
- The flannel board increases the child's learning abilities .

From the above, we can conclude that the flannel board is useful for teaching picture composition.

**59(C).** Realia refers to the objects associated with everyday life to be used in the classroom. Realia can be used as props for dialogues to teach new lexical or structural items as it is a tangible teaching-learning object.
- It includes coin, newspaper, map, tickets, fruits, vegetables, etc.
- It makes learning more interesting and enliven by bringing the class to life.
- It ensures the use of accurate and realistic materials in the teaching-learning process.
- It encourages healthy classroom interaction and helps in meeting individual differences.

So, we conclude that realia can be used as props for dialogues to teach new lexical or structural items.

**60(B).** Remedial teaching: During learning, a child makes mistakes willingly-unwillingly or due to some alternative conceptions. It is the job of a teacher to help students to correct those mistakes after diagnosing them. The method so followed is known as remedial teaching. The following are its characteristics:
- It can be used for improving language skills
- To rectify a particular problem area, it can be used. For example, a student is confused among the pronunciation of 'no' and 'know', he can be taught the concept of silent letters.
- It is carried out after the identification of problems and challenges faced by students.
- A teacher should be well aware of students' strengths and weaknesses to apply this method.
- It is a systematic process as the teacher first diagnoses the problem of students and then applies appropriate remedial methods.

So, we conclude that remedial teaching is a systematic process.

**61(B).** Given,
The length of a pendulum $= 60cm$ and an arc of length $= 16.5cm$

Length of arc $= \frac{\theta}{360°} \times 2\pi \times$ Radius

$\Rightarrow 16.5 \times 360° = 2 \times \frac{22}{7} \times 60 \times \theta$

$\Rightarrow \theta = \frac{63°}{4}$

$\Rightarrow \theta = 15°45'$

$\therefore$ The angle through which it swings $= 15°45'$

**62(D).** Given,
Dimensions of the box:
Length $= 10$ cm

Breadth $= 6$ cm
Height $= 5$ cm
Thickness $= 2$ cm
As we know,
Volume of cuboid $=$ Length $\times$ Breadth $\times$ Height
Volume of material used when thickness is given $=$ Outer volume $-$ Inner volume

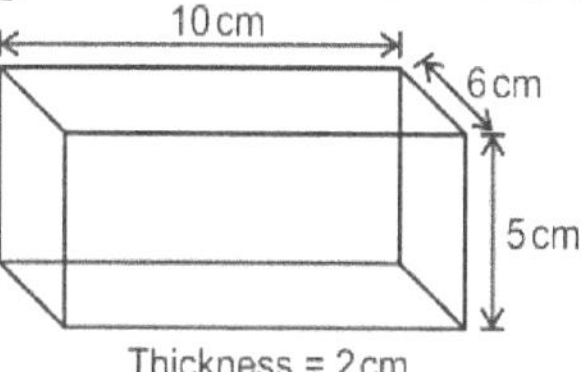

Inner length $= 10 - 2\times$ thickness $= 10 - 4$ $= 6$ cm
Inner breadth $= 6 - 2\times$ thickness $= 6 - 4$ $= 2$ cm
Inner height $= 5 - 2\times$ thickness $= 5 - 4$ $= 1$ cm
Inner volume $= 6 \times 2 \times 1 = 12$ cm$^3$
Outer volume $= 10 \times 6 \times 5 = 300$ cm$^3$
Volume of wood used $=$ Outer volume $-$ Inner volume
$= 300 - 12$
$= 288$ cm$^3$
$\therefore$ Volume of wood used $= 288$ cm$^3$

**63(B).** Given,
Circumference of the base $= 44m$
High conical tent $= 9m$
As we know,
Circumference of circle $= 2\pi r$
Volume of cone $= (\frac{1}{3})\pi r^2 h$

$\Rightarrow 2\pi r = 44$
$\Rightarrow r = 7m$
Volume of air contained
$= (\frac{1}{3}) \times (\frac{22}{7}) \times 7 \times 7 \times 9$
$= 462m^3$
$\therefore$ The volume of air contained $= 462m^3$

**64(D).** Given,
Sum of 5 consecutive integers is $S$.
Let the smallest of these 5 numbers be $x$.
5 consecutive numbers will be $x, x+1, x+2, x+3, x+4$.
According to the question,
$x + x + 1 + x + 2 + x + 3 + x + 4 = S$
$\Rightarrow 5x + 10 = S$
$\Rightarrow 5x = S - 10$
$\Rightarrow x = \frac{(S-10)}{5}$
Largest of these 5 number
$= x + 4 = [\frac{(S-10)}{5}] + 4$
$= \frac{(S+10)}{5}$

**65(C).** Given,
$13\frac{1}{5} + 15\frac{4}{5} + 12\frac{2}{3} + 13\frac{1}{3}$
$= \frac{66}{5} + \frac{79}{5} + \frac{38}{3} + \frac{40}{3}$
$= \frac{145}{5} + \frac{78}{3}$
$= 29 + 26$
$= 55$

**66(A).** Given,

Speed of man $= \frac{2}{5}$ of his original speed
He is late by 15 minutes.
As we know,
Distance $=$ Speed $\times$ Time
Let the original speed of man be $5x$ and time taken by him be $t$ minutes.
Distance $=$ Speed $\times$ Time
Distance $= 5x \times t = 5xt$ ...(1)
Reduced speed $= \frac{2}{5}$ of $5x$
Reduced speed $= 2x$
New time taken $(t') = t + 15$
Distance $=$ Reduced speed $\times t'$
$\Rightarrow$ Distance $= 2x \times (t + 15)$
$\Rightarrow$ Distance $= 2xt + 30x$ ...(2)
By equating (1) and (2) we'll get
$5xt = 2xt + 30x$
$\Rightarrow 3xt = 30x$
$\Rightarrow t = \frac{30x}{3x}$
$\Rightarrow t = 10$
$\therefore$ Time taken with original speed is 10 minutes.

**67(D).** Given,
Rohit : Sahil ( 1 year ago) $= 6 : 7$
Rohit : Sahil ( 4 year after) $= 7 : 8$
Let Rohit's age 1 year ago be $6x$, and Sahil's age 1 year ago be $7x$.
Time difference $= 4 + 1 = 5$ years
According to the question,
$\frac{(6x+5)}{(7x+5)} = \frac{7}{8}$
$\Rightarrow 8 \times (6x + 5) = 7 \times (7x + 5)$
$\Rightarrow 48x + 40 = 49x + 35$
$\Rightarrow 49x - 48x = 40 - 35$
$\Rightarrow x = 5$
Sahil's age 1 year ago $= 7x$
$= 7 \times 5$
$= 35$ years
Sahil's present age $= 35 + 1 = 36$ years
$\therefore$ The present age of Sahil is 36 years.

**68(B).** Given series,
$23, 48, 99, 203, 413$ ___
The pattern followed here is;
Second term $=$ First term $\times 2 +$ (Addition of prime numbers)

| 23 | 48 | 99 | 203 | 413 | 837 |
|----|----|----|-----|-----|-----|
| ×2+2 | ×2+3 | ×2+5 | ×2+7 | ×2+11 | |

The next term is determined by multiplying the previous term by 2 and the addition of series of prime numbers.
So, 837 is the missing term.

**69(A).** Sum of the imports in 2015 and 2018 $= 390 + 450 = 840$ crore
Sum of the exports in 2014 and 2017 $= 300 + 420 = 720$ crore
$\therefore$ The required ratio $= 720 : 840$
$= 6 : 7$

**70(A).** Given,
The scheduled time of Jadu's flight $= 02 : 14$ pm
Jadu wants to go to the airport 65 minutes before the scheduled time of the flight.
Jadu arrives at the airport $= 02 : 14$ pm $-75$ minutes

$= 02 : 14\,\text{pm} - 1\,\text{hour}\,5\,\text{minutes}$
$= 01 : 09\,\text{pm}$
Jadu completes his lunch in 25 minutes.
He completes his lunch $= 01 : 09\,\text{pm} + 25$ minutes
$= 01 : 34\,\text{pm}$
Total time before the scheduled time of flight, Jadu completes his lunch $= 02 : 14$ pm $-01 : 34$ pm
$= 40\,\text{minutes}$
∴ Jadu completes his lunch 40 minutes before the scheduled time of his flight.

**71(D).**
Given,
Weight of oranges $= 4\,\text{kg}\,455\,\text{gm}$
Weight of mangoes $= 3\,\text{kg}\,100\,\text{gm}$
Difference $=$ Weight of oranges $-$ Weight of mangoes

|  | Kg | gm |
| --- | --- | --- |
| Weight of Oranges | 4 | 455 |
| Weight of Mangoes | 3 | 100 |
| Difference | 1 | 355 |

∴ The weight of oranges is 1 kg 355 gm more than the weight of mangoes.

**72(A).** As we know,
$1km = 1000m$
Checking option (A):
$6km = (6 \times 1000)m = 6000m$
$5.6km = (5.6 \times 1000)m = 5600m$
$4\frac{3}{4}km = \frac{19}{4}km = 4.75km = (4.75 \times 1000)m = 4750m$
The descending order of these lengths:
$6km > 5.6km > 5455m > 4\frac{3}{4}km$

**73(D).** Given,
Denominator $= 2 +$ Numerator
Let the numerator be $a$.
The denominator be $2 + a$.
As per the question,
$\frac{a \times 3}{(2+a) \times 2} = \frac{1}{2}$
$\Rightarrow \frac{3a}{(2+a)} = 1$
$\Rightarrow 3a = 2 + a$
$\Rightarrow 2a = 2$
$\Rightarrow a = 1$
Numerator $= 1$
Denominator $= 1 + 2 = 3$
∴ The required fraction $= \frac{1}{3}$

**74(C).** The nature of Mathematics is enlisted in the following points:
- Mathematics is based on understanding.
- Mathematics has its own language.
- Mathematics puts great emphasis on the child's own methods of calculating and solving problems and rejects the previous practice of heavy emphasis on standard written algorithms.
- Mathematics is a science of discovery and logical reasoning.
- Mathematics is regarded as a powerful tool for interpreting the world and therefore should be rooted in real experience across the whole curriculum. Mathematics is brought out of the child's everyday situations.
- Mathematics is an exact science.
- Mathematics with reason is rooted in action – learning through doing.
- Mathematics with reason puts less emphasis on representing numbers on paper as 'sums' and more emphasis on developing mental images in the child.

Thus, it is concluded that Mathematics is changeable in the universe is incorrect about nature of mathematics.

**75(D).** The nature of mathematics highly influences the nature of the teaching-learning process in mathematics.
Nature of mathematics:
- Mathematics should be visualised as the vehicle to train a child to think, reason, analyse, and articulate logically. Apart from being a specific subject, it should be treated as a concomitant to any subject involving analysis and meaning.
- 'Mathematics' is a broad term that encompasses many branches and components. It is a science that involves dealing with numbers, measurement of shapes and structures, organisation and interpretation of data and establishing relationship among variables, etc.
- Mathematics is a way of thinking and it is related to our life on daily basis. Mathematics, as an expression of the human mind, reflects the active will, the contemplative reason, and the desire for aesthetic perfection.
- Mathematics is the "queen of all sciences" and its presence is there in all the subjects. Mathematics acts as the basis and structure of other subjects. Its basic elements are logic and intuition, analysis and construction, generality and individuality".

So, it is concluded that all of the above are correct in the context of nature of Mathematics.

**76(C).** Mathematics is the study of numbers, shape, quantity, and patterns. Mathematics is the 'queen of all sciences' and its presence is there in all the subjects. It acts as the basis and structure of other subjects.
- Mathematics is an important subject and is not hard in comparison to other subjects.
- It is just a myth that boys easily grasp problems in mathematics while girls take more time.
- It is the same for all and everyone can learn and succeed in mathematics by practicing.
- It is also a myth that mathematics takes a lot of time to be understood in comparison to other subjects.

So, from the above-mentioned points, it becomes clear that everyone can learn and succeed in mathematics.

**77(D).** Mathematics is one of the few subjects that have the practical, cultural and disciplinary value . Mathematics has the potential to range across all the three values, but due to inappropriate teaching-learning process, its potential is not being utilized to its optimum level.
- Mathematics provides an effective way of building mental discipline and encourages logical reasoning and mental rigour and moral development .
- In addition, mathematical knowledge plays a crucial role in understanding the contents of other school subjects such as science, social studies, Cultural Studies.
- Mathematics has always been praised for its usefulness and significance in life. It plays a key role in deciding how individuals deal with various problems of life.
- According to National Curriculum Framework-2005, the main goal of Mathematics education in school is the mathematisation of the child's thought process.
- Mathematics relies on logic, reasoning, problem-solving, creativity and mathematical way of thinking. These skills can be useful in many other subjects.

So, we conclude that the important role of Mathematics in the syllabus is all the above points.

**78(D).** Mathematics is the study of numbers , shape , quantity and patterns . It relies on logical thinking and connects learning with children's day to day life.
The subject Mathematics is important in the curriculum since it:
- Improves logical thinking.
- Helps in the study of science subjects.
- Connects learning with children's day to day life.
- Develops skills such as speed, accuracy, estimation.
- Improves reasoning power, analytical and, critical thinking.
- Enhances scientific attitude like estimating, finding and verifying results.

So, we conclude that the subject Mathematics is important in the curriculum for the above-mentioned reason.

**79(D).** The main characteristics of mathematical language are
- the simplicity of the concepts so that the learner can easily understand them.
- accuracy is also needed in mathematics so that students can learn to commit fewer mistakes and be accurate in doing calculations.
- through precision, students learn exactly how to use formulas and under what situations these formulas are correct.

On the other hand, ordinary language can be ambiguous, vague, and emotive.

So, we conclude that all the above points are characteristics of the language of mathematics.

**80(D).** Language of mathematics refers to the language that used to express mathematical thoughts, expressions, and ideas.

- Language of mathematics makes learners able to reason logically, assimilate mathematical terms, and recognize and employ patterns of mathematical thought.
- Mathematical language should be well defined, clear, and should be highly compact and focussed.

Language of Mathematics Includes:

- Sign , symbol, graphs
- Formulae , syntax
- Number variable
- Greek alphabet
- Letter convention

So, we can conclude that it does not require other ordinary languages for its use is not one of the merits of mathematical language.

**81(D).** Error analysis is a method commonly used to identify the cause of student errors when they make consistent mistakes. It is a process of reviewing a student's work and then looking for patterns of misunderstanding. Errors in mathematics can be factual, procedural, or conceptual, and may occur for a number of reasons.

The most probable reason for writing 0.50 is larger than 0.5 is a misconception regarding the significance of zero in ordering decimal .

- They would not have a clear concept about dealing with zero right to the decimal.
- The only time you would want to keep zeros is when dealing with money. Monetary amounts require two place values after the decimal to indicate cents to the Hundredth place.
- Writing .5 cents is not appropriate; it should be Rs0.50.
- The concrete experience of representation of decimal numbers on a number line is required for abstract problems.
- Such misconceptions can be cleared by several examples.

So, we can conclude that students often make a mistake in comparing decimal numbers. For example, 0.50 is larger than 0.5. The most probable reason for this error is a misconception regarding the significance of zero in ordering decimal.

**82(A).**

Diagnostic Assessment: It is the assessment that is conducted along with formative assessment during the instructional process.

- It is carried out based on the data obtained from the formative assessment. Diagnostic assessment is specially conducted for investigating and removing the learning permanent difficulties of learners.
- For example, if it is found that a learner has not understood certain concepts in a particular subject, then to help him/her understand these concepts, diagnostic assessment is conducted and remediation is provided.
- This is conducted by diagnostic remedial test. The keyword in diagnostic assessment is an assessment of learning difficulties.

So, we can conclude that a learner has not understood certain concepts in a maths subject, to help him/her understand these concepts, the teacher will conduct diagnostic assessment.

**83(C).** Diagnostic teaching: It is a process of informal teaching and using different methodologies for enough practice until they get mastery over the topic.

- After diagnosing the learning gaps or errors of children, the teacher teaches those concepts or topics again by using different techniques or methods.
- In this type of test, no scores are made for a right answer, only wrong answers are taken into view in the sequence of contents.
- The main purpose of diagnostic teaching is to identify the areas of learning difficulties of children which helps to find out the weakness or deficiency of a child in learning.
- A diagnostic test helps us to identify the trouble spots and discovered those areas of students' weakness that are unresolved by formative test.
- It works as an effective tool in planning remedial teaching as during remedial teaching, teacher provides learners with necessary help and guidance to overcome the problems which are determined during diagnostic teaching.

So, it can be concluded that We may say that Diagnostic testing implies a detailed study of learning difficulties to locate and identify the areas of learning difficulties.

**84(D).** Given,

$$\sqrt{324} + 9^2 - 7^2 = 2 \times (?)^2$$
$$\Rightarrow 18 + 81 - 49 = 2 \times (?)^2$$
$$\Rightarrow 50 = 2 \times (?)^2$$
$$\Rightarrow \frac{50}{2} = (?)^2$$
$$\Rightarrow 25 = (?)^2$$
$$\Rightarrow ? = \sqrt{25}$$
$$\Rightarrow ? = 5$$

$\therefore$ The value of $(?)$ is $5$ .

**85(B).** As we know,

$$\Rightarrow \text{Divisor} = \frac{(\text{Dividend} - \text{Remainder})}{\text{Quotient}}$$

$$\Rightarrow \text{Divisor} = \frac{(13501 - 7)}{78}$$
$$= \frac{13494}{78}$$
$\therefore$ Divisor $= 173$

**86(A).** Mathematics is commonly perceived as the most difficult subject at all stages in the school curriculum. Further, its abstractness is highlighted in the textbooks and classroom transactions, although all the concepts included in the mathematics curriculum are r elated to the real-life experiences of the child. It is a common belief that mathematics concepts cannot be learned without being taught.

- A teacher asked the students to collect leaves and to identify symmetry patterns. This task reflects the teacher's efforts to relate a real-life experience with mathematical concepts.
- We can connect mathematics in our daily life. There are many activities and maths exercises which are directly or indirectly connected with our daily routine life.
- Certain qualities that are nurtured by mathematics are the power of reasoning, creativity, abstract or spatial thinking, critical thinking, problem-solving ability, and even effective communication skills.
- Maths puzzles and riddles encourage and attract an alert and open-minded attitude among students and help them develop clarity in their thinking. Emphasis should be laid on the development of the clear concept in mathematics which reflects daily life experience in a child, right from the primary classes.

So, we can conclude that through the above activity or task, the teacher wants to relate a real-life experience with mathematical concepts.

**87(D).** Evaluation in Mathematics refers to a process of making value judgments based on both qualitative and quantitative data collected over a period of time.

Evaluation in mathematics is necessary as it helps in:

- making reliable decisions about educational planning.
- determining the effectiveness of the learning process or program.
- providing constructive feedback to both the students and the teachers.
- provides qualitative and quantitative information.
- assessing both scholastic and co-scholastic aspects of a child's growth.
- evaluating teaching methodology regarding the expected learning objectives.
- emphasis should be on testing of mathematization abilities rather than procedural knowledge.

So, it could be concluded that all of the above are true in the context of mathematical evaluation.

**88(A).** Essay type test:
- The math essay question type is subjective and cannot be auto-scored.
- In this type of test, the teacher assesses communication skills besides logical ability and precision in thinking in mathematics.
- For example definition of a Mathematics term, to prove a theorem all comes under essay type test.
- Essay items are no doubt valuable exercises for students but they consume a lot of testing time.
- Essay question type allows students to input text and advanced math equations within the same answer, allowing them to clarify their thought process to teachers and pinpoint any areas with which they've struggled.

Thus from the above-mentioned points, it is clear that in essay type test the teacher assess communication skills besides logical ability and precision in thinking in mathematics.

**89(B).** Assessment is the process of collecting, reviewing and using data for improvement in the learning process. One of the ways of collecting data about student's learning is by taking test.

Evaluation is described as the process of passing judgement based on some set standards. It is the decision making process.

Types of Assessment:
- Formative assessment: Assessment during instruction, immediate assessment or feedback during instruction or on-going programme. In this situation, a student is asked to draw a cube which is recently taught (this can be understood from the question) to test the understanding of the student and to make sure if diagnosing of problem or re-teaching is required hence it is a formative assessment which is done time to time to assess the understanding of the students.
- Summative Assessment: Assessment after the instruction. For example, after completion of a class, the teacher gives questions to students to assess their learning of the entire class, students give feedback after the class.

So, we conclude that the above statement is of formative assessment .

**90(B).** Assessment is integral to the teaching-learning process which helps in facilitating student learning and improving instruction. It is a process of collecting relevant information on student learning.

Formati ve assessment:
- For mative assessment is goal-centered that is, it focuses attention on successful teaching and learning of important learning goals and standards.
- It gives feedback on learning regularly within a short interval of time.
- This approach involves students in the teaching/learning process and offers opportunities for them to take responsibility for learning by setting personal goals and selecting strategies for meaningful learning.
- Through formative assessment, students compete with themselves rather than with other students.

So, we can conclude that the above situation is reflecting formative assessment.

**91(A).** Mammals have glandular skin with hairs.
- Mammals or Mammalia class of animal kingdom are found in a variety of habitats – polar ice caps, deserts, mountains, forests, grasslands and dark caves.
- Some of them have adapted to fly or live in water.
- The most unique mammalian characteristic is the presence of milk-producing glands (mammary glands) by which the young ones are nourished.
- They have two pairs of limbs, adapted for walking, running, climbing, burrowing, swimming or flying.
- The skin of mammals is unique in possessing hair. External ears or pinnae are present. Different types of teeth are present in the jaw. The heart is four-chambered. They are homoiothermous. Respiration is by lungs. Sexes are separate and fertilisation is internal.

**92(A).** The crops depends on the onset of South-West monsoon are known as Kharif crops.

Kharif crops are those which require monsoonal rains for their growth. They are grown in the beginning of the first rain in july i.e., during the south west monsoon season. The common kharif crops are maize and rice. They require rains for their cultivation.

**93(C).** Indian Satellite Series 'INSAT' is an example of a Meteorological Satellite.
- INSAT or the Indian National Satellite System is a series of multipurpose geostationary satellites launched by ISRO to satisfy the telecommunications, broadcasting, meteorology, and search and rescue needs of India.
- It was commissioned in 1983.
- It is the largest domestic communication system in the Asia Pacific Region.
- It has nine operational communication satellites and 200 transponders placed in Geo-stationary orbit.
- The satellite is monitored and controlled by Master Control Facilities that exist in Hassan and Bhopal.
- INSAT-3D is a multipurpose geosynchronous spacecraft with main meteorological payloads (imager and sounder).
- The main objectives for this mission are to provide an operational, environmental and storm warning system to protect life and property.

**94(C).** The tusks of an elephant which are part of the upper teeth are modified incisors in the upper jaw.

They replace the deciduous milk teeth when the elephant reaches about six to twelve months of age and continue growing at about seventeen centimetres a year.

**95(A).** The pitcher plant is an insectivorous plant.
- It has a Pitcher-like structure that is the modified part of the leaf.
- The apex of the leaf forms a lid that can open and close the mouth of the pitcher.
- Inside the pitcher, there are hairs that are directed downwards.
- When an insect lands in the pitcher, the lid closes and the trapped insect gets entangled into the hair.
- The insect is digested by the digestive juices secreted in the pitcher.

**96(B).** Statements A and C are correct.
- In Uttar Pradesh, people enjoy eating a vegetable made of kachnar flowers.
- In Kerala and West Bengal, people cook a vegetable made of banana flowers.
- People who are from Maharashtra love pakoras made of drumsticks (sahjan) flowers.

**97(B).** Vermicompost is an o rganic biofertilizer.

Vermicomposting: It is the scientific method of making compost, by using earthworms. They are commonly found living in soil, feeding on biomass and excreting it in a digested form.

**98(B).** Gibberellins:
- Gibberellins (GAs) are plant hormones that regulate various developmental processes, including stem elongation, germination, dormancy, flowering, flower development, and leaf and fruit senescence.
- It is a plant hormone, that helps in controlling stem elongation and provides desired crop yield.
- It induces stem elongation in genetic dwarf and rosette dwarf plants; these plants, though genetically predisposed to be dwarfs, undergo stem elongation with the help of gibberellins.
- It was first discovered from a fungus due to its effect on rice causing elongated stem.
- This compound was later shown to be an endogenously synthesized hormone that regulates stem cell elongation . Gibberellin acts through its nucleus-localized receptor and stem elongation often occur quickly.

- One outcome of this quick development is that there is exceptional contention for minerals and nutrients, and this may result in the death of some shoots in a few sections of the plant.

**99(D).** There are three adverse effects of burning fossil fuels: air pollution, water pollution, and climate change. These effects are caused by the products released when fossil fuels are burned.

**100(C).** Irrigation is defined as the science of artificial application of water to the land, in accordance with the crop water requirement throughout the crop period for full fledged nourishment of the crops.
- The term consumptive use implies the total water required for all plant processes.
- In drip irrigation system , precise amount of water that is equal to the daily consumptive use of the plant or the depleted soil water that change with crop growth stages and whether conditions is applied.
- Drip irrigation is also called as Trickle Irrigation .
- Drip irrigation is the method of applying filtered water (also water soluble fertilizers) onto or into the soil near the plant roots at a low discharge rate with the help of drippers or emitters .
- The operating pressure of drip irrigation system is small compared to sprinkler irrigation method and it varies from 1-2 $kg/cm^2$ or 20-200 Kpa.
- Apart from Drip irrigation, Sprinkler irrigation system also delivers water for consumptive use .

**101(C).** Macronutrients or Primary nutrients are essential for plant growth and a good overall state of the plant. The primary macronutrients are Nitrogen (N), Phosphorus (P), and Potassium (K).
- Potassium is involved in the regulation of water and the transport of the plant's reserve substances.
- It increases photosynthesis capacity, strengthens cell tissue , and activates the absorption of nitrates.
- Potassium stimulates flowering and the synthesis of carbohydrates and enzymes.
- This, in turn, provides an increase in the plant's ability to withstand unfavorable environments such as low temperatures and prevents withering.
- Therefore, a lack of potassium reduces plant resilience to dry spells and frosts or to a fungus attack.
- This, in turn, results in a lack of balance among other nutrients, such as calcium, magnesium, and nitrogen.
- When there is a potassium insufficiency, dark spots appear on the leaves.

**102(A).** Rainwater harvesting helps for flood mitigation.
Appropriate designed recharges in open public spaces will help to keep the roads from flooding. When water is not allowed to leave the premises there is less chance for choking up of the roads.

**103(D).** Kala-azar is transmitted by Sand fly.
People get the disease from the bites of sandflies which themselves got a parasite from drinking blood of another person infected with the parasite. Globally there are more than 20 different Leishmania parasites which cause the disease and 90 species of sandfly which spread those parasites.

**104(A).** Integrated Teaching: Integrated Teaching refers to a way of connecting skills and knowledge from multiple sources and experiences or applying skills and practice in various settings
- The EVS curriculum is thematic in nature; therefore, the content of EVS needs to be drawn from the child's life experiences.
- At the primary level , social studies and social science are taught in an integrated manner based on the real-life situations as Environmental Studies (EVS) that includes six themes (Family and Friends, Food, Shelter, Water, Travel, Things we make and do).
- To make the EVS learning more experiential, the teaching-learning strategies need to:
- It must be designed so that all the senses (touch, feel, taste, smell, sight, auditory) are involved.
- It provide freedom to children to express themselves.
- Teaching strategies must be developmentally appropriate and diverse.
- Different lesson or units can be taught by various methods to create interest in studies.
- Integrated approach of EVS helps in connected and interrelated understanding to think in the multiple directions that develops divergent thinking.
- This approach includes both conceptual and process approach that will lead to better learning of child.
- It should provide opportunities for sharing of experiences/ideas (rather than the correct answer) and reflection.
- It must provide freedom to children to express themselves.
- It is expected that the teachers would adapt and use appropriate transactional processes, based on the resources available, the interests and aptitude levels of children, as well as their geographical locations and the socio-economic and cultural contexts.

So, concept of environmental study should be integrated which includes integration of teaching methods.

**105(C).** The aim of E.V.S.(environmental studies) is:
- To develop an attitude of concern and awareness about the environment.
- To help social groups and individuals to acquire a set of values for environmental protection.
- To help social groups and individuals to acquire knowledge of the environment beyond the immediate environment including the distant environment.
- Linkage with children's real-life experiences and context to the surrounding environment.
- To inculcate values among children and the right attitude towards the environment.

So, it is clear that memorizing maximum concepts in EVS should not be encouraged by EVS teachers while teaching at the primary level.

**106(A).** Gardening at school: Gardens are important to the planet because, despite being human-made, they represent a natural environment.
- Encourage healthy eating: School gardening provides children with opportunities to gain extra outdoor exercise whilst teaching them useful development skills. Gardens containing fruit and vegetables can help to revise attitudes about particular foods - students are more likely to try eating vegetables they have grown themselves and to ask for them at home. When this influence is taken back home, it can help improve their family's shopping and meal choices.
- Environmental appreciation: By deepening children's sense of connection with nature, school gardening can inspire environmental stewardship. Children are able to learn about water and energy cycles, the food chain, and the individual needs of different species, meaning they will have more of a desire to explore outside. Gardening can also offer insights into the long-term human impact on the natural environment.
- Provide unique experience: Gardening activities are fantastic for helping children engage in a way that is more difficult in the classroom. It allows for surprises to arise, for example, when plants are afflicted with fungus, how the weather and seasons can impact the growth of different crops and how different insects are enticed by different plants.

So, it is concluded that to improve the school garden area we need gardening activities in school.

**107(B).** Child centred curriculum should

be borne in mind while constructing curriculum for Environmental Studies as:
- It promotes the value of freedom from fear and prejudice.
- It requires learners to view the subject as a social enterprise.
- It emphasizes more on the process of teaching and learning.
- It helps children to explore their surroundings and to get connected.
- It provides children opportunities to express, experiment, and ask questions.
- It contains real-life incidents and everyday challenges to make learning enliven.

So, it could be concluded that Child centred curriculum should be borne in mind while constructing curriculum for Environmental Studies.

**108(B).** ADHD (attention deficit hyperactivity disorder) is one of the most common neurodevelopmental disorders of childhood.
- It is usually first diagnosed in childhood and often lasts into adulthood. Children with ADHD may have trouble paying attention like Rashmi, controlling impulsive behaviors (may act without thinking about what the result will be), or being overly active.
- The child who is constantly in motion, tapping fingers, poking others for no apparent reason, talking out of turn, and fidgeting is often called hyperactive.
- These children also have difficulty in concentrating i.e., they would not be able to pay attention in class for long. So, they may not be able to complete the task on time and shy away from taking independent charge of doing tasks.
- They will continuously face problems like restlessness and impulsiveness. Their activities and movements seem haphazard which can be observable through their behavior in the classroom.

Therefore, it can be concluded that Rashmi is suffering from ADHD.

**109(D).** EVS course is designed so that students can:
- Develop a deep understanding of the concepts as it includes several activities and approaches. They all help the students to understand all the concerned topics of environmental studies.
- Develop an understanding of morality. As EVS also deals with society and how one should behave ethically and morally in order to be a responsible member of society.
- To provide knowledge and importance of environment so that the students can learn and become aware of their surrounding environment.
- Develop appropriate learning situations with a focus on interactive and experimental learning.

- Assess the learning levels, learning difficulties of each child and design appropriate strategies for the future environment.

Thus, it is concluded that all of the above are correct.

**110(D).** EVS has organized around three broad principles:
- Learning about the environment
- Learning through the environment
- Learning for the environment

The scope of EVS is very wide. It ranges from using the environment as a medium of learning to all that one can do to protect and conserve it.
- The contents are spirally organized starting with the immediate experience of the child (known) moving out to the world she/he inhabits (unknown), leading to an analysis of some of the factors that influence life on this planet.
- The focus of EVS enlarges from the personal to the national and global (local to global), from a physical dimension to the aesthetic dimension.
- The teaching-learning of EVS is thus just not a study area for primary stage children but is a training ground for developing environmentally friendly attitudes, values, habits, and behaviors among the children.

EVS is believed to be a permanent investment in creating a sustainable society. Thus, the scope of EVS lies in not only helping children explore and understand their environment but also in:
- developing positive attitudes, values, and practices such as respect and care for all life on earth, compassion, caring for self and others, conservation of natural resources, appreciation of cooperative learning, sense of belonging, social responsibility, valuing culture, etc.
- generating positive and proactive actions in improving the quality of the environment
- promoting a conservation ethic and adoption of environment-friendly practices and habits

From the above, it is clear that developing positive values for non-living things is not a scope of EVS.

**111(C).** A map is a representation or a drawing of the earth's surface or a part of it drawn on a flat surface according to a scale. There are three Components of Maps – distance, direction and symbol.

Direction on map:
- Most maps contain an arrow marked with the letter 'N' at the upper right-hand corner.
- This arrow shows the northern direction. It is called the north line.
- Using this north line, we can find out other directions, for example east, west and south.
- There are four major directions, North,

South, East, and West.
- They are called cardinal points.
- The other four intermediate directions are north-east (NE), southeast (SE), south-west (SW), and north-west (NW).
- We can locate any place more accurately with the help of these intermediate directions.

In a map
- North direction: at the top of the map
- South direction: at the bottom of the map
- East direction: towards your right hand
- West direction: towards your left hand

Thus, if a map is in front of you, the East direction is shown towards your right hand of the map.

**112(D).** Continuous and Comprehensive Evaluation (CCE) aims to evaluate 'all aspects of the development of the child' as it ensures all-around development of students including cognitive, psychomotor, and affective domains.

Continuous and comprehensive evaluation are necessary as:
- It reduces stress and anxiety, which often builds up among young students during and after the examination.
- It reduces the dropout rate as there will be less fear and anxiety among learners related to their examination and school performance.
- In CCE, greater focus is given to learning rather than on conducting tests and examinations. It contributes to the holistic development of learners.
- CCE is used as an instrument of preparing learners for future life by making them physically fit, mentally alert, emotionally balanced, and socially adjusted.
- Learners get more time to develop their interests, hobbies, and personalities through CCE. It promotes a learner-friendly environment, thereby optimizing student learning.

So, it could be concluded that all of the above-mentioned options are correct.

**113(A).** 'Resource' means something that can be used to help achieve an aim. As a teacher, you must already be using a number of resources like a dictionary, a map or a model, etc. to help you transact EVS lessons better.
- A textbook is one of the learning resources and not only resource both for children as well as teachers.
- Other learning resources such as family members and community, newspapers, books and worksheets, etc. should be used for better learning.
- While interacting with parents/elders, children collect past information and also get the opportunity to develop discussion/ questioning skills.

EVS learning supports working outside the school walls because it :

- promotes peer learning.
- improves social interaction.
- ensures the active participation of all children.
- boosts brainstorming and critical thinking skills.
- promotes hands-on experience.
- promotes real-life experience.
- promotes learning on the basis of previous and home knowledge of the child.
- encourage native or acquired language called mother tongue.
- discourage rote learning and encourage self-learning, experiment, curiosity, questioning, exploration from the surroundings that include people, society, culture, and environment.
- develops communication and lifelong learning skills.
- increases the ability to understand other's perspectives.
- allows collaboration and cooperation of maximum children.

So, we conclude that children should be encouraged to tap sources other than textbooks and teachers in EVS.

**114(A).** In the above-mentioned situation, the following ways should be attempted by the teacher to address problems related to EVs learning:
- Encourage children to take initiative and take ownership of their own learning.
- Ensure that students' ideas are respected, encourage independent thinking among children.
- Facilitate children to frame questions and identify issues, gather and analyze information, and create new knowledge, ask open-ended questions.
- Allow them time to reflect and build on the ideas of others, Promote higher-level thinking, challenge children to reach beyond factual answers.
- Encourage children to connect and summarize concepts by analyzing, predicting, justifying, and defending their ideas,
- Inculcateproblem solving abilities, promote children to justify and defend their ideas and encourage children to discuss their concrete experiences.
- Involve children in experiences that challenge hypotheses and arrive at solutions, ensuring that children are involved in real-world situations from which they can generate abstract concepts.

So, it could be concluded that encouraging children to discuss their concrete experience and ensure that children are involved in real-world situations is the way that should be attempted by the teacher to address problems related to EVs learning.

**115(A).** Principle of learning: Principles of learning serve as a foundation for making learning more practical and meaningful.

These are the practical and comprehensive learning laws that affirm the rule of action. Principle of learning followed in EVS:
- Concrete to Abstract- For children, abstract concepts are difficult to understand. As a result, the teacher should begin with teaching about concrete things that we can see and touch. The teacher employs this strategy by displaying models, photos, and other visual aids to help the student visualize abstract concepts.
- Known to Unknown- Whatever children know should be related to new information. Learning gets clearer and more precise when we combine new knowledge with previous knowledge.
- Other principles are local to global, easy to difficult, etc.

So, we conclude that the concrete to the abstract principle of learning is followed in EVS.

**116(B).** According to the National Curriculum Framework (NCF-2005)
- Unequal gender relations not only perpetuate domination but also create anxieties and stunt the freedom of both boys and girls to develop their human capacities to their fullest.
- Gender discrimination (giving more importance to one gender over another) will have an adverse effect on the performance and achievement of students.
- As it is perceived that only boys can perform well in mathematics, science, and sports (gender stereotype) and girls only in artistic and humanistic subjects. They will take interest in only the activities which are according to their gender roles and not try to improve themselves.
- The belief is that the girls do not play motorsports including bike and car racing. The EVS teacher conducts a discussion on discrimination in games on the basis of gender, caste, and class. It is showing that our society has gender stereotypes.
- The teacher tries to remove these by conducting a discussion on this with the main aim of removing such gender stereotypes from our society.
- If the teacher will not try to remove these gender biases, then the students will never be able to overcome them.
- It is the responsibility of a teacher, school, family, and community to remove these gender roles and biases in order to give equal opportunities to both genders.

So, it is concluded that the main aim of the discussion is to remove gender stereotypes.

**117(A).** Environmental education: It includes the study of the relationship of humans with other aspects affecting their life for the development of human life. It is

also known as environmental studies which include the study of different ecosystems.
- Through teaching about the environment, the teacher should sensitize the children about the protection and conservation of the environment.
- If we want to sustain on the Earth in the future then we must preserve our environment as its resources are limited.

Environment protection is a fundamental value for a sustainable future because:
- Natural resources are the heritage of future generations and we must save these resources for them.
- Nature is the common heritage of all living beings as each of us irrespective of our differences equally dependent on nature for fulfilling our needs.
- A healthy, beautiful, and clean environment is both a right and a duty as it will increase the life of the people on Earth. Because dirty environment will spread dangerous diseases and pollution at a global level which should be stopped.

Thus, we can conclude that Both (A) and (R) are correct and (R) is the correct explanation of (A).

**118(A).** Social Science is a branch of science that deals with human behavior and social relationships, which rely primarily on empirical approaches.

Aims of teaching Social Science includes:
- involving with complexities rather than information.
- using the natural and physical basis of scientific inquiry.
- encouraging the learners into a study of their own region, state, and country in the global context.
- developing an understanding about the earth as the habitat of humankind and other forms of life.
- introducing the learner to the functioning and dynamics of social and political institutions and processes of the country.
- initiating the learner into a study of India's past, with references to contemporary developments in other parts of the world.

Here the statements (B) and (C) are false because:
- Social Science teaching has the responsibility towards preparing students to grow up as an active, responsible, and effective member of society but not towards value education only.
- Social Science uses scientific methods as well as other methods, so different methodology is used to teach different disciplines of Social Science, not the same one.

So, it could be concluded that the statements 'The teaching of Social Science has responsibility for value education only' and 'The same methodology can be used to teach different disciplines of Social Science' are false in the context of Social Science.

**119(A).** The social studies are concerned with man and his interaction with his social and physical environment; they deal with human relationships.

- Social sciences are a term that refers to a wide range of academic disciplines related to human interaction. Among the common social science, disciplines are history, psychology, sociology, economics, political science, and sometimes philosophy and religion.
- According to U.S American National Council for the Social Studies, "Social studies, is the integrated study of the social sciences and humanities to promote civic competence."
- Social studies are subjects most frequently taught to school students to help them understand how to be effective citizens of society.
- The core difference between social science and social studies exists in their purpose; in social science, you study the society and social life of human groups while in social studies, you study both social science and humanities in order to promote effective citizenry.

Thus, it is concluded that Social studies is integrated study of social sciences is correct about the relationship between social studies and social sciences.

**120(B).** Section 25 of The Indian Forest Act 1927 deals with power to stop ways and water-courses in reserved forests.

Power to stop ways and water-courses in reserved forests: The Forest-officer may, with the previous sanction of any state government officer duly authorised by it in this behalf, stop any public or private way or water-course in a reserved forest, provided that a substitute for the way or water-course so stopped, which the State Government deems to be reasonably convenient, already exists, or has been provided or constructed by the Forest-officer in lieu thereof.

## Child Development and Pedagogy

**1. You must have heard people saying that any person learns from his own mistakes, on which principle of teaching is it based?**
(a) Theory of insight
(b) Adjustment principle
(c) Theory of Error and Trial
(d) Formal contract theory

**2. What is the difference between the work that can be done independently by the child and the work done with help?**
(a) Adaption with learning parameters
(b) Total teaching learning done
(c) Modernization of society
(d) Zone of proximal development

**3. Social inheritance in infancy comes from:**
(a) parents
(b) chromosome
(c) media
(d) All of the Above

**4. Assertion (A): Ram is an active and creative student in his classroom as compared with other students.**
**Reason (R): Society and culture play an important role in the development of the child.**
(a) Both (A) and (R) are true and (R) is the correct explanation of (A).
(b) Both (A) and (R) are true but (R) is not the correct explanation of (A).
(c) (A) is true but (R) is false.
(d) Both (A) and (R) are false.

**5. Which of the following skills involves the use of large muscles in the body and involves extensive activities such as walking and jumping?**
(a) Fine motor skills
(b) Gross motor skills
(c) Gross motor skills
(d) None of the above

**6. The child of Mr. Sharma tries to solve a problem by analyzing the situation and finding the way to solve the problem then concludes. According to Piaget's theory of cognitive development, the child falls in:**
(a) Concrete operational stage
(b) Formal operational stage
(c) Pre-operational stage
(d) Sensory motor stage

**7. Assertion (A): A child of age 4 years, learns their primary language by their cognitive approach.**
**Reason (R): Language can learn without an environment only through cognition.**
(a) (A) and (R) both are true, and (R) is the correct explanation of (A).
(b) (A) is true but (R) is false.
(c) Both (A) and (R) are false.
(d) (A) and (R) both are true, but (R) is not a correct explanation of (A).

**8. Man is a social animal, according to you, at what stage does the child socialize?**
(a) Pre-childhood
(b) Pre-adolescence
(c) Adolescence
(d) All of the above

**9. Which of the statements are true about creativity and intelligence?**
**(i) The relationship between creativity and intelligence is positive.**
**(ii) Intelligence does not ensure creativity.**
**(iii) Creativity tests involve divergent thinking whereas intelligence tests involve convergent thinking.**
(a) (i) and (ii)
(b) (i) and (iii)
(c) (ii) and (iii)
(d) (i), (ii) and (iii)

**10. Which of the following is not true regarding the speech community?**
**(I) Speech community is the group of people who speaks a common language.**
**(II) The dictionary of a language is independent of it's speech community.**
(a) Only I
(b) Only II
(c) Both I & II
(d) None of these

**11. What are the measures to avoid gender discrimination in school?**
(a) Male teacher and female teacher have a respect for themselves
(b) Make school rules even tighter
(c) Giving girls a chance to speak more than boys

(d) All of the Above

**12. What would be appropriate to say about talented children?**
(a) They do not need a teacher
(b) He does not talk much to other colleagues
(c) They are capable of taking decisions themselves
(d) All of the Above

**13. What does the theory of graded patterns represent under the theory of language teaching?**
(a) Selection of language material to be taught is the first requirement of good teaching. Selection of language material is done with respect to grammatical items and vocabulary and composition structures.
(b) In order to fulfill the purpose of learning a language, it is necessary to develop systems of various habits as well as to achieve that habits, for this language patterns should be taught slowly.
(c) Vocabulary should be kept under control. Vocabulary should be taught and practiced only in the context of actual situations.
(d) None of these

**14. Direction: Given below are two statements, one leveled as Assertion (A) and the other leveled as Reason (R):**
**Assertion (A): The school-based assessment (SBA) is a systematic process held under the full control of school organizations.**
**Reasoning (R): The school-based assessment (SBA) helps in predicting the future success of learners.**
(a) Both (A) and (R) are correct and (R) is the correct explanation of (A).
(b) Both (A) and (R) are correct, but (R) is not the correct explanation of (A).
(c) (A) is correct, but (R) is not the correct.
(d) (A) is not correct, but (R) is correct.

**15. Which statement is not correct regarding continuous and comprehensive evaluation?**
(a) The system of school-based assessment of students, which includes all aspects of student development, is to keep away

from the evaluation of the child.

(b) "Continuing" refers to the emphasis on evaluating the identified aspects of "growth and development" of students, which is a continuous process rather than an event.

(c) "Comprehensive" means that the scheme seeks to include both academic and co-educational aspects of student growth and development.

(d) These objectives are in the continuity of broad based learning and on the other hand the evaluation and determination of behavioral outcomes.

**16. Vygotsky has said about the development of the child that:**

(a) It is caused by heredity. There is no importance of society in this.

(b) The most important in a child's development is his morality

(c) Social end play has special importance in the development of a child

(d) All of the above

**17. A teacher also has to face many difficulties in teaching children by Inductive Method, which of the following is not included in that difficulty?**

(a) The knowledge gained by this method itself is the discovered knowledge of the children. Therefore, such knowledge becomes part of their brain.

(b) It takes both power and time to learn by this method.

(c) This method is incomplete in itself. The incorporation method is necessary to test the truth discovered by it.

(d) Only the general rules can be discovered by Inductive Method. Therefore, not every subject can be taught by this method.

**18. Which of the following is not appropriate regarding formative assessment?**

(a) Enables to adjust teaching keeping in mind the convenience of teachers.

(b) Develops on the foundation of students' prior knowledge and experience to conceptualize what is to be taught.

(c) Provides students with the opportunity to improve their work after feedback.

(d) Helps students to assist, and be assisted by their counterparts.

**19. Which one of the following methods would be best for understanding the thinking of a child?**

(a) Psychoanalytic method

(b) Inductive method

(c) Qualitative method

(d) Synthesis method

**20. After analyzing a problem a student tries to understand/explain it in his mind, In which type of speech he is involved?**

(a) Debate Speech

(b) Private Speech

(c) Silent/Inner Speech

(d) Social Speech

**21. What will you do if a student in your school is studying well and presenting positive behavior?**

(a) Find the boy's shortcomings and ask him to fix it.

(b) Will behave harshly towards this child so as not to fall asleep.

(c) Will give many kinds of reward to that child.

(d) Praise that child for good progress and encourage him to do better in future.

**22. A child tries to learn and built about himself through experience and interaction with others. He wants to involve in:**

(a) Primary socialization

(b) Secondary socialization

(c) Developmental socialization

(d) Resocialization

**23. Which of the following is the most important task for a successful teacher to improve the teaching learning process?**

(a) Helping children to pass the exam

(b) Helping boys to be good players

(c) Developing awareness abilities in children

(d) Developing love for children in books

**24. Which of the following statements is not true?**

(a) Development is a biological process

(b) Development is a quantitative process

(c) Development is a goal-oriented process

(d) Learning is a process of behavior change

**25. Which of the following is factor affecting motivation?**

(a) Requirements

(b) Aspiration level and interest

(c) Emotional state

(d) All of the above

**26. We all know that sports have special importance in the development of children, what kind of ability of the child is mainly developed by sports?**

(a) Sports develop social skills of children

(b) Sports develop mental skills of children

(c) Sports develop physical skills of children

(d) All of the above

**27. If instructed to the goal of teaching that by looking at this picture and describing its characteristics, which of the following is it related to?**

(a) Abstract thinking

(b) Direct Perceptual

(c) Indirect intelligence

(d) None of these

**28. Which of the following is not a guiding principle of NCF 2005?**

(a) Knowledge should be linked to life outside school.

(b) Link study to rote system.

(c) Text discussion should not remain textbook-centric.

(d) The classroom should be linked to activities and it should be made flexible.

**29. Which of the following stages is not the part of Bruner's Cognitive Development Theory?**

(a) Enactive stage

(b) Iconic stage

(c) Intuitive stage

(d) Symbolic stage

**30. Groups of learning strategies that are more task-specific are called ____________.**

(a) Cognitive

(b) Positive attitude

(c) Drafting

(d) Metacognitive



**Ques (31-39): Direction** : Read the passage given below and answer the question by choosing the correct/most appropriate options.

Padma lives with her mother, a retired

anganwadi teacher, and four brothers who are farmers. Her family doesn't mind that she travels at odd hours or is in the company of male colleagues, which in her community was once taboo. They understand the value of her service, she says. One common thread among these young girls is that all their mothers have either worked in or taught at the village anganwadis, and they insisted that their daughters be educated.

"Initially, the people were cold and sceptical," says Padma, "but over the past couple of years, attitudes have changes. They trust us, they have our phone numbers pasted on their walls so that they can reach out when need to."

Possibly the most important change these young women have brought to the valley is getting their tribes to move from traditional medicine to modern medicine. They repeatedly visited families, explained the need for better healthcare and hygiene, and taught them to eat well.

The women earn between Rs. 10,000 and Rs. 18,000 a month based on their experience. A few of them went as far as Vishakapatnam to study, but chose to return home since working in the community was important to them.

The outcome is evident in the figures. According to the 2011 census, the maternal mortality rate in Araku valley was over 400 per 100,000 live births, more than double the national average. In the last two years, however, there have been no deaths during pregnancy or childbirth. While all these years, women gave birth in their homes, aided by the elderly in the institutional deliveries reaching 68% of women.

**31. Read the following statements:**
A. The girls who work in cities earn an amount ranging from Rs. 10,000/- to 18,000/-
B. Padma's family is unhappy with the odd hours that her job imposes on her.
C. These young girls have brought about a change in attitude among their tribes with regard to medical treatment.
D. The child mortality rate in the Araku Valley has increased.
1. Both A and C are true.
2. Both B and C are false.
3. A is true and C is false.
4. Both B and C are true.

(a)  1          (b)  2
(c)  3          (d)  4

**32. Which of the following statements is correct?**
1. Padma's family is not averse to her travelling at odd hours or working with male colleagues.
2. Padma and other tribal girls insist on the use of traditional

medicines.
3. The women went to big cities to earn name and fame.
4. Despite the services of these women, the number of child deaths has remained static.

(a)  1          (b)  2
(c)  3          (d)  4

**33. Which of the following words cannot be associated with Padma?**
1. Innovative
2. Progressive
3. Bold
4. Orthodox

(a)  1          (b)  2
(c)  3          (d)  4

**34. Which of the following was once considered taboo among the tribals?**
1. Young girls engaged in social work.
2. Anganwadi workers visiting strangers.
3. Tribal girls studying in cities.
4. Tribal girls working with male colleagues.

(a)  1          (b)  2
(c)  3          (d)  4

**35. What is common among the young anganwadi women workers?**
1. They belong to educated families.
2. Their mothers have worked in anganwadis in different capacities.
3. They are all thrilled by the idea of earning money.
4. They are all interested in working in cities.

(a)  1          (b)  2
(c)  3          (d)  4

**36. Which of the following words has the same meaning as the word 'mortality' used in the passage?**
1. sanctuary
2. transience
3. temporal
4. death

(a)  1          (b)  2
(c)  3          (d)  4

**37. Which of the following words is the antonym of the word 'Traditional' used in the passage?**
1. Customary
2. Established
3. Conventional
4. Modern

(a)  1          (b)  2
(c)  3          (d)  4

**38. Which part of speech is the underlined word in the sentence.**
"She travels at <u>odd</u> hours"?
1. Adjective

2. Adverb
3. Conjuction
4. Pronoun

(a)  1          (b)  2
(c)  3          (d)  4

**39. Which part of the following sentence contains an error?**
No sooner (a)/ did I reached the station (b)/ than (c)/ the train departed.(d)

(a)  a          (b)  b
(c)  c          (d)  d

**Ques (40-45): Direction:** Read the following poem and answer the questions by choosing the correct/most appropriate options:

Out of the night that covers me
Black as the pit from pole to pole,
I thank whatever gods may be
For my unconquerable soul.
In the fell clutch of circumstance,
I have not winced nor cried aloud.
Under the bludgeonings of chance
My head is bloody, but unbowed.
Beyond this place of wrath and tears
Looms but the horror of the shade,
And yet menace of the years
Finds, and shall find, me unafraid
It matters not how strait the gate,
How charged with punishment the scroll,
I am the master of my fate
I am the master of my soul.

**40. The poem is about:**
1. Passive suffering
2. A cry against the gods.
3. The hostile circumstances that the narrator is facing.
4. Determination and courage in the face of suffering.

(a)  1          (b)  2
(c)  3          (d)  4

**41. The poem is a picture of:**
1. deepening gloom.
2. a journey from despair to hope.
3. man's eternal and irreversible suffering.
4. a grudging acceptance of suffering.

(a)  1          (b)  2
(c)  3          (d)  4

**42. The poem underlines the:**
1. prevalence of all-encompassing sorrow.
2. cheerful and courageous acceptance of sorrow.
3. the hostility of gods towards the narrator.
4. a painful reminder of advancing age

(a)  1          (b)  2
(c)  3          (d)  4

**43. The overall tone of the poem is:**

1. Gloomy
2. Challenging
3. Bitter
4. Optimistic
(a)  1          (b)  2
(c)  3          (d)  4

44. Which figure of speech has been used in the line 'Black as the pit from pole to pole'?
1. Alliteration
2. Metaphor
3. Simile
4. Epigram
(a)  1          (b)  2
(c)  3          (d)  4

45. Which figure of speech has been used in "Under the bludgeonings of chance?"
1. Synecdoche
2. Paradox
3. Personification
4. Metonymy
(a)  1          (b)  2
(c)  3          (d)  4

46. If Hindi language is to be taught to those children whose mother tongue is somewhat different from Hindi, which one would you give importance to?
(a)  Only the mother language of the child
(b)  For multilingualism
(c)  Hindi language only
(d)  All of the above

47. The language teacher gives the children to write essays for the purpose of assessing their writing ability. The important aspect to be assessed by the language teacher in the essay written by the children is:
(a)  Accuracy of Spelling
(b)  Organization of the thought elements.
(c)  Beauty of writing
(d)  Grammatical Knowledge

48. Who said that "creative is synonymous with the power of human mind to develop relationships by creatively creating new subject matter by transforming relationships"?
(a)  Spearman      (b)  Barlett
(c)  Skinner       (d)  Levine

49. Arrange the steps of the Inductive method in sequence.
1. Conclusion/Regulation
2. Analysis/Inspection
3. Practice/Test
4. Example
(a)  1, 2, 3, 4      (b)  4, 2, 1, 3

(c)  2, 3, 4, 1      (d)  2, 1, 4, 3

50. Tools such as rich language environment, natural speaking, social interaction, home environment are related to which aspect of language?
(a)  Acquisition   (b)  Learning
(c)  Testing       (d)  Grammatical

51. The correctness of spelling in writing is responsible for:
(a)  Grammar
(b)  Language
(c)  Stationery
(d)  Teacher's skills

52. The purpose of grammar-teaching is:
(a)  To memorize grammar definitions
(b)  To understand and analyze the systematic nature of language
(c)  Overemphasizing the normative nature of language
(d)  To memorize the nature, functions and grammatical rules of language

53. At the primary stage a Hindi speaking child makes spelling errors related to E-E because:
(a)  Errors are a stop in the learning process.
(b)  The child does not know the language.
(c)  The way of teaching of the teacher is not right.
(d)  The child is retarded.

54. Directions: Select the correct/most appropriate answer to the question given below.
Which of the following statements indicates an important objective of language learning at the primary stage?
(a)  Participate in speeches, debates and poetry readings
(b)  To make language a medium for children to understand their environment and experience
(c)  Knowing Numbers in Hindi as per Mathematics Syllabus
(d)  Correct identification of nouns, pronouns, adjectives and verbs

55. The activities chosen in the assessment of children should be:
(a)  Engaging children in concrete experiences at the primary level.
(b)  Any one method is sufficient for assessment.
(c)  Selection of activities based on child bias.

(d)  Encouraging an answer

56. Writing skills are initiated by:
(a)  Operational skills
(b)  With letter practice
(c)  Through word practice
(d)  By practicing sentences

57. Enriched linguistic environment in the school/classroom means:
(a)  More opportunities for speaking, listening, reading and writing.
(b)  Availability of a dictionary for more than one language
(c)  Teacher's knowledge of more than one language
(d)  More opportunities to listen to the mainstream language

58. The steps required to make Hindi language learning interesting are:
(a)  Using traditional methods
(b)  Use of new teaching methods and information and communication methods
(c)  Extend the period
(d)  Change time table

59. To develop a reading culture:
1. The reading material should be standard.
2. Must consist of all letters to assess the identity of the letters.
3. Pronunciation requires special attention.
4. The ability to understand is assessed.
The point to read is:
(a)  1 and 4
(b)  1, 2 and 4
(c)  1, 3, and 4
(d)  All of the above

60. What is the purpose of the pictures given in the lesson?
(a)  Pictures make textbook attractive
(b)  Pictures beautify the textbook
(c)  painting is in vogue
(d)  Pictures in text book help in understanding abstract concepts

## Mathematics

61. A circle touches all four sides of a quadrilateral $PQRS$. If $PQ = 11$ cm. $QR = 12$ cm and $PS = 8$ cm. Then what is the length of $RS$?
(a)  7 cm          (b)  15 cm
(c)  9 cm          (d)  7.3 cm

62. An angle of $89°$ is _______ angle.
(a)  Acute

(b)  Right
(c)  Obtuse
(d)  All of the above

**63.** **What is the perimeter of the given figure if all the measures are in cm?**

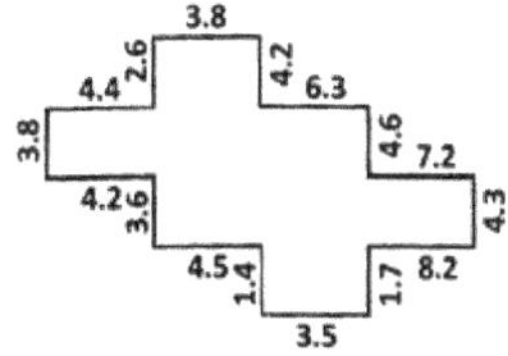


(a)  68.2 cm          (b)  68.1 cm
(c)  86.3 cm          (d)  68.3 cm

**64.** **How many cuboidal bricks are required to build a wall of** 20 m **long,** 5 m **high and** 30 cm **thick. The dimensions of each brick is** 20 cm × 5 cm × 3 cm **.**
(a)  20000          (b)  100000
(c)  10000          (d)  200000

**65.** **How many angles are there in a pentagon?**
(a)  3          (b)  4
(c)  5          (d)  6

**66.** **A number that is divisible by** 6 **will be divisible by which of the following?**
(a)  2 and 3          (b)  5 and 3
(c)  2 and 5          (d)  2 and 4

**67.** **The associative property is applicable to:**
(a)  Addition and subtraction
(b)  Multiplication and division
(c)  Addition and Multiplication
(d)  Subtraction and Division

**68.** $56 \div 4 \times \_\_ = 56$ **, Fill in the blank.**
(a)  4          (b)  3
(c)  2          (d)  5

**69.** **Sreetama wants to collect Rs.** 5 **coins. In the year** 2021 **, she accumulated** 2 **notes of Rs.** 500 **,** 4 **notes of Rs.** 200 **,** 3 **notes of Rs.** 100, 23 **notes of Rs.** 50, 14 **notes of Rs.** 20 **and** 18 **coins of Rs.** 10 **. If she gave all the money to her father to get all Rs.** 5 **coins in exchange. How many coins Sreetama can get from her father in exchange for the money?**
(a)  736 coins          (b)  738 coins
(c)  740 coins          (d)  742 coins

**70.** $0.2 \,\text{kg} =$
(a)  200000 mili-gram
(b)  2000 mili-gram
(c)  200 mili-gram

(d)  None of these

**71.** **The sum of ages of** 5 **children born at the intervals of** 3 **years each is** 50 **years. What is the age of the youngest child?**
(a)  4 years
(b)  8 years
(c)  10 years
(d)  None of these

**72.** **In the given below options which is the largest fraction?**
(a)  $\dfrac{6}{8}$          (b)  $\dfrac{4}{5}$
(c)  $\dfrac{2}{9}$          (d)  $\dfrac{7}{8}$

**73.** **Convert** 2 **hours** 30 **minutes to seconds.**
(a)  90000 seconds
(b)  90 seconds
(c)  900 seconds
(d)  9000 seconds

**74.** **Direction:** The rates of various fruits in the market are given below:

| Fruit's name | Price |
| --- | --- |
| Apple | Rs. 80/ kg |
| Orange | Rs. 75/ kg |
| Mango | Rs. 60/ kg |
| Pineapple | Rs. 50/ kg |
| Grapes | Rs. 65/ kg |

Ranjit buys $2,5$ **kg of apples,** 3 **kg of mangoes,** 1.6 **kg of orange,** 500 **grams of pineapples, and** 800 **grams of grapes from the market. How much would he be required to pay?**
(a)  Rs. 575          (b)  Rs. 577
(c)  Rs. 580          (d)  Rs. 585

**75.** **Direction:** Select the option that will fill in the blank and complete the given series.
$9, 11, 14, 18, 23, ?$
(a)  25          (b)  29
(c)  36          (d)  27

**76.** **A car completes a journey in seven hours. It covered half of the distance at** 40 km / hr **and the remaining half at** 60 km / hr **speed. Then, the distance (in km) covered is:**
(a)  280          (b)  300
(c)  336          (d)  420

**77.** **Which of the following is not one of the methods of coordinating student discussion and analysing their solutions in Mathematics?**
(a)  Gallery walk
(b)  Bansho
(c)  Math Congress

(d)  Remedial Teaching

**78.** **The nature of mathematics is:**
(a)  Ornamental
(b)  Logical
(c)  Difficult
(d)  Not for common

**79.** **A close relationship between the growth of thinking and the development of mathematical concepts is established in:**
(a)  Theory
(b)  Intervention
(c)  Research
(d)  Demonstration

**80.** **Why we need mathematics in society?**
(a)  For transaction
(b)  For business
(c)  For calculation
(d)  All of the above

**81.** **Curriculum of mathematics in primary level in school education should be:**
(a)  Job oriented
(b)  Teacher centered
(c)  Content centered
(d)  Objective centered

**82.** **Which of the component helpful in translating verbal language to the language of mathematics?**
(a)  Mode-Building
(b)  Word-Building
(c)  Concept-Building
(d)  None of the above

**83.** **Identify the symbol that is unique to the mathematics language.**
(a)  %          (b)  ?
(c)  &          (d)  /

**84.** **The assessment of what children learn in mathematics in primary classes should not focus on:**
(a)  Development of reasoning skills
(b)  Understanding of the mathematical concepts
(c)  Development of mathematical language
(d)  Preciseness in answering mathematics problems

**85.** **Which of the following strategies can be used to assess learners' interest in and attitude to mathematics?**
(a)  Check List, Portfolio, Paper Pencil Test
(b)  Oral Test, Paper Pencil Test Class Participation

(c) Check list, Portfolio, Project Class Participation

(d) Portfolio, Project, Paper Pencil Test

**86.** **What are the difficulties do mathematics teacher face while teaching in classroom?**

(a) Problem in teaching mathematics due to poor mathematics background of students

(b) Difficulty on teaching mathematics because of difference in social, cultural and family environment of students

(c) Lack of information about new instructional techniques and invention

(d) All of the above

**87.** **Which of the following could be a contributing factor towards underachievement in mathematics?**

(a) Gender

(b) Socio-Cultural background

(c) Nature of Mathematics

(d) Innate ability of person

**88.** **The functioning process of evaluation is:**

(a) Marking

(b) Decision making

(c) Error finding

(d) All of the above

**89.** **One of the major reasons for errors in mathematics is due to:**

(a) Over-emphasis on procedural skills

(b) Lack of teaching resources

(c) Absenteeism of students

(d) Hierarchical nature of the subject

**90.** **______ demonstrates the importance of incorporating cultural elements in the teaching of mathematics.**

(a) Context (b) Community

(c) Language (d) Diversity

## Environmental Studies

**91.** **Cuttlefish belongs to phylum ________.**

(a) Echinodermata

(b) Mollusca

(c) Annelida

(d) Pisces

**92.** **Which section of The Indian Forest Act 1927 deals with the Powers of Forest Settlement-officer?**

(a) Section 12 of The Indian Forest Act 1927

(b) Section 8 of The Indian Forest Act 1927

(c) Section 14 of The Indian Forest Act 1927

(d) Section 9 of The Indian Forest Act 1927

**93.** **"Slash and burn" agriculture is a type of ________.**

(a) Shifting agriculture

(b) Intensive agriculture

(c) Commercial agriculture

(d) Subsistence Farming

**94.** **Who invented Jet Engine?**

(a) Sir Frank Whittle

(b) Gottlieb Daimler

(c) Roger Bacon

(d) Lewis E. Waterman

**95.** **Select from the following a group of animals which is able to recognize their areas by the smell of urine and stool.**

(a) Tigers, Monkeys and Buffaloes

(b) Elephants, Cats and Lions

(c) Dogs, Tigers, Lions

(d) Cats, Dogs, Cows

**96.** **Transfer of pollen grains from the anther to the stigma of another flower of the same plant is called:**

(a) Autogamy

(b) Geitonogamy

(c) Xenogamy

(d) None of the above

**97.** **Boiled tapioca with any curry made using coconut is a preferred food of the people of:**

(a) West Bengal (b) Bihar

(c) Tamil Nadu (d) Kerala

**98.** **The process in which earthworms are used to degrade organic wastes is:**

(a) Compost bedding

(b) Humus forming

(c) Vermicomposting

(d) None of these

**99.** **Altitude sickness occurs due to________.**

(a) Changing pressure and reducing oxygen levels

(b) Changing pressure and increasing oxygen levels

(c) Increasing oxygen levels and higher altitude

(d) All of the above

**100.** **Apart from sugarcane (most commonly Saccharum officinarum) which among the following plants is widely known in the world as a commercial source of table sugar?**

(a) Toona cilata

(b) Gloriosa superba

(c) Asparagus pulmosus

(d) Beta vulgaris

**101.** **When coal burns in air then which of the following greenhouse gases is present in very high quantities?**

(a) Carbon dioxide

(b) Sulphur dioxide

(c) Carbon monoxide

(d) Hydrogen gas

**102.** **The minimum furrow grade to assure surface drainage is:**

(a) 0.09% (b) 0.02 %

(c) 0.07 % (d) 0.05 %

**103.** **Which part of plant is called food factory?**

(a) Fruits (b) Seeds

(c) Leaves (d) Flowers

**104.** **Why should people implement rainwater harvesting?**

(a) In order to play with the water

(b) In order to use during scarcity of water

(c) In order to pour the rain water directly to the sewage

(d) In order to time pass

**105.** **Plague is caused by:**

(a) Leishmania donovani

(b) Yersinia pestis

(c) Salmonella typhimuium

(d) Trichinella spiralis

**106.** **National tourism includes:**

(a) Domestic tourism

(b) Outbound tourism

(c) Domestic & Outbound tourism

(d) None of these

**107.** **Environmental Studies curriculum may lead to holistic learning of children if it is:**

(a) Integrated

(b) Inclusive

(c) Thematic

(d) All of the above

**108.** **Environmental education is important only at:**

(a) Primary school stage

(b) Secondary school stage

(c) Undergraduate stage

(d) All of the above

**109. Which of the following is not one of the six broad themes of EVS in the present syllabus?**
(a) Shelter
(b) Things we make and do
(c) Work and Play
(d) Food

**110. The human activity, among the following, which causes maximum environmental pollution having regional and global impact, is:**
(a) Industrialization
(b) Urbanization
(c) Agriculture
(d) Mining

**111. The science that deals with the relationship of various organisms with their environment is known as:**
(a) Anthropology
(b) Economics
(c) Ecology
(d) Geology

**112. One of the important pedagogical l earning principle of environmental studies is:**
(a) Maximum use of environment related books
(b) Use of environment as learning resource
(c) Maximum homework to students
(d) All the above

**113. EVS curriculum at primary stage has been developed to include pure science as well as social science concepts. This has been done primarily to:**
(a) Enable a learner look at environment in a holistic manner.
(b) Reduce the number of subjects to be studied.
(c) Reduce the load of school bag.
(d) Reduce the requirement of subject teachers.

**114. Which subject of social science is very closely related to science?**
(a) Geography
(b) Economics
(c) Political science
(d) History

**115. Teaching of EVS should encourage process skills, which are the core of inquiry-based, hands-on learning. Which one of the following is not such a skill?**
(a) Predicting
(b) Determination
(c) Inferring
(d) Observation

**116. Providing services includes in which human activities?**
(a) Primary activities
(b) Tertiary Activities
(c) Secondary Activities
(d) Nutrient Cycling

**117. The basic objective of educational excursion in EVS is:**
(a) To develop the energy of children
(b) First hand experience to the students
(c) Promote socialisation
(d) Promote team spirit

**118. Which of the following is a desirable practice for an EVS teacher?**
(a) Addressing multicultural dimensions of diverse classrooms.
(b) Encouraging children to provide important information related to the concepts of EVS.
(c) Linear arrangement of six themes of EVS.
(d) Relying only in textbooks.

**119. The term 'Comprehensive ' in continuous and comprehensive evaluation means:**
(a) Scholastic development
(b) Co-scholastic development
(c) Academic skills
(d) Both (A) and (B)

**120. Continuous and comprehensive evaluation should be adopted by all schools because:**
(a) It affords teachers opportunities to test learners frequently.
(b) It is the latest development in the field of education.
(c) Traditional pen-paper tests do not assess and enhance all the attributes and abilities of learners.
(d) It frees the learners from studies and hard work.

**// Hints and Solutions //**

**1(C).** If any person learns from his own mistakes, it is based on the theory of error and trial.
Trial and Error is a method of learning in which various responses are tentatively tried and some discarded until a solution is attained. E.L.Thorndike (1874-1949) was the chief exponent of the theory of connectionism or trial and error. He was an American Psychologist who conducted Stimulus - Response(S-R) theory experiment with the help of animals. Thorndike was the first to study the subject of learning systematically using standardized procedure and apparatus. All learning, according to Thorndike is the formation of bonds or connections between stimulus-response.

**2(D).** The difference between the work that can be done independently by the child and the work done with help is zone of proximal development.
The zone of proximal development (sometimes abbreviated ZPD), is the difference between what a learner can do without help and what he or she can do with help.
For example, A student is able to perform simple addition when working with a teacher or parent but is frustrated when performing the task alone. By guiding the student to use tools and strategies, and by asking questions about why he/she is using each tool or strategy, the student is able to fortify knowledge and eventually add independently.

**3(A).** Social inheritance in infancy comes from parents.
Social inheritance is a collection of ideas and prejudices instilled in you as a child by your parents, schools, and society as a whole, and which explains to your developing brain "How the world truly works."
Parents have a social inheritance. Social inheritance is a collection of ideas and prejudices instilled in you as a child by your parents, relatives, and society as a whole, and which explains to your developing brain "How the world truly works." The notion of social inheritance should be explored and conveyed in the framework of social psychology and developmental psychology, with the guiding hypothesis that socio-psychological processes transmit attitudes, linguistic constructions, and familial connections into the child's mind.
Social inheritance has evolved into an important social component. Social inheritance may be thought of in two ways. The first is the common level, which is linked to a variety of personal characteristics such as social identification and ethnic identity, both of which are historically defined. Institutions that incorporate the same values in subsequent generations are the conductors of social inheritance from that level on. The parents, on the other hand, compress reality to their own, integrating the general reality as it was experienced.

**4(A).** "Ram is more active and creative"

because his development is done in all the social and cultural aspects.

Lev Vygotsky was a Russian psychologist, He emphasized the role of society and culture in the development of the child. According to Vygotsky, the main needs in the development of a child are:

- Social interaction
- Culture
- Language

Society: An enduring social group living in a particular place whose members are mutually interdependent and share interests and other institutions, and a common culture. Society and Culture helps in the develoopment of the child as:

- Child can be interacted easily.
- Development is done in all the aspects.
- Make child more active and creative.
- Help the child to gain knowledge of different views.

**5(B).** Gross motor skills involves the use of large muscles in the body and involves extensive activities such as walking and jumping.

Gross motor abilities entail the use of the body's major muscles and include tasks such as walking and leaping. The major muscles in the arms, legs, and torso are involved in gross motor skill development. Walking, running, throwing, lifting, kicking, and other daily physical tasks need gross motor skills. Gross motor abilities make use of the body's vast muscles to provide balance, coordination, response time, and physical strength, allowing us to do larger actions. Sitting, crawling, sprinting, leaping, tossing a ball, and climbing stairs are just a few examples of gross motor abilities.

**6(A).** The child of Mr. Sharma tries to solve a problem by analyzing the situation and finding the way to solve the problem then concludes. According to Piaget's theory of cognitive development, the child falls in concrete operational stage.

Jean Piaget made a systematic study of cognitive development among children of different age groups and he categorized it into different developmental stages. These stages are:

- Sensory-motor stage (0 to 2 years)
- Pre-operational stage (2 to 6 years)
- Concrete operational stage (6 to 11 years)
- Formal operational stage (11+ years to adolescence)

Concrete operational stage: There are many changes found in the child during the concrete operation stage (6 to 11 years) such as:

- Reversibility: Reversibility comes in a child, he/she can change their views by thinking diversely.
- Logics mapping: Logical mapping begins in a child so they analyze the problem, then think critically about it then comes to conclusion.

- Classification: The child is able to classify things.

**7(A).** Jean Piaget made a systematic study of cognitive development among children of different age groups and he categorized it into different developmental stages. These stages are-

- Sensory-motor stage (0 to 2 years)
- Pre-operational stage (2 to 6 years)
- Concrete operational stage (6 to 11 years)
- Formal Operational stage (11+ years to adolescence)

Pre-operational stage (2 to 6 years): The children at this stage use a symbolic representation that is the ability to make one thing - a word or an object - stand for something other than itself. It means that the child begins to use language to represent his thoughts and ideas symbolically which gives birth to his thinking. This stage also explains that a child develops the notion about the irreversibility of thoughts means he believes that an action performed cannot be undone falsely.

**8(D).** The child socialize at pre-childhood, pre-adolescence and adolescence.

Socialization is the process in which an individual tries to adopt the norms, rules, and skills so that he is accepted by society. It is the continuous process of negotiating identities and shaping one's concept of self, identity, various attitudes, and behaviors.

- In pre-childhood, the child becomes socialized through the family. For example, a very young child in a family has little knowledge of his culture. It is through the family that the child gets to know what is accepted and what is not in a particular society.
- In pre-adolescence and adolescence, the child gets socialized through other agents of socialization like the school and peers' group begin to play a role in socializing the child. For example, Schools help children in learning the importance of social cohesion and unity and inculcating the informal cues about social roles through interaction.

**9(D).** Statement, "The relationship between creativity and intelligence is positive, Intelligence does not ensure creativity and Creativity tests involve divergent thinking whereas intelligence tests involve convergent thinking" are true about creativity and intelligence.

Creativity is the ability to come up with or generate creative ideas and possibilities. It involves thinking in new and original ways to reach a solution Intelligence refers to the capacity to acquire and apply knowledge. It is the ability to solve problems, learn from experiences, and apply knowledge to deal with new situations.

The relationship between creativity and

intelligence is positive: Creativity and intelligence are positively correlated because high ability is a component of creativity. A highly intelligent person may not be creative but all creative persons are definitely high in intelligence. All creative persons require some ability to acquire, knowledge, and the capacity to comprehend.

Intelligence does not ensure creativity: Researchers have found that both high and low levels of creativity can be found in highly intelligent children and also in children of average intelligence. The same person can be creative as well as intelligent but it is not necessary that intelligent ones, in the conventional sense, must be creative. Intelligence, therefore, does not ensure creativity.

Creativity tests involve divergent thinking whereas intelligence tests involve convergent thinking: Creativity involves divergent thinking in contrast to convergent thinking. Divergent thinking refers to thinking out of the box. Divergent thinking is having divergent ideas and possibilities. Convergent thinking refers to thinking in a conventional set pattern, intelligence tests involve this thinking.

**10(B).** The dictionary of a language is independent of it's speech community, is not true regarding the speech community.

Speech Community: A speech community is a group of people who share rules, values, and attitudes about language use and practices. The speech community is the only vital part of language and its usage. A speech community is formed by people who speak a given language and give the given language a shape or standard. A speech community is a group of people who speaks a common language. There is no doubt that language developed as humans developed in a certain process through various phases. Had there been no society or speech community, the dictionaries and grammar would have had no value. The dictionary of a language is dependent on its speech community.

**11(A).** The measures to avoid gender discrimination in school are male teacher and female teacher have a respect for themselves.

Gender discrimination is older than any kind of social discrimination. It can be avoided by adopting certain methods in school:

Create an open school environment with books, toys, sports equipment, and musical instruments that cater to everybody. Be aware of current gender bias. Male and female teachers should have respect for each other, as it is said children adapt and learn what they see. Think about your own conduct. Make sure expectations are the same for all of your students.- Both genders can succeed at math, science, language arts, and reading. Use examples that are gender-balanced. If there are none in your textbooks, do some research to find some.

**12(C).** Talented children are capable of taking decisions themselves.

Talented children are born with innate skills that are above average. Children that are gifted have honed their innate skills to a great degree. Children that are gifted have much greater intellectual talents than ordinary children. Children with exceptional abilities are capable of making their own judgments. Children with exceptional natural abilities have refined their skills to a high level. Children can be gifted and/or talented in a variety of areas, including sport, art, music, intelligence, and more. To make the most of their gifts, gifted and talented youngsters require encouragement and assistance. Schools are increasingly assessing a wide range of skills, including linguistic, mathematical, spatial-visual, musical, and interpersonal abilities, using several measures of giftedness.

**13(B).** The theory of graded patterns represents the theory of language teaching order to fulfill the purpose of learning a language, it is necessary to develop systems of various habits as well as to achieve those habits, for this language patterns should be taught slowly.

As language is the medium of communication, through language we express our emotions, thoughts and feelings. To make the child listen, speak, read and write, language teaching is necessary.

Theory of graded patterns: "To teach a language is to impart a new system of complex habits, and habits are acquired slowly." So, language patterns should be taught gradually, in cumulative graded steps. This means the teacher should go on adding each new element or pattern to previous ones. New patterns of language should be introduced and practiced with vocabulary that students already know.

**14(A).** Both (A) and (R) are correct and (R) is the correct explanation of (A).

The school-based assessment (SBA) is a systematic process held under the full control of school organizations and teachers to help the students in their individual learning. SBA helps a teacher in diagnosing the learning problems of a child as well as his achievements that will help to decide the further action i.e., the child should be taken to the next level of learning or he needs to go through the remediation to remove the learning errors. It is completely run by the teachers who interact with the children on daily basis and share a unique bond with them. Thus, it is clear that the assertion is correct.

The school-based assessment (SBA) helps in predicting the future success of learners. SBA provides information/reports on the progress of students in scholastic and co-scholastic areas and thus helps in predicting the future success of learners. The external examiner will only come to examine the students on a specific day with a special purpose of evaluation. He will be unaware of students' capabilities and weaknesses. It shows that the given reasoning is also correct.

**15(A).** Statement, "The system of school-based assessment of students, which includes all aspects of student development, is to keep away from the evaluation of the child" is not correct regarding continuous and comprehensive evaluation.

The term 'continuous' refers to regularity in assessment. The development of a child is a continuous process. Therefore, students' development should be assessed continuously. Evaluation has to be completely integrated with the teaching and learning process. It is also considered an assessment as learning because it helps in evaluating the identified aspects of growth and development of students in a continuous process rather than an event. The term comprehensive refers to the evaluation of the learner's performance in both scholastic and co-scholastic areas. The performance of the students in scholastic and co-scholastic activities is assessed as it aims to reduce the stress of the curricular load so that students improve in their overall abilities through the process of the evaluation. It integrates assessment with the teaching and learning process; emphasizing assessment of learner abilities in scholastic areas along with the co-scholastic areas.

**16(C).** Vygotsky has said about the development of the child that social end play has special importance in the development of a child.

Vygotsky, a Russian psychologist, believed that social interactions play a key role in development. According to him, learning occurs when children interact with people and the environment.

The theory of socio-cultural development was given by the Lev Vygotsky. He believes that every development in the child appears on two levels first on the social level and second on the individual. Lev Vygotsky said the children first create the experience with the interaction with others and then they take that information and use them with themselves. Lev Vygotsky believe that the ways child interacts with others and the culture they live in gives shape to the mental abilities of the child, he believed that the parents, relative, peers and society all have an important role in developing higher mental abilities in a child. Vygotsky believed that play promotes cognitive, social, and emotional development in children.

**17(A).** The inductive method helps in gaining knowledge by themselves and through the discovery method.

Inductive Method: Induction is a form of reasoning in which a general law is derived from a study of particular objects or specific processes. The child can use measurement. manipulator or constructive activities, patterns, etc. to discover a relationship which he shall himself, later, formulated in symbolic form as a law or rule. The law, rule, or definition formulated by the child is the summation of all the particular or individual instances. In all inductions. the generalization that is evolved is regarded as a tentative conclusion.

It proceeds from particular to general, concrete to abstract. I t takes care of the needs and interests of children, it is a developmental process. I t increases discovery and stimulates the thinking process. T he generalization or rule is formed by the child, so it is easily remembered by the child. T he how and why of the process are made clear with the reasoning. I t starts from experience and observation, which ends in the development of a rule. It encourages child participation and group work.

**18(A).** Enables to adjust teaching keeping in mind the convenience of teachers, is not appropriate regarding formative assessment.

Formative assessment is typically conducted during the development or improvement of a program or product (or person) and it is conducted, often more than once. The term formative assessment is used for the first time in the year 1967 by Michel Scriven.

The purpose of conducting the formative assessment is to monitor the learning progress of the learner; it is also conducted to know whether the learning objectives have been achieved or not and to provide feedback on the teaching-learning process. It is considered the second stage of assessment which is conducted during the teaching-learning process. It is carried out from the very beginning of instruction and continues till the end of the course. It enables to adjust teaching keeping in mind the convenience of students. It helps students to assist, and be assisted by their counterparts. It develops on the foundation of students' prior knowledge and experience to conceptualize what is to be taught.

**19(A).** Psychoanalytic method would be best for understanding the thinking of a child.

Psychoanalysis is a way of treating mental problems that is based on psychoanalytic theory and stresses unconscious mental processes. It is also known as "depth psychology." Sigmund Freud, an Austrian psychiatrist who created the word psychoanalysis, started the psychoanalytic movement with his clinical findings and formulations. Psychoanalysis is divided into three parts:

- A technique of studying the mind and how people think
- A formalized collection of hypotheses about human nature
- A method of treating psychological or emotional disorders

**20(C).** After analyzing a problem a student tries to understand/explain it in his mind, In which type of speech he is involved silent/inner speech.

Lev Vygotsky argues that communication is the driving force behind speech in both adults and children. According to Vygotsky, there are mainly three types of speech are there:

- Social Speech (From 2 years)
- Private Speech (From 3 years)
- Silent/Inner Speech (From 7 years)

Silent/Inner Speech: This is a speech in which the use of words or word images in thinking without audible or visible speaking. The ability of this type of speech comes when a child is about 7 years or above. Characteristics of Silent/Inner Speech:

- Helps the student to think about all the aspects without saying a single word.
- Gives purity to the thought process.

Example: During writing answered in an exam hall.

**21(D).** If a student in your school is studying well and presenting positive behavior praise him for good progress and encourage him to do better in future.

Positive behavior techniques are proactive ways to change problematic student behavior that are evidence-based. Pre-correcting, urging, and nonverbal messages are examples of positive behavior methods. For promoting Positive Student Conduct Create and stick to simple procedures. Have a good time together. Set clear goals and stick to them. Encourage good habits to develop. Educate and practice coping mechanisms. Recognize your emotions, Concentrate on the behavior rather than the child, and reward excellent conduct. At any age, you may praise and encourage your child. Rewards promote the desired behavior, but they should not be used excessively. One of the simplest methods to reinforce your child's positive conduct is to praise them. However, effective praise entails more than just saying "excellent work."

**22(A).** A child tries to learn and built about himself through experience and interaction with others. He wants to involve in primary socialization.

The process of learning to internalize the values and norms into itself or the mode of learning to live in society is called the process of socialization. It may be defined more comprehensively as a life-long process of inculcation whereby an individual learns the principles, values, and symbols of the social system in which he participates and the expression of those values and norms in the roles he enacts. Socialization may be classified into two broad groups:

Primary socialization: Inculcation of norms and values within the family is called primary socialization. Here children want to know themselves and try to find their identity and learn the daily routine tasks of humans.

- Example: Hygiene training, Eating food with utensils, toilet training, etc.

Secondary socialization: The process of imbibing norms, values, and behavior patterns of school may be called secondary socialization.

- Example: How to behave in a church, How to behave in a school, etc.

**23(C).** Developing awareness abilities in children is the most important task for a successful teacher to improve the teaching learning process.

The teaching-learning process is a combined process in which a teacher examines students' understanding requirements, sets specific learning targets, formulates teaching and memorization tactics, implements a work plan, and evaluates the instruction's outcomes.

- Teachers educate to support the growth and learning of all children by offering a mix of adult-guided and child-guided experiences for all children. Teachers design curricula to help students attain critical learning objectives through play, small groups, big groups, interest centers, and routines.
- A good teacher is one who has a long-term influence on his or her students' life, develops children's awareness abilities, and maintains the ability to motivate them to achieve greater achievement.
- Teachers are in charge of influencing a child's destiny and making him or her a better person. A teacher instills in students information, good values, tradition, modern-day issues, and solutions to them.

**24(B).** Statement, "Development is a quantitative process" is not true.

Development refers to the process by which an individual's potentialities unfold and appear as new abilities, qualities, and characteristics. Development is a progressive series of coherent changes.

Development is a biological process: It is a biological process like an individual's physical attributes, inherited diseases, and temperament level. Genes inherited from parents, the development of the brain, height. and weight gains are all examples of biological processes that affect development.

Development is a qualitative process:- Development implies qualitative change. This means that development is just not adding inches to one's height or refining one's ability but it is a complex process that involves the integration of many structures and functions.

Development is a goal-oriented process: There may be the individual goals of the learner, the institutional goals, or the social goals. Being goal-oriented means you are focused on reaching or completing specific tasks or stages to achieve a planned outcome.

Learning is a process of behavior change: Learning is defined as "any relatively permanent change in behavior that occurs as a result of experience". It is a continuous process and human beings are always undergoing the process of learning as a result of their interactions with the environment in which they operate.

**25(D).** The factors affecting motivation are r equirements, aspiration level and e motional state.

Motivation is a state of mind that may help pupils keep their focus and conduct while also providing them with the extra energy they need to finish activities. As a result, it can aid in the long-term maintenance of activities. Motivation has a wide range of implications on students' behaviors, choices, interests, and outcomes in education.

Individual members' willingness to set and achieve difficult goals, accept responsibility and obligations, engage in work, and be happy at work are all instances of motivation. It's a process that begins with a physiological or psychological need or deficit and concludes with behavior or a desire to achieve a goal or get an incentive. If a student develops a negative sentiment toward their teachers, such as fear or dislike, it might alter their attitude about the topic in general. When a teacher favors specific pupils or uses insulting and demeaning words, it might affect their willingness to learn.

**26(D).** Sports develops the all social, mental, and physical skills of children.

Development- When the new abilities and characteristics get exhibited and there is a progressive change in the behaviour of the individual. Abilities develop by sports:

The overall development takes place while the child plays sports. When a child plays individual sports or team sports he comes into the contact with the various other players he meets with them, shares information and details interacts with other players this helps the child in socializing thus social skills such as communication are developed. Development of mental skills of the child, as in sports when the child wins he builds his confidences when he loses his game it gives him aim to perform in next game. He is able to build his self-esteem and confidence which helps in the mental development of the child. Physical skills such as coordination of the body parts are improved like running, jumping swimming.

**27(B).** If instructed to the goal of teaching that by looking at this picture and describing its characteristics, it related to direct perceptual.

The goals of teaching include the objective of teaching and learning. These goals involve the motive that helps in the ultimate achievement of learning goals. Perception stands for the knowledge of an object or its qualities that we obtain by means of our sensations. Direct perception consists of the activity of getting information from the ambient array of light, i.e. a process of "information pickup" through the exploratory activities of looking at things by looking around and moving around.

**28(B).** Link study to rote system, is not a guiding principle of NCF 2005.

The National Curriculum Framework 2005 (NCF 2005) is the fourth National Curriculum Framework published in 2005 by the National Council of Educational Research and Training (NCERT) in India. Its predecessors were published in 1975, 1988, and 2000. It was developed by the government of India for renovating the curriculum for students' education to cope up with the development in the global issues.

Guidelines provided by the NCF 2005:
- Connecting knowledge to life outside the school
- To create flexible examination by integrating the classroom learning and activities
- To enrich the curriculum so that it goes beyond textbooks:-
- To shift from rote learning to the creation of experience while learning.
- Nurturing an overriding identity informed by caring concerns within the democratic polity of the country.

**29(C).** Intuitive stage is not the part of Bruner's cognitive development theory.

Jerome Bruner, an American psychologist has made crucial contributions in the field of human cognitive psychology. He has identified three stages of cognitive representation which includes:

Enactive stage:
- It refers to the representation of knowledge through actions.
- Learning by doing is the main principle.
- They learn by physical actions and storing things in memory.

Iconic stage:
- It refers to the visual summarization of images.
- The learner stores sensory images which are visual ones.

Symbolic stage:
- It refers to the use of words and other symbols to describe experiences.
- The experience stored in memory in the form of symbols i.e., language.

**30(A).** Groups of learning strategies that are more task-specific are called " Cognitive ".

Bloom's Taxonomy: It is a hierarchical ordering of cognitive, affective, and psychomotor domains and each domain has some objectives that can help teachers teach and students learn.

Cognitive domains: In this domain, a child deals with knowledge and hence, learns to create, evaluate, analyze, apply, understand, remember.

The revised model lays out the components nicely so they can be considered and used, and so cognitive processes as related to chosen instructional tasks can be easily documented and tracked.

**31(A).** According to the line:- "The women earn between Rs. 10,000 and Rs. 18,000 a month based on their experience". It can be concluded that statement (A) is true.

According to the line:- "Her family doesn't mind that she travels at odd hours or is in the company of male colleagues, which in her community was once taboo". It can be concluded that statement (B) is false.

According to the line:- "Possibly the most important change these young women have brought to the valley is getting their tribes to move from traditional medicine to modern medicine". It can be concluded that statement (C) is true.

According to the line:- "According to the 2011 census, the maternal mortality rate in Araku valley was over 400 per 100,000 live births, more than double the national average. In the last two years, however, there have been no deaths during pregnancy or childbirth". It can be concluded that statement (D) is false.

**32(A).** According to the line:- "Her family doesn't mind that she travels at odd hours or is in the company of male colleagues, which in her community was once taboo." It can be concluded that statement (1) is correct.

**33(D).** Orthodox is the word which is not associated with Padma.

Orthodox means following or conforming to the traditional or generally accepted rules or beliefs of a religion, philosophy, or practice.

**34(D).** Tribal girls working with male colleagues was once considered taboo among the tribals.

According to the line: "Her family doesn't mind that she travels at odd hours or is in the company of male colleagues, which in her community was once taboo".

**35(B).** Their mothers have worked in anganwadis in different capacities, is common among the young anganwadi women workers.

According to the paragraph, "One common thread among these young girls is that all their mothers have either worked in or taught at the village anganwadis". It is directly giving a sense that either the young anganwadi women workers are working or being taught by somebody at the village anganwadi.

**36(D).** Death has the same meaning as the word 'mortality' used in the passage.

Mortality: T he fact that nobody can live for ever.

Example: He didn't like to think about his own mortality.

Death: The action or fact of dying or being killed, The end of the life of a person or organism.

Example: The police do not know the cause of death.

**37(D).** Modern is the antonym of the word 'Traditional' used in the passage.

Traditional: Existing in or as part of a tradition, long-established.

Example: T he traditional roles of men and women have changed in the last generation .

Modern: Relating to the present or recent times as opposed to the remote past.

Example: Modern buildings are made of concrete .

**38(A).** Odd is an adjective as it is modifying the noun 'hours'.

Adjectives are the words that describe the qualities or states of being' noun'.

For example: Red, quick, happy, and obnoxious.

**39(B).** The error lies in the usage of 'reached' instead of 'reach'.

"did I reached the station" is an incorrect phrase as reached is in the past tense form. We need to use the v1 form of 'reached' as we know that 'did' is followed by v1 form of verb not v2 or v3.

**40(D).** The poem is about determination and courage in the face of suffering.

The poet describes hardships at the beginning of each stanza.

For example: Out of the night that covers me
Black as the pit from pole to pole,

Here he is using the metaphor of night for difficulties he is facing.

However, he ends the stanza with words of courage.

For example I thank whatever gods may be
For my unconquerable soul.

He is thanking the gods for providing him

with unshakable resilience.

**41(C).** The poem is a picture of man's eternal and irreversible suffering.
It matters not how strait the gate,
How charged with punishment the scroll,
By alluding to the Bible, the poet doesn't care how difficult life becomes or it is full of punishment.
He continues, I am the master of my fate
I am the master of my soul.
He is the master of his fate and his inner life i.e the soul.

**42(B).** The poem underlines the cheerful and courageous acceptance of sorrow.
In the third stanza of the poem, the poet describes the certainty of death in life:
Beyond this place of wrath and tears
Looms but the horror of the shade,
Death is the only certainty of the future that hangs like a horrifying shadow over the oresent.
However, in the next lines poet describes his courage:
And yet menace of the years
Finds, and shall find, me unafraid
He affirms that any difficulty will find him unafraid and courageous.

**43(D).** The poem is about the optimistic nature of the poet in the face of adversities.
The mood of the poem is dark and gloomy which is also the kind of situation the poet is facing. for example:
In the fell clutch of circumstance,
I have not winced nor cried aloud.
Poet never complained whenever he found himself in difficulty.
However, the poet is optimistic no matter what the hardship is:
Under the bludgeonings of chance
My head is bloody, but unbowed.
The poet was impacted by the beatings of his life but he always stood with pride and kept facing the challenges.

**44(C).** Simile has been used in the line 'Black as the pit from pole to pole'.
Simile: a figure of speech comparing two unlike things that is often introduced by 'like' or 'as'.
Ex: As red as a rose.
In the line "Black as the pit from pole to pole," the poet compares black and pit with the use of 'as'.

**45(C).** Personification has been used in "Under the bludgeonings of chance.
Personification is a figure of speech where human-like qualities are attributed to inanimate objects or to abstract concepts.
The word bludgeonings mean to hit someone with heavy impact.

**46(B).** If Hindi language is to be taught to those children whose mother tongue is somewhat different from Hindi, then we will give importance to multilingualism.
Multilingual classroom refers to a class where children from different languages receive the same education together. During the teaching process in a multilingual classroom, the teacher always provides opportunities to the students to speak in their mother tongue.
Features of multilingual classroom:
- Gives children the freedom to listen in their home language.
- Accelerates the cognitive and educational development of children.
- In a multilingual classroom, the mother language of the child is given a place in the classroom.
- Expands linguistic skills in children by connecting them to the environment of the room.
- Provides children with the ability to cope with interactive situations.

**47(B).** The language teacher gives the children to write essays for the purpose of assessing their writing ability. The important aspect to be assessed by the language teacher in the essay written by the children is the organization of the thought elements.
In the case of assessment of writing skills, children should be given an opportunity to indulge in such activities so that originality can be incorporated in their ideas because through the expression of original ideas, children:
- Ensure the development of spontaneous expression with efficiency.
- Will grasp linguistic skills easily with actual experience.
- Express your views by connecting facts with your own personal experiences.
- You will keep your views open by getting opportunities for free and original expression.

**48(C).** Skinner said that "creative is synonymous with the power of human mind to develop relationships by creatively creating new subject matter by transforming relationships".
Skinner's Theory- This principle is called the principle of obstetric contract because it is based on actions. All the principles of classical conditioning are found in this theory. Significance of Skinner's theory in language:
- This principle makes the language easy to learn.
- There should be immediate reinforcement of tasks so that recurrence of errors can be prevented and interest can be generated in the works.

**49(B).** Inductive method- It is a psychological method in which general rules are constructed through specific experiences and examples. Through this, students become more active and communicate new knowledge with the help of simple concepts.
Steps of Inductive Method:

4. Example- In this step many examples of the same type are presented to the child.
2. Analysis/Inspection- In this step the children inspect the examples presented and after that the teacher asks analytical questions related to the examples.
1. Conclusion/Regulation- In this step children draw general rules. This step is also known as generalization of rules.
3. Practice/Test- The rules drawn in this step are tested.

**50(A).** Tools such as rich language environment, natural speaking, social interaction, home environment are related to acquisition aspect of language.
Language teaching is a rich system in itself. There are many aspects to it which all together make up the language teaching. Language learning becomes more effective through acquisition. Language teaching includes the following aspects:
Enriched Language Environment- The environment in which the child learns his language expression by doing this is called his linguistic environment. This includes the mother tongue or spoken language of the child.
Natural colloquial- It is mainly the language of the family. By nature the language we use becomes our innate language. In some places it is also called dialect.
Social Interaction- After the family environment, the interaction through which a child learns a language is his society. Children's language development is enhanced through exposure to social interactions.
Domestic environment- The home environment is formed by the family and close members. The mother's linguistic development of the child starts from her womb itself. The language development of the child will also be similar to the domestic environment.

**51(A).** The correctness of spelling in writing is responsible for grammar.
Grammar is the systematic system of rules for speaking and writing a language, that is, grammar works to organize the language. Teaching grammar brings correctness, discipline, and stability to the language. In the context of grammar-teaching, it is most important to emphasize the practical side of grammar because the knowledge of the practical side of grammar:
- Makes possible the pure speaking or writing of the language.
- Introduces the homogeneity and correctness of the language.
- It serves to give pure and clear form to the various forms of language.
- Provides knowledge of the principles of letters, words, and syntax in language.
- Emphasizes on learning grammar by referring to the grammatical rules contained in the text.

**52(B).** The purpose of grammar-teaching is to help understand and analyze the systematic nature of language.

Grammar is the systematic system of rules for speaking and writing a language, that is, grammar works to organize the language. The purpose of teaching grammar is to help understand and analyze the systematic nature of language. Language is bound by rules at the level of words, sentences and proverbs, some of which are already in our innate language ability but are mostly formed through communication in the social environment. Recognizing, understanding and analyzing these rules through teaching grammar will expand the language skills of children to a higher level.

**53(A).** At the primary stage a Hindi speaking child makes spelling errors related to E-E because errors are a stop in the learning process.

Errors are an important stop in the learning process that give insight to children's thinking. Mistakes decide the way of helping children and can also be called a step in the learning process. Errors make the teacher aware of the learning needs of the children so that the teacher can meet them as needed. By diagnosing the difficulties of the children through pedagogical diagnosis, the teaching methods adopted by the teachers to overcome those difficulties are called remedial teaching. Errors in children's language use help teachers in remedial teaching because remedial teaching requires that teachers come to know about the shortcomings of the children, which are possible due to their errors. Errors do not mean language ignorance or lack of teacher at all because it is also considered a process in the process of acquiring knowledge which is very important.

**54(B).** An important objective of language learning at the primary stage is to make language a medium for children to understand their environment and experience, i.e., language teaching should be such that children can easily relate it to their surroundings. They are successful in using language in a variety of contexts and they acquire linguistic skills easily with actual experience.

Language teaching is concerned with developing communication skills and originality in children and making them successful in using language in different contexts. The basic skills acquired through language at the primary level are helpful in understanding the concepts of other areas. The aim of language teaching is to develop understanding and expression of language.

**55(A).** The activities chosen in the assessment of children should be engaging children in concrete experiences at the primary level.

All children have their own different way of learning. Therefore, the activities selected for assessment should also be child-friendly. The activities selected for assessment should be free from bias and aimed at being inclusive of all children. The activities should give opportunities to the children to show their potential. Assessment based questions asked to the children should be related to the child's cognition. Should be of the child's level and speed. They should not be based on any one answer, but should be the ones that expand the thoughts of the children. It should be according to the interest of the child.

**56(A).** Writing skills are initiated by operational skills.

Operational skill- Operational skill means to develop the ability to sit, hold the pen, etc., before teaching the child to write. Many skills require coordination before learning to write. A child is considered ready to learn writing when he has developed operational ability (the ability to hold fingers). Operational skills can be developed with the help of the following activities or games:

- Drawing- Painting develops operational skills in children and also entertains them.
- Pour water in a pot
- Flower garland
- Making clay

**57(A).** Enriched linguistic environment in the school/classroom means more opportunities for speaking, listening, reading and writing.

Enriched linguistic environment refers to an environment in which there are maximum opportunities for the use of language. Language use refers to the presence of a language in some form or the other in the school/classroom. This presence can be in any form of language such as speaking, listening, reading or writing. The main objective of a enriched linguistic environment is to make the child proficient in all the four language skills (listening skills, reading skills, reading skills and writing skills).

**58(B).** The steps required to make Hindi language learning interesting are the use of new teaching methods and information and communication methods.

Efforts should be made to bring awareness about employment opportunities in the government and non-government institutions working for the upliftment of Hindi language so that students and teachers can be aware of those opportunities. Students nowadays want to study only those subjects which are employable and which enable them to earn their livelihood.

To make Hindi teaching interesting, instead of traditional methods, new methods of teaching like problem solving method, project method, etc., should be used properly. In the context of Hindi language, the employment generating aspects of the language are translation, editing courses, creative writing in Hindi, purposeful Hindi, etc. Students can be attracted towards Hindi language by giving them a place in the curriculum. Information and communication technology should also be used in the work of teaching Hindi.

**59(A).** To develop reading culture, the reading material should be standard and the ability to understand is assessed.

Reading is a creative activity. No text-material explains its whole thing by itself, that is, the whole thing is not contained in it. The reader uses his prior knowledge about the subject matter of the text to understand any text material. Must be truly fluent in reading. Recognition of words is the basis of reading fluently. Every learner of reading has to assimilate that 'code' so that relationships can be established between spells, words and meanings. In the skill of reading comprehension, only those children come forward who start recognizing words accurately and quickly in the first grade. Readers must have the ability to decode words at a fast speed. Only then they can harmonize this process with the process of making meaning of any text material. Skilled readers make no mistake in reading concocted words. What separates skilled and ordinary readers in this situation is the speed, not the accuracy. Skilled readers do not recognize unfamiliar words according to the rules that govern the relationship between spellings and pronunciation. Their identification is based on the congruence of a truly unfamiliar word with already familiar words.

**60(D).** Purpose of the pictures given in the text The pictures in the text book are helpful in understanding the abstract concepts.

The objectives of the pictures given in the lesson at the primary level are to:

- Make practice interesting.
- Enhances the imagination power of children.
- It helps in increasing the teaching ability of the children.
- Helps in connecting children's learning with their surroundings.
- Helps to make education attractive.
- Enrich the intellectual development of children.
- Helps in increasing the power of imagination.
- Make the subject matter interesting.
- Through pictures, children's abstract conceptual power is enriched.
- Provide opportunities for use of writing skills through pictures.

**61(C).** Given,

A circle touches all four sides of a quadrilateral $PQRS$ . If $PQ = 11$ cm, $QR = 12$ cm and $PS = 8$ cm.

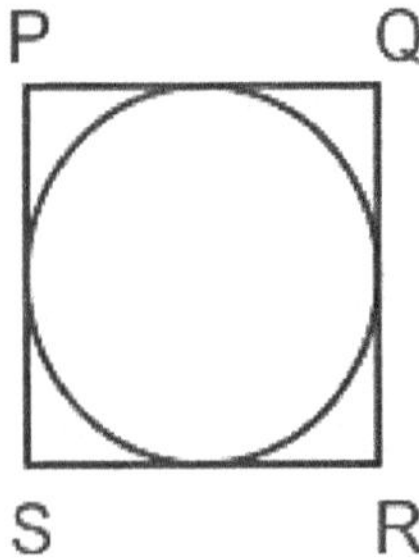


If a circle touches all four sides of quadrilateral $PQRS$ then,
$PQ + RS = SP + RQ$
So,
$\Rightarrow 11 + RS = 8 + 12$
$\Rightarrow RS = 20 - 11$
$\Rightarrow RS = 9$

**62(A).** An angle of 89° is " Acute " angle.
An angle which is measuring less than 90 degrees is called an acute angle. This angle is smaller than the right angle (which is equal to 90 degrees).
For example:
$\angle 30°, \angle 45°, \angle 60°, \angle 75°, \angle 33°, \angle 55°, \angle 85°$ , etc.

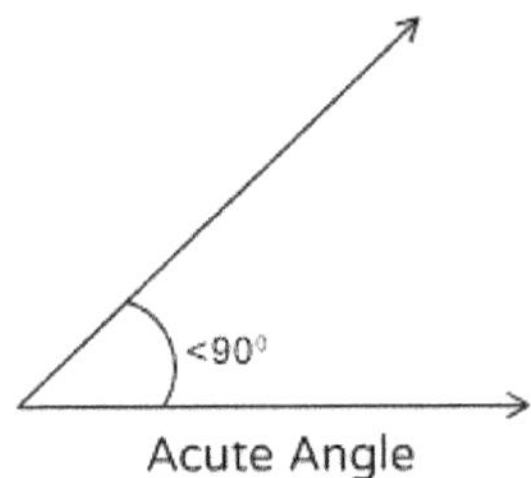


**63(D).** Given:
$3.8, 4.2, 6.3, 4.6, 7.2, 4.3, 8.2, 1.7, 3.5, 1.4,$
$4.5, 3.6, 4.2, 3.8, 4.4, 2.6$
A perimeter is a closed path that encompasses, surrounds, or outlines either a two dimensional shape or a one-dimensional length.
So,
Perimeter =
$3.8 + 4.2 + 6.3 + 4.6 + 7.2 + 4.3 + 8.2 +$
$1.7 + 3.5 + 1.4 + 4.5 + 3.6 + 4.2 + 3.8 +$
$4.4 + 2.6$
$= 68.3$ cm

**64(B).** Given,
The dimensions of the Wall
$= 20\,m \times 5\,m \times 0.3\,m$
The dimensions of the bricks
$= 0.2\,m \times 0.05\,m \times 0.03\,m$
As we know,
The volume of the cuboid (V) = Length × Width × Height
The number of bricks $= \dfrac{\text{Volume of wall}}{\text{Volume of bricks}}$
Volume of wall
$= 20\,m \times 5\,m \times 0.3\,m = 30\,m^3$
Volume of brick
$= 0.2\,m \times 0.05\,m \times 0.03\,m = 0.0003\,m^3$

$= \dfrac{30}{0.0003}$
$= 100000$

**65(C).** There are 5 angles in a pentagon. A pentagon is a flat 2D shape that has 5 sides, 5 angles and 5 vertices. The word "pentagon" comes from the greek word "pentagonos", which means 5-angled". A regular pentagon has five internal angles that form corners.

**66(A).** A number that is divisible by 6 will also be divisible by 2 and 3 .
Numbers which are divisible by both 2 and 3 are divisible by 6 . That is, if the last digit of the given number is even and the sum of its digits is a multiple of 3 , then the given number is also a multiple of 6 .
Example:
630 , the number is divisible by 2 as the last digit is 0 .
The sum of digits is $6 + 3 + 0 = 9$ , which is also divisible by 3 .
So, 630 is divisible by 6 .

**67(C).** The associative property is applicable to " Addition and Multiplication ".
As per associative property:
$A + (B + C) = (A + B) + C$
$A \times (B \times C) = (A \times B) \times C$

**68(A).** Given,
$56 \div 4 \times \_\_ = 56$
Solving the equation, we get
$\Rightarrow (\frac{56}{4}) \times \_\_ = 56$
$\Rightarrow 14 \times \_\_ = 56$
Now to equate the equation we must multiply it by 4 .
Thus the new equation becomes
$56 \div 4 \times 4 = 56$
So, in the place of blank 4 will come.

**69(D).** Given,
Total number of Rs. 500 notes $= 2$
Total numbers of Rs. 200 notes $= 4$
Total number of Rs. 100 notes $= 3$
Total number of Rs. 50 notes $= 23$
Total number of Rs. 20 notes $= 14$
Total number of Rs. 10 coins $= 18$
Total amount of the money
$= (500 \times 2) + (200 \times 4) + (100 \times 3) + (50 \times 23)$
$+ (20 \times 14) + (10 \times 18)$
$= 1000 + 800 + 300 + 1150 + 280 + 180$
$= 3710$
Total number of Rs. 5 coins for exchange of the money $= \dfrac{3710}{5}$
$= 742$

**70(A).** Given:
0.2 kg
As we know,
1 Kilogram (kg) = 1000000 mili-gram
$0.2\,kg = 0.2 \times 1000000$
$= 200000$ mili-gram

**71(A).** Let the ages of children be $x, (x+3), (x+6), (x+9)$ and $(x+12)$

years.
Then,
$x + (x + 3) + (x + 6) + (x + 9) + (x + 12) = 50$
$\Rightarrow 5x = 20$
$\Rightarrow x = 4$
$\therefore$ Age of the youngest child $= x = 4$ years

**72(D).** Given,
Fractions are $\dfrac{6}{8}, \dfrac{4}{5}, \dfrac{2}{9}, \dfrac{7}{8}$
As we know,
If the denominator of two or more fractions are same .
Then greater the numerator greater will be the fraction.
At first, take the LCM of denominator,
$LCM\,(8, 5, 9, 8) = 360$
Now, We have to make denominator of fractions equal.
So, We will multiply the suitable number in the numerator or denominator so that the denominator will be 360 in all fractions.
$\dfrac{6}{8} = \dfrac{6}{8} \times \dfrac{45}{45} = \dfrac{270}{360}$
$\dfrac{4}{5} = \dfrac{4}{5} \times \dfrac{72}{72} = \dfrac{288}{360}$
$\dfrac{2}{9} = \dfrac{2}{9} \times \dfrac{40}{40} = \dfrac{80}{360}$
$\dfrac{7}{8} = \dfrac{7}{8} \times \dfrac{45}{45} = \dfrac{315}{360}$
Now, we can see that
$315 > 288 > 270 > 80$
So, $\dfrac{7}{8} > \dfrac{4}{5} > \dfrac{6}{8} > \dfrac{2}{9}$
$\therefore$ The greatest fraction is $\dfrac{7}{8}$ .

**73(D).** Given,
2 hours 30 minutes
We know that,
1 hour = 60 minutes
Then,
2 hours $= 2 \times 60 = 120$ minutes
Now, we will add 30 minutes.
2 hours 30 minutes $= 120 + 30 = 150$ minutes
1 minute = 60 seconds
Then,
$150 = 150 \times 60$ minutes
$= 9000$ seconds

**74(B).** Given,
The price of Apple = Rs. 80/ kg
The price of Orange = Rs. 75/ kg
The price of Mango = Rs. 60/ kg
The price of Pineapple = Rs. 50/ kg
The price of Grapes = Rs. 65/ kg
As we know,
1 gram $= \dfrac{1}{1000}$ kg
Total amount of apples = 2.5 kg
Total amount of orange = 1.6 kg
Total amount of mangoes = 3 kg
Total amount of pineapples = 500 grams
$= \dfrac{500}{1000}\,kg = 0.5$ kg
Total amount of grapes
$= 800\,grams = \dfrac{800}{1000}\,kg = 0.8$ kg
Total price
$= (80 \times 2.5) + (75 \times 1.6) + (60 \times 3) + (50 \times 0.5) + (65 \times 0.8)$
$= 200 + 120 + 180 + 25 + 52 = 577$

**75(B).** The logic followed here is:

$$9 \quad 11 \quad 14 \quad 18 \quad 23 \quad \boxed{29}$$
$$\quad +2 \quad +3 \quad +4 \quad +5 \quad +6$$

**76(C).** Given,

Total time of journey = 7 hours

Speed of car for half distance = 40 km / hr

Speed of car for remaining distance = 60 km / hr

As we know,

Distance = Speed × Time

Let total distance be $2x$.

$\text{Time }_1 = \dfrac{\text{Distance}}{\text{Speed}}$

$\Rightarrow \dfrac{x}{40}$ hours

$\text{Time }_2 = \dfrac{\text{Distance}}{\text{Speed}}$

$\Rightarrow \dfrac{x}{60}$ hours

Total time = $\text{Time }_1 + \text{Time }_2$

$\Rightarrow 7 = \dfrac{x}{40} + \dfrac{x}{60}$

$\Rightarrow 7 = \dfrac{(3x+2x)}{120}$

$\Rightarrow 7 = \dfrac{5x}{120}$

$\Rightarrow x = 7 \times 24$

$\Rightarrow x = 168$ km

$\Rightarrow$ Total distance = $2x$

$= 2 \times 168$

$= 336$ km

**77(D).** Remedial Teaching is not one of the methods of coordinating student discussion and analysing their solutions in Mathematics.

Gallery Walk, Math Congress and Bansho provide students with organized and facilitated time to talk about and listen actively to one another's mathematical thinking, justify their thinking to others and reflect on what they are learning. In fact, this organized and safe discussion forum encourages students to share and challenge ideas. Importantly, students are reassured that their voices, ideas, and experiences are valued and contribute directly to the whole class learning.

During Gallery Walk, Math Congress, and Bansho, it becomes evident to the students and teacher that mathematical communication is not about "answering the question using words, numbers, pictures, and symbols." Instead, they realize that these forms of communication are selected and applied in order to create a precise mathematical argument, where labeled diagrams and/or numeric expressions and equations are viewed as being more precise, concise, and persuasive forms than descriptive narratives.

- Gallery Walk is an interactive discussion technique that gets students out of their chairs and into a mode of focused and active engagement with other students' mathematical ideas. The purpose of the Gallery Walk is to have students and the teacher mathematically engage with a range of solutions through analysis and response.

- Math Congress is a mathematics instructional strategy developed by Fosnot and Dolk. Preparation for and participation in a Math Congress occurs over two lesson periods. The purpose of the congress is to support the development of mathematicians in the classroom learning community, rather than fixing mistakes in the children's work or getting agreement on answers.

- Bansho, in Japanese, literally means board writing. The purpose of Bansho is to organize and record mathematical thinking derived from and collectively produced by students on a large-size chalkboard or dry erase board.

**78(B).** The nature of mathematics is logical.

Mathematics is the study of numbers, shape, quantity, and patterns. Mathematics is the 'queen of all sciences' and its presence is there in all the subjects. It acts as the basis and structure of other subjects. The Nature of Mathematics is Logical as it relies on:

- Evaluation of truth or likelihood of statements
- It visualized as the vehicle to train a child to think, reason, analyze, and articulate logically
- Development of skills like speed, accuracy, estimation
- Improvement of reasoning power, analytical and, critical thinking
- Enhancement of scientific attitude like estimating, finding and verifying results

**79(C).** A close relationship between the growth of thinking and the development of mathematical concepts is established in " Research ".

The three basic groups of mathematical concepts that are essential in all topics included in the mathematics curriculum at the elementary school level are number and operations on numbers, spatial thinking and measurement. The mathematical concepts and processes at different levels, especially at the primary level, are arranged from simpler to complex order. Research has established a close relationship between the growth of thinking and the development of mathematical concepts. As a teacher, one should be aware of such relationship so that one can develop an understanding of the strength and difficulties of every child in one's class in their learning of mathematics. concepts and can take appropriate facilitating steps in that direction. So, we conclude that a close relationship between the growth of thinking and the development of mathematical concepts is established in Research.

**80(D).** We need mathematics in society for counting, business, calculation, transaction, measurement, making budget, financial analysis.

Mathematics is the study of numbers, shape, quantity, and patterns. The nature of mathematics is logical as it relies on logic and connects learning with children's day to day life. Mathematics plays an important role in society, be it the intellectual, vocational, moral, and cultural development of the members of the society.

**81(C).** Curriculum of mathematics in primary level in school education should be content centered.

One of the major objectives of teaching primary mathematics is to enable children to solve speedily and accurately the numerical and spatial problems which they encounter at home, in the school and in the community. It should help children develop an understanding of key mathematical concepts through appropriate experiences with the physical world and the immediate environment. For maintaining the relevance of the mathematics curriculum to the societal and personal needs of the learners, it should continuously undergo a change in light of changing national goals and priorities. Mathematics curriculum in order to be realistic, relevant and meaningful has to be in tune with the pedagogical goals and the nature of the mathematical content. It should be based on systematic research about the nature of the learner, the learning process and the presentation of the mathematics curriculum to the learners.

**82(A).** Mode-Building component helpful in translating verbal language to the language of mathematics.

Mode-Building: Translating verbal language to the language of mathematics, that is solving a word problem, involves three stages: (i) encoding (ii) operations (iii) decoding

- Encoding is the process of building a mathematical model from a given verbal statement. Suppose we say that "a father's age is 5 years more than twice his son's age". If we assume the two ages to be x and y years respectively, then the corresponding mathematical model is: x=2y+5.

- Operations: After a model has been set up, we operate on it according to given conditions, obtain a solution, and then translate it back into verbal language.

- The skill of model-building requires a clear understanding of the mathematical equivalent of words that have mathematical meanings. Words such as more, less, times, difference, is equal to, square, etc., have to be identified and used in the model for the verbal statement.

**83(A).** The % symbol is unique to the mathematics language.

Language helps an individual to

communicate with others in an effective way with words, symbols, and expressions as the mediums. As mathematics is considered a nonlinguistic subject but still possess similarities with the language. It uses symbols and expressions to describe the lengthy problems in a precise and accurate manner which makes it an economical language.

- With the help of language, one individual can express mathematics in terms of mathematical equations, laws, and principles.
- Also, to express any mathematical fact, theorem, or statement, we need to use the language.
- Just like we use letters, alphabets, and words to write or speak a language, mathematical language uses symbols, numbers, diagrams, and graphics to express, define, or prove the mathematical statements and concepts.
- The symbols that are generally used in mathematics are 'x', '÷', '+', '-', '%' etc.

**84(D).** Assessment in mathematics refers to the process of collecting, receiving, and using data for improvement of the mathematical learning process. The assessment of mathematics learning at primary stage should be focus on:

- Development of reasoning skills
- Development of mathematical language
- Development of the social personal qualities of the children
- The understanding of how children learn mathematics
- Development of the mathematical concept and their application in daily life
- Use suitable method to solve mathematical problems and answers the questions

**85(C).** Check list, portfolio, project class participation strategies can be used to assess learners' interest in and attitude to mathematics.

National Curriculum Framework 2005 talks about the importance of integrating assessment with the teaching-learning process. Consequently, Continuous and Comprehensive Evaluation has been implemented in the school education system. The basic tenet of this assessment is that it should be integrated with classroom activities. There are various tools and techniques used to assess learned performance in Mathematics which are as follows:

- Checklist: It is an observational technique. It offers systematic ways of collecting data about specific behavior, knowledge, performance and skills. Checklists have two parts, in the first column statement; and the latter is response yes/no related to the statement.
- Portfolio: It is a collection of learner's work. It can be designed to represent many things in relation to children's Mathematics learning experiences. It compiles academic work and other forms of educational evidence assembled for the purpose of evaluating the curriculum quality, learning progress, academic achievement, etc. It also helps in determining whether the learners have met learning standards, helping the learners to reflect on their academic goals and progress as learners.
- Project Class Participation: A project relates to issues concerning the learner which is carried to completion in its natural setting. In order to complete a project, the learners, preferably work in groups, are required to combine all their knowledge and experience relating to different disciplines in order to solve a real-life problem.

**86(D).** Problems and challenges do mathematics teacher face while teaching in the classroom:

- Difficulty in classroom management because of individual differences, different intellectual abilities, and age.
- Difficulty in teaching mathematics because of differences in the social, cultural, and family environment of students.
- The problem in teaching mathematics due to poor mathematics background of students at the secondary level.
- Lack of information about new instructional techniques and inventions.
- Lack of opportunity to participate in the interactions, workshops related to the subject matter.
- Difficulty in managing classroom teaching-learning activities due to large class sizes.

**87(B).** Socio-Cultural background could be a contributing factor towards underachievement in mathematics.

Underachievement is defined as a large discrepancy between the child's performance (at school) and his innate ability. When a child with a high I.Q. level is performing poorly, he is said to be an underachiever. A child who has average intelligence, but whose performance is below average is also said to be a low achiever. Factors are those related to the underachievement in mathematics, which surrounds the individual as well as to his unique persona (e.g., socio-economic level and educational background of the family, the school climate, the language background, and students' attitudes toward mathematics). Among social variables, the factors which were considered very widely are socioeconomic status, parental involvement, and parent's education.

**88(D).** The functioning process of evaluation is marking, decision making and error finding.

Evaluation plays a vital role in teaching-learning experiences. It is an integral part of the instructional programmes. It provides information's on the basis of which many educational decisions are taken. We are to stick to the basic function of evaluation which is required to be practised for pupil and his learning processes. And find out the error of learner by giving marks and grades. Functions of Evaluation:

- A planned evaluation helps a teacher in deciding and developing the ways, methods, techniques of teaching.
- Helps to formulate and reformulate suitable and realistic objectives of instruction.
- Helps to improve instruction and to plan appropriate and adequate techniques of instruction.
- Helps in the improvement of curriculum.

**89(A).** One of the major reasons for errors in mathematics is due to over-emphasis on procedural skills.

Errors are incorrectness made by the child during learning. Error analysis is one of the common ways to find out the reasons for the student's mistakes or errors. They are accepted as an essential part of the mathematics learning process. The child, freed from the fear of criticism, will more readily experiment.

Errors in mathematics can be factual, procedural, or conceptual. There are a number of reasons for errors done by students in mathematics like careless attitude, lack of interest in the subject, improper understanding of the concept etc. Over-emphasis on procedural skills can be one of the major reasons for errors in mathematics.

Procedural skill is a series of steps that must be followed to solve mathematical problems. This knowledge includes knowledge of techniques, and methods. The teacher's main emphasis is on procedural skill rather than conceptual understanding. Concepts are not clear of the students that is why they commit mistakes. It is very important for the students to have conceptual as well as procedural knowledge to get a deeper understanding of the mathematics concepts.

**90(B).** Community demonstrates the importance of incorporating cultural elements in the teaching of mathematics.

Mathematics can be referred to as the study of patterns, numbers, geometrical objects, data, and information. It deals with data analysis, integration of various fields of knowledge, involves proofs, deductive and inductive reasoning, and generalizations. Community participation is important for a number of reasons:

- It strengthens the link between home, school, and community; it strengthens the link between school and the cultural diversity of students.

- It demonstrates the importance of incorporating cultural elements in the teaching of mathematics, all of which motivates students to learn about their culture and that of others while also learning mathematics.
- Students should be contributions of members of their own and other cultures can help them gain confidence, self-esteem and a sense of belonging as well as respect for the mathematical thinking of other cultures".
- Culturally relevant pedagogy validates students' cultural backgrounds, and ethnic history and provides ways for educators to support cultural connections between the school and the community.

**91(B).** Cuttlefish or cuttles are marine Molluscs of the Phylum- Mollusca, Class- Cephalopoda, Subclass- Coleoids, Order- Sepiida, Kingdom- Animalia.

Examples of Molluscs are squid, octopuses, colossal squid, gastropods (snails and slugs), etc. Cuttlefish are the most intelligent creatures in the ocean without backbones. It also has 8 arms like an octopus.

**92(B).** Section 8 of The Indian Forest Act 1927 deals with the Powers of Forest Settlement-officer.

Powers of Forest Settlement-officers: For the purpose of such inquiry, the Forest Settlement-officer may exercise the following powers, that is to say:

- Power to enter, by himself or any officer authorised by him for the purpose, upon any land, and to survey, demarcate and make a map of the same.
- The powers of a Civil Court in the trial of suits.

**93(A).** "Slash and burn" agriculture is a type of shifting agriculture.

Slash and burn/shifting agriculture is a type of primitive farming in which the farmer cultivates on a plot of land temporarily. When he finds the land infertile to grow due to soil exhaustion, they move on to another plot. It is largely practised in the north-eastern region of India, including Assam, Manipur, Mizoram, Nagaland, etc. This way of farming is also known as "Jhum Kheti". It is a shifting cultivation practice. It is also known as fire-fallow cultivation. Forest land is cleaned and ashes are added to the soil. Cultivated spots/ areas are usually small. Short periods of crop occupation alternate with long fallow periods. Field rotation is practised instead of crop rotation.

**94(A).** Jet Engine was invented by Sir Frank Whittle.

A jet engine is a type of reaction engine discharging a fast-moving jet that generates thrust by jet propulsion. While this broad definition can include rocket, water jet, and hybrid propulsion, the term jet engine typically refers to an internal combustion airbreathing jet engine such as a turbojet, turbofan, ramjet, or pulse jet. In general, jet engines are internal combustion engines.

Air Commodore Sir Frank Whittle, OM, KBE, CB, FRS, FRAeS (1 June 1907 – 8 August 1996) was an English engineer, inventor and Royal Air Force (RAF) air officer. He is credited with inventing the turbojet engine. A patent was submitted by Maxime Guillaume in 1921 for a similar invention; however, this was technically unfeasible at the time. Whittle's jet engines were developed some years earlier than those of Germany's Hans von Ohain, who designed the first-to-fly (but never operational) turbojet engine.

**95(C).** Dogs, tigers, and lions are able to recognize their areas by the smell of urine and stool.

Many animals use scent marking to advertise their territory. They urinate at strategic locations to communicate their social status and ownership. These markings serve to attract females and potentially warn off competitors.

- Dogs mark out their own area on the road. They can make out if another dog has come into their area by the smell of its urine or potty (stool).
- A tiger can see six times better at night than most of us. The tiger's whiskers are very sensitive and can sense the movements or vibrations in the air. A tiger's sense of hearing is so sharp that it can make out the difference between the rustling of leaves and the sound of an animal moving on the grass. The ears of the tiger can move in different directions and this helps to catch the sounds from all around. Tigers make different sounds for different purposes like when it is angry or to call out to a tigress. It can also roar or snarl. Tigers mark their area with their urine. A tiger can at once come to know if there is another tiger in its area by the smell of the urine.
- Lions have an excellent sense of sight, they can see at night. Their sense of smell is well developed. Lions mark their territories by means of scent deposits.

**96(B).** The transfer of pollen grains from the anther to the stigma of another flower of the same plant is called geitonogamy. Geitonogamy is the process of pollination between two flowers of the same plant. Honeybee helps with the pollination of sunflowers. Bats help with the pollination in banana.

The transfer of pollen grains from the anther to the stigma of a flower is called pollination. Pollens are produced by the male part of a flower called the stamen. Pistil is the female part of a flower with stigma at its top.

**97(D).** Boiled tapioca with any curry made using coconut is a preferred food of the people of Kerala. They like to eat especially two things, tapioca and coconut. Both of these foods grow in their courtyard.

**98(C).** The process in which earthworms are used to degrade organic wastes is vermicomposting.

During the vermicomposting process, earthworms play an important role in converting biodegradable organic matter into high quality manure. Earthworm gut microorganisms produce exoenzymes that help to degrade organic matter into forms of nutrients that are available for plant growth.

Hence, the correct option is (C)

**99(A).** Altitude sickness occurs due to " Changing pressure and reducing oxygen levels ".

Altitude sickness is a group of symptoms which occur when we climb to a higher altitude. Since we did not give our body the time to adapt to the changing pressure and reducing oxygen levels at the high altitudes. The symptoms of altitude sickness occur too quickly. Nevertheless, our fascinating body responds by increasing the breathing rate, which, in turn, not only, increases the oxygen levels in the blood but also changes the blood acidity levels, lung pressure, electrolyte levels, and salt balance.

**100(D).** Apart from sugarcane (most commonly Saccharum officinarum) Beta vulgaris plants is widely known in the world as a commercial source of table sugar.

Beta vulgaris is a species of flowering plant in the subfamily Betoideae of the family Amaranthaceae. Red beet (Beta vulgaris) is a swollen root, dark red–purple in color, consumed either raw as salad or further processed. Red beet gets its distinctive color due to the presence of nitrogen-containing water-soluble pigments betalains. It is widely used as a natural food colorant and labeled as E-162.

**101(A).** When coal burns in air then " Carbon dioxide " is present in very high quantities.

Carbon dioxide has the highest concentration among the greenhouse gases, the concentration ranges from 9 to 26% , another important gas methane constitutes about 4 to 9% whereas ozone constitutes about 3 to 7% .

**102(D).** The minimum furrow grade to assure surface drainage is 0.05%.

Furrow is a long, narrow irrigation trench made in the ground used for an optimal supply of water. Furrows can be level and are very similar to long narrow basins. However, a minimum grade of 0.05% is recommended so that effective drainage can occur following irrigation or excessive rainfall.

**103(C).** Plant l eaves part is called food factory.

Leaves prepare food by the process of photosynthesis. So, they are called the food factories of plants. Photosynthesis is the process by which green plants and some other organisms use sunlight to synthesize food in the form of glucose using carbon dioxide and water. Glucose is either used up by the different parts of the plant or stored in the form of starch.

**104(B).** In order to use during scarcity of water people should implement rainwater harvesting.

Rainwater harvesting helps to store the rain water and it can be used during the scarcity of water. We can use as per convince either directly or for recharging groundwater as the rain falling on the surface to flow away fast.

**105(B).** Plague is caused by Yersinia pestis.

Plague is a disease that affects humans and other mammals. It is caused by the bacterium, Yersinia pestis. Humans usually get plague after being bitten by a rodent flea that is carrying the plague bacterium or by handling an animal infected with plague.

**106(C).** National tourism includes domestic & outbound tourism.

Domestic Tourism is concerned with travelling within the country. It does not need a passport and visa or conversion of one currency into another. Domestic tourism has greater scope in countries of large dimensions such as India as compared to smaller countries. From a geographical viewpoint, domestic tourism may range from local excursion, regional trips to national level travels.

Outbound tourism comprises the activities of residents of a given country travelling to and staying in places outside their country of residence and outside their usual environment for not more than 12 consecutive months for leisure, business and other purposes.

**107(D).** Environmental Studies curriculum may lead to holistic learning of children if it is integrated, inclusive and thematic.

Learning Environmental Studies can lead to holistic learning with the following curriculum:

- Integrated curriculum: It emphasizes purposeful and relevant learning by interconnecting different themes and ignore traditional subject barriers.
- Inclusive curriculum: It refers to that content that should be accessible to as many learners as possible to fulfill their specific educational needs.
- Thematic curriculum: Its content is arranged around themes that are familiar to the children. It includes familiar area language as the medium of instruction to make them feel connected with.

**108(D).** Environmental education is important only at primary school stage, secondary school stage and undergraduate stage.

Environmental education: It includes the study of the relationship of humans with other aspects affecting their life for the development of human life. It is also known as environmental studies which include the study of different ecosystems.

- At the primary level, children must be taught through an integrated approach rather than teaching in parts. At the primary level, we shouldn't teach students the concepts in isolation.
- At the secondary level, they are taught environment through different subjects such as science and social science to make them understand the different aspects of their environment in detail in co-relation with other subjects such as science, history, civics, etc.
- At the undergraduate level, they are taught environment education as a completely isolated subject in the form of its sub-branches such as physical science, life science, social science, and environmental science. Its aim at the primary level is to make students aware of their surroundings to develop knowledge and skills about their environment.
- At the higher level, its aim is to provide knowledge and develop skills among students to conserve the natural environment and to develop the conscience to deal with the issues and problems related to the environment.

**109(C).** Work and Play is not one of the six broad themes of EVS in the present syllabus.

In the EVS syllabus of class III to V, there are six broad themes that begin with key questions in a language suitable for children's conceptual understanding.

Broad Themes of EVS:

1. Family and Friends: It encompasses four sub-themes:
- Relationships
- Work and Play
- Animals
- Plants

2. Water: It deals with the important issue of water and with the availability and storing of water.

3. Travel: This theme suggests traveling through deserts, hills, forests, or big cities. It also suggests resources to be brought into classrooms like the experiences of the children of migrating families and discussion of problems faced in starting a new life in a new city.

4. Food: it includes cooking, eating in family and about what we eat and what others eat, what animals eat, etc.

5. Shelter: It evolves into Habitat, which is subsumed in the world of the Living. It deals with the differences in urban and rural houses. It also deals with a variety of houses in different topographical regions.

6. Things we Make and Do: We humans make things not only to meet our needs but also to express ourselves in a variety of ways and to transcend our limitations. We also comprehend better when we do things ourselves.

**110(A).** The human activity, among the following, which causes maximum environmental pollution having regional and global impact, is industrialization.

Industrialization is the process by which an economy is transformed from a primarily agricultural one to one based on the manufacturing of goods. Individual manual labor is often replaced by mechanized mass production, and craftsmen are replaced by assembly lines.

The combustion of fossil fuels like coal, petroleum and other factory combustibles is a major cause of air pollution. These are generally used in power plants, manufacturing facilities (factories) and waste incinerators, as well as furnaces and other types of fuel-burning heating devices.

**111(C).** The science that deals with the relationship of various organisms with their environment is known as ecology. In this, study life processes, biodiversity of organisms, adaptations and habitats etc. In this, try to develop an understanding of these interactions at the levels of organism, population, community, biosphere and ecosystem. The subject of ecology is further divided into global ecology, landscape ecology, community ecology, population ecology, ecosystem ecology and organismal ecology.

**112(B).** One of the important pedagogical learning principle of environmental studies is " Use of environment as learning resource ".

Learning environment increases students' attention and focus, promotes meaningful learning experiences, encourages higher levels of student performance, and motivates students to practice higher-level critical thinking skills. Students who study in a positive learning environment have been shown to be more motivated, engaged, and have a higher overall learning ability.

**113(A).** EVS curriculum at primary stage has been developed to include pure science as well as social science concepts. This has been done primarily to enable a learner look at environment in a holistic manner.

A young child's world is organized not as neatly organized bodies of knowledge, but rather it is a body of integrated experience of interacting and making sense of the world around. While organizing the revised curriculum and the new textbooks the key concern has been to look at the environment as a totality and avoid approaching it in compartmentalized subjects like different streams of "science" and "social science". Therefore that concepts that are typically dealt in biology like plants, or animals that are studied in zoology, or botany, or which are at the primary stage framed in the categories of 'living and non-living, are introduced not as categories but through the child's familiar experiences and surroundings.

**114(A).** Geography subject of social science is very closely related to science.
Geography: Geography is concerned with the description and explanation of the areal differentiation of the earth's surface.It is the field of science. Geography as an integrating discipline has an interface with numerous natural and social sciences. All the sciences, whether natural or social, have one basic objective, understanding reality. Geography attempts to comprehend the associations of phenomena as related in sections of reality. Geography is essentially a science because, in its modern development, it deals with the man, his distribution, and his activities. It is more related to the social environment. All the social science disciplines, viz. sociology, political science, economics, and demography study different aspects of social reality. The branches of geography, viz. social, political, economic, and population and settlements are closely linked with these disciplines as each one of them has spatial attributes.

**115(B).** Teaching of EVS should encourage process skills, which are the core of inquiry-based, hands-on learning. Determination is not such a skill. We observe objects and events using all our five senses, and this is how we learn about the world around us. The ability to make good observations is also essential to the development of the other science process skills: communicating, classifying, measuring, inferring, and predicting.

**116(B).** Providing services includes in tertiary activities.
The tertiary sector of the economy, generally known as the service sector, is the third of the three economic sectors in the three-sector model. The others are the primary sector and the secondary sector. The tertiary sector consists of the provision of services instead of end products.

**117(B).** The basic objective of educational excursion in EVS is first hand experience to the students.
Educational excursions are powerful, positive teaching tools that help enhance the social, personal, and emotional development of all learners. The basic objective of educational excursions in EVS is to provide first-hand experience to the students by engaging them with real situations. It is the appropriate tool to engage children effectively in EVS learning due to the active participation of students in the learning process. It introduces such concepts, ideas, and hands-on experiences that can't be provided in a classroom environment. It provides opportunities to bridge the gap between the theoretical and practical aspects of learning.

**118(A).** " Addressing multicultural dimensions of diverse classrooms " is a desirable practice for an EVS teacher.
India is a multilingual, multicultural, and multireligious country and the effect of this diversity could also be seen in the classroom. So, addressing the multicultural dimensions of diverse classrooms is a desirable practice for an EVS teacher.

**119(D).** The term 'Comprehensive ' in continuous and comprehensive evaluation means " Scholastic development " and " Co-scholastic development ".
CCE or Continuous and Comprehensive Evaluation is a process of evaluating the child's development in all the school-related activities. This proposal was directed under the Right to Education Act in 2009 by the Central Board of Secondary Education of India and the state governments in India. Using CCE, teachers can diagnose learners' deficiencies using a variety of assessment activities. After completing the assessment activities, learners are given valuable feedback. The teacher guides and supports them to identify the problems.

**120(B).** Continuous and comprehensive evaluation should be adopted by all schools because i t affords teachers opportunities to test learners frequently.
Continuous and Comprehensive Evaluation (CCE) aims to evaluate the 'All aspects of the development of the child' as it ensures all-round development of students including cognitive, psychomotor, and affective domains . Other Objectives of CCE: Emphasizing continuity and regularity of assessment.

## Child Development and Pedagogy

1. Sudipta works tirelessly to help children escape the inhuman conditions she had witnessed in Uttar Pradesh. She does this because she believes it is the right thing to do even though she often finds herself in life-threatening situations when helping these children. Sudipta demonstrates which of Kohlberg's stages of moral development?
   (a) Individualism, purpose, and exchange
   (b) Social systems morality
   (c) Social contract
   (d) Universal ethical principles

2. All babies learn to turn over, crawl, stand, and then walk. They may skip a particular stage, but the order or pattern will remain the same. What development principle is this?
   (a) Development leads to integration
   (b) Development is continuous
   (c) Development follows a pattern
   (d) Individuals differ with respect to the rate of development

3. Some parents think that if they leave their children among their friends, there is strong probability for them to deviate on some wrong path. What do you think about this?
   (a) This is not correct. On the contrary, if a child does not get the company of his companions, there is more probability of his behavior to be distorted.
   (b) It is correct that if a child is left in bad company, there is more possibility of going in a wrong direction. Hence, the parents should themselves select the company.
   (c) To make the child, a part of society, he should be left in good or bad company. because he should get every type of experience in this tender age.
   (d) Socialization of the children should be in a free and natural way. There should be no intervention of the parents.

4. Hindrance in Socialization is caused by:
   (a) Religion      (b) Equality
   (c) Politics      (d) Prejudices

5. Before going to give a speech on teacher's day, Raman practices by giving speech in front of the mirror. Vygotsky described this activity as ______.
   (a) Private Speech
   (b) Distorted speech
   (c) Make-Believe Play
   (d) Ego-centric Speech

6. A teacher evaluate the students in terms of the marks scored by them in a test and their interest in the subject. Which of the following types of the evaluation was done by the teacher?
   (a) Formative
   (b) Comprehensive
   (c) Summative
   (d) Diagnostic

7. Direction: Given below are two statements, one leveled as Assertion (A) and the other leveled as Reason (R):
   Assertion (A): Mother Teresa, Mahatma Gandhi, Sarvepalli Radhakrishnan, Raja Rammohun Roy, Sri Sri Ravi Shankar, and Mata Amritanandamayee have good Interpersonal Intelligence.
   Reason (R): Intrapersonal Intelligence is the ability to understand oneself and know one's thoughts, emotions, feelings, motives, and desires, and how these influence their behavior.
   (a) Both (A) and (R) are correct and (R) is the correct explanation of (A).
   (b) Both (A) and (R) are correct, but (R) is not the correct explanation of (A).
   (c) (A) is correct, but (R) is not the correct.
   (d) (A) is not correct, but (R) is correct.

8. Theory of multiple intelligence emphasize that:
   (a) Intelligence in one domain ensures intelligence in all other domains.
   (b) There are several forms of intelligence.
   (c) There are no individual differences in intelligence.
   (d) Intelligence Quotient (IQ) can b measured only by objective tests.

9. Direction : Given below are two statements, one leveled as Assertion (A) and the other leveled as Reason (R):
   Assertion (A): A print-rich environment in a primary classroom is essential for the language development of children.
   Reason (R): Emotions play an important role in learning.
   Choose the correct option.
   (a) Both (A) and (R) are true and (R) is the correct explanation of (A).
   (b) Both (A) and (R) are true but (R) is not the correct explanation of (A).
   (c) (A) is true but (R) is false.
   (d) Both (A) and (R) are false.

10. In order to maintain gender equality in the classroom, a teacher should:
    (a) Provide the same opportunity to both the boys and girls.
    (b) Discourage the girls to take part in curricular activities.
    (c) Provide analytical work to the girls.
    (d) None of the above

11. The main objective of Continuous and Comprehensive Evaluation (CCE) is ______.
    (a) to assess the scholastic aspects of a child.
    (b) to recording the methods of learning in order to make the required improvements.
    (c) to focuses on quantitative evaluation.
    (d) to assess the achievement only.

12. Rahul, a language teacher is planning to evaluate the language proficiency of his student. He can evaluate the proficiency level of a learner from his:
    (a) Repertoire of words
    (b) Ability to construct sentences
    (c) Ability to use the language effectively
    (d) Love for poetry

13. One of the tools of Formative assessment is ______.
    (a) Conventions of writing
    (b) Reading comprehension
    (c) Project work
    (d) Grammar

14. Ruhi is shown three pencils and she observes that pencil A is longer than pencil B and pencil B is longer than pencil C. When Ruhi infers

that A is a longer pencil than C, which characteristic of Jean Piaget's cognitive development is she demonstrating?

(a) Seriation

(b) Conservation

(c) Transitive thought

(d) Hypothetico – deductive reasoning

**15. In an inclusive classroom with diverse learners, cooperative learning and peer-tutoring:**

(a) Should not be practiced and students should be segregated based on their abilities.

(b) Should be used only sometimes since it promotes comparison with classmates.

(c) Should be actively discouraged and competition should be promoted.

(d) Should be actively promoted to facilitate peer-acceptance.

**16. Choose the description that best represents diversity from among the following.**

(a) It accepts differences among people.

(b) It accepts inequality among people.

(c) It leads to discrimination among people.

(d) It leads to similarity of people.

**17. In learning disabilities, the name for mathematical disorder is:**

(a) Dyspraxia

(b) Dyslexia

(c) Dysphasia

(d) None of the above

**18. Method for identifying gifted children is:**

(a) Observation

(b) Intelligence test

(c) Personality test

(d) All of the above

**19. Out of following which is not the enrichment programme for Gifted children?**

(a) Enrichment of curriculum

(b) Grade acceleration

(c) Arrangement of special classes

(d) Special residential school

**20. Insightful theory of learning is given by:**

(a) Thorndike

(b) Gardener

(c) Kohler

(d) Hull and Tollman

**21. A student is tried to learn new knowledge in such a way that he/she is tried to modified and elaborate concepts and principles already learnt. This type of learning is known as what?**

(a) Combinational learning

(b) Subordinate learning

(c) Subordinate learning

(d) Correlative leaning

**22. Identify the sequence which correctly indicates the order for ensuring teaching-learning activities in a constructivist approach:**

(a) Explore, Explain, Engage, Extend and Evaluate

(b) Evaluate, Extend, Engage, Explain and Explore

(c) Explain, Engage, Explore, Evaluate and Extend

(d) Engage, Explore, Explain, Extend and Evaluate

**23. Which of the following step is not included in problem solving?**

(a) Accumulation of data

(b) Formulating hypothesis

(c) Verification and making generalization

(d) Responding to the stimulus

**24. Which of the following factors affect learning?**
A. Motivation of the learner
B. Maturation of the learner
C. Teaching strategies
D. Physical and emotional health of the learner

(a) A, B and C    (b) A, B, C and D

(c) A and D    (d) A and C

**25. Which of the following is teacher related factor affecting learning?**

(a) Maturation & Motivation

(b) The socio-emotional climate of the class

(c) Structure of the discipline

(d) Leadership style of teacher

**26. Primary objective of analysing errors in student's work is -**

(a) to rank students and segregate them in ability-based groups.

(b) to understand children's thinking.

(c) to reprimand students for making any kind of mistakes.

(d) to compare the efficiency of teachers at the school.

**27. Which of the following is a** hindrance in effective problem-solving?

(a) Activating the right schema

(b) Response set

(c) Identification of the real problem

(d) Application of heuristics or general problem solving strategies

**28. Nowadays there is a tendency to refer to 'wrong concepts' of children as 'alternative conceptions'. This could be attributed to__________**

(a) children's understanding being nuanced and their being passive in their own learning.

(b) recognition that children are capable of thinking and their thinking is different from that of adults.

(c) using fancy terms to describe children's errors.

(d) children being thought of as adult-like in their thinking.

**29. According to the stages of cognitive development suggested by Piaget, the earliest period is called as:**

(a) Formal operational

(b) Existential

(c) Sensori motor

(d) Verbalizer

**30. In Individual difference we find:**

(a) Variability

(b) Normality

(c) Both (A) and (B)

(d) None of the above

## Language - I: English

**Ques (31-39): Direction:** Read the passage and answer the questions that follow.

The Biden administration warned on Wednesday that a Russian invasion of Ukraine would trigger "high impact" U.S. sanctions that would surpass any previously imposed on Moscow. Secretary of State Antony Blinken, speaking in the Latvian capital of Riga after meeting with his NATO counterparts, said Russia's large-scale troop buildup on Ukraine's border and other pressure tactics resembled steps Moscow took before it invaded Ukraine in 2014 and seized the Crimean peninsula. "Now, we've seen this playbook before in 2014, when Russia last invaded Ukraine. Then as of now they significantly increased combat forces along the border. Then as now, they intensified disinformation to paint Ukraine as the aggressor to justify pre-planned military action," Blinken said. But it remained unclear if Russian President Vladimir Putin planned to order an invasion, Blinken told reporters.

"Now, we don't know whether President Putin has made the decision to invade," he said. "We do know that he's putting in place the capacity to do so in short order should he so decide. So despite uncertainty about intentions, and time, we must prepare for all contingencies while working to see to it that Russia reverses course." CIA Director William Burns recently travelled to Moscow to convey Washington's concerns, to urge a return to diplomacy to resolve the conflict between Russian-backed separatists and the Ukraine government, and to make clear "the severe consequences should Russia follow the path of confrontation in military action," Blinken said.

"We've made it clear to the Kremlin that we will respond resolutely, including with a range of high impact economic measures that we have refrained from pursuing in the past," Blinken said. Russia has deployed tens of thousands of combat troops on Ukraine's border but has denied any aggressive plans toward Ukraine, saying it is only responding to what it calls provocative actions by Ukraine and NATO countries. Blinken said the U.S. is urging Russia to reverse its troop buildup, pull back heavy weapons and recommit to the diplomatic process set up to resolve the conflict in eastern Ukraine.

"That's how we can turn back from a crisis that will have far-reaching and long-lasting consequences for our bilateral relations with Moscow, for Russia's relations with Europe, and for international peace and security," Blinken said. NATO Secretary-General Jens Stoltenberg said earlier that Russia would face serious political and economic consequences if it invades Ukraine.

**31. The U.S. is urging Russia to reverse its troop buildup because:**
(a) They want to support a crisis that will have far-reaching and long-lasting consequences.
(b) They want to publish a crisis that will have far-reaching and long-lasting consequences.
(c) They want to avoid a crisis that will have far-reaching and long-lasting consequences.
(d) They want to demonstrate a crisis that will have far-reaching and long-lasting consequences.

**32. Which one of the following words is most similar in meaning to the word 'peace' as used in the passage (Para 4)?**
(a) Discord      (b) Conflict
(c) Tranquillity      (d) Hostility

**33. What would trigger "high impact" U.S. sanctions that would surpass any previously imposed on Moscow?**
(a) Ukrainian invasion of Russia
(b) Russian invasion of the U.S.
(c) Russian invasion of Ukraine
(d) Ukrainian invasion of the U.S.

**34. Russia has denied:**
(a) any aggressive plans toward Ukraine
(b) any aggressive plans toward U.K.
(c) any aggressive plans toward U.S.
(d) any aggressive plans toward Moscow

**35. Which part of speech is the underlined word in the following sentence?**
**Russia has deployed tens of thousands of combat <u>troops</u> on Ukraine's border.**
(a) Adverb      (b) Verb
(c) Adjective      (d) Noun

**36. Blinken said they will respond resolutely including with:**
(a) A range of high impact cognitive measures
(b) A range of high impact economic measures
(c) A range of high impact social measures
(d) A range of high impact political measures

**37. Read the following sentences.**
**A. According to Blinken, it is definite that President Putin has made the decision to invade.**
**B. Jens Stoltenberg said that Russia would face serious political and economic consequences if it invades Ukraine.**
(a) A is true, B is false.
(b) B is true, A is false.
(c) Both A and B are true.
(d) Both A and B are false.

**38. Which one of the following words is the most opposite in meaning to the word 'invaded' as used in the passage (Para 1)?**
(a) Conquered      (b) Liberated
(c) Captured      (d) Annexed

**39. Which one of the following words is most similar in meaning to the word ' consequences ' as used in the passage (Para 2)?**
(a) Result
(b) Consideration
(c) Determinant
(d) Factor

**Ques (40-45): Directions: Read the poem and answer the questions that follow.**
The Snow Fairy
BY CLAUDE MCKAY
Throughout the afternoon I watched them there,
Snow-fairies falling, falling from the sky,
Whirling fantastic in the misty air,
Contending fierce for space supremacy.
And they flew down a mightier force at night,
As though in heaven there was revolt and riot,
And they, frail things had taken panic flight
Down to the calm earth seeking peace and quiet.
I went to bed and rose at early dawn
To see them huddled together in a heap,
Each merged into the other upon the lawn,
Worn out by the sharp struggle, fast asleep.
The sun shone brightly on them half the day,
By night they stealthily had stol'n away.

**40. The snow-fairies had come to the earth for:**
(a) playing
(b) dancing
(c) peace and quietness
(d) hiding

**41. Name the figure of speech used in 'Snow-fairies falling, falling from':**
(a) Personification
(b) Alliteration
(c) Simile
(d) Metaphor

**42. The expression 'snow-fairies falling' refers to:**
(a) fairies of snow falling down
(b) the snowfall
(c) angels descending from heaven
(d) a thunderstorm

**43. Which literary device is being used in 'And they, frail things had taken panic flight'?**
(a) Enjambment
(b) Synecdoche
(c) Personification
(d) Simile

**44. Which of the following statements is <u>NOT</u> true?**
**The poet watched the snow-fairies falling**
(a) Throughout the afternoon.
(b) Whirling fantastic in the misty air
(c) Contending fierce for space supremacy

(d) And they flew down a mightier force the next morning

**45. Which of the adjectives does not apply to the snow-fairies?**
(a) White          (b) Fierce
(c) Frail          (d) Warm

**46. In which of the following learning skills, action and meaning formation are possible simultaneously?**
(a) Reading-reading
(b) Writing-reading
(c) Listening-writing
(d) Reading-listening

**47. Discussion-debate have special importance in building various skills. Points to be noted during the discussion-debate are:**
(a) The topic of discussion should be related to the experience and environment
(b) Instead of asking yes or no questions, children have opportunities to speak
(c) Listen carefully to the children
(d) All of the above

**48. Ideal reading has special importance in bringing accuracy in pronunciation. Whose views does this statement correspond to?**
(a) Skinner          (b) Vygotsky
(c) Chamsky          (d) Jean Piaget

**49. At the primary stage, a child uses mother tongue words while speaking. As a language teacher you will:**
(a) Hit the child immediately
(b) You forbid him from doing so
(c) Accept mother tongue words
(d) Will force him to use Hindi words

**50. The best way to assess listening and writing skills is to:**
(a) Listening to poetry and writing answers to questions
(b) Write the story you heard in your own words
(c) Write the story you heard verbatim
(d) Poetry listening and writing verbatim

**51. "The planet Venus is also called the 'morning star' and the 'evening-star'." How would it be appropriate to explain to a child the different meanings of the usages of these three from the point of view of the eclipse?**

(a) For contextually only
(b) For perception only
(c) Both contextually and perception
(d) None of these

**52. What is it called a person who gives accurate knowledge of written and oral forms of a language?**
(a) Ethology          (b) Art
(c) Grammer          (d) Skills

**53. What is the fundamental process that includes planning, implementation and evaluation?**
(a) Computing     (b) Access
(c) Teaching       (d) Considerate

**54. At what age a child is well acquainted with the basic structure of language and can communicate well?**
(a) Seven          (b) Three
(c) Five           (d) Six

**55. The skills required for a teacher to implement inclusion in the classroom are:**
(a) the skill to recognize the need of the child.
(b) Knowledge of language skills
(c) Correct pronunciation
(d) Thorough knowledge of the subject

**56. There are four language skills. Just as it is important to organize ideas in writing and give form to writing, in the same way it is important to make _______ in reading skills.**
(a) Character recognition
(b) Pronunciation of words
(c) Fast reading
(d) Meaning and inference

**57. Rhythmic words, last-letter-first dictation and pictorial story writing are innovative methods of learning in which of the following?**
(a) Reading          (b) Writing
(c) Recitation       (d) Listening

**58. How will you as a language teacher involve the visually impaired child in the non-availability of Braille books?**
(a) will teach them with special sympathy
(b) Will wait for material to be available in Braille
(c) You will not involve the child in the activity
(d) Will expand the description of the text by reading it in slow motion

**59. Audio-visual aids make learning:**
(a) Easy
(b) Interesting
(c) Effective
(d) All of the above

**60. The word growth purely represents which sense of the person?**
(a) General          (b) Political
(c) Logical          (d) Physical

**Mathematics**

**61. If $A$ is $26°$ more than its complementary angle and $B$ is $30°$ less than its supplementary angle, then find the value of $(A - B)$.**
(a) $17°$          (b) $-17°$
(c) $-15°$         (d) $15°$

**62. If the angles, in degrees, of a triangle, are $x, 3x + 20$ and $6x$, the triangle must be:**
(a) Acute          (b) Right
(c) Isosceles      (d) Obtuse

**63. Two cubes each of volume $729$ cm$^3$ are joined end to end. The total surface area of the resulting cuboid is:**
(a) $841$ cm$^2$          (b) $729$ cm$^2$
(c) $810$ cm$^2$          (d) $720$ cm$^2$

**64. Find the volume of cube whose edge is $5\ m$.**
(a) $128 m^3$          (b) $75\ m^3$
(c) $125 m^3$          (d) $225\ m^3$

**65. If we add two irrational numbers the resulting number:**
(a) Is always an rational number
(b) Is always an irrational number
(c) May be a rational or an irrational number
(d) Always an integer

**66. The cube root of $2197$ is:**
(a) $23$          (b) $17$
(c) $19$          (d) $13$

**67. Match the following:**

| List - I | List - II |
| --- | --- |
| (a) Cuboid | (i) Square |
| (b) Cube | (ii) Circle |
| (c) Sphere | (iii) Triangle |
| (d) Cone | (iv) Rectangle |

(a) (a) - (i), (b) - (iv), (c) - (iii), (d) - (ii)
(b) (a) - (iv), (b) - (i), (c) - (ii), (d) - (iii)
(c) (a) - (iii), (b) - (i), (c) - (iv), (d) - (ii)

(d)  (a) - (ii), (b) - (iii), (c) - (i), (d) - (iv)

68.  What is the value of $12\frac{1}{2} + 12\frac{1}{3} + 12\frac{1}{6}$?

(a)  36          (b)  37

(c)  39          (d)  38

69.  A rectangular playground of length 125 m and width 75 m, has a walking strip of width 5 m in the middle of the ground and parallel to shorter side. What is the area of the ground without the walking strip?

(a)  9375 sq.m     (b)  9000 sq.m

(c)  9750 sq.m     (d)  8625 sq.m

70.  Choose the incorrect conversion from the following.

(a)  1 tonne $= 100$ kg

(b)  1000 mg $= 1$ g

(c)  1 g $= 10^{-3}$ kg

(d)  1 mg $= 1000$ kg

71.  Shaurya said his brother, "I was as old as you are at present at the time of your birth. "If the Shaurya age is 38 now, the brother age 5 years back was:

(a)  31          (b)  13

(c)  21          (d)  14

72.  Which of the following is true?

(a)  $\frac{9}{16} < \frac{13}{24}$     (b)  $\frac{9}{16} = \frac{13}{24}$

(c)  $\frac{9}{16} > \frac{13}{24}$     (d)  $\frac{9}{16} \leq \frac{13}{24}$

73.  Bincy reads a newspaper daily for approximately 3 hours. She took 2 hours and 55 minutes to read the newspaper today. How many seconds did she read this newspaper?

(a)  10200        (b)  10500

(c)  10800        (d)  10850

74.  Direction : What should come in place of the question mark ' ? ' in the following number series?
$9, 19, 40, 83, ?, 345, 696$

(a)  162          (b)  170

(c)  175          (d)  166

75.  Direction:  In the following alphanumeric series, one term is missing as shown by the question mark (?). Select the missing term from the given options.
$5E, 7F, 11H, 17K, ?$

(a)  $25P$         (b)  $20Q$

(c)  $30J$         (d)  $25O$

76.  A car travels some distance at a speed of 8 km/hr and returns at a speed of 12 km/hr. If the total time taken by the car is 15 hours, then what is the distance (in km)?

(a)  48          (b)  60

(c)  56          (d)  72

77.  Which one of the following is an important characteristic of a good mathematics textbook at primary level?

(a)  concepts should be introduced through contexts

(b)  It should only contain numerous exercises to give rigorous practice

(c)  It should be attractive and colorful

(d)  It must be thick and large

78.  Which of the following should be avoided in a good mathematics textbook?

(a)  linking the mathematics that students do (in their textbooks) to the mathematics they see and experience all around

(b)  Introducing concepts through situations of life in which they are placed

(c)  beginning concept formation with definitions and mathematical terminology

(d)  arriving at concepts and ideas by observing patterns, exploring them, and providing children opportunities to define them in their own words

79.  Who said that "Mathematics is the science that draws necessary conclusions"?

(a)  Hogben

(b)  Benjamin Peirce

(c)  Locke

(d)  None of them

80.  Which of the following statements is/are true regarding teaching 'Numbers' at the primary level?
A.  Intuitive understanding of numbers should be encouraged.
B.  Writing numbers should be taught in a sequence.
C.  Writing of numbers as Numerals should proceed to count.
D.  Order irrelevance of numbers should be encouraged.

(a)  B and C        (b)  A and D

(c)  C and D        (d)  A and B

81.  Identify the correct statement with respect to the mathematics curriculum.

(a)  The concept of fractions should be introduced only at upper primary level.

(b)  The concept of negative numbers should be introduced at the primary level for better understanding.

(c)  The concept of area-measurement should be introduced only at upper primary level.

(d)  The foundation of algebraic thinking can be laid at primary level.

82.  Who is regarded as the father of Demonstrative Geometry?

(a)  Euclid

(b)  P. Samuel

(c)  Cunning Ham

(d)  Bertrand Russel

83.  Displaying sentence strips in the classroom throughout the school year to provide continual reminders of key vocabulary in mathematics teaching is known as:

(a)  Labelling

(b)  Word wall

(c)  Construction

(d)  Diagramming

84.  In order to monitor students' progress and to modify teaching accordingly, the best method of evaluation is:

(a)  Formative evaluation

(b)  Summative evaluation

(c)  Qualitative evaluation

(d)  Objective-based evaluation

85.  The purpose of formative evaluation is to:

(a)  Monitor progress and plan remedial instruction

(b)  Know the understanding of students

(c)  Know that teacher's objectives are fulfilled

(d)  Assign grades

86.  Which of the following teaching-learning resources in mathematics cannot be used for visually challenged students?

(a)  Tiles

(b)  GeoBoard

(c)  GeoGebra

(d)  Taylor's abacus

87.  __________ are accepted as essential part of the mathematics learning process.

(a)  Errors        (b)  Numbers

(c)  Calculations  (d)  Theories

88.  If a learner is having problem with numbers and calculations, he may be having disability known as:

(a) Dysgraphia

(b) Dyslexia

(c) Dyscalculia

(d) Visual-spatial organization disability

89. **How will you cater to the needs of visually challenged students of your classroom in an inclusive school?**

(a) Use alternate teaching-learning methods and resources.

(b) Send them to special educator.

(c) Provide them extra time for practice.

(d) Make them sit with high achievers.

90. **Remedial teaching is used for which kind of children?**

(a) Fast learners

(b) Slow learneres

(c) Gifted children

(d) Creative learners

## Environmental Studies

91. **The bodies of penguins are ______ and their feet have webs, making them good swimmers.**

(a) heavy          (b) feathery

(c) streamlined  (d) oily

92. **Rice is a Kharif crop that requires high temperature (above 25°C) and high humidity with annual rainfall above ____.**

(a) 100 cm        (b) 200 cm

(c) 150 cm        (d) 50 cm

93. **'Artemis 1' is the flagship program of which space agency?**

(a) ISRO          (b) NASA

(c) ESA           (d) JAXA

94. **Which of the following plants is carnivorous?**

(a) Cypress Vine

(b) Pink turasawa

(c) Venus Flytrap

(d) Amaryllis

95. **A flower with both male and female reproductive parts is called a______.**

(a) Bisexual flower

(b) Pistillate flower

(c) Staminate flower

(d) Unisexual flower

96. **Select from the following a group of eatables each member of which is rich in iron.**

(a) Amla, Spinach, Jaggery

(b) Amla, Cabbage, Tomato

(c) Cabbage, Amla, Spinach

(d) Jaggery, Amla, Tomato

97. **Choose the incorrect pair from the following.**

(a) Vermicompost → earthworms

(b) Farm compost → farm waste

(c) Farmyard manure → Cattle dung, urine and litter

(d) Green manures → Chemical compound

98. **Which of the following part of cinchona tree is used to treat malaria ?**

(a) Root          (b) Bark

(c) Leaves        (d) Seed

99. **What is the chemical name for Vitamin B7?**

(a) Panotothenic Acid

(b) Cobalamin

(c) Biotin

(d) Folic Acid

100. **Burning of fossil fuels is the main cause of:**

(a) Nitrogen oxide pollution

(b) Nitrous oxide pollution

(c) Nitric oxide pollution

(d) Both (A) and (C)

101. **Water for irrigation supplied as per crop requirement throughout the crop period / year is called:**

(a) Perennial irrigation

(b) Lift irrigation

(c) Drip irrigation

(d) Inundation irrigation

102. **How many methods of rainwater harvesting are there?**

(a) One            (b) Two

(c) Three          (d) Four

103. **What vector is used to transmit encephalitis and yellow fever to humans?**

(a) Ticks          (b) Sandflies

(c) Mosquitoes    (d) Rodents

104. **Which section of The Indian Forest Act 1927 deals with the Extinction of rights?**

(a) Section 7 of The Indian Forest Act 1927

(b) Section 9 of The Indian Forest Act 1927

(c) Section 4 of The Indian Forest Act 1927

(d) Section 5 of The Indian Forest Act 1927

105. **Nutrients which are present in**

plant tissues in large quantities are known as ______.

(a) essential element

(b) macronutrients

(c) micronutrients

(d) non-essential elements

106. **When a visitor travels in his country of residence, he is a ______visitor.**

(a) Domestic

(b) International

(c) Inbound

(d) Out bound

107. **Environmental studies is defined as the branch that deals with the:**

(a) Design, study, and discovery of new materials.

(b) The study of humanities, social, biological, and physical sciences.

(c) Incorporate the information and physical sciences.

(d) Approach about the natural world and the impact of humans on its integrity.

108. **According to NEP, what is the main reason for including environmental science as an integral part of education?**

(a) Making students aware of their environment.

(b) Making students aware of environmental issues.

(c) Preparing students for future environmental hazards.

(d) To teach students the value of protection and conservation of the environment.

109. **Which of the following is a broad theme of EVS in the present syllabus?**

(a) Relationships

(b) Plants

(c) Family and friends

(d) work and play

110. **Chipko Movement was strengthened under the leadership of:**

(a) A.K. Banerjee

(b) Sunder Lal Bahuguna

(c) Amrita Devi Bishnoi

(d) Medha Patkar

111. **Direction: The underlying purpose of environmental education is to:**
A. Adjust to environmental challenges
B. Help face environmental hazards

C. Promote individual's critical-thinking about emerging issues
D. Increase public awareness and knowledge of environmental issues.
E. Enhance problem-solving and decision-making skills in respect of handling environmental issues.
Choose the correct answer from the options given below:

(a) A, B, C only    (b) B, C, D only
(c) C, D, E only    (d) D, E, A only

**112.** Which of the following is an example of a psychological trait?

(a) Anxiety enduring for months or years

(b) Anxiety over just seeing a spider

(c) Shyness when meeting a stranger for the first time

(d) Depression caused by the loss of a ball game

**113.** What is the nomenclature change suggested by the National Curriculum Framework (NCF), 2005 for Civics?

(a) Geography

(b) History

(c) Social and Political Life

(d) Economics

**114.** Mr Raj is highlighting the relevance of social science to his elementary school students.
A. 'It would enable you to develop analytical skills.'
B. 'An inter-dependent world required you to adjust and appreciate various cultures'
C. 'You have to be equipped with contemporary realities'
Choose the statements that is/are appropriate for the topic of his discussion.

(a) Only A and B    (b) Only B and C
(c) Only A and C    (d) A, B and C

**115.** The idea of showing a sample of air ticket to child is to:

(a) provide information regarding fare

(b) enhance the skills of student to arrive at conclusion

(c) provide the knowledge about different things listed on the ticket

(d) provide an opportunity to interact with the real information and develop the skill of observation

**116.** Which one of the following is not a suitable activity at primary stage to sensitise students to the concepts of conservation of trees?

(a) organizing a slogan-writing competition on trees

(b) encouraging every student to adopt a tree and look after it

(c) showing children storage of logs of wood

(d) organizing a poster-making competition on trees

**117.** A teacher gives pictures of different animals to his students and asks them to color the animals that do not live in their houses. The objective of this activity is to develop:
A. Creativity
B. Observation
C. Classification skill
D. Data collection
Which of the above are correct?

(a) A, C and D    (b) A, B and C
(c) A, B and D    (d) B, C and D

**118.** Which of the following is true w.r.t. EVS ?

(a) EVS is a subject taught from classes I to V.

(b) For classes I and II, EVS is taught through language and Mathematics.

(c) For classes II, III and IV, issues and concerns of EVS are taught through language and Mathematics.

(d) For classes I and II, concerns and issues of EVS are taught through Science and Social science.

**119.** Which of the following method of assessment includes both formative and summative tests?

(a) Computer based test

(b) Placement evaluation

(c) Continuous and Comprehensive Evaluation

(d) Term end test

**120.** Which of the following is/are important in constructing knowledge in EVS by the children?
A. Active participation of children.
B. Community members of children
C. Text books of EVS
D. Description and definition given in the textbook of EVS

(a) A, B and C    (b) A and C only
(c) A, C and D    (d) C only

---

### // Hints and Solutions //

**1(D).** Sudipta demonstrates the Universal ethical principles stage of moral development. Because she believes it is the right thing to do even though she often finds herself in life-threatening situations when helping these children.

Lawrence Kohlberg, an American psychologist, has propounded the 'Theory of Moral Development'. He has made a systematic study of moral development in his theory that is categorized into 3 levels and 6 stages.

Level (1): Pre-moral stage/Pre-conventional Morality:
- Stage 1: The Obedience & Punishment Orientation - behaviour driven by avoiding punishment.
- Stage 2: Individualism & exchange orientation- behaviour driven by self-interest and rewards.

Level (2): Conventional Morality:
- Stage 3: Interpersonal concordance orientation/Good Boy - Nice Girl Orientation - behaviour driven by social approval.
- Stage 4: The Law & Order Orientation: behaviour driven by obeying authority and conforming to social order.

Level (3): Post-conventional Morality:
- Stage 5: Social contract legalistic orientation: behaviour driven by a balance of social order and individual rights.
- Stage 6: The Universal Ethical Principle Orientation: behaviour driven by internal moral principle.

**2(C).** All babies learn to turn over, crawl, stand, and then walk. They may skip a particular stage, but the order or pattern will remain the same. This development principle follows a pattern.

Development is a process by which an individual grows and changes throughout its life span. This change may be defined as a progressive series of changes that are orderly and coherent and which lead towards the goal of maturity. Although all individuals grow and develop in their own unique way and in their own contexts, some basic principles underlie the process of development and can be observed in all human beings. These are called the principles of development.

The development follows a pattern: In human beings, development takes place in an organised, orderly and patterned fashion. Every species has a specific pattern that all its members follow. The sequence of development is also the same. For example, all babies learn to turn over, crawl, stand, and then walk. They may skip a particular stage, but the order or pattern will remain the same.

**3(A).** "Some parents think that if they leave their children among their friends, there is a strong probability for them to deviate on some wrong path." This is not correct. On the contrary, if a child does not get the company of his companions, there is more probability of his behavior to be distorted.

Friends are important for the emotional and moral growth of children. It comes under the part 'Socialization' which helps children to manage their emotions, feelings, needs, understanding others, and communicating with others in a respectful and mature way. So, interaction with friends or peer groups helps in the overall development of the child. It also helps in developing social skills like cooperation, interaction, and many more.

**4(D).** Hindrance in Socialization is caused by prejudices.

Socialization is the process through which communities transact or educate their members about the norms and values of society to be socially acceptable. Hindrance in Socialization is caused by Prejudices as:

- Prejudice refers to a negative attitude or unreasonable opinion for a specific group of people.
- It is a preconceived opinion that is not based on concrete experience or reality.
- The already held negative attitudes can't let the individual understand the societal norms, values, and beliefs.
- For example, a negative attitude against someone just because of gender, race, religion, or beliefs.

**5(A).** Before going to give a speech on teacher's day, Raman practices by giving speech in front of the mirror. Vygotsky described this activity as private speech.

In Vygotsky theory of Socio-Cultural Development, he states that the skills children learn first are related to interactions with others and they then take that information and use it within themselves. In his theory, Vygotsky mentioned three key areas:

Private Speech: It takes place when children talk to themselves. Children spoke to themselves as a way of guiding themselves through action.

Zone of Proximal Development: It is the gap between the actual developmental level of a person as determined by independent problem solving, and the levels of potential development as determined through problem-solving under adult guidance or in collaboration with more capable peers. It also includes scaffolding.

**6(B).** A teacher evaluate the students in terms of the marks scored by them in a test and their interest in the subject. In this "Comprehensive" evaluation was done by the teacher.

Evaluation is done to assess or evaluate someone's performance in a specified field. It is a component of assessment in education.

Comprehensive evaluation:

- The comprehensive evaluation involves the assessment of the all-round development of a student's personality.

It evaluates the development of students in two areas – scholastic and co-scholastic.

- The activities based on core subjects taught at the schools constitute scholastic areas and other co-curricular activities comprise co-scholastic areas. The term "scholastic" refers to those aspects which are related to the intellectual exercise of the students in curricular subjects. They include assignments, practicals, projects, and different types of tests conducted in schools.
- The components of assessment covered under co-scholastic areas are life skill development of students, their attitudes, self-concept, personality, emotional intelligence, etc. It also involves developments in the areas of art, crafts, health, physical education, yoga, and peace education, etc.
- For example, scores or grades in Mathematics represent the scholastic competency and attitude towards the subject, interest in the subject represents co-scholastic competency. Both the aspects are interrelated and are in line with the goals of education.

**7(B).** For the assertion "Mother Teresa, Mahatma Gandhi, Sarvepalli Radhakrishnan, Raja Rammohun Roy, Sri Sri Ravi Shankar, and Mata Amritanandamayee have good Interpersonal Intelligence" the correct reasoning would be Interpersonal Intelligence refers to the ability to understand others and social interactions.

Interpersonal Intelligence refers to the ability to understand others and social interactions. They can understand the emotions and the perspectives of others and relate well to others. They are able to establish good interpersonal relationships with others. They have good and effective communication skills. They also show sensitivity and empathic understanding towards others. People with high interpersonal intelligence tend to be social workers, managers, psychologists, nurses, counselors, politicians, leaders, teachers, reformers, and spiritual gurus. Some examples of such people are Mother Teresa, Mahatma Gandhi, Sarvepalli Radhakrishnan, Raja Rammohun Roy, Sri Sri Ravi Shankar, and Mata Amritanandamayee.

Intrapersonal Intelligence is the ability to understand oneself and know one's thoughts, emotions, feelings, motives, and desires, and how these influence their behavior. It includes awareness about one's strengths, limitations, goals, and ambitions in life. Such intelligence includes one's introspective and self-reflective capacities. Such people are usually introverted, intuitive type, love to work alone, and are least affected by any external events.

Various people-oriented careers require intrapersonal intelligence, e.g., psychologists and spiritual leaders like Swami Vivekananda, Ramakrishna Paramahansa, and Sri Aurobindo. Philosophers and writers also have strong intrapersonal intelligence

**8(B).** Theory of multiple intelligence emphasize that there are several forms of intelligence.

The 'Theory of Multiple Intelligence' or 'Multidimensional Intelligence Theory' was propounded by an American psychologist 'Howard Gardner' in his book 'Frames of Mind'. This theory describes eight different kinds of intelligence and emphasizes that:

- Intelligence is of several kinds.
- Intelligence can't be tied to a single domain.
- Each individual has his/her own unique abilities.
- Intelligence is not dominated by a general factor.

**9(B).** Both statements, A print-rich environment in a primary classroom is essential for the language development of children and Emotions play an important role in learning are separate from each other.

(A) The print-rich environment in the classroom: A print-rich environment is one where young children get many different opportunities to interact with many different forms of print. That is, in order to be truly print-rich, a classroom needs to display and use print meaningfully during teaching and learning. This exploration of print in meaningful contexts and observing adults around the use of print is critical for literacy development because it shows children that print carries meaning and that reading and writing serve real, everyday purposes. Over time, children become motivated to try to read and write themselves and they can develop language. "A print-rich environment is one in which "children interact with many forms of print, including signs, labeled centers, wall stories, word displays, labeled murals, bulletin boards, charts, poems, and other printed materials. A print-rich environment in a primary classroom is essential for the language development of children.

(B) Emotions play an important role in learning: Emotions impact learning in four ways. They impact our levels of motivation (motivational impact).

Positive emotions can help a student engage with learning longer because they stay motivated. Emotions during learning also impact our feelings toward education (psychological impact). If we have positive experiences, we are more likely to enjoy our schooling and develop a love of learning. Emotions can also make group work run much more smoothly (social impact). However, we need to keep in mind that learning sometimes requires confusion and frustration when we are learning difficult but necessary concepts (cognitive impact).

**10(A).** In order to maintain gender equality in the classroom, a teacher should provide the same opportunity to both the boys and girls.

Gender equality is when people of all genders have equal rights, responsibilities, and opportunities. Everyone is affected by gender inequality - women, men, trans, and gender diverse people, children, and families. Societies that value women and men as equal are safer and healthier. Gender equality is a human right.

As young children begin to notice the differences in social expectations for gender roles, the ways teachers interact with students stand to have a great impact on their ability to participate in their education. These interactions also create long-lasting effects in other areas of their lives, at times limiting their self-image and their perception of the opportunities that are available or appropriate for them. Following are a few ways by which a teacher should be able to maintain gender equality in the classroom:

- Be reflective and objective.
- Use gender-neutral language when appropriate.
- Use project-based learning.
- Provide equal opportunity to both boys and girls.
- Seat and group students intentionally.

**11(B).** The main objective of Continuous and Comprehensive Evaluation (CCE) is to recording the methods of learning in order to make the required improvements.

Continuous and Comprehensive Evaluation, commonly know as 'CCE' has been introduced as a school-based system of evaluation by the CBSE in 2009 with the enactment of the Right to Education Act. The main objective of Continuous and Comprehensive Evaluation (CCE) is to lay emphasis on the thought process and de-emphasize memorization as CCE includes all aspects of students' development. Other objectives of CCE:

- Emphasizing continuity and regularity of assessment.
- Assessing both scholastic and co-scholastic aspects of a child's growth.
- Focusing on both quantitative and qualitative academic growth of the students.
- Recording the methods of learning in order to make the required improvements.
- Making evaluation an integral part of learning through diagnostic and remedial teaching.
- Ensuring all-around development of students including cognitive, psychomotor, and affective domains.

**12(C).** Rahul, a language teacher is planning to evaluate the language proficiency of his student. He can evaluate the proficiency level of a learner from his ability to use the language effectively.

Evaluation is a systematic way to assess learner's abilities, analyze performance, provide appropriate feedback to each learner and help them to progress. It is one of the crucial components of the teaching-learning process. In the above-mentioned situation, the teacher can evaluate the proficiency level of a learner from his ability to use the language effectively as:

- To achieve proficiency in a language, one must be able to use the basic skills of any language and be a good communicator in it.
- L anguage proficiency means that an individual must be skillful to use the four basic skills of a language that are listening, speaking, reading, and writing.
- When we will evaluate the language proficiency of an individual then his level of acquired vocabulary can be tested from it.
- T he different types of words he uses, the way of his speaking, reading, and writing are enough to tell us about his level of language proficiency.
- T he evaluation of language must include the proficiency of an individual in that specific language that is he must be able to use the language smoothly and effectively.

**13(C).** One of the tools of Formative assessment is project work.

Formative assessment is also known as assessment for learning, used to evaluate student learning progress and achievement. It helps teachers to identify problem-facing areas and to understand the learning needs of students to ensure their academic growth. It is considered an Informal Method of assessment as it can be conducted at any time or during teaching also.

Project work, oral testing, anecdotal records, portfolios, class test, etc. are the tools of formative assessment. Projects refer to a series of task that needs to be done by a group of students in order to achieve a particular goal. Projects are purpose-oriented and provide a rich experience to the pupils.

**14(C).** Ruhi is shown three pencils and she observes that pencil A is longer than pencil B and pencil B is longer than pencil C. When Ruhi infers that A is a longer pencil than C, then Ruhi is demonstrating the transitive thought characteristic of Jean Piaget's cognitive development.

According to Piaget, cognitive development takes place at different rates at different stages of development. When Piaget talks about cognition, he means the mental process which can systematize, organize and utilize knowledge.

Transitive thought: In Piaget's theory of cognitive development, the third stage is called the Concrete Operational Stage. During this stage, the child shows increased use of logic or reasoning. One of the important processes that develop is that of transitivity, which refers to the ability to recognize relationships among various things in a serial order. For example, when a child is told to put away his books according to height, the child recognizes that he starts with placing the tallest one on one end of the bookshelf and the shortest one ends up at the other end.

Example: Ruhi is shown three pencils and she observes that pencil A is longer than pencil B and pencil B is longer than pencil C. So, she is showing the ability of transitive thought.

**15(D).** In an inclusive classroom with diverse learners, cooperative learning and peer-tutoring should be actively promoted to facilitate peer-acceptance.

Inclusive classroom refers to an education system that includes children regardless of physical, intellectual, social, linguistic, or other differently-abled conditions. In an inclusive classroom with diverse learners, cooperative learning and peer-tutoring should be actively promoted to facilitate peer-acceptance.

- Cooperative learning: It refers to a heterogeneous group where students work collaboratively to achieve learning outcomes. It develops critical thinking, brainstorming, communication, and life long learning skills.
- Peer tutoring: It refers to the learning process where fellow students teach each other. In this strategy, a higher-performing student is paired with a lower performing student to teach specific skills.

An inclusive classroom is not limited to children with a disability but also gifted children, economically disadvantaged children, children from remote populations, children belonging to ethnic, linguistic, or cultural minorities or children from other marginalized groups.

**16(A).** The statement, "It accepts differences among people" best represents diversity.

Diversity means that each individual is unique having individual differences. These differences may be because of personal qualities, physical features, social or economic background or cultural factors. India has always been a country with diversity. People belonging to different religions, cultural backgrounds, caste and regions have been living here in harmony for several centuries. People come from various backgrounds which are cultural, religious, and from regional backgrounds.

**17(D).** Learning disabilities, the name for mathematical disorder is 'Dyscalculia'.
Learning disability refers to a neurological disorder that causes cognitive impairment. Dyslexia, dysgraphia, dyscalculia, etc. are the most common learning disability.
'Dyscalculia' is a type of mathematics-related learning disability which:
- Hinders learner's basic understanding of numbers.
- Affects learner's ability to perform mathematical calculations.
- Makes learners unable in identifying mathematical symbols like +, x, >, etc.

**18(D).** A gifted child is the one who displays consistently remarkable performance in various physical or cognitive aspects and exhibits superiority in general intelligence levels. There are different kinds of method to identify gifted children some of them includes:
- Observation: Observation refers to the act of observing something carefully. It is used to identify gifted children by observing them while asking, drawing, discussing, and behaving individually as well as in groups.
- Intelligence test: Intelligence test is a test designed to determine the relative mental capacity of a person. It identifies gifted children by measuring their intelligence.
- Personality test: These tests are designed to reveal those central aspects of the personality of gifted children that lie in the unconscious mind of an individual.

**19(D).** 'Special residential school' is not an enrichment program for Gifted children.
Special Residential School refers to the school which cares for the most vulnerable children of society. It facilitates children with complex special education need or disabilities. Exceptional children are those who deviate from the normal population and need special education services to meet their needs. It includes children who are gifted, backward, creative, learning disabled, etc.
A gifted child is the one who displays consistently remarkable performance in various physical or cognitive aspects and exhibits superiority in general intelligence levels. Enrichment program for Gifted children includes:
- Grade acceleration: It refers to advancing gifted students to more challenging and higher-level classes in a shorter amount of time than usual.
- Enrichment of curriculum: It refers to include programs that are designed to give students the opportunity to try new things and explore and develop interests outside of the classroom.
- Arrangement of special classes: It refers to the 'Congregated Gifted Classes' which congregate gifted students together to receive specialized instruction and training.

**20(C).** The insightful theory of learning was given by Kohler.
According to Kohler, insight doesn't take place with trial & error, rather than it is a sudden reorganization of experience. 'Insightful Theory of learning' implies that:
- The solution to a problem arrives 'all of a sudden' flash of insight when a person is struggling.
- Insight enhances an individual's ability to perceive and understand something or someone instinctively.
- Insight doesn't rely on behavior or observation, it is the sudden realization of a problem's solution using intuition.

**21(A).** A student is tried to learn new knowledge in such a way that he/she is tried to modified and elaborate concepts and principles already learnt. This type of learning is known as 'Combinational Learning'.
Combinational Learning: In this type of learning students could think as learning by analogy. It describes a process by which the new idea is derived from another idea that comes from his previous knowledge. In combinational learning, students try to modify and elaborate on already learned concepts and principles. It consists of sensible combinations of previously learned ideas that can be modified or elaborate on the generally relevant content in cognitive structure.

**22(D).** Identify the sequence which correctly indicates the order for ensuring teaching-learning activities in a constructivist approach-Engage, Explore, Explain, Extend and Evaluate.
Constructivist-based Teaching and Learning: There are many different models of constructivist classroom learning however, the model developed by Roger Bybee is widely used by teachers. This model is best known as the "5Es". It provides a planned sequence of instruction that places learners at the centre of their learning experiences. These 5Es are:
1. Engage: This stage provides the opportunity for the teachers to discover what students know by capturing the learners' attention, stimulating their thinking and helping them to access prior knowledge.
2. Explore: This stage allows students to plan, investigate and collect information and to think and reflect on the data to organize it, to make preliminary meaning. This is facilitated by the teachers through organizing various activities such as group work, discussion etc.
3. Explain: This stage provides an opportunity for students to connect their previous experiences, to analyse the data gathered and begin to make conceptual sense of the main ideas within the unit of study.
4. Elaborate/Extend: In this stage, students are guided by the teacher to apply or extend their understanding of the concepts in new situations and relate their previous experiences to a realworld situation. Teachers facilitate and guide learners in expanding their understanding and developing interpretative abilities as well as reflective and critical thinking.
5. Evaluate: Evaluation of students' conceptual understanding and ability to use skills begins at the Engage stage and continues throughout the model.

**23(D).** Responding to the stimulus is not included in problem solving.
Problem-solving is a child-centered approach that emphasizes learner's active involvement in the learning process. In this approach, teachers create a problematic situation for students and then assist them in perceiving, defining, and stating the problems in a fear-free environment. Steps Involved in the Problem-solving Method:
- Recognizing a problem
- Accumulation of data
- Formulating a hypothesis
- Testing the hypothesis
- Making a generalization

**24(B).** All the factors affect the learning.
Learning is the acquisition of new behaviour or the strengthening or weakening of old behaviour as a result of experience. It represents progressive changes in behaviour. It also involves the acquisition of knowledge, habits, and attitude.
The main factors affecting learning are Motivation of the learner, Maturation of the learner, Teaching strategies, and Physical and emotional health of the learner.
- To have a safe and productive learning environment, students must feel motivated, supported, and energetic.
- The factor of interest and maturation of the learner is very closely related in nature to that of symbolic drive and reward. A favourable mental attitude and maturity facilitate learning.
- Readiness is essential for students. It will help to develop a positive attitude in learners.
- Effective pedagogy strategies, teaching methods, goal-oriented instruction must be used to create a positive effect on learning.
- Concentration needs the emotional and physical health of the learner otherwise it may cause anxiety that leads to a lack of concentration. Some children find it difficult to prepare for the examinations, simply because of fear of the examination and anxiety neurosis.

**25(D).** Leadership style of teacher is teacher related factor affecting learning.

Learning is a process by which behaviour is either modified or changed through experience or training. Learning is thus a relatively permanent change in response potentiality which occurs as a function of reinforced practice. Teacher-related factors affecting learning:

- Teacher's Knowledge over the subject matter: Teachers who are firmly rooted in their subject knowledge make clearer presentations and recognize students' difficulties readily. He/she should be able to undertake application-oriented teaching as well.
- The leadership style adopted by the teacher in terms of whether it is authoritarian, democratic, benevolent, or indifferent greatly influences how the students will respond and involve themselves in the learning tasks.
- The relationship which teachers have with their students also sets the tone and climate of the classroom.
- The evaluative comments which teachers make either verbally or in writing also have a great bearing on students learning. They have the power to motivate and encourage or stifle and discourage.
- Apart from expectations, there are many other characteristics related to teachers that influence their learners and the teaching-learning process. The most significant among these are modeling, enthusiasm, caring, and positive expectations.
- Research indicates that teachers who present information enthusiastically, increase learners' self-efficacy, attributions of effort and ability, self-confidence, and achievement.
- The caring attitude of a teacher and how he/she communicates it is another important factor, Caring refers to a teacher's ability to emphasize and invest in the protection and development of her learners.

**26(B).** An error is an incorrect form and a sure indication that the learner has not mastered the core of the selective topic in a learning process.

The primary objective of analyzing errors in students' work is to understand children's thinking or thought processes since they are a window to children's thinking.

Errors are necessary for the learning process to give insight into children's thinking. It helps the teacher to be aware of learners' learning styles and to cater to them according to their needs.

Making an error cannot be just due to negligence and carelessness. It may be so that students are thinking about it in a different manner other than what is the right process.

To understand this, a teacher should analyze what mistake the students are doing, how the mistake is generated, and where exactly they tend to make mistakes.

It is clear that the primary objective of analyzing errors in students' work is to understand children's thinking.

**27(B).** Ways of effective problem-solving:

- Activating the right schema helps the problem solver to think openly with their minds. With the right schema, they can predict all the probable root causes that can generate the problem.
- Identification of the real problem helps the problem solver to become aware of the problem and to explore many possible solutions and limitless approaches to any given problem.
- Application of heuristics or general problem-solving strategies helps the problem solver to solve the problem effectively by following the steps including a selection of problems, the formation of hypotheses, collection of data, analysis of data, and verification of hypotheses.
- Good problem solvers tend to have a lack of response set as they will think divergently and try to analyze every possible outcome of the given problem before responding or solving a problem.
- Thus, it is concluded that the response set is a hindrance in effective problem-solving.

**28(B).** When teachers provide instruction on concepts in various subjects, they are teaching students who already have some pre-instructional knowledge about the topic. Student knowledge, however, can be erroneous, illogical, or misinformed. These erroneous understandings are termed alternative conceptions or wrong concepts. Purpose of Alternative Conceptions:

- These concepts are a normal part of the learning process.
- Through this process, the teacher recognizes that children are capable of thinking and their thinking is different from that of adults.
- They naturally form ideas from our everyday experience, but not all the ideas we develop are correct concerning the most current evidence and scholarship in a given discipline.
- This helps the students to interpret new experiences through these erroneous understandings for being able to correctly grasp new information.
- The teacher used instructional strategies to be effective in achieving conceptual change and helping students leave their alternative conceptions.

Hence, we can conclude that nowadays there is a tendency to refer to 'wrong concepts' of children as 'alternative conceptions'. This could be attributed to the recognition that children are capable of thinking and their thinking is different from that of adults.

**29(C).** Stages of Cognitive Development suggested by Jean Piaget:

- Sensorimotor stage: Birth to 2 years- During this earliest stage of cognitive development, infants and toddlers acquire knowledge through sensory experiences and manipulating objects. A child's entire experience at the earliest period of this stage occurs through basic reflexes, senses, and motor responses.
- Preoperational stage: Ages 2 to 7- The foundations of language development may have been laid during the previous stage, but the emergence of language is one of the major hallmarks of the preoperational stage of development.
- Concrete operational stage: Ages 7 to 11- While children are still very concrete and literal in their thinking at this point in development, they become much more adept at using logic.
- Formal operational stage: Ages 12 and up The final stage of Piaget's theory involves an increase in logic, the ability to use deductive reasoning, and an understanding of abstract ideas.

So, According to the stages of cognitive development suggested by Piaget, the earliest period is called the Sensorimotor stage.

**30(C).** The following attributes are:

- Variability and Normality: Individual differences include both variations and similarities among individuals as every individual differs from the others on important psychological aspects such as intelligence, personality, interest, etc.
- Differential Rate of Growth and Learning: Every human being follows the same procedure when it comes to growth, however, the rate of growth is different in each individual.
- The interrelation of Traits: We can find many people of the same height or the same eye-colour, this resembles the interrelation of traits.
- It becomes clear that in the individual difference, we find variability and normality.

**31(B).** The U.S. is urging Russia to reverse its troop buildup because they want to publish a crisis that will have far-reaching and long-lasting consequences.

According to the passage, 'Blinken said the U.S. is urging Russia to reverse its troop buildup, pull back heavy weapons and recommit to the diplomatic process set up to resolve the conflict in eastern Ukraine.'

'That's how we can turn back from a crisis that will have far-reaching and long-lasting consequences for our bilateral relations with Moscow, for Russia's relations with Europe, and for international peace and security," Blinken said.

**32(C).** The word peace is used to mean

'freedom from disturbance or tranquillity.'
'Tranquility' is the quality or state of being tranquil or calm.
Example: Passing cars are the only noise that disturbs the tranquillity of rural life.

**33(C).** Russian invasion of Ukraine would trigger "high impact" U.S. sanctions that would surpass any previously imposed on Moscow.
According to the passage, 'The Biden administration warned on Wednesday that a Russian invasion of Ukraine would trigger "high impact" U.S. sanctions that would surpass any previously imposed on Moscow. '

**34(A).** Russia has denied any aggressive plans toward Ukraine.
According to the passage, 'Russia has deployed tens of thousands of combat troops on Ukraine's border but has denied any aggressive plans toward Ukraine, saying it is only responding to what it calls provocative actions by Ukraine and NATO countries.'

**35(D).** The word 'troops' is a noun.
The word 'troops' is being used for soldiers or armed forces.
Example: UN peacekeeping troops have been deployed.
Nouns are words that are used to name a person, place, animal, thing, state or emotion.
Example: Youth these days are eager to learn.

**36(B).** Blinken said they will respond resolutely including with a range of high impact economic measures.
According to the passage, "We've made it clear to the Kremlin that we will respond resolutely, including with a range of high impact economic measures that we have refrained from pursuing in the past," Blinken said.'

**37(B).** According to the passage, "But it remained unclear if Russian President Vladimir Putin planned to order an invasion, Blinken told reporters." So, A is false.
According to the passage, "NATO Secretary-General Jens Stoltenberg said earlier that Russia would face serious political and economic consequences if it invades Ukraine." So, B is true.
So, it is concluded that B is true, A is false.

**38(B).** The word opposite in meaning to 'invaded' in meaning is 'liberated'.
Invaded is used to mean 'entering into a country or region by an armed force so as to subjugate or occupy it.'
'Liberated' is used to mean 'set someone free from imprisonment, slavery, or oppression.'
Example: They liberated all war prisoners from the concentration camp.
According to the passage, 'and other

pressure tactics resembled steps Moscow took before it invaded Ukraine in 2014 and seized the Crimean peninsula.'

**39(A).** The meaning of the given words:
- Consequences: something that happens or follows as a result of something else
- Result: something that happens because of something else; the final situation at the end of a series of actions
- Consideration: an act of thinking about something carefully or for a long time
- Determinant: an element that identifies or determines the nature of something or that fixes or conditions an outcome
- Factor: one of the things that influences a decision, situation, etc.

So, from the meaning of the given word, we can say that Result is the synonym of consequences.

**40(C).** The snow-fairies had come to the earth for peace and quietness.
Panic means sudden uncontrollable fear or anxiety, often causing wildly unthinking behaviour.
Example: Her calm expression hid her inward panic.
According to the poem:
'And they, frail things had taken panic flight Down to the calm earth seeking peace and quiet.'

**41(B).** The figure of speech being used is alliteration.
Alliteration is the occurrence of the same letter or sound at the beginning of adjacent or closely connected words. Here, the letter 'f' is being repeated in 'faires falling, falling'.

**42(B).** According to the given lines,
"Throughout the afternoon I watched them there,
Snow-fairies falling, falling from the sky,"
So, from the given lines it is concluded that the expression 'snow-fairies falling' refers to the snowfall.

**43(C).** The literary device being used here is personification.
In the given lines, they refer to the snow. Snow being non-human is incapable of 'panicking'.
Personification is the attribution of a personal nature or human characteristics to something non-human, or the representation of an abstract quality in human form.

**44(D).** According to the given lines,
"Contending fierce for space supremacy.
And they flew down a mightier force at night,"
From the given lines it is concluded that the snow-fairies flew down a mightier force at night and not the next morning.
So, 'and they flew down a mightier force the next morning' is not true.

**45(D).** Warm is not suitable as snow is never warm and it is in this poem

personified as the 'snow-fairies'.
The adjectives that are suitable for the snow-faires are 'white', 'fierce' and 'frail'.
An adjective describes or modifies noun/s and pronoun/s. It normally indicates quality, size, shape, duration, feelings, contents, and more about a noun or pronoun.

**46(B).** In writing-reading learning skills, action and meaning formation are possible simultaneously.
Reading or reading is one of the four language skills. It is a meaningful, purposeful and thought-provoking process that develops semantic and heuristic skills during reading. Taking the meaning of the read object, reading it with a definite purpose and guessing the facts that come next, it proves to be truly meaningful.
Importance of Reading Process:
- In the process of reading, the child reads written or printed words and acquires their feelings.
- Seeing a written language or picture and getting the meaning of its meaning is called reading.
- In this verb, along with speaking, meaning is also created.

**47(D).** Discussion-debate means to exchange views with each other. This group based learning is the simplest method of teaching technique. Things to note while discussing:
- The topic of discussion should be related to experience and should be environmental.
- Not only questions should be questions, but there should be discussion on this topic as well.
- There should be no 'yes' or 'no' questions, but a suitable environment for the children to speak.
- Treat children with kindness, so that their expression is easy.
- Do things that prompt the child to ask themselves. Inspire them for this.
- Listen patiently to the whole story of the children.

**48(A).** Ideal reading has special importance in bringing accuracy in pronunciation. This statement corresponds with Skinner's views.
Model reading - When the teacher himself presents the reading to the students, it is called model reading. The teacher presents it in the class keeping in mind the speed of his reading, yati, ascension, accentuation and stress. It has special importance in bringing correctness of pronunciation in children. According to Skinner, language is learned by imitation. Skinner in his book Verbal Behavior gave more importance to imitation medium in language learning.

**49(C).** At the primary stage, a child uses mother tongue words while speaking. As a language teacher you will accept mother tongue words.

The word language is derived from the root language (verb) which literally means to express an idea. Therefore, language is a process of exchange of ideas. At the primary stage, children are taught mother tongue because mother tongue is the first language that a child learns after birth. It is completely natural for children to use their mother tongue while learning Hindi language in the first and second grades because through the use of mother language, children:

- Able to connect with the classroom environment.
- Cognitively and linguistically develop.
- Best learn the concepts being taught.
- Able to interpret their experiences effectively.
- They are able to express their opinions, experiences and feelings with ease.
- Acquire the ability to cope with interactive situations.

**50(B).** The best way to assess listening and writing skills is to write the story you heard in your own words.

Listening and speaking form essential roles for reading and writing abilities. In fact these four abilities are mutually cooperative parts of language. The importance of the role of speaking in language development is as follows:

- Speaking is of great importance in evaluating the knowledge gained by listening in children, through this a teacher checks language errors in children, he can evaluate the teaching process in the classroom.
- Children's hesitation ends by speaking, they learn to express their point in front of others through reading
- Reading is the act of speaking and reading is followed by the act of writing. Speaking develops dexterity, proficiency and skill in language fluency. There is also a grasp on the language.
- When the child speaks a poem or story, the ability to present it in an emotional way develops.

**51(C).** "The planet Venus is also called the 'morning star' and the 'evening-star'." From the point of view of the eclipse, it would be appropriate to explain the meaning-variety of the usages of these three to a child both contextually and in perception.

Grammar in context: It is concerned with clarifying the grammatical point in the context of the lesson being taught. Explains the meaning of words, their grammatical form during the lesson. In the context of the above sentence, many grammatical information is available about noun, compound, type of sentence, meaning of adjective used for star, etc.

Perception: Collecting information about a subject or thing comes under understanding. The information about the

celestial body is being obtained from the above sentence. This gives us the sense that the planet Venus is near our earth and it looks like a star in the morning and evening. After reading these three experiments, we become aware of this, but if we are not clear about the concepts of planet, dawn and evening, then we will not be able to understand the information related to the planet. Therefore, language plays an important role in clarifying the concepts of any subject.

**52(C).** The one who gives accurate knowledge of written and oral forms of a language is called grammar.

Grammar is said to be that scripture, in which the correct rules of the language have been told. The analysis and analysis of the parts of any language is called grammar. Grammar is the knowledge by which a language is spoken, read and written correctly. There are definite rules for writing, reading and speaking any language. Grammar is the systematic system of rules for speaking and writing a language, that is, grammar works to organize the language. Grammar keeps the language stable. It makes a meaningful arrangement of the nature of the language. It is the physiology of language and conducts behavioral analysis. The pedagogical implication of 'grammar in context' is that grammar is taught in the context of the text.

**53(C).** Teaching is the fundamental process that includes planning, implementation and evaluation.

While planning, the educational objectives are also set. Teaching is done only to achieve the set objective. Teaching methods are used to make teaching easy and accessible.

Learning Options- There are many different ways of learning. Some of the text can be taught well by the deductive method, some by the inductive method. In some, the subject matter can be clarified by showing the model, some require real experience. Acting is required for the development of some skills, while for some, discussion is needed. Therefore, the selection of options for teaching-learning depends on the discretion and experience of the teacher.

Evaluation- Evaluation is the final stage of the teaching process. Through evaluation, knowledge is obtained about how successful the teaching-learning process has been. To what extent have we achieved the objectives which we had set in our plan. If the child is facing any difficulty, then it is the responsibility of the teacher to diagnose that problem and take proper treatment.

**54(B).** At age three a child is well acquainted with the basic structure of language and can communicate well.

Chomsky recognized that every human

child had an inherent and innate pattern of grammatical structures, which he termed universal grammar.

'Vygotsky' in his 'Socio-Cultural Theory' presented the socio-cultural perspective of language development. He has emphasized "social interaction" in the context of language development because he believed that children assimilate linguistic rules during social interaction.

According to Piaget, language, like any other cognitive system, develops through interaction with the environment.

**55(A).** The skills required for a teacher to implement inclusion in the classroom the skill to recognize the need of the child.

Every teacher should have the skill to recognize the need of the child. The teacher should have the skill to choose the method of teaching according to the needs of the child. The assessment of the child should be flexible according to the capacity of the child. The teacher should be able to provide various resources to support the learning activity of the children. The low cost learning material made by the teacher is the best to use in teaching. The teacher should be proficient in using different learning materials.

**56(D).** There are four language skills. Just as it is important to organize ideas in writing and give form to writing, in the same way it is important to make meaning and inference in reading skills.

Importance of Reading Process: In the process of reading, the child reads written or printed words and gets their sense. Seeing a written language or picture and getting the meaning of its meaning is called reading. Reading is the process of reading and understanding expressions and thoughts, expressions through written language. Apart from languages, the reading process is also very important for the understanding of other subjects.

**57(B).** To make writing learning interesting, rhyming words, last-syllable-first dictation and pictorial story writing method are used.

Many skills require coordination before learning to write. A child is considered ready to learn writing when he or she has developed operational ability (the ability to hold fingers). Operational skills can be developed with the help of the following activities or games:

- Drawing - Painting develops operational skills in children and also entertains them.
- Pour water in a pot
- Flower garland
- Making clay

**58(D).** In the non-availability of Braille books, it is an appropriate activity to expand the description of the text by reading it at a slow motion.

Things to consider when teaching language to visually impaired children:
- Have opportunities for conversation and discussion in your own language.
- To present the experience of hearing different types of sounds (eg- rain, train, bus, hawker etc.), the experience of taste of an object etc. in one's own way in oral or sign language.
- Discussing your travel experience in a group.
- Visually impaired children should have access to language learning opportunities in an inclusive classroom. Inclusive classroom means a classroom in which all the children sit together, participate equally in all the activities and learn the same curriculum.
- Expand the description of the text by reading it slowly.
- To learn long passages or paragraphs with tactile or audio-visual information, i.e. verbal information.
- Make more use of spoken language.

**59(D).** Audio-Visual Aids: These are sensory devices, they provide a sensory experience to the learner, and i.e. the learners can see and hear simultaneously using their senses. These are instructional devices that are used to communicate messages more effectively through sound and visuals. For example, LCD project, Film projector, TV, Computer, VCD player, Multimedia, etc.
Benefits of using Audio-Visual Aids in Learning:
- Audio-Visual aids can enhance your presentations, they can increase the learner's understanding of the topic.
- Audio-visual aids activate the sense of both hearing and vision to enrich learner's knowledge by providing information about different subjects and boost their self-confidence and independence.
- It helps to present the lesson effectively involving both sound and pictures for heightening learner's intellectual abilities to make learning easy and interesting.
- Audio-visual aids are the types of learning equipment that maximizes learning with the help of auditory and visual system including LCD Projector, TV computer, video, multimedia, etc.

So, from the above-mentioned points, it becomes clear that audio-visual aids make learning easy, interesting, and effective.

**60(D).** The word growth purely represents the physical sense of the person. Growth and development are the basis of human life. Growth is a part of the developmental process as development in its quantitative aspect is referred to as growth. Growth occurs when there are gradual and progressive changes in human beings due to maturation and experience whereas growth refers to structural and physiological changes.
Growth refers to a quantitative change that results in an increase in a child's height, weight, and length. Growth refers to a qualitative change that results in improved and enhanced functioning of organs. Growth can happen without development. Growth is development but not vice versa. Growth and development are a product of the interaction of heredity and environment. They play a vital role in determining the growth and development of an individual.

**61(B).** Given:
$A$ is $26°$ more than its complementary angle.
$B$ is $30°$ less than its supplementary angle.
Complementary angles are those angles whose sum is $90°$
$A + A - 26° = 90°$
$\Rightarrow 2A = 116°$
$\Rightarrow A = 58°$
Supplementary angles are those whose sum is $180°$.
$B + B + 30° = 180°$
$\Rightarrow 2B = 150°$
$\Rightarrow B = 75°$
So,
$A - B = 58° - 75°$
$= -17°$
$\therefore$ Required value is $-17°$.

**62(D).** Given:
Angles, in degrees, of a triangle, are $x, 3x + 20$ and $6x$,
As we know,
Sum of all three angles of triangles is $180°$.
According to the question
$\Rightarrow x + 3x + 20° + 6x = 180°$
$\Rightarrow 10x + 20° = 180°$
$\Rightarrow 10x = 180° - 20°$
$\Rightarrow 10x = 160°$
$\Rightarrow x = \dfrac{160°}{10}$
$\Rightarrow x = 16°$
First angle $= x = 16°$
Second angle $= 3x + 20° = 3 \times 16° + 20° = 48° + 20° = 68°$
Third angle $= 6x = 6 \times 16° = 96°$
So, this is the obtuse angled triangle.

**63(C).**

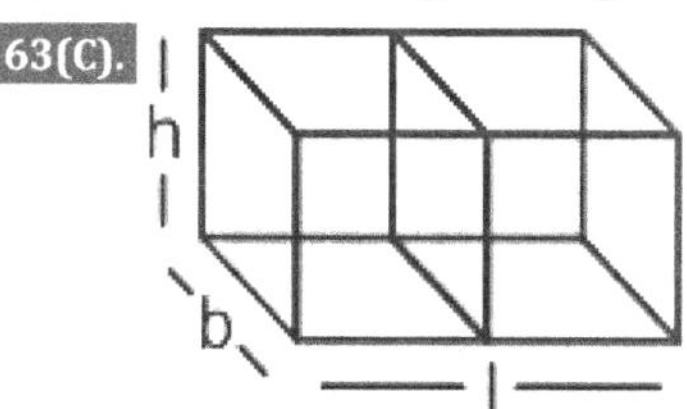

Volume of cube $= a^3$
$a^3 = 729$
$\Rightarrow a = 9$ cm
Length of cuboid $= 9 + 9 = 18$ cm
Breadth $= 9$ cm
Height $= 9$ cm
Total surface area of cuboid $= 2lb + 2bh + 2hl$ or $2(lb + bh + hl)$

Here $l, b$ and $h$ are length, breadth and height.
Total surface area of cuboid $= 2(18 \times 9 + 9 \times 9 + 9 \times 18) = 810$ cm$^2$
$\therefore$ Total surface area of the cuboid is $810$ cm$^2$.

**64(C).** Given:
Edge of the cube $= 5\ m$
Surface area of cube $= 6 \times (\text{edge})^2$
$6 \times (5)^2\ m^2 = 150\ m^2$
$\therefore$ Volume of cube $= (\text{edge})^3 = (5\ m)^3$
$= 125\ m^3$

**65(C).** Case 1:
Take two irrational numbers $\pi$ and $1 - \pi$
$\Rightarrow$ Sum $= \pi + 1 - \pi = 1$
Which is a rational number.
Case 2: Take two irrational numbers $\pi$ and $\sqrt{2}$
$\Rightarrow$ Sum $= \pi + \sqrt{2}$
Which is an irrational number.
So, a sum of two irrational numbers may be a rational or an irrational number.

**66(D).** Given number is $2197$:
Prime factoriztion of $2197 = (13 \times 13 \times 13)$
To Find Cube Root we need to find a pair set of 3 numbers
$\Rightarrow \sqrt[3]{13 \times 13 \times 13} = 13$
$\therefore$ The cube root is $13$.

**67(B).**

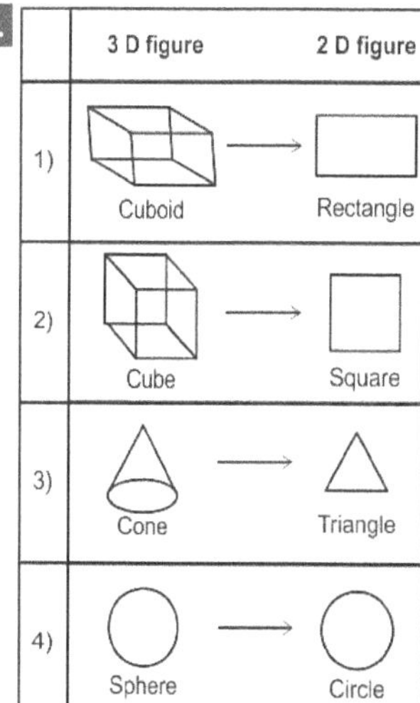



**68(B).** Given:
$12\frac{1}{2} + 12\frac{1}{3} + 12\frac{1}{6}$
$= \dfrac{25}{2} + \dfrac{37}{3} + \dfrac{73}{6}$
$= \dfrac{(75 + 74 + 73)}{6}$
$= \dfrac{222}{6}$
$= 37$

**69(B).** Given:
A rectangular playground of length 125 m and width 75 m.
Walking strip of width 5 m is in the middle of the ground, parallel to shorter side.
Area of a rectangle $=$ length $\times$ breadth
As per the given data:

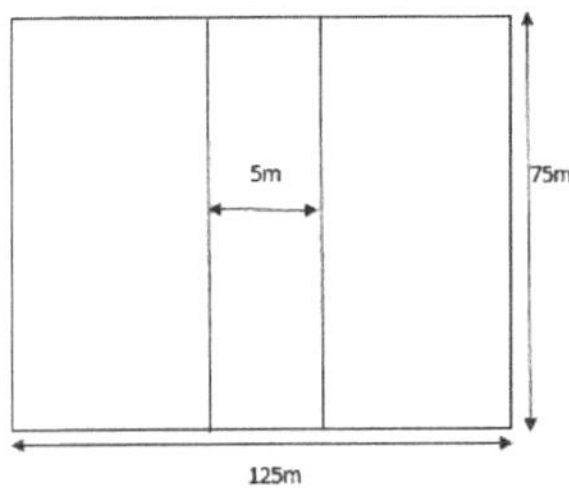



Area of the ground without the walking strip:
$$= (125 \times 75) - (5 \times 75)$$
$$= 9000 \text{ sq.m}$$

**70(A).**

| 1 gram | 1000 mg |
|---|---|
| 1 kg | 1000 gram |
| 1 tonne | 1000 kg |

From the table , 1 g = 1000 mg
1 kg = 1000 g = 1 g = $10^{-3}$ kg
1 mg = 1 mg = $1 \times 10^6$ g = $1000 \times 10^3$ g
= 1000 kg = 1 tonne
So, the incorrect conversion is 1 tonne = 100 kg.

**71(D).** Given:
Shaurya age is 38 ,
Let the brother's present age be $x$ years.
According to Question statement,
$$(38 - x) = x$$
$$\Rightarrow 2x = 38$$
$$\Rightarrow x = \frac{38}{2}$$
$$\Rightarrow x = 19$$
$\therefore$ Brother's age 5 years back
= (19 − 5) = 14 years

**72(C).** Concept:
$\frac{a}{b}$ and $\frac{c}{d}$ are two numbers,
then $(a \times d)$ and $(b \times c)$ are need to be compared.
Calculation:
We have, $\frac{9}{16}$ and $\frac{13}{24}$
$$\Rightarrow 9 \times 24 = 216$$
$$\Rightarrow 13 \times 16 = 208$$
$$\Rightarrow 216 > 208$$
$$\Rightarrow \frac{9}{16} > \frac{13}{24}$$

**73(B).** Given:
Total time is taken to read newspaper = 2 hours 55 minutes
1 hours = 3600 seconds
1 minute = 60 seconds
Bincy read a newspaper in 2 hours 55 minutes
2 hours 55 minutes
$$= (2 \times 3600) + (55 \times 60)$$
$$= 7200 + 3300 = 10500 \text{ seconds.}$$
$\therefore$ Bincy read this newspaper for 10500 seconds.

**74(B).** The pattern followed here is:
$$\Rightarrow 9 \times 2 + 1 = 19$$
$$\Rightarrow 19 \times 2 + 2 = 40$$
$$\Rightarrow 40 \times 2 + 3 = 83$$
$$\Rightarrow 83 \times 2 + 4 = 170$$
$$\Rightarrow 170 \times 2 + 5 = 345$$

$$\Rightarrow 345 \times 2 + 6 = 696$$
So, 170 will come in place of question mark.

**75(D).** The given series follows two series: Alphabetical and numeric
In the alphabetical series:
$$E + 1 = F$$
$$F + 2 = H$$
$$H + 3 = K$$
So, $K + 4 = O$
In the numeric series:
$$5 + 2 = 7$$
$$7 + 4 = 11$$
$$11 + 6 = 17$$
So, $17 + 8 = 25$
Thus $25O$ will come in the place of ?.

**76(D).** Given:
A car travels some distance at a speed of 8 km/hr and returns at a speed of 12 km/hr.
Total time taken by the car = 15 hours
Let the distance be $d$ km.
We know that,
Distance = Speed $x$ Time
$$\Rightarrow \frac{d}{8} + \frac{d}{12} = 15$$
$$\Rightarrow \frac{3d+2d}{24} = 15$$
$$\Rightarrow d = 72 \text{ km}$$

**77(A).** Concepts should be introduced through contexts is an important characteristic of a good mathematics textbook at primary level.
Textbook should be well illustrated and there should be a diagram and figures wherever needed. The content should be up-to-date. It should provide sufficient materials to motivate the students to solve problems in the classroom as well as in daily life.

**78(C).** beginning concept formation with definitions and mathematical terminology should be avoided in a good mathematics textbook.
It is critical for students to understand and use math terminology in daily math lessons. Math has a language of its own. Sometimes it uses symbols and sometimes the written word, but there is no denying that Math is a language. Math terminology plays a critical part in understanding math concepts.

**79(B).** " Benjamin Peirce " said that "Mathematics is the science that draws necessary conclusions".
In the philosophy of mathematics, he became known for the statement that "Mathematics is the science that draws necessary conclusions ". Peirce's definition of mathematics was credited by his son, Charles Sanders Peirce, as helping to initiate the consequence-oriented philosophy of pragmatism.
Mathematics is a science of structure, order, and relation that has evolved from counting, measuring, and describing the shapes of objects. It deals with logical reasoning and quantitative calculation.
So, Benjamin Peirce said that Mathematics

is the science that draws necessary conclusions.

**80(B).** Mathematics plays a vital role in the education system as it has universal applicability. Mathematical knowledge is used in almost every aspect of our everyday life such as money exchange, etc.
- The mathematical understanding will develop best when the learners learn by doing only.
- The teacher should try to engage every child in the classroom activities, quizzes, and experiments.
Teaching 'Numbers' at the primary level:
- At the primary level, the teacher expects the children to develop a positive attitude and a liking towards mathematics.
- The concept of "numbers" is taught in the primary classes in which they learn the sub-topics of counting, numerals, face value, place value, etc.
- It is not necessary that writing of numbers is taught in a sequence i.e., children might learn to write 9 first and then they learn to write 2.
- Also, writing numbers in numerals i.e., 9 as IX is not encouraged at the primary level.
- Numerals should be introduced only after the learners have experience with counting.
- Intuitive understanding of numbers should be encouraged at the primary level i.e., children will be able to identify the number of objects before counting them.
- Order irrelevance of numbers should be encouraged at the primary level.
- For example, children should first practice writing numbers and then move to number names.
So, we can conclude that statements A and D are true regarding teaching 'Numbers' at the primary level.

**81(D).** A good mathematics curriculum should present suitable learning experiences to foster common needs as citizens and special needs as an individual. The main consideration should be given to desirable pupil growth within the overall purposes of all levels of education.
- The negative numbers concept should be introduced at the upper primary level for better understanding.
- The concept of area measurement should be introduced at both levels as per the conceptual understanding and difficulty level.
- The foundation of algebraic thinking can be laid at the primary level.
- The concept of fractions should be introduced only at the primary level.
- Natural numbers, whole numbers, properties of numbers (commutative, associative, distributive, additive identity, multiplicative identity),

number line.
- Seeing patterns, identifying and formulating rules to be done by children. (As familiarity with algebra grows, the child can express the generic pattern.)

So, we can conclude that the foundation of algebraic thinking can be laid at primary level is correct concerning the mathematics curriculum.

**82(A).** 'Elucid', a great Greek mathematician is the father of Demonstrative Geometry which is a branch of Mathematics deals with questions of different shape, size and figures. He has proposed many methods in Geometry including intuitional, informal, observational, creative, intentional, constructive, experimental based on pure reasoning and geometrical truths.

**83(B).** Displaying sentence strips in the classroom throughout the school year to provide continual reminders of key vocabulary in mathematics teaching is known as word wall.

It is creating an evolving word wall in your classroom, by posting up useful words and expressions reminders of key vocabulary in mathematics terminology such as triangle, quadrilaterals, Pythagoras theorem, etc. It seeks out opportunities to invite your students to contribute new words. It involves the use of different-coloured pens or cards displaying sentence strips in the classroom throughout the school year to provide continual reminders of key vocabulary in mathematics, as with the labels.

**84(A).** In order to monitor students' progress and to modify teaching accordingly, the best method of evaluation is formative evaluation.

Evaluation refers to a process of making value judgments based on both qualitative and quantitative data collected over a period of time. CCE describes two different types of evaluation which include 'formative' and 'summative' evaluation.

'Formative evaluation' is a type of evaluation which refers to monitor the child's progress throughout the teaching-learning process. Oral testing, anecdotal records, portfolios, class test, etc are the tools of formative evaluation.

**85(A).** The purpose of formative evaluation is to monitor progress and plan remedial instruction.

Evaluation is a systematic way to assess learners' abilities, analyze performance, provide appropriate feedback to each learner and help them to progress. The formative evaluation assesses the performance of students, tests comprising various types of questions are constructed and administered during the period of instruction.

Purpose of Formative Evaluation:

- Its main objective is to provide continuous feedback to both teacher and student concerning learning successes and failures while instruction is in process.
- It is used to monitor the learning progress of students during the period of instruction .
- Feedback to students reinforces successful learning and identifies the specific learning errors that need correction.
- Feedback to the teacher provides information for max living instruction and for prescribing group and individual remedial work.
- The formative evaluation depends on tests, quizzes homework, classwork, oral questions prepared for each segment of instruction.

**86(C).** Learning resources are texts, audio-video materials and digital aids that assist you in the effective transaction of curricular content. Resources that can be used for visually impaired children are:

- Taylor's Abacus: Once the child learn that how to calculate the problems mentally or when the child can do mental calculations i.e. addition, subtraction, division, multiplication, etc. then the child can verify his answer with the use of an Abacus.
- Geoboard It is a rectangular or square board in shape with nails at equal distance. This can be used for showing geometrical figures and graphs. Rubber bands can be used to show various shapes.
- Tiles: It can also be used as a TLM for showing dimensions of two different rectangles and squares.

So, we conclude that all the GeoGebra can not be used for visually challenged students.

**87(A).** Errors are accepted as essential part of the mathematics learning process.

Mathematics is a branch of science which deals with counting, calculating, and studying numbers, shapes, and structures. Among all the school subjects, maximum emphasis is attached to learning mathematics. You must have experienced, during your student days and also being a teacher, the extent of pressure exerted on children to perform at a higher level in mathematics in comparison with other subjects. Sue Atkinson in her book "Mathematics with Reason" has provided an introduction to her book.

**88(C).** Learning disability refers to a neurological disorder that causes cognitive impairment. Dyslexia, dysgraphia, dyscalculia, etc. are the most common learning disability.

**Learning disability:**
- Learning disability is intrinsic and due to central nervous system dysfunction.
- It is a variable state which can be addressed by appropriate comprehensible input.
- It can't be attributed to cultural deprivation as it can present in children of any culture.
- It can't be attributed to educational deprivation as it can also present in children with average or above-average IQ.

'Dyscalculia' is a type of mathematics-related learning disability which:
- hinders learner's basic understanding of numbers.
- affects learner's ability to perform mathematical calculations.

**89(A).** An inclusive school is a platform where all students irrespective of any differences sit and learn together.

Here, the needs of visually challenged students can be catered by a number of ways.

Teachers can use alternate teaching-learning methods like:
- Asking students to clap or raise hand.
- Proper seating arrangements
- Avoiding gestures, always verbalize whatever is written in blackboard
- Helping students to visualize/imagine the theme taught.

**90(B).** The teaching-learning process aims to develop the overall personality of a child. The teacher uses various different types of resources to facilitate the learning and to increase the learning pace of students.

Remedial teaching for showing lower than average performance or slow learner:
- The students who show below-average performance require remedial teaching in order to improve their performance.
- They usually does mistakes because of their wrong contextual understanding or lack of interest in learning.
- The teacher has to re-teach the concepts using different techniques to make them understand the concepts in the right way so that their mistakes can be omitted.

So, we can conclude that remedial teaching is used for slow learners.

**91(C).** The bodies of penguins are streamlined and their feet have webs, making them good swimmers.

The penguin's body is adapted for swimming. Its body is fusiform (tapered at both ends) and streamlined. A penguin has a large head, short neck, and elongated body. The legs and webbed feet are set far back on the body, which gives penguins their upright posture on land.

**92(A).** Rice is a Kharif crop that requires high temperature (above 25°C) and high humidity with annual rainfall above 100 cm.

It is the staple food crop of a majority of the people in India. Our country is the second largest producer of rice in the world after China. It is a kharif crop which requires high temperature, (above 25°C) and high humidity with annual rainfall above 100 cm.

**93(B).** 'Artemis 1' is the flagship program of NASA, which aims to establish a long-term, sustainable human presence on the moon by the end of the 2020s.
NASA's Artemis 1 moon mission will be the agency's first big step toward returning astronauts to the lunar surface. Formerly known as Exploration Mission 1 (EM-1), Artemis 1 will be the first test flight of the agency's new Space Launch System megarocket and the Orion crew capsule.

**94(C).** Venus Flytrap plants is carnivorous.
- Venus Flytrap is a carnivorous plant.
- Carnivorous plants are adapted to capture and digest insects and protozoa.
- These plants derive most of their required nutrients by these insects.
- Examples of insectivorous plants are Venus Fly Trap, Pitcher plant, Drosera capensis etc.

**95(A).** A flower with both male and female reproductive parts is called a bisexual flower.
- A flower that includes both a male and a female reproductive structure (stamen and pistil) is considered a bisexual flower.
- Bisexual or complete flowers have both male (androecium) and female (gynoecium) reproductive structures, including stamens and ovaries.

**96(A).** Amla, spinach and jaggery are a group of eatables each member of which is rich in iron.
- Amla, spinach and Jaggery are rich sources of iron for the human body.
- There, these sets of eatables are rich in iron. Green vegetables are a rich source of iron.
- Iron helps in making the haemoglobin in the blood.
- The deficiency of Iron causes the disease called Anaemia.

**97(D).**
"Green manures → Chemical compound" is the incorrect pair.
In agriculture, a green manure is a crop specifically produced to be incorporated into the soil while still green. Typically, the green manure's biomass is incorporated with a plow or disk, as is often done with (brown) manure. The primary goal is to add organic matter to the soil for its benefits.

**98(B).** "Bark" of cinchona tree is used to treat malaria.
Malaria is a disease caused by Plasmodium parasites that are transmitted to humans through the bites of infected female Anopheles mosquitoes. High fever with a shiver, headache, vomiting, and nausea are common symptoms of malaria.
Quinine medicine was made from the bark of the cinchona tree. Quinine is a medication used to treat malaria and babesiosis. Quinine was first isolated in 1820 from the bark of a cinchona tree. It is an antimalarial drug that is made from Cinchona bark. Cinchona is used in eye lotions to numb pain, kill germs, and as an astringent.

**99(C).** Biotin is the chemical name for Vitamin B7.
- Biotin, also called Vitamin B7, is one of the B vitamins.
- It is involved in a wide range of metabolic processes, both in humans and in other organisms, primarily related to the utilization of fats, carbohydrates, and amino acids.
- The name biotin derives from the Greek word "bios" (to live) and the suffix "-in" (a general chemical suffix used in organic chemistry).
- Biotin deficiency can be caused by inadequate dietary intake (rare) or the inheritance of one or more inborn genetic disorders that affect biotin metabolism.
- The most common among these is biotinidase deficiency.
- The low activity of this enzyme causes a failure to recycle biotin from biocytin.

**100(D).** Burning of fossil fuels is the main cause of Nitrogen oxide pollution and Nitric oxide pollution.
The major harmful gas which is released upon burning of fossil fuel is nitrogen oxide. Release of nitrogen oxide contributes in the formation of smog and acid rain. Additionally when fuels are burnt at high temperature, a highly reactive gas called nitric oxide is also released in the environment. Various automobiles release these gases leading to air pollution.

**101(A).** Water for irrigation supplied as per crop requirement throughout the crop period / year is called perennial irrigation.
In this system assured supply of water throughout the crop period to irrigation requirement of the crops is made available to the command area through storage of water done at dam or diversion supply made by means of head works at the off take point of the canal. Perennial irrigation may be either direct (e.g reservoir or tank), storage (indirect) or combined.

**102(B).** There are two ways of harvesting rainwater.
- Surface runoff harvesting: In urban area rainwater flows away as surface runoff, this runoff can be used for recharging aquifers.
- Roof top rainwater harvesting: It is a system of catching rainwater where it falls.

**103(C).** Mosquitoes vector is used to transmit encephalitis and yellow fever to humans.
Arboviruses, which are one of the most common causes of encephalitis, are spread by blood-sucking insects like mosquitoes and less commonly, ticks. Avoiding being bitten is the greatest strategy to avoid becoming infected with a mosquito-borne virus.

**104(B).** Section 9 of The Indian Forest Act 1927 deals with the Extinction of rights.
The Act classified the forests into three categories – Reserved Forests, Protected Forests and Village Forests. It attempted to regulate the collection of forest produce by forest dwellers, and the policy introduced certain activities declared as offenses and imprisonment and fines to establish state control over forests.

**105(B).** Nutrients which are present in plant tissues in large quantities are known as " Macronutrients ". Macronutrients play a very important role in the growth and development of plants.
- Macronutrients are usually present in large amounts in plant tissue i.e. more than 10 mm kg$^{-1}$ of dry matter.
- Macronutrients have various applications, including in the yield, growth and quality of crops.
- Macronutrients include carbon, hydrogen, oxygen, nitrogen, sulfur, phosphorous, potassium, calcium and magnesium.
- Of these, carbon, hydrogen, and oxygen are derived mainly from $CO_2$ and $H_2O$, while others are absorbed as mineral nutrition from the soil.

**106(A).** When a visitor travels in his country of residence, he is a domestic visitor.
Domestic tourism is travel within your own nation. For example, if a Canadian from Alberta decided to spend a few days at Niagara Falls, as you're staying in your own country of residence, this is domestic or internal tourism.

**107(D).** Environmental studies is defined as the branch that deals with the Approach about the natural world and the impact of humans on its integrity.
Environmental studies deal with the issues that affect the life of a living organism. It can be various factors that relates to the natural world and the human impact on it. The other three options are related to material science, general studies, and environmental science.

**108(D).** According to NEP, " To teach students the value of protection and conservation of the environment " is the main reason for including environmental science as an integral part of education.

A framework of educational policy analysis involves a process in which various stakeholders analyze, generate, implement, assess and redesign policies. Educational policy is directly related to an ideal educational standard such as that which suits the manpower requirements of the economy.

**109(C).** Family and friends is a broad theme of EVS in the present syllabus.

The National Curriculum Framework (NCF) had recommended in the 1975 policy document "The Curriculum for the Ten-year School: A Framework", that a single subject "Environmental Studies" be taught at the primary level. It had proposed that in the first two years (class I and II), EVS will look at both the natural and the social environment, while in class III to V, there would be separate portions for social studies and general science called Part I and Part II. It should be noted that the syllabus for class 3-5 has six common themes.

**110(B).** Chipko Movement was strengthened under the leadership of Sunder Lal Bahuguna.

It is primarily a forest conservation movement. It was started in 1970 aimed at protecting trees. It was started in the northern Himalayan segment i.e. Uttarakhand.

**111(C).** Environmental education is a process that allows individuals to explore environmental issues, engage in problem-solving, and take action to improve the environment. As a result, individuals develop a deeper understanding of environmental issues and have the skills to make informed and responsible decisions.

The components of environmental education are:

- Awareness and sensitivity to the environment and environmental challenges
- Knowledge and understanding of the environment and environmental challenges
- Attitudes of concern for the environment and motivation to improve or maintain environmental quality
- Skills to identify and help resolve environmental challenges
- Participation in activities that lead to the resolution of environmental challenges

Environmental education does not advocate a particular viewpoint or course of action. Rather, environmental education teaches individuals how to weigh various sides of an issue through critical thinking and it enhances their own problem-solving and decision-making skills.

**112(A).** " Anxiety enduring for months or years " is an example of a psychological trait.

A trait is a prominent psychological aspect of a person that is stable across situations. Such a behaviour, emotion, or pattern of thinking may have been learnt and this becomes part of character. Some traits may be biological in origin and are said to be traits of temperament.

It's a relatively stable way of thinking and behaving that can be used to describe a person and compare and contrast that person with others. Some examples of traits include impulsivity/reflectivity, intelligence, sensation seeking, aggression, and dependency.

**113(A).** Geography is the nomenclature change suggested by the National Curriculum Framework (NCF), 2005 for Civics.

The National Curriculum Framework for School Education, 2005 discussed the need for the social science curriculum to be comprehensive but not loaded with information. The present National Focus Group (NFG) recognizes the efforts made in the past to create an ideal social studies curriculum. To ensure that the curricular recommendations are adequately translated into textbooks, the NFG has also highlighted the main issues to be addressed in order to make the social sciences an intellectually and professionally valuable subject of study. recommendations are given for the subject of social science in 2005.

**114(D).** The social sciences encompass diverse concerns of society and include a wide range of content, drawn from the disciplines of history, geography, political science, economics, and sociology.

Following points are highlighted for the relevance of social science in elementary class:

- To develop analytical skills.
- To adjust and appreciate various cultures.
- To be equipped with contemporary realities.
- To initiate the learner into a study of India's past, with references to contemporary developments in other parts of the world.
- To initiate the learner into a study of her/ his own region, state, and country in the global context.

Thus, it is concluded that A, B, and C options are correct.

**115(D).** The idea of showing a sample of air ticket to child is to provide an opportunity to interact with the real information and develop the skill of observation.

Observation skills refer to the ability to use all five of your senses to recognize, analyze and recall your surroundings. This practice is often associated with mindfulness because it encourages you to be present

and aware of the details of your daily life.

**116(C).** showing children storage of logs of wood is not a suitable activity at primary stage to sensitise students to the concepts of conservation of trees.

Showing children storage of logs of wood is not a suitable activity at primary stage to sensitize students to the concept of conservation of trees. Because at the primary stage they are not much more sensible to understand this phenomena.

**117(B).** Learning activities are activities designed by the teacher to enhance learning. Using different activities with flexibility will make learning more interesting for students.

This activity will develop observational and classification skills and will make the learners creative because by getting involved in it, they will classify the animals by observing the pictures and will create a new understanding of the animals that don't live/live in their surroundings.

Such activities help students become confident and learn to enquire themselves.

- This activity is aimed at boosting learners' confidence generally and creating a positive learning environment.
- By doing this activity students will invent their hidden strength.
- They will become confident while talking to others during the survey.
- Their Communication skill will be improved.
- They can work in pairs or teams if they find that easier.
- They will learn to enquire themselves.

So, we can conclude that statements A, B, and C are correct.

**118(B).** Environmental Studies is a multidimensional subject that covers important principles from various academic fields. It is a broad field that studies the basic principles of EVS as well as associated subjects such as social science, science, language, mathematics, etc.

In class I and II, the concepts of Environmental Science are integrated into Language and Mathematics. The teaching of language and mathematics are woven around the child's immediate environment to ensure contextual learning. National Curriculum Framework-2005, has prescribed Environmental Studies as a separate subject at Classes III-V.

So, we conclude that for classes I and II, EVS is taught through language and Mathematics.

**119(C).** " Continuous and Comprehensive Evaluation " method of assessment includes both formative and summative tests.

Continuous and Comprehensive Evaluation: The aim of education is all round development of the children. Keeping this in mind, the Central Board of Secondary

Education (CBSE) introduced the CCE (Continuous and Comprehensive Evaluation) format for secondary classes in 2009-2010. It was introduced under the Right to Education Act 2009 to provide quality education to the students in the age group of 6-14 years.

Continuing states that assessment should be done every day in the classroom during teaching and also after teaching, so that difficulties faced by students can be diagnosed regularly.

Comprehensive states that assessment has to cover all aspects- cognitive, emotional and functional. The CCE format consists of two different tests- Formative and Summative. Formative testing includes student's class performance, class work, homework, submission of assigned projects and active participation in various activities conducted in the classroom. Summative consists of a three-hour written test to test the academic insight of the student.

In the CCE format, students are marked based on their level of estimation in situations, its correlation with real-life experiences and events, and the method of solving information technology situations.

So, continuous and comprehensive evaluation is the correct answer here.

**120(A).** Environment Studies is a subject which is concerned with the development of learner's awareness about environmental issues. Children actively construct their own knowledge and understanding of the world by observing and interacting with the real content and situation.

Activities or things which are important in constructing knowledge in EVS by the children:

- Textbook of EVS.
- Hands-on activities.
- Organization of field visit.
- Linking classroom to real-life.
- Conduction of creative activity.
- Active participation of children.
- Community members of children.

So, we conclude that the above-mentioned points are important in constructing knowledge in EVS by the children.

**1. Which one of the following statements best sums up the relationship between development and learning?**

(a) Learning and development are synonymous terms.

(b) Learning and development are inter-related in a complex manner.

(c) Development is independent of learning.

(d) Learning trails behind development.

**2. Which one of these is not a principle of development?**

(a) Development is Life-Long

(b) Development is influenced by both heredity and environment

(c) Development is modifiable

(d) Development is governed and determined by culture alone

**3. For optimum development of an individual:**

(a) Only heredity is essential

(b) Both heredity and environment are essential

(c) Only environment is essential

(d) Neither heredity nor environment is essential

**4. Process of primary socialisation begins from ______.**

(a) infancy    (b) childhood

(c) adolescence    (d) adulthood

**5. According to Piaget the child is able to apply logical thoughts to all classes of problems, this development occurs in which of the following periods?**

(a) The sensory motor period

(b) The pre-operational period

(c) The formal operational period

(d) The concrete operational period

**6. Which of the following is a sub-stage in Kohlberg's 'conventional state's of Moral Development?**

(a) Instrumental purpose and exchange

(b) Universal ethical principles

(c) Morality of contract, rights and law

(d) Social concern and conscience

**7. Child centered system of education lays major emphasis on:**

(a) Learning without burden

(b) Incidental learning and self expression

(c) Activity based learning

(d) Learning under free environment

**8. Gardner's Multiple Intelligences Theory support the idea that:**

(a) Most students can be considered "intelligent" in some way

(b) Intelligence changes multiple times across the life span

(c) Creative individuals are considered to be more intelligent

(d) Intelligence can be multiplied through academic and non-academic tasks

**9. Shorya is a renowned dancer. So he must posses with ________.**

(a) Linguisitc Intelligence

(b) Body-kinesthetic Intelligence

(c) Musical Intelligence

(d) Inter-personal Intelligence

**10. The cause of downfall of a particular language is:**

(a) Acceptance of language other than the native language

(b) Narrow thinking

(c) Intolerance

(d) Both (B) and (C)

**11. Gender is a/an:**

(a) Social Construct

(b) Biological Determinant

(c) Economic Concept

(d) Psychological Entity

**12. Which of the following is NOT an effective strategy to cater to individual differences in the class?**

(a) Reflect on one's verbal and non-verbal communication

(b) Recognize and respect differences

(c) Use diverse pedagogical strategies

(d) Identify deficits in students and correct them

**13. Which one of the following is not a social-personal quality assessed under Continuous and Comprehensive Evaluation (CCE)?**

(a) Cleanliness    (b) Painting

(c) Co-operation    (d) Discipline

**14. In absolute grading, the reference point for an assessment of students performance happens to be a:**

(a) Pre-determined standard

(b) Standard determined on the basis of a normal probability curve

(c) Standard determined on the basis, of dividing the equal percentage of cases from top to bottom

(d) Standard determined on the basis of arbitrarily chosen percentages of cases for various grading groups

**15. A teacher has to enhance the readiness level of his students. Which will be the best way to do so?**

(a) By organizing a creational activity in the classroom related to the particular topic

(b) By organizing an indoor game in classroom

(c) By story telling method

(d) By giving monitoring to one of the student of the class

**16. Hearing impaired children exhibit:**

(a) Barriers in communication by language

(b) Barriers in moving around

(c) Barriers in individuals self-care skills

(d) Barriers in tactile skills

**17. In inclusive term, exceptional children means ______.**

(a) the children with mental disabilities

(b) the children with low IQ

(c) the children with maladjustment problem

(d) the gifted, intelligent, backward, mentally retarded childrens

**18. Children with special needs should be:**

(a) Given no education at all.

(b) Given only vocational training.

(c) Segregated and put in separate institutions.

(d) Included in 'regular' set-ups with special provisions.

**19. A creative learner refers to one who is:**

(a) Capable of scoring consistently good marks in tests

(b) Good at lateral thinking and problem-solving

(c) Very talented in drawing and painting

(d) Highly intelligent

**20. The gifted children:**

(a) Are always calm and quiet

(b) Always behave extraordinarily

(c) Solve the problem quickly

(d) Perform any task quickly

21. **Which one of the following is the last stage of learning?**
(a) Acquisition  (b) Adaptation
(c) Fluency  (d) Maintenance

22. **Rohini, a newly admitted student, is unable to adjust to the classroom, as a teacher you will:**
(a) Give her small group work and supervise.
(b) Will try to find out the reason.
(c) Will leave her on time.
(d) Will call the guardians

23. **Which one of the following statements about teaching is not correct?**
(a) Teaching is an interactive process.
(b) Teaching is a tripolar process.
(c) Teaching is an effect - directed process.
(d) Teaching is a process confined only to the classrooms.

24. **Children's errors and misconceptions:**
(a) Are a hindrance and obstacle to the teaching-learning process.
(b) Should be ignored in the teaching-learning process.
(c) Signify that children's capabilities are far inferior to that of adults.
(d) Are a significant step in the teaching-learning process.

25. **Errors made by children are indicative of:**
(a) Poor intelligence
(b) Low ability
(c) Their inability to reproduce knowledge
(d) Children's thinking process which is qualitatively different from that of adults

26. **What is the definition of cognition?**
(a) The process of acquiring and understanding knowledge through our thoughts, experience and sense
(b) The process of biological and psychological changes
(c) Developing attitude and interest
(d) Structural and physiological changes

27. **Motivation and learning are inter-related. Which among the following is not true about the principle of motivation?**
(a) Depends on curiosity
(b) It provides a purpose for learning
(c) Helps to get a higher position
(d) Skills and knowledge

28. **Which of the following is an environmental factor which impact learning?**
(a) Attitude
(b) Motivation
(c) Personality traits
(d) School

29. **Learning is influenced by:**
i. Psychological factors
ii. Socio-Cultural factors
iii. School-related factors
iv. Teacher related factors
Choose the correct option.
(a) i  (b) i, ii
(c) i, ii, iii  (d) i, ii, iii, iv

30. **How should teachers promote motivation to learn among their students?**
(a) Use incentives to help students learn.
(b) Give the students things to study that will be tested rather than things that won't.
(c) Give easier tests.
(d) Let the students make the test.

## Language - I: English

**Ques (31-39): Direction** : Read the given passage and answer the questions that follow.

The move by the government to demonetize Rs.500 and Rs.1000 notes by replacing them with new Rs.500 and Rs.2000 notes has taken the country by surprise. The move by the government is to tackle the menace of black money, corruption, terror funding, and fake currency. From a market perspective, we think that this is a very welcome move by the government and which has taken the black money hoarders by surprise. The total value of old Rs.500 and Rs.1000 notes in circulation is to the tune of Rs.14.2 trillion, which is about 85% of the total value of the currency in circulation. This means that the total cash has to now pass through the formal banking channels to get legitimacy. The World Bank in July 2010 estimated the size of the shadow economy for India at 20.7% of the Gross Domestic Product (GDP) in 1999 and rose to 23.2% in 2007. Assuming that this figure has not risen since then (quite unlikely though) and that the cash component of the shadow economy is also proportional (it could be higher), the estimated unaccounted value of the currency could be to the tune of Rs.3.3 trillion. Now, post the announcement of demonetization by the government this money would have to either account for by paying the relevant tax and penalties or would get extinguished. There are higher chances of a larger proportion of this unaccounted currency getting extinguished as the tax rate and subsequent legal issues could be prohibitively high for such money.

This move by the government is likely to have long-term benefits for the economy. The extinguishing of the major proportion of unaccounted currency would reduce the liabilities of the government and would add to its finances. This move is likely to lead to better tax compliance, raise the Tax to GDP ratio and improved tax collection. The move is also likely to have a habit-changing impact on the Indian populous and there could be an increased belief in keeping cash in the banks rather than stashed at home and using formal banking channels for their spending needs. It will improve the medium to long-term Current Account and Savings Account (CASA) ratio of the banks. Another element of the demonetization would be a reduction in cash transactions in real estate which has been acting like a cash cow for the corrupt. This is likely to reduce real estate prices and make it affordable to some extent. This may be visible more in the rural belt, where many non-farming entities purchase fertile farmland, not for farming but for money parking purposes. The demonetization and consequent reduction in the shadow economy would bring the demand for such farmlands down.

31. **How will the demand for fertile farmlands be brought down by demonetization?**
(a) Lack of cash flow in the shadow economy
(b) Higher investments in real estate
(c) Cash hoarding
(d) Low agricultural output

32. **What percentage of the total value of currency in circulation is made up by the old Rs.500 and Rs.1000 notes?**
(a) 80%  (b) 85%
(c) 75%  (d) 60%

33. **What does cash cow mean?**
(a) Cash that buys cows
(b) People with low income from land
(c) Approximate estimate of cost of land
(d) A product or service that is a

regular source of income for someone

**34. Why will the demonetization move have a habit-changing impact on the Indian population?**

(a) Indians will stop using black money for their daily needs and rely more on white money for day to day transactions.

(b) The Indian population generally uses mostly UPI for transactions and is not in the habit of saving. Demonetisation will make them wary of the future and grow their expanding habits altering their lifestyles.

(c) Demonetisation will affect the spending habits of the foreigners.

(d) The demonetization has affected all Indians and in the future, the scheme would make them wary and help to create an atmosphere where banks and other legalized avenues will make their savings secure and easily accessible.

**35. What is the main idea discussed in the passage?**

(a) How black money is hid in the economy.

(b) The effects of demonetization on the Indian economy.

(c) Demonetization and its effect on the next elections.

(d) Demonetization and common man's woe.

**36. Choose the correct synonym of the word 'formal'.**

(a) Official  (b) Ceremonial

(c) Informal  (d) Traditional

**37. What is the full form of CASA?**

(a) Current action and Savings Action

(b) Current Affirmation and Savings Affirmation

(c) Current Account and Savings Account

(d) Current Act and Savings Account

**38. According to World Bank estimates what percentage of the GDP did the shadow economy have in 2007?**

(a) 20.7%  (b) 21.4%

(c) 22.6%  (d) 23.2%

**39. Choose the correct antonym of the word 'compliance'.**

(a) Agreement  (b) Assent

(c) Defiance  (d) Consensus

**Ques (40-45): Direction** : Read the poem given below and answer the questions that follow.

I was angry with my friend;
I told my wrath, my wrath did end.
I was angry with my foe:
I told it not, my wrath did grow.
And I waterd it in fears,
Night & morning with my tears:
And I sunned it with smiles,
And with soft deceitful wiles.
And it grew both day and night.
Till it bore an apple bright.
And my foe beheld it shine,
And he knew that it was mine.
And into my garden stole,
When the night had veild the pole;
In the morning glad I see;
My foe outstretched beneath the tree.

**40. What did the poet water with his fears?**

(a) Tree  (b) Plant

(c) Poison  (d) Anger

**41. Which device is used in the following lines?**
**And I sunned it with smiles,**
**And with soft deceitful wiles.**
**And it grew both day and night.**

(a) Consonance

(b) Anaphora

(c) Satire

(d) Personification

**42. What does the poet mean when he says 'My foe outstretched beneath the tree.'?**

(a) Poet's enemy was using the tree

(b) Poet's enemy was trying to steal the fruits from the tree

(c) The enemy was relaxing under poet's tree

(d) The enemy was lying dead under the tree

**43. ' night had veild the pole' means:**

(a) Tree covered the pole

(b) The dark night covered the pole

(c) Night had covered the pole

(d) The dark night was all around the tree

**44. Which literary device is used throughout the poem?**

(a) Personification

(b) Simile

(c) Extended Metaphor

(d) Assonance

**45. What does the garden refer to in the poem?**

(a) Anger  (b) Kindness

(c) Forgiveness  (d) Apology

**46. Consider the correct statements regarding language learning.**
**I. Input-rich communicational** environments are a prerequisite for language learning.
**II. It helps in bridging the gap between the burden of incomprehension and language learning.**

(a) Only I

(b) Only II

(c) Both I & II

(d) None of these

**47. The 'acquired system' or 'acquisition' of a language is the:**

(a) Formal skills development

(b) Subconscious process of learning

(c) Input output process

(d) Self monitoring of learning

**48. One of the principles of materials preparation for language learning is that:**

(a) Complex materials should be chosen for each age group

(b) Materials need to be graded appropriately.

(c) Any kind of materials can be selected.

(d) Materials should be short and limited.

**49. Principles of sequencing in teaching a foreign language, does not include:**

(a) Grammatical sequence

(b) Lexical sequence

(c) Semantic sequence

(d) Phonetic sequence

**50. Grammatical rules are________ for learning a language.**

(a) important

(b) compulsory

(c) not important

(d) mandatory

**51. Given below are two statements, one leveled as Assertion (A) and the other leveled as Reason (R).**
**Assertion (A): Grammar is the backbone of any language, it is the womb that gives birth to sentences.**
**Reasoning (R): Grammar rules are made easier if the teacher t eaches grammar using a standard textbook.**

(a) Both (A) and (R) are correct and (R) is the correct explanation of (A).

(b) Both (A) and (R) are correct, but (R) is not the correct explanation of (A).

(c) (A) is correct, but (R) is not correct.

(d) (A) is not correct, but (R) is correct.

**52. When child has difficulties in understanding or expressing language that is called:**
(a) Grammatical language problem
(b) Delayed Language
(c) Language Disability
(d) All of the Above

**53. The order advocated for learning the language skills is:**
(a) writing, reading, speaking, listening
(b) reading, writing, listening, speaking
(c) listening, speaking, reading, writing
(d) speaking, listening, reading, writing

**54. Through which of the following language skills should be taught?**
(a) Through imitation
(b) In isolation
(c) Through detailed explanation
(d) In an integrated manner

**55. Rohit, a English teacher, is planning to evaluate the speaking skills of his students. Which of the following should be the main focus for evaluating speaking skill?**
(a) Accuracy of pronounciation
(b) Adequacy of fluency
(c) Communicative competence
(d) Accuracy of pronounciation and adequacy of fluency

**56. Decoding in evaluating language proficiency refers to:**
(a) The ability to enhance reading error.
(b) The ability to hear sounds to build and write words.
(c) The ability to read individual words and to sound out unfamiliar words accurately.
(d) The ability to provide remedial classes.

**57. A smartboard is a:**
(a) A visual aid
(b) An audio aid
(c) An audio-visual aid
(d) None of these

**58. ________ is of great utility in teaching English pronunciation, accent and intonation.**
(a) Epidiascope (b) Films
(c) Linguaphone (d) Radio

**59. The objective of remedial teaching in English language is/are:**
(a) Provides learning activities and practical experiences to pupils according to their abilities and requirements.
(b) Designs individualized teaching with intensive remedial support
(c) Help the pupils to get rid of their common or specific weaknesses.
(d) All of the above

**60. The main purpose of using oral drill is:**
(a) To assess the comprehension skills of learners
(b) To improve pronunciation and accuracy
(c) To enhance the speaking skills of learners
(d) To improve retention capacity of learners

## Mathematics

**61. The area of four walls of a room is $660m^2$ and length is twice the width, height being $11m$. Find the area of ceiling of the room?**
(a) 200 (b) 190
(c) 210 (d) 220

**62. A rectangular field of length $242m$ has an area of $4840m^2$. What will be the cost of fencing if the cost of fencing is 50 paise/meter?**
(a) Rs 262 (b) Rs 270
(c) Rs 320 (d) Rs 258

**63. Ratio of two complementary angles is $1:5$. What is the difference between them?**
(a) $60°$ (b) $90°$
(c) $120°$ (d) $160°$

**64. Direction : What will come in the place of the question mark '?' in the following question?**
$$18\tfrac{1}{3} + 9\tfrac{2}{3} - 10\tfrac{1}{3} = 1\tfrac{2}{3} + ?$$
(a) 10 (b) 15
(c) 18 (d) 16

**65. The sum of the radius and height of a cylinder is $19m$. The total surface area of the cylinder is $1672m^2$. What is the volume of the cylinder?**
(a) $3080m^3$ (b) $2940m^3$
(c) $3420m^3$ (d) $2860m^3$

**66. The rational number lying between $\sqrt{2}$ and $\sqrt{3}$ is:**
(a) $\frac{49}{28}$ (b) $\frac{56}{35}$
(c) $\frac{63}{45}$ (d) $\frac{85}{66}$

**67. The numbers $x, x+2, x+4$ are all prime numbers. What is the value of $x$ ?**
(a) 3 (b) 2
(c) 11 (d) 17

**68. If $\sqrt[3]{\left[\frac{x}{27}\right]} = \frac{5}{3}$, then the value of $x$ is:**
(a) 125 (b) 12
(c) 11 (d) 17

**69. Boating at $\frac{6}{7}^{th}$ of regular speed in a lake, the tourist got late by 30 minutes. How much time will it take while boating at usual speed?**
(a) 2 hr
(b) 3 hr
(c) 1.5 hr
(d) None of these

**70. The age of $x$ is six times that of $y$. After 4 years, $x$ is 4 times elder of $y$. What is the present age of $y$ ?**
(a) 4 years (b) 5 years
(c) 6 years (d) 7 years

**71. Direction : In the following question a number of series is given with one term missing. Choose the correct alternative that will continue the same pattern.**
$2, 3, 5, 7, 11, \_\_, 17$
(a) 12 (b) 13
(c) 14 (d) 15

**72. Direction : Study the histogram that shows the marks obtained by students in an examination and answer the question that follows.**

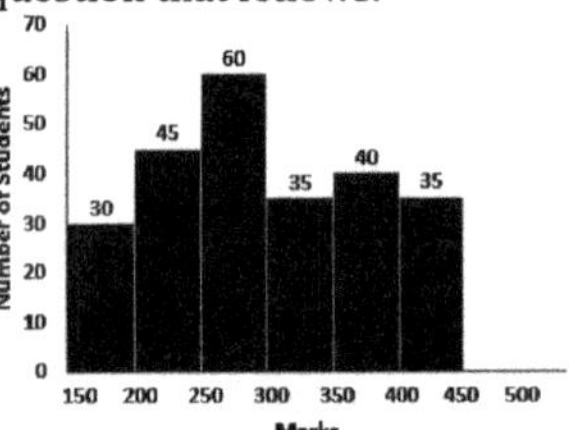


By what percentage is the number of students who obtained marks between 200 and 300 more than the number of students who obtained 350 or more marks?
(a) 55% (b) 25%
(c) 30% (d) 40%

**73. Divyanka reaches her office for a meeting 15 minutes before $11:20$ am. If she reached half an hour after the scheduled time of the meeting. Her colleague Rajia reached 25 minutes after the scheduled time of the meeting. When Rajia reached her office?**

(a) $10:30$ am  (b) $11:00$ am
(c) $10:40$ am  (d) $11:45$ am

74. **Rama has gone to a sweet shop to buy laddus for her birthday. The weight of 35 laddus is 1 kg 400 g. If 12 laddus can be packed in one box then how many boxes are needed to pack a total of 96 kg laddus?**
(a) 180  (b) 200
(c) 220  (d) 240

75. **Which of the following statement is/are not correct?**
**(1) 5 L 40 ml = 540 ml**
**(2) 56 paisa = Rs. 0.56**
**(3) 3.5 km = 3500 meter**
**(4) One and half dozen = 16**
(a) (1) and (2)  (b) (2) and (3)
(c) (3) and (4)  (d) (1) and (4)

76. **Which of the following is the largest?**
(a) $\frac{3}{8}$  (b) $\frac{5}{7}$
(c) $\frac{16}{21}$  (d) $\frac{19}{25}$

77. **The nature of Mathematics is:**
(a) Ornamental
(b) Difficult
(c) Logical
(d) Unsystematic

78. **Learning maths is a means to develop logical and _____ thinking abilities.**
(a) qualitative  (b) quantitative
(c) inductive  (d) deductive

79. **Which one is not related to the nature of Mathematics?**
(a) Exactness
(b) Specific sequence
(c) Expanded expression
(d) Pattern

80. **As per NCF 2005, the goal of mathematics teaching in school curriculum is that children learn "Important Mathematics". Important Mathematics implies:**
(a) Understanding appropriate use of learnt mathematical techniques.
(b) Verifying geometrical theorems in Maths Lab.
(c) Knowing mathematical procedures and algorithms.
(d) Solving mathematical games and puzzles.

81. **Which one of the following does not match curricular expectations of teaching mathematics at the primary level?**

(a) Analyse and infer from representation of grouped data
(b) Develop a connection between the logical functioning of daily life and that of mathematical thinking
(c) Develop language and symbolic notations with standard algorithms of performing number operations
(d) Represent part of whole as a fraction and order simple fractions

82. **Mathematics is itself a language with its own symbols, words, and rules of syntax. Which of the following is not a part of mathematical language?**
(a) $>,<$  (b) $*,!$
(c) $\#,\&$  (d) $[],\{\}$

83. **Which mathematical topic that is best seen as a compact language and a means of succinct expression is introduced at the upper primary stage?**
(a) Mensuration
(b) Differential equations
(c) Number notation
(d) Algebra

84. **Which of the following is/are the problems in teaching and learning of mathematics?**
(a) Inadequate of training for upgradation of learning strategies
(b) Attitude towards mathematics relating fear of mathematics
(c) Mathematical Anxiety
(d) All of the above

85. **Which of the following is not true regarding the problems in teaching and learning mathematics?**
(a) Positive attitude towards mathematics
(b) Focus on problem solving approach
(c) Cramming of all mathematical formulas
(d) Connecting real life problems to mathematics

86. **Which of the following is NOT acceptable with regard to teaching students to solve problems based on mathematical operations?**
(a) The problems chosen should be realistic
(b) Simple examples with smaller numbers should be taken up first
(c) Concrete materials may be used

to support students' understanding of the steps of the algorithm
(d) Only one method of solving a particular type of problem should be emphasised

87. **The maximum success of remedial teaching depends on:**
(a) Time and duration
(b) The correct identification of causes of problem
(c) Knowledge of linguistic rules
(d) Remedial teaching materials

88. **Which is the main remedial teaching strategy?**
(a) Tutorial
(b) Supervised
(c) Both (A) and (B)
(d) None of these

89. **Which of the following assessment strategies can be used to make connections of Mathematics with real life and promote inter-disciplinarily?**
(a) Field trip, oral test, drill worksheet
(b) Survey, project, checklist
(c) Field trip, oral test, checklist
(d) Field trip, survey, project

90. **In a class text, to the question, find out 23% of 200, two students answered in following ways:**
**Student A:** $23\%$ of $200 = 23\%$ of $(100+100) = 23+23 = (20+20)+(3+3) = 46$
**Student B:** $23\%$ of $200 = 200 \times \frac{23}{100} = 2 \times 23 = 46$
(a) Since student B has used the standard algorithm, teacher gives full marks to student B and zero to student A
(b) Teacher gives full marks to both the students as they have attempted the question using their own algorithms. Both formal and informal algorithms are integral to solving problems in mathematics.
(c) Teacher gives zero marks to student A and directs him to redo the question using the algorithm taught in the Class
(d) Teacher accepts both the responses but directed student A to refrain from using informal algorithm

## Environmental Studies

91. **Which of the following is a "living fossil"?**

(a) Spider    (b) Moth
(c) Limulus    (d) Scorpion

**92.** A pulse crop is grown between two cereal crops to compensate for the:
(a) Loss of water
(b) Loss of nitrogen
(c) Loss of sulphur
(d) Loss of phosphate

**93.** The revolver was invented by ____.
(a) Theodor Bergmann
(b) Henry Deringer
(c) John Browning
(d) Samuel Colt

**94.** In cockroaches, air enters the body through:
(a) Lungs    (b) Gills
(c) Spiracles    (d) Skin

**95.** Read the description given below and identify the dish.
1. It is a vegetable stew.
2. All the vegetables are put into a clay pot, along with fresh spices.
3. The pot is placed upside down.
(a) Khichdi
(b) Undhiya
(c) Thukpa
(d) Vegetable curry

**96.** _____ is apt for vermicomposting.
(a) Algae
(b) Nitrifying bacteria
(c) Earthworms
(d) Fungus

**97.** Which of the following strategies are useful for preventing oxidation of foodstuffs?
(i) Addition of antioxidants
(ii) Keeping food in an airtight container
(iii) Use of flush bags containing inert gases
(iv) Addition of buffer solutions
(a) (i), (ii) and (iv)
(b) (i), (ii) and (iii)
(c) (ii), (iii) and (iv)
(d) All of the above

**98.** Wood, coal, petroleum release unburnt carbon particles in the environment are called what type of fuels?
(a) Fossil fuels
(b) Carbon fuels
(c) Nitrogen fuels
(d) Unburnt fuels

**99.** Consider the following statements about Irrigation.
1. Irrigation is the artificial process of applying controlled amounts of water to land to assist in the production of crops.
2. Irrigation helps to grow agricultural crops, maintain landscapes, and revegetate disturbed soils in dry areas.
Select the correct answer using the code given below.
(a) 1 only
(b) 2 only
(c) Both (A) and (B)
(d) Neither (A) nor (B)

**100.** The crop nutrients available in fertilizers are:
(a) Nitrogen, potassium and iron
(b) Nitrogen, phosphorus and potassium
(c) Nitrogen, phosphorus and iron
(d) Nitrogen, sodium and potassium

**101.** Which of the following is not a vector-borne disease?
(a) Yellow fever
(b) Dengue fever
(c) Viral fever
(d) Malaria

**102.** Rina stays in Delhi. She wants to visit her aunt in Gwalior. In which direction should she travel?
(a) East    (b) West
(c) South    (d) North

**103.** Which of the following is not true w.r.t EVS?
(a) EVS is based on child-centred learning.
(b) EVS provides opportunities to learners to explore their environment.
(c) EVS emphasizes descriptions and definitions.
(d) Nature of EVS is integrated.

**104.** Section 10 of The Indian Forest Act 1927 deals with:
(a) Power to reserve forests
(b) Power to declare forest no longer reserved
(c) Treatment of claims relating to practice of shifting cultivation
(d) Protection of forests at request of owners

**105.** ______is a traditional rainwater harvesting technique indigenous to the Thar desert region of Rajasthan.
(a) Taanka
(b) Khadin
(c) Bavadi
(d) All of the above

**106.** Consider the sense of hearing of the following animals.
I. Bat
II. Tiger
III. Dolphin
IV. Whale
Which of the above animal(s) use echolocation?
(a) I only    (b) II and III
(c) I, II and IV    (d) I, III and IV

**107.** Which is the principle of Learning Environment Study?
(a) Principle of necessity
(b) Principle of utility
(c) Principle of relationship with life
(d) All of the above

**108.** EVS is organised around three broad principles, one of them is:
(a) Learning through the environment
(b) Learning beyond the environment
(c) Learning inside the environment
(d) Learning without the environment

**109.** A teacher tells her students to collect garbage from school playground. Anup, a student, separates wet garbage in one bucket while dry garbage in another. He does so:
(a) He does it willingly unwillingly
(b) He knows the concept of Reduce, Reuse and Recycle
(c) He is emotional towards cleaning environment
(d) None of these

**110.** As an EVS teacher, you plan to take the students to the zoo. Which of the following activities would you not allow the students to undertake?
(a) Collect photographs of the animals they expect to see at the zoo
(b) Take their drawing books along with them to draw what they see at the zoo
(c) Take along lots of eatables for the animals at the zoo
(d) Try to find out the food taken up by different animals at the zoo

**111.** Soni, a student of class 3rd, understands the concept of EVS very well but faces problems while writing. The problem she suffers is a symptom of:
(a) Dyslexia    (b) Dysphasia

(c) Dyscalculia    (d) Dysgraphia

**112.** ______ **mandated CCE as a process of assessment.**
(a) NCF 2005
(b) RTE 2009
(c) NPE 1986
(d) Kothari commission

**113. What are the essential TLM for teaching Social Studies/ Environmental Studies?**
(a) Pedagogy, Syllabus and Assessment
(b) Curriculum, Syllabus and Textbook
(c) Textbook, Pedagogy and Assessment
(d) Curriculum, Language and Syllabus

**114. EVS teacher should:**
(a) focus exclusively on experiments
(b) focus exclusively on books and tests
(c) accept and respect perception of children
(d) accept and respect views of parents

**115. Shalini has planned a field trip for Class IV students to the Science Center. Which one of the following general instructions given to the students is irrelevant for the trip?**
(a) Do not go anywhere without informing me
(b) Carry your full schoolbag for the day
(c) Ask question for your doubts on displays
(d) Take notepad and pen with you

**116. EVS curriculum at primary stage has been developed to include pure Science as well as Social Science concepts. This has been done primarily to:**
(a) Reduce the requirement of subject teachers
(b) Enables a learner look at environment in a holistic manner
(c) Reduce the load of schoolbag
(d) Reduce the number of subjects to be studied

**117. Children can be effectively engaged in EVS learning through:**
**A. Narratives**
**B. Stories**
**C. Effective explanation of concepts by the teacher**
**D. Effective demonstration and explanation of concepts by the**

**teacher**
(a) A, C, D
(b) A and B only
(c) C and D only
(d) A, B and C

**118. The concept of 'seed germination' can be taught best by:**
(a) Showing germinated seeds to the class and explaining the process of germination
(b) Presenting the germination stages through drawings on the board
(c) Asking the students to perform an activity to sow seeds, observe different stages and draw them
(d) Showing photographs of speed germination

**119. The method that can be useful while teahcing EVS in an integrated manner is:**
(a) Synthesis method
(b) Lecture method
(c) Analysis method
(d) Deductive method

**120. What are the major barriers to implementing environmental education?**
**a. Shortage of Qualified Trained Environmental Teacher**
**b. Rigorous expertise**
**c. Shortage of teachers**
**d. Inter-disciplinary nature**
(a) a, b, and c
(b) b, c, and d
(c) a, c, and d
(d) a, b, and d

---

**// Hints and Solutions //**

**1(B).** Development and learning are inter-related and inter-dependent and contribute to each other.
- Development is a product of maturity and learning.
- Learning and development are inter-related in a complex manner.
- Maturity is more or less automatic, unfolding biological potential which is an irreversible sequence and entails biological changes.
- Such changes are relatively independent of environmental factors as long as environmental factors remain normal.
- There is a more or less permanent change in human behaviour from the individual's experience in the environment.
- Learning occurs across the entire life span, which differs from maturity.
- However, learning depends on the process of maturing i.e. individual readiness (mental and physical) for certain activities.

So, we conclude that l earning and development are inter-related in a complex

**2(D).** Principles of development include:
- Development is Life-Long/Principle of continuity: This principle defines that development is a life-long process as it does not stop at maturation and continues gradually until reaching its maximum growth.
- Development is modifiable: Development may be explained as the series of overall changes in an individual due to the emergence of modified structures and functions that are the outcome of the interactions and exchanges between the organism and its environment.
- Development follows a pattern: Prenatal (before birth) and postnatal (after birth) development of human beings follow a pattern or a predictable sequence. Physical development, motor or language development and intellectual development take place in definite sequences.
- Product of hereditary and environment: Hereditary and environment play a vital role in determining the development of an individual as all the mental and social traits depend on the environment and all the inborn traits, instincts, potentials, and I. Q. depends on heredity.

So, it could be concluded that development is governed and determined by culture alone is not a principle of development.

**3(B).** Heredity and environment are the elements that play a vital role in determining the personality development of an individual. How a person will develop depends on the environment but how far a person can develop depends on heredity.
- Heredity and environment play an important role in the development of the personality and other qualities in the individual.
- From the earliest moments of life, the interaction of heredity and the environment works to shape who children are and who they will become.
- While the genetic instructions a child inherits from his parents may set out a road map for development, the environment can impact how these directions are expressed, shaped or event silenced.
- In order to understand child development, it is important to look at the biological influences that help shape child development, how experiences interact with genetics and some of the genetic disorders that can have an impact on child psychology and development.
- The complex interaction of Heredity and the environment does not just occur at certain moments or at certain periods instead it is persistent and lifelong.

Thus, it can be concluded that for optimum

development of an individual both heredity and environment are essential.

**4(A).** Primary socialization: Inculcation of norms and values within the family is called primary socialization. Here children want to know themselves and try to find their identity and learn the daily routine tasks of humans.

Characteristics of primary socialization:

- Primary socialization begins from the age of infancy.
- Self-identity formed.
- Children start to go familiar with their innate abilities and disabilities.
- Children start learning their daily needs, such as toilet training.

So, it is concluded that process of primary socialisation begins from infancy.

**5(C).** According to Piaget, in the 'Formal Operational Period', the child is able to apply logical thoughts to all classes of problems as in this period:

- Mental capabilities develop to the maximum level.
- Metacognition and problem-solving skills develop in children.
- Children understand world through abstract & scientific thinking.
- Children become capable of hypothetical and deductive reasoning.

So, it could be concluded that according to Piaget the child is able to apply logical thoughts to all classes of problems, this development occurs in 'Formal Operational Period'.

**6(D).** Stages of Moral Development : Kohlberg's theory is broken down into three primary levels. At each level of moral development, there are two stages.

Level 1. Preconventional Morality (4 to 10 years) : Preconventional morality is the earliest period of moral development. At this age, children's decisions are primarily shaped by the expectations of adults and the consequences of breaking the rules. There are two stages within this level:

- Stage 1 (Obedience and Punishment): Children at this stage see "rules as fixed and absolute". Obeying the rules is important because it is a way to avoid punishment. In this children ignore the intention of others and instead focus on the fear of authority and negative consequences.
- Stage 2 ( Instrumental purpose and exchange ) : At the individualism and exchange stage of moral development, children account for individual points of view and judge actions based on how they serve individual needs.

Level 2. Conventional Morality (10 to 13 years) : The next period of moral development is marked by the acceptance of social rules regarding what is good and moral . During this time, adolescents and adults internalize the moral standards they have learned from their role models and from society.

- Stage 3 (Good-Boy Good-girl orientation ) : This stage of the interpersonal relationship of moral development is focused on living up to social expectations and roles. There is an emphasis on conformity, being "nice" and consideration of how choices influence relationships.
- Stage 4 ( Social concern and conscience ) : This stage is focused on ensuring that social order is maintained. The focus is on maintaining law and order by following the rules, doing one's duty, and respecting authority.

Level 3. Postconventional Morality (13 to 16 years) : At this level of moral development, people develop an understanding of abstract principles of morality. The two stages at this level are:

- Stage 5 (Social Contract and Individual Rights): At this stage, the people believe that rules of law are important for maintaining a society, but members of society should agree upon these standards.
- Stage 6 ( Universal Ethical Principles ): Kohlberg's final level of moral reasoning is based on universal ethical principles and abstract reasoning. At this stage, people follow these internalized principles of justice, even if they conflict with laws and rules.

So, we can conclude that social concern and conscience is a sub-stage in Kohlberg's 'conventional state's of Moral Development.

**7(C).** A child-centered system of education is designed to develop the individual and social qualities of a student rather than providing generalized information or training by way of the prescribed subject matter.

Characteristics of the child-centered education system:

- More focus is being placed on the holistic development of a child.
- To help the child become independent, responsible, and confident.
- Child-centered teachers engage in an 'active learning' process.
- Students actively engaged in their own learning.
- They have opportunities to investigate and discover.
- Continuous evaluation.
- Gives respect to the individuality of the child.

Thus, it can be concluded that the child-centered system of education lays major emphasis on activity-based learning.

**8(A).** Gardner's Multiple Intelligences Theory supports the idea that", Most students can be considered Intelligent" in some way.

For example: as all individuals have some different strengths, so the Intelligence. Fish different strengths, so the Intelligence. Fish is not a good climber as that of a monkey but has strength in swimming, so we cannot expect the fish to be good climbers instead we should recognize the natural potential otherwise they may lose their essence.

- The Teachers should be aware that every class has different learners, and they learn in different ways, including their own intelligence profile.
- Should practice content using several points of entry and various strategies.
- Knowing the learners in your current teaching context, what intelligences do they have and what activities can you implement to maximize their learning potential
- Students should be encouraged to practice their strengths and opposed to practicing one universal strength.

**9(B).**

| Bodily-Kinesthetic Intelligence | Persons who said to be good at body movement, performing actions, and physical control. People have excellent hand-eye coordination, Physical movement, and motor control. | - Dancer<br>- Builder<br>- Sculptor<br>- Actor |
| --- | --- | --- |

So, we can conclude that Shorya is a renowned dancer. So he must possess Body-kinesthetic Intelligence.

**10(D).** Our attitude towards diversity in languages influences the existence of linguistic diversity or multiline quality.

- If we have a positive attitude to linguistic diversity, we help in the existence and growth of all the languages spoken in the environment.
- On the contrary, intolerance and narrow thinking towards languages other than one's own may result in discord and disagreement.
- For example, there are 21 sub-castes in the Naga community and about the same numbers of languages are spoken in the community. People of a particular sub-group speak to the other members of their sub-group in their mother tongue. When people of one sub-group need to

talk to people of the other sub-group they use Nagameez language and when they have to speak to people outside their community (i.e. people outside Nagaland and Manipur) they use Hindi and English. This is an example of the positive attitude that Naga people have towards linguistic diversity and this is what makes them multilingual.

- On the other hand, residents of Goa keep fighting over the existence of Marathi and Konkani. Similarly, residents of Belgaon in Karnataka are arguing over the existence of Kannada and Marathi.

So, we conclude that the cause of the downfall of a particular language is intolerance and narrow.

**11(A).** Gender refers to the socially constructed differences between men and women. It refers to the masculine and feminine qualities, behavior, roles, and responsibilities that society upholds. Gender can be changed / re-oriented.

- Gender is such a familiar part of life that it usually takes a deliberate disruption of our expectations of how women and men are supposed to act to pay attention to how it is produced.
- Transvestites and transsexuals construct their gender status of dressing, speaking, walking, gesturing in the way of prescribed for women or men whichever they want to be taken for and so does any normal person.
- Gendering is legitimated by religion, law, science, and society's entire set of values.

So, from the above-mentioned points, it becomes clear that Gender is a social construct.

**12(D).** Individual differences are characteristic of all living organisms. It refers to the difference which distinguishes an individual from another on the basis of psychological characteristics.

Effective strategies to cater to individual differences in the class:

- Recognize and respect differences: Teachers should recognize individual differences in their classroom, fulfill students' needs and respect the diversity and individual differences of learners.
- Use diverse pedagogical strategies: Teachers should use diverse pedagogical strategies to teach students because every student learns in their style, some learn by reading, some learn by doing, etc.
- Reflect on one's verbal and non-verbal communication: While communicating with students teachers should pay attention to their verbal and non-verbal communication to provide required guidance.

So, we can conclude that identifying deficits in students and correcting them is not an effective strategy to cater to individual differences in the class.

**13(B).** Continuous and Comprehensive Evaluation (CCE) has been introduced as a school-based system of evaluation by the CBSE in 2009 with the enactment of the 'Right to Education Act.

- CCE refers to all-around development including both scholastic and co-scholastic aspects of a child's growth.
- It never assesses students according to their economic status rather it emphasizes the continuity of assessment.

The list of personal-social qualities (PSQ) that are assessed under Continuous and Comprehensive Evaluation:-

- Regularity and Punctuality
- Neatness (cleanliness)
- Discipline, Co-operation, and Responsibility
- Physical health
- Emotional stability and leadership qualities
- Consciousness with a spirit of social service
- Positive attitude towards school, teachers, peers, studies, and society
- Entrepreneurship, etc.

So, it becomes clear that painting is not a social-personal quality assessed under CCE.

**14(A).** In absolute grading, the reference point for an assessment of a student's performance is a pre-determined standard.

- Each point value is assigned a grade represented by a letter with each grade assigned based on a predetermined or predefined standard that corresponds to the level of performance by a student
- The grades are associated with that fixed standard irrespective of the distribution of grades in the class
- For example, all students who score 95% and above are collectively grouped under outstanding category and awarded an A grade the categories like outstanding, excellent, very good etc are predetermined and each grade specifically assigned are associated only with that predetermined standard
- This system is used to evaluate students under scholastic areas.

So, we can conclude that in absolute grading, the reference point for an assessment of students' performance happens to be a pre-determined standard.

**15(A).** A teacher can enhance the readiness level of his students by organizing a creational activity in the classroom related to the particular topic as:

- Inclusion of purposeful creational activities makes learning meaningful and fruitful. It is best for teaching students of class three.
- Creative expressions in learning ensure the active involvement of the child and develop the ability to assimilate the concept efficiently by building creative thinking skills.

Form of Creational Activities in Teaching-learning Process:

- Writing: Poetry, songs, dramas, etc.
- Graphic Arts: Designing posters, banners, etc.
- Music: Songs related to environmental messages.
- Movement and dance: Performing non-verbal arts.
- Puppetry: Transmitting environmental messages.

So, it could be concluded that organizing a creational activity in the classroom related to a particular topic will be the best way to enhance the readiness level of his students.

**16(A).** Hearing impairment refers to hearing loss that prevents a person from totally receiving sounds through the ear. If the loss is mild, the person has difficulty hearing faint or distant speech.

Language and Speech Development Barrier in Children with Hearing Impairment:

- Hearing impairment is a great barrier to the normal development of language; the child with such impairment is at a severe disadvantage in virtually all aspects of language development.
- A considerable number of educators of deaf individuals believe that many of the problems of people who are hearing-impaired related to social and intellectual development are primarily due to their deficiencies in language.
- When the child meets other hearing-impaired children and realizes other people face similar challenges and manage fine, regardless of language or level of hearing, it supports identity development and increases confidence.

So, we can conclude that Hearing-impaired children exhibit barriers in communication by language.

**17(D).** Exceptional Children refer to deviated children as they are the ones:

- who deviate significantly from the normal children in respect to social, mental, physical, and emotional characteristics.
- who show deviations falling far above or extremely below from the average which limits their participation in normal activities.

Exceptional types of children include:

- Gifted children: It refers to the children who perform tasks extraordinarily when compared with others of their peer group. They are independent in their judgments as they possess advanced logical and creative thinking.
- Intelligent children: These categories of children have divergent thinking, curious in nature, and are able to find solutions for different problems on their own.

- Backward children: These are those children who are low in achieving academic skills. Backward learners not only lag behind other students in academics but in areas of social, emotional, and psychological well-being.
- Mentally Retarded children: The mentally retarded are those whose normal intellectual growth is arrested before birth, during the birth process, or in the early years of development.
- Physically handicapped learner: These categories of children can not participate in educational, social, and vocational activities on fairly equal terms with their peers due to physical disabilities.
- Disabled child: Disabled children are again divided into different groups based on types of disabilities. They can be learning, cognitive, developmental, intellectual, mental, physical, sensory, or some combination of these.

So, it could be concluded that in inclusive term, exceptional children means the gifted, intelligent, backward, mentally retarded children.

**18(D).** Children with special need are disabled ns any restriction or lack (resulting from an impairment) of ability to perform an activity in a manner or within the range considered normal for a human being.

- Special education is individualized education for children with special needs. Special education means, "Specially designed instruction , to meet the unique needs of a child with special needs including instructions conducted in the classrooms.
- Inclusive education , as an approach, seeks to address the learning needs of all children (disabled and non-disabled) with a specific focus on those who are vulnerable to marginalization and exclusion.
- Inclusion emerged as a result of the social justice movement in the field of disability which emphasizes that schools should create an environment in which students with special needs are seen as valuable members of the social community.

Thus from above-mentioned points, it is clear that children with special needs should be included in 'regular' set-ups with special provisions.

**19(B).** Characteristics of Creative learner:
- A creative learner can make unusual associations or connections between seemingly unrelated or remote ideas They can rearrange elements of thought to create new ideas or products.
- Also, they pose many ideas or solutions to problems.
- They display intellectual playfulness, fantasize, imagine, and daydream. Also,

a creative learner doesn't need to have a high IQ.
- They are good at lateral thinking and problem-solving. Creativity is associated with lateral thinking for the generation of new ideas.
- These children have divergent thinking and are very curious in nature that's why sometimes the classroom seems monotonous to them because they grab things fastly than their age-peers.
- Divergent thinking in creativity leads to a broadening of the definition and criteria of the problem to generate a wide variety of possible solutions.
- The creative learner has personality traits such as sensitivity to problems, fluency, flexibility, originality, ability to transform meaning, and ability to elaborate.

So, we can conclude that a creative learner refers to one who is good at lateral thinking and problem-solving.

**20(C).** Gifted children are those who show consistently remarkable performance in educational endeavours. They possess superior intellectual ability within the range of the upper two to three per cent of the population. Characteristics of Gifted Children:
- Learning commensurate with that expected of older students, often reading at an earlier than average age.
- Gifted child solve the problem quickly
- Knowing about things of which other students are unaware.
- They have a high ability for abstract and symbolic thinking.
- Curiosity indicated by asking serious questions.
- They have a large vocabulary and mature, expressive ability.
- They require limited exposure and fewer repetitions to learn. They have extra-ordinary memory.
- They can apply knowledge to unfamiliar situations.

So, from the above explanation, it can be concluded that gifted children solve the problem quickly.

**21(B).** 'Learning' means a relatively permanent change in behaviour that occurs as a result of experience with the environment.

Learning, in the case of all persons, proceeds through five stages. These are as follows :
1. Acquisition: During this stage, the person learns a new task.
2. Fluency/Proficiency: During this stage, the person learns to perform the new task to a higher degree of accuracy.
3. Maintenance: During this stage, the person is able to perform the task independently, even after teaching has ended.
4. Generalization: During this stage, the

person learns to generalize the learned skills/tasks to other situations or environments; in ' other words, he is able to perform the task in situations other than the ones in which he had learnt it.
5. Adaptation: During this stage, the learner applies a previously learnt skill in a new area of application without direct instruction or guidance.

So, we can conclude that the fifth and last stage is "Adaptation".

**22(B).** The teacher is a friend, philosopher, and guide to the students.
- If a new student is unable to adjust in the classroom, the teacher will make the classroom environment comfortable.
- The teacher will try to find out the reason by talking to her and try to resolve it.
- The teacher can introduce the new student to old students to make her comfortable.
- The teacher tells the other students to help her with all the work.

Thus, it is concluded that Rohini, a newly admitted student, is unable to adjust to the classroom, as a teacher, will try to find out the reason.

**23(D).** Teaching is a process related to the effective transmission of knowledge and skills in an individual. It limits or enhances the ways the learners learn and assimilate concepts and ideas.
- Teaching becomes much more effective when 'Learner-centered instruction' and 'Interactive methods' are used which provides autonomy to students to control their own work.
- In these approaches, students work in flexible, cooperative groupings to solve problems and analyze texts to demonstrate an understanding of a task.

Characteristics of teaching:
- Teaching is a tripolar process . This process of education considers that the development of the child takes place in and through the society , in which the teacher and the child live together.
- Active engagement and student participation are fostered by the teachers through a series of interactive processes in the form of debate, group tasks, projects, etc.
- Teaching is a purposeful and effect-directed process that ends at desired changes of learners' behavior. When the desires and goals are fulfilled teaching is effective.

So, we can conclude that teaching is a process confined only to the classroom's statements about teaching is not correct.

**24(D).** Error: When a learner can't master a topic, he/she is vulnerable to make errors. Errors are nothing but incorrectness made by a child during learning.

Misconceptions: It takes place due to the mismatch in previously assimilated and the newly accommodated knowledge.

Children's errors and misconceptions:

- Are a significant step in the teaching-learning process.
- Are necessary in the learning process to give insight into children's thinking.
- Help the teacher to be aware of learners' learning styles, to cater them according to their needs.
- Are considered as a part of the teaching-learning process as it helps to understand the child.

So, it could be concluded that children's errors and misconceptions are a significant step in the teaching-learning process.

**25(D).** All learners make mistakes. As someone has said: "You can't learn without goofing". Whether you are learning how to ride a bicycle, how to fly a kite or learn a language, everyone does make mistakes.

- An error is an incorrect form and a sur e indication that the learner has not mastered the core of the selective topic in a learning process.
- The qualitative difference in children's thinking as compared to adults is reflected in the type of errors made by the children.
- Errors can occur in adults as well as children. The qualitative effect of errors can be observed through the type of error.
- Adults tend to make silly mistakes that may not be serious as they tend to overlook minor details and focus on bigger things.
- Whereas children may make a significantly big error as they may not have the experience of the concept.

Thus, it is concluded that errors made by children are indicative of children's thinking process which is qualitatively different from that of adults.

**26(A).** The term 'cognition' refers to all processes by which the sensory input is transformed, reduced, elaborated, stored, recovered, and used. Cognitive development refers to the development of the ability to think and reason.

- Cognition develops in the learners through the interaction of innate power (heredity), environment and maturation.
- Cognition is the process of acquiring and understanding knowledge through our thoughts, experiences, and senses .
- Cognition embraces all those aspects of human intelligence that we use to adapt to and make sense of the world and the emotional environment around him has an impact on his cognitive thinking.
- Cognitive skill s are used to comprehend, process, remember, and apply incoming information.
- Cognition describes how mental

processes i.e. learning, remembering, problem-solving, and thinking develop from birth until adulthood. Understanding cognitive development is useful in determining the kind of thinking children are capable of at different age levels.

- It develops the ability to solve problems, learn from experiences, and apply knowledge to deal with new situations. It is a mental process that facilitates obtaining , transform, store, retrieve, and use information.

So, it becomes clear that cognition is a process of acquiring and understanding knowledge through our thoughts, experience, and sense .

**27(C).** Motivation is something that makes the person to action and continues him in the course of action already initiated. There are two identifiable components of motivation. These are needed and drive.

Important principles of motivation in learning are as follows :

- All learning must have a purpose.
- Students need skills and knowledge.
- Specific directions empower students.
- Students want to have fun while they learn/work.
- Curiosity
- A blend of praise and Encouragement
- A combination of intrinsic and extrinsic rewards.
- Involvement in collaborative activities.

Thus from the above-mentioned points, it is clear that helps to get a higher position is not true about the principle of motivation.

**28(D).** Learning is the process by which skills, attitudes, knowledge, and concepts are acquired, understood, applied, and extended. All human beings, whether grown-ups or children engage in the process of learning, either consciously, or subconsciously.

Environmental factors that impact learning:

- Environmental factors refer to the combination of all external and environmental factors that affect the learning process.
- Some schools operate in dilapidated buildings with leaking roofs. They may not have a lab, library, toilets, or drinking water facilities which creates a barrier in the path of learning.
- On the other hand, a well-designed school environment fosters positive peer relationships, promotes pleasant interactions between teachers and children, and allows teachers to assist children in achieving their objectives.

So, school is an environmental factor that impacts learning.

**29(D).** Learning is a proces s by which behavior is either modified or changed through expe rience or training. Learning is thus a relatively permanent change in

response potentiality which occurs as a function of reinforced practice. There are many factors that influence learning.

Learning is influenced by:

Psychological factors:

- Psychological aspects are the elements of one's personality that limit or enhance the ways that one learns and thinks.
- Several psychological factors such as intelligence, personality, attitude, interest, and aptitude have considerable influence on the learning of a child.

Socio-Cultural factors:

- Socio-cultural factors refer to the combination of social and cultural factors. These factors play a vital role in shaping the abilities and behaviors of a child.
- The immediate environmental structure of social culture is where an individual has direct interaction with their significant others such as parents, siblings, teachers, and peers.

School-related factors:

- Overcrowding classrooms is another contributing factor. In some big cities, houses are converted into English medium schools. In small rooms, sixty to seventy children are made to sit and are unable to benefit from highly verbal instruction.
- The condition of the setting where the learning process takes place can also enhance or interfere with the intake of information.

Teacher-related factors:

- Learning problems may occur because of inadequate or inappropriate teaching. The child may have difficulty in learning because the teacher does not provide adequate or appropriate instruction.
- If the teacher is a poor communicator or uses monotonous and uninteresting methods, the children are put at a disadvantage.

So, it is clear that learning is influenced by all Psychological, Socio-Cultural, School-related, and Teacher related factors.

**30(A).** One of the major approaches to understand motivation is the behavioural approach.

- The behavioural approach considers the role of external rewards and punishment in motivation in the classroom. According to this approach, the role of positive and negative stimuli as incentives is very important in encouraging or discouraging a particular behaviour. The role of reinforcement is also considered important in teaching and learning. This approach promotes the use of grades, stars, rewards, certification, appreciation, etc., for enhancing the motivation of learners.
- Incentives motivate students to be more productive, as they create a sense of

pride among students.
- The incentive is an amazing way to ensure that students stay motivated to do their work and learning.

Thus from the above-mentioned points, it is clear that teachers should promote motivation to learn among their students by using incentives to help students learn.

**31(A).** According to the passage, "This may be visible more in the rural belt, where many non-farming entities purchase fertile farmland, not for farming but for money parking purposes. The demonetization and consequent reduction in the shadow economy would bring the demand for such farmlands down."

The paragraph clearly states that most black money hoarders utilize their hoarded cash to buy fertile agricultural land as means of turning the black to white, which is a part of the shadow economy.

**32(B).** According to passage, "The total value of old Rs.500 and Rs.1000 notes in the circulation is to the tune of Rs.14.2 trillion, which is about 85% of the total value of the currency in circulation."

So, it is concluded that 85% of the total value of currency in circulation is made up by the old Rs.500 and Rs.1000 notes.

**33(D).** The idiom 'cash cow' refers to any products or services that yield a profit or income on a regular basis.

**34(D).** According to the passage, "The move is also likely to have a habit-changing impact on the Indian populous and there could be an increased belief in keeping cash in the banks rather than stashed at home and using formal banking channels for their spending needs."

As per the paragraph, Indians are well-known for not availing of proper banking services and since people have been mightily inconvenienced because of this move, the future may change the lackadaisical habits.

**35(B).** The passage deals with the act of demonetization taken up by the Indian government and its effect on the economy.

**36(A).** The meaning of the given words:
- Formal: Officially sanctioned or recognized
- Official: relating to an authority or public body and its activities and responsibilities
- Ceremonial: relating to or used for formal religious or public events
- Informal: 'unorthodox' or 'unofficial'
- Traditional: existing in or as part of a tradition; long-established

So, from the meaning of the given word we can say that official is the correct synonym of the word 'formal'.

**37(C).** According to passage, "It will improve the medium to long-term "Current

Account and Savings Account (CASA)" ratio of the banks."

The full form of CASA is Current Account and Savings Account.

**38(D).** According to passage, " The World Bank in July 2010 estimated the size of the shadow economy for India at 20.7% of the Gross Domestic Product (GDP) in 1999 and rising to 23.2% in 2007."

**39(C).** The meaning of the given words:
- Compliance: the state or fact of according with or meeting rules or standards
- Defiance: open resistance; bold disobedience
- Agreement: harmony or accordance in opinion or feeling.
- Assent: the expression of approval or agreement:
- Consensus: a general agreement

So, from the meaning of the given word we can say that defiance is the correct antonym of the word 'compliance'.

**40(D).** According to the given lines, "And I waterd it in fears"

Here the 'it' refers to wrath which means anger. The poet is comparing suppressed anger to a tree that kept growing over years into a garden.

Therefore, the poet watered 'anger' with his fears.

**41(B).** The poet is representing two scenarios in his poem.
- First, when he confessed his anger to his friend and it subsides.
- Second, when he suppressed his anger and how it kept growing over years and became poisonous.
- If we read both the lines carefully, we will easily notice the repetition of And I.
- Such repetition of the same phrase at the beginning of multiple consecutive lines is called Anaphora.

**42(D).** The meaning of difficult words in the line:
- Foe: Enemy
- Outstretched: It means that something is stretched to its capacity.

When a person is outstretched it means they are lying on the floor.

But in the last stanza of the poem, the poet is narrating how his enemy sneaked into his garden.

Since the tree and its fruit were poisonous, the enemy died and that's why he was outstretched under the tree.

Therefore, from all the points given above, we can infer that the last line of the poem means 'The enemy was lying dead under the tree.'

**43(D).** The line given in the question is from the last stanza of the poem.
- Velid is an archaic use of the word veiled which means to cover.
- The word pole refers to the tree of wrath

that the poet has cultivated.
- So, through this line, the poet is describing the nighttime.

Therefore, the expression When the night had veild the pole means 'The dark night was all around the tree.'

**44(C).** The poem uses simple language to present its readers with a powerful message.
- The poet believes that anger that stays with an individual for a long time is dangerous.
- A metaphor is when two things are compared directly.
- An extended metaphor is simply a metaphor that extends over lines, paragraphs or stanzas.
- In this poem, the extended metaphor is a tree and it is used for anger.

Therefore, from all the points given above, we can infer that the literary device used throughout the poem is 'Extended Metaphor'.

**45(A).** In the whole poem, the poet is actively cultivating his anger with fears, tears and smiles:
- And I waterd it in fears,
- Night & morning with my tears:
- And I sunned it with smiles

Eventually, his tree turned into a garden as he expressed in the last stanza " And into my garden stole"

Therefore, from all the points given above, we can infer that the garden in the poem refers to anger.

**46(C).** Language teaching is the process in which a child gains communicative comprehension or fluency over a language. It involves practice by learners where facilitation is provided by a teacher.

Language learning:
- It is a result of deliberate and conscious effort for a better understanding of the foundational skills of a specific language. It refers to have a basic knowledge of grammatical rules and their use in communication.
- Input-rich communicational environments are a prerequisite for language learning. It arouses the interest and curiosity of learners to learn a specific language.
- Inputs include textbooks, learner-chosen texts, and class libraries allowing for a variety of genres. For example, Big Books for young learners, parallel books and materials in more than one language, radio/audio cassettes, and "authentic" materials.
- Also, these inputs and the environment that is enriched with these types of resources can help to minimize the gap between incomprehension and language learning i.e., the disability to interpret and comprehend a language and the ability to comprehend and use a

language practically.
So, both statements regarding language learning are true.

**47(B).** Language is a symbolic, rule-governed system, shared by a group of people to express their thoughts and feelings. In a child, language development takes place through language acquisition and language learning.

Language acquisition:
- It refers to the subconscious process of learning a native or second language because of the innate capacity of the human brain.
- It is a natural process whereby children acquire language by observing and repeating what they hear in their native environment.
- Language acquisition does not require any formal instruction, children acquire the language without being taught.
- Language acquisition is a natural process so, one does not forget one's native language.

Language learning:
- It refers to the result of deliberate and conscious effort for a better understanding of foundational skills of language learning.
- It refers to have a basic knowledge of grammatical rules and their use in communication.

So, it could be concluded that the 'acquired system' or 'acquisition' of a language is the subconscious process of learning.

**48(B).** Language teaching is less about the school and more about the process of learning English. The modern approach to all language learning and teaching is the scientific one and is based on sound linguistic principles.
- Principle of Graded Patterns is one of the principles of materials preparation for language learning that emphasizes that materials need to be graded appropriately.
- "To teach a language is to impart a new system of complex habits, and habits are acquired slowly." So, language patterns should be taught gradually, in cumulative graded steps.
- This means the teacher should go on adding each new element or pattern to previous ones. New patterns of language should be introduced and practiced with vocabulary that students already know.

So, we can conclude that one of the principles of materials preparation for language learning is that materials need to be graded appropriately.

**49(D).** Language teaching is the process whereby a child gains communicative comprehension or fluency over a language. It involves practice by learners where facilitation is provided by a teacher. Some of the Principles of Language Teaching are the

Principle of Graded Patterns, the Principle of Selection and graduation, etc.
Principle of Selection and Gradation:
Selection of the language material is considered as the first requisite of good teaching. It should be done in respect of grammatical items and vocabulary and structures.
Gradation of the language material means placing the language items in order. It involves grouping and sequence.
- Grouping the system of language means what sounds, words, phrases, and meanings are to be taught. Thus we have Phonetic grouping, Lexical grouping, Grammatical grouping, Semantic grouping, and Structure grouping.
- Sequence means what comes after what. In teaching a foreign language, the sequence should be there in the arrangement of phrases (grammatical sequence) words (lexical sequence), and meaning (semantic sequence).

So, we can conclude that the principles of sequencing in teaching a foreign language, do not include phonetic sequence.

**50(C).** Grammar is defined as a theory of language. We consider language as rule-governed behavior, relating to sounds, word formation, and structure. Here grammar constitutes a subset of rules relating to morphology and syntax.
- It takes time to learn a language, even if it is by acquisition. It requires context to learn a language, for example, children speak the language when they have previous knowledge or experience.
- Grammatical Rules instruct a language user that how language should be used correctly and clearly. But it is widely known that effective language learning takes place from practicing it in real context rather than following the accurate rule.

So. it could be concluded that grammatical rules are not important for learning a language.

**51(C).** Grammar is the backbone of any language. It is the womb that gives birth to sentences. These sentences are fertilized using grammar to form correct and appropriate speech.
- Grammar is defined as a theory of language. We consider language as rule-governed behavior, relating to sounds, word formation, and structure. Here grammar constitutes a subset of rules relating to morphology and syntax.
- Grammar rules are made easier if they are given in a context using examples and teaching grammar in context provides accuracy in the target language.
- Learning grammar in context using examples will allow learners to see how rules can be used in sentences.
- Providing the chance to practice

grammar in context will allow learners to understand how language works and this will improve their communication skills.

Thus, it is concluded that (A) is correct, but (R) is not correct.

**52(C).** Language is the rule-based use of speech sounds to communicate. Language disorders or language disabilities involve the processing of linguistic information.
- Problems that may be experienced can involve grammar (syntax and/or morphology), semantics (meaning), understanding or expressing language, or other aspects of language.
- Disordered language may be due to a receptive problem , that is, a difficulty in understanding speech sounds (involving impaired language comprehension).
- It can also be due to an expressive problem , i.e., a difficulty in producing the speech sounds (involving language production), that follow the arbitrary rules of a specific language.
- The disorders that come under language disorders/disabilities include Stuttering, Specific Language Impairment, Developmental Phonological Disorders, Aphasia, Dyspraxia, etc.

Thus, it is concluded that when a child has difficulties in understanding or expressing language that is called language disability.

**53(C).** Language skills are necessary for effective communication in any environment and to interact with others. It allows an individual to comprehend and produce language for proper and effective interpersonal communication.
The four basic language skills and their natural order are listening-speaking-reading-writing. These foundational skills of language are divided into two categories which are receptive and productive skills.
Productive skills:
- The productive skills of language are speaking and writing because these skills can measure learner's ability to produce language.
- Both skills are concerned with language product or output through speech or written tests.

Receptive skills:
- The receptive skills of language are listening and reading because these skills don't require the production of language.
- These skills focus on an individual's ability of understanding and comprehending language.

So, from the above-mentioned points, it becomes clear that the order advocated for learning the language skills is listening, speaking, reading, writing.

**54(D).** Language is a purely human and non-instinctive method of communicating ideas, emotions, and desires by means of voluntarily produced symbols.

- Language skills should be taught in an integrated manner. In order to provide more focused and significant learning situations, teachers must integrate the four language skills while teaching and practicing the language.
- When we speak, we also listen simultaneously. When we write we are also reading. This engagement with language enables us to internalize the underlying grammaticality of the language.

Thus, it is concluded that language skills should be taught in an integrated manner.

**55(C).** Communicative competence refers to a learner's ability to use language to communicate successfully. This competence can be oral, written, or even nonverbal.

- It is an inclusive term that refers to possessing the knowledge of the language as well as the skill to use the language in real-life situations for fulfilling communicative needs.
- It includes the ability to use grammatical structures in different situations to convey and interpret messages and to negotiate meanings.
- Teachers can use information gap and role-play activities to evaluate learners' competence for speaking. It includes accuracy, fluency, complexity, appropriateness, and capacity.

Thus, it is concluded that communicative competence should be the main focus for the evaluation of speaking skills.

**56(C).** Decoding: This refers to the ability to read individual words and to sound out unfamiliar words accurately and automatically. Most reading problems are related to difficulty with decoding.

Decoding should be evaluated in three ways:

- Decoding of word lists to eliminate context clues for the reader,
- Reading of nonsense words to eliminate memorization of words,
- Reading in context.

So, we can conclude that decoding in evaluating language proficiency refers to the ability to read individual words and to sound out unfamiliar words accurately.

**57(C).** A smartboard is an audio-visual aid that maximizes learning with the help of the auditory and visual systems.

- Smartboards in classrooms allow teachers and students to access a wide range of educational resources that are available online, from videos to texts to animations and apps.
- Audio-visual aids activate the sense of both hearing and vision to enrich learner's knowledge by providing information about different subjects and

boost their self-confidence and independence.

- Being an audio-visual learning aid video is used to present the lesson effectively involving both sound and pictures for heightening learner's intellectual abilities to make learning meaningful.

So, from the above-mentioned points, it becomes clear that smartboard is an audio-visual aid.

**58(C).** Linguaphone: Speaking a language is an active skill, something you learn by doing, not just studying. This is the practical approach taken by Linguaphone to language learning. Linguaphone enables understanding of the language and is able to converse with and understand real people speaking the language. It helps in teaching pronunciation, accent and intonation.

So, it becomes clear that Linguaphone is a utility in teaching English pronunciation, accent and intonation.

**59(D).** Remedial Teaching is an integral part of the teaching-learning program, also known as compensatory or corrective teaching.

Objectives of Remedial Teaching in the English language:

- To eliminate ineffective habits
- To make learners learn better by giving additional help
- To provide learning activities and practical experiences to pupils according to their abilities and requirements.
- To teach again the language items not properly learned
- To arise learners' interest in learning with stimulating approaches
- Help the pupils to get rid of their common or specific weaknesses.
- To transmit practical experiences to learners according to their diverse needs
- To provide individualized teaching with intensive remedial support.

So, we can conclude that all of the above are the objectives of remedial teaching in the English language.

**60(B).** The main purpose of using oral drill is that they help students gain confidence, and they help the teacher draw learners' attention to phonological features (i.e., accuracy and pronunciation) of the target language.

**61(A).** Given,

Area of four walls of a room $= 660m^2$

Height of the room$( h ) = 11m$

Length $=$ twice the width

As we know,

Area of four walls of a room $= 2(l + b) \times h$

where ' $l$ ' is length of the room and ' $b$ ' is breadth of the room and $h$ is the height of the room.

Area of ceiling of a room $- (l \times b)$

Let the length and breadth of the room be $2x$ and $x$ respectively.

Area of four walls of a room $= 2(l + b) \times h$

$\Rightarrow 2 \times (2x + x) \times 11 = 660$

$\Rightarrow 2 \times (3x) \times 11 = 660$

$\Rightarrow x = 10$

Area of ceiling of a room $= (l \times b)$

$= (2x \times x)$

$= 200$

$\therefore$ The area of ceiling of the room is $200m^2$.

**62(A).** Given,

Length of the rectangular field $= 242m$

Area of the rectangular field $= 4840m^2$

Cost of fencing $= 0.50$ Rs.per meter

Area of the rectangular field $= ($ length $\times$ breadth $)$

$\Rightarrow 4840 = (242 \times$ breadth $)$

$\Rightarrow$ breadth $= 20m$

Perimeter of the rectangular field $= 2 \times$ (length $+$ breadth)

$= 2 \times (242 + 20)$

$= 524m$

Total cost of fencing of the rectangular field $= ($ Perimeter $\times$ cost of fencing per meter $)$

$= (524 \times 0.50)$

$= 262$

$\therefore$ The total cost of fencing of the rectangular field is Rs. $262$.

**63(A).** Given,

Ratio of two complementary angles is $1 : 5$.

As we know,

Sum of two complementary angles is $90°$.

Let the two angles be $1x$ and $5x$.

Sum of two complementary angles is $90°$.

$\Rightarrow (1x + 5x) = 90°$

$\Rightarrow x = 15°$

$\Rightarrow (5x - x) = 60°$

$\therefore$ The difference between two complementary angles is $60°$.

**64(D).** Given,

$18\frac{1}{3} + 9\frac{2}{3} - 10\frac{1}{3} = 1\frac{2}{3} + ?$

$\Rightarrow 18 + 9 + \frac{1}{3} + \frac{2}{3} - \left(10 + 1 + \frac{1}{3} + \frac{2}{3}\right) = ?$

$\Rightarrow 28 - 12 = ?$

$\Rightarrow ? = 16$

$\therefore$ The value of (?) is $16$.

**65(A).** Given,

Surface area of the cylinder $= 1672m^2$

As we know,

Surface area of the cylinder $= 2\pi r(r + h)$

According to the question,

$\Rightarrow 2\pi r(r + h) = 1672m^2$

$\Rightarrow 2 \times \frac{22}{7} \times r \times 19 = 1672m^2$

$\Rightarrow r = \frac{(1672 \times 7)}{(2 \times 22 \times 19)}$

$\Rightarrow r = 14$

$\therefore h = 19 - 14$

$= 5m$

Volume of the cylinder $= \pi r^2 h$

$= \frac{22}{7} \times 14 \times 14 \times 5$

$= 3080m^3$

**66(B).** Decimal values of the given

numbers:
$\sqrt{2} = 1.42 \quad \sqrt{3} = 1.73$
So the number inserted must be between 1.42 and 1.73.
Now checking the options:
(A): $\frac{49}{28} = 1.75$
(B): $\frac{56}{35} = 1.6$
(C): $\frac{63}{45} = 1.4$
(D): $\frac{85}{66} = 1.28$
We can see that only $\frac{56}{35}$ can be put between $\sqrt{2}$ and $\sqrt{3}$.

**67(A).** Given,
$x, x + 2$ and $x + 4$ are all prime numbers.
As we know,
A number divisible by 1 and itself only is known as a prime number.
Checking the options:
Put $x = 3$, then the numbers are $3, 5, 7$
Put $x = 2$ then the numbers are $2, 4, 6$
Put $x = 11$ then the numbers are $11, 13, 15$
Put $x = 17$ then the numbers are $17, 19, 21$
After analyzing the options we can see that at $x = 3$ all numbers are coming prime.
$\therefore$ The value of $x = 3$

**68(A).** Given,
$\sqrt[3]{\left[\frac{x}{27}\right]} = \frac{5}{3}$
$\Rightarrow (\frac{x}{27})^{(\frac{1}{3}) \times 3} = (\frac{5}{3})^3$
$\Rightarrow (\frac{x}{27}) = (\frac{5}{3})^3$
$\Rightarrow (\frac{x}{27}) = \frac{125}{27}$
$\Rightarrow x = 125$

**69(B).** Given,
Boating at $\frac{6}{7}^{th}$ of regular speed in a lake, the tourist got late by 30 minutes.
Let regular speed and changed speed be $7x$ and $6x$ respectively.

| Speed | Distance | Time |
|---|---|---|
| $7x$ | 42x Km/hr | 6 hours |
| $6x$ | | 7 hours |

Difference of time is 60 minutes $= 30$ minutes
1 minute $= (\frac{1}{2})$ minutes
Regular time $= 6$ hours $\times (\frac{1}{2})$
$= 3$ hours
$\therefore$ The time taken at usual speed is 3 hours.

**70(C).** Given,
$x = 6 \times y \,...(1)$
$(x + 4) = 4 \times (y + 4) \,...(2)$
Put the value of eq. (1) in eq. (2), we get
$\Rightarrow 6y + 4 = 4y + 16$
$\Rightarrow 6y - 4y = 16 - 4$
$\Rightarrow 2y = 12$
$\Rightarrow y = 6$
$\therefore$ The present age of $y$ is 6 years.

**71(B).** Given series,
$2, 3, 5, 7, 11, \_\_\_ 17$
The given series is of prime numbers.
The prime numbers are those which are only divisible by 1 or by itself. example;

$2, 3, 5, 7$ etc.
After 11, 13 is the next prime number.
So, 13 is the missing term.

**72(D).** Given,
No of students who obtained marks between 200 and 300 $= 45 + 60 = 105$
No of students who obtained marks between 350 or more marks $= 40 + 35 = 75$
$\therefore$ The required percent $= \frac{(105-75)}{75} \times 100$
$= \frac{30}{75} \times 100$
$= 40\%$

**73(B).** Given,
Divyanka reaches her office for a meeting 15 minutes before 11 : 20 am.
She reached half an hour after the scheduled time of the meeting.
Rajia reached 25 minutes after the scheduled time of the meeting.
Divyanka reaches her office $= 11 : 20$ am $-15$ minutes $= 11 : 05$ am
She reached half an hour after the scheduled time of the meeting.
The scheduled time of the meeting $= 11 : 05 - 30$ minutes $= 10 : 35$ am
Rajia reached her office $= 10 : 35$ am $+25$ minutes $= 11 : 00$ am
$\therefore$ Rajia reached her office at 11 : 00 am.

**74(B).** Given,
The weight of 35 laddus $= 1$ kg 400 g
The total number of laddus can be packed in one box $= 12$
The total quantity of needed laddus $= 96$ kg
As we know,
1 kg $= 1000$ g
The weight of 35 laddus $= 1$ kg 400 g $= (1000 + 400)$ g $= 1400$ g
The weight of one laddu $= \frac{1400}{35} = 40$ g
The weight of one box that are packed with 12 laddus $= 12 \times 40 = 480$ g
The total quantity of needed laddus $= 96$ kg $= (96 \times 1000)$ g $= 96000$ g
Total number of box needed $= \frac{96000}{480} = 200$
$\therefore$ A total number of 200 boxes are needed to pack a total of 96 kg laddus.

**75(D).** As we know,
1 Litre $= 1000$ ml
1 Paisa $= $ Rs. $0.01$
1 km $= 1000$ meter
One dozen $= 12$
(1): 5 L 40 ml $= (5 \times 1000 + 40)$ ml $= 5040$ ml
The statement (1) is not correct.
(2) 56 Paisa $= 56 \times 0.01 = $ Rs. $0.56$
The statement (2) is correct.
(3) 3.5 km $= (3.5 \times 1000)$ meter $= 3500$ meter
The statement (3) is also correct.
(4) One and half dozen $= 1.5 \times 12 = 18$
The statement (4) is not correct.
Therefore, statements (1) and (4) are not correct.

**76(C).** According to the question,
$\frac{3}{8} = 0.375$
$\frac{5}{7} = 0.714$
$\frac{19}{25} = 0.76$
$\frac{16}{21} = 0.761$
Clearly, $\frac{16}{21}$ is largest number.

**77(C).** Mathematics is the study of numbers, shape, quantity, and patterns. Mathematics is the 'queen of all sciences' and its presence is there in all the subjects. The Nature of Mathematics is Logical as it relies on:
- evaluation of truth or likelihood of statements.
- development of skills like speed, accuracy, estimation.
- improvement of reasoning power, analytical and, critical thinking.
- enhancement of scientific attitude like estimating, finding and verifying results.

So, it becomes clear that the nature of Mathematics is logical.

**78(B).** Learning mathematics serves both as a means and an end. It is a means to develop logical and quantitative thinking abilities. At the early grades, children's learning of mathematics should be a natural outgrowth from children themselves. Such experiences must be interesting and should challenge their imagination, so that while observing any natural phenomena they can think mathematically Let us now discuss in detail regarding the nature of mathematics:
- Mathematics is logical
- Mathematics is symbolic.
- Mathematics is precise.
- Mathematics is the study of structures.
- Mathematics aims at abstraction.

So, we conclude that learning maths is a means to develop logical and quantitative thinking abilities.

**79(C).** Mathematics : Mathematics is a systematized, organized, and exact branch of Science. It plays an important role in accelerating the social, economical, and technological growth of a nation. It helps in solving problems of life that need enumeration and calculation.
The nature of Mathematics can be made explicit by understanding the chief characteristics of Mathematics:
- Mathematics is a science of discovery.
- Mathematics is an intellectual game.
- It deals with the art of drawing conclusions.
- It is a tool subject.
- It involves an intuitive method.
- It is the science of exactness, precision, and accuracy.
- It is the subject of a logical and specific sequence.
- It requires the application of rules and concepts to new situations.

- It is a logical study structure and patterns.

Thus, it is concluded that expanded expression is not related to the nature of Mathematics .

**80(A).** Role of Mathematics in School Curriculum: National Curriculum framework, 2005 recommends that teaching of mathematics at the primary level should focus on:

- Children understand the basic structure of Mathematics like Arithmetic, algebra, geometry, and trigonometry, the basic content areas of school mathematics, all offer a methodology for abstraction, structuration, and generalization.
- Mathematics implies understanding of the appropriate use of learned mathematical techniques.
- Teachers engage every child in the class with the conviction that everyone can learn mathematics and enrich them with examples of achievements and contributions of mathematicians from different regions and different social groups.
- Helping students to connect classroom learning with everyday life.
- Children learn to enjoy Mathematics rather than fear it.
- Children pose and solve meaningful problems.

So, from the above-mentioned points, it becomes clear that important Mathematics implies understanding the appropriate use of learned mathematical techniques.

**81(A).** Teaching-learning of mathematics takes account of well-defined objectives. Some Curricular Expectation of Teaching Mathematics at the Primary Level are as follows:

- To ensure a good start for the students in learning mathematics.
- To give clarity on the fundamental concepts and processes of the subject.
- To develop a connection between the logical functioning of daily life and that of mathematical thinking.
- To create love, faith and interest for learning mathematics.
- To develop in them a taste and confidence in mathematics.
- To develop language and symbolic notations with standard algorithms of performing number operations.
- Represent part of whole as a fraction and order simple fractions.
- To develop an appreciation for accuracy.
- To acquaint them with the relation of mathematics with their present as well as future life.
- To develop in them the habits like regularity, practice, patience, self-reliance and hard work.
- To link mathematics with other subjects.

So, we conclude that analysing and inferring from the representation of grouped data is not curriculum expectation at the primary level.

**82(C).** Like any language, the mathematics language is made up of concepts, terminology, symbols, algorithms, and syntax which is peculiar to it.

- The components of a language give meaning, bring organization, and make its structure well defined.
- Mathematical language has its components in the form of concepts, terminologies, and algorithms.

Some commonly used mathematical symbols are:

- <, used for showing inequality, less than 8 < 10.
- [ ] , { } brackets calculate expression inside first [5×5] + 7 = 32 , {2×5} =10.
- = equals sign equality 4 = 2 + 2.
- + plus sign shows addition 4 + 5 = 9.
- * asterisk shows multiplication 2 * 3 = 6.
- ! is the symbol for factorial.
- % percent means part of hundred

(#): This symbol is known as the hashtag that is not a mathematical symbol but is used in the language before relevant or important terms like people usually hashtag in social media while blogging or writing anything important or to give tags. (&): It is the ampersand symbol that is used to denote the "and" in short form in the English language.

So, it is concluded that #, & are not a part of mathematical language.

**83(D).** Algebra is generalized arithmetic where letters are used as symbols to represent numbers . Every number is a constant and every symbol can be assigned different values in different situations. Algebraic expressions are formed using symbols and constants. Four fundamental operations on the symbols and constants to form expressions are used. Terms are parts of an expression which are separated by '+' or '_' sign. It may be a constant, a variable or combination of both. The algorithm (method) involved in solving real-life problems is to:

- Understand the situation expressed in the word problem
- Choose a symbol and substitute it for the unknown to be determined
- Write an equation from the given relation in the problem
- Solve the equation and find the value of the unknown
- Verify the correctness of the solution

So, we conclude that the above statement is of algebra.

**84(D).** Problems in teaching and learning of mathematics:

- Teacher Related: It is found less than half of mathematics teachers having a mathematics background is available in higher-level but the majority were given training. Some teachers who are actually from other backgrounds have to teach mathematics and maximum math teacher have to teach other subjects like physics, chemistry, social science, religion, and physical education class as there is a shortage of teachers. More than half of teachers agreed with the fact that all teachers are not having sufficient training and therefore the quality of education failing to upgrade for all these problems.
- Attitude towards Mathematics: Mathematics is an important subject, but many of them do not at all like this subject at all. The reasons for disliking the subjects mentioned by the students were dissatisfactory results; lack of interest in the subject and in some cases complicacy with the subject contents. According to teachers, there are negative attitudes towards mathematics relating to fear of mathematics, examination system, and memorization. Students' attitudes towards mathematics have a great influence on their decision-making of choosing streams.
- Mathematical Anxiety: Most students mentioned that their poor result of mathematics creates lots of anxiety. Teachers' views also indicate this fact as problems for students. anxiety about getting zero if they solved their problems in a different way or through another method than those followed by teachers.

So, we can conclude that all of the above factors creating problems in teaching and learning mathematics.

**85(C).** Problems of Teacher's attitude in teaching and learning of mathematics:

- It is the responsibility of a teacher to develop a liking and positive attitude for mathematics among the students.
- The attitude of students towards mathematics plays a significant role in their achievement. If the students learn mathematics with a positive attitude, interest, and liking then their level of achievement will go up.
- The teacher should encourage the students to use a problem-solving approach to solve mathematical problems i.e., where teachers create a problematic situation for students and then assist them in perceiving, defining, and stating the problems.
- The teacher tries to raise a problem in the minds of students so that it can stimulate purposeful reflective thinking to arrive at a solution.
- Also, it is necessary to connect real-life problems with mathematics to make the students familiar with the use of mathematics in their daily life.
- The teaching of mathematics is mainly focused on the practical usability of mathematics i.e., to enable the children to apply mathematics in their daily life

situations.
So, it is concluded that cramming all mathematical formulas is not true regarding the problems in teaching and learning mathematics.

**86(D).** Problem-solving - Problem-solving method involves reflective thinking, reasoning,, and results from the achievement of certain abilities, skills,, and attitudes. The teacher should provide such situations and activities from which a problem emerges. It involves a definite procedure of confronting the problem and finding out its solution inductively.

Principles for teaching problem-solving:
- Using real-world problems- It enhances mental skill and also develops logical analysis and creative thinking in students.
- Simple examples should be taken first- When children have just understood the chapter, solving hard problems will give them the wrong answer and discourage them. Instead,, they should start with simple ones.
- Concrete materials should be used- These are the physical objects that children can pick up and manipulate to improve their mathematical knowledge. There are plenty of mathematical tools that can help students picture abstract math concepts in the real world. For example,, using an abacus for counting and base ten blocks etc.
- Providing various methods to solve a problem- A problem can have multiple ways of solution in mathematics as it helps students to develop flexibility and support the understanding of concepts.

So, it is concluded that "only one method of solving a particular type of problem should be emphasized" is not acceptable about teaching students to solve problems based on mathematical operations.

**87(B).** Teaching, evaluation, and remedial measures are the three steps in any teaching-learning process. So the teacher is not only meant to teach and test but to take necessary remedial measures when required. The aim of this step is not just revision of earlier work and check on it but to find errors and then apply the remedial measures.
- The main objective of remedial teaching is to solve the problems students are facing. Diagnosis, weakness of the students, and individual differences are the basis of remedial teaching.
- To solve the problem it is important to identify the problem, then the teacher can use different methods for remedial teaching.

**88(C).** Remedial teaching refers to the teaching which is intended to improve the ability of slow learners to learn something. It is an integral part of the teaching-learning program, also known as compensatory or corrective teaching.

The Most Effective Strategies of Remedial Teaching:
- Tutorial: In this strategy, the teacher conducts remedial tutorial sessions for the students who have learning difficulties.
- Supervised: By using this strategy, the teacher supervises the learning of the students and guides them in which they suffer in learning the concepts.
- Action research: It is an interactive method of collecting information that's used to explore topics of teaching, curriculum development, and student behavior in the classroom. It refers to the integration of practice-based experiences in the learning process to help learners with difficulties in developing a better understanding of the concept.
- Programmed test: It refers to a test in which the items are so presented that they depend upon the earlier response of the learners, thus helps to design a test suited to the learning ability of the learners.
- Individual Teaching: It is characterized by the teacher in the educational process with individual students works individually, based on their intellectual characteristics.

So, we can conclude that tutorial and supervision both are the main remedial teaching strategies.

**89(D).** These methods can be used in assessment to make connections of Mathematics with real life:
- Field trip refers to a learning approach which ensures the active involvement of learners in the learning process by taking them to a certain place where they can earn knowledge by engaging with real situations.
- Survey: This is used on a large population. But instead of studying the whole of the population, a sample is studied. The sample is generally large in size. It is generally used in descriptive studies.
- A project is an educational method where students working individually or in small groups analyze and develop "real-life" problem or tackle a present-day theme within a preset time limit, working independently and with the division of tasks clearly defined.

So, we conclude that Field Trip, survey, Project methods can be used in assessment strategies in mathematics to make connection with real-life.

**90(B).** In this question, both the students have solved the problems according to their understanding of algorithms which is correct, so the teacher assigns full marks to both the students.

- There is not a fixed pattern or method to solve a problem in mathematics. This enhances divergent thinking.
- Mathematics increases logical thinking.
- The students should be taught in a way so that they will think mathematically and use their logical thinking in their daily life.
- The teaching-learning process should not focus on robotic learning of steps of solving any question.
- The questions which only check the procedural learning, rote memorization, and drill do not initiate the mathematical thinking of students.
- Another aim is to develop numeracy skills in the students.

Thus, we can conclude that teacher gives full marks to both the students as they have attempted the question using their own algorithms. Both formal and informal algorithms are integral to solving problems in mathematics.

**91(C).** A living fossil is a species t hat cosmetically resemble ancestral species known only from the fossil record.
- These species have remained largely unchanged over billions of years and are mainly used for describing the similarities and differences between the living organisms and fossils of extinct specimens.
- Though all fossils provide evidence of evolution, the living fossils are one of the best evidence from which various living species can be proved to be identical.
- Few examples of living fossils are - Elephant shrew, Red pandas, Koala, Hagfish, Platypus, Tuatara, Olive Ridley Turtle, Limulus, etc.
- Limulus is also known as the king crab or horseshoe crab, it belongs to the phylum "Arthropoda".
- It has remained unchanged for the last 190 million thereby it is considered a living fossil.

Spider , Moth & Scorpion all belong to the phylum arthropoda but these are not living fossils.

**92(B).** Pulses are considered to be nitrogen-fixing crops as they have root nodules onto which symbiotic nitrogen-fixing bacteria like Rhizobium get attached and fix atmospheric nitrogen.

Whereas, Cereals are the crops that demand a lot of nitrogen thus after harvest the soil becomes deficient in nitrogen, so to compensate for this deficiency a pulse crop is grown between two cereal crops.

This practice of growing different food crops alternatively in the same field is called Crop Rotation.

**93(D).** Samuel Colt was an American industrialist and businessman who is credited with the invention of the revolver.

| Scientist | Product |
| --- | --- |

| | |
|---|---|
| Theodor Bergmann | Firearms, Bergmann Pistol |
| Henry D eringer | Derringer pistol |
| John Bro wning | Military and civilian firearms, cartridges, and gun mechanisms |

**94(C).** The respiratory system of cockroaches:
- The respiratory system of the cockroach consists of a network of the trachea, that opens through 10 pairs of small holes called spiracles present on the lateral side of the body.
- Thin branching tubes (tracheal tubes subdivided into tracheoles) carry oxygen from the air to all the parts. air enters the body through spiracles.
- When air through external openings, enters into its respiratory system, spiracles serve as muscular valves paving the way to the internal respiratory system. The respiratory organ of the cockroach is referred to as the tracheae.
- The trachea is a dense array of a network of air tubes found in the internal system.
- Tracheae are known to balance the pressure inside the system.
- When oxygen-rich air enters the body of the cockroach via spiracles into the tracheal tubes, it diffuses into various tissues and cells of the body. Here, oxygen is used up to liberate energy.
- Likewise, carbon-dioxide rich air passes into the trachea and moves outwards through the spiracles.
- Carbon dioxide is given out as a result of the respiratory process.

**95(B).** The dish is named Undhiya or upside down, in Gujrati.
- This dish is a regional speciality of Surat.
- A little-known fact is that the name Undhiyu comes from the Gujarati word Undhu, which means being upside down.
- The upside-down is here because the pot in which this food is made is placed upside down.
- There are a total of eight vegetables are stirred upside down and cooked over a wood fire in large earthen (clay) pots along with fresh spices to give Undhiyu its distinctive texture and flavour.
- The pot was sealed and kept between hot coals.
- Undhiya would be eaten with bajra rotis, freshly cooked on chulha.

**96(C).** Earthworms is apt for vermicomposting.
Vermicomposting is the scientific method of making compost, by using of earthworms which are commonly found living in soil, feeding on biomass and excreting it in a digested form. Vermiculture means "worm-farming".

**97(D).** An antioxidant can be defined as a substance which prevents the reaction of various food constituents with oxygen.
- This protective effect is desirable because many foods become discoloured or spoiled when oxidation takes place
- Keeping food in the airtight container helps to slow down the oxidation process.
- Manufacture usually flushes bags of chips with an inert gas such as nitrogen to prevent the chips from getting oxidized.
- Buffers maintain the physical, chemical and microbiological stability of foods .
- Specialised buffers are also used extensively in the food industry as food additives.
- These additives are usually weak acids or their respective salts already naturally present in some foods.

So, all the above strategies are useful for preventing the oxidation of foodstuffs.

**98(B).** Wood, coal, petroleum release unburnt carbon particles in the environment are called Carbon fuels.
Carbon fuels such as wood, coal, petroleum release unburnt carbon particles in the environment. These particles are very dangerous pollutants and cause respiratory diseases for example asthma. When fuels are incompletely burnt, they release carbon monoxide gas into the atmosphere.

**99(C).** Irrigation is the artificial process of applying controlled amounts of water to land to assist in the production of crops , but also to grow landscape plants and lawns, where it may be known as watering. So, statement 1 is Correct .
Irrigation helps to grow agricultural crops, maintain landscapes, and revegetate disturbed soils in dry areas and during periods of less than average rainfall. So, statement 2 is Correct .

**100(B).** Fertilisers are very rich in plant nutrients like nitrogen, phosphorus & potassium.
- Fertilisers are chemical substances that are rich in a particular nutrient.
- Some examples of fertilisers are— urea , ammonium sulphate , superphosphate , potash , NPK (Nitrogen, Phosphorus, Potassium ).
- They are used to ensure good vegetative growth (leaves, branches and flowers), giving rise to healthy plants.
- The use of fertilisers leads to a better yield of crops such as wheat , paddy and maize . But excessive use of fertilisers also makes the soil less fertile.
- Fertilisers have also become a source of water pollution.

**101(C).** Viral fever is not a vector-borne disease.
- Yellow fever is an acute viral haemorrhagic disease transmitted by infected mosquitoes.
- Dengue (DENG-gey) fever is a mosquito-borne illness that occurs in tropical and subtropical areas of the world.
- Malaria is a mosquito-borne infectious disease that affects humans and other animals.

**102(C).** Direction is divided into 8 sections, 4 cardinal directions, and 4 ordinal directions.
- The four cardinal directions are the directions north, east, south, and west, commonly denoted by their initials N, E, S, and W.
- East and west are perpendiculars (at right angles) to north and south.
- East is in the clockwise direction of rotation from north and west is directly opposite east.
- The ordinal directions are northeast (NE), southeast (SE), southwest (SW), and northwest (NW).
- NE, SE, SW, and NW lie in between the cardinal directions north and east, south and east, south and west, and north and west respectively.

Thus, Rina should travel south.

**103(C).** Environmental Studies is a multidimensional subject that covers important principles from various academic fields. It is a broad field that studies the basic principles of EVS as well as associated subjects such as social science , science , language , mathematics , etc.
EVS emphasizes the following points:
- The contents of EVS are organised thematically. Topics of both social studies and science are integrated.
- Contents of the EVS are drawn from the children's own environment.
- Provides scope for children's expressions–oral and written and other creative expressions, etc.
- Children learn about their environment through exploring and experiencing it, gathering and analysing information based on their observations and experiences, and constructing their own knowledge, enriching and enhancing it.
- Learning is planned to progress from

what the child already knows, to what is to be learnt, from local to global, or from the immediate environment to community and society and beyond.

- Chapters begin with key questions initiating children into thinking and constructing their own knowledge .

So, we conclude that EVS does not emphasize descriptions and definitions.

**104(C).** Section 10 of The Indian Forest Act 1927 deals with treatment of claims relating to practice of shifting cultivation. According to Section 10, If an individual claims the right to shifting agriculture over a piece of land, the forest settlement officer will record a statement setting forth the claims to the state government. These claims will be subject to approval or disapproval of the state government.

**105(A).** Taanka is a traditional rainwater harvesting technique indigenous to the Thar desert region of Rajasthan.

A Taanka A taanka, also known as a tanka or kund, is a traditional rainwater harvesting technique, common to the Thar desert region of Rajasthan, India. It is meant to provide drinking water and water security for a family or a small group of families.

**106(D).** Echolocation is a two-part process: the animal makes a sound, and the animal listens to the rebounding sound waves to identify where items are located.

- Animals like bats, dolphins, shrews, moth, elephants, owl, rat, dog, cat, horse, pigeon, whales, and some birds all use sound echolocation to see in the dark.
- A well-known trait of the bat is the exceptional hearing they have.
- Using echolocation, a bat can squeak whilst in flight and navigate their way to where they need.
- The sound vibrations they emit through squeaking bounces off any nearby surfaces back to the bat, allowing them to know where is the surface.

So, we may say that tigers are sensing the origin of sound differently than other echolocators like a bat, whale, and dolphin which are capable to see in the dark and feel the vibration around them.

**107(D).** The environment described as a composite of natural conditions, circumstances, and influences, and sociocultural contexts in which an individual is situated.

Guiding Principles of Environment Education laid by UNESCO:

- Environmental education should have an interdisciplinary approach.
- It should take into account the historical perspective also.
- It should emphasize the importance of sustainable development .
- It should emphasize the necessity of seeking international cooperation.
- It emphasizes the principle of utility and

principle of relationship with life.

- It should lay more stress on practical activities .

So, from the above-mentioned points, it becomes clear that all the given principles are the principle of learning environment study.

**108(A).** EVS is organised around three broad principles – Learning about the environment; Learning through the environment and Learning for the environment. Hence the scope of EVS is very wide.

- It ranges from using the environment as a medium of learning to all that one can do to protect and conserve it.
- The contents are spirally organized starting with the immediate experience of the child (known) moving out to the world she/he inhabits (unknown), leading to an analysis of some of the factors that influence life on this planet.
- The focus of EVS enlarges from the personal to the national and global (local to global), from the physical dimension to the aesthetic dimension.

Thus it is clear that one of the broad principles of EVS is 'Learning through the environment'.

**109(B).** A teacher tells her students to collect garbage from the school playground. Anup, a student, separates wet garbage in one bucked while dry garbage in another. Here the student knows the concept of Reduce, Reuse, and Recycle and applies it in his real-life.

- Schools and teachers should provide excellent educational opportunities for creating awareness about environmental concepts, so they can apply them in their real-life.
- It also provides numerous opportunities for the students to understand this issue and its implications on the local environment.
- Teachers should plan and give importance to co-curricular activities of EVS as the students can learn several skills and competencies from these activities in a real-life situation in a joyful environment. For the holistic development of students' learning, these are considered essential.

So, we can conclude that He knows the concept of reduce, reuse and recycle.

**110(C).** Co-curricular activities in EVS teaching are those activities that are usually organized outside the classroom to provide opportunities for students to develop their special talents and to creatively express themselves through various forms.

| Activities allowed | Activities not allow |
| --- | --- |
| Collect photogr aphs of animals | Do not feed the animals |
| Take drawing b | Do not touch the anima ls |
| ook and draw p ictures | Do not throw any thing s on animals (stones, pl astic bottles, etc.) |
| Notes making | |
| Collect informa tion about diffe rent animals | Do not take eatables for the animals |

Eatables will attract the animals towards the students which can be dangerous for students. So, it should not be allowed.

So, it becomes clear that taking along lots of eatables for the animals at the zoo should not be allowed to students.

**111(D).** **Dysgraphia refers to a learning disability which:**

- affects learners' ability to write coherently.
- hinders in organizing letters, numbers, or words on papers.
- leads to problems with poor spelling, impaired handwriting, etc. are the problems someone faces while suffering from dysgraphia.

Teachers can give the following remedies for treating young students with Dysgraphia:

- giving extra time for writing assessment, will reduce the copying activity and will emphasize the importance of writing original answers.
- dividing tasks into small steps will enable the learners to assimilate the idea easily and will help them in putting their thoughts on paper.
- providing low-stress opportunities will allow the learners to learn and write at their own pace and to foster their own strategy of learning and writing.

So, we can conclude that in the above scenario, the problem of writing she suffers is a symptom of Dysgraphia.

**112(B).** 'Continuous and Comprehensive Evaluation' also known as 'CCE' has been introduced as a school-based system of evaluation by the CBSE in 2009 with the enactment of the "Right to Education Act" .

CCE refers to all-around development including both scholastic and co-scholastic aspects of a child's growth. The objective of CCE is to make evaluation an integral part of learning through diagnostic and remedial teaching.

**113(B).** Teaching-learning materials provide a range of learning experiences to learners from direct to indirect. It includes textbooks, curriculum, syllabus, novels, lectures, pictures, radio, verbal, visual symbols, etc.

- Syllabus covers the list of topics and units to be covered while teaching a specific subject over a period of time.
- Curriculum refers to the overall subject matter to be taught in a course. It includes all the co-curricular and recreational activities.
- Textbooks are the important pedagogical tool of teaching which

introduce concepts through contexts to ensure facilitation of contextual learning.

So, Curriculum, Syllabus and Textbook are the essential TLM for teaching Social Studies/Environmental Studies.

**114(A).** EVS aims at developing in children a holistic or integrated perspective of our environment as a composite of natural and human-made surroundings with the intricate interactions and interdependence that exist.

The approach in EVS goes beyond the single-subject approach and helps children to use the contents and methods of science and social sciences and the environment to solve environmental problems/issues in the future.

So, EVS teachers should focus exclusively on experiments.

**115(B).** The teacher should give clear instructions to all the students before going on field trips. These instructions should include what is expected from them in the trip and the things that they can and cannot bring along with them. They would not be expected to take the full schoolbag on field trips because it won't be required there.

**116(B).** EVS curriculum at primary stage has been developed to include pure Science as well as Social Science concepts. This has been done primarily to enable a learner look at environment in a holistic manner.

**117(B).** Children can be effectively engaged in EVS learning through narratives and stories as these are the effective tools of the teaching-learning process that broadens children's reading choices. Narratives and stories are used as a method of teaching in EVS at the primary level to engage children effectively in EVS learning.

- providing the contextual learning environment to children.
- promoting imaginative and creative ability in the children.
- developing interest and providing fun and enjoyment to children.
- increasing children's vocabulary, listening and critical thinking skills.
- making children able to construct meaning based on their own experiences.

So, it could be interpreted that narratives and stories are the tools that can engage children successfully in EVS learning.

**118(C).** The concept of 'seed germination' can be taught best by asking the students to sow seeds, notice their different stages, and draw them as learning by doing and experiencing the consequences of one's own actions helps learners in:

- retaining information and concepts for a longer period.
- enhancing skills and better understanding of the concept.
- nurturing their curiosity and interest in the learning process.
- gaining concrete experience by actively engaging with content.
- assimilating practical knowledge by applying theoretical knowledge.

So, it could be concluded the concept of 'seed germination' can be taught best by asking the students to sow seeds, notice their different stages, and draw them.

**119(A).** The integrated nature of EVS means the teacher aims to develop different dimensions of one's personality (social, emotional, mental, moral) by teaching one or two subjects together in a collective manner.

- At the primary level, children must be taught through an integrated approach rather than teaching in parts. At the primary level, we shouldn't teach students the concepts in isolation.
- We should teach them concepts and processes in an integrated manner so that they could explore the other aspects of a specific subject matter and could find the connection among them.
- It feels less burdened as the learners can learn more comprehensively and able to connect subjects or topics with each other in several domains.
- It helps to integrate the knowledge of different disciplines by using a real process of synthesis.
- This approach creates holistic knowledge by integrating knowledge from different disciplines.
- This approach is student-centred where a learner gets the opportunity to achieve unified knowledge, which is meaningfully used in real-life experience

gained from different disciplines.

- Integrating the concepts or issues of social sciences with other disciplines like mathematics, general sciences, languages, etc. is an example of an interdisciplinary or integrated approach to the concepts or issues of environmental sciences.

Therefore, the method that can be useful while teaching EVS in an integrated manner is the synthesis method.

**120(D).** Environmental education includes the study of the environment and its attributes. It provides an approach towards understanding the environment and the impact of human life on it.

Barriers in implementing environmental education:

- Shortage of qualified trained environmental teachers: This is a problem that arises due to lack of resources, as a teacher is a key to the successful implementation of environmental education in the classroom he should be well trained.
- There should be qualified trained environmental teachers so that they can effectively implement and use all the teaching strategies leading to the enhancement and development of children.
- Rigorous expertise: It is always a barrier in implementing environmental education in the classroom as one teacher can learn skills easily but to achieve rigorous expertise in one's subject is quite difficult. Not everyone is capable of handling child pedagogy along with having expertise in one's subject matter.
- Interdisciplinary nature: Interdisciplinary studies are when two or more academic disciplines are combined into one activity. For example, EVS combines science, geography, history, political science, etc. It provides a direct connection for students between the study of science and the world around them.

So, we can conclude that options a, b, and d are the major barriers to implementing environmental education.

## Child Development and Pedagogy

1. At which stage, children become an active member of the peer group?
   - (a) Early childhood
   - (b) Later childhood
   - (c) Adolescence
   - (d) Adulthood

2. Critical developmental tasks adolescence is: -
   (i) Social Competence
   (ii) Development of adult body
   (iii) Attain sexual maturity
   (iv) Acquire mature thinking and planning
   - (a) (i) and (ii)
   - (b) (ii) and (iii)
   - (c) (iii) and (iv)
   - (d) All of the above

3. ___________ assessment is conducted prior to the teaching of any content or topic.
   - (a) Summative   (b) Formative
   - (c) Formal     (d) Initial

4. In a progressive classroom, assessment of learners during the process of teaching-learning –
   - (a) is helpful in identifying 'high', 'low' and 'non' achievers for the purposes of giving feedback to the parents.
   - (b) is very important since it gives insights into children's understanding and helps the teacher to reflects on her pedagogy.
   - (c) is not at all helpful in children's learning.
   - (d) creates a hindrance in the process of children's learning.

5. A teacher giving ample opportunities to each of her children. It is an example of –
   - (a) Progressive classroom
   - (b) Gender equality
   - (c) Inclusive classroom
   - (d) All of the above

6. Curriculum is focused on needs, experiences, interests and ability of the students. Which method of the following is fully satisfied of this statement?
   - (a) Project Method
   - (b) Demonstration method
   - (c) Scientific method
   - (d) Heuristic method

7. Who among the following has propounded the seven primary mental abilities?
   - (a) Gardner    (b) Thurston
   - (c) Sternberg   (d) Thorndike

8. In which stage of moral development children's moral judgement is based on self-interest and considerations of what others can do for them in return?
   - (a) Stage 1- Obedience and Punishment orientation
   - (b) Stage 4- Maintaining the social order
   - (c) Stage 5- Social Contract and individual rights
   - (d) Stage 2- Individualism and change

9. "Development is a never-ending process.". This idea is associated with which of the following principles of development.
   - (a) principle of interaction of maturation and learning
   - (b) principle of continuity
   - (c) principle of interaction of heredity and environment
   - (d) principle of orderly development

10. Which of the following refers to traits and behaviour that a particular culture judges to be appropriate for men and women?
    - (a) Sex
    - (b) Gender
    - (c) Gender identity
    - (d) Gender orientation

11. Individual differences in a progressive classroom should be treated as:
    - (a) criteria for making ability-based groups.
    - (b) important for planning of teaching-learning process.
    - (c) a hindrance to the process of learning.
    - (d) a failure on the part of teacher.

12. Both ________ and ________plays a decisive role in the growth and development of the child.
    - (a) change, stability
    - (b) assimilation, orientation
    - (c) challenges, limitations
    - (d) heredity, environment

13. Multilingualism in a classroom needs to be understood as _____ by the teachers.
    - (a) a problem
    - (b) a systemic issue
    - (c) an asset and resource
    - (d) a hindrance

14. In which type of socialisation, a child learns the values, attitudes, cultures etc.
    - (a) Formal Socialisation
    - (b) Informal Socialisation
    - (c) Primary Socialisation
    - (d) Secondary Socialisation

15. which of the following steps can be taken to deal with a child with hearing impairment?
    - (a) They should be sent to a special school for them.
    - (b) They should be given vocational training since academic education is of no use to them.
    - (c) They should be trained to compete with students of regular schools.
    - (d) Regular schools should cater suitable facilities and resources for them.

16. The term "Dyslexia" is associated with -
    - (a) Mathematical disorder
    - (b) Reading disorder
    - (c) Mental disorder
    - (d) Behavioral disorder

17. What should be done to make education system more inclusive in nature?
    i. Separate school for learners with SEN
    ii. Considering wide range of learning modalities (drawing, oral, writing, acting)
    iii. Use of Home Language
    - (a) Only i and ii
    - (b) Only ii and iii
    - (c) Only i
    - (d) i, ii and iii.

18. A teacher can respond effectively to the needs of the students from a disadvantaged section of the society by-
    - (a) ensuring that the students of different sections sit separately so that there is no chance of the disadvantaged section getting bullied
    - (b) asking the other students to cooperate with the

disadvantaged section and help them learns the ways in school

(c) making other students sensitize by telling them about the different struggles faced by disadvantaged group people.

(d) reflecting on herself and the school system about various ways in which stereotypes surface

**19.** Which of the following are principles of inclusive education system?
A. Principle of individual difference
B. Principle of no rejection
C. Principle of individualized education programme
D. Principle of restricted environment

(a) A and B     (b) B, C and D
(c) A, B and C     (d) A, B, C and D

**20.** The Wheel of Emotions was given by:
(a) Paul Eckman
(b) Piaget
(c) Robert Plutchik
(d) Vygotsky

**21.** ______ is also known as the ethical-moral arm of the personality.
(a) Ego
(b) Super-ego
(c) Id
(d) None of these

**22.** Which out of the following justifies the concept of scaffolding as explained by Vygotsky in his theory?
(a) Intrinsic motivation
(b) Extrinsic motivation
(c) Dependency on teacher
(d) Little guidance from the teacher

**23.** The most effective way to encourage conceptual learning is:
(a) Correcting the mistakes of students
(b) Let students learn and understand new concepts on their own without any reference to the old ones
(c) Give extra work to practice
(d) Give students different examples and encourage them to use reasoning

**24.** To enhance effective learning a teacher should:
(a) Adopt that method of teaching in which maximum number of senses are utilized
(b) Correlate learning in one area with that of another
(c) Use that method of teaching in which he/she is comfortable
(d) Both (A) and (B)

**25.** The problem-solving method in which multiple attempts are made to reach a solution is:
(a) Demonstration method
(b) Inductive method
(c) Trial and error method
(d) Lecture cum demonstration method

**26.** Motivation to learn can be sustained by:
(a) giving very easy tasks to children
(b) focusing on rote-memorization
(c) punishing the child
(d) focusing on mastery-oriented goals

**27.** In a class, the teacher demonstrates to a student how to hold a pencil or write capital 'A'. This can be known as the effect of:
(a) Modeling
(b) Conceptualization
(c) Understanding
(d) Reflection

**28.** Which of the following factors has least effect on learning?
(a) Fatigue
(b) Age
(c) Illness
(d) Gender difference

**29.** Identify the factor that does not influence student difficulty in learning.
(a) Intellectual factor
(b) Social factor
(c) Economic factor
(d) None of the above

**30.** The 'Laws of learning' were given by:
(a) Pavlov     (b) Skinner
(c) Thorndike     (d) Kohler

## Language - I: English

**31.** Ravi, a English teacher, is planning remedial teaching for his student who faces problems in expressing his view while talking with someone. Remedial work for spoken English involves:
(a) Drill and studying
(b) Revision, drill, situation communicative practice and reviewing
(c) Going through situational practice
(d) Revision and practice

**32.** A teacher divides the class in small groups and asks them to discuss and present their views on "Save Environment".
Students are free to plan and present their choice and creativity. The teacher is facilitating them as and when required. Which approach/method is followed in the class?
(a) Structural approach
(b) Natural approach
(c) Deductive approach
(d) Constructivist approach

**33.** A language teacher, while teaching grammar, writes some examples on the blackboard and with the help of students tries to point out some of the rules. She tries to stimulate the power of thinking and reasoning. Which method of teaching grammar is she adopting?
(a) Direct method
(b) Inductive method
(c) Inductive deductive method
(d) Translation method

**34.** Teaching grammar should focus on ____.
(a) rules of language
(b) forms and structures of language
(c) communicative functions of language
(d) both structures and rules of language

**35.** Direction: Answer the following questions by selecting the most appropriate option.
Students of Class IV can recognize flawed usage or sentence construction when the teacher.
(a) tells them something is wrong
(b) gives alternatives as possible corrections
(c) lets them find the corrections
(d) focuses on certain surface errors

**36.** Direction: Given below are two statements, one as Assertion (A) and the other Reason (R) read it carefully and answer the question:
Assertion (A): At first, the child starts listening to the sounds then observes how people speak, and then later development of reading and writing skills takes place.
Reasoning (R): The four basic language skills and their natural

order are reading-writing-listening-speaking.

(a) (A) is correct and (R) is incorrect

(b) (A) is incorrect and (R) is correct

(c) Both (A) and (R) are correct

(d) Both (A) and (R) are incorrect

**37. At upper primary level, the language/languages used by children in a multilingual classroom is/are:**

(a) resource

(b) puzzle

(c) complex challenge

(d) difficult problem

**38. A teacher found an advertisement pamphlet for sale of biscuits. She uses it for reading and speaking activities in her class. What do you call the pamphlet?**

(a) Realia

(b) An authentic text

(c) Extra materials

(d) Newspaper clipping

**39. A Hindi - speaking teacher gets posted in a primary school which is situated in a remote area of Rajasthan. Since she doesn't known the local language, she faces lots of problems. She should:;**

(a) focus on the textbook as a source of standard Hindi.

(b) use the child's language as a resource while teaching

(c) encourage the community to learn standard Hindi

(d) try to get a positing to a Hindi speaking area.

**40. Fluency in English can be developed through:**

(a) Creating opportunities to use the language for communication among learners

(b) The teacher talking for most of the time

(c) The teacher being alert to spot the errors and correcting them

(d) Allowing students who are not confident to have the freedom to be quiet

**41. Continuous comprehensive evaluation emphasises ______evaluation.**

(a) process　　(b) product

(c) term end　　(d) formation

**42. According to National Curriculum Framework 2005, which one of the following is NOT an objective of language teaching-learning?**

(a) The competence to understand what one hears

(b) Ability to read with comprehension

(c) Effortless expression

(d) To know the history of languages

**43. Reading longer texts usually for one's own pleasure is known as:**

(a) Skimming

(b) Scanning

(c) Extensive Reading

(d) Intensive Reading

**44. Which language is a part of the personal, social and cultural identity of a child?**

(a) First language

(b) Second language

(c) School language

(d) Foreign language

**45. Which one of the following is an essential characteristic of a good textbook in English?**

(a) Every lesson should have a proper introduction at the beginning and a conclusion at the end.

(b) It should be based on the guiding principles of curriculum and syllabus.

(c) No difficult words should be given in the textbook at primary level.

(d) The maximum number of textual exercises should be given to practise at the end of the lesson.

**Ques (46-54): Direction:** Read the passage given below and answer the questions by choosing the correct/most appropriate options.

1. Today when we pick up a daily newspaper, we invariably find an increased incidence of vandalism, fraud, theft, robbery, rape, child spouse, battered spouses, murders, hate crimes, genocide (now termed as "ethnic cleansing") along with a multitude of other senseless violent acts that have become disturbingly common. These are not the actions of people who like themselves.

2. The solution to a great many problems, whether personal, national or global, lies in improving our feelings about ourselves both as individuals and members of society. When the significance of good self-esteem is well understood and it achieves the prominence it deserves, a transformation will begin, for as the people will learn they are deserving of self-respect, their respect for others will automatically increase.

3. Most of our behaviour has been shaped by our parent's caregivers and authority figures who played an important part in our early springing and were responsible for crystallizing our ideas about ourselves and the world. While everyone has self-esteem, only a small percentage of us have high self-esteem. High self-esteem denotes that we accept ourselves unconditionally exactly as we are, we appreciate our value as a human being. When, on the other hand, we have low self-esteem, we believe that we have little intrinsic worth.

4. We believe our personal value is in direct proportion to the value of our accomplishments. If we cannot accomplish certain results, we tend to feel low about ourselves. Some of us try too hard and become workaholics and over-achievers. With a few genuine feelings of self-worth, we try to create some and prove that we are somebody by our successes and achievements. Because our desire for perfection is so great, we tend to set unrealistic goals and place unreasonable demands on ourselves. Failing, rather than encouraging us to have realistic aspirations, only leads to a mere punishing round of self-blame and a resolve to drive ourselves harder next time. If we do finally achieve our goals we are disappointed; despite everything we have done, we still feel empty inside.

5. Vulnerable to the opinions of others, we desperately try to gain their recognition and approval sometimes through risky and dangerous behaviour. Thus, we are at the mercy of our emotions, instead of controlling them, we permit them to control us. Since we allow circumstances to influence our feelings, we are inclined to be moody. The insecurity we feel as a result of devaluing ourselves makes us react with jealousy, envy and possessiveness. Fear makes us greedy and acquisitive, and feelings of self-hate alternate with those of futility, unhappiness and depression.

**46. Which of the following are the things the newspapers are full of these days?**

(a) news about the development of the country.

(b) news about politics.

(c) news about acts of crime and violence.

(d) news about educational matters and employment.

**47. Identify the parts of speech of the underlined segment in the given sentence.**
When the <u>significance</u> of good self-esteem is well understood.

(a) Adverb　　(b) Pronoun

(c) Noun　　(d) Conjunction

**48. Find the word from the passage which is the antonym of the word,**

'futility' as used in the passage(para 5)?

(a) Pointlessness
(b) Vanity
(c) Usefulness
(d) Failure

**49. Why is good self-esteem stressed upon?**

(a) It is essential in solving many problems.
(b) It builds up self-confidence.
(c) It increases one's reputation.
(d) It helps one respect others.

**50. Find the word from the passage which means the same as the word, 'vandalism' as used in the passage(para 1)?**

(a) Construct    (b) Destruction
(c) Build    (d) Mend

**51. Find the error in a part of the sentence:**

**The solution to a great many problems (a)/ , whether personal, national and global (b)/ , lies in improving our feelings (c)/ No error. (d)**

(a) (a)      (b) (b)
(c) (c)      (d) (d)

**52. Which of the following statements is true?**

**A. We need to accept ourselves unconditionally exactly as we are.**
**B. We give permission to others to control our emotions.**
**C. All the non violent acts are the actions of those who like themselves.**

(a) Only A
(b) Only B
(c) Both A and B
(d) All of the above

**53. According to the passage, when does a person start feeling empty inside?**

(a) When we gets involved in crimes.
(b) When we push ourselves towards achieving goals and prove that we are somebody by our successes and achievements.
(c) When others start influencing our behaviour.
(d) None of the above

**54. Identify the part of speech of the underlined word:**

**We tend to set <u>unrealistic</u> goals and place unreasonable demands.**

(a) Noun      (b) Adverb
(c) Adjective    (d) Pronoun

**Ques (55-60): Direction:** Read the extract given below and answer the question.

There is a Reaper, whose name is Death,
And, with his sickle keen,
He reaps the bearded grain at a breath,
And the flowers that grow between.
"Shall I have naught that is fair?" saith he;
"Have naught but the bearded grain?
Though the breath of these flowers is sweet to me,
I will give them all back again."
He gazed at the flowers with tearful eyes,
He kissed their drooping leaves;
It was for the Lord of Paradise
He bound them in his sheaves.
"My Lord has need of these flowerets gay,"
The Reaper said, and smiled;
"Dear tokens of the earth are they,
Where He was once a child.
"They shall all bloom in fields of light,
Transplanted by my care,
And saints, upon their garments white,
These sacred blossoms wear."
And the mother gave, in tears and pain,
The flowers she most did love;
She knew she should find them all again
In the fields of light above.
Oh, not in cruelty, not in wrath,
The Reaper came that day;
'T was an angel visited the green earth,
And took the flowers away.

**55. The poem presents death in a:**

(a) gloomy light
(b) positive light
(c) fearful light
(d) negative light

**56. According to the poet, the mother will meet her flowers in _____ .**

(a) Garden    (b) Playground
(c) Home      (d) Paradise

**57. Who were the flowers for?**

(a) Death     (b) Satan
(c) God       (d) The mother

**58. Identify the figure of speech in the line:**

**She knew she should find them all again**

(a) Alliteration
(b) Personification
(c) Metaphor
(d) Simile

**59. Who wears the flowers in the new world?**

(a) angels    (b) cherubs
(c) saints     (d) God

**60. How did Death gaze at the flowers?**

(a) happy eyes    (b) fearful eyes
(c) angry eyes    (d) tearful eyes

## Mathematics

**61. Which of the following is correct about the nature of mathematics?**

(a) The results of mathematics theorems and theories are not significant and useful.
(b) Precision is the nature of mathematics that deals with accuracy and exactness.
(c) Mathematics is science of concrete objects and there is no place for logic or creativity.
(d) Mathematics deals with qualitative facts and relationships as well as problem solving.

**62. Ensuring a good start to the students in learning mathematics, creating love, faith and interest for learning mathematics are:**

(a) Broader Aims
(b) Narrower Aims
(c) Specific Aims
(d) All of the above

**63. Which of the following statements is NOT correct with regard to nature of mathematics?**

(a) Mathematics aims at abstraction.
(b) Mathematics is illogical.
(c) Mathematics is precise.
(d) Mathematics is symbolic.

**64. Which of the following is the most appropriate strategy for teaching students to solve mathematical problems?**

(a) Multiple perspective approach
(b) Rigidness in problem solving
(c) Hit and trial method
(d) Memorization of formula

**65. To enjoy Mathematics, a teacher must ensure that the students:**

(a) Must practice their exercise
(b) Have sense of competence and fear
(c) Must do exactly as is written in their textbooks
(d) Must memorise all the formula and steps

**66. Which of the following is the major problem of teaching Mathematics?**

(a) Teaching methods of Mathematics teacher
(b) Ability to use Mathematical tools.
(c) Class Room operations
(d) Knowledge of teaching methods

**67. What is not there in mathematics text book?**
(a) Worked out problems
(b) Practice problems
(c) Methods of learning
(d) Geometrical figures and graphs

**68. Which of the following is most likely to impact teaching-learning in mathematics?**
(a) Providing complete solutions to students wrong answers
(b) Crude methods of assessment.
(c) Memorization and rote learning in mathematics.
(d) Providing feedback via formative assessment.

**69. Mathematics can be used in-**
(a) the truths that are discovered
(b) the methods used to discover truths
(c) Both (A) and (B)
(d) None of the above

**70. Which among the following is true regarding Van Hiele Theory?**
(a) Van Hiele Theory describes the evaluation of learner in geometry
(b) Van Hiele Theory describes how people learn geometry
(c) Van Hiele Theory describes how people learn algebra.
(d) Van Hiele Theory describes the evaluation of learner in algebra.

**71. One of the important aims of teaching mathematics to children is to comprehend mathematical language. Which one of the following statements is not correctly stated in context to mathematical language?**
(a) "<" used for showing inequality
(b) "*" asterisk shows multiplication
(c) "!" is the symbol for factorial
(d) "%" percent means part of ten

**72. In a Mathematics classroom, emphasis is placed on:**
(a) mathematical content
(b) mathematical content, process and reasoning
(c) problem solving strategies
(d) mathematical algorithms and processess

**73. In Mathematics, word problems help to:**
(a) develop ability to convert real life problems into mathematical problems
(b) learn mathematical language

(c) remove fear from the child
(d) None of the above

**74. Remedial teaching is required for-**
(a) Mentally retarded children
(b) Weak students
(c) Average students
(d) All of these

**75. Difference between achievement test and diagnostic test is**
(a) of objectives
(b) of nature
(c) of level difficulty
(d) none of these

**76. The length (in meter, correct to one decimal place) of the longest pole that can be fitted in a room of dimensions $12m \times 6m \times 4m$ is :**
(a) 14.0
(b) 7.2
(c) 12.6
(d) 13.4

**77. The area of the triangle whose vertices are given by the coordinates $(1, 2)$ , $(-4, -3)$ and $(4, 1)$ is:**
(a) 7 sq. units
(b) 20 sq. units
(c) 10 sq. units
(d) 14 sq. units

**78. A circle touches all four sides of a quadrilateral $PQRS$ . If $PQ = 11$ cm. $QR = 12$ cm and $PS = 8$ cm. then what is the length of $RS$ ?**
(a) 7 cm
(b) 15 cm
(c) 9 cm
(d) 7.3 cm

**79. Find the sum of the factors of $3240$ .**
(a) 10890
(b) 11000
(c) 10800
(d) 10190

**80. Rs. 720 was divided among $A, B, C, D, E$ . The sum received by them was in ascending order and in arithmetic progression. $E$ received Rs. 40 more than $A$ . How much did $B$ receive?**
(a) Rs. 134
(b) Rs. 154
(c) Rs. 144
(d) Rs. 124

**81. What will come in the place of question mark (?) in the following question?**
$$? = \sqrt[5]{(243)^2}$$
(a) 3
(b) 7
(c) 6
(d) 9

**82. Conversion of 1 kWh to Joule is equal to?**
(a) $36 \times 10^6 J$
(b) $3.6 \times 10^{-6} J$
(c) $36 \times 10^{-6} J$
(d) $3.6 \times 10^6 J$

**83. If the weight of 18 sheets of paper is 50 grams, how many sheets of the same paper will weigh $3\frac{3}{4}$ kg?**

(a) 1350
(b) 1314
(c) 1386
(d) 1836

**84. A car completes a journey in seven hours. It covered half of the distance at 40 kmph and the remaining half at 60 kmph speed. Then, the distance (in km) covered is:**
(a) 280
(b) 300
(c) 336
(d) 420

**85. Direction: The following question is based on the number series given below.**
P 3 6 T U 7 C 8 B M 2 X 0 W 1 R 5 S V A
**If all the numbers are dropped out from the above arrangement, which element will be 10 th from the left side?**
(a) V
(b) S
(c) R
(d) M

**86. The fractions $\frac{44}{49}, \frac{33}{38}, \frac{22}{25}$ and $\frac{24}{29}$ are written in descending order as:**
(a) $\frac{22}{25}, \frac{24}{29}, \frac{33}{38}, \frac{44}{49}$
(b) $\frac{44}{49}, \frac{22}{25}, \frac{33}{38}, \frac{24}{29}$
(c) $\frac{44}{49}, \frac{33}{38}, \frac{24}{29}, \frac{22}{25}$
(d) $\frac{24}{29}, \frac{33}{38}, \frac{22}{25}, \frac{44}{49}$

**87. A playground is in the form of a rectangle of length 46 m and breadth 44 m. Aman starts running around it at the rate of 3.6 km/hr. The time taken by him to go three rounds of the playground will be -**
(a) 8 minutes
(b) 9 minutes
(c) 10 minutes
(d) 7 minutes

**88. By walking $\frac{5}{3}$ of the usual speed a student reaches school 20 minutes earlier. Find his usual time.**
(a) 60 minutes
(b) 50 minutes
(c) 40 minutes
(d) 30 minutes

**89. The ratio of ages of Rahul and his wife after 7 years from now will be $7 : 6$ . If his wife was born 23 years ago, find the age of Rahul after 2 years?**
(a) 25
(b) 30
(c) 28
(d) 40

**90. What is the minimum number of straight lines that is needed to construct the figure?**

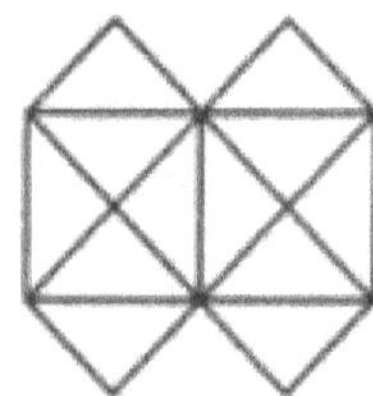

(a) 11      (b) 13
(c) 15      (d) 21

## Environmental Studies

91. Environmental Studies curriculum may lead to holistic learning of children if it is—
    (a) Integrated
    (b) Inclusive
    (c) Thematic
    (d) All of the above

92. Some birds can see four times as far as we can see. These birds are:
    (a) Crows, Kites, Nightingales
    (b) Eagles, Pigeons, Parrots
    (c) Kites, Eagles, Vultures
    (d) Doves, Crows, Peacocks

93. Which among the following is a way of cooking food by exposing it to dry radiant heat over open fire?
    (a) Baking    (b) Frying
    (c) Roasting    (d) Boiling

94. Direction: Study the following statements about the Jhoom farming practiced in Mizoram:
    A. After cutting one crop, the land is left as it is for some years.
    B. The bamboo or weeds which grow on that land are cut and burnt.
    C. The land is deeply ploughed before sowing the seeds.
    D. In one farm three or four different types of crops are grown.
    E. Chemical fertilizers and pesticides are also used as per need.
    The correct statements are
    (a) A, B and D    (b) Only A and B
    (c) Only B and D   (d) A,B, C, D

95. Direction: Answer the following question by selecting the most appropriate options.
    A class V teacher provides her students with a Neem leaf and a Mango leaf and asks them to state in which way they are similar to and different from each other. Which one of the following process skills will be used in answering this question?
    (a) Hypothesizing

(b) Predictiing
(c) Observing
(d) Measuring

96. Ramesh a teacher of class VII engages his students in a fun activity before beginning a new lesson. The purpose behind this activity is to:
    (a) Motivate and energize the students
    (b) Reduce the workload of the teacher
    (c) Discipline the students before starting the class
    (d) Reduce the tension of students

97. Syllabus of EVS has been divided into________themes to inculcate every aspect of learning which are considered important for child of primary level.
    (a) 2       (b) 4
    (c) 5       (d) 6

98. Direction: Answer the following question by selecting the most appropriate options.
    A teacher organizes a group discussion on the topic, "Save Water" in class V. The purpose of organizing this discussion is :
    (A) to give an opportunity to all students to speak.
    (B) to develop multiple perspectives.
    (C) to manage the class-room effectively.
    Which one of the following is correct?
    (a) (A) only
    (b) (B) only
    (c) (C) and (B) only
    (d) (A) and (B) only

99. The EVS textbook has a chapter on snake charmer. It is intended to make children aware and be sensitized-
    (a) for snake charmers as children do not see them often these days
    (b) that snake charmers may not harm snake and they need to be provided with alternatives before depriving them of their livelihoods
    (c) that animal keeping is good source of livelihood
    (d) that it is an illegal act

100. "People who have been living in the forest for at least 25 years have a right to the forestland and what is grown on it." This is mandated by :

(a) The Indian Forest Act, 1927
(b) The Right to Forest Act, 2007
(c) The Land Acquisition Act, 1894
(d) The Consitution (Scheduled Castes) Orders (Amendment) Bill, 2012

101. Reema took a test after teaching the lesson 'Experiments with water' to class IV students. She observed that most of the students got very less marks . This happens because -
    (a) the environment of the school was not suitable for their cognitive level.
    (b) The environment of the school was not suitable for their learning
    (c) Students did not pay attention in the class
    (d) The teacher did not use the appropriate method to teach and assess the topic

102. 'Family and friends' are a predominant theme in the EVS syllabus divided into four sub-themes. Which of the following is not one of the sub-themes?
    (a) Relationships
    (b) Houses
    (c) Animals
    (d) Work and play

103. Which one of the following four teaching methodologies followed by four different EVS teachers for teaching the topic "Water pollution" is most appropriate?
    (a) Dictating the answers to all the questions
    (b) Showing a documentary film on "Water pollution"
    (c) Asking the students to collect different water sample from their locality
    (d) Organize a Seminar on the topic.

104. The instrument ______ is used for detecting electric current .
    (a) Galvanometer
    (b) Tube tester
    (c) Altimeter
    (d) Fathometer

105. Plant stores glucose in the form of ______.
    (a) Glycogen
    (b) Starch
    (c) Monosaccharide
    (d) Cellulose

106. A doctor tells the following to the

mother of a child.
I. The bones of her child have become soft.
II. The child is suffering from a deficiency of vitamin D.
III. The child's body needs minerals like calcium and phosphorus.
IV. Calcium comes from milk and its products.
The child may be suffering from _____.

(a) Anaemia    (b) Kwashiorkor
(c) Goitre    (d) Rickets

107. Which of the following methods uses earthworms during composting?
(a) Vermicomposting
(b) Vertical composting
(c) Windrow composting
(d) Burning

108. In a multi-cylinder diesel engine, the cylinders are fired in a particular sequence:
(a) To reduce fuel consumption
(b) To reduce knocking
(c) To reduce engine vibrations
(d) All of the above

109. The minimum grade of groove to assure surface drainage is_____.
(a) 0.09%    (b) 0.02%
(c) 0.07%    (d) 0.05%

110. Which among the following is an insectivorous plant?
(a) Cuscuta    (b) Pitcher plant
(c) China rose    (d) Rose

111. Which of the following structures are traditional methods of water harvesting?
(a) Khadins    (b) Kulhs
(c) Bundhis    (d) All of these

112. Narcolepsy is a disease related to:
(a) Compulsive stealing habits
(b) Forgetting disorder
(c) Frequent attacks of epilepsy
(d) Excessive sleeping disorder

113. Amarbel (Cuscuta) is an example of:
(a) Autotroph    (b) Parasite
(c) Saprotroph    (d) Host

114. Athlete's Foot or Tinia Pedis is caused by which of the following ?
(a) Bacteria    (b) Virus
(c) Fungi    (d) Protozoan

115. Which of these layers of the atmosphere consists of the ozone layer that is responsible for absorbing the Ultra-Violet (UV) light?
(a) Troposphere
(b) Mesosphere
(c) Stratosphere
(d) None of these

116. Helping individuals and social groups acquire social values, contributes to development of:
(a) Environmental awareness
(b) Environmental knowledge
(c) Environmental perspective
(d) Environmental skills

117. The teaching of EVS should encourage process skills, which are the core of inquiry-based, hands-on learning. Which one of the following is not such a skill?
(a) Determination
(b) Inferring
(c) Observation
(d) Predicting

118. Which of the following approaches have been considered while developing social and political life textbooks?
A. Learning through use of concrete examples and experiences.
B. Learning through retention based on facts and data.
(a) Only A
(b) Only B
(c) Both A and B
(d) Neither A nor B

119. Continuous and Comprehensive Evaluation mainly aims at promoting:
(a) Competition among children
(b) Competition among teachers
(c) Academic excellence among children
(d) Inclusive education

120. Which of the following types of radiation do Greenhouse gases emit?
(a) Ultraviolet (UV)
(b) Visible
(c) Infrared (IR)
(d) Gamma

### // Hints and Solutions //

**1(C).** Adolescence is a crucial period and the period of transition between childhood and adulthood. Children when enters in adolescents period goes through many changes, such as – physical, intellectual, mental, personality, and social development. At this stage, children want to be independent and they are very close to their friends and share many things with the friends. Children understand the actual meaning of peer/friend at this stage.

**2(D).** A development task is a task that arises in a certain period of life. In Adolescence there are lots of chances in their behavior, social life, physical appearance, some of developmental tasks of adolescence are:-
• Learning to get along with friends of both sexes
• Accepting one's physical body
• Preparing for career
• Acquiring a set of values to guide behavior
• Take social responsibilities.

**3(D).** Initial Assessment is conducted before any teaching. The initial assessment is the process where a teacher identifies the individual's learning and support. Initial learning mainly takes place at the time of transition into a new learning program. It works as a holistic process where the teacher makes the achievement, interest, skills, previous learning experience, and the learning needs associated with the learning goals. It takes 10-20 minutes before the teacher starts teaching the concept.

**4(B).** In a progressive classroom, assessment of learners during the process of teaching-learning is very important since it gives insights into children's understanding and helps the teacher to reflects on her pedagogy. In a progressive classroom, teachers adapt their pedagogy and vary assessment to cater to individual students.
In order to develop a progressive classroom culture, a teacher must provide ample opportunities to all students for construction of knowledge. A progressive classroom does not allow for any discrimination among learners. The philosophy of progressive education is based on the idea that children should be taught how to think rather than just cramming facts.

**5(D).** Progressive classroom is where the teacher does not believe in the concept of spoon-feeding either the lecture method. In progressive classroom teacher targets to reach the last child by giving as many opportunities as she can give.
Gender equality is when the teacher gives equal opportunities to both the gender. Inclusive Education is when all students get the same opportunity in a classroom regardless of their strength and weaknesses.

**6(C).** The scientific method is used by teachers so students can study matter and events systematically with their own hands. Students are an active learner that test idea by experimentation. Learning is experienced through the questions of the students and active participation. The other three methods are included in the scientific method and the part of the scientific method.

**7(B).** The theory of Multi-Dimensional was propounded by Thurstone. Thurstone believes that intelligent behaviour does not raise from a general factor rather emerges from seven independent factors and he called them the primary abilities. The seven primary mental abilities are – verbal comprehension, word fluency, number facility, spatial visualization, associative memory, perceptual speed, and reasoning.

**8(B).** In this stage of the pre-moral level, children's moral judgement is based on self-interest and consideration of what others can do for them in return. They value things because those things have some practical utility for them.

**9(B).** Development begins from birth and continues till death. Earlier it was believed that all the developmental, milestones are achieved before adulthood. But now it is known, that development is an ongoing process that happens at every stage of life.

**10(B).** Gender refers to traits and behaviour that a particular culture judges to be appropriate for men and women.

**11(B).** Knowledge of individual differences helps a teacher to know variables in students like their ability, learning styles, perception, understanding, intelligence and attitude. knowledge of all these helps a teacher to plan the teaching-learning process so that the learning is personalized for the students.

**12(D).** Heredity is the biological mechanism from where a child gets his traits and characteristics. The environment of the child also influences the potential of healthy development in the child. Therefore, Both heredity and the environment plays a decisive role in the growth and development of the child.

**13(C).** Multilingualism in a classroom needs to be understood as an asset and resource by the teachers. Multilingualism can be described as a person speaking more than one language. It can also be described as a community of speakers where the use of more than one language is common. The perfect example of a multilingual society is provided by India where more than 1600 languages are spoken. It is found that children with knowledge of more than one language show more creativity and develop better problem-solving skills.

**14(C).** Socialisation means providing an individual with the skills and habits required to participate in the society. There are basically two types of Socialisation: Primary and secondary. Primary Socialisation is important for the child because in this, it learns attitudes, values, actions, culture and all these things are mostly influenced by the family and friends. In secondary Socialisation, child learn different type of skills outside their home.

**15(D).** If a child is not allowed to be in a normal/regular school and sit with normal students, they might develop a sense of inferiority complex and their confidence may get shattered. Thus regular schools should cater suitable facilities and resources for them to develop academically.

**16(B).** Dyslexia is a learning disorder that involves difficulty in reading due to the problem of speech and sound clarity. Dyslexia affects that part of the brain which processes language. Dyslexia doesn't mean an abnormal child. Dyslexia can occur to anyone, to a bright child as well as to an abnormal child.

**17(B).** Inclusion should be not be limited to only placing learners with special educational needs in normal schools or providing a separate quota to them. A learning environment that promotes to the full personal, academic, and professional development of all learners is a basic requirement for inclusive education. Therefore, adjustment in pedagogical means is required to bring inclusion. Teachers in inclusive schools should be promoted to use wide range of learning modalities (drawing, oral, writing, acting). Use of home language will also make learners from deprived communities welcome and they would be able to learn more.

**18(D).** The best way a teacher can effectively respond to the needs of the disadvantaged students is by reflecting on herself and the school system that they believe that it is a mistaken idea to judge people with the look on the outside. making them sit separately will increase the differences. Asking other students to cooperate will make them feel different from the disadvantaged group of students.

**19(C).** Principles of Inclusive education are: Principle of individual difference, Principle of No rejection, Principle of individualized education program and Principle of parental co-operation. Principle of restricted environment is not applicable in Inclusive education.

**20(C).** According to Paul Eckman, there are six basic types of emotions. They are fear, disgust, anger, surprise, happiness, and sadness. These six emotions are universally accepted in all cultures. Another classification of emotions was given by Robert Plutchik. This was called Wheel of Emotions. In this classification, Robert demonstrated a variety of emotions by mixing the basic emotions.

**21(B).** Super-ego represents the ethical and moral aspect of the psyche and usually develops in the child at the age of five and referred to as conscience. It is idealistic in nature and seated in the unconscious mind.

**22(D).** Scaffolding is an instructional method where the teacher demonstrates the process of problem-solving and explains each step or guides them step by step and after few initial explanations, she allows students to do it on their own and offers help only when required.

**23(D).** The most effective method to encourage conceptual learning in students is to give multiple examples and encourage them to use reasoning. The students develop logical problem-solving skills and analyze possible alternative actions and provide solutions with a rationale for their choices.

**24(D).** A teacher can enhance effective learning in classroom by: Utilization of maximum number of senses, correlating learning in one area with that of another, Revision and practice, feedback and reinforcement, linking the recent learnings with those of the past.

**25(C).** The trial and error method is the method in which multiple attempts are made to reach a solution. It is a basic method of learning that essentially all organisms use to learn new behaviors. E.L. Thorndike was the chief exponent of the trial and error method.

**26(D).** Motivation to learn can be sustained by focusing on mastery-oriented goals. Mastery orientation goals are self-set standards in which the learner is self-motivated to develop new skills, improving and acquiring additional knowledge. Giving the easy task to child, focusing on rote memorization or punishing the child does not motivate a child to learn.

**27(A).** Bandura's modeling effect can be seen when a teacher demonstrates to a student how to hold a pencil or write capital 'A' etc. while teaching in class and this shows a new behavior by which a student learns new kinds of response pattern.

**28(D).** Learning is a comprehensive process that refers to a change in behaviour, knowledge, and skills as a result of practice and experience.
**Gender difference** is the factor that has the least effect on learning as gender refers to the socially constructed differences between men and women.
There are many factors affecting learning and physical factor is one of them. It is the

elements of one's physical body that limit or enhance the ways one learns and thinks.

**29(D).** Learning is an active process, transferable, measurable and goal-oriented. It is the desired change or modification of behaviour attained through experience and environment. It is both a formal and informal process, it is universal and continuous. From birth, every child should have access to high-quality learning opportunities for language, literacy and mathematics. These should be available in all early years settings, including the home, and facilitated by parents.

**30(C).** The 'Laws of learning' were given by thorndike.
Edward Thorndike developed the first three laws of learning readiness, exercise, and effect. He set also the law of effect which means that any behavior that is followed by pleasant consequences is likely to be repeated, and any behavior followed by unpleasant consequences is likely to be avoided.

**31(C).** A great teacher is warm, accessible, enthusiastic, and caring. This is the teacher to whom students know they can go with any problems or concerns.
- Effective teachers strive to motivate and engage all their students in learning rather than simply accepting that some students cannot be engaged and are destined to do poorly.
- They believe every student is capable of achieving success at school and they do all they can to find ways of making each student successful.

**32(D).** **Approach:** The practices in language teaching are based on the theories concerning the nature of language and language learning. These theories together form the first component of a method.
**Constructive approach:** One of the most important principles in the constructivist approach to language teaching is action orientedness. Another principle of constructive approach refers to content-oriented language teaching and usually takes place in bilingual classes. A constructive approach to language teaching is based on the foundation that knowledge is constructed. Students are given the freedom to plan their choice and to be creative.
**Structural Approaches:** Structural approach is a scientific study of the fundamental structures of the English language, their analysis and logical arrangement. Every structure expresses an important grammatical point. A sentence needs a grammatical background. The different arrangements or patterns of words are called structures.
**Natural approaches:** It is the theory that is based on the notion that we learn the language in the same way as we acquire our first language. It doesn't force to utter words or phrases, much less pronounce them correctly. There are no endless drills on correct usage and no mentions of grammar rules or long lists of vocabulary to wrap the head around.
**Deductive approaches:** Deductive approaches refer to developing a Hypothesis. It is testing of Existing theory.

**33(C).** **Language teaching:** It is the process whereby a child gains communicative comprehension or fluency over a language. It involves practice by learners where facilitation is provided by a teacher.
- The teaching rules at the initial stage do not lend much to language learning.
- Grammar teaching should move from meaning to form.
- Grammar teaching at the initial stage doesn't lend much to language learning and has focused on meaning before form. While teaching grammar, the activities should be designed in a way that requires the Inductive and creative reasoning of the child.

**34(C).** The ultimate aim of every language learner is to acquire the ability to speak and write the language correctly. In order to do this, she requires knowledge of grammar in some form or the other. Grammar is defined as a theory of language. We consider language as rule-governed behavior, relating to sounds, word formation, and structure. Here grammar constitutes a subset of rules relating to morphology and syntax.

**35(B).** Children learn various lessons of learning the English language throughout their school life. At various stages/standards, children learn different difficulty levels of English.

**36(A).** Language skills are necessary for effective communication in any environment and to interact with others. It allows an individual to comprehend and produce language for proper and effective interpersonal communication.

**37(A).** Multilingualism is the ability to use more than two languages, it refers to using the language of learners as a strategy in school.
- Multilingualism is constitutive of the identity of a child and a typical feature of the Indian linguistic landscape must be used as a resource, classroom strategy, and a goal by a creative language teacher.
- Multilingualism as a resource means using the languages of learners as a strategy in school.
- It is used as a resource to teach a new language to the child with the help of a mother tongue or other known language.

**Benefits of Multilingualism (NCF - 2005):**
- It emphasizes on the significance of a smooth transition between the home and school language.
- Multilingualism encourages children to believe in themselves.
- It improves cognitive flexibilities to express thought in multiple ways.
- Multilingual children are capable of greater cognitive flexibility and creativity and perform better academically than monolingual.
- It helps in the development of various language skills that lead to language development.

So, from the above points, we can conclude that at the upper primary level, the language/languages used by children in a multilingual classroom is a resource.

**38(B).** Teaching aids or teaching-learning material which is used by teachers to help learners to learn concept with ease and efficiency. It can be an artificial or real object which makes learning more effective.

**39(B).** Different teachers would face different challenges in their regular teaching – in terms of the curriculum, classroom transactions, time and resource management, as well as dealing with individual students. These may change from time to time.

**40(A).** The teaching of English must be done in a way so that it reduces the errors and compels students to use English in their daily life and gives them confidence and satisfaction while using the language. The main purpose of teaching a language in education is to make a child proficient in that specific language.

**41(A).** Continuous Comprehensive Evaluation refers to a school-based evaluation, which covers all aspects of school activities related to a child's development.
- It emphasizes two-fold objectives such as continuity of evaluation and assessment of learning outcomes in a comprehensive manner.
- It covers all the domains of learning i.e. cognitive, affective, and psychomotor domains.

**42(C).** NCF (National Curriculum Framework) 2005 is one of the four NCFs published in India by NCERT. It seeks to provide a framework for the betterment of educational purposes and experiences.
- Language is a medium through which human beings tend to communicate with each other by using various attributes of a language that are symbols, gestures, words, etc.
Hence, the correct option is (D).

**43(C).** Reading can be defined as the ability to make sense of written or printed words. The reader uses the symbols to activate the information from his memory and subsequently uses the information to arrive at a plausible interpretation of the written words.

- It is a multifaceted and layered process in which a reader by actively interacting with the text , tries to decode what has been encoded by the writer.

**44(A).** Language is essentially a means of communication among the members of society. In the expression of culture, language is a fundamental aspect. It is the tool that conveys traditions and values related to group identity.

**45(B).** A textbook is a tool to be used in the teaching process to facilitate effective learning. A good English textbook's every lesson should have a proper introduction at the beginning and a conclusion at the end to develop a good understanding of the concept for a better educational experience. It should be based on the guiding principles of the curriculum and syllabus.

**46(C).** The correct answer is 'news about acts of crime and violence.'
As we can see in the first paragraph of the passage, it is clearly mentioned that "when we pick up a daily newspaper, we invariably find an increased incidence of vandalism, fraud, theft, robbery, rape, child spouse, battered spouses, murders, hate crimes, genocide (now termed as "ethnic cleansing") along with a multitude of other senseless violent acts that have become disturbingly common".
Thus, it is concluded that the newspapers are full of news about acts of crime and violence these days.

**47(C).** The underlined word significance is a noun which means a word (other than a pronoun) used to identify any of a class of people, places, or things (common noun), or to name a particular one of these (proper noun).
It can be defined as any member of a class of words that typically can be combined with determiners to serve as the subject of a verb, can be interpreted as singular or plural, can be replaced with a pronoun, and refer to an entity, quality, state, action, or concept.
Significance can be defined as the quality of being important.

**48(C).** **Futility** means the quality or state of being futile; uselessness.
**Usefulness** means the quality or fact of being useful.
From the above meanings it is evident that **usefulness** is the correct antonym of the word futility.

**49(D).** The correct answer is 'It helps one respect others'.
As we can see in the second paragraph of the passage, it is clearly mentioned that "when the significance of good self-esteem is well understood and it achieves the prominence it deserves, a transformation will begin, for as the people will learn they are deserving of self-respect, their respect for others will automatically increase".
Thus, it is concluded that good self-esteem is stressed upon because it helps one to respect others.

**50(B).** **Vandalism** means an action involving deliberate destruction of or damage to public or private property.
**Destruction** means the action or process of causing so much damage to something that it no longer exists or cannot be repaired.
From the above meanings it is evident that destruction is the correct synonym of the word vandalism.

**51(B).** The error is in part (b).
Whether- or is a correlative conjunction.
Example: I didn't know whether you'd want the cheesecake or the chocolate cake, so I got both.
So, in part (b), and should be replaced by or.
Correct part: whether personal, national or global
Correct sentence: The solution to a great many problems(a)/, whether personal, national or global(b)/, lies in improving our feelings(c)/ No error. (d)

**52(C).** Let's refer to the lines:
- High self-esteem denotes that we accept ourselves unconditionally exactly as we are , we appreciate our value as a human being.
- Vulnerable to the opinions of others, we desperately try to gain their recognition and approval sometimes through risky and dangerous behaviour. Thus, we are at the mercy of our emotions, instead of controlling them, we permit them to control us.
- Today when we pick up a daily newspaper, we invariably find an increased incidence of vandalism, fraud, theft, robbery, rape, child spouse, battered spouses, murders, hate crimes, genocide (now termed as "ethnic cleansing") along with a multitude of other senseless violent acts that have become disturbingly common. These are not the actions of people who like themselves.
Upon the perusal of the above lines, it can be concluded that statement A and B are true, C is false.

**53(B).** The correct answer is When we push ourselves towards achieving goals and prove that we are somebody by our successes and achievements.
If we cannot accomplish certain results, we tend to feel low about ourselves. Some of us try too hard and become workaholics and over-achievers. With a few genuine feelings of self-worth, we try to create some and prove that we are somebody by our successes and achievements.
If we do finally achieve our goals we are disappointed; despite everything we have done, we still feel empty inside.
Upon the perusal of the above lines, it can be concluded that a person starts feeling empty inside when he pushes himself towards achieving goals and prove that he is somebody by his successes and achievements.

**54(C).** The correct answer is **Adjective** .
**Adjectives** are words that are used to describe or modify nouns or pronouns.
**Goals** is a noun. Unrealistic is a word that is modifying that word 'goals'. Thus, unrealistic is an adjective.
So, the part of speech of the underlined word is adjective, making option (C) the correct answer choice.

**55(B).** The correct answer is **positive light.**
Look at the lines:
- There is a Reaper, whose name is Death,
  _And, with his sickle keen
The poem **subverts** the meaning of **death** .
**Death** is a character in the **poem** .
**Death** may seem **merciless** on the surface but it takes loved ones to a new world.
Therefore, death is not gloomy or fearful.
Gloomy means dark or poorly lit, especially so as to appear depressing or frightening.
Thus, **death** is shown in a **positive light.**

**56(D).** The correct answer is **paradise** .
Let us take a look at the line, 'And the mother gave, in tears and pain,/_The flowers she most did love;/She knew she should find them all again/_In the fields of light above.'
It says the mother will meet her flowers in **fields of light** .
'Fields of light' is an allegory for **Paradise** .
Paradise is the garden of Eden.
Thus the mother will meet her flower in **Paradise** .

**57(C).** The correct answer is God.
Let us take a look at the line, 'It was for the **Lord of Paradise** '.
The lines state that the flowers are for the 'Lord of Paradise'.
'Lord of Paradise' refers to **God** .
Thus, the flowers are for **God** .

**58(A).** The figure of speech is ' **Alliteration** '.
'A figure of speech' is a word or phrase that is used in a non-literal way to create an effect.
'Alliteration' is a literary device that reflects repetition in two or more nearby words of initial consonant sounds.
For example:
- rocky road.
- big business.
Similarly in expression 'She knew she should find them all again', the figure of speech 'Alliteration' is used as consonant

sound 's' is being repeated in she, she and should.

**59(C).** The answer is saints.
Let us take a look at the line, 'And saints, upon their garments white, _These sacred blossoms wear.'
It is stated that saints wear the blossoms.
**Blossoms** are a kind of flower.
Thus, saints wear flowers over their white garments.

**60(D).** The correct answer is **tearful eyes.**
- Let us take a look at the line, 'He gazed at the flowers with tearful eyes'.
- It is stated that Death gazed at the flowers with tearful eyes .
- Thus, Death gazed at the flowers with tearful eyes.

**61(B).** Mathematics is a study of patterns, numbers, geometrical objects, data, and information. It deals with data analysis, integration of various fields of knowledge, deductive and inductive reasoning, and generalizations.
- The teaching of mathematics should be done in the way, in which a student learns the best i.e., following the child-centered approach by engaging students actively in the learning process.
- The teacher should focus more on providing practical exercises and abstract knowledge to students to foster their individualized discovery-oriented learning.

**62(C).** The specific aims of mathematics education help to design suitable methods for planning effective classroom learning process, curriculum, guide to prepare TLMs, prepare evaluation procedures, etc. Thus it is desirable to write the specific aims in action verbs, pinpointed, short, achievable, etc. The following are some of the specific aims of mathematics education:
- To ensure a good start for the students in learning mathematics.
- To give clarity on the fundamental concepts and processes of the subject. To create love, faith, and interest in learning mathematics.
- To develop in them a taste and confidence in mathematics.
- To develop an appreciation for accuracy.
- To acquaint them with the relation of mathematics with their present as well as future life.
- To see aesthetics in mathematics.
- To develop in them the habits like regularity, practice, patience, self-reliance, and hard work.
- To apply mathematics in other subjects.
- To acquaint them with mathematical language and symbolism.
- To prepare them for the learning of mathematics of higher classes.
- To prepare them for mathematical exhibitions.

So, we conclude that the above points are specific aims of mathematics.

**63(B).** The basic structure of mathematics includes arithmetic, algebra, geometry, and trigonometry that helps in learning the techniques to handle abstractions and structures.
- The teaching of mathematics must develop attitudes to think, reason, analyze, and articulate logically.
- The nature of mathematics highly influences the nature of the teaching-learning process in mathematics.

**64(A).** Mathematics is a subject matter of complex abstractions that mainly deals with patterns, shapes, sizes, figures, and data analysis. It is based on practical usability in all aspects of life.

**65(A).** The teaching and learning of mathematics have always been a major concern in education. The National Policy of Education (1986) lays down the importance of "Mathematics" as a vehicle for developing creativity.
- The old methods of mathematics teaching heavily depended upon rote learning which have been replaced by methods that depend upon discovery and problem-solving approaches.
- The teacher should use effective teaching methods of mathematics so that individualized discovery-oriented (or problem-solving) learning could be fostered.

**66(C).** In a math class, a teacher follows a proper sequence in teaching which is usually practically followed in any classroom. This is known as classroom operations. It plays a major role in Mathematics learnings and one of the challenges that teacher face in a classroom depending on different factors i.e., nature of the content, the learning style of the students, knowledge of teaching methods and also depends on the ability to use mathematical tools. This is what exactly done in mathematics class.

**67(C).** Mathematics: Mathematics is a science of number and space. It has its own language, signs, symbols, terms, etc. The scope of mathematics in our daily life is immense. For example: building houses or purchase anything involves the use of numbers, geometry, measures, and space.

**68(D).** Mathematics focuses on developing an understanding of numbers, shapes, and patterns by using the techniques of problem-solving and logical reasoning.
The mathematical curriculum treats mathematics both as a tool for practical utility as well as a discipline that develops reasoning and analytical abilities.

**69(C).** Throughout the centuries, mathematics has been recognised as one of the central strands of human intellectual activity. From the very beginning, mathematics has been a living and growing intellectual pursuit. It has its roots in everyday activities and forms the basic structure of our highly advanced technological developments. Math's has grown largely as a result of
- social needs, as shown in everyday life, commerce, science and technology
- the intellectual need to connect together existing mathematics into a single logical framework or proof structure

Thus, the word mathematics can be used in two distinct and different senses:
- the truths that are discovered
- the methods used to discover truths

So, we conclude that mathematics can be used in both distinct and different senses.

**70(B).** Van Hiele was famous for his theory that describes how students learn geometry, he was born in 1909 and died November 1, 2010. It postulates five levels of geometric thinking.

**71(D).** Language helps an individual to communicate with others in an effective way with words, symbols, and expressions as the mediums.
- As mathematics is considered a non-linguistic subject but still it possess similarities with the language.
- It uses symbols and expressions to describe the lengthy problems in a precise and accurate manner which makes it an economical language.

**72(B).** Mathematics is a branch of science which deals with counting, calculating, and studying numbers, shapes, and structures. Effective Mathematics teaching should aim to promote students' confidence in mathematics, curiosity, freedom, and belief in doing mathematics.
In a mathematics class , students enjoy learning, solving problems, develop mathematical curiosity, and become confident in using mathematics to analyze and solve problems.
Mathematics Classroom Emphasise on:-
According to National Curriculum Framework-2005, the main goal of Mathematics education in school is the mathematisation of the child's thought process.

**73(A).** Word problems in mathematics are those questions which are given in the form of statements, which, after comprehension, is solved using mathematical operations.
Word problems help to develop the ability to convert real-life problems into mathematical problems and find out a solution.
Although, they help in understanding the language of mathematics, yet their ultimate aim is to connect children with real-life, so that they can visualize a math problem.
It develops thinking skills by letting

students know how to convert a 'mathematical language statement' to 'symbolic statement'.

So, we conclude that in Mathematics, word problems help to develop ability to convert real-life problems into mathematical problems.

**74(D).** Remedial teaching refers to the method of teaching that helps the teacher to provide learners with the necessary help and guidance to overcome the problems which are determined through diagnosing them.

Remedial teaching is required for all weak, average and mentally retarded children with the purpose:

- to eliminate their ineffective habits.
- to reteach them the items not properly learnt.
- to arise their interest in learning with stimulating approaches.
- to make them learn better by providing necessary help and guidance.
- to transmit practical experiences to them according to their diverse needs.

**75(A).** **An Achievement test** is used to measure the relative accomplishment of pupils in specified areas of learning.

While the **Diagnostic test** is the test to know the strength, weaknesses, knowledge, and skill of a student prior to the instructions. It is used to diagnose the difficulties and to guide accordingly as a result.

**76(A).** Given:

Length $= 12m$

Breadth $= 6m$

Height $= 4m$

Formula:

Length of the longest pole $= \sqrt{l^2 + b^2 + h^2}$

Calculation:

The length of the longest pole that can be fitted in a room of dimensions

$= 12m \times 6m \times 4m$

$\Rightarrow \sqrt{(12^2 + 6^2 + 4^2)}$

$\Rightarrow \sqrt{(144 + 36 + 16)}$

$\Rightarrow \sqrt{196}$

$\Rightarrow 14m$

$\therefore$ The length of the largeat pole is $14.0m$.

**77(C).** Given:

$(1, 2), (-4, -3)$ and $(4, 1)$

Formula:

Area of triangle whose vertices are $(x_1, y_1), (x_2, y_2)$ and $(x_3, y_3) = \frac{1}{2}[x_1(y_2 - y_3) + x_2(y_3 - y_1) + x_3(y_1 - y_2)]$

Calculation:

$\Rightarrow$ Area of triangle

$= \left(\frac{1}{2}\right) \times [1(-3 - 1) + (-4)(1 - 2) + 4\{2 - (-3)\}]$

$= \left(\frac{1}{2}\right) \times \{(-4) + 4 + 20\}$

$= \frac{20}{2}$

$= 10$ sq. units

**78(C).** Given:

A circle touches all four sides of a quadrilateral $PQRS$. If $PQ = 11$ cm. $QR = 12$ cm and $PS = 8$ cm.

Calculation :

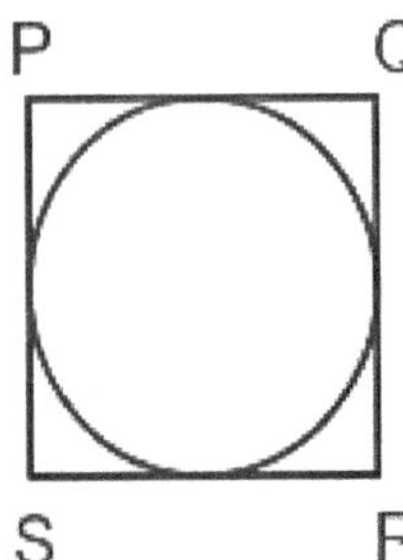

If a circle touches all four sides of quadrilateral $PQRS$ then,

$PQ + RS = PS + QR$

So ,

$\Rightarrow 11 + RS = 8 + 12$

$\Rightarrow RS = 20 - 11$

$\Rightarrow RS = 9$

**79(A).** Given: 3240

Concept:

If $k = a^x \times b^y$, then

$a$, and $b$ must be prime number

Sum of all factors $= \left(a^0 + a^1 + a^2 + \ldots + a^x\right)\left(b^0 + b^1 + b^2 + \ldots + b^y\right)$

Solution:

$3240 = 2^3 \times 3^4 \times 5^1$

Sum of factors $= \left(2^0 + 2^1 + 2^2 + 2^3\right)\left(3^0 + 3^1 + 3^2 + 3^3 + 3^4\right)\left(5^0 + 5^1\right)$

$\Rightarrow (1 + 2 + 4 + 8)(1 + 3 + 9 + 27 + 81)(1 + 5)$

$\Rightarrow 15 \times 121 \times 6$

$\Rightarrow 10890$

$\therefore$ required sum is $10890$.

**80(A).** Let $A$ receive Rs. $a$ and let the difference between each consecutive person be Rs. $d$.

$\Rightarrow$ Amount received by $E = a + 4d$

According to question,

Amount received by $E =$ Amount received by $A + 40$

$\Rightarrow a + 4d = a + 40$

$\Rightarrow 4d = 40$

$\Rightarrow d = 10$

Also,

Total amount $= a + (a + d) + (a + 2d) + (a + 3d) + (a + 4d)$

$\Rightarrow 720 = 5a + 10d$

$\Rightarrow 720 = 5a + 100$

$\Rightarrow a = 124$

$\Rightarrow$ Amount received by $B = a + d = 124 + 10 =$ Rs. $134$.

**81(D).** Given:

$? = \sqrt[5]{(243)^2}$

Calculation:

$? = \sqrt[5]{(243)^2}$

$\Rightarrow ? = (243)^{\left(\frac{2}{5}\right)}$

$\Rightarrow ? = (3 \times 3 \times 3 \times 3 \times 3)^{\left(\frac{2}{5}\right)}$

$\Rightarrow ? = \left(3^5\right)^{\left(\frac{2}{5}\right)}$

$\Rightarrow ? = 3^2$

$\therefore ? = 9$

**82(D).** Concept:

Joule is a S.I unit of energy or work done which is represented by J

Watt is a S.I unit of Power and it is represented as W

$\text{Power ( Watt )} = \dfrac{\text{Work ( Joule )}}{\text{time } (sec)}$

Work done $(J) =$ power ( Watt )$\times$ time (sec)

1 joule = 1 watt. Sec

Calculation:

Since 1 kW = 1000 W = $10^3$ Watt or W

And 1 hour = 60 min $\times$60 sec = 3600 sec

$\therefore$ 1 kWh = $10^3 \times 3600 = 3.6 \times 10^6 J$.

**83(A).** Using Unitary method,

Weight of 18 sheets of paper = 50 gm

1 gm $= \dfrac{18}{50}$ sheet

$3\dfrac{3}{4}$ kg = 3 kg +750 gm = 3750 gm

$\Rightarrow \dfrac{15}{4}$ kg has $\dfrac{18}{50} \times 3750 = 1350$ sheets

**84(C).** Given:

Total time of journey = 7 hours

Speed of car for half distance = 40 km/hr

Speed of car for remaining distance = 60 km/hr

Concept:

Distance $=$ Speed $\times$ Time

Calculation:

Let total distance be $2x$.

$\text{Time }_1 = \dfrac{\text{Distance}}{\text{Speed}}$

$\Rightarrow \dfrac{x}{40}$ hours

$\text{Time }_2 = \dfrac{\text{Distance}}{\text{Speed}}$

$\Rightarrow \dfrac{x}{60}$ hours

Total time $=$ Time $_1+$ Time $_2$

$\Rightarrow 7 = \dfrac{x}{40} + \dfrac{x}{60}$

$\Rightarrow 7 = \dfrac{(3x + 2x)}{120}$

$\Rightarrow 7 = \dfrac{5x}{120}$

$\Rightarrow x = 7 \times 24$

$\Rightarrow x = 168$ km

$\Rightarrow$ Total distance $= 2x$

$\Rightarrow 2 \times 168$

$\Rightarrow 336$ km

$\therefore$ Total distance covered by the car is 336 km.

**85(B).** Given series: Left side P 3 6 T U 7 C 8 B M 2 X 0 W 1 R 5 S V A Right side.

If all the numbers are dropped, the new series will be:

Left side P T U C B M X W R S V A Right side

So, the 10 th letter from the left side is S.

**86(B).** Given:

$\dfrac{44}{49}, \dfrac{33}{38}, \dfrac{22}{25}$ and $\dfrac{24}{29}$

Calculation:

Converting the fractions in decimal forms,

$\Rightarrow \frac{44}{49} = 0.89$

$\Rightarrow \frac{33}{38} = 0.86$

$\Rightarrow \frac{22}{25} = 0.88$

$\Rightarrow \frac{24}{29} = 0.82$

So, correct descending order is $\frac{44}{49}, \frac{22}{25}, \frac{33}{38}, \frac{24}{29}$.

**87(B).** Given:

Length of playground = 46 m

Breadth of playground = 44 m

Speed of Aman = 3.6 km/hr

Concept:

Distance covered in 1 round = Perimeter of the palyground

Perimeter of rectangle = 2 × ( length + breadth )

$1 \text{ km/hr} = \left(\frac{5}{18}\right) \text{ m/s}$

1 minute = 60 seconds

Formula:

Time taken = $\frac{\text{Distance}}{\text{Speed}}$

Calculation:

Distance covered in 1 round

$= 2 \times (46 + 44)$

$= 180$ m

Distance covered in 3 rounds $= 180 \times 3$

$= 540$ m

Speed in m/s $= 3.6 \times \left(\frac{5}{18}\right)$

$= 1$ m/s

$\therefore$ Time taken $= \frac{540}{1}$

$= 540$ s

$\because 60$ s $= 1$ minute

$\Rightarrow 540$ s $= \left(\frac{1}{60}\right) \times 540$

$= 9$ minutes

**88(B).** Calculation:

Let the man's usual speed be $x$ km/hr and the distance to be covered $= y$ km.

We know that,

Time $= \frac{\text{Distance}}{\text{Speed}}$

So,

His usual time is $\left(\frac{y}{x}\right)$ hours.

When his speed is $\frac{5}{3}$ his usual speed the time taken is $\left(\frac{3y}{5x}\right)$ hours

$\because$ Time is inversely proportional to speed when distance is constant.

Now, $\left(\frac{y}{x}\right) + \frac{20}{60} = \left(\frac{3y}{5x}\right)$

$\Rightarrow \left(\frac{y}{x} - \frac{3y}{5x}\right) = \frac{20}{60}$

$\Rightarrow \frac{(5y - 3y)}{5x} = \frac{1}{3}$

$\Rightarrow \frac{2y}{5x} = \frac{1}{3}$

$\Rightarrow \frac{y}{x} = \frac{5}{6}$

इसलिए, $\frac{5}{6}$ घंटे को मिनट में बदलने पर

$= \left(\frac{5}{6}\right) \times 60$

उसका सामान्य समय 50 मिनट है।

**89(B).** Given:

Wife was born 23 years ago (which means her present age is 23 years)

Ratio of ages of Rahul and his wife 7 years from now will be 7 : 6

Calculation:

Let the present age of husband be $x$ years.

Age of husband 7 years hence $= x + 7$

Present age of wife = 23 years

Age of wife after 7 years = 30 years

According to the question,

Ratio of ages of husband and wife 7 years from now = 7 : 6

$\Rightarrow \frac{(x+7)}{30} = \frac{7}{6}$

$\Rightarrow x + 7 = 35$

$\Rightarrow x = 28$ years

$\therefore$ Age of Rahul after 2 years = 30.

**90(B).** The figure may be labeled as shown.

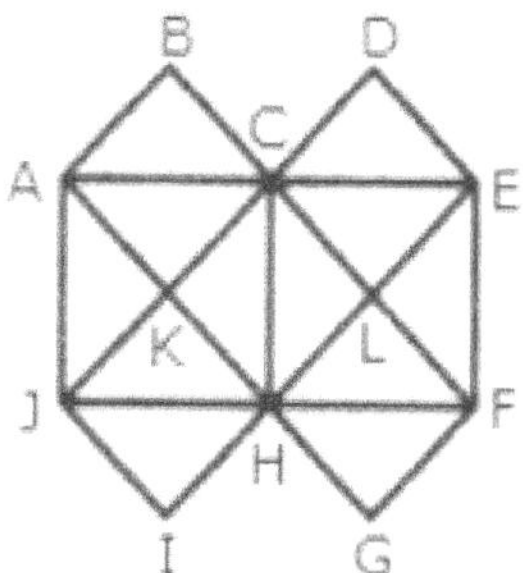

The horizontal lines are AE and JF i.e. 2 in number. The vertical lines are AJ, CH and EF i.e. 3 in number.

The slanting lines are AG, BF, JD, IE, AB, DE, JI and FG i.e. 8 in number.

Total number of straight lines needed to construct the figure $= 2 + 3 + 8 = 13$.

**91(D).** Environmental Science is the study of interrelationships between human activities and the environment.

* Environmental Science is an unusual academic discipline in that it requires scientific knowledge about the natural world, as well as an understanding of ways in which humans interact with the natural world.

* It examines the effects of human actions on the environment and the means by which policies, regulations, and decisions influence human actions.

* Environmental Studies learning could lead to holistic learning with the following curriculum.

**92(C).** There are some birds such as Eagle, Kites, Vultures which can see distinctly the object four times as far as we can see. These birds can see objects from distance of eight meters what we can see from a distance of two meters.

**93(C).** Roasting is a way of cooking food by exposing it to dry radiant heat over open fire, in oven, or at times within surrounding hot embers, sand, or stones. Vegetables, meat, corn, potatoes, and sweet potatoes are cooked by roasting.

**94(B).** In this type of farming after cutting one crop, the land is left as it is for some years. Nothing is grown on the land

The bamboo or weeds (small or waste plants) which grow on the land are not pulled out. They are cut and burnt because ash makes the land fertile

When the land is ready for farming it is lightly dug up not plowed

This type of farming is being done in Mizoram

The main crop here is rice

People celebrated when the crop is ripened, and they do Cheraw dance holding bamboos.

**95(C).** Observation is the active acquisition of information from a primary source. In living beings, observation employs the senses and since the student are observing the two leafs, they are performing observational activity. So, Observing process skills will be used in answering this question.

**96(A).** By conducting a fun activity before starting a new lesson, a teacher tries to motivate students for learning new concepts with interest. It will increase their attention and curiosity level in the class while attending the lecture.

**97(D).** Syllabus of EVS has been divided into 6 themes to inculcate every aspect of learning which are considered important for child of primary level.

1. Family and friends (i. Relationships, ii. Plants, iii. animals, iv. work and play)
2. food
3. Shelter
4. travel
5. Water
6. Things we make and do

**98(D).** The purpose of teacher to give an opportunity to all students to speak and to develop multiple perspectives. This will help student to providing the opportunities to synthesize their knowledge and illustrate it thereby communicating graphically. This will also give students the opportunity to discover spatial and temporal trends and patterns.

**99(B).** Option (B) is correct as the chapter is intended to make children aware and be sensitized that snake charmers may not harm snake and they need to be provided with alternatives for their livelihoods. People with less earning opportunities are forced to rely on animals as their livelihood sources.

**100(B).** According to the Right to Forest act 2007, people who have been living in the forest for at least 25 years, have a right over the forest land and what is grown on it. They should not be removed from the forest. The work of protecting the forest should be done by their Gram Sabha.

**101(D).** If most of the students are unable

to perform well in a test, then there could be a problem in the way of making students understand a particular concept and the way of assessing those students for that concept. Different topics are needed to be evaluated in ways that are specific for them.

**102(B).** Relationships, work and play and animals along with plants are the sub themes of the main theme of family and friends. Houses is not one of the sub themes of family and friends however shelter is one of the other main themes of EVS syllabus.

**103(B).** Showing a documentary film on "Water pollution" is most appropriate for teaching the topic. A documentary film is a nonfictional motion picture intended to document some aspect of reality, primarily for the purposes of instruction, education, or maintaining a historical record. It help to understanding the concept of given topic and also enhance their learning.

**104(A).** **Galvanometer:**
- A galvanometer is used for detecting current in an electric circuit.
- The galvanometer is the device used for detecting the presence of small currents and voltage or for measuring their magnitude.
- The galvanometer is mainly used in the bridges and potentiometer where they indicate the null deflection or zero current.
- The potentiometer is based on the premise that the current sustaining coil is kept between the magnetic field experiences a torque.

From the above, it is clear that the galvanometer is the instrument used for detecting the presence of electric current in a circuit.

| Instrument | Used to |
|---|---|
| Altimeter | Measure the altitude of an object. |
| Tube tester | Used to test characteristics of vacuum tubes. |
| Fathometer | Measure the depth of water. |

**105(B).** Starch is a polymeric carbohydrate consisting of numerous glucose units joined by glycosidic bonds. Starch is a polysaccharide comprising glucose monomers. Glucose is a simple sugar having the molecular formula $C_6H_{12}O_6$. Glucose circulates in the blood of animals in the form of blood sugar. Glucose is stored as a polymer. In plants, it is stored as starch and in animals as glycogen.

**106(D).** The child may be suffering from rickets. Vitamin D helps the body to use calcium from the diet and makes the bones strong. Its deficiency causes rickets that is characterized by softening of bones, skeletal deformities and inadequate mineralization of bone matrix.

**107(A).** Vermicomposting methods uses earthworms during composting. Vermicomposting is a method that uses earthworms during composting by degrading the organic wastes present in the bulk waste material, in vertical reactor, waste flows vertically and that is called as Vertical composting, in windrow composting there is a direct contact between the waste and the atmosphere, whereas, burning is not a composting process.

**108(C).** Firing order: The order or sequence in which the firing takes place, in different cylinders of a multi-cylinder engine. Most commonly used firing order for different engines are as followed :-
3-cylinder engine: 1-3-2
4 Cylinder engine (inline): 1-3-4-2
4-cylinder horizontal opposed engines: 1-4-3-2
6-cylinder inline engine: 1-5-3-6-2-4 or 1-4-2-6-3-5 or 1-3-2-6-4-5 or 1-2-4-6-5-3
8-cylinder inline engine: 1-6-2-5-8-3-7-4 or 1-4-7-3-8-5-2-6
Advantages of proper firing order:
- Reduced engine vibrations
- Proper balancing of engine
- Even flow of power

**109(D).** The minimum grade of groove to assure surface drainage is 0.05%. Furrow is a long, narrow irrigation trench made in the ground used for an optimal supply of water. Furrows can be level and are very similar to long narrow basins. However, a minimum grade of 0.05% is recommended so that effective drainage can occur following irrigation or excessive rainfall.

**110(B).** Concept:
- Insectivorous plants are the plants that obtain their nutrients by trapping or consuming animals (insects and other arthropods).
- Insectivorous plants grow in nitrogen-deficient soils.
- They obtain nitrogen from different insects, e.g. Drosera, Nepenthes, Dionnea, Utricularia, Pitcher plant, etc.
- The pitcher plant is an insectivorous plant.

| Cuscuta | Parasite |
|---|---|
| China rose | Autotroph |
| Rose | Autotroph |

**111(D).** Khadins, Bundhis, Ahars , Kulhs and Kattas are ancient structures of water harvesting. Water harvesting is a term which means storage of water during rains. Traditionally, small dams and other reservoirs were built so that rainwater could be stored for later use.

For example, Khadins and nadis in Rajasthan, bundhis in Madhya Pradesh and Uttar Pradesh, ahars and pynes in Bihar, and kattas in Karnataka are some of the ancient water harvestings, including water conveyance, structures. These are still in use in many places. These structures were not having any adverse effect on the local natural balance and had no environmental costs.

**112(D).** Narcolepsy is a disease related to excessive sleeping disorder. Narcolepsy is a chronic sleep disorder characterized by overwhelming daytime drowsiness and sudden attacks of sleep. People with narcolepsy often find it difficult to stay awake for long periods of time, regardless of the circumstances. Narcolepsy can cause serious disruptions in your daily routine.

**113(B).** Cuscuta is a parasitic plant. Since Cuscuta does not have chlorophyll, it cannot synthesize its own food by photosynthesis. It uses the nutrients of host plants for its growth. Other parasitic plants are - Rafflesia, Viscum, Nuytsia floribunda. Parasitic plants cause damage to the host plant.

**114(C).** Athlete's foot is a fungal infection that affects the upper layer of the skin of the foot, especially when it is warm, moist, and irritated. Athlete's foot is contagious and can spread through contact with an infected person or from contact with contaminated surfaces, such as towels, floors and shoes. You can also spread it from the foot to other parts of the body, especially if you scratch or pick the infected parts of your foot.

**115(C).** An atmosphere can be defined as the blanket of gas on the surface of a planet. The Earth's atmosphere is the mixture of gases that surrounds the planet. The Earth's atmosphere contains mainly 5 layers which are troposphere, stratosphere, mesosphere, thermosphere and exosphere.
**Stratosphere** :
The stratosphere extends from the top of the troposphere to about 50 km (31 miles) above the ground. The famous ozone layer is found within the stratosphere. Ozone molecules in this layer absorb high-energy ultraviolet (UV) light from the Sun, converting the UV energy into heat.

**116(C).** Helping individuals and social groups acquire social values, contributes to the development of Environmental perspective.
- Environmental perspective are a psychological tendency expressed by evaluative responses to the natural environment with some degree of favor or disfavor.
- Environmental perspective are latent (i.e. hidden) construct; therefore we

cannot observe them directly. We can only infer it from overt responses.

- Research has identified a few factors that influence Environmental perspective. The factors influencing Environmental perspective can be broadly classified into socio-demographic, psychological, and environmentally related variables.
- Based on this value orientation, there are three environmental perspective and they are categorized as rooted in a concern for the self (egoistic concern), for other people (altruistic concern), or for the biosphere (biospheric concern).

Therefore, Helping individuals and social groups acquire social values, contributes to development of Environmental perspective.

**117(A).** **Inquiry-based approach:** It emphasizes to connect the child with their own experiences by posing questions and making decisions in the search of new understanding.

**Hands-on learning:** It emphasizes the child's effective involvement in the learning process rather simply listening to the teacher's lecture. It promotes learning by doing and active learning.

**The above-mentioned techniques should be promoted since:**

- It develops the learner's ability to discover and explore.
- It emphasizes the use of learner's five sense organs in learning.
- It requires the learner's involvement mentally, physically and intellectually.
- It includes inferring, observing, predicting, classifying, questioning, measuring, analyzing, and interpreting.

Hence, we conclude that inferring, observing and predicting are the process skills which are the core of inquiry-based, hands-on learning, while determination is not one of them.

**118(A).** Social and Political Life is a new subject area in middle school social science that has replaced the earlier subject of Civics . NCF 2005 strongly argues that Civics should be discontinued and its focus on government institutions and functioning should be tempered in the new subject that replaces it.

S ocial and Political Life , as its name suggests, focuses on topics related to social, political, and economic life in contemporary India. This subject recognizes that children learn best through concrete experiences.

Approaches like learning through use of concrete examples and experiences should have been considered while developing social and political life textbooks as Social and Political Life:

- focuses on real situations to teach concepts.
- develops learners' abilities of critical understanding.
- uses case studies and narratives to explain concepts.
- avoids the use of definitions to sum up a concept.
- uses material that draws upon experiential understanding.

So, it could be concluded that learning through use of concrete examples and experiences is the best approach in the context of the question.

**119(D).** Continuous and Comprehensive Evaluation, commonly know as 'CCE' has been introduced as a school-based system of evaluation by the CBSE in 2009 with the enactment of the Right to Education Act.

- Continuous and comprehensive Evaluation mainly aims at promoting Inclusive education.
- CCE can be incorporated in the inclusive classroom while engaging in teaching through a variety of activities.
- Incorporating strategies for attending to diverse needs in classrooms would be particularly useful in developing CCE processes for the classroom.

**120(C).** Infrared (IR) types of radiation do Greenhouse gases emit.

Greenhouse gases such as methane and carbon dioxide in the atmosphere prevent the rays of the Sun reflected from the Earth's surface to escape the atmosphere thus trapping the radiations.

The trapped radiations warm the Earth's atmosphere, causing increases in the global temperature. This is called the greenhouse effect. Because of the increase in temperature, icy bodies start melting and increase the sea level.

Water vapor, carbon dioxide, methane, and other trace gases in Earth's atmosphere absorb the longer wavelengths of outgoing infrared radiation from Earth's surface. These gases then emit infrared radiation in all directions, both outward toward space and downward toward Earth.

## Child Development and Pedagogy

1. **In this context, Sachin is committed to discrimination against the child in his school, what is the right thing to do to avoid the problem of gender stereotyping in the classroom?**
   (a) Both boys and girls should try to be in non-traditional roles.
   (b) Appreciate the good work of the students by saving 'good girl' or 'good boy'.
   (c) Girls should be discouraged from talking to boys.
   (d) Encourage boys to be bold to face troubles.

2. **A child responds to a new situation based on responses made in the same situation in the past, this is related to which law?**
   (a) Law of assimilation
   (b) Law of effect
   (c) Law of disposition
   (d) Law of Readiness

3. **Finding out the child's ability through multiple-choice questions in competitive exams is considered a better way to test a lot of children in a short time, which of the following options is NOT appropriate in relation to multiple-choice questions.**
   (a) Any teacher can make these questions whether he has experience or not.
   (b) In this type of question, the child has difficulty in finding the right option out of the options.
   (c) The way a child can be evaluated is through an OMR sheet.
   (d) In such questions, mainly one answer is correct.

4. **Which of the following is true in the context of school based assessment?**
   (a) It reduces the responsibility of the teacher.
   (b) The standard complies with NCERT obliges children to check.
   (c) Helps students learn more through diagnostic tests.
   (d) It reduces the burden of students' studies.

5. **According to Kohlberg, a teacher can instill moral values in children by:**
   (a) Giving importance to religious teachings
   (b) Laying clear rules of behaviour
   (c) Involving them in discussions on moral issues
   (d) Giving strict instructions on 'how to behave'

6. **Mukesh does what his parents tell him to do because he knows that if he doesn't, his parents will punish him. Mukesh is in which of Piaget's stages of moral development?**
   (a) Heteronomous morality
   (b) Individualism, purpose and exchange
   (c) Social systems morality
   (d) Social contract

7. **All teachers, including the school headmaster, must respect the individual diversity of children in order to advance children of all classes to an educational level, which of the following options gives an opportunity to advance children's learning regardless of variation?**
   (a) As a teacher, you should follow a child-centered curriculum and provide students with many learning opportunities.
   (b) To remove individual differences in students, all possible measures should be implemented so that all children become equal.
   (c) Make provision for sending children with slow learning to special school.
   (d) Continue your teaching process by treating all children as equal.

8. **A preferred teacher told another newly appointed teacher that to understand learning difficulties we should assess the factors affecting a child's learning, what are they discussing about?**
   (a) Physical disability
   (b) Emotional Disability
   (c) Economic troubles
   (d) Learning Disability

9. **Manisha is employed as a teacher employed in an elementary school, which of the following is most important to attend to her responsibilities?**
   (a) If children make any mistakes then strict action should be taken on them.
   (b) Children who often answer questions correctly should ask other children to be like them.
   (c) When any child is talking, he should be not be corrected at the same time.
   (d) We should try to tell as much of the child as possible from the teacher.

10. **Rashi said to Rani that if you help me, maybe I will help you sometimes. The above-mentioned statement is related to:**
    (a) Pre-conventional level
    (b) Conventional level
    (c) Pre-operational level
    (d) Post-conventional level

11. **Which of the following statements regarding assessment and evaluation is correct?**
    1. Assessment is an interactive and constructive process.
    2. Assessment is a summative process.
    3. Educational achievement is made by evaluation of any pre-made educational program.
    4. The academic achievement of the students is determined by the assessment at the end of the course.
    5. Through assessment, the teacher knows whether the student is getting proper learning or not.
    (a) 1, 2 and 3    (b) 1, 3 and 4
    (c) 1, 2, 3 and 5   (d) 2, 3, 4 and 5

12. **Which would be the best example to challenge students' stereotypes regarding 'gender and occupation'?**
    (a) Male pastry chef
    (b) Male space scientist
    (c) Male Bharatanatyam Dancer
    (d) Male playback singer

13. **Children of different classes are present in our school, why is it important to understand the individual variation among these children?**
    (a) To reduce the difference between students
    (b) To enhance students' abilities and performance
    (c) To find out why students are able or unable to learn.
    (d) To make some children feel special

14. **If a student in your school is motivated by the things inherent in a task or activity in itself and concentrates on learning processes**

personally instead of focusing on the end result, then how would they be considered motivated?

(a) Motivated by learning motivation

(b) Inspired by social motivation

(c) Inspired by external motivation

(d) Inspired by intrinsic motivation

**15. Suresh is a Class 5 teacher in a school who wants to create a conducive learning environment for his children, which of the following is appropriate for this?**

(a) Teaching students the interpretation method

(b) Prolonging class time

(c) All children do their own work and also check for problem resolution with self assessment

(d) Understand the students' expressions of what and how they want to learn and design the teaching accordingly

**16. A teacher tells the process of problem solving to children for the development of problem solving technique in children, which of the following does not come in the major stages of problem solving?**

(a) Telling children how to identify any problem

(b) After knowing the problem, a technique plan to solve it is necessary.

(c) Analyze the problem solution logically to make it easier to find solutions in detail

(d) Think about the results after solving the problem and hope that you will get the desired solution.

**17. Which one of the following is true?**

(a) Development and learning are unaffected by socio-cultural contexts

(b) Students learn only in a certain way

(c) Play is significant for cognition and social competence

(d) Questioning by teachers constrains cognitive development

**18. What type of motivation does not apply to young children?**

(a) Intrinsic motivation

(b) Extrinsic motivation

(c) Achievement motivation

(d) None of the above

**19. Which of the following is true in the context of social inheritance?**

(a) Along with heredity, environment also contributes equally to the development of the learner.

(b) Wisdom is the result of heredity (nature) and environment i.e. complex interaction of environment.

(c) Both of the above

(d) None of these

**20. Suman is working as a teacher in primary school and wants to run the class room on an ongoing basis, understanding the individual differences of the children. Which of the following options should Suman follow?**

(a) Suman should try to know the ability and interest of children

(b) Suman should try to adjust the classroom curriculum to the children's needs

(c) Both (A) and (B)

(d) None of these

**21. When some people live together and influence each other by staying together, then what kind of group is formed?**

(a) Criminal group

(b) Social group

(c) Merchant group

(d) Political group

**22. Which of the following is correct about the implications of the concept of progressive education in a classroom?**

(a) It enhances skills and understanding of the learners by engaging with the textual material in classroom

(b) It provides 'learning by doing' to make children self-reliant and productive to use their knowledge in real-life situations

(c) It ensures the participation of students by working individually

(d) All of the above

**23. Which of the following is appropriate in the context of an inclusive class?**

(a) Every child has the right to proceed despite the different status of the child.

(b) Inclusive class distinguishes between students.

(c) Sets less challenging achievement targets, especially for children with disabilities.

(d) The inclusive class believes that children with disabilities will take more time in any task.

**24. In school, telling a teacher about the type of thinking, a teacher says that it does not require realization of real subjects or actions. It uses concepts and generalized ideas. Language has a big hand in the development of this type of thinking. What is the teacher talking about?**

(a) Tangible thinking

(b) Abstract thinking

(c) Divergent thinking

(d) Convergent thinking

**25. A teacher gives a half done example to child while teaching a particular concept. According to Lev Vygotsky's which of the following strategies is the teacher using?**

(a) Observational learning

(b) Scaffolding

(c) Conflict teaching

(d) Conditioning

**26. Direction: Given below are two statements : One is labelled as Assertion (A) and the other is labelled as Reason (R).**
**Assertion (A): The purpose underlying modern and ICT based support system in teaching is to optimise learning outcomes.**
**Reason (R): An effective instructional support system has to be linked with enhancement of learning conditions.**
**In the light of the above statements, choose the correct answer from the options given below.**

(a) Both (A) and (R) are true and (R) is the correct explanation of (A).

(b) Both (A) and (R) are true but (R) is not the correct explanation of (A).

(c) (A) is true but (R) is false.

(d) (A) is false but (R) is true.

**27. As a teacher how can you facilitate problem solving abilities in your students?**

(a) Generating fear amongst your students

(b) Encouraging a fixed way of solving problem

(c) Encouraging use of analysis

(d) Emphasizing on use of passive memorization strategies

**28. Individuals who have the ability to understand the motives, feelings and behaviors of others to bond with them are high on_____intelligence in Howard Gardner's theory.**

(a)  naturalistic
(b)  interpersonal
(c)  intrapersonal
(d)  spatial

29.  **The crowd always walks on the path which seems easy, but this does not mean that the crowd always walks on the right path. Choose your path yourself because no one knows you better than you, for which work is this line important for a child?**
(a)  Physical development
(b)  Goal-oriented Behavior
(c)  Measures of Disability
(d)  None of these

30.  **Radha asks her child Advik to complete a chore around the house, he ask what the benefit would be to him. As per Kohlberg, the Advik is lying at which stage of development?**
(a)  Obedience and Punishment Orientation
(b)  Maintaining the Social Order
(c)  Individualism and Exchange
(d)  Social Contract and Individual Rights

## Language - I: English

**Ques (31-39): Direction** : Read the passage given below and answer the questions that follow by choosing the correct/most appropriate options.

For the past two weeks, China has locked down Shanghai, its financial center. Many of its 26 million residents, confined to their apartments, have complained of acute food shortages. The government has struggled to supply every household with daily necessities, with the supply chain paralyzed by China's stringent measures under which every COVID-19 case, even if asymptomatic, is confined in government-run quarantine facilities. Food shortages are not the only problem. Many have said they are running out of medicines. Children who tested positive have been separated from their parents. The crisis has now ignited a debate on whether this strategy that enabled China to avoid a major second wave, still remains relevant when much of the rest of the world has returned to some form of normalcy thanks to vaccines. China is the only country still closed off from the rest of the world.

Signs are Beijing has no intention of changing course. The official Xinhua news agency on Sunday rebutted criticism over the policy saying "a dynamic zero-COVID approach remains crucial..." and "the repercussions of lowering the guard could be disastrous for... 1.4 billion people,

including 267 million aged 60 or above". With those numbers, it argued, China's medical system "would risk a collapse". Chinese officials point to Hong Kong's experience. After two successful "zero COVID" years that allowed for normalcy, an Omicron outbreak this year led to 8,000 deaths there. Most were unvaccinated elderly residents. Beijing now finds itself in a bind. Opening up, it is feared, would mean many deaths among the elderly who have refused to get vaccinated. However, experts say one major reason for vaccine hesitancy is the "zero COVID" strategy, with the wide perception that risks from vaccines outweigh the risk of catching COVID. Zero COVID, in a sense, has become a victim of its own success. Politics is also as much a factor as public health. For two years, China's government has hailed its model as a contrast to the West which saw high deaths and continues to tell its population that COVID is a dangerous disease that requires everyone to be hospitalized. Changing course now would not suit that narrative, particularly with President Xi framing China's COVID response as one of his big legacies. Continuing on the current path, however, will bring rising economic and social costs. Rather than trumpet zero COVID and criticize living with the virus as irresponsible, China would be better served looking at the examples of countries that have successfully opened up and followed the science, as in Singapore, which aggressively vaccinated its population and incentivized it to do so by setting a timetable for opening. Otherwise, as the continued suffering in Shanghai has shown, the cure risks becoming worse than the disease.

31.  **According to the passage, how China's "zero COVID" strategy could backfire?**
(a)  It will bring rising economic and social costs.
(b)  It will bring increase the use of the medicines and vaccines.
(c)  It will make every person in China opportunistic.
(d)  It will bring a huge increase in the price of vaccines.

32.  **Read the sentence to find out whether there is any grammatical error in it.**
**Children who tested (A)/ positive have been (B)/ separated from (C)/ their parent. (D)**
(a)  A
(b)  B
(c)  C
(d)  D

33.  **Which of the following is/are correct according to the given passage?**
**A. China has agreed to change its**

zero COVID strategy.
**B. Chinese government has extolled its zero COVID strategy.**
**C.  Singapore has aggressively vaccinated its population.**
(a)  Only A
(b)  Both A and B
(c)  Only B
(d)  Both B and C

34.  **What is the central theme of the passage?**
(a)  China should continue its zero COVID strategy.
(b)  India should learn the zero COVID strategy from China.
(c)  The cure risks becoming worse than the disease in China.
(d)  The zero COVID strategy has become a success throughout China.

35.  **Choose the antonym of the word ' Stringent '.**
(a)  Draconian
(b)  Rigorous
(c)  Strict
(d)  Lenient

36.  **Which of the following is/are incorrect according to the given passage?**
**A. Asymptomatic persons are also confined in China.**
**B.  People confined to their apartments in China have complained of the shortage of medicines.**
**C. The Chinese government has taken care of every household with daily necessities.**
(a)  Only A
(b)  Both A and B
(c)  Only B
(d)  Only C

37.  **What is the insight behind the refusal to get vaccinated?**
(a)  The vaccines consist of many toxic chemicals.
(b)  The risks from vaccines outweigh the risk of catching COVID.
(c)  The vaccines are painful and non-effective.
(d)  China is running out of vaccines.

38.  **Choose the synonym of the word ' Hesitancy '.**
(a)  Reluctance
(b)  Resolution
(c)  Willingness
(d)  Certainty

39.  **Identify the part of speech of the underlined word:**
**Many of its 26 million residents, confined to their apartments, have complained of <u>acute</u> food shortages.**
(a)  Adverb
(b)  Adjective
(c)  Noun
(d)  Verb

**Ques (40-45): Direction** : Read the poem

and answer the questions carefully:
1. The apes yawn and adore their fleas in the sun.
The parrots shriek as if they were on fire, or strut
Like cheap tarts to attract the stroller with the nut.
Fatigued with indolence, tiger and lion
2. Lie still as the sun. The boa-constriktor's coil
Is a fossil. Cage after cage seems empty, or
Stinks of sleepers from the breathing straw.
It might be painted on a nursery wall.
3. But who runs llike the rest past these arrives
At a cage where the crowd stands, stares, mesmerized,
As a child at a dream, at a dream, at a jaguar hurrying enraged
Through prison darkness after the drills of his eyes.

**40. Which of the following statements describes Parrots' behaviour as expressed in the poem?**
(a) Parrots scream as of they were set alight
(b) They lie still as Sun
(c) They parade before passers-by hoping for a snack
(d) Both (A) and (C)

**41. Which poetic device is used in the following line?**
"Stinks of sleepers from the breathing straw"
(a) Oxymoron  (b) Alliteration
(c) Consonance  (d) Simile

**42. The expression 'As a child at a dream' refers to:**
(a) Jaguar and his antics
(b) Spectators who encounter the cage of Jaguar
(c) People who take their time to look at every cage
(d) Children who like to visit the zoo

**43. Which of the following animals is not mentioned in the first stanza?**
(a) Lion  (b) Parrot
(c) Jaguar  (d) Apes

**44. Which figure of speech is used in the following line:**
"tiger and lion/ Lie still as the sun".
(a) Simile
(b) Metaphor
(c) Personification
(d) Alliteration

**45. Why poet had described Boa-constricter as a fossil?**
(a) Because it resembles a fossil
(b) Because the Boa is too old

(c) Because it's in the shape of a fossil
(d) The Boa cannot move in the cage

**46. Which of the following practice is the most helpful in developing oral language skill?**
(a) Reciting poems - individually and in group
(b) Participating in role play
(c) Group reading a chapter from the textbook
(d) Practicing correct pronunciation of words

**47. Poetry teaching is ____**
(a) to learn words and phrases.
(b) to learn poetic devices.
(c) for enjoyment and appreciation.
(d) to write a critical commentary.

**48. Which of the following is most important when it comes to language learning?**
(a) Use of teaching-learning method (TLM)
(b) Social interaction
(c) Book reading
(d) Watching a play or a movie

**49. A child learns the first language through:**
(a) Speech  (b) Reading
(c) Writing  (d) Mistakes

**50. The National Curriculum Framework – 2005 proposes which of the following objective for language teaching-learning?**
(a) The competence to understand what she hears
(b) Ability to read with comprehension, and not merely decode
(c) Effortless expression
(d) All of the above

**51. When the teacher asks the students to repeat some words or sentences several times, it is called:**
(a) Recalling
(b) Acquiring
(c) Inferring meaning
(d) Drilling

**52. Which assessment is the ability of a person to accurately evaluate or assess his/her performance, and his/her strengths and weaknesses?**
(a) Self-assessment
(b) Peer assessment
(c) Group assessment
(d) CCE assessment

**53. Which of the following is not among**

the aims of teaching English?
(a) Four skills development
(b) To learn a text by-heart
(c) To motivate students to learn more
(d) To create interest in reading

**54. For students to gain language skills from textbooks, the textbook learning should:**
(a) Correlate with assessment and achievement
(b) Lead to using the textbook sparingly
(c) Expose them to more literary reading
(d) Become more cost-effective compared to technologically supported courses

**55. With which of the following the students acquire language?**
(a) By using language in natural interactive environment
(b) By analyzing the syntax of a language
(c) By analyzing the syntax of a language
(d) By being aware of the culture of the speakers of the language

**56. What does multilingualism as a source mean?**
(a) Multiple language teaching
(b) To stress on every word of a child's language
(c) Teaching language through the syllabus
(d) Using student's language as a strategy

**57. Which of the following is not one of the principles of Interactive language teaching?**
(a) The student is the language learner.
(b) Classroom relations reflect individual liking and respect.
(c) Language learning and teaching are shaped by student needs.
(d) Language learning and teaching are based on normal uses of language, with communication of meanings.

**58. In a language class, students are expected to be accurate in whatever she says or writes and this grammatical accuracy is to be realized through constant drills and construction of correct sentences. The teacher is following the:**
(a) Oral approach

(b)  Communicative approach

(c)  Structural approach

(d)  Situational approach

**59. What is the main purpose of continuous and comprehensive evaluation?**

(a)  Written test

(b)  Testing students more than one time

(c)  Identify the mistakes made by children

(d)  Develop students' ability to use the language

**60. A language teacher wants to meet the demand of the style of learning of all the students. He can overcome this challenge by:**

(a)  Teaching every words

(b)  Assessing children continuously

(c)  Encouraging students to study seriously

(d)  Using various teaching methods and strategy

## Mathematics

**61. Which of the following options is equal to:**
$$16 \div 4 \times 2 - 5 + 1 = ?$$

(a)  $\{(16 \div 4) \times 2\} - (5 + 1)$

(b)  $[\{(16 \div 4) \times 2\} - 5] + 1$

(c)  $\{16 \div (4 \times 2)\} - (5 + 1)$

(d)  $[\{16 \div (4 \times 2)\} - 5] + 1$

**62. What is the correct ascending order for the given fractions?**

$A.\ \dfrac{22}{7}, \dfrac{13}{17}, \dfrac{11}{19}, \dfrac{2}{3}$

$B.\ \dfrac{11}{19}, \dfrac{2}{3}, \dfrac{13}{17}, \dfrac{22}{7}$

$C.\ \dfrac{2}{3}, \dfrac{11}{19}, \dfrac{13}{17}, \dfrac{22}{7}$

$D.\ \dfrac{2}{3}, \dfrac{13}{17}, \dfrac{11}{19}, \dfrac{22}{7}$

(a)  $D$            (b)  $B$

(c)  $C$            (d)  $A$

**63. What minimum value must be given to $x$ to make $6357x5$ exactly divisible by $9$ ?**

(a)  8            (b)  1

(c)  9            (d)  3

**64. The perimeter of a triangle is $600$ m. If the ratio of sides is $12 : 13 : 15 :$ then find the longest side.**

(a)  195            (b)  180

(c)  220            (d)  225

**65. Consider the following statements:**
**(i) 1 km = 1 lakh millimeter**
**(ii) $1\ m^3 = 1000$ litres**
**(iii) 1 decameter = One-tenth hectometer**

**(iv) $1\ cm^3 = 1000$ millilitre**
**Which of the following statement(s) are true?**

(a)  (i), (ii) and (iv)

(b)  (ii), (iii) and (iv)

(c)  (i), (iii) and (iv)

(d)  (i), (ii) and (iii)

**66. Consider the following data:**
$13, 15, 9, x, 4, 17, y$
**If the mean of the above data is $12$ and given that $(y - x) = 6$ , then**
$xy =$

(a)  610            (b)  63

(c)  160            (d)  48

**67. The ratio of present ages of Meena and Sina is $4 : 3$ . After $6$ years, Meena's age will become $26$ years. What is the present age of Sina?**

(a)  12 years

(b)  19 years 6 months

(c)  15 years

(d)  21 years

**68. To tell the password of a lock, Aman uses an expression which was $12 - 3 \times 8 \div 4 + 3$ . The result of this expression is to be added to the largest 2 digit prime number to get the password. The password is-**

(a)  104            (b)  105

(c)  106            (d)  107

**69. A worker works $4$ hours per day for the first week, $5$ hours per day for the second week, and $6$ hours per day for the third and fourth week. If his salary is calculated on the basis of Rs. $100$ for every $30$ minutes, then the amount he would receive at the end of four weeks is (there is no holiday on any day of the week)-**

(a)  Rs. 29400        (b)  Rs. 29600

(c)  Rs. 29450        (d)  Rs. 30000

**70. I am a plane figure which has-**
- **Two pairs of equal adjacent sides.**
- **One pair of equal opposite angles.**
- **2 unequal diagonals that intersect each other at right angles.**

**Out of the given options I can be-**

(a)  Parallelogram

(b)  Kite

(c)  Square

(d)  Rectangle

**71. In a marathon conducted by a social welfare organization, an athlete starts running at $09:05$ am. He took a $15$ minutes rest in between and then ran continuously till $02:18$ pm. Then the total time during**

which he was running is:

(a)  5 hours 13 minutes

(b)  4 hours 58 minutes

(c)  5 hours 28 minutes

(d)  4 hours 43 minutes

**72. Direction: Consider the following statements-**
**Statement A: All prime numbers are odd numbers.**
**Statement B: Natural numbers that are not prime numbers are composite numbers.**
**Which of the following options is TRUE regarding the statements?**

(a)  Statement A and B both are correct.

(b)  Statement A is incorrect but Statement B is correct.

(c)  Statement A and B both are incorrect.

(d)  Statement A is correct but Statement B is incorrect.

**73. The quantity of different vegetables sold by a vegetable seller during a week is given in the table together with the unit price of each.**

| Vegetable name | Quantity sold (in kg) | Price per kg (in Rs) |
|---|---|---|
| Potato | 98 | 14.50 |
| Tomato | 75 | 18.80 |
| Onion | 65 | 22.30 |
| Ladyfinger | 114 | 12.20 |

**The total revenue generated by each type of vegetable in ascending order is-**

(a)  Potato,  Tomato,  Onion, Ladyfinger

(b)  Onion,  Potato,  Tomato, Ladyfinger

(c)  Onion,  Tomato,  Potato, Ladyfinger

(d)  Ladyfinger,  Tomato,  Potato, Onion

**74. Raman tells his brother that he saves Rs. $180$ everyday from the day he took a loan to pay only in one installment in future. The amount of loan increases by Rs. $10$ everyday from the day the loan was taken. If Raman had take a loan of Rs. $7650$ , then after how many days he will be able to pay the loan completely by saved money?**

(a)  30 days        (b)  45 days

(c)  50 days        (d)  54 days

**75. Which is the next number in the series?**
$5, 25, 125, \_\_\_$

(a) 625          (b) 650
(c) 675          (d) 600

**76. Nature of Mathematics is:**
(a) Abstract      (b) Illogical
(c) Non-specific  (d) Un-arranged

**77. "Failure to recognize place value leads to failure in four operations in mathematics." The given statement indicates which of the following problems in teaching and learning of mathematics?**
(a) Fear and failure
(b) Crude assessment
(c) Inadequate learning materials
(d) Disappointing curriculum

**78. Effective learning of mathematical concepts depends on:**
(a) How far teachers are successful in developing mathematical language
(b) Generalization in different areas
(c) Number, measurement, places and base of mathematics
(d) Monitoring responses to questioning

**79. The nature of mathematical understanding is:**
(a) Ornamental   (b) Behaviourist
(c) Logical       (d) Simple

**80. Community mathematics:**
(a) Collection of resources for engaging the students to learn mathematics.
(b) Provide opportunities to learner to justify their reasoning skills.
(c) Help in gaining the insight to learner to solve a problem.
(d) All of the above

**81. According to Van Hiele levels of Geometry, at level 3 a child is able to:**
(a) Perceive the relationships
(b) Differentiate between a square and a rectangle on the basis of their properties
(c) Prove an abstract statement on geometric properties to conclude
(d) Recognize and classify the shapes

**82. Which of the following is the basic cause of problems occurring in teaching and learning mathematics?**
(a) A sense of fear and failure among children
(b) A disappointing curriculum

(c) Lack of teacher preparation
(d) All of the above

**83. Which of the following is not responsible for lack of interest of a child in mathematics**
(a) The fear of failure in mathematics and examination system
(b) Inefficient teaching of mathematics by the teacher
(c) Assessment based problems and structure of mathematics
(d) Gender differences in mathematics classroom

**84. _____ is necessary to find out mathematical errors in children.**
(a) Remedial test
(b) Diagnostic test
(c) Oral test
(d) Benchmark test

**85. The term evaluation is closely related to?**
(a) Marks
(b) Measurement
(c) Difficult
(d) Fear

**86. Which one of the following is true about Formative Evaluation?**
(a) Which one of the following is true about Formative Evaluation?
(b) It does not provide teaching.
(c) It does not provide feedback.
(d) Its focus is on measurement of pupils' achievement.

**87. Importance of diagnostic test is-**
(a) in teaching
(b) in counseling and guidance
(c) in the arrangement of remedial teaching
(d) All of the above

**88. Which of the following is the objective of a diagnostic test in mathematics?**
(a) To find out the weakness or deficiency of a child in learning.
(b) To fill progress report of children.
(c) To give feedback to the parents.
(d) None of these

**89. In remedial teaching, the teacher is __________**
(a) required to prepare instructional material for quality learning and adopting different methodologies.
(b) expected to devise some strategy

to remove problems in learning.
(c) provide pupils clear instructions to avoid confusion, summarize the main points and encourage pupils' active participation in class activities.
(d) All of the above

**90. The Van Hiele's theory describes the thinking levels of?**
(a) The Van Hiele's theory describes the thinking levels of?
(b) Geometry
(c) Face and Place value
(d) Numbers concept



**91. Which are the two major natural disasters of India?**
(a) Flood and Drought
(b) Fire and Tsunami
(c) Earthquake and Fire
(d) None of these

**92. I have sharp curved teeth. I don't chew my food, but swallow it. Who am I?**
(a) Cow           (b) Rat
(c) Dolphin       (d) Snake

**93. The game of Kabaddi is played with seven members in each team. How long does a kabaddi game lasts?**
(a) 40 minutes with 5 minute break
(b) 60 minutes with 10 minute break
(c) 60 minutes with 5 minute break
(d) 40 minutes with 10 minute break

**94. Things that are learned to live in a Joint family-**
(1) children learn good manners from elders
(2) children learn to be stubborn
(3) children learn to share things with others
(a) Only (1)
(b) Only (2) and (3)
(c) Only (1) and (3)
(d) All of the above

**95. Section 25 of The Indian Forest Act 1927 deals with______.**
(a) Record of plants and trees
(b) Power to stop ways and watercourses in reserved forests
(c) Power to declare forest no longer reserved
(d) Protected forests

**96. 'Undhiya' a famous food for farmers in-**

(a) Rajasthan

(b) Gujarat

(c) Madhya Pradesh

(d) Chhattisgarh

**97. Which country has launched its first military exercise 'AsterX' in space?**

(a) France    (b) Russia

(c) Germany    (d) India

**98. Which animal has poor eyesight but have an excellent sense of smell, touch and taste?**

(a) Monkey, Elephant and Rat

(b) Rat, Dog and Elephant

(c) Elephant, Dog and Monkey

(d) Dog, Rat and Monkey

**99. Dengue is caused by:**

(a) Female Anopheles

(b) Male Anopheles

(c) Female Aedes

(d) None of these

**100. The following are few measures of water conservation. Which one is the most suitable method for domestic purposes?**

(a) Rain water harvesting

(b) Watershed development

(c) Recycle and reuse

(d) Monitoring water quality index

**101. Match list-I with list-II and select the correct answer using the codes given below:**

| List-I (Animal) | List-II (Characteristic) |
|---|---|
| **(a) Sloth** | **(i) can find his partner by smell** |
| **(b) Eagle** | **(ii) sleeps for 17 hrs** |
| **(c) Silkworm** | **(iii) have eyes in the front like humans** |
| **(d) Owl** | **(iv) can see four times than humans** |

(a) (a) - (iii), (b) - (ii), (c) -(iv), (d) - (i)

(b) (a) - (ii), (b) - (iv), (c) -(i), (d) - (iii)

(c) (a) - (iii), (b) - (i), (c) -(iv), (d) - (ii)

(d) •
    (a) - (i), (b) - (ii), (c) -(iv), (d) - (iii)

**102. Which state does not touch the boundary of Mizoram:**

(a) Assam    (b) Tripura

(c) Manipur    (d) Nagaland

**103. A farmer in Karnataka uses which of the following tools to make his soil soft:**

(a) Khunti    (b) Illige

(c) Kurige    (d) Khurpi

**104. Which one of the following resources can be recycled?**

(a) Petroleum

(b) Coal

(c) Iron

(d) None of these

**105. What is vermiculture?**

(a) The science of raising worms

(b) The science of studying animals

(c) The science of studying fishes

(d) The science of killing worms

**106. Which of the following is not the main theme of the thematically designed curriculum of EVS at the primary level?**

(a) Food    (b) Community

(c) Water    (d) Travel

**107. One can describe Environment science as a permanent investment in creating a ____ society.**

(a) changing    (b) positive

(c) sustainable    (d) (A) and (C)

**108. The main objective(s) of CCE is/ are:**

(a) Making evaluation an integral part of the teaching-learning process

(b) Maintaining desired standard of attainment

(c) Providing scope for self-evaluation

(d) All of the above

**109. Which of the following activities can help the learners of EVS in encouraging group work and peer learning?**

(a) Project on EVS topic on any theme

(b) Test on any topic of EVS

(c) Stamp collection

(d) Group discussion on EVS topic

**110. To make students think 'out of the box', which of the following method is appropriate in EVS?**

(a) Demonstration

(b) Group Discussion

(c) Lecture

(d) All of the above

**111. Which of the following will help to shape an enabling learning environment for each child in EVS classroom?**

(a) Teachers

(b) Textbook

(c) Materials and classroom activities

(d) All of the above

**112. Which of the following is not correct regarding the scope of EVS?**

(a) To inculcate problem-solving and critical thinking skills.

(b) To enable the children in gathering and analyzing information.

(c) To help the children in enrichment and enhancement of their own knowledge.

(d) To conduct paper-pencil test to assess the performance of children.

**113. An ideal textbook of EVS should involve:**

(a) Formal language

(b) Activities to gain scientific knowledge

(c) Informal language only

(d) Activities to connect them with real life

**114. Which activities are encouraged by a teacher in the constructivist classroom?**
**I. Experimentation**
**II. Project work**
**III. Field trips**
**IV. Visuals**
**V. Class discussion**

(a) II, III, IV and V

(b) I, III, IV and V

(c) I, II, III and V

(d) I, II, III, IV and V

**115. Choose the most suitable for introducing class discussion on a EVS topic.**

(a) It tests what students have learnt from media.

(b) It keeps students busy.

(c) It enables students to relate to the topic and express themselves.

(d) It reduces the time teachers have to speak.

**116. Group discussion is one of the techniques that can facilitate ______.**

(a) individual learning

(b) school learning

(c) cooperative learning

(d) None of the above

**117. The teaching-learning process of EVS must not:**

(a) Address the individual needs of each child.

(b) Focuses on assessing children to provide them with reasonable marks.

(c) Engages children in various meaningful learning activities.

(d) Begins with the child's immediate environment.

**118. In the primary level, environmental studies are integrated with:**

(a) Social studies and economics

(b) Social studies and science

(c) Social studies and geography

(d) Social studies and civics

**119. Which method of teaching is about 'finding the most appropriate way' to achieve the learning objective?**

(a) Lecture method

(b) Project method

(c) Problem solving method

(d) Play method

**120. Which of the following is not the techniques of assessing learners in EVS in Class I?**

(a) Oral tests, as children may not be able to write

(b) Drawing, as children enjoy it

(c) Teachers' observation and recording

(d) There is no need of assessment in view of 'no detention policy'

*// Hints and Solutions //*

**1(A).** We can avoid gender stereotyping in the classroom and at home by these steps:

- Providing equal opportunities for both boys and girls.
- Implying the idea that an equal balance of man and women is required in all aspects of life.
- Putting girl and boys in non-traditional roles and will also promote a sense of gender equality among people.
- Removing the stereotype that certain activities are only meant to be done by men and not by women and vice versa.
- Encourage boys to participate in singing, rangoli, cooking, etc. competitions and girls to participate in sports, science, model, etc.
- Use non-biased language like chairman to chairperson, policeman to police officer, etc.

- Teacher should do non-traditional activities themselves so that students learn by watching them.

So, we can say that teachers can avoid the problem of gender stereotyping in the classroom by providing non-traditional roles for both boys and girls.

**2(A).** A child responds to a new situation based on responses made in the same situation in the past, this is related to the law of assimilation.

**Law of Analogy and Assimilation:** In this, a person accepts knowledge becomes part of his foreknowledge and uses that knowledge in future learning.

**3(A).** A multiple-choice question (MCQ) has two parts: a stem that defines the question or problem, and a set of alternatives or possible replies that includes a key, which is the best solution to the question, and several distractors, which are reasonable but erroneous answers to the question.

- Multiple-choice questions in competitive examinations are seen to be a superior approach to assessing a large number of pupils in a short amount of time. Any instructor, regardless of expertise, may create these questions. When it comes to multiple-choice questions, this option isn't acceptable.
- Learners must pick the best solution from various possibilities in multiple-choice questions. Because multiple-choice questions are short and crisp, more of them may be asked in a test environment to provide a more complete evaluation to a student.
- Introduction One of the most effective kinds of assessment is the multiple-choice exam. Due to its flexibility and impartiality in scoring, this is the most valuable and extensively used format in standardized tests.
- Multiple-choice questions are frequently employed, in which a variety of choices are presented, but only one is right.

As a result, we may infer that any instructor, regardless of expertise, can create these questions. However, alternatives are not acceptable in connection to multiple-choice questions.

**4(C).** Assessment is the second step of evaluating students' performance. It makes students' performance more meaningful. Unless we interpret, analyze, rank-order, and compare one's individual score with the average score of the group, we cannot find out one's relative position in a group. Assessment and evaluation occupy a very important position in the teaching-learning process. They help teachers, students, and others in the following ways:

- It helps students to know their progress in learning, and learning difficulties in different subject areas.

- It not only assigns students grades or marks but also develops their learning habits.
- It helps in diagnosing learning difficulties of students.
- It helps in planning new learning experiences.
- It facilitates teachers to make a decision about promoting students to the next class, grouping them, and grading them based upon their special abilities.
- It assists students in their problems of adjustment.
- It helps a teacher to prepare a student cumulative record card (CRC) or report card.
- It helps teachers to decide whether to continue with their teaching methodology or to change it.
- It helps the curriculum developers to modify the curriculum.
- It helps the parents to provide proper guidance and timely assistance to their children.

Thus, from the above points, we can conclude that School-based assessment helps students learn more through diagnostic tests.

**5(C).** According to Kohlberg, a teacher can instill moral values in children by involving them in discussions on moral issues.

**Role of teacher in facilitating moral development of children:**

- The teacher or the school has a major role in facilitating the moral development of children once they are enrolled in the school.
- Schools should have an activity-oriented program for the moral development of children.
- The school plays a very important role in the moral development of the students. Through the organization of various curricular and co-curricular activities, the teacher can foster among students various moral qualities.
- In the teaching of different subjects like languages and social studies, etc., the teacher may stress moral qualities like love, sacrifice, self-control, truthfulness, uprightness, etc.

**6(A).** Moral development refers to the process through which children develop the standards of right and wrong within their society, based on social and cultural norms, and laws.

- Lawrence Kohlberg describes moral development as a process of discovering universal moral principles and is based on a child's intellectual development.
- Piaget conceptualizes moral development as a constructivist process, whereby the interplay of action and thought builds moral concepts.

**Piaget (1932) suggested two main types of moral thinking:**

**Heteronomous morality (5-9 yrs):**

- The stage of heteronomous morality is also known as moral realism
- Morality is imposed from the outside.
- Children regard morality as obeying other people's rules and laws, which cannot be changed.
- They accept that all rules are made by some authority figure (e.g. parents, teacher, God) and that breaking the rules will lead to immediate and severe punishment (immanent justice).

**Autonomous morality (moral relativism):**

The stage of autonomous morality is also known as moral relativism – morality based on your own rules. Children recognize there is no absolute right or wrong and that morality depends on intentions not consequences.

**7(A).** As a teacher, you should follow a child-centered curriculum and provide students with many learning opportunities. This gives an opportunity to advance children's learning regardless of variation. Integrated education means providing the least restrictive environment to disabled children so that they may grow and develop like other children. It promotes a healthy social relationship between normal and disabled children of all levels and reduces the physical distance between them, though equal participation in social activities. It provides equal educational opportunities to the disabled and prepares them for life like other members of society.

- To cater to children with varying individual differences one must adopt a child-centered curriculum to fulfill all the needs and requirements of the learner.
- The intellectual maturity and the receptiveness of the student is an important point to be considered. The teacher needs to know the background of her students. This may be achieved through self-introduction; preparation of a class roster with a few pertinent facts about each student, giving of frequent short class assignments early in the class, etc., and it will help the teacher to learn something about the academic ability of each student.

**8(D).** In the above scenario, a preferred teacher told another newly appointed teacher that to understand learning difficulties we should assess the factors affecting a child's learning, they are discussing about the learning disabilities occurring in the classroom and what are the strategies should be adopt to cater the needs of children.

Learning Disability is an umbrella term that encompasses a variety of specific kinds of learning problems. Children with learning disabilities experience difficulty in learning and using certain skills namely reading, writing, listening, reasoning and mathematics.

- Usually learning disability is not identified until they enter school.
- A child with a learning disability has difficulty mastering one or more academic subjects, has normal intelligence, and is not suffering from any sensory impairment or inadequate instructions. Learning disability is an invisible disability.
- The child usually appears normal in every aspect except that his learning difficulties limit his progress in school.

**9(B).** Teaching is a complex activity. It is a process in which students are provided with a controlled environment for interaction with the purpose to promote definite learning in them.

- Children who often answer the question correctly should ask other children to be like them because due to peer guidance the students will be able to learn properly.
- Manisha should make the children learn from their classmates as all children are in the same class.
- The socialization process will be increased when they will interact with each.

**10(A).** The above-mentioned statement is related to the 'pre-conventional level' of Kohlberg's moral development as according to Kohlberg, in the pre-conventional level of moral development:

- Child shows no internalization of moral values.
- Moral reasoning of the child is controlled externally.
- Child's morality is influenced by rewards and punishment.
- Right action is one that instrumentally satisfies one's needs and occasionally the needs of others.
- Elements of fairness of reciprocity and of equal sharing are present but they are always interpreted in terms of expediency.

**11(D).** The term "evaluation" refers to a student's feedback to an instructor on their learning. Evaluation incorporates methodologies and metrics to assess student learning and understanding of content for grading and reporting. Evaluation refers to the instructor's assessment of a student's progress.

- Summative assessments, measure student learning, knowledge, competency, or accomplishment at the end of a learning period, such as a unit, course, or program. Summative evaluations are nearly always assessed formally and are sometimes significantly weighted (though they do not need to be).
- The examination of any pre-made educational curriculum determines

academic accomplishment. A program assessment assesses a program's success by looking at its student achievement targets, implementation level, and external considerations such as limits set and community support.

- Educational accomplishment is determined by evaluating any pre-made education program. Assessment is a participatory and constructive process, and it is a summative process.

As a result, assessment is a summative method that entails the examination of any premade educational program. Options 2, 3, 4 and 5 are correct in terms of assessment and evaluation.

**12(A).** Male pastry chef would be the best example to challenge students' stereotypes regarding 'gender and occupation'.

- Male pastry chef: we can see that in our society cooking-related activities are performed by females only. A male pastry chef is the best example to challenge the stereotype of students.
- Male space scientists may be both a boy and a girl so, this is not the best example to give.
- Male Bharatnatyam dancers can be of both gender, this is also not related to gender occupation stereotypes.
- Male playback singer: this profession can be performed by both gender. so, this is also not the best option to select.

**13(B).** Children of different classes are present in our school, t o enhance student's abilities and performance it is important to understand the individual variation among these children.

**Individual difference-** Individual difference/variation means no two individuals are alike. There are mental, physical, emotional, etc. many differences among the individual.

**Importance to understand individual differences/variations:**

- Helps in classifying children as per their needs.
- Helpful in providing personalized instructions.
- Helpful for teachers to know how can we enhance students' abilities and performance.
- Helpful in choosing teaching methods.
- Helpful in creating curriculum as per individual needs.

**14(D).** If a student in your school is motivated by the things inherent in a task or activity in itself and concentrates on learning processes personally instead of focusing on the end result, then inspired by intrinsic motivation they be considered motivated.

**Intrinsic motivation-** When the learner is interested in the process rather than the end result, where he starts enjoying the process as it provides happiness this kind of motivation is called intrinsic motivation. **Example of intrinsic motivation-** When a learner read the storybook for enjoying the process of reading, where is neither evaluated nor awarded, but for the sake of his own happiness the learner is reading because it gives joy to the learner, The learner is said to be intrinsic motivated.

**15(D).** Understand the students' expressions of what and how they want to learn and design the teaching accordingly is an appropriate way for Suresh who wants to create a conducive learning environment for his children.

**Conducive learning:** The conducive school environment is one in which teachers establish a learning environment where students feel physically, psychologically, socially, and culturally secure. In a conducive school environment teachers work independently and cooperatively to make their classrooms and school stimulating learning environments. A conducive school environment helps in creating a favorable atmosphere to ensure an effective teaching and learning process takes place.

**16(D).** Think about the results after solving the problem and hope that you will get the desired solution that does not come in the major stages of problem solving .

**Problem solving technique-** It is the process of solving the problem by identifying, analyzing, evaluating and implementing.

**Identification of problem-** Before solving the problem first we need to identify the problem.

**Analyzing the problem-** After the identification of the problem, analyzing problem is necessary. because by doing this process, we figure out the steps to solve the problem.

**Evaluating-** After analyzing the problem, the evaluation of the correct step is required.

**Implementation-** Once the Evaluation is completed execute the steps if the result doesn't come, again start by analyzing the problem.

**In the whole problem-** Solving technique importance is given to the identification of the problem and ideas which we are going to follow to solve our problems rather than finding the solution.

**17(C).** Play is an important part of a child's development and growth which ensures:-

- The development of self-confidence and a healthy brain.
- To make children learn teamwork and communication skills too.
- To make the child socialized and to keep the child fit and fight diseases.
- The overall development of the child such as physical, social, and cognitive.

- - the active engagement of children with their surroundings for meaningful learning.
- - Cognitive competence: It consists of the ability to solve problems, learn from experiences, and apply knowledge to deal with new situations.
- Social competence: It consists of social, cognitive, emotional, and behavioral skills that are necessary for a person to be socially acceptable.

Remaining options are not true because:

- Development and learning are influenced and affected by socio-cultural context.
- Students learn in different ways as every student has their own learning needs.
- Questioning by teachers and students facilitates learning in a meaningful and constructive way.

Therefore, from the above-mentioned points, it becomes clear that play is significant for cognition and social competence.

**18(A).** Intrinsic motivation does not apply to young children.

Motivation refers to a drive or motive to do something. These are factors that activate, direct and sustain goal-directed behavior. It can be either intrinsic or extrinsic.

**Intrinsic motivation:** It is defined as doing an activity for inherent satisfaction rather than for some reward. When a child engages in activities due to his personal interest or an element of joy in doing the activity, then the child is said to be intrinsically motivated. Intrinsically motivated children do things for the fun or challenge also he/she displays a high level of enthusiasm and energy while working.

**19(C).** Both of the above statements are correct about social inheritance.

**Social Inheritance :** Social inheritance is the set of beliefs and prejudices that you are taught as you grow up, by your parents, schools, and the wider society. The human infant comes into the world as a biological organism with animal needs. Social inheritance is a complex combination of both Heredity and Environment.

**Heredity or Nature-** Heredity covers all factors that are present in the individual. when he/she begins life not at birth, but at the time of conception. Each child is born with certain hereditary endowments, i.e., the characteristics transmitted to the child through his parents, germplasm which itself is the legacy of a long line of ancestors. Heredity and environment are in dynamic interaction and hence, one can not be separated from the other. Every growing organism is not exclusively dependent on only heredity or only environment but on heredity and environment. Every individual is born with wisdom but the degree to which you use intelligence depends on nurture. This is because the environment

may shape your intelligence or any ability associated with it, but it cannot push it to the maximum limit, which has to be done by the individuals themselves.

**20(C).** Suman is working as a teacher in primary school and wants to run the classroom on an ongoing basis, understanding the individual differences of the children. Suman should try to know the ability and interests of children and Suman should try to adjust the classroom curriculum to the children's needs.

In psychology, individual differences refer to the extent and kind of variations or similarities among people on some of the important psychological aspects such as intelligence, personality, interest, and aptitude. In the given problem, Suman should also try to know the ability and interests of the children. Individual differences occur due to the interaction of genetic and environmental factors. The differences in psychological characteristics are often consistent and form a stable pattern. This consistency and stability in behavior are unique to every person.

The role of the teacher is to observe his / her students and reveal the individual differences that exist in them and arrange the learning environment accordingly. Suman should try to adjust the classroom curriculum to the children's needs. The teacher influences the class interaction by considering the individual differences of the students by manifesting a fairly values inside the classroom. The teacher doesn't discourage her students whenever responding to her wrong answer to the question.

**21(B).** When some people live together and influence each other by staying together, then a s ocial group is formed.

A social group thus refers to a collection of continuously interacting persons who share common interests, cultures, values, and norms within a given society.

- The group in which the people live together and influence each other by staying together is a social group.
- W hen people come and interact with one another who share the same characteristics and collectively have a sense of duty , they form a social group.
- As the human wants to socialize, he always tries to l ive in a group where the needs like safety and social security are fulfilled, so he tries to live together with other humans.

**22(B).** John Dewey, an American philosopher proposed the concept of 'Progressive Education' which emphasizes that learning takes place only through 'hands-on' approach so the students must interact with their environment to adapt and learn.

Belief in the capability and potential of

every child is central to the concept of progressive education as it promotes:

- Emphasizes to enhance skills and understanding of the learners by engaging with the contents and experiences.
- Promotes 'learning by doing' to make children self-reliant and productive to use their knowledge and talents effectively.
- Ensures the active participation of students by working in a group and applying practical knowledge to complete an activity.

Therefore, it could be concluded that lt promotes 'learning by doing to make children self-reliant and productive to use their knowledge in real-life situations is correct about the implications of the concept of progressive education in a classroom.

**23(A).** Statement "Every child has the right to proceed despite the different status of the child." is appropriate in the context of an inclusive class.

**Inclusive classroom :** An inclusive classroom is a general education classroom where students with and without learning differences learn together. Inclusive classrooms are welcoming and support the diverse academic, social, emotional, and communication needs of all students.

- Inclusive education is the most effective way to give all children a fair chance to go to learn and develop the skills they need to thrive.
- Inclusive education means all children are in the same classrooms, in the same schools.
- It means real learning opportunities for groups who have traditionally been excluded – not only children with disabilities but speakers of minority languages too.
- Inclusive systems value the unique contributions students of all backgrounds bring to the classroom and allow diverse groups to grow side by side, to the benefit of all.
- Inclusion is cost-effective.
- Inclusion for social cohesion.

**24(A).** In the above-mentioned situation, t he teacher is discussing tangible thinking. Convergent or analytical thinking, divergent thinking, critical thinking, and creative thinking are the four categories of "thinking talents." These abilities assist us in comprehending the world around us, thinking critically, solving issues, making rational decisions, and forming our own values and views.

When a student describes this style of thinking to a teacher in school, the instructor responds that it does not necessitate the reality of real subjects or activities. It makes use of concepts and broad notions. The formation of this style of thinking is heavily influenced by language. The instructor is discussing tangible thinking.

When someone travels from idea to thought but never appears to get to the primary issue, this is known as tangential thinking. Instead, the concepts are related in some manner, but only on a surface or tangential level. Tools for 'concrete thinking' can be used to materialize how individuals perceive and comprehend systems, especially when it comes to concerns of (inter) disciplinarily.

**25(B).** A teacher gives a half done example to child while teaching a particular concept.

According to Lev Vygotsky's the teacher is using scaffolding in the above-mentioned phenomenon.

- Scaffolding is a technique to provide the right kind of support in the right amount at right time to increase a child's competence.
- When a teacher starts supporting the learner initially for learning, and gradually reduces the support till the learner reaches a situation, where she/ he can develop his/ her own meaning and understanding independently. The teacher is scaffolding the learner.

**Examples:**

- The teacher explicitly describes how the new lesson builds on the knowledge and skills students were taught in a previous lesson.
- A teacher gives a half-done example to a child while teaching a particular concept so that they can understand the concept well.

**26(A).** **Assertion (A):** The purpose underlying modern and ICT-based support system in teaching is to optimize learning outcomes.

- In schools, classroom teaching constitutes the primary means of impacting student learning.
- While organizing teaching-learning, the teacher makes use of a host of learning support systems available in school.
- These learning support systems supplement what the teacher teaches in the classroom.
- Some of these learning systems are libraries, laboratories , etc.
- Although these learning support systems have been contributing to student learning in conventional ways, their efficiency and effectiveness have increased with the use of ICT.

**Reason (R):** An effective instructional support system has to be linked with the enhancement of learning conditions.

- A learning support system refers to any system which provides academic resources to support student learning in educational institutions.
- Learning support systems in schools such as a library, laboratory, etc. have been greatly transformed with the use of ICT.
- ICT-based learning support services such as a digital library, virtual laboratory, e-content repository, e-mail, Internet, etc. are increasingly being used by schools. Such methods lead to enhanced learning conditions.

**27(C).** As a teacher encouraging the use of analysis can facilitate problem-solving abilities in students.

As a teacher, it is necessary to facilitate problem-solving to help the children in becoming successful in life. To do so, a teacher should encourage the students to develop a habit of analyzing things.

To solve a problem means to eliminate the source of problem generation. And this can only be done by analyzing each and every probable root cause of the problem, simulating the effect of the probable cause, and then concluding the solution by eliminating the source of the problem or by enforcing a regular check on the source of the problem so that the problem does not get out of control. Analysis helps a person predict the situations in advance and allows a person to take necessary action against the source of problem generation.

**28(B).** Individuals who have the ability to understand the motives, feelings and behaviors of others to bond with them are high on interpersonal intelligen ce in Howard Gardner's theory.

**Interpersonal intelligence:** In this type of intelligence people have the ability to understand others' feelings, wishes, expectations, and needs & others' behavior. These people have better social communication skills and the ability to relate well with others and manage relationships.

**29(B).**

Goal-oriented Behavior work in the above-mentioned line is important for a child.

Behavior refers to the response made by an individual. It is determined by both the heredity and environmental factors. The behavior of one individual differs from others. Several factors like demographic, abilities and skills, perception, attitudes, personality, etc. influence the individual difference and patterns of behavior. Therefore, understanding of individual's behavior is very important for managers to elicit a favorable response from subordinates.

The above-mentioned situation states that one should always be goal-directed and should not follow the crowd.

Goal-directed behavior is behavior that is oriented toward attaining a particular goal. Effective goal-directed behavior requires the cognitive system to be:

- Stable enough to maintain behavior

consistent with the current goal.
- Relevant task-set active while monitoring the context and controlling interference from irrelevant sources.
- Also flexible enough to rapidly adapt to contextual information that indicates the need to modify the goal.
- Goal-directed behavior requires an effective balance between stability and flexibility.

**30(C).** As per Kohlberg, the Advik is lying at the individualism and exchange stage of development.
Lawrence Kohlberg , an American psychologist, has propounded the 'Theory of Moral Development' . He has made a systematic study of moral development in his theory that is categorized in 3 levels and 6 stages.
**Individualism and Exchange** : This stage observes how children begin to adopt the views taught, but also recognize that there is more than one point of view for each matter. Each person is different and will, therefore, have a unique outlook according to their interests. In terms of our example above, they may reason that "he may think that it is right to take the drug, but the pharmacist would not."

**31(A).** According to the passage, "Continuing on the current path, will bring rising economic and social costs".
From the above sentence, we can say that according to the passage , China's "zero-covid" will bring rising economic and social costs .

**32(D).** In the fourth part of the given sentence, the singular form of the noun 'parent' is incorrect.
- In the given sentence, the pronoun 'their' is a plural possessive pronoun.
- We know that a plural pronoun always takes a plural noun .
- The plural form of the noun ' parents ' should be used with the plural possessive pronoun 'their' .
- Therefore, the plural form of the noun ' parents ' should be used in place of the singular form of the noun 'parent' .

**33(D).** The first sentence of the second paragraph says "Signs are Beijing has no intention of changing course." From the above sentence, we can say that statement A is incorrect according to the given passage.
The second paragraph says " For two years, China's government has hailed its model as a contrast to the West which saw high deaths, and continues to tell its population that COVID is a dangerous disease that requires everyone to be hospitalized" and the second-last sentence of the second paragraph says "Rather than trumpet zero COVID and criticize living with the virus as irresponsible, China would be better served looking at the examples of countries that

have successfully opened up and followed the science, as in Singapore, which aggressively vaccinated its population and incentivized it to do so by setting a timetable for opening".
From the above sentences, we can say that statements B and C are correct according to the given passage.

**34(C).** The second-last sentence of the first paragraph says " The crisis has now ignited a debate on whether this strategy that enabled China to avoid a major second wave, still remains relevant when much of the rest of the world has returned to some form of normalcy thanks to vaccines ", the second-last sentence of the second paragraph says " Rather than trumpet zero COVID and criticize living with the virus as irresponsible, China would be better served looking at the examples of countries that have successfully opened up and followed the science, as in Singapore, which aggressively vaccinated its population and incentivized it to do so by setting a timetable for opening " and the last sentence of the passage concludes " Otherwise, as the continued suffering in Shanghai has shown, the cure risks becoming worse than the disease ".
From the above sentences, we can say that the central theme of the passage is " The cure risks becoming worse than the disease in China ".

**35(D).** The antonyms of the word ' Stringent ' is "Lenient".
**Stringent:** The word 'Stringent' means Not allowing for any exceptions or loosening of standards; very strict.
**Example:** Stringent safety regulations were introduced after the accident .
**L enient -** More merciful or tolerant than expected; not as strict as expected.
**Example:** The police are sometimes more lenient with female offenders .

**36(D).** The first paragraph says "The government has struggled to supply every household with daily necessities, with the supply chain paralyzed by China's stringent measures under which every COVID-19 case, even if asymptomatic, is confined in government-run quarantine facilities" And first paragraph says "Many have said they are running out of medicines".
From the above sentences, we can say that statements A and B are correct according to the given passage.
The first paragraph says "The government has struggled to supply every household with daily necessities, with the supply chain paralyzed by China's stringent measures under which every COVID-19 case, even if asymptomatic, is confined in government-run quarantine facilities".
From the above sentence, we can say that statement C is incorrect according to the given passage.

**37(B).** The ninth sentence of the second paragraph says " However, experts say one major reason for vaccine hesitancy is the "zero COVID" strategy, with the wide perception that risks from vaccines outweigh the risk of catching COVID" .
From the above sentence, we can say that according to the passage , the insight behind the refusal to get vaccinated is that t he risks from vaccines outweigh the risk of catching COVID .

**38(A).** The synonyms of the word ' Hesitancy ' is "Reluctance .
**Hesitancy** : The word 'Hesitancy' means A lack of willingness or desire to do or accept something.
**Example:** I noticed a certain hesitancy in his voice .
**Reluctance** : Unwillingness or disinclination to do something.
**Example:** He showed great reluctance to reveal his whereabouts .

**39(B).** The underlined word 'acute' is an adjective.
Here, in this given question, food shortages is a noun, and acute is qualifying it. Therefore, from the above explanation, the correct answer should be 'adjective'.
Adjective: Adjectives are the words that qualify a noun or a pronoun.
**Example:** The music was really melodious. (melodious is qualifying the noun 'music')

**40(D).** The poem "The Jaguar" is by Ted Hughes and was published in 1957. The poet visits a zoo and describes the lifelessness of the animals inside the confinement. In the first stanza, he mentions Apes, Parrots, Lions and Tigers.
The beginning lines of the first stanza are:
The parrot's shriek as if they were on fire,
or strut
Like cheap tarts to attract the stroller with the nut.
Let's look at some difficult words:
- Shriek: high-pitched scream
- Strut: walk in a way to gain attention
- Stroller: Leisurely walk
The given lines mean that Parrots were screaming as if they were on fire or walking leisurely to get the attention of spectators that might offer them some food.
Therefore, from all the points given above, we can conclude that both statements (A) and (C) are correct.

**41(B).** As we can see that the letter s is getting repeated in multiple words such as stinks and sleepers and straw. When words begin with the same sound and are placed next to one another are called alliteration. It's a literary device commonly used to make the poem sounds better and also to make provide a natural rhythm to poetry.
**A few examples of alliteration are:**
- 'From forth the fatal loins of these two foes.'
- Smart lad, to slip betimes away

Therefore, the device used in the given lines is alliteration.

**42(B).** The given phrase can be found in the last stanza of the poem:
'At a cage where the crowd stands, stares, mesmerized, as a child at a dream, at a dream, at a jaguar hurrying enraged.'
- In these lines, the poet describes a crowd of people.
- The crowd is standing at the Jaguar's cage and completely mesmerised by it.
- They are engrossed in the Jaguar's movement like a child dreaming.
Therefore, 'As a child at a dream' refers to 'spectators who encounter the cage of Jaguar'.

**43(C).** The poem is titled 'The Jaguar' by Ted Hughes. It describes the pitiful state of animals in the zoo. The poet begins by describing the lethargic state of the animals and contrasts it with the energetic Jaguar. The poet begins with Apes who are inspecting for fleas:
- The apes yawn and adore their fleas in the sun.
He also described the Parrots who are either shrieking or trying to get food from spectators:
- The parrots shriek as if they were on fire, or strut
  Like cheap tarts to attract the stroller with the nut.
In the final line of the stanza, he mentioned the lions and tigers who are in deep sleep and completely still.
- Fatigued with indolence, tiger and lion/ Lie still as the sun.
The Jaguar is not mentioned till the third stanza.
Therefore, from all the points given above, we can infer that The animal that is not mentioned in the first stanza is 'Jaguar'.

**44(A).** Here the poet is comparing the state of sleep of lions and tigers with the stillness of the sun.
The given line can be found at the end of the first stanza: "tiger and lion/ Lie still as the sun".
The literary device that uses as or like to compare two entities or concepts is known as Simile.
A few examples of simile are:
- Fits like a glove
- Love is like the wild rose-briar
Therefore, the literary device used in tiger and lion/Lie still as the sun is simile.

**45(D).** The Boa is mentioned at the beginning of the second stanza:
Lie still as the sun. The boa-constrictors coil/Is a fossil.
- Similarly, Boa is also coiled and completely still.
- The stillness is emphasised by comparing it with a fossil.
- Since the Boa is in the cage it doesn't have the space to move or hunt.

Therefore, the Boa is compared to a fossil because 'The Boa cannot move in the cage'.

**46(B).** Participating in role play is the most helpful in developing oral language skills.
- Receptive oral language (comprehension), which is the first area of development and the largest subset of the language, forms the base of the child.
- Oral skills can be best developed by participating in role-playing. It provides concrete experiences as it mainly aims at enhancing communication skills.
- Role-play is a speaking activity where a child gets an opportunity to speak in an expressive way and can build their creative ideas.
- In this method, students play the role of the character that has come in the story to dramatize the story. It develops communication and observational skills.

**47(C).** Poetry teaching is for enjoyment and appreciation.
Poetry is a form of literature in which thoughts and feelings are expressed through aesthetic qualities of language. Poetry teaching is done for enjoyment and appreciation as poetic words and phrases are always a source of keen pleasure to the learners to develop a genuine feeling and real enjoyment.
**Aims of teaching poetry:**
- Developing interest and providing fun to learners.
- Promoting imaginative and creative ability in the learners.
- Making learners aware of ethics, norms, and values of society.
- Increasing learners' vocabulary, listening, and critical thinking skills.

**48(B).** Social interaction is most important when it comes to language learning.
' Lev Vygotsky ', a Soviet psychologist, has propounded the " Socio-cultural Theory ". This theory implies the idea that social interaction is the most important part of language learning and plays a crucial role in the learner's cognitive development.
Social interaction is the primary cause of learners' development as his theory emphasizes that children learn through interaction and collaboration with skilled and knowledgeable people.

**49(A).** A child learns the first language through s peech.
Language is a symbolic, rule-governed system, shared by a group of people to express their thoughts and feelings. It provides a bank of memories and symbols inherited from one's fellow speakers and created in one's lifetime.
- Learning a language requires the operation of an innate capacity processed by all human beings. The child starts using language in the form of

smiling, crying, weeping, etc.
- The children learn the first language informally by speaking from their societal environment. They only need to practice a lot by speaking in the natural environment continuously so that they can have a good grasp of the language.
- The meaningful practice facilitates language learning as it gives confidence and also helps in the enhancement of language skills which makes a person proficient in a specific language.

**50(D).** Objectives of language teaching should enable the learners at the end of ten-year schooling to develop skills and competencies to use the language for real-life purposes in a social situation as well as to use the language for academic or higher-order thinking purposes. The National Curriculum Framework – 2005 proposes the following objectives for language teaching-learning for the school:
- The competence to understand what she hears
- Ability to read with comprehension, and not merely decode
- Effortless expression
- Coherent writing
- Control over different registers
- Scientific study of language
- Creativity
- Sensitivity

**51(D).** When the teacher asks the students to repeat some words or sentences several times, it is called drilling.
**Drilling:** It is a technique that is used in structuralism to master the structure of language by practicing and repeating the concept again and again .
- Drilling emphasizes practicing to learn something effectively.
- It involves mastering specific skills through repetition.
- For example, listening to a person and repeating what he said. It can repeat more than one time to gain specific skills in speaking.
- It includes activating the knowledge through application.
- So, when the teacher asks the students to repeat some words or sentences several times, it is called drilling.
- Through drilling, the teacher can improve the language skills of students and make them confident while speaking.

**52(A).** Self-assessment is the ability of a person to accurately evaluate or assess his/her performance, and his/her strengths and weaknesses.
Self-assessment is when students examine their own language skills rather than having a teacher do it. Learner portfolios frequently include a type of self-assessment, such as a checklist for completing the learning objectives.

- Student instructors make judgments about their own work and the amount to which they have satisfied criteria and standards during self-assessment . Student instructors are primarily responsible for determining the criteria and standards that must be applied to their own performance. Self-evaluation can lead to fresh ideas or knowledge of areas that need improvement, and it can also help aspiring teachers take greater control and responsibility for their own professional growth.
- Self-monitoring is a method of constantly examining one's practice in order to obtain a better knowledge of one's work performance and identify strengths and deficiencies.

**53(B).** To learn a text by-heart is not among the aims of teaching English.

In India, English is a second language and it should be taught as a language and not as literature .

Language is authentically called a "skill" rather than a "subject". The four skills, namely, listening, speaking, reading, and writing are required to use the language, the language is a skill.

**54(C).** For students to gain language skills from textbooks, textbook learning should expose them to more literary reading.

Textbook is a tool to be used in the teaching-learning process to facilitate effective and meaningful learning. It contains questions that promote exploration and divergent thinking.

To gain language skills from textbooks, textbook learning should expose the learner to more literary texts as it would allow them to learn the technicalities of the language. It will help them in understanding not only the structure of the language but will also help them in understanding the usage of the language.

**55(A).** The students acquire language by using language in natural interactive environment.

The Indian educationists are in a strong belief that the very aim of teaching English in India is to prepare the students to acquire practical command of English . Teachers need to employ different methods and approaches to achieve this aim. More care is needed when selecting a method of teaching a foreign language like English as a second language. Some of the methods and approaches are the Direct method, oral approach, grammar-translation method, and communicative approach.

**56(D).** Multilingualism as a source means u sing student's language as a strategy.
•

**Multilingualism:** Multilingualism is the ability to use more than two languages. Multilingualism is constitutive of the identity of a child and a typical feature of the Indian linguistic landscape must be used as a resource, classroom strategy, and a goal by a creative language teacher.

**Multilingualism as a source aims at:**
- Using languages of all children for teaching-learning.
- Increasing the better innate understanding of how language works.
- Enhancing creativity, divergent thinking and appreciation of local languages.
- Ensuring the inclusion of all students irrespective of their linguistic background.
- Connecting the classroom with real-life to make learners familiar with the content.

**57(B).** Interactive language teaching- It is the method of teaching the language in school so that the students are able to understand the language and its usage because by interaction students will be able to use the language and speak properly.

Principle of the Interactive language principle:
- The student is the language learner.
- The control over the language is proceed through creativity, which is developed by doing interactive participation activities.
- The language learner and teaching are to be shaped as per the students' needs and objectives.
- Language learning and teaching are based on normal uses of language.

Therefore, Classroom relations reflect individual liking and respect is not the principles of Interactive language teaching.

**58(C).** In a language class, students are expected to be accurate in whatever she says or writes and this grammatical accuracy is to be realized through constant drills and the construction of correct sentences. The teacher is following the s tructural approach.

**Structural approach :**
- It is a language tool that helps the learner to master the structure or pattern of sentences and improves the fundamental skill of language learning and corrects learner's speech habits.
- A learner in this approach is expected to be accurate in whatever s/he says or writes and this grammatical accuracy is to be realized through constant drills and construction of correct (error-free) sentences.
- In this method, to teach a language (English in the present context) a particular pattern or structure is presented and practiced thoroughly before the learner goes on to a new one.
- It is the descriptive approach that gives more importance to speech only without reference to meaning and it gives priority to pupils' activity, spoken language, multiskill approach,

situational teaching, etc.

**59(D).** Develop students' ability to use the language is the main purpose of continuous and comprehensive evaluation.

Continuous and comprehensive evaluation' also known as 'CCE' has been introduced as a school-based system of evaluation by the CBSE in 2009 with the enactment of the "Right to Education Act". Continuous and comprehensive evaluation refers to all-around development including both scholastic and co-scholastic aspects of a child's growth. It makes evaluation an integral part of learning through diagnostic and remedial teaching.

**Purposes of Continuous and comprehensive evaluation :**
- Enhancing the thought process and de-emphasizing memorization.
- Develop students' ability to use the language in different situations.
- Developing student's cognitive, psychomotor and affective domains.
- Making evaluation an integral part of diagnostic and remedial teaching.

**60(D).** A language teacher wants to meet the demand of the style of learning of all the students. He can overcome this challenge by using various teaching methods and strategy.

**Learning style:**
- Each of us has a style of learning as an individual and as our own personality. These styles could be categorized as visual (reading), aural (listening), and physical (actively doing things).
- Each classroom is likely to include students whose styles of learning vary widely. Teachers should try to cater to the diverse needs of students to ensure effective learning.
- Each student has his\her own specific preference. Some like to hear lectures, some prefer discussion, and some would rather personally experience the thing being studied.
- Teachers can use various methods and strategies and modes of assessment to meet the demand of every individual. It gives learners customized techniques to learn through the best strategies.
- When teachers use various methods according to their learning style, students will take more interest in learning and it leads to better performance of the students.

**61(B).** According to the question;
$$16 \div 4 \times 2 - 5 + 1$$
$$= 4 \times 2 - 5 + 1$$
$$= 8 - 5 + 1$$
$$= 4$$
Now from the given options;
Option (B): $[\{(16 \div 4) \times 2\} - 5] + 1$
$$= [\{(16 \div 4) \times 2\} - 5] + 1$$
$$= [\{4 \times 2\} - 5] + 1$$
$$= [8 - 5] + 1$$

$= 4$

**62(B).** On dividing the numerator by denominator,

$\Rightarrow \frac{11}{19} = 0.57$

$\Rightarrow \frac{2}{3} = 0.66$

$\Rightarrow \frac{13}{17} = 0.76$

$\Rightarrow \frac{22}{7} = 3.14$

$\Rightarrow 0.57 < 0.66 < 0.76 < 3.14$

$\therefore \frac{11}{19} < \frac{2}{3} < \frac{13}{17} < \frac{22}{7}$

**63(B).** As we know,
The rule of divisibility of 9 is:
If the sum of digits of the number is divisible by 9 , then the number itself is divisible by 9 .
The given number is $6357x5$ .
The sum of digits of the number
$= 6 + 3 + 5 + 7 + x + 5$
$= 26 + x \quad \cdots (1)$
Now, put the value of $x$ from each option one by one in equation (1) ,
Option (A): $x = 8$
$= 26 + 8$
$= 34$
34 is not divisible by 9 . So, 635785 is not divisible by 9 .
Option (B): $x = 1$
$= 26 + 1$
$= 27$
27 is divisible by 9 . So, 635715 is divisible by 9 .
Option (C): $x = 9$
$= 26 + 9$
$= 35$
35 is not divisible by 9 . So, 635795 is not divisible by 9 .
Option (D): $x = 3$
$= 26 + 3$
$= 29$
29 is not divisible by 9 . So, 635735 is not divisible by 9 .

**64(D).** Given,
Perimeter of triangle $= 600$ m
Ratio of sides of triangle $= 12 : 13 : 15$
As we know,
Sum of all sides of triangle $=$ Perimeter of triangle
Sum of all sides of triangle,
$\Rightarrow 12x + 13x + 15x = 40x$
$\Rightarrow 40x = 600$
$\Rightarrow x = 15$
Longest side $= 15x$
$= 15 \times 15$
$= 225$ cm
$\therefore$ The longest side is 225 cm.

**65(D).** As we know,
$1$ km $= 1000$ m
$1$ m $= 1000$ mm
$\Rightarrow 1$ km $= 1000 \times 1000$
$\Rightarrow 1$ km $= 1,00,000$ mm, (i) is true,
$1$ cm$^3 = 1$ ml, (iv) is false,
$1$ L $= 1000$ ml
$\Rightarrow 1$ m$^3 = 1,00,000$ cm$^3$
$\Rightarrow 1$ m$^3 = 1000$ L, (ii) is true,

$1$ decameter $= 10$ meter
$1$ hectometer $= 100$ meter
$\Rightarrow 1$ decameter $= \frac{1}{10} \times 100$ m
$\Rightarrow 1$ decameter $= \frac{1}{10} \times 100 =$ One-tenth hectometer, (iii) is true,

**66(C).** Given,
Data $= 13, 15, 9, x, 4, 17, y$
$y - x = 6$
As we know,
Mean $= \dfrac{\text{(Sum of all observations)}}{\text{(Number of all observations)}}$
Sum of all observations
$= 13 + 15 + 9 + x + 4 + 17 + y$
$= x + y + 58$
Number of all observations $= 7$
Mean $= \dfrac{(x+y+58)}{7}$
$\Rightarrow 12 = \dfrac{(x+y+58)}{7}$
$\Rightarrow x + y = 26 \dots$ (i)
Also given that $y - x = 6$
Solving two equations, we get
$x = 10, y = 16$
$\therefore xy = 160$

**67(C).** Given,
The ratio of present ages of Meena and Sina
$= 4 : 3$
After 6 years, Meena's age will become 26 years.
Let the present of Meena and Sina be $4x$ and $3x$ respectively.
$\Rightarrow 4x + 6 = 26$
$\Rightarrow 4x = 20$
$\Rightarrow x = 5$
Now,
The present age of Sina $= 3x$
$= (3 \times 5)$ years
$= 15$ years
$\therefore$ The present age of Sina is 15 years.

**68(C).** Given,
Expression is $12 - 3 \times 8 \div 4 + 3$ .
As we know,
To solve these type of expressions we use BODMAS rule.
A prime number is a number that has exactly two factors.
$12 - 3 \times 8 \div 4 + 3$
$\Rightarrow 12 - 3 \times 2 + 3 \quad$ (Division done)
$= 12 - 6 + 3 \quad$ (Multiplication done)
$= 15 - 6 \quad$ (Addition done)
$= 9 \quad$ (Subtraction done)
Also, the largest 2 -digit prime number is 97
.
$\therefore$ Password is $(9 + 97)$
$= 106$

**69(A).** Given,
Hours worked per day in first week $= 4$
Hours worked per day in second week $= 5$
Hours worked per day in third and fourth week $= 6$
Rate $=$ Rs. 100 for every 30 minutes
As we know,
In these type of questions we calculate total hours worked and multiply them by the

rate.
Amount $=$ Total hours $\times$ Price per hour
Hours worked in first week $= 4 \times 7$
$= 28$ hours
Hours worked in second week $= 5 \times 7$
$= 35$ hours
Hours worked in third week $= 6 \times 7$
$= 42$ hours
Hours worked in fourth week $= 6 \times 7$
$= 42$ hours
$\therefore$ Total hours worked $= 28 + 35 + 42 + 42$
147 hours
Rate $=$ Rs. 100 for every 30 minutes
$=$ Rs. $100 \times 2$ for every hour
$=$ Rs. 200 per hour
$\therefore$ Amount that the worker will receive
$= 147 \times 200$
$=$ Rs. 29400

**70(C).** Given,
A plane figure with two pairs of equal adjacent sides, one pair of equal opposite angles and 2 unequal diagonals that intersect each other at right angles.
Kite:

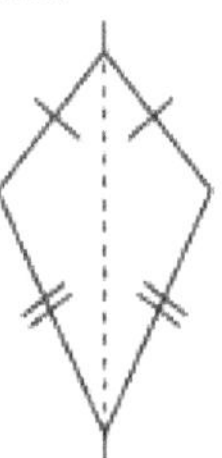

**On checking options-**
Option (B) True, because all the above properties are true in case of Kite.
Option (A) False, because the property that pair of adjacent sides are equal does not hold true.
Option (C) False, because diagonals of a square are equal.
Option (D) False, because for unequal diagonals of a rectangle they can not intersect at right angles.

**71(B).** Given,
Running start time $= 09 : 05$ am
Running end time $= 02 : 18$ pm
Rest time $= 15$ minutes
As we know,
One hour $=$ Sixty minutes
One minute $=$ Sixty seconds
We can use 24 hour clock time while subtracting am time from pm time,
Total time from $09 : 05$ am to $02 : 18$ pm is,
$= 14$ h $18$ m $- 09$ h $05$ m
$= 5$ h $13$ m
Subtracting rest time from above time, we get,
$= 5$ h $13$ m $- 15$ m
$= 4$ h $73$ m $- 15$ m
$= 4$ h $58$ m

**72(C).** Given,
Statement A: All prime numbers are odd numbers.
Statement B: Natural numbers that are not

prime numbers are composite numbers.
As we know,
A prime number is a number that has exactly two factors.
A composite number is a number that has more than two factors.
Set of natural numbers is $1, 2, 3, \ldots$.
Statement A is incorrect because 2 is a prime number as it has exactly two factors but it is an even number.
Statement B is incorrect because 1 is a natural number but is neither prime nor composite number.

**73(D).** Given,
The quantity of each type of vegetable together with its unit price.
As we know,
Total revenue by each type of vegetable = quantity $\times$ price per unit
Revenue by Potato = $98 \times 14.50$
= Rs. 1421
Revenue by Tomato = $75 \times 18.80$
= Rs. 1410
Revenue by Onion = $65 \times 22.30$
= Rs. 1449.50
Revenue by Ladyfinger = $114 \times 12.20$
= Rs. 1390.80
$\therefore$ Revenues in ascending order is Ladyfinger < Tomato < Potato < Onion.

**74(B).** Given,
Loan amount = Rs. 7650
Money saved daily = Rs. 180
Increase in loan amount everyday = Rs. 10
Let the required days be $x$.
According to question,
$(180 \times x) = 7650 + 10x$
$\Rightarrow 180x = 7650 + 10x$
$\Rightarrow 170x = 7650$
$\Rightarrow x = \dfrac{7650}{170}$
$\Rightarrow x = 45$

**75(A).** Given,
$\Rightarrow 5 \times 5 = 25$
$\Rightarrow 25 \times 5 = 125$
$\Rightarrow 125 \times 5 = 625$
$\therefore$ The next number is 625.

**76(A).** Nature of Mathematics is Abstract. Learning mathematics serves both as a means and an end. It is a means to develop logical and quantitative thinking abilities.
- At the early grades, children's learning of mathematics should be a natural outgrowth from children themselves.
- Such experiences must be interesting and should challenge their imagination, so that while observing any natural phenomena they can think mathematically.
Let us now discuss in detail regarding the nature of mathematics:
- Mathematics aims at abstraction.
- Mathematics is logical.
- Mathematics is symbolic.
- Mathematics is precise.
- Mathematics is the study of structures.

**77(A).** "Failure to recognize place value leads to failure in four operations in mathematics." The given statement indicates Fear and failure of the problems in teaching and learning of mathematics.
**Problems in teaching and learning of mathematics:**
- **Fear and Failure:** Most of the students, peers, teachers, parents, etc. have given priority to teaching and learning mathematics at the elementary level although most of them thought that it is a difficult subject. Lack of awareness of objectives is also another cause of fear and failure. Failure to recognize place value leads to failure in four operations in mathematics.
- **Disappointing Curriculum:** Unattractive and Loaded mathematics curriculum created disappointment among the students.
- **Inadequate Learning Materials:** For the majority of children in elementary schools textbook in mathematics is the only resource material available to them.
- **Crude Assessment:** Most of our mathematics curriculum emphasized on memorization of formulas. Our classroom teaching process is also examination-oriented. In our school, different tests are designed to assess student's knowledge of procedure and memory of formulas and facts. Questions are set not to expose student's experiences but to get a fixed answer.
- **Inadequate teacher preparation:** Teaching and learning of mathematics in the elementary level are purely depends on the preparation of teachers, her own understanding, the preparation of teachers on pedagogic techniques, and the student's preparedness.
- **The teaching-learning process:** The teaching-learning process in mathematics at the elementary level are not attractive because,
- (i) Bookish knowledge in the class creates dissatisfaction,
- (ii) School mathematics learning becomes charmless, dull, uninteresting, and stereotype,
- (iii) Emphasis on rote learning,
- (iv) Emphasis on teaching, not on learning,
- (v) Development of Understanding, Application and skill are ignored.
- **Lack of interest:** Most of the school children find learning of mathematics difficult and lose their confidence in mathematics.

**78(A).** Effective learning of mathematical concepts depends on how far teachers are successful in developing mathematical language.
Effective learning of mathematical concepts does not result from mastery over activities alone. It depends on how far teachers are successful in developing mathematical language or other symbolic representations, building links with past experiences to formulate. corresponding abstractions or laws. The transition from concrete to abstraction depends upon explanations written in mathematical terms.
Mathematical language distinguishes between things and names of things. Number and numeral, and fraction and fractional numbers are a few examples. Mathematical solutions emphasize a specific arrangement of steps in the solution, i.e., an algorithm to develop accuracy of thought and precision In quantitative matters.

**79(C).** The nature of mathematical understanding is l ogical.
The nature of mathematics includes mathematical ideas that progress from concrete to abstract; grow from particular to general and its knowledge is conceptual as well as procedural.
- Mathematics is based on logic and reasoning because mathematicians need to prove theorems, formulas that are based on logical principles and rules.
- Mathematics relies on both logic and creativity, and it is pursued both for a variety of practical purposes and for its intrinsic interest.
- Learning mathematics is concerned with both comprehending the facts, theories, rules, and laws that are based on logic.
- Children do come across situations to solve problems, and for the same, mathematical reasoning and logic are used. To arrive at a solution, either inductive or deductive reasoning is used. While reasoning, children organize data, evaluate situations, formulate relations, solve problems and identify situations that have practical applications.

**80(D).** Mathematics has a great social significance. It helps in the maintenance and organization of our society. To live a balanced social life in harmony with the community, mathematics is very essential. Great Napoleon once said, 'The progress and the improvement of mathematics are linked with the prosperity of the state'.
**Community mathematics:** Connecting mathematics to community and culture is community mathematics. In a very simplified way community, mathematics is mathematics we use in our daily lives while living in a society. Each and every aspect of mathematics used in our lives while living in a community is included in community mathematics.
- It is a collection of resources for engaging the students to learn mathematics.
- It provides opportunities for the learner to justify their reasoning skills.
- It helps in gaining insight to the learner

to solve a problem in mathematics.

- In addition to this, mathematics is also able to provide a livelihood. In addition to all other subjects, mathematics contributes the most in providing livelihood in the era of technology.
- It also helps in the development of psychological aspects like a child learning from learning by doing, learning from experience, logical thinking, creativity, curiosity etc.

**81(C).** According to Van Hiele levels of Geometry, at level 3 a child is able to p rove an abstract statement on geometric properties to conclude.

The Van Hiele's levels originated in 1957 given by Pierre Van Hiele and his wife from the Utrecht University in the Netherlands. It helped in shaping the curriculum throughout the world that especially influenced the learning of geometry at a large level.

It provides an insight to the teacher about how the students learn geometry at different levels. It describes how the students learn at each level and pass to another level.

**82(D).** There are causes related to the classroom and home environment associated with the creation of fear towards mathematics learning. Some very common causes of mathematics phobia are:

- Prior negative experiences with mathematics: These may be related to one or more of the following:
  1. Unfavorable school climate
  2. Lack of encouragement from parents and/or teachers or lack of teacher's preparation
  3. Lack of positive role models
  4. Ethnic and/or gender stereotypes
  5. Mathematics problems being used as punishment in school
- The pressure of taking timed tests
- A disappointing curriculum
- The fear of looking or feeling "stupid" in front of others

**83(D).** Gender differences in mathematics classroom is not responsible for lack of interest of a child in mathematics.

**Lack of interest:** Most school children find learning mathematics difficult and lose their confidence in mathematics.

- The teaching-learning process in mathematics is not joyful and attractive.
- Even the students don't know what benefit they will get after learning mathematics. So, students lack their interest and attitude towards mathematics.
- NCF-2005 states that the fear of failure and examination system is responsible for the lack of interest of a child in mathematics.
- Mathematics should be taught in a way

that children learn to enjoy mathematics rather than fear it.

- Another main issue that brings the lack of interest among learners is the assessment-based problem and the structure of mathematics .
- The teaching of mathematics should be done in the way, in which a student learns the best i.e., following the child-centered approaches by engaging students actively in the learning process.
- The teacher should provide the students more opportunities to experience typical processes of mathematical activity like looking for patterns, making quizzes, puzzles, and proving arguments, etc.

**84(B).** Diagnostic test is necessary to find out mathematical errors in children.

Different types of tests are required for different purposes. Different tests can be used to measure the knowledge and skills of students, to identify problems, to change teaching methods, etc.

**There are different types of tests-**
- Diagnostic test
- Placement test
- Progress test
- Oral test
- Benchmark test
- Proficiency test etc.

**Characteristics of a diagnostic test:**
- A diagnostic tes t is an evaluation of the student's specific strengths, weaknesses, knowledge, and skills. It is used to find out specific learning deficiencies.
- The essential steps in diagnostic testing are:
  1. Identifying the students who are having trouble or need help.
  2. Locating the errors or learning difficulties.
  3. Discovering the causal factors of slow learning.
- The purpose of diagnostic testing is to find out the errors or to locate and identify the areas of learning difficulties in learning particular content.
- Here the teacher starts from basics and slowly goes on increasing the difficulty level of the test.
- After identifying the areas where the error lies, you have to find out the reasons due to which the particular child/group of students have not responded well.

**85(B).** Evaluation may be considered as an umbrella term which includes measurement and assessment . This relationship can be further explained as measurement focuses mainly on quantifying the variable, assessment bring in qualitative descriptions and when value judgment is added to these, it becomes evaluation.

"Measurement is a process of assigning

numbers to individuals or their characteristics according to specific rules." It is a process of quantifying the degree to which someone or something possessed a given trait, i.e., quality, characteristics, or features. The term evaluation is closely related to measurement. It is in some respect, inclusive including the informal and intuitive judgment of pupil's progress. Evaluation is describing something in terms of selected attributes and judging the degree of acceptability or suitability of that which has been described.

For Example: Rakesh has scored 65 marks in Mathematics in the final year examination, which is above average performance but he has not performed well on test items related to Trigonometry. Rakesh has improved significantly with compared to his half-yearly examination. In this, 65 marks measurement indicator, like above average performance, identification of area of improvement comes under assessment and judgment of his performance in relation to half yearly examination is evaluation.

Evaluation is a process of value judgment. It is also used to refer to the product or outcome of the process. You can say that "measurement and assessment are the means and evaluation is the end". In the process of evaluation, measurement is the first step, assessment comes next and when value judgment is added to it, it becomes evaluation.

**86(A).** Formative evaluation provides information to teachers for modifying instructions and teaching.

**Formative evaluation ( evaluation for Learning):**
- It is also known as evaluation for learning, used to evaluate student learning progress and achievement.
- The goal is to collect detailed information like strengths, weaknesses, knowledge, skills, etc., and then plan the next lesson in a way to improve the performance of the students.
- It helps teachers to identify problem-facing areas, to understand and learning needs for achieving academic growth .
- It is considered an Informal Method of assessment as it can be conducted at any time or during teaching also.
- E xample: Discussions, Class tests, homework, assignments, debate, plays, etc.

**87(D).** Diagnostic test is a comprehensive test that provides feedback to teachers and students on their strengths and weaknesses. It is specially conducted for removing the learning difficulties of learners.

**Importance of diagnostic test:**
- It makes learning and teaching meaningful by improving the achievement level of students through

remedial teaching.
- It is used to locate and identify the areas of learning difficulties.
- It is used in counseling and guidance.
- Diagnostic test is an arrangement of remedial teaching.
- It used in guiding lesson and curriculum planning.
- It used in removing barriers to learner's understanding.
- Diagnostic test is used in determining learner's strength and weakness.

**88(A).** To find out the weakness or deficiency of a child in learning is the objective of a diagnostic test in mathematics.
**Diagnostic testing:**
- The diagnostic test takes up where the formative test leaves off.
- A diagnostic test is a means by which an individual profile is examined and compared against certain norms or criteria.
- The diagnostic test focuses on an individual's educational weakness or learning deficiency and identifies the gaps in pupils.
- A diagnostic test is more intensive and acts as a tool for analysis of Learning Difficulties.
- A diagnostic test is more often limited to low ability students.
- Diagnostic tests pinpoint the specific types of error each pupil is making and searches for underlying causes of the problem.
- A diagnostic test helps us to identify the trouble spots and discovered those areas of students' weaknesses that are unresolved by the formative test.

**89(D).** In remedial teaching, the teacher is:
- Required to prepare instructional material for quality learning and adopting different methodologies.
- Expected to devise some strategy to remove problems in learning.
- Provide pupils clear instructions to avoid confusion, summarize the main points and encourage pupils' active participation in class activities.

The word 'remedial' means 'to rectify, improve or remedy something.' Remedial teaching is teaching which is designed to bring students who are lagging behind up to the level of achievement realized by their peers. Remedial teaching means necessary learning support will be provided to pupils who need pedagogical or didactic assistance. There are often children who receive a lower grade because of certain learning or behavioral problems/disorder. The ultimate aim of remediation or remedial teaching is to help pupils who have fallen behind to learn to the best of their ability and to bring them back into the mainstream of the teaching-learning process as far as possible.
- Remedial teaching in which a t eacher is required to prepare instructional material for quality learning and adopting different methodologies as per the needs of the learner or a particular group.
- During the process of remediation, a teacher is expected to devise some strategy to remove problems in learning and the causes due to which the learner has faced the difficulties.
- Teachers provide pupils clear instructions to avoid confusion, summarize the main points and encourage pupils' active participation in class activities.
- Teachers should prepare a rich, pleasant and comfortable learning environment for pupils during remedial classes.

**90(B).** Van Hiele is a model that describes how students learn geometry. It was originated in 1957.
It postulates five levels of geometrical thinking which are visualization, analysis, abstraction, formal deduction, rigor.
- Level 0 (Visualization): In this level, they can recognize shapes by their appearance, but not by properties.
- Level 1 (Analysis): At this level, students can describe the properties of shapes. Eg: Students at this level can classify shapes according to their properties.
- Level 2 (Abstraction/Informal Deduction): Students will be able to participate and understand informal deductive discussions about shapes and their characteristics.
- Level 3 (Formal Deduction): Students will be able to work with an abstract statement about geometric properties and can make conclusions.
- Level 4 (Rigor): This is the last level, Students will be able to compare geometric results in different axiomatic systems.

**91(A).** Flood and Drought are the two major natural disasters of India.
**Disaster:** A Disaster is a serious disruption of the functioning of a society involving widespread human, material, economic or environmental losses & impacts which exceeds the ability of the affected community or society to cope using it's own resources. A natural disaster is a major adverse event that occurs as a result of Earth's natural processes such as floods, volcanic eruptions, earthquakes, tsunamis and other geological processes, resulting in loss of life and property.
**Flood:** A flood is an overflow of water that submerges land, can occur as an overflow of water from water bodies, such as a river or lake, into which the water rises. It results in some of that water escaping it's usual boundaries or it may occur due to accumulation of rainwater on saturated ground in an areal flood. Floods often cause damage to livelihood & structures.
**Draught:** A drought or drouth is a natural disaster of below-average precipitation in a given region. It results in prolonged shortages in the water supply, whether atmospheric, surface water or ground water.

**92(D).** I have sharp curved teeth. I don't chew my food, but swallow it. I am a snake.
**Snake:**
- A snake has two hollow teeth (fangs).
- Snakes have sharp curved teeth, but they do not chew their prey.
- Snakes always swallow their food whole.
- When it bites, the poison enters the person's body through the fangs.
- There is a medicine for snake bites.
- The medicine is made from the snake's poison and is available in all government hospitals.
- Of the many kinds of snakes found in our country, only four types of snakes are poisonous.
- They are Cobra, Common Krait, Russel's Viper (Duboiya), Saw-scaled Viper (Afai).
- Python is not a poisonous snake.

**93(A).** The game of Kabaddi is played with seven members in each team. It lasts for 40 minutes with 5-minute break.
**Kabaddi :**
- Kabaddi is a popular contact sport in Southern Asia that first originated in Ancient India.
- It is played across the country and is the official game in the states of Punjab, Tamil Nadu, Bihar, Telangana, and Maharashtra.
- In the kabaddi game, each side has 7 players when the game starts.
- There will be 5 substitutes for each side as well.
- The games in Kabaddi are 40 minutes long.
- Each side gets alternating tu r ns to send any one player to the opponent's side.
- This player is called the raider and each player on the opposing team is called a defender.
- The two teams alternate between raiding and defending for two halves of twenty minutes each (with a five-minute break between halves and newly introduced small timeouts for teams are used to generate advertisement revenue).
- After halftime, the two teams switch sides of the court.
- The Lobby is the area of the court which is considered active only when contact has been made between the raider and a defender.
- Else, it is considered out of bounds for both raider and the defenders.
- The team with the most points at the end of the game wins.

**94(C).** Joint family: A family which lives together with all family members up to the second generation like grandparents, parents, uncle, aunts and their children is called a joint family. The most aged man is the head of the family. Such a type of family arrangement is especially common in India. Joint family, is a family in which members of a unilineal descent group (a group in which descent through either the female or the male line is emphasized) live together with their spouses and offspring in one homestead and under the authority of one of the members. The joint family is an extension of the nuclear family (parents and dependent children), and it typically grows when children of one sex do not leave their parents' home at marriage but bring their spouses to live with them.

The several advantages of staying in a joint family are:

- It develops a sense of respect when you grow up in a family with so many elders.
- Sharing and caring is another fundamental of a joint family.
- It is always beneficial for the working parents to live in a joint family.
- Children inherit good manners and etiquette from the elders.

Therefore, we conclude that Only (1) and (3) options are correct.

**95(B).** Section 25 of The Indian Forest Act 1927 deals with p ower to stop ways and water-courses in reserved forests.

**Section 25 in The Indian Forest Act, 1927:**

The Forest-officer may, with the previous sanction of the 1[State Government] or of any officer duly authorised by it in this behalf, stop any public or private way or water-course in a reserved forest, provided that a substitute for the way or water-course so stopped, which the 1[State Government] deems to be reasonably convenient.

**96(B).** 'Undhiya' is a famous food for farmers in Gujarat.

**Undhiya:**

- The dish is named Undhiya or upside down , in Gujrati.
- This dish is a regional specialty of Surat .
- A little-known fact is that the name Undhiyu comes from the Gujarati word Undhu , which means being upside down.
- The upside-down is here because the pot in which this food is made is placed upside down.
- In the wintertime enjoy the undhiya (a kind of stew).
- There are a total of eight vegetables that are stirred upside down and cooked over a wood fire in large earthen (clay) pots along with fresh spices to give Undhiyu its distinctive texture and flavor.
- The pot was sealed and kept between hot coals.
- The vegetables are cooked slowly in this special cooker, on the fields.
- Undhiya would be eaten with bajra rotis, freshly cooked on chulha.

**97(A).** France has launched its first military exercise 'AsterX' in space.

**AsterX:** To bridge the gap with rivals China and Russia, France plans to develop anti-satellite laser weapons and strengthen surveillance capabilities.

**Aim:** To keep an eye on a potentially deadly space object as well as dangers to its own satellite from another country with a strong space force.

**98(B).** Rat, dog and elephant have poor eyesight but have an excellent sense of smell, touch and taste.

**Rat:** Rats have poor eyesight. They have an excellent sense of smell, touch and taste.

**Elephant:** Elephants have a keen sense of smell, touch and taste. They have poor eyesight.

**Dog:** Dogs have an excellent sense of smell, touch and taste. They have poor eyesight and are colour blind.

**99(C).** Dengue is spread by several species of mosquito of the female Aedes type, principally Aedes aegypti.

Dengue fever is a mosquito-borne tropical disease caused by the dengue virus. Symptoms include high fever, headache, vomiting, muscle and joint pains, characteristic skin rash, bleeding, low levels of blood platelets and blood plasma leakage.

**100(C).** **Water conservation and management:** Since there is a declining availability of fresh water and increasing demand, the need has arisen to conserve and effectively manage this precious life-giving resource for sustainable development. Besides developing water-saving technologies and methods, attempts are also to be made to prevent pollution. There is a need to encourage watershed development, rainwater harvesting, water recycling and reuse, and conjunctive use of water for sustainable water supply in long run.

**Recycle and reuse water:**

- Water recycling and reuse is the process of collecting, treating, and using wastewater, particularly from municipalities, industry, and agriculture.
- The recycled water can be used for irrigation or industrial purposes, as well as domestic purposes if properly treated.
- The terms "reused" and "recycled" are often used interchangeably depending on where you are geographical.
- Reclaimed water is not reused or recycled until it is put to some purpose.

**101(B).**

| List-I (Animal) | List-II (Characteristic) |
|---|---|
| (a) Sloth | (ii) sleeps for 17 hrs |
| (b) Eagle | (iv) can see four times than humans |
| (c) Silk worm | (i) can find his partner by smell |
| (d) Owl | (iii) have eyes in the front like humans |

**Sloth:** Sloths sleep for almost 17 hours per day. That leaves only nine hours to lumber through the trees. They maintain a low body temperature of about 86°F-93°F. They move in and out of shade to regulate their body temperature. Sloths live for about 40 years.

**Eagle:** Eagles are large birds of prey, meaning that they hunt and eat animals for food. They fly high in the sky and aim at their prey.

**Silkworm:** The silkworm is the larva or caterpillar of the Bombyx mori moth. It is entirely dependent on humans, and it no longer lives in the wild. Silkworms eat mulberry leaves and are native to northern China.

**Owl:** An owl is a nocturnal bird, which means it sleeps during the day and is awake at night. They have eyes on the front of their head. Owls are carnivores. They eat rodents, small and medium-sized mammals, insects, fish, and other birds. Owls can rotate their neck back up to 270 degrees.

**102(D).** Nagaland state does not touch the boundary of Mizoram.

**Mizoram:** Mizoram lies in the northeastern part of India. Its capital city is "Aizawl". The domestic bordering states of Mizoram are Manipur, Assam and Tripura. While the international borders of Mizoram are Bangladesh and Myanmar. Thus, the states around Mizoram are Tripura, Assam and Manipur.

**103(A).** A farmer in Karnataka uses a khunti to make his soil soft.

**Khunti:**

- Khunti is an iron rod to dig the soil, loosen it and make it soft.
- It is called a khurpi in north India.
- In south Indian states, it is called a Khunti.

**104(C).** Iron can be recycled.

Recycling:

- The process of transforming waste resources into new materials and things is known as recycling.
- The ability of a substance to reclaim the qualities it had in its original form determines its recyclability.
- It's a greener alternative to "traditional" garbage disposal that saves resources and reduces greenhouse gas emissions.

- Recycling reduces energy consumption, air pollution (from incineration), and water pollution by preventing the waste of potentially valuable materials and minimising the use of fresh raw resources (from landfilling)
- Recycling is the third component of the "Reduce, Reuse, and Recycle" waste hierarchy and is an important part of modern waste reduction.
- By substituting raw material inputs and moving waste outputs out of the economic system, recycling tries to achieve environmental sustainability.
- A recyclable resource is thus a material that can be used repeatedly after going through a process to make it ready for reuse.
- The process can be induced by humans or occur naturally or spontaneously.
- Examples of recyclable materials: Iron scraps like keys, sheets, kitchen pans or pots or tins etc; aluminium; certain plastics; old newspapers etc.

**105(A).** Vermiculture is the science of raising worms.
- Vermiculture is the scientific process of cultivating worms or artificial rearing of worms to decompose organic food wastes into a nutrient-rich material.
- It is a process of utilization of some species of earthworms to create some kind of vermicompost.

**106(B).** Community is not the main theme of the thematically designed curriculum of EVS at the primary level.
At the primary level, social studies, and social science are taught in an integrated manner as Environmental Studies (EVS) which includes six themes: family and friends, food, shelter, water, travel, things we make and do. The textbook of environmental studies at the primary level is based on these themes which refer to the thematic approach. It is also known as a multi-disciplinary approach where many concepts/topics are being taught in a collective manner.
The primary level students must be taught about their immediate surroundings first (family, school, neighborhood) and then about their wider surroundings (society, community). If we teach them social studies and social science separately, they will not be able to develop the inter-related understanding that is needed to develop an insight over a specified concept which may include various components of the environment. So, in order to develop divergent thinking and to understand each and every component of a particular matter students need to be taught in an integrated manner.

**107(C).** One can describe environment science as a permanent investment in creating a sustainable society.

The teaching-learning of environmental science is just not a study area for primary-stage children but is a training ground for developing environmentally friendly attitudes, values, habits, and behaviors . One can describe environment science as a permanent investment in creating a sustainable society .
Therefore, the scope of environmental science lies in not only helping children explore and understand their environment but also in:
- Developing positive attitudes, values, and practices such as respect and care for all life on earth, compassion, caring for self and others, conservation of natural resources, appreciation of cooperative learning, sense of belonging, social responsibility, valuing culture, etc.
- Generating positive and proactive actions in improving the quality of the environment
- Promoting a conservation ethic and adoption of environment-friendly practices and habits.

**108(D).** All of the above are the objectives of CCE.
CCE, commonly known as continuous and comprehensive evaluation was introduced in 2009 by CBSE as a school-based evaluation sys tem. Continuous means assessment on a regular basis while comprehensive stands for scholastic and co scholastic aspects of evaluation. Continuous and Comprehensive Evaluation aims to evaluate the 'All aspects of the development of the child' as it ensures all-around development of students including cognitive, psychomotor, and affective domains.
Main objectives of CCE :
- Providing scope for learner for self evaluation.
- Teaching and learning should be learner centered.
- Emphasizing continuity and regularity of assessment.
- Enhancing learning through diagnostic and remedial teaching.
- Assessing both scholastic and co-scholastic aspects of a child's growth.
- Laying emphasis on thought processes and de-emphasize memorization.
- Making evaluation an integral part of the teaching-learning process.
- Maintaining desired standard of attainment through detection and correction.

**109(D).** Group discussion on EVS topic can help the learners of EVS in encouraging group work and peer learning.
Group Learning is a learning in which students work collaboratively and involves in active learning. It serves as an important tool to make learning meaningful by working together. In EVS learning, working in groups (or group discussion) is

encouraged because group learning:
- Promotes peer learning.
- Improves social interaction.
- Ensures the participation of all children.
- Boosts brainstorming and critical thinking skills.
- Develops communication and life long learning skills.
- Increases the ability to understand other's perspectives.
- Allows collaboration and cooperation of maximum children.

**110(B).** To make students think 'out of the box', group discussion method is appropriate in EVS.
**Discussion method:** Discussion takes place whenever there is a difference of opinion concerning the situation. It involves an interchange of questions and ideas among the students/peers.
- EVS is a multidisciplinary area of study. Group discussions are effective in breaking 'subject boundaries' related to a problem or a concern. For example, even when the topic of discussion may appear to be a scientific/technical one, like pollution of soil, water and air, the discussion will provide an opportunity to bring in social aspects, economic aspects or even political aspects related to the topic. Thus, group discussions are suitable for EVS.
- In complex socio-economic and environmental scenarios, no single answer seems to satisfy all stakeholder groups. On needs to generate multiple possibilities and think for 'out-of-the-box' solutions. Groups discussions make it possible.
- Different viewpoints to the same concern, based on different beliefs, priorities, culture and context, get generated. Children learn to respect and appreciate diversity.
- Such learning processes develop divergent thinking, reflective thinking, listening abilities and inter-personnel skills among children.
- Helps to bring real-life situations in the classroom.
- Helps to inculcate positive inter-relationships.
- Children do not have the rigidity of subject in their mind. Gradually they will develop subject boundaries from a broad platform of Environmental Studies. Group discussion provides their scope to express their views from a subject free area and gradually get familiarised with the existence of different subject boundaries.

**111(D).** All of the above will help to shape an enabling learning environment for each child in EVS classroom.
How can Environmental Studies help all our children, all those who struggle to go to school, and even all those who still cannot

do so; those for whom the main purpose in life is going to school, as well as those who aspire for a school that can support life, with meaning and dignity? It is up to the teachers and textbook writers to translate this into books, materials and classroom activities, to shape an enabling learning environment for each child, wherever she may be located.

For each thematic area related key concepts, skills and activities have been clearly indicated at appropriate places. However, schools must ensure that these activities or discussions will be conducted because only then can it be ensured that learning will happen. For instance, at several places, the activities indicate that children need to conduct specific observations. We know that even young children's senses are sharp and they are able to detect small differences between fairly similar objects, though not always the similarities.

**112(D).** Statement " To conduct paper-pencil test to assess the performance of children. " is not correct regarding the scope of EVS.

The environment studies make us aware about the importance of the protection and conservation of our mother earth and about the destruction due to the release of pollution into the environment. The scope of environmental studies is very wide.

- Developing an awareness and sensitivity to the total environment and its related problems.
- Motivating people for active participation in environmental protection and improvement.
- To inculcate problem-solving and critical thinking skills.
- Developing skills for active identification and development of solutions to environmental problems.
- Imbibe and inculcate the necessity for the conservation of natural resources.
- To enable the children in gathering and analyzing information.
- Evaluation of environmental programmes in terms of social, economic, ecological, and aesthetic factors.
- To help the children in enrichment and enhancement of their own knowledge.

**EVS deals with many areas like:**
- Conservation of natural resources,
- Ecological aspects
- Pollution of the surrounding natural resources,
- Controlling the pollution,
- Social issues connected to it, and
- Impacts of human population on the environment.

**113(D).** An ideal textbook of EVS should involve a ctivities to connect them with real life.

Environmental Studies is a subject that deals with a human's interaction with the environment. It gives the children a lot of freedom to explore their physical and social surroundings. A good textbook always helps a teacher as a resource.

**The following are the good qualities of an EVS book:**
- Link their daily life experiences and existing knowledge to develop new learning
- Construct meanings of the world around them
- It includes real-life examples that connect their learning not only to facts but also to experience.
- EVS, as a subject does not focus on abstract concepts as the concepts covered in it, are more scientific and concrete.
- EVS as a subject does not just concern physical surroundings but also the social surrounding of an individual therefore it has to cater to different backgrounds from which students come.
- A good textbook contains true stories and incidents to enhance learning.
- Natural and socio-cultural surroundings are in reality integrated. For eg- In certain tribal communities, the forests are considered sacred and worshipped; the wild animals are considered as siblings of the humans.
- A good textbook always keeps the interest of the learner alive
- It provides ample opportunities to explore their knowledge.
- It always discourages rote learning and makes the whole process better by including hands-on-experiences.
- It includes maps, diagrams, charts, which helps them to understand better.

**114(D).** All the above activities are encouraged by a teacher in the constructivist classroom.

**Characteristics of Social constructivist approach:**
- It emphasizes on collaboration with others for learning.
- It ensures active involvement of learners and promotes peer tutoring.
- It involves experimentation, project work, field trips, visuals and class discussions.
- It allows learners to foster their own strategy of learning to perform an activity.
- It views learners as makers of meaning and creators of knowledge through social interaction.

**115(C).** **Class Discussion-** Discussion is one of the widely used group-centered learning techniques. Its value lies chiefly in the fact that it represents a type of intellectual teamwork, resting on the principle that the pooled knowledge, ideas, and feelings of several persons have greater merit than those of a single individual. The strength of the discussion lies in the broad participation of members of the group.

It is a process of thinking together that breaks down if one member or group dominates it. It is the responsibility of the teacher to encourage the more relevant students to participate. It enables students to relate to the topic and express themselves. The skills develop in this process are as follows-
- Listen attentively when others are speaking.
- Be open-minded, respect and accept the contributions of others, but think independently.
- Ask for clarification of ideas and ask for evidence to substantiate ideas/ statements.
- Recognize the problem of semantics in arriving at group decisions or in discussing a controversial issue.

**116(C).** Group discussion is one of the techniques that can facilitate cooperative learning.

Group discussion is one of the techniques that can facilitate cooperative learning among children. Group discussions provide learning opportunities to students in developing analytical and communication skills. As the name says, small group discussions are group exercises used as a teaching strategy to influence learning through the engagement of peer groups.

**117(B).** The teaching-learning process of EVS must not focus on assessing children to provide them with reasonable marks.

**The teaching-learning process of EVS must:**
- Address the individual needs of each child.
- Engage children in various meaningful learning activities.
- Focusing on assessing children to provide them constructive feedback.
- Gathering and analyzing information based on their observations and experiences, and constructing their own knowledge, enriching and enhancing it.
- Begin with the child's immediate environment.
- Sensitize learners towards environmental issues and different people.
- Nurture the curiosity and creativity of the child regarding the natural environment.

**118(B).** In primary level, Environmental Studies is integrated with Social Studies and Science because at early childhood:
- Children look at their environment in a holistic manner .
- Children couldn't compartmentalize any topic into 'science' and 'social science'.
- Children are not mature enough to interpret the aspects of science and social science in a graded manner.

**Integrated approach:**
- EVS in the primary level is visualized as an integrated approach as the EVS syllabus has been made in an integrated manner including science, and social studies as well.
- It helps children to explore and connect to their surroundings.

**119(C).** Problem solving method of teaching is about 'finding the most appropriate way' to achieve the learning objective.

**Problem-solving approach:** Problem-solving is a learner-centered approach that emphasizes learner's active involvement in the learning process. It helps the children to learn better by catering totality of their experiences that occur in the educational process.

Teachers can model different aspects of problem-solving and engage students in activities and discussions around the concept. These are some ways by which teacher help children to become better problem solver-
- By providing multiple potential solutions for any problem
- By giving children a variety of problems to solve and support while solving them.
- By 'do-it-yourself' projects
- By teaching basic problem-solving steps
- By Continous and Comprehensive Evaluation

**120(D).** **Assessment:** Assessment is a vital part of a student's learning environment in school. Assessment is the process of gathering, interpreting, recording, and using information about a learner's responses to an educational task. EVS objectives aim at creating a close bond between a student and her surroundings. Assessment in EVS must serve as an appropriate aid in the creation of this bond.

**Oral tests:**
- The teacher may use oral , written and performance modes to assess child learning .
- She will need to sometimes assess each child individually, but at other times assess groups or assess the whole class together.
- The teacher should not overemphasize any one form of assessment, be it written or oral, or activity-based.
- Such a verse and balanced assessment make assessment comprehensive.

**Some of oral , written, and performance modes-**
- Self-assessment
- Peer assessment
- Cumulative anecdotal records
- Assessment through projects
- Extent and quality of participation

**Teachers' observation and recording:** On different occasions, different types of incidences are noted by the teacher. Such observation s, on each child, get accumulated in the teacher's diary. At the end of the year, different notings for every child make a cumulative anecdotal record for that child.

**Drawing (Maps & Motor Skills):** A student can also access by providing a variety of work within an assignment (e.g., making charts, maps, or flags; drawing pictures; etc.).

## Child Development and Pedagogy

1. In this the child starts to understand the shapes, size, space and figure visualisation. Which type of intelligence is reflected here?
   - (a) Personal-self intelligence
   - (b) Spatial intelligence
   - (c) Naturalistic intelligence
   - (d) None of the above

2. Match column A to column B perfectly. Column A represents the type of intelligence and column B represents the professionals who are gifted with a certain kind of intelligence.

| | A | B |
|---|---|---|
| a) | Body-kinesthetic intelligence | i. Botanist |
| b) | Naturalistic intelligence | i i. Architect |
| c) | Existentialistic intelligence | ii Neurosurgeon / i. |
| d) | Spatial intelligence | i v. Philosophers |

   - (a) a-iii,b-i,c-iv,d-ii
   - (b) a-ii,b-iii,c-iv,d-i
   - (c) a-iii,b-iv,c-ii,d-i
   - (d) a-ii,b-i,c-iv,d-iii

3. Which type of intelligence is added to Gardner's theory of multiple intelligence after the amendment of 2000?
   - (a) Personal-self intelligence
   - (b) Naturalistic intelligence
   - (c) Existentialistic intelligence
   - (d) Body-kinesthetic intelligence

4. According to Sternberg which of the following is not a type of intelligence found in humans?
   - (a) Analytical intelligence
   - (b) Creative intelligence
   - (c) Logical intelligence
   - (d) Practical intelligence

5. In criticism of Guilford's theory who said that it is better to call his theory 'classification of taxonomy', instead of theory?
   - (a) Thurstone
   - (b) Spearman
   - (c) Phares
   - (d) Cattell

6. Which among the following does not show intellectual development in early childhood?
   - (a) Interpretation of logical concepts
   - (b) An increase span of attention
   - (c) Distinction between past, present and future
   - (d) Exploration of environment

7. Who said "intelligent parent will have intelligent children while dull parents will have dull children" in context of heredity?
   - (a) Peterson
   - (b) Godard
   - (c) Dugwell
   - (d) Both (A) and (B)

8. In context of progressive education the appropriate statement among the given below is:
   - (a) Knowledge is generated through direct experience and collaboration.
   - (b) Examination is norm centered and external.
   - (c) Teachers are the originator of information and authority.
   - (d) Education is teacher centered.

9. If Rachna learns from her family about how to be a good daughter, sister, friend, wife and mother. This learning results from the process of:
   - (a) Adaptability
   - (b) Change
   - (c) Maturity
   - (d) Socialisation

10. There are lot of debates all around whether girls and boys have specific set of abilities due to their genetic materials. In this context which among below option is most agreeable?
    - (a) All girls have inherent talent for arts, while boys genetically programmed to be better at aggressive sports.
    - (b) Girls are socialised to be caring, while boys are discouraged to show emotions such as crying.
    - (c) Boys cannot be caring since they are born this way.
    - (d) After puberty, boys and girls cannot play with each other since their interest are completely opposite.

11. In a class individual learners differ from each other in terms of:
    - (a) Sequence of development
    - (b) Principles of growth and

development

(c) General capacity for development

(d) Rate of development

12. **Which among the following not supported the word 'comprehensive' in the scheme of continuous and comprehensive evaluation ?**
   (a) L.L. Thurstone's theory of primary mental abilities
   (b) J.P. Guilford's theory of structure of intellect
   (c) Howard gardener theory of multiple intelligence's
   (d) G. Miller theory of information processing

13. **Which among the following is not a factor affecting language development of a child?**
   (a) Social    (b) Emotion
   (c) Educational    (d) Biological

14. **Suppose a child learns the name of a bird as parrot he/she starts referring to all the birds as parrots. What is this called?**
   (a) Assimilation
   (b) Accommodation
   (c) Schema
   (d) Adaptation

15. **Which among the following are the parameters for measuring the validity of a test?**
   **(A) Construct**
   **(B) Stability**
   **(C) Criterion**
   **(D) Content**
   (a) A, B only
   (b) A, B, C
   (c) A, C, D
   (d) All of the above

16. **According to Piaget's cognitive theory of learning, identify the process among the following by which the cognitive structure is modified.**
   (a) Perception
   (b) Assimilation
   (c) Schema
   (d) Accommodation

17. **According to Kohlberg's moral development model, If a child obeys orders to avoid being scolded by his/her teacher. This depicts the stage of-**
   (a) Reward orientation
   (b) Punishment and obedience orientation

(c) Social contract orientation

(d) Universal ethical principle orientation

18. **According to Vygotsky, 'the relationship between development and learning' summarizes best by which among the following option given below:**
   (a) Development is synonymous with learning
   (b) Development is independent of learning
   (c) Development process lags behind learning process
   (d) Learning and development are parallel process

19. **Government agencies have taken many measures at the institutional level to check out the drop out cases in the government schools. identify an institutional reason for children dropping out of these schools:**
   (a) Teachers do not have appropriate qualifications and are paid lesser salaries.
   (b) Teachers have not been sensitized about the need of treating children well.
   (c) There is no alternative curriculum for children who reject the compulsory curriculum offered.
   (d) Teachers have appropriate qualifications and are paid lesser salaries.

20. **Learners with special educational needs (SEN) does include which among the following?**
   (a) Children belongs to SC and ST families
   (b) Children with locomotor disabilities
   (c) Children's from backward classes
   (d) All of the above

21. **If a child leaves the words unfinished or omitting them when writing sentences then he/she is suffering from:**
   (a) Dyspraxia    (b) Dysgraphia
   (c) Dysclaculia    (d) Dyslexia

22. **Which among the following is correct regarding ability grouping?**
   (a) Ability grouping of student should be encouraged as it promotes competition among students.
   (b) Ability grouping of students should be discouraged as it gives

the message that ability is valued more than effort.

(c) Ability grouping of student should be encouraged as it maximizes learning using special methods.

(d) Both (A) and (C)

23. **Thinking processes in children are not based upon:**
   (a) Manifestation
   (b) Imitation
   (c) Perception
   (d) Logic and reasoning

24. **If a child fails to perform well in the class test leads us to believe that-**
   (a) There is no need to reflect upon the syllabus, pedagogy and assessment process
   (b) Children are born with certain capabilities and deficits
   (c) There is a need to reflect upon the syllabus, pedagogy and assessment processes
   (d) Some children are deemed to fail irrespective of how hard the system tries

25. **Kavya engages her students in a number of group activities such as group discussion projects, role plays, etc. The learning dimension highlighted by Kavya is-**
   (a) Competition-based learning
   (b) Learning as social activity
   (c) Language-guided learning
   (d) Learning through recreation

26. **In context of learning theories scaffolding refers to which among the following?**
   (a) Ascertaining the causes of mistakes committed by students
   (b) Simulation teaching
   (c) Temporary support in learning by adults
   (d) Recapitulation of previous learning

27. **According to Aristotle Emotional catharsis is:**
   (a) Feeling highly depressed
   (b) Bringing out emotional repression
   (c) Increasing the ability to tolerate emotional repression
   (d) Suppression of emotions

28. **How a teacher can enhance the learning as per the context of motivation theories?**
   (a) By setting uniform standards of expectation

(b) By not having any expectation from students

(c) By setting extremely high expectation from students

(d) By setting realistic expectations from students

29. **Which among the following is not a personal factor influencing learning?**

(a) Sensation or perception

(b) Needs

(c) Cultural demands

(d) Emotional conditions

30. **Which among the following is an autocratic strategy of teaching?**

(a) Heuristic method

(b) Discovery method

(c) Brain storming method

(d) Demonstration method

## Language - I : English

31. **Direction** : Read the passage given below and answer the question that follow by selecting the most appropriate option.

One day in 1924, five men who were camping in the Cascade Mountains of Washington saw a group of huge apelike creatures coming out of the woods. They hurried back to their cabin and locked themselves inside. While they were in, the creatures attacked them by throwing rocks against the walls of the cabin. After several hours, these strange hairy giants went back into the woods. After this incident the men returned to the town and told the people of their adventure. However, only a few people accepted their story. These were the people who remembered hearing tales about footprints of an animal that walked like a human being. The five men, however, were not the first people to have seen these creatures called Bigfoot. Long before their experience, local Native Americans were certain that a race of apelike animals had been living in the neighboring mountain for centuries. They called these creatures Sasquatch. In 1958, workmen, who were building a road through the jungles of Northern California often found huge footprints in the earth around their camp. Then in 1967, Roger Patterson, a man who was interested in finding Bigfoot went into the northern California jungles with a friend. While riding, they were suddenly thrown off from their horses. Patterson saw a tall apelike animal standing not far away. He

managed to shoot seven rolls of film of the hairy creature before the animal disappeared in the hushes. When Patterson's film was shown to the public, not many people believed his story. In another incident, Richard Brown, a music teacher and also an experience hunter spotted a similar creature. He saw the animal clearly through the telescopic lens of his rifle. He said the creature looked more like a human than an animal. Later many other people also found deep footprints in the same area. In spite of regular reports of sightings and footprints, most experts still do not believe that Bigfoot really exists.

**What did the five campers do when they saw a group of apelike creatures?**

(a) They ran into the woods and hid there for several hours.

(b) They quickly ran back into their cabin and locked the cabin door.

(c) They threw rocks against the walls of their cabin to frighten the creatures away.

(d) They attacked the creatures by throwing rocks at them.

**Ques (32-39): Direction:** Read the passage given below and answer the question that follow by selecting the most appropriate option.

One day in 1924, five men who were camping in the Cascade Mountains of Washington saw a group of huge apelike creatures coming out of the woods. They hurried back to their cabin and locked themselves inside. While they were in, the creatures attacked them by throwing rocks against the walls of the cabin. After several hours, these strange hairy giants went back into the woods. After this incident the men returned to the town and told the people of their adventure. However, only a few people accepted their story. These were the people who remembered hearing tales about footprints of an animal that walked like a human being. The five men, however, were not the first people to have seen these creatures called Bigfoot. Long before their experience, local Native Americans were certain that a race of apelike animals had been living in the neighboring mountain for centuries. They called these creatures Sasquatch. In 1958, workmen, who were building a road through the jungles of Northern California often found huge footprints in the earth around their camp. Then in 1967, Roger Patterson, a man who was interested in finding Bigfoot went into the northern California jungles with a friend. While riding, they were suddenly thrown off from their horses. Patterson saw a tall apelike animal standing not far away. He

managed to shoot seven rolls of film of the hairy creature before the animal disappeared in the hushes. When Patterson's film was shown to the public, not many people believed his story. In another incident, Richard Brown, a music teacher and also an experience hunter spotted a similar creature. He saw the animal clearly through the telescopic lens of his rifle. He said the creature looked more like a human than an animal. Later many other people also found deep footprints in the same area. In spite of regular reports of sightings and footprints, most experts still do not believe that Bigfoot really exists.

32. **Did the town people believe the story of the five men about their meeting with Bigfoot ?**

(a) No, not everyone believed their story.

(b) Only those who had heard the same tale the second time believed them

(c) Some said the five men were making up their own story.

(d) All the people believed what they said..

33. **Who were the first people to have seen these apelike creatures before the five campers?**

(a) The workers who built the road in the jungles of Northern California.

(b) Roger Patterson and his friend.

(c) The local Native Americans.

(d) Richard Brown, a music teacher and a hunter.

34. **The word neighbouring would BEST be replaced with**

(a) Far-off          (b) Nearby

(c) Remote          (d) Far-away

35. **Who gave the name 'Sasquatch' to the apelike creatures?**

(a) The five campers

(b) Roger Patterson

(c) The local Native Americans

(d) Richard Brown

36. **Which of the following pairs is INCORRECT ?**

(a) Creatures -- animals

(b) Woods -- jungles

(c) Spotted -- saw

(d) Huge -- hairy

37. **The BEST title for this passage would be**

(a) The adventures of the five campers.

(b) The experts and the existence of Bigfoot.

(c)   The creature called Bigfoot.

(d)   The adventures of Bigfoot.

**38.  Who has seen the telescopic lens?**

(a)   Roger Patterson

(b)   Richard Brown

(c)   The five adventures men

(d)   Robert Brown

**39.  How many photo shot had been taken by Roger Patterson of hairy creature?**

(a)   Four        (b)   Five

(c)   Six         (d)   Seven

**Ques (40-45): Direction :** Read the given poetry and answer the question that follow by selecting the most appropriate option.

Weavers, weaving at break of day,
Why do you weave a garment so gay?
Blue as the wing of a bluebird wild,
We weave the robes of a new-born child.
Weavers, weaving at fall of night,
Why do you weave a garment so bright?
Like the plumes of a peacock, purple and green,
We weave the marriage-veils of a queen.
Weavers, weaving solemn and still,
What do you weave in the moonlight chill?
White as a feather and white as a cloud,
We weave a dead man's funeral shroud.

**40.  What do the weavers weave in the early morning?**

(a)   A dull grey cloth

(b)   A bright blue cloth

(c)   A soft white cloth

(d)   A red coloured veil

**41.  The _______ is purple and green coloured.**

(a)   The queen's marriage veil

(b)   The robe of a king

(c)   Dress of the weavers

(d)   Dress of a newborn child

**42.  Whom does the poet address in the poem?**

(a)   Weavers      (b)   Queens

(c)   Children     (d)   All the above

**43.  What do the weavers weave in the chilly moonlight?**

(a)   A garment to wrap a newborn child in

(b)   A garment to keep away the chill

(c)   A garment light as a feather

(d)   A garment meant to cover a dead man

**44.  The three stages of life mentioned in the poem are**

(a)   Infancy, childhood and senility

(b)   Infancy, youth and death

(c)   Infancy, adolescence, middle age

(d)   Childhood,   adulthood   and senility

**45.  What is the synonym of the word 'solemn'?**

(a)   Deliberate    (b)   Excited

(c)   Cheerful      (d)   Trivial

**46.  Which of the following should be the characteristic of the textbooks included in the curriculum?**

(a)   The   introduction   at   the beginning and conclusion at the end of the chapter should be given in the textbook.

(b)   It should be content oriented

(c)   A standardized language should be used

(d)   All of the above

**47.  Grammar-translation method of teaching English heavily relies on :**

(a)   form-focussed teaching

(b)   meaning-focussed teaching

(c)   direct teaching as a strategy for learning

(d)   language use as the main focus

**48.  Which one of the following is not accepted in association with multimedia and its pedagogical strengths?**

(a)   It helps in problem solving by means of learning by doing.

(b)   It facilitates individualized and cooperative learning.

(c)   It proves to be time consuming and not so effective for slow learners.

(d)   It facilitates mastering basic skills of a student by means of drill and practice.

**49.  Which of the following programme helps students to reinforce their knowledge and develop their communication and co-operation skill as well as good interpersonal relation?**

(a)   Reward scheme

(b)   Handling   pupils   language acquisition problems

(c)   Peer support programme

(d)   None of these

**50.  What are the things that as a teacher should follow before, during or after the parent teacher meeting?**

(a)   Start the meeting by showing that you care and know something positive about their child.

(b)   Do use materials from the student's work folder.

(c)   Do use clear and descriptive terms.

(d)   All of these

**51.  Direction: Answer the following question by selecting the correct/ most appropriate option.**
When a child learns a language naturally, without much practice, it is called

(a)   Language adaptation

(b)   Language learning

(c)   Language acquisition

(d)   Language generalization

**52.  Direction: Answer the following question by selecting the most appropriate option :**
The study of 'chunks of language' which are bigger than a single sentence is :

(a)   Discourse     (b)   Morphology

(c)   Syntax        (d)   Semantics

**53.  A teacher asks the questions in the class to:**

(a)   Keep students busy

(b)   Attract student's attention

(c)   Maintain discipline

(d)   For curriculum

**54.  Micro teaching focuses on the competency over**

(a)   Methods

(b)   Skills

(c)   Contents

(d)   None of these

**55.  Why oral composition is useful in development of child.**

(a)   It provides fluency in language

(b)   It correct grammar

(c)   It build self confidence

(d)   All of the above

**56.  What is the importance of reading?**

(a)   It increase vocabulary

(b)   It makes pupil knowledge

(c)   It helps in getting information

(d)   All of the above

**57.  What is the usage of language laboratory**

(a)   It   makes   education   child centered

(b)   It reduce the burdon on the teacher

(c)   It provides mass education

(d)   The student can hear his own mistake for himself

**58.  Direction : Answer the following question by selecting the most appropriate option.**

The material on opaque sheet is projected with the help of _____ hardware.

(a) Episcope

(b) Audio player

(c) Video cassette player

(d) Board, charts and graphs

59. **Direction: Answer the following question by selecting the most appropriate option.**
_ is the backbone of learning a language.

(a) Listening skill

(b) Speaking skill

(c) Reading skill

(d) Writing skill

60. **Direction: Answer the following question by selecting the most appropriate option.**
Evaluation covers _____ domains of behavior.

(a) Four   (b) Three

(c) Two    (d) Five

## Mathematics

61. **What will be the mode of numbers:**
$5, 7, 9, 12, 10, 15, 7, 8, 7, 25$?

(a) 5    (b) 7

(c) 9    (d) 12

62. **The mean, mode and median of**
$6, 15, 50, 120, 80, 100, 15, 10, 10, 8, 15$.

(a) $39, 15, 17$    (b) $15, 15, 39$

(c) $39, 15, 15$    (d) $37, 15, 15$

63. **A train leaves a station at $6 : 14$ a.m. and reaches its destination after $13$ hours $48$ minutes. The time at the destination is:**

(a) $7 : 12$ p.m.    (b) $8 : 02$ p.m.

(c) $7 : 02$ p.m.    (d) $8 : 12$ p.m.

64. **Length of each side of a rhombus is 13 cm and one of the diagonal is 24 cm. What is the area (in cm$^2$) of the rhombus?**

(a) 60    (b) 120

(c) 300    (d) 240

65. **On subtracting $8$ metric tonne (mt) $50$ kilogram from $12$ metric tonne $8$ quintals we get:**

(a) 3 mt 8 quintal

(b) 4 mt 7 quintal 50 kilogram

(c) 4 mt 8 quintal 50 kilogram

(d) 3 mt 8 quintal 50 kilogram

66. **Look carefully for the pattern, and then choose which pair of numbers comes next.**
**13 29 15 26 17 23 19**

(a) 21 23    (b) 20 21

(c) 20 17    (d) 25 27

67. **The area of a rectangular sheet is $480$ cm$^2$. If its width is $12$ cm, then the perimeter of the sheet will be:**

(a) 105 cm    (b) 94 cm

(c) 160 cm    (d) 104 cm

68. **The product of two numbers is $48$. The sum of their squares is $100$. Find the sum of these two numbers.**

(a) 14    (b) 16

(c) 19    (d) 24

69. $1.66 \times 1.66 + 0.66 \times 0.66 - 1.32 \times 1.66$
**is equal to:**

(a) $0.1$    (b) 1

(c) 10    (d) 101

70. **What is the area (in $sqcm$) of a rhombus if the lengths of its diagonals are $25cm$ and $20cm$?**

(a) 500    (b) 250

(c) 125    (d) 200

71. **A 7 year old boy recognizes all four sided regular figures as squares. According to Van Hiele's, he is at which stage of geometrical thinking?**

(a) Level 4-Deduction

(b) Level 3-Informal deduction

(c) Level 2-Analysis

(d) Level 1-Visualization

72. **A teacher makes a teaching method more effective by using devices known as _______.**

(a) Technique of teaching

(b) Principle of teaching

(c) Methodology of teaching

(d) Aim of teaching

73. **Direction : Match List- 1 with List- 2 and select the correct answer using the codes given below the lists.**

|    | List- 1 |    | List- 2 |
|----|---------|----|---------|
| P. | Deductive method | 1. | B.F Skinner |
| Q. | Inductive method | 2. | Aristotle |
| R. | Project method | 3. | David Hume |
| S. | Auto-instructional teaching | 4. | William Heard Kilpatrick |

(a) P-3; Q-2; R-4; S-1

(b) P-2; Q-3; R-4; S-1

(c) P-4; Q-3; R-2; S-1

(d) P-2; Q-4; R-1; S-3

74. **To decide whether a two digit number is divisible by 3, add the two digit number. If the sum of the digit is multiple of 3. This is an example of a/an:**

(a) Rational    (b) Relational

(c) Algorithm    (d) Prototype

75. **In Diagnostic test in Mathematics, both background and performance of the students is needed for helping them in:**

(a) Getting first position in the class

(b) Crack competitive exam like JEE, NEET etc

(c) Acquisition of intellectual habits and enhances learning

(d) Become a politician

76. **Which one of the following is not a principle of helping pupils with learning difficulties in Mathematics?**

(a) Devise various learning activities related to mathematics

(b) Design meaningful learning situations

(c) Teacher provides home tuitions in mathematics

(d) Teaching preparations

77. **What can not be a perfect step to conduct error analysis?**

(a) Interview the students by asking him/her to explain how he/she solved the problem.

(b) Record all the responses made by the students.

(c) Always analyse the responses made by the learners.

(d) None of these

78. **What are the objectives that makes the inclusion of mathematics in the curriculum prominent?**

(a) To prepare for the future vocation or occupation.

(b) To develop their intellectual powers and discipline.

(c) Both (A) and (B)

(d) None of these

79. **Sequence the following tasks as they are taken up while developing the concept of measurement:**
a. Learners use standard units to measure length.
b. Learners use non-standard units to measure length.
c. Learners verify objects using simple observation.
d. Learners understand the relationship between metric units.

(a) a, b, d, c    (b) b, a, c, d

(c) c, b, a, d    (d) d, a, c, b

80. **Which of the following is the**

organization of **Remedial teaching in Mathematics?**

(a) Tutorial teaching

(b) Auto-instructional teaching

(c) Informal teaching

(d) All of these

**81.** In an exercise, the question was-Measure the lengths of the line segments

P•———•Q and R•———•S

The child answered
length of AB = 5 cm
length of AB = 3 cm
This refers to

(a) Conceptual error

(b) Procedural error

(c) Error due to habit of naming line segment as AB

(d) Reading error

**82.** According to NCF 2005, school Mathematics takes place in a situation where:

(a) Mathematics is part of children's life experience.

(b) Children are forced to learn all concepts by daily practice.

(c) Children are listeners and the teacher is an active narrator.

(d) Children are involved in chorus drill of formulae and pressure of performance in examination.

**83.** Kumar belongs to a very poor and conservative family, what teacher can do to help him?

(a) A special school and classes may be opened for him

(b) Special training may be given to the teacher

(c) He should be treated as a normal pupil

(d) He should be sympathized

**84.** What are the steps of the construction of diagnostic test?
1) Analyse the content into subtopics and its elements.
2) Formulate the objectives and outline of the content.
3) Identify the difficulties in the orders and subtopics, prepare the final draft of the test.
4) Remedial devices and measures.
5) Prepare manual of test.

(a) 2, 1, 3, 5, 4      (b) 4, 3, 5, 2, 1

(c) 2, 1, 4, 5, 3      (d) 2, 3, 4, 5, 1

**85.** Twice the age of $X$ is thrice the age of $Y$. 8 years back, the difference between the ages of $X$ and $Y$ was 8 years. What is the present age of $X$ ?

(a) 24      (b) 54

(c) 56      (d) 91

**86.** If the fractions $\frac{7}{13}, \frac{2}{3}, \frac{4}{11}, \frac{5}{9}$ are arranged in ascending order, then the correct sequence is:

(a) $\frac{2}{3}, \frac{7}{13}, \frac{4}{11}, \frac{5}{9}$

(b) $\frac{7}{13}, \frac{4}{11}, \frac{5}{9}, \frac{2}{3}$

(c) $\frac{4}{11}, \frac{7}{13}, \frac{5}{9}, \frac{2}{3}$

(d) $\frac{5}{9}, \frac{4}{11}, \frac{7}{13}, \frac{2}{3}$

**87.** Two bikers $A$ and $B$ start at same time and ride at $75\,km/hr$ and $60\,km/hr$ respectively towards each other. They meet after 20 minutes. How far (in $km$ ) were they from each other when they started?

(a) 60      (b) 45

(c) 30      (d) 15

**88.** 2 cubes each of volume $64\,cm^3$ are joined end to end. Find the surface area of the resulting cuboid.

(a) $128\,cm^3$

(b) $130\,cm^3$

(c) $160\,cm^3$

(d) None of these

**89.** A closed wooden rectangular box made of 1 cm thick wood has the following outer dimensions: length 22 cm, breadth 17 cm, and height 12 cm. It is filled with cement. What is the volume of the cement in the box?

(a) 1488 cu. cm      (b) 3000 cu. cm

(c) 4488 cu. cm      (d) 2880 cu. cm

**90.** The speed of a bus is 54 km/hr excluding stoppage and 45 km/hr including stoppages. For how many minutes does the bus stop per hour?

(a) 12 min      (b) 10 min

(c) 8 min      (d) 6 min

## Environmental Studies

**91.** The term **Golden Quadrilateral** refers to:

(a) The road connects Delhi-Mumbai, Kolkata and Chennai

(b) Road connects the capital cities of different state and important cities

(c) These roads are present in border areas

(d) None of the above

**92.** Identify the bird who makes its nest on the top of tree with grass and lays its eggs between stones.

(a) Barbet      (b) Weaver bird

(c) Indian Robin  (d) Dove

**93.** Which among them is the form of learning in which a child learn to organize information and fact about anything in logical structure?

(a) Appreciative learning

(b) Associative learning

(c) Conceptual learning

(d) Perceptual learning

**94.** Identify the problems in EVS teaching which are not related to lack of resources?

(a) Lack of experienced teachers

(b) Problems related to environmental education syllabus

(c) EVS is closely related to science

(d) Difficulty in making use of public resources

**95.** Which of the following has the largest brain in proportion to its body size?

(a) Ant

(b) Elephant

(c) Dolphin

(d) Human Being

**96.** When did The Indian Forest Act 1927, come into force?

(a) 01 April 1927

(b) 01 March 1927

(c) 21 September 1927

(d) 23 April 1927

**97.** The region where farmers specialize in vegetables only, this type of farming is known as:

(a) Cooperative farming

(b) Mixed farming

(c) Truck farming

(d) Collective farming

**98.** The first pico satellite of India is:

(a) INSAT      (b) STUDSAT

(c) GSAT-4      (d) ANUSAT

**99.** Which of the following is called vaccinia in Latin?

(a) Cowpox      (b) AIDS

(c) Smallpox      (d) Malaria

**100.** Which of the following plant follows both autotrophic and heterotrophic modes of nutrition?

(a) Insectivorous

(b) Algae

(c) Fungi

(d) Parasites

**101.** 'Dhokla' is a delicacy of which state of India?

(a) Gujarat  (b) Odisha
(c) Karnataka  (d) Maharashtra

**102. Which type of fertilizer is useful for gardening?**
(a) Urea
(b) Sodium phosphate
(c) DAP
(d) Vermi Compost

**103. What does the sum total of the population of the same kind of organisms known as?**
(a) Kingdom  (b) Class
(c) Phylum  (d) Species

**104. Combustion that takes place at high speed is called______.**
(a) Spontaneous burning
(b) Explosion
(c) Incomplete burning
(d) Rapid combustion

**105. Which of the following is a plantation type of crop?**
(a) Ground nut  (b) Tea
(c) Fodder  (d) Sugarcane

**106. Which of the following rivers does not originate in India?**
(a) Ganga
(b) Yamuna
(c) Brahmaputra
(d) Godavari

**107. Khadins, Bundhis, Ahars and Kattas are ancient structures that are examples for:**
(a) Soil conservation
(b) Wood storage
(c) Grain storage
(d) Water harvesting

**108. Insects responsible for transmitting diseases are called:**
(a) Vector  (b) Drones
(c) Transmitter  (d) Conductor

**109. Which of the following is a subtheme under the theme suggested in the EVS syllabus?**
(a) Family and Friends
(b) Food
(c) Animals
(d) Things we make and do

**110. The nature of environmental studies does not advocate that:**
(a) Children make fewer mistakes
(b) Children get space to learn by doing
(c) Children ask a lot of questions
(d) Children get a lot of space to explore

**111. A good assignment in EVS should primarily aim at:**
(a) Revise the lesson for effective learning.
(b) Ensure better utilization of time.
(c) Keep the students engaged and disciplined.
(d) Provide extended learning opportunities.

**112. Supreme Court was directed in the judgment given in 1991, to make the subject _____ compulsory in the college curricula.**
(a) women study
(b) environmental study
(c) information technology
(d) value education

**113. International Environmental Education Programme (IEEP) has been launched by:**
(a) UNESCO  (b) ILO
(c) UNICEF  (d) UNO

**114. Which of the following principle of learning is followed in EVS?**
(a) Global to local
(b) Abstract to concrete
(c) Unknown to known
(d) Known to unknown

**115. Which subject is not included in social science at the upper primary level?**
(a) Philosophy
(b) Political Science
(c) Geography
(d) History

**116. Which of the following activity/ activities can be given to the students to teach about 'cultural diversity in India'?**
I. Asking one student to read about cultural diversity in the class.
II. Asking the students to list the different cultures of India and write their features.
III. Asking students to write about the different dimensions of cultures of India and prepare a chart on it.
(a) Only I
(b) I, II and III
(c) Both II and III
(d) Only III

**117. New knowledge is acquired through:**
(a) Transmission of knowledge
(b) Memorization
(c) Experience and searching new meanings
(d) None of the above

**118. What is the standard time duration of a micro-teaching cycle?**
(a) 06 Min  (b) 12 Min
(c) 24 Min  (d) 36 Min

**119. Milk turns into curds faster in summer because:**
(a) The growth of bacteria increases with the increase in temperature
(b) The growth of bacteria increases with the decrease in temperature
(c) The growth of bacteria decreases when the temperature remains normal
(d) The temperature will have no effect on the growth of bacteria

**120. In rural areas, cow dung is used to coat the floors and walls of huts to __________.**
(a) to smooth them
(b) to thicken them for friction
(c) to give a natural color to walls and floors
(d) keep insects away

**// Hints and Solutions //**

**1(B).** In "Spatial intelligence" child starts to understand the shapes, size, space and figure visualisation.
Spatial intelligence is the concept of being able to successfully perceive and derive insight from visual data . This cognitive process is known as an aptitude for understanding visual information in the real and abstract word as well as an innate ability to envision information.

**2(A).** Body-kinesthetic Intelligence : In this type of intelligence person learns to control his/her physical activities perfectly and skillfully.
**Naturalistic Intelligence :** According to Gardner in naturalistic intelligence a person knows well how to observe and utilize the patterns and symmetry present in the nature.
**Existentialistic Intelligence :** With this type of intelligence the person develops the curiosity to know and question the facts related to human life and existence.
**Spatial Intelligence:** In this type of intelligence the person develops the ability to deal with the figures, shapes, structures, etc.

**3(C).** Initially Gardner propounded 7 types of intelligence. Later in 1998 and 2000 he added 8th and 9th type of intelligence i.e., Naturalistic intelligence, Existentialistic intelligence respectively. Existential intelligence involves an individual's ability to use collective values and intuition to understand others and the world around them . People who excel in this intelligence typically are able to see the big picture.

**4(C).** According to Sternberg " Logical intelligence " is not a type of intelligence found in humans.
According to Sternberg there are three types of intelligence found in humans, which are : Analytical intelligence, Creative intelligence and Practical intelligence. Being practical means you find solutions that work in your everyday life by applying knowledge based on your experiences. Analytical intelligence is closely aligned with academic problem solving and computations. Creative intelligence is marked by inventing or imagining a solution to a problem or situation.

**5(C).** In 1984, while criticising Guilford's theory Phares said that instead of being called as a theory, Guilford's theory should be called as a system of classification of taxonomy.
Guilford's Structure of Intellect (SOI) Model is a multiple intelligences theory . He believed that intelligence wasn't a monolithic, global attribute but a combination of multiple abilities, that were relatively independent. He applied the factor analytical method to learn these mental abilities.

**6(A).** " Interpretation of logical concepts " does not show intellectual development in early childhood.
In the early childhood phase, a child acquires only basic communication skills, such as speaking, reading, listening and writing. Around this age a child does not develop the capacity of reasoning, problem solving and thinking.
Early childhood generally refers to the period from birth through age 5. A child's cognitive development during early childhood, which includes building skills such as a pre-reading, language, vocabulary, and numeracy, begins from this moment a child is born.

**7(B).** Both Peterson and Godard said "intelligent parent will have intelligent children while dull parents will have dull children" in context of heredity.
As per Godard specific genetic traits are responsible for intelligence of a child and associate IQ levels of parents and siblings. The ability of effective learning, analysis and decision making capacity develops from the level of intelligence that a child inherits.
As per Peterson, heredity may be defined as "what one gets from his ancestral stock through his parents".

**8(A).** Progressive education focuses on learning that is both experiential and collaborative.
Some of the progressive educations qualities are:-
- Emphasis on learning by doing
- Integrated curriculum focused on thematic units
- Strong emphasis on problem solving and critical thinking
- Group work and development of social skills
- Collaborative and cooperative learning projects
- Education for social responsibility and democracy
- Emphasis of lifelong process and social skills

**9(D).** If Rachna learns from her family about how to be a good daughter, sister, friend, wife and mother. This learning results from the process of socialisation.
Socialisation is a life long process of inheriting norms, customs and philosophies from prevailing environment . It provides an individual with the necessary skills and habits that help him/her get accustomed to the given social environment.

**10(B).** Girls are socialised to be caring while boys are discouraged to show emotions such as crying, is a gender-biased thought of the society. Girls are considered to be more caring as they are quick in showing emotions than boys who are not expected to act emotionally in front of others.

**11(D).** In a class individual learners differ from each other in terms of rate of development.
The rate of development of an individual child is different from that of another child. This principle is known as the 'principle of individual differences'. For instance, some children may learn to walk in 8 months, while some may take more than a year to start walking.
It is important for teachers to know variables such as physical characteristics, intelligence, perception, gender, ability, learning styles, which are individual differences of learners. An effective and productive learning-teaching process can be planned by considering these individual differences of students.

**12(D).** The word 'comprehensive' in the scheme of continuous and comprehensive evaluation (C.C.E) is not supported by the theory of information processing. This theory is actually based on computer analogy.
Continuous and comprehensive evaluation was a process of assessment, mandated by the Right to Education Act, of India. The main aim of C.C.E is to evaluate every aspect of the child during their presence at school.

**13(B).** " Emotion " is not a factor affecting language development of a child.
The three factors which affects the language of a child are -
Social - a child's development directly depends on its social interactions with its parents, siblings, peers and caretakers the socio economic conditions also affects the language development of a child, poor socio-economic background speak much lesser number of words than children from professional families.
Educational - language development is boosted by correct exposure to reading and listening to correct language being spoken. Attending school exposes a child to a variety of learning experiences.
Biological - some children are slow in language and speech development is due to a biological problem like autism (mental defect making communication slow), cleft lip/palate (from birth), attention deficit hyperactivity disorder (ADHD- a brain defect), brain injury during birth etc.

**14(A).** Suppose a child learns the name of a bird as parrot he/she starts referring to all the birds as parrots. It is this called " Assimilation ".
In assimilation, new information is incorporated in the existing ideas. Our mentally guided behaviors or schemas, are modified as we take in more new information or experiences.
Assimilation is a cognitive process that manages how we take in new information and incorporate that new information into our existing knowledge.

**15(C).** To have confidence that a test is valid, and thus the inferences we make based on the test scores are valid, three kinds of validity evidence are:
**Construct** - It is the extent to which the content of the test matches the instructional objectives.
**Criterion** - It is the extent to which scores on the test are in agreement with or predict an external criterion.
**Content** - It is the extent to which an assessment corresponds to other variables, as predicted by some rationale or theory.

**16(D).** According to Piaget's cognitive theory of learning, identify the process among the following by " Accommodation " the cognitive structure is modified.
There is accommodation when a child either modifies an existing schema or forms an entirely new schema to deal with a new object or event. This concept was developed by Jean Piaget, a Swiss developmental psychologist who is best known for this theory of cognitive development in children.

**17(B).** According to Kohlberg's moral development model, If a child obeys orders to avoid being scolded by his/her teacher. This depicts the stage of " Punishment and obedience orientation ".

The theory of moral development that in the first stage in the preconventional level, a child will make moral decisions based on rules from an authority figure. Such obedience is simply to avoid punishment. When a child does an action, not because of their conscious decision about it, but simply to avoid punishment for not doing it, that is an example of punishment and obedience orientation.

**18(C).** "Development process lags behind learning process" best summarizes the relationship between development and learning as proposed by Vygotsky.

According to Vygotsky, learning is a process that occurs anytime in everyday life and that isn't just an external phenomenon. His theory of Zone of Proximal Development (ZPD) expanded learning and development, which posits that learning precedes development processes.

- Development: It refers to a progressive and systematic series of changes that occur in the life of an individual he/she grows from infancy to old age.
- Learning: The process by which a person alters his responses and behavior in order to adjust himself to the changing environment is called learning.

**19(C).** Children dropout from school because they feel disconnected from their teachers and peers. As a measure against this issue, schools need to increase and diversify their resources to meet the complex academic and emotional needs of such children.

The cause of dropout from school is solely due to cultural disadvantaged characteristics of low cast and rural background. Other reasons for dropouts:
- Poverty, accessibility and availability
- The school and teachers
- Lack of interest
- Excessive academic pressure from school and parents
- Frequent change of school
- Bullying
- Constant failure
- To support family
- Delinquency
- Education not considered necessary
- The community they belong to

**20(D).** Learners with special educational needs (SEN) does include children belongs to SC and ST families, children with locomotor disabilities and children's from backward classes.

Education of learners with special needs (SEN) is a powerful instrument of social change, and often initiates upward movement in the social structure, thereby helping to bridge the gap between different sections of society. However, much still needs to be done, as studies in government schools have shown that in the classroom, such disadvantaged and deprived children are subject to various form of discrimination and humiliation, both by the teachers and the other students, which severely affects their self respect and self confidence.

**21(B).** If a child leaves the words unfinished or omitting them when writing sentences then he/she is suffering from Dysgraphia.

This disorder may cause learner to be tense and awkward when holding a pen or pencil, and even twist its body. Such learners have very poor handwriting and they are not able to improve. Learners with Dysgraphia often show other condition. These may include:
- A strong dislike of writing and drawing
- Problems with grammar
- A quick loss of energy and interest while writing
- Trouble writing down thoughts in a logical sequence
- Saying words out loud while writing

**22(B).** Sorting of students according to their talents in a classroom is ability grouping. It should be discouraged as it gives the message that ability is of more value than effort.

Ability grouping is the practice of placing student of similar academic ability level within the same age group for instruction as opposed to placement on age and grade level. Ability grouping can be implemented in regular and special education classrooms. Groups are typically small, consisting of ten and fewer students.

**23(C).** Thinking processes in children are not based upon perceptions.

Manifestation- When children observe objects and situations in their physical and psychological environment, they increase their knowledge and develop thinking.

Imitation- When children observe others taking some actions and the result of such actions, they try to imitate the same and increase their power accordingly.

Logic and reasoning- This is the highest level of thinking and it develops as the child's language develops. Children follow two kinds of reasoning: deductive and inductive.

**24(C).** If a child fails to perform well in the class test leads us to believe that t here is a need to reflect upon the syllabus, pedagogy and assessment processes.

The failure of a child is also the failure of the syllabus pedagogy and assessment. So we need to reflect upon all these points before making any judgment about the students.

To avoid failure or to tackle it when it looks likely, both parents and teachers must get involved. They can do this by involvement of parents, skill development, increase in the motivation.

**25(B).** Kavya engages her students in a number of group activities such as group discussion projects, role plays, etc. The learning dimension highlighted by Kavya is " Learning as social activity ".

Socialisation plays an important role in learning. Doing activities that include tasks based on discussion or interaction with others will boost social learning. Social learning develops the feeling of cooperation among the students.

**26(C).** In context of learning theories scaffolding refers to temporary support in learning by adults.

In the scaffolding process, students are given the needed support while learning something new. Thus, they stand a better chance of independently using that knowledge. Psychologist and instructional designer Jerome Bruner first used the term 'scaffolding'. The theory is that when students are given the support they need while learning something new, they stand a better chance of using that knowledge independently.

**27(B).** According to Aristotle Emotional catharsis is bringing out emotional repression.

Aristotle describes the catharsis as the purging of the emotions of pity and fear that are aroused in the viewer of a tragedy. The concept is linked to the positive social function of tragedy by Aristotle. Catharsis is the process of venting aggression as a way to release or get rid of emotions in general terms.

**28(D).** According to the theories of motivation, a teacher can enhance learning by setting realistic expectation from students. This is because a teacher's expectation have a strong effect on the performance of his/her students. The expectation of a teacher from his/her students works as a motivational force for them which in turns results of better performance.

**29(C).** Cultural demand is an environmental factor influencing the learning.

Learning-centred education focuses on the learning process. Although its primary concern is on the learning of the students, all those involved in the education of students such as teachers are also co-learners with the students in the learning-centred education. It is basically learner-centred but includes teachers in the process of learning in a classroom situation. Learner-related factors affecting learning are:

Following are the factors affecting individual learning:
- Physical health
- Sensation or perception
- Needs
- Emotional conditions

- Mental health
- Willingness to learn
- Learning time
- Readiness to learn
- Student's basic ability
- Intelligence level
- Interest
- Motivation level

**30(D).** Demonstration method- it is the autocratic strategy of teaching. Teacher shows all the activities given in a lesson to the students as an action and explains the important points before them during demonstration. It is a teaching method used in technical and training colleges and in teacher education. This strategy focuses to achieve psychomotor and cognitive objectives.

Heuristic method- it is a democratic strategy of teaching. Students learn themselves as teachers raise problem before the students and ask them to discover the answer.

Discovery method- this method is used in social science to clarify the facts and concepts. This is democratic style of teaching.

Brain storming- a problem is given to the students and they are asked to put forward their views one by one, conclusion is drawn after evaluating their jumbled ideas.

**31(B).** Five men who were camping in the Cascade Mountains of Washington saw a group of huge apelike creatures coming out of the woods. They hurried back to their cabin and locked themselves inside.

**32(A).** After the incident when five men saw the big foots they returned to the town and told the people of their adventure. However, only a few people accepted their story.

**33(C).** The local native Americans were the first people to have seen these apelike creatures before the five campers.
Then in 1967, Roger Patterson, a man who was interested in finding Bigfoot went into the northern California jungles with a friend. While riding, they were suddenly thrown off from their horses. Patterson saw a tall apelike animal standing not far away. Therefore the first people to have seen these apelike creatures before the five campers was Roger Patterson and his friend.

**34(B).** Neighbouring means: a person or place which is adjacent with the given person of place. Therefore nearby will be correct option which can replace the word 'neighbouring'

**35(C).** The local Native Americans were certain that a race of apelike animals had been living in the neighboring mountain for centuries. They called these creatures Sasquatch.

**36(D).** Animals are the creatures, woods are found in jungles and after seeing the objects are spotted. But there is no relation between huge and hairy.
Therefore Huge – hairy is not correct pair.

**37(C).** After carefully reading the passage the best title of the passage would be "The creature called Bigfoot."

**38(B).** Richard Brown, a music teacher and also an experience hunter spotted a similar creature. He saw the animal clearly through the telescopic lens of his rifle. He said the creature looked more like a human than an animal.

**39(D).** Roger Patterson managed to shoot seven rolls of film of the hairy creature before the animal disappeared in the hushes.

**40(B).** From the lines 'Blue as the wing of a bluebird wild, We weave the robes of a new-born child' it is clear that the weavers weave a bright blue cloth in the early morning.

**41(A).** From the lines 'Like the plumes of a peacock, purple and green, We weave the marriage-veils of a queen'. The queen's marriage veil is purple and green coloured.

**42(D).** The poet addresses to the weavers, queen and children all in the poem.

**43(D).** From the lines 'white as a feather and white as a cloud, We weave a dead man's funeral shroud'. It is clear that the weavers weave a garment meant to cover a dead man in the chilly moonlight.

**44(B).** As in the weavers weaving; cloths for new born baby, marriage-veils of a queen and dead man's funeral shroud. Therefore in the poem infancy, youth and death stages of life are discussed.

**45(A).** The synonym of the word 'Solemn' is " Deliberate ".
**Solemn** : D one or said in a formal way.
**Example** : He wore a very solemn expression on his face.
**Deliberate** : To think about or discuss issues and decisions carefully.
**Example** : The jury deliberated for two days before reaching a verdict .

**46(A).** Textbook is the area in which the language material presented prescribed for teaching and learning. A good textbook not only teaches but it also tests. The content of the book should be very clear, a proper beginning is required to prepare the learners for the upcoming content and a perfect conclusion is required to assemble the entire learning.

**47(A).** Grammar-translation method of teaching English heavily relies on form-focussed teaching. The grammar–translation method is a method of teaching foreign languages derived from the classical (sometimes called traditional) method of teaching Greek and Latin. In grammar–translation classes, students learn grammatical rules and then apply those rules by translating sentences between the target language and the native language.

**48(C).** Multimedia provides a technology based constructivist learning environment where students are able to solve a problem by means of self exploration, collaboration and active participation. This approach provides various opportunities to the learners and provides a platform to the learners to be an avtive individual performer. It is helpful for each kind of learner.

**49(C).** In this type of programme teachers may teach and train students who perform better in a particular subject and also helps to maintain their teaching learning difficulties within group teaching and self study itself. This programme helps students to reinforce their knowledge and develop their communication and co-operation skill as well as good interpersonal relation.

**50(D).** Keeping in mind teachers has many children demanding their time and attention; a good conference can help a busy teacher to focus on what your child needs. Review reports and check your files from previous conferences to see if they remind you of important topics you may have missed. Be clear in your own mind about each child's strengths, weaknesses and appropriate goals.

**51(C).** When a child learns a language naturally, without much practice, it is called language acquisition. It is the process by which humans acquire the capacity to perceive and comprehend language, as well as to produce and use words and sentences to communicate. It is one of the quintessential human traits, because non-humans do not communicate by using language.

**52(A).** The study of 'chunks of language' which are bigger than a single sentence is Discourse. It denotes written and spoken communications. It is a conceptual generalization of conversation within each modality and context of communication.

**53(B).** Children need frequent changes of

activity: they need activities which are exiting and stimulate the curiosity, they need to be involved in something active, and they need to be appreciated by the teacher, an important figure for them. Question answer activity is an example to attract student's attention. In this activity, teachers can give examples of question and answer. Teachers can start to train students by Yes/No question. Furthermore, teachers can give Wh-question. It is expected the students can give relevant and suitable answers based on real situation.

**54(B).** Interaction analysis based on practice teaching training in teaching skills using micro-teaching approach and simulated teaching exercise are some of innovative technologies through which effective training program can be transacted. The present mode also pointed out each one of these technologies, its major emphasis on the use of micro-teaching in Indian situation for developing the required skills of teaching at the mastery level.

**55(D).** Oral compositions have been very popular in English language teaching for some time. The idea is for the teacher and students working together to build up a narrative orally before writing it. The process of building up the composition with the whole class allows the teacher and students to focus in on a variety of language items from tense usage to cohesive elements, etc. Oral composition develop much influencing grammar, once a child communicate orally to other self confidence also develop on him. After making such practice he get fluency in language too.

**56(D).** Reading is i mportant because it increases vocabulary, makes pupil to gain knowledge and helps them in getting information.
Reading affects our attitudes, beliefs, standards, morals, judgments, and general behavior. It shapes our thinking and our actions. The purpose of reading is to correlate the ideas on the text to what you have already known. The reader must understand about the subject that he/she read to connect the ideas. Learning to read is about listening and understanding as well as working out what's printed on the page. Through hearing stories, children are exposed to a wide range of words. This helps them build their own vocabulary and improve their understanding when they listen, which is vital as they start to read. Reading is important because it makes you more empathetic, knowledgeable and stimulates your imagination. Reading allows one to develop a better understanding of the subject and gain conceptual clarity. It is one of the simplest entertainment entities for humans.

**57(D).** Language laboratory is the place where the learners have to listen on headphone. It is an audio or audio-visual installation used as an aid in modern language teaching. Here, the student can hear his own mistake for himself and also the student's active speaking time is increased considerably.
Hence, the correct option is D.

**58(A).** The material on opaque sheet is projected with the help of episcope hardware. The opaque projector, epidioscope, epidiascope or episcope is a device which displays opaque materials by shining a bright lamp onto the object from above. A system of mirrors, prisms and/or imaging lenses is used to focus an image of the material onto a viewing screen.

**59(A).** In any language, attending to and interpreting the oral rendition is termed as listening. The student imitates and memorizes linguistic items, such as words, idioms, phrases, tone, etc. and thus learns speaking the language. Listening skill forms the backbone of learning a language, irrespective of the fact that it is a first language or a second language.

**60(B).** Evaluation encompasses more aspects than measurement, but proper evaluation is not possible without the process of measurement. Evaluation covers all the three domains of behavior which are; cognitive domain, affective domain and psychomotor domain.

**61(B).** Given:
The given numbers are $5, 7, 9, 12, 10, 15, 7, 8, 7, 25$
In the given numbers the frequency of occurrence of 7 is maximum i.e., 3 times, therefore the mode of the numbers is $7$.

**62(C).** The given observations are:
$6, 15, 50, 120, 80, 100, 15, 10, 10, 8, 15$
Arranging the given observations in ascending order:
$6, 8, 10, 10, 15, 15, 15, 50, 80, 100, 120$
Number of observations $= 11$ (odd)
$$\text{Mean} = \frac{\text{Sum of the observations}}{\text{Number of the observations}}$$
$$= \frac{6+8+10+10+15+15+15+50+80+100+120}{11}$$
$$\Rightarrow \frac{429}{11} = 39$$
$$\text{Median} = \frac{n+1}{2} \text{ th terms}$$
$$= \frac{11+1}{2} \text{ th terms}$$
$$= \frac{12}{2} \text{ th terms}$$
$$= 6 \text{ th terms}$$
$$= 15$$
Now, in the given observations, 15 repeated most frequently, that is 3 times. Therefore, mode of the given observations is $15$.

**63(B).** Given:
Train leaves at 6 : 14 a.m.
$= 6$ hours 14 minutes
$= 6 \times 60 + 14 = 360 + 14 = 374$ minutes

Time of reaching $= 13 \times 60 + 48 = 828$ minutes
Therefore, adding the two, $828 + 374 = 1202$ minutes,
$= \frac{1202}{60} = 20.02$ hours
So,
6 : 14 a.m. $+20.02 = 8 : 02$ p.m.

**64(B).** Calculation:
Let the other diagonal of rhombus = q
$13 = (\sqrt{24^2 + q^2}) \div 2$
$\Rightarrow 262 = 576 + q^2$
$\Rightarrow 676 - 576 = q^2$
$\Rightarrow q = \sqrt{100} = 10$
$\therefore \text{Area} = \frac{1}{2} \times 24 \times 10 = 120 \text{ cm}^2$

**65(B).** Given,
1 metric tonne $= 1000$ kilogram
1 quintals $= 100$ kilogram
8 metric tonne 50 kilogram
$= 8 \times 100 + 50 = 850$ kilogram
12 metric tonne 8 quintals
$= 12 \times 1000 + 8 \times 100 = 12800$ kilogram
Difference $= 12800 - 8050 = 4750$ kilogram
$= 4$ mt 7 quintal 50 kilogram

**66(B).** There are two series here:
(1): 13, 15, 17, 19
(2): 29, 26, 23
The pattern followes here is:
$13 + 2 = 15$
$15 + 2 = 17$
$17 + 2 = 19$
$19 + 2 = 21$
And
$29 - 3 = 26$
$26 - 3 = 23$
$23 - 3 = 20$
Pair of numbers that comes next is = 20 21

**67(D).** Given:
Area $= 480 \text{ cm}^2$
Width $= 12$ cm
Area of rectangular sheet $= l \times b$
$l = \frac{480}{12} = 40$ cm
Therefore perimeter of rectangular sheet
$= 2 \times (l + b)$
$= 2 \times (40 + 12) \text{ cm}$
$= 104 \text{ cm}$

**68(A).** Let $x$ and $y$ be two numbers.
Therefore,
$x \times y = 48 \ldots . . (1)$
and
$x^2 + y^2 = 100 \ldots . (2)$
We have,
$(x + y)^2 = x^2 + y^2 + 2xy$
$(x + y)^2 = 100 + 2 \times 48$
$(x + y)^2 = 100 + 96$
$x + y = \sqrt{196} = 14$

**69(B).** Given:
$1.66 \times 1.66 + 0.66 \times 0.66 - 1.32 \times 1.66$
$= 1.66 \times 1.66 + 0.66 \times 0.66 - 2 \times 0.66 \times 1.66$
Let $a = 1.66$ and $b = 0.66$, then
$= a \times a + b \times b + 2 \times a \times b$
$= a^2 + b^2 + 2ab$

$$= (a - b)^2$$
$$= (1.66 - 0.66)^2$$
$$= (1.0)^2 = 1$$

**70(B).** Given:
Length of diagonals $= 25cm$ and $20cm$
Area of rhombus $= \frac{1}{2} \times$ p r o d u c t o f i t s
d i a g o n a l s
Area                of            rhombus
$= \frac{1}{2} \times 25 \times 20 = 250 sqcm$

**71(D).** A 7 year old boy recognizes all four sided regular figures as squares. According to Van Hiele's, he is at Level 1-Visualization stage of geometrical thinking.
According to Van Hiele's, at this level, the focus of a child's thinking is on individual shapes, which the child is learning to classify by judging their holistic appearance. Children simply say, "That is a circle," usually without further description. Children identify prototypes of basic geometrical figures. According to this theory, if students do not teach at the proper Hiele level that they will face difficulties and they cannot understand geometry. According to Van Hiele's theory, the development of student's geometrical thinking considered regarding the increasingly sophisticated level of thinking. These levels are hierarchies and able to predict future students' enactment in geometry. This model consists of five levels of understanding, which numbered from 0 to 4.

**72(C).** A teacher makes a teaching method more effective by using devices known as methodology of teaching. They are determined partly on subject matter to be taught and partly by the nature of the learner. For making particular teaching method to be appropriate and efficient it should to be in relation with the characteristic of the learner. Commonly used teaching methods may include class participation, demonstration, recitation etc.

**73(B).** The correct answer is P-2; Q-3; R-4; S-1.
Deductive method is discovered by Aristotle. Inductive method is discovered by David Hume. Project method is discovered by William Heard Kilpatrick. Auto-instructional teaching is discovered by B.F Skinner.
Deductive method: It is a logical process in which a conclusion is based on the concordance of multiple premises that are generally assumed to be true . Deductive reasoning is sometimes referred to as top-down logic. Deductive reasoning relies on making logical premises and basing a conclusion around those premises.
Inductive reasoning: It is a method of drawing conclusions by going from the specific to the general . It's usually contrasted with deductive reasoning,

where you go from general information to specific conclusions. Inductive reasoning is also called inductive logic or bottom-up reasoning.
Project method: It is a medium of instruction which was introduced during the 18th century into the schools of architecture and engineering in Europe when graduating students had to apply the skills and knowledge they had learned in the course of their studies to problems they had to solve as practicians of their trade.
Auto-instructional teaching: With auto-instructional methods, a student is allowed to go on to the next phase only after he has mastered the preceding phase . Thus, a grade shows how far a student has progressed. An A might indicate that he has mastered the whole course; a B, the first three-quarters of the course; a C, half of the course.

**74(C).** This is an example of an algorithm. In mathematics and computer science, an algorithm is an unambiguous specification of how to solve a class of problems. Algorithms can perform calculation, data processing and automated reasoning tasks.

**75(C).** In Diagnostic test, both background and performance of the students is needed for helping them in acquisition of intellectual habits and various powers as discipline. Diagnostic test in Mathematics are used by the teachers to detect the errors committed by the student during mathematical operations like addition, subtraction, multiplication, division. These tests are qualitative in nature not quantitative. These tests find the errors made by students and correct the so that help in their learning.

**76(C).** "Teacher provides home tuitions in mathematics" is not a principle of helping pupils with learning difficulties in Mathematics.
The principal of teaching mathematics in school describe the mathematical understanding, knowledge, and skills that students should acquire from lower primary section to upper primary section. It also provides proper guidance for teacher as well as students in making their decisions. Therefore, providing home tuitions in mathematics is not a principle of helping pupils with learning difficulties in Mathematics.

**77(D).** Identification of student's specific error is especially important for students with learning disabilities and low performances. The teacher plays a crucial role in the process of identification, and for that a close check is highly required of the performances of the learners.
Four steps for the analysis of error:
• Collecting samples of learner language
• Identifying the errors
• Describing the errors

• Explaining the errors
• Evaluating/correcting the errors

**78(C).** The objectives that makes the inclusion of mathematics in the curriculum prominent are "To prepare for the future vocation or occupation" and "To develop their intellectual powers and discipline".
Mathematics provides an effective way of building mental discipline and encourages logical reasoning and mental rigor . In addition, mathematical knowledge plays a crucial role in understanding the contents of other school subjects such as science, social studies, and even music and art.

**79(C).** According to the National Council of Teachers of Mathematics (2000), "Measurement is the assignment of a numerical value to an attribute of an object, such as the length of a pencil.
The correct sequence of developing the concept of measurement is as:
c. Learners verify objects using simple observation.
b. Learners use non-standard units to measure length.
a. Learners use standard units to measure length.
d. Learners understand the relationship between metric units.

**80(D).** Tutorial teaching, Auto-instructional teachingn, Informal teaching are the organization of remedial teaching in Mathematics.
Tutorial teaching is a remedial teaching session given to one student or a small group of students.
Auto-instructional programs are educational material from which students learn by themselves. The teaching technique based on auto-instructional programs. Its purpose is to enable the learner to progress through a pre-arranged sequence of experiences to the acquisition of knowledge or skill.
Informal teaching encompasses student interests within a curriculum in a regular classroom but is not limited to that setting. It works through conversation and the exploration and enlargement of experience.

**81(C).** The student is answering in terms of 'AB' where the line segments are given 'PQ' and 'RS'. It is possible that the student has the habit that he mentions all line with AB. Therefore error due to habit of naming line segment as AB.

**82(A).** According to NCF 2005, school Mathematics takes place in a situation where Mathematics is part of children's life experience.
The National Curriculum Framework (NCF 2005) is one of the four National Curriculum Frameworks published in 1975, 1988, 2000 and 2005 by the National Council of Educational Research and Training NCERT in India. The Framework

provides the framework for making syllabii, textbooks and teaching practices within the school education programmes in India.

**83(C).** Kumar belongs to a very poor and conservative family, a teacher can "Treated him as a normal pupil" to help him.

A teacher should treat him like a normal pupil so that he can't feel the inferior complexity among the other students in the classroom. According to inclusive education, all students should be treated equally. It rejects but still provides the use of special schools or classrooms to separate students with disabilities from students without disabilities.

**84(A).** While performing a diagnostic test you have a specific aim to analyse the exact nature of the progress made by the learner. The main of diagnostic testing is to analyse not to assess , so while preparing this kind of test the objectives have to be focused upon. The steps of the construction of diagnostic test are as:

2) Formulate the objectives and outline of the content.

1) Analyse the content into subtopics and its elements.

3) Identify the difficulties in the orders and subtopics, prepare the final draft of the test.

5) Prepare manual of test.

4) Remedial devices and measures.

**85(B).** Given:

2 times the age of $X$ = 3 times the age of $Y$

Difference between $X$ and $Y$, 8 years back = 18 years

$2X = 3Y$

$\Rightarrow X : Y = 3 : 2$

Let present age of $X$ and $Y$ be $3R$ and $2R$ respectively.

$3R - 2R = 18$

$\Rightarrow R = 18$

$\Rightarrow 3R = 3 \times 18 = 54$

$\therefore$ The present age of $X$ is 54 years.

**86(C).** Given:

$(\frac{7}{13}) = 0.538$

$(\frac{2}{3}) = 0.666$

$(\frac{4}{11}) = 0.3636$

$(\frac{5}{9}) = 0.5555$

Out of $\frac{2}{3}, \frac{7}{13}, \frac{4}{11}, \frac{5}{9}$

$\frac{2}{3}$ is the largest number followed by $\frac{5}{9}$ then $\frac{7}{13}$ and the smallest is $\frac{4}{11}$ .

$\therefore$ The ascending order will be $\frac{4}{11}, \frac{7}{13}, \frac{5}{9}, \frac{2}{3}$ .

**87(B).** Given:

Speed of bikers $A = 75 \ km/hr$

Speed of bikers $B = 60 \ km/hr$

Time taken to meet = 20 minutes

Let the distance between bikers = $D \ km$

$\because$ Bikers ride in opposite directions:

Relative speed of bikers = $75 + 60 = 135 \ km/hr$

Time taken by them = $\frac{20}{60} hr = \frac{1}{3} hr$

Distance $(D)$ = speed $\times$ time

$\Rightarrow D = 135 \times \frac{1}{3}$

$\therefore$ Initial distance between bikers = $45 \ km$

**88(C).** Volume of cubes = 64 cm$^3$

$($ Edge $)^3 = 64$

Edge = 4 cm

If cubes are joined end to end, the dimension of the resulting cuboid will be 4 cm, 4 cm, 8 cm .

Therefore,

Surface area of cuboids = $2(lb + bh + hl)$

$= 2(16 + 32 + 32) = 2 \times 80$

$= 160$ cm$^3$

**89(B).** Given:

Thickness of wood = 1 cm

Length of box = 22 cm

Breadth of box = 17 cm

Height of box = 12 cm

Calculation:

Inner length of the box = (22 – 2) = 20 cm

Inner breadth of the box = (17 – 2) = 15 cm

Inner height of the box = (12 – 2) = 10 cm

Inner volume of the box = (20 × 15 × 10) = 3000 cu. Cm

$\therefore$ Volume of cement in the box is 3000 cu. cm

**90(B).** L.C.M. of 54 and 45 = 270

$\therefore$ Time taken by bus to cover 270 km excluding stoppages = $\frac{270}{54} = 5$ hours

Time taken by bus to cover 270 km including stoppages = $\frac{270}{45} = 6$ hours

$\therefore$ Time for which the bus stops per hour = $\frac{6-5}{6}$ hours = $\frac{1}{6} \times 60$ min = 10 min .

**91(A).** The term Golden Quadrilateral refers to the road connects Delhi-Mumbai, Kolkata and Chennai.

The golden quadrilateral is a highway network connecting many of the major industrial, agricultural and cultural centres of India. It forms a quadrilateral connecting Chennai, Kolkata, Delhi and Mumbai. It is the largest highway project in India, the Golden Quadrilateral project was launched in 2001 as part of National Highways Development Project (NHDP).

**92(C).** Indian Robin- it makes its nest on the top of tree with grass, soft twigs, roots, wool, hair and cotton wool. It lays its eggs between the stone.

Different birds use different techniques and different materials to build their nests. Indian robins are diurnal birds. It lays eggs between stones. Their nest is made of grass. On top, they have soft twigs, roots, wool, wall and cotton. The baby robin bird has a red mouth on the inside. Their nest is soft and comfortable.

**93(C).** Conceptual learning is the form of learning in which a child learn to organize information and fact about anything in

logical structure.

Conceptual learning is a kind of learning about the subject matter in detail about its principle or ideas but after learning student start thinking in abstract term. Through this, students learn to organize information and facts about anything in logical structure. It provides analytical character to a student.

**94(B).** Problems related to environmental education syllabus in EVS teaching is not related to lack of resources p roblem.

Problems related to environmental education system - the subject matter of EVS is complex and difficult for learners at primary level . How to make the subject matter easily comprehensible? It is the major challenge while teaching small children.

The resource based problems are:

- Difficulty in making use of public resources
- EVS closely related to science
- Lack of experienced teachers

**95(C).** Dolphin has the largest brain in proportion to its body size.

- Dolphins have the highest brain-to-body weight ratio of all cetaceans.
- Bottlenose dolphins have bigger brains than humans, and they have a brain-to-body-weight ratio greater than great apes do.
- Monitor lizards, tegus, and anoles, and some tortoise species have the largest among reptiles.
- Among birds, the highest brain-to-body ratios are found among parrots, crows, magpies, jays, and ravens.

**96(C).** The Indian Forest Act 1927, come into force in 21 September 1927.

The main objective of the Indian Forest Act (1927) was to secure exclusive state control over forests to meet the demand for timber. Most of these untitled lands had traditionally belonged to the forest dwelling communities. This Act classified the forests into three - reserved forests, protected forests and village forests. It attempted to regulate the collection of forest produce by forest dwellers and some activities declared as offences and imprisonment and fines were imposed in this policy to establish the state control over forests.

**97(C).** The region where farmers specialize in vegetables only, this type of farming is known as Truck farming.

- In the regions where farmers specialize in vegetables only, the farming is known as Truck farming, and the distance of truck farms from the market is governed by the distance that a truck can cover overnight, hence the name truck farming.
- Vegetable farms are in some regions

known as truck farms: "truck" is a noun for which its more common meaning overshadows its historically separate use as a term for "vegetables are grown for the market".

- The production of crops of some vegetables on an extensive scale in regions especially suited to their culture primarily for shipment to distant markets known as Truck farming.
- The major truck-farming areas are in California, Texas, Florida, along the Atlantic Coastal Plain, and in the Great Lakes area.
- Centers for specific crops vary with the season. Among the most important truck crops are tomatoes, lettuce, melons, beets, broccoli, celery, radishes, onions, cabbage, and strawberries.

**98(B).** The first pico satellite of India is STUDSAT.
- STUDSAT stands as an acronym for Student Satellite.
- It is the first pico-satellite developed in the country by a consortium of seven engineering colleges from Karnataka and Andhra Pradesh.
- The mission is an experimental one and was launched on 12th July 2010.
- The satellite, since it was a pico satellite, weighs less than 1 kg.
- The satellite was placed in the polar sun synchronous orbit.
- The satellite had the primary objective of promoting space technology in educational institutions and encouraging research and development in miniaturized satellites.
- The satellite and the project also aimed to establish a communication link between the satellite and ground station.
- The satellite also captured the image of earth with a resolution of 90 meters and transmitted the payload and telemetry data to the earth station.

**99(A).** In Latin, "cow" is "vacca" and "cowpox" is "vaccinia". From these roots, the term 'vaccination' has come into our usage.
- Vaccinia Virus is also the name of a poxvirus (species Vaccinia virus of the genus Orthopoxvirus) that differs from but is closely related to the viruses causing smallpox and cowpox and that includes a strain used in making vaccines against smallpox.
- Famously in 1796, Edward Jenner, an English physician realized that milkmaids who had had cowpox did not catch smallpox even during epidemics.
- Jenner tried deliberately giving cowpox to people, and found that they were now resistant to smallpox.
- This was because the smallpox virus is closely related to the cowpox virus.
- It was the first successful vaccine to be developed.

**100(A).** Insectivorous plants follow both autotrophic and heterotrophic modes of nutrition.
They are carnivorous plants that derive nutrition by the consumption of insects, animals, protozoans, and Arthropoda. They generate energy by the process of photosynthesis. They are found on all continents except Antarctica and also found on many pacific islands. Venus trap, Drosera capensis, California pitcher plant, etc are examples of insectivorous plants.

**101(A).** Dhokla is a delicacy of Gujarat.
Dhokla is a savoury cake made out of Bengal gram flour and is steamed to get a fluffy texture. The dish occupies pride of place in its state of origin Gujarat, and has become a favourite across the country. It's a low-calorie, healthy and protein-packed snack.

**102(D).** " Vermi Compost " is useful fertilizer for gardening.
Vermi Compost is the excreta of earthworms, which is rich in humus and hence acts as a fertilizer. It is produced by earthworms when they decompose the organic matter and excrete the waste. The castings of earthworms are then separated from the undecomposed matter and vermin compost is obtained. It is an organic fertilizer that has no harm to either environment or human beings.

**103(D).** The sum total of the populations of the same kind of organisms is called species.
Species are often defined as a group of individuals with similar characteristics, where they can interbreed to produce fertile offspring's.

**104(D).** Combustion that takes place at high speed is called Rapid combustion.
When a combustible burns rapidly to produce heat and light, this type of combustion is called rapid combustion. Example: LPG, CNG, Petrol etc. combust rapidly. That is, burning of LPG, CNG, petrol etc. are some examples of rapid combustion. Combustible substances cause rapid combustion.

**105(B).** Tea is a plantation type of crop.
The plantation crop refers to those crops which are cultivated on an extensive scale in an area. In this type of agriculture, single crop is raised on a large area. These crops include tea, coffee, rubber, cocoa, coconut, oil palm and cashew etc.

**106(C).** The Brahmaputra river does not have its origin in India.
- Origin: Chemayungdung glacier of the Kailash range near the Mansarovar lake in Tibet.
- In Tibet, it is known as the Tsangpo, which means 'the purifier.'
- The Rango Tsangpo is the major right-bank tributary of this river in Tibet.
- It enters India west of Sadiya town in Arunachal Pradesh.
- Flowing southwest, it receives its main left-bank tributaries, viz., Dibang or Sikang, and Lohit; thereafter, it is known as the Brahmaputra.
- The Brahmaputra enters Bangladesh near Dhubri and flows southward.
- In Bangladesh, the Tista joins it on its right bank from where the river is known as the Jamuna.
- It finally merges with the river Padma, which falls in the Bay of Bengal.

**107(D).** Khadins, Bundhis, Ahars and Kattas are ancient structures that are examples for water harvesting.
Water harvesting is a term which means storage of water during rains. Traditionally, small dams and other reservoirs were built so that rainwater could be stored for later use. For example, Khadins and nadis in Rajasthan, bundhis in Madhya Pradesh and Uttar Pradesh, ahars and pynes in Bihar, and kattas in Karnataka are some of the ancient water harvestings, including water conveyance, structures. These are still in use in many places. These structures were not having any adverse effect on the local natural balance and had no environmental costs.

**108(A).** Insects responsible for transmitting diseases are called V ectors.
Vectors are frequently arthropods, such as mosquitoes, ticks, flies, fleas, and lice. The diseases transmitted through vectors:
- Elephantiasis is transmitted by mosquitos.
- Malaria is transmitted by mosquitos.
- Rabies is transmitted by mad dogs.

**109(C).** "Animals" is a subtheme under the broad theme "Family and Friends" suggested in the EVS syllabus while remaining are the broad themes of the EVS syllabus for class III to V.

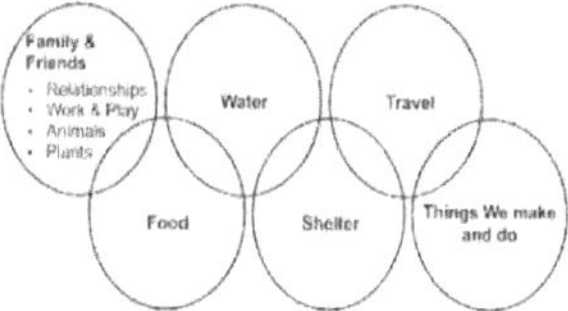


**110(A).** Children making fewer mistakes is not advocated by EVS.
Environmental Studies is a subject that deals with a human's interaction with the environment. It gives the children a lot of freedom to explore their physical and social surroundings.
The following are the ways of learning EVS:
- They should be provided with opportunities that provide hands-on experience.
- Children are curious that's why they ask a lot of questions.

- It should be remembered that mistakes are a part of the learning process.
- They also get to clear their doubts and learn from their mistakes by exploring their surroundings.

**111(D).** A good assignment in EVS should primarily aim at providing extended learning opportunities because learning opportunities make learners independent and constructivist in learning.

The Other Aims of an EVS Assignment:
- Locating and comprehending relationships between the natural, social, and cultural environment.
- Studying inter-relationship between the human and natural systems.
- Drawing attention to different people, cultures, and communities.
- Developing understanding, critical thinking, and problem-solving skills.
- Addressing environmental issues and making plans to bring improvements.

**112(B).** Supreme Court was directed in the judgment given in 1991, to make the subject of environmental study compulsory in the college curricula.

The University Grants Commission (UGC) has instructed its affiliated universities and colleges to introduce a compulsory six-module course on Environmental Studies at all branches of an undergraduate degree. The module, however, has been existent since 2013. The decision to create a six-module course on Environmental Studies was taken by the Supreme Court in 1991 after a Public Interest Litigation (PIL) filed by an advocate, MC Mehta. According to the court order, UGC had to prescribe a course on the environment as a mandatory subject in colleges.

**113(A).** International Environmental Education Programme (IEEP) has been launched by UNESCO.
- IEEP came into existence in the year 1975.
- For two decades, UNESCO and UNEP led the International Environmental Education Program (1975-1995) that set out a vision for and gave practical guidance on how to mobilize education for environmental awareness.
- In 1976 UNESCO launched an environmental newsletter Connect as the official organ of the UNESCO-UNEP International Environmental Education Program (IEEP).
- Until 2007, it served as a clearinghouse to exchange information in general and to promote the aims and activities of the IEEP in particular, as well as being a network for institutions and individuals that are interested and active in environmental education.

**114(D).** Known to Unknown is the principle of learning that is followed in teaching EVS.
- In this principle the teaching and learning process starts from previous knowledge to new content to be taught, the learner does not find difficulty in moving from known to unknown.
- The contents are spirally organized starting with the immediate experience of the child (known) moving out to the world she/he inhabits (unknown), leading to an analysis of some of the factors that influence life on this planet.
- The focus of EVS enlarges from the personal to the national and global (local to global), from the physical dimension to the aesthetic dimension.

**115(A).** The Philosophy subject is not included in social science at the upper primary level.

Social Science at Upper Primary Level:
- Social Science must link a child's life at school with life outside the classroom.
- It helps to initiate the learner into a study of India's past, with references to contemporary developments in other parts of the world.
- It includes disciplines of History, Geography, Political Science, Economics, and Sociology.
- The objective of teaching the social sciences is to develop an understanding of the earth as the habitat of humankind and other forms of life.

**116(C).** Both II and III activity/activities can be given to the students to teach about 'cultural diversity in India'.

India is a country incredible for its diversity. Ethnic origins, religions and languages are the major sources of cultural diversity. Despite maintaining distinct identities several Jatis, sects, and communities have organic links with other segments of the population of the region. They have constantly maintained cultural linkages, particularly by sharing resources, traits, and space. A teacher can do the following activities to teach students about cultural diversity:
- Giving pictures of different places and asking them to differentiate based on religion and asking names of those religions.
- Asking them to write an essay with proper elaboration, how India experiences these differences in different times and at different places.
- Presenting them different situations the way people travel, live, eat.
- Asking them to differentiate among them in regard to their relation to an urban area and rural area.
- Asking them to make a list of cultural differences we find in India.
- Asking them castes existing in our country and their opinion on it.

**117(C).** New knowledge is acquired through e xperience and searching new meanings.

Knowledge is a result of many processes like knowing, perceiving, thinking, remembering, reflecting, observing, finding out, inferring, proving, and so on. Knowledge has three elements which are:
- Existence of a group of ideas and phenomena,
- These ideas and phenomena correspond to things which exist
- The correspondence is supported by beliefs.

**118(D).** 36 Min is the standard time duration of a micro-teaching cycle.

The standard time duration of a micro-teaching cycle is:
- Teach - 6 minutes
- Feedback - 6 minutes
- Re-plan - 12 minutes
- Re-teach - 6 minutes
- Re-feedback - 6 minutes
- Total - 36 minutes

There are six steps of micro-teaching which are as follows -

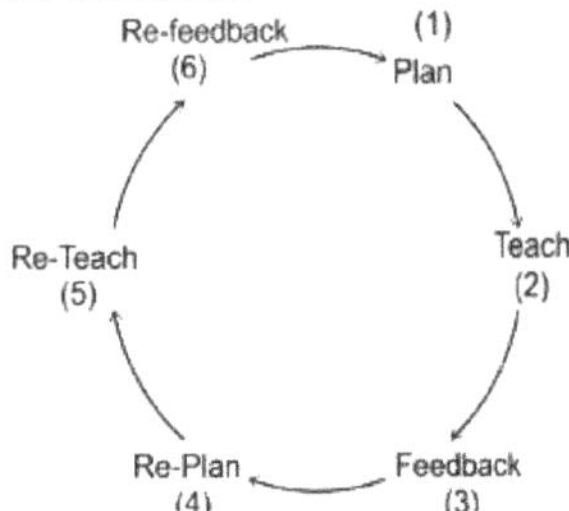


**119(A).** Milk turns into curds faster in summer because the growth of bacteria increases with the increase in temperature. High-temperature conditions are favorable for bacterial growth. Curd contains several microorganisms, the bacterium Lactobacillus promotes the formation of curd. Bacteria are also involved in the making of cheese, pickles, and many other food items. The use of oil and vinegar prevents spoilage of pickles because bacteria cannot live in such an environment.

**120(D).** In rural areas, cow dung is used to coat the floors and walls of huts to keep insects away.

People in rural areas use cow dung to coat the floors and walls of huts as it acts as a cheap heat insulator. It is also used to repel insects. Dung contains bacteria that are not harmful to humans. Dung is rich in minerals and has antibacterial properties to protect people from various diseases and health problems. It acts as a repellent for mosquitoes and other poisonous creatures like scorpions, millipedes, snakes, etc. In addition, the floors and walls remain warm in winter and cool in summer.